KU-536-345

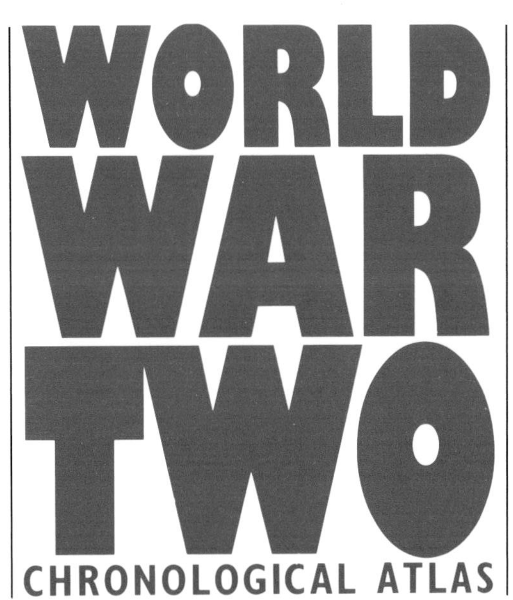
WORLD
WAR
TWO
CHRONOLOGICAL ATLAS

WORLD WAR TWO

CHRONOLOGICAL ATLAS

When, Where, How and Why

CHARLES MESSENGER

BLOOMSBURY

CONT

ENTS

SECTION 7

JANUARY 1943 to AUGUST 1943

SLOWLY BUT SURELY

SECTION 8

AUGUST 1943 to JANUARY 1944

EUROPE RE-ENTERED

SECTION 9

FEBRUARY 1944 to SEPTEMBER 1944

LIBERATION

SECTION 10

SEPTEMBER 1944 to FEBRUARY 1945

CLOSING IN

SECTION 11

FEBRUARY 1945 to MAY 1945

VICTORY IN EUROPE

SECTION 12

JUNE 1945 to SEPTEMBER 1945

THE ULTIMATE WEAPON

SECTION 13

1945 to the Present

THE LEGACY

First published in Great Britain in 1989 by Bloomsbury Publishing Ltd, 2 Soho Square, London W1V 5DE.

British Library Cataloguing in Publication Data:
Messenger, Charles, *1941–*
World War 2: chronological atlas
1. World War 2
I. Title
940.53
ISBN 0-7475-0229-3

Jacket illustration by courtesy of the Imperial War Museum, London; jacket designed by David Gibbons; colour simulation by Rober W. Phasey.

Designed and edited by DAG Publications Ltd.
Cartography by Micromap Ltd, Romsey, Hampshire.
Designed by David Gibbons.
Edited by Michael Boxall.
Typeset by Typesetters (Birmingham) Ltd.
Camerawork by M&E Reproductions, North Fambridge, Essex.
Design consultant: Roger Walton.

Printed and bound in Spain by Printer Industria Grafica s.a., Barcelona.

Introduction

Many millions of words have already been written about the Second World War. This is not surprising since it was the largest and most intensive conflict that the world has ever known. Now that the 50th anniversary of its outbreak is upon us, we can expect to be deluged with many more publications, not to mention programmes on radio, television, film and video.

There is still a generation alive that fought and experienced that war at first hand. Another was born during it. To subsequent generations it is mere history. Yet all these generations, and those in between, retain an interest in the years 1939 to 1945, and for a variety of reasons. The more senior among us, who were of an age to fight or endure those years as teenagers or adults, have a desire to put the individual roles they played into perspective and, given the inevitably restricted vantage points available to them at the time, to establish what really happened and why. For the rest of us it is a mixture of curiosity, a desire to understand what our grandparents and parents went through, to comprehend why the world is as it is today, or simply because we have to study it at school and college.

A major frustration, however, about studying a global war is the difficulty of placing a particular campaign or event into the context of the war as a whole. There is also the problem of trying to identify on the map where events occurred; quickly to establish when and why they happened; and to understand the effects, sometimes far-reaching, which they had not just within but also outside the geographic theatre of war in which they took place. Moreover, it is the very complexity of global war that is often difficult to comprehend. This is why I have kept to a fairly strict chronological approach rather than cover each theatre of war as a finite block. Breaking the book down into chronological sections and building the opening spread of each as much as possible around a major Allied conference in order to create an overview of the war at a specific point in time enables the reader to draw a large number of threads together and to comprehend the overall strategy of the war and how it evolved.

There are a number of reference aids that will help the reader use the book in a variety of ways. The top of each spread gives a timescale both in words and in the form of a bar-chart, as well as the geographic area being addressed. The bottom left-hand page refers back to the last relevant spread and the bottom right-hand page the next spread dealing with the same topic. There is also a comprehensive index and a list of recommended books covering almost every aspect of the war. Finally, presenting the text in diary form will, I hope, make it easier for the reader quickly to pin-point particular facts.

This book is the result of much work by a small, close-knit team, each member playing a vital and distinct role. DAG Publications Ltd, in the form of David and Beryl Gibbons and Anthony Evans, were at the centre of the web in co-ordinating the whole project, as well as undertaking the design. Richard and Hazel Watson drew all the maps with admirable *sangfroid*, let alone accuracy and imagination, and Michael Boxall was the painstaking and patient editor. Finally, Kathy Rooney of Bloomsbury Publishing Ltd was the driving force behind us. I am deeply grateful to them all.

London,
January 1989

CHARLES MESSENGER

1918 TO 1920

The Treaty of Versailles

The causes of the Second World War had their origins in what was called the Great War of 1914–18, which was popularly believed at the time to be the 'war to end all war'. The year 1918 had begun disastrously for the Allies when Russia, consumed by revolution, made a separate peace with Germany in March. The Germans were therefore able to reinforce in the west and launch a series of offensives in France and Flanders designed to defeat the British and French before the American troops arrived there in force. The Allies held, and by the end of July the Germans had shot their bolt. In August the Allies began to attack, and this was mirrored on the other fronts – Italy, Salonika and the Middle East. While the armies of the Central Powers and Turkey fought on, their peoples, exhausted by the rigours of the war, saw defeat staring them in the face. Their governments therefore began to sue for peace. First to fall by the wayside was Bulgaria which agreed an armistice on **30 September**. A month later, on **30 October**, Turkey followed suit. This left just Germany and Austria-Hungary in the field.

3 November 1918 Sailors from the German Grand Fleet based at Kiel, who had previously refused to put to sea, demonstrated for peace. Sailors' and Workers' Councils were set up, and the idea quickly spread among the German forces.

4 November Austria-Hungary signed an armistice.

8 November In view of the growing unrest, Chancellor Prince Max of Baden persuaded Kaiser Wilhelm to abdicate; he went into exile in Holland. A new government was formed in Berlin under the Socialist, Friedrich Ebert.

9 November German peace delegates met the Allies in a railway carriage in the Forest of Compiègne, France. The Allies demanded German agreement to immediate evacuation of occupied territories, including Alsace-Lorraine (in German hands since 1871), demilitarization of the Rhineland, surrender of substantial war *matériel* and annulment of Treaty of Brest-Litovsk (signed with Russia in March 1918) before they would sign an armistice.

11 November German delegation informed the Allies that the German government had agreed to the demands. The armistice was signed in the railway carriage at Compiègne at 5 a.m. and all firing stopped on the Western Front at 11 a.m. German troops began their withdrawal to the Rhine.

25 November Last German troops left Belgium and France.

1 December Allied troops began to cross the Rhine to occupy the Rhineland and Saarland.

6–11 January 1919 Growing unrest in Germany culminated in the Spartacist Revolt in Berlin, when Russian-backed Communists attempted to seize power. It was put down with some brutality by the *Freikorps* (Free Corps), organized groups of anti-Communist officers and soldiers.

18 January Conference of the Allies began in Paris to agree the terms on which peace should be granted to their defeated enemies.

19 January Elections held in Germany. A government was formed, led by Ebert's majority Socialists and selected as its seat Weimar, 150 miles southwest of Berlin. The Weimar Republic was thus born.

January Further left wing insurgencies in Bremen and elsewhere in Germany were crushed by the *Freikorps* on whom the Weimar Government was becoming increasingly reliant. Spartacist survivors flocked to Bavaria, which had, as early as **8 December 1918** declared itself an independent socialist republic.

4 March Comintern (Communist International), the agency for exporting Communist revolution abroad, founded in Moscow. On the same day the Spartacists declared a General Strike in Germany. Further fighting broke out in Berlin, but by the 13th the *Freikorps* were once more in control.

21 March Bela Kun declared a Hungarian Socialist Republic.

20 April–3 May Civil war in Bavaria. Forces of the left were crushed by the *Freikorps*.

7 May Allies presented their terms for peace to Germany. She was given fifteen days to comment, but the government was horrified by their harshness and submitted a stream of objections, especially over the clauses concerning loss of territory and war reparations.

16 June Allies rebutted the German counter-proposals and presented a seven-day ultimatum for signing the treaty.

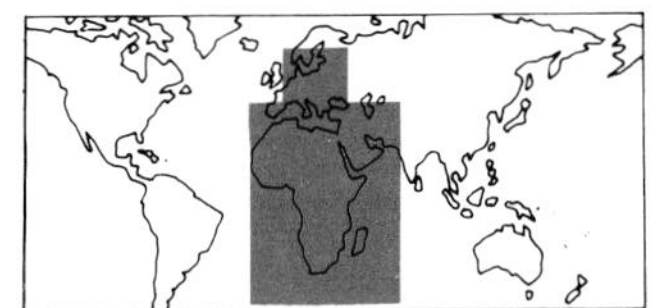

CENTRAL EUROPE AFTER VERSAILLES

THE AFRICAN MANDATES

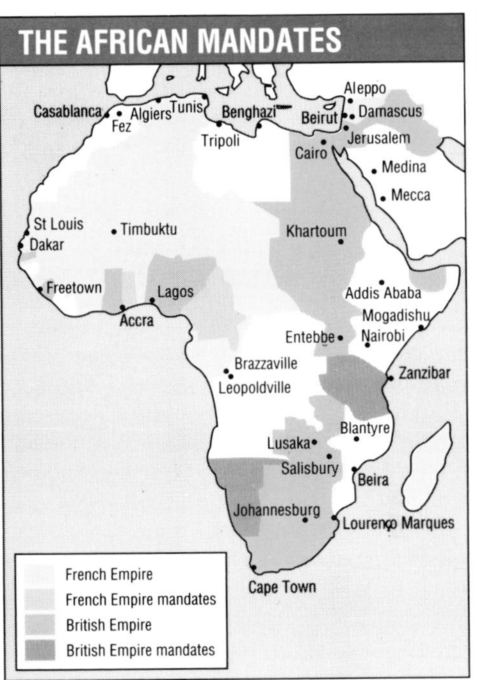

28 June Germany signed the Treaty of Versailles with the Allies. Under it she lost territory (see map) and her colonial possessions in Africa, which were ceded to Britain, France and South Africa; those in the Pacific were given to Japan, Australia and New Zealand (see page 14). Germany was to pay the Allies £6,600 million ($33 billion) by 1 May 1921, even though the eminent economist John Maynard Keynes warned that Germany could not possibly meet this demand. Her army was to be restricted to a 100,000-man long-service force (so as to prevent sizeable reserves being built up as would be the case if soldiers enlisted on short engagements); she was to be allowed no air force, or 'offensive' weapons such as tanks; and her war industry was to be dismantled under Allied supervision. The valuable coal-mining region of the Saarland was handed over to France under the auspices of the League of Nations. (This further aggravated the problem of reparations payments, and Keyne's warnings fell on deaf ears.) This situation was to remain for fifteen years when a plebiscite of the Saarlanders would be called so that they could decide their own future. The German territory on the west bank of the Rhine was to be occupied by Allied troops, also for fifteen years, and Germany was not allowed to have any form of military installation within 50 kilometres (28 miles) of the right bank of the river. These terms were to cause growing resentment in Germany and to make life very difficult for the Weimar Government which had been forced to agree to them.

10 September Austria signed the Treaty of St-Germain with the Allies who, believing that the desire for self-determination of many of the ethnic groupings that had constituted the old Austro-Hungarian Empire had been a major cause of the Great War, created three new states – Czechoslovakia, Poland and Yugoslavia. Austria had to cede territory to these new states (see map) as well as to Italy and Roumania. She also had to pay reparations and had her army restricted to 30,000 men. Finally, she was forbidden to form any sort of union with Germany.

27 November Bulgaria signed the Treaty of Neuilly with the Allies. By this she surrendered territory to Greece and Roumania, was to pay reparations and had her army limited to 20,000 men.

4 June 1920 Hungary signed the Treaty of Trianon with the Allies. In March Bela Kun had been overthrown by Admiral Miklos Horthy, who established a virtual right-wing dictatorship, and it was he who was forced to sign. Between them, Roumania, Czechoslovakia and Yugoslavia took virtually two-thirds of Hungary's territory, and her population dropped from 18 to 7 millions.

10 August Turkey, the last of the belligerents formally to make peace, signed the Treaty of Sévres with the Allies. The old Ottoman Empire in the Middle East was broken up. France was given Syria and Britain Palestine, Transjordan and Iraq as League of Nations Mandates. The Dodecanese Islands were ceded to Italy, and Greece was allowed to occupy parts of western Turkey on both sides of the Bosphorus. The straits between the Black Sea and the Mediterranean were demilitarized.

The Great War was now formally at an end, but the Allied peace terms, which their erstwhile enemies had been forced to accept, contained seeds of future conflict. Discontent over the severity of the terms and squabbles over the newly drawn national borders of Europe would help to nurture these seeds. In addition, the spectre of the spread of Soviet Marxist-Leninism and the rise of Fascism in Europe were to increase the uncertainty of the future.

To counter this and to ensure that a lasting peace, especially in Europe, could be maintained, the Allies had two strings to their bow – the League of Nations and Disarmament.

The League of Nations and Disarmament

The death toll during 1914–18 of both combatants and non-combatants had been awesome. In addition, many survivors were maimed both physically and mentally. Everyone agreed that never again should humankind be put to such suffering: ways must be found to prevent a major war breaking out in the future.

The idea of a League of Nations as an international organization dedicated to the maintenance of world peace had begun to be explored on both sides of the Atlantic as early as 1914. US President Woodrow Wilson was its most enthusiastic proponent, much more so than Britain and France, who initially believed that the war would need to be won before the concept could be considered seriously.

8 January 1918 President Wilson announced his 14 Points setting forth America's war aims.
The climax to this was his conclusion: 'A general association of nations must be formed under specific covenants for the purpose of affording mutual guarantees of political independence and territorial integrity to great and small States alike.' This concept was supported by his allies, and when the Paris Peace Conference began its deliberations in January 1919 the League was high on the agenda. After much discussion it was the Anglo-US view, that the League should be a free association of nations, rather than the French idea of a military alliance of the victorious countries that won through. It was agreed that the functions of the League would be to maintain peace among its own members and in the world at large. It would do this by encouraging disarmament, mutual guarantees among nations of territorial integrity, international agreement not to resort to war until peaceful means to resolve disputes had been exhausted, and to provide machinery for the latter. The League could not, however, dictate to nations; it could only suggest and encourage. It was to have a council consisting of five permanent members – Britain, France, Japan, Italy and the USA – plus four smaller nations, initially Belgium, Brazil, China and Spain, who were elected on a periodic basis. A permanent secretariat and an assembly, both of which were to be based in Geneva, Switzerland, completed the infrastructure.

The League Covenant was written into each peace treaty, but none of the vanquished nations was invited to become a member.

19 November 1919 US Senate refused to ratify the Treaty of Versailles.
President Wilson had paid too little attention to US domestic policies in his efforts to set up the League of Nations. Many Americans never wanted their country to be involved again in European affairs. There was also suspicion that the League would threaten traditional US independence in foreign policy and jealousy that Britain and her Dominions had six votes in the League to America's one. The US Senate confirmed its attitude in another vote taken on **19 March 1920**, and the final blow fell when the Democrats, using the League as a platform, were decisively defeated in the presidential election of that November. The US failure to join the League robbed it of much of its teeth and was to prove a fatal flaw.

November 1920 First session of the League of Nations Assembly.
Forty-four countries were represented. Apart from the USA, Germany, Austria, Hungary, Turkey and Bulgaria were absent from Geneva; Russia did not attend, having not been invited to join.

18 March 1921 Treaty of Riga signed between Poland and Russia.
In April 1920 the Poles, taking advantage of the fact that Russia had been severely weakened by two years of civil war between the Reds and Whites, invaded, intending to extend their territory eastwards. This caught the League by surprise, and it was unable to intervene. The Russians counter-attacked, driving the Poles back to the gates of Warsaw. Britain and France, fearful that Poland would go under, sent military advisers, but a Polish counterstroke drove the Russians back, and a cease-fire came into effect in October. By the Treaty of Riga, Poland was able to retain most of her initial gains.

11 November 1921 Naval Conference opened in Washington, DC.
Even though the USA had withdrawn from the League, she was still concerned about world peace, especially in the Pacific. President Harding therefore invited the major powers to a disarmament conference. By the Washington Naval Treaty of **6 February 1922** it was agreed that all capital warship building should be halted for ten years and that existing numbers of US, British, Japanese, French and Italian capital ships should remain in the proportion 5:5:3:1.75:1.75 respectively. In order to prevent increased rivalry in the Pacific, the USA, Britain, France and Japan agreed to maintain the status quo.

16 April 1922 Germany and Russia signed the Treaty of Rapallo.
A treaty of friendship between the two 'outcasts of Europe'. Its secret clauses enabled the Germans to set up arms factories in Russia and eventually to begin training selected officers there as pilots and in tank warfare. This was in direct contravention of the Treaty of Versailles. In May 1922, however, the Allies did allow Germany to begin manufacturing civil aircraft of limited performance.

24 July 1923 Treaty of Lausanne between Turkey and the Allies.
Kemal Atatürk had overthrown the Sultan of Turkey in early 1921 and then had begun to drive the Allies out of mainland Turkey. By September 1922 he had decisively defeated the Greeks at Smyrna and had isolated the British garrison at Chanak. This was withdrawn in October. By the treaty the Allies dropped all claims to mainland Turkey; this marked the first major revision of the Treaty of Versailles.

1 December 1925 Locarno Treaties.
Britain and Italy agreed, through the Locarno Treaties, to act as guarantors of the national borders within western Europe.

10 September 1926 Germany allowed to join the League of Nations.

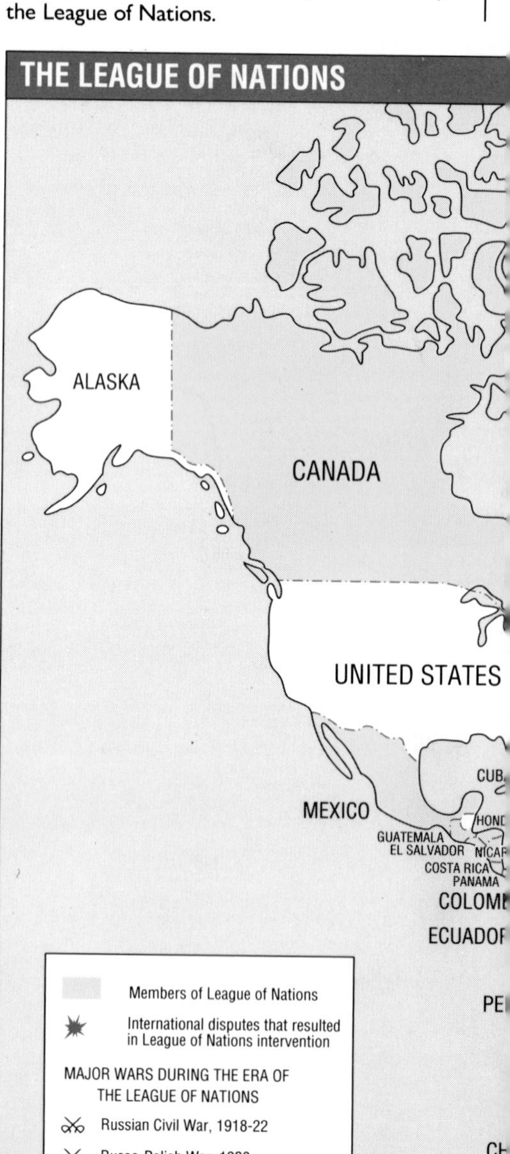

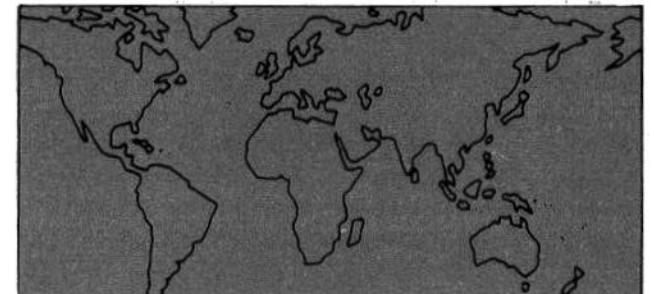

June–August 1927 International Naval Conference at Geneva.
The USA failed to get Britain and Japan to agree that all classes of warship should be reduced to the same 5:5:3 ratio as capital ships.

27 August 1928 Kellogg-Briand Pact.
More than sixty nations signed a pledge to outlaw war.

22 April 1930 London Naval Treaty.
President Hoover had revived the question of naval disarmament in 1929. Britain, USA and Japan agreed to restrict tonnages in cruisers, destroyers and submarines along the lines of the 5:5:3 ratio. A five-year embargo on capital ship construction was agreed. France and Italy also attended the conference, which opened in January, but could not agree how to resolve rival claims and therefore remained outside the treaty.

2 February 1932 International Disarmament Conference opened in Geneva.
This was an effort to get all European nations to disarm to the same level as Germany. It ran until May 1934, but failed to achieve anything, mainly because France saw the proposal as too great a threat to her security and Germany demanded to be allowed to re-arm if there was no agreement to disarm to her level.

The League of Nations had enjoyed some success in the field of naval disarmament and in encouraging international treaties in order to maintain peace. It also succeeded in preventing a number of conflicts from breaking out. These included a dispute between Britain and Turkey over Mosul in 1924, Bulgaria and Greece in 1925, Poland and Lithuania in 1927, and Peru and Colombia in 1932. By the early 1930s, however, cracks were beginning to appear in the plaster of global peace. Japanese militarism, Italian Fascism and, from 1933, Nazi Germany became increasingly strident in their demands. The League's lack of executive powers to impose peaceful solutions became more and more apparent.

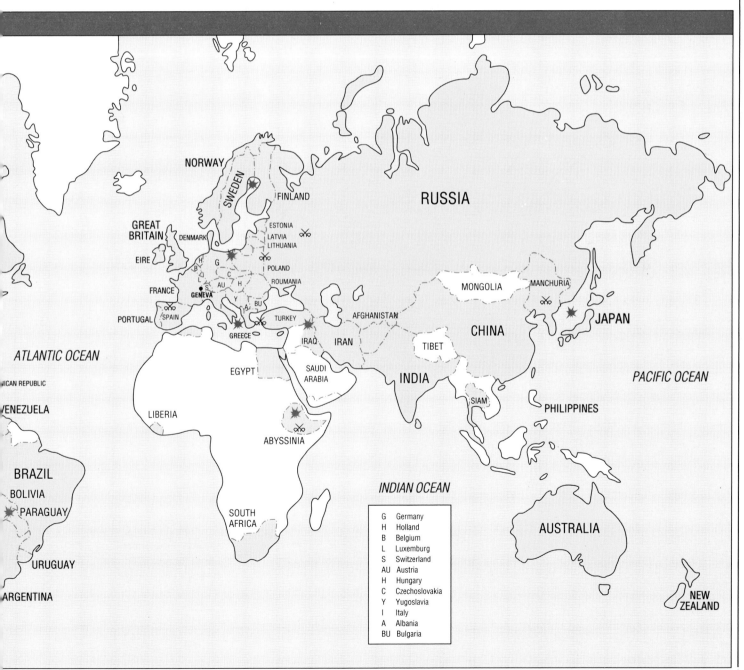

G Germany
H Holland
B Belgium
L Luxemburg
S Switzerland
AU Austria
H Hungary
C Czechoslovakia
Y Yugoslavia
I Italy
A Albania
BU Bulgaria

The Rise of the Dictators

ITALY

Although one of the victors, Italy had been disappointed by Versailles since she did not achieve the territorial gains she had hoped for. At the same time she suffered from a series of weak governments. Fears of a revolution by the left were fanned by a number of strikes called by the Socialists and their continued denouncement of the war, even after it was over. This inflamed many of the soldiers.

23 March 1919 First *Fascio di Combattimento* formed, in Milan.
These ex-officers, students and patriots adopted the *fasces* or axe and bundle of rods, which was the symbol of state authority in ancient Rome, and they became known as Fascists or Blackshirts after their distinctive uniform. One of their leaders was Benito Mussolini, a former Socialist who had campaigned for Italy's entry into the war in 1915 and had himself fought in it. He had then founded his own newspaper, *Popolo d'Italia*, to propagate his ideas.

15 April 1919 Fascists broke up a Socialist demonstration in Milan.
This was one of the few Fascist successes during their early days. They failed to attract mass support and fared disastrously in the 1919 national elections, from which the Socialists emerged as the largest party. During 1920 they made better progress, especially in the Po Valley, where the landowners, farmers and professional classes increasingly resented the way in which the government was giving in to workers' demands for higher wages. The Fascists often used terror as a weapon against their opponents.

May 1921 Fascists won 35 seats in the national election.
Mussolini was one of the new deputies.

September 1921 Fascists seized control of Ravenna.
This marked the start of a new phase: Fascist bands would move into a city and take control of all the public utilities. Ferrara and Bologna fell in the same way in May 1922.

August 1922 The Socialists declared a general strike.
Since the government appeared unwilling to take the necessary steps to break it, the Fascists took over the railways and trams.

28 October 1922 Mussolini began his march on Rome.
Frustrated by the weakness of the central government, the Fascists decided to seize power. They occupied all public buildings in northern and central Italy and began to converge on Rome. The government would have declared a state of emergency, but King Victor Emmanuel, fearful of a civil war, refused to sign the proclamation. On 30 October Mussolini arrived by train in Rome. The King invited him to form a government, and the Fascists staged a victory march through the capital. This marked the beginning of Mussolini's dictatorship of Italy.

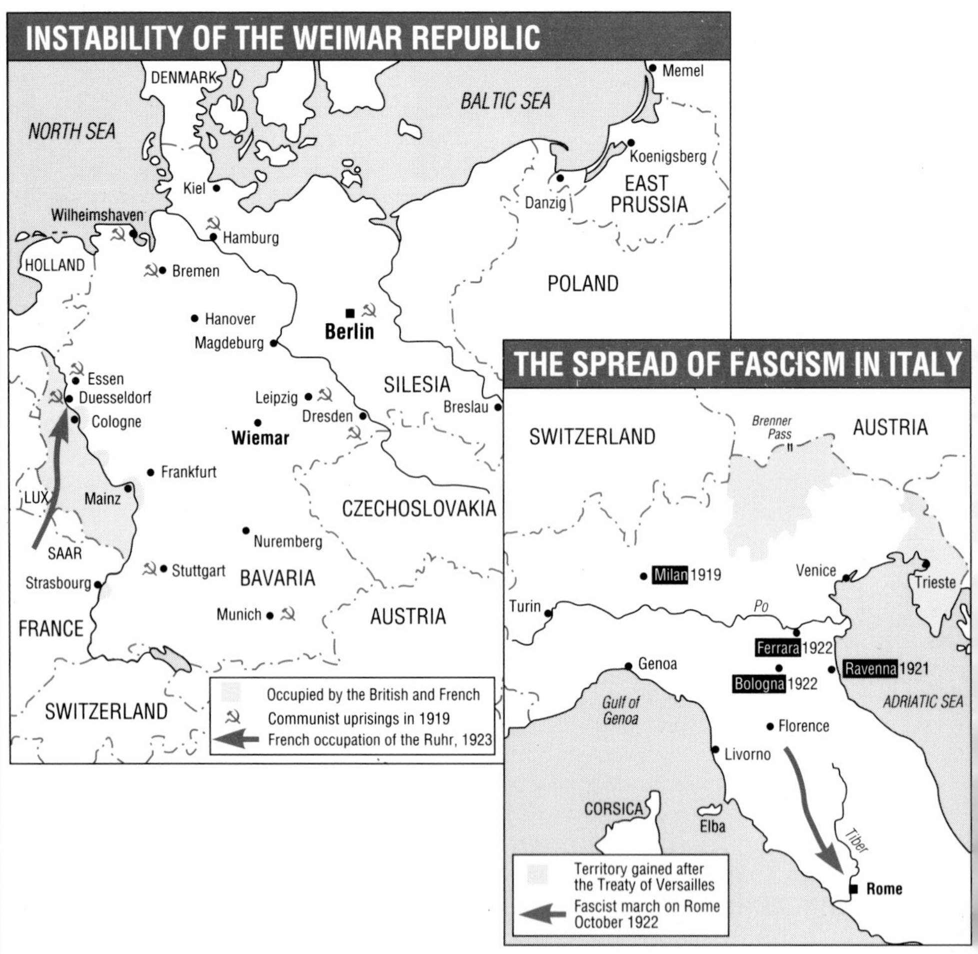

GERMANY

There was widescale resentment in Germany over the fact that the Weimar Government had acquiesced with the terms of Versailles. Indeed, many Germans argued that their army had not been defeated in the field but had been betrayed by the politicians – the so-called 'stab in the back'.

24 February 1920 Adolf Hitler announced his party's policies.
The small German Workers' Party (*Deutsche Arbeiterpartie*), had been founded in Munich in 1919 by Anton Drexler, Dietrich Eckart and Karl Harrer. Hitler had originally been sent by the army to check on the subversive activities of the party – and promptly joined it. He was soon head of propaganda, and the policy statement was contained in a speech made by him in the Hofbrauhaus in Munich. The main points were demands for a union of Germans in a Greater Germany, denial of citizenship for Jews, centralized power and the abrogation of the treaties of Versailles and St-Germain.

13 March 1920 *Freikorps* elements attempted a *putsch*.
Under Wolfgang Kapp and General von Luettwitz, they occupied Berlin in an attempt to overthrow the Weimar Government. The army refused to support the government, which fled to Dresden. The workers declared a general strike, and Kapp and von Luettwitz fled the country. The Communists tried to take advantage of the Kapp *Putsch* through uprisings of their own in various parts of the country, but these were quickly put down by the army and *Freikorps*. The *putsch* demonstrated how weak the government was; it was determined to do away with the *Freikorps*, but merely succeeded in driving them underground.

1 April 1920 German Workers' Party renamed National Socialist German Workers' Party (*Nationalsozialistische Deutsche Arbeiterpartei* or NSDAP).
Hitler left the army on this same day and took control of the NSDAP.

April 1921 Allies presented their reparations bill to Germany.

The Deutschmark began to slide.

3 May 1921 **Polish irregulars attempted to seize Upper Silesia.**
Under the Versailles terms this region was to be handed over to Poland, but in the face of German objections the Allies had agreed to a plebiscite of the population. Held in March, this revealed that 60 per cent wanted Upper Silesia to remain part of Germany. France refused to allow the German Army to turn back the Poles, and the Weimar Government had to rely on the *Freikorps*. In early July, after some fierce fighting, the Poles were forced to withdraw, but the *Freikorps* were once more driven underground which increased their loathing for the government. This manifested itself in the murder of a number of Weimar politicians, culminating on 24 June 1922 with that of Foreign Minister Walter Rathenau.

January 1923 **French troops occupied the Ruhr.**
This was due to Germany's failure to maintain reparations payments. The hijacking of Germany's key industrial region not only increased resentment against the Allies and gave the *Freikorps* another focus of attention, but also aggravated inflation, which rose from 7,000 marks to the dollar to 18,000, and by 1 August one million marks to the dollar.

26 September 1923 **State of emergency declared.**
The new chancellor, Gustav Stresemann, declared an end to passive resistance to the French in the Ruhr, a resumption of reparations payments and a state of emergency. Stresemann realized that Germany had reached economic breaking point and could no longer resist the Allies. He had support of all parties except the extreme left and right. In view of Stresemann's policy, the French had evacuated the Ruhr at the end of August. Resistance to Stresemann was strongest in Bavaria, and Hitler took advantage of this by forming an alliance of rightist groups dedicated to overthrowing Weimar and tearing up the Treaty of Versailles.

9 November 1923 **The Beer Hall *Putsch*.**
Hitler, supported by the eminent soldier, Erich Ludendorff, attempted a *coup d'état* in Munich. It misfired and was quickly suppressed by the army and police. The NSDAP was banned, and Hitler and some of his followers were put on trial. Hitler was sentenced to five years' imprisonment, later reduced to nine months, which he spent in the fortress of Landsberg, west of Munich. It was here that he wrote his political testimony, *Mein Kampf* (My Struggle). His 'martyrdom' provoked much sympathy for him in Bavaria.

April 1924 **Dawes Plan for repayment of reparations introduced.**
Named after Charles G. Dawes, Director of the US Bureau of the Budget, this eased the rate of payment, but it was still very high. Nevertheless, the German economy began to recover and support for the right began to fall.

20 December 1924 **Hitler released on probation from Landsberg.**
A month later the Bavarian Government removed the ban on the NSDAP. It was relaunched at a rally addressed by Hitler in Munich on **27 February 1925**. As a result the Bavarian Government banned Hitler from speaking in public. This, and lack of funds, severely restricted the growth of the NSDAP. The ban lasted until May 1927.

January 1927 **Inter-Allied Disarmament Commission withdrawn from Germany.**
This, together with Germany's admittance to the League of Nations, marked a further Allied easing of attitude towards her.

May 1928 **NSDAP won 12 seats out of 491 in the elections to the *Reichstag* (German parliament).**
This marked a major move in Hitler's policy away from extra-parliamentary means of gaining power to playing the Weimar Republic at its own game. He himself did not stand since technically he was still an Austrian citizen.

August 1929 **Allies agreed to the Young Plan.**
This further eased Germany's reparation payments; they also undertook to evacuate the Rhineland by June 1930. The period of repayment was extended until 1988, but this was attacked by the right in Germany, who saw it as merely prolonging Germany's 'enslavement'. The reverberations of the Wall Street Crash of October 1929, however, dramatically worsened Germany's economy leading to a resurgence of unrest.

14 September 1930 **The Nazis won 107 seats in the Reichstag elections.**
The election had been precipitated by controversy over how the economic crisis should be solved. The election campaign was marked by much violence between the Nazis and the Communists. Chancellor Heinrich Bruening managed to keep the Nazis out of government, but his deflationary policies dramatically increased unemployment and swelled the ranks of Nazi and Communist supporters. The Nazis were now the second largest party in the Reichstag.

13 March 1932 **Presidential elections.**
Hitler came second after Field Marshal Paul von Hindenburg; now finally a German citizen, he gained 30 per cent of the national vote. Because von Hindenburg failed to gain an outright majority, a second election was held on **10 April**. Von Hindenburg won 53 per cent, Hitler 36.8 per cent, the balance going to the Communist leader, Ernst Thaelmann.

16 June–9 July 1932 **Lausanne Conference.**
It was agreed that German reparations payments should be ended.

31 July 1932 **NSDAP became the largest party in Germany.**
Chancellor Bruening had been forced to resign because of his refusal to come to terms with Hitler. He was succeeded by Fritz von Papen, an unpopular choice with all parties, and an election had to be called. The NSDAP won 230 of the 609 seats. Hitler, however, refused to join any coalition. This forced another election, held on **6 November**. The NSDAP vote fell to 196 seats, reflecting an improved economic situation and von Papen's tough line at the Geneva Disarmament Conference. Von Hindenburg appointed General Kurt von Schleicher as Chancellor on 2 December 1932 after the latter asserted that the army would not support von Papen. Von Schleicher tried to split the more left-leaning Nazis under Gregor Strasser away from Hitler. He failed.

30 January 1933 **Hitler appointed Chancellor.**
Hitler isolated von Schleicher by making overtures to von Papen. Unable to form a government, von Schleicher was forced to rule by decree. Von Hindenburg, seeing the Hitler–von Papen alliance as a means of finally forming a government, sacked von Schleicher and appointed Hitler in his place, with von Papen as Vice-Chancellor.

27 February 1933 **The Reichstag Fire.**
The new government contained only two Nazis besides Hitler, and von Papen still hoped that he could isolate the Nazis. Hitler now called fresh elections for 5 March. On the evening of 27 February the Reichstag was set on fire. A half-crazed Dutchman, Marianus van der Lubbe, was accused, but the finger of suspicion has since been pointed at the Nazis. Hitler used the incident to claim that a Communist uprising was imminent and persuaded von Hindenburg to restrict civil and political liberties severely.

23 March 1933 **Enabling Act passed by the Reichstag.**
The Nazis secured only 44 per cent of the vote in the 5 March election, but enough to seize total power. Using the Communist scare, Hitler was able to get the Enabling Act passed. It virtually outlawed all political parties other than the NSDAP, and by the summer all official political opposition to Hitler had ceased. A dictatorship now existed in all but name.

2 August 1934 **Death of von Hindenburg.**
Hitler had now achieved absolute power.

Dress Rehearsals – Abyssinia and Spain · P16

Japanese Militarism

Japan had not played a major part in the First World War. True, in 1914 she had helped the Allies in capturing the German concessions in China and had seized the Marshall, Mariana and Caroline Islands in the Pacific; otherwise she had contributed little to victory over the Central Powers. The truth was that her victory over Russia in 1905 had made her determined, to use the words of Count Okuma, her premier in 1914, to become one of the 'governing nations' of the world. She saw the way to achieve this was through gaining administrative and economic control of China, already weakened by constant civil war. By threatening to leave the war she managed to persuade Britain, France and the USA to allow her to retain the former German concessions in the Shantung area on the Yellow Sea. This was confirmed, albeit with much heartsearching, at Versailles; Chinese protests were in vain. In America itself the surrender of Shantung to Japan was viewed with disgust, especially since Japan's attitude was beginning to appear to threaten US interests in the Pacific, and it was one reason why the USA did not join the League of Nations.

It was largely these fears that brought about the Washington Naval Conference of 1921–2, after which the USA felt well satisfied that a naval

JAPANESE AMBITIONS IN THE PACIFIC

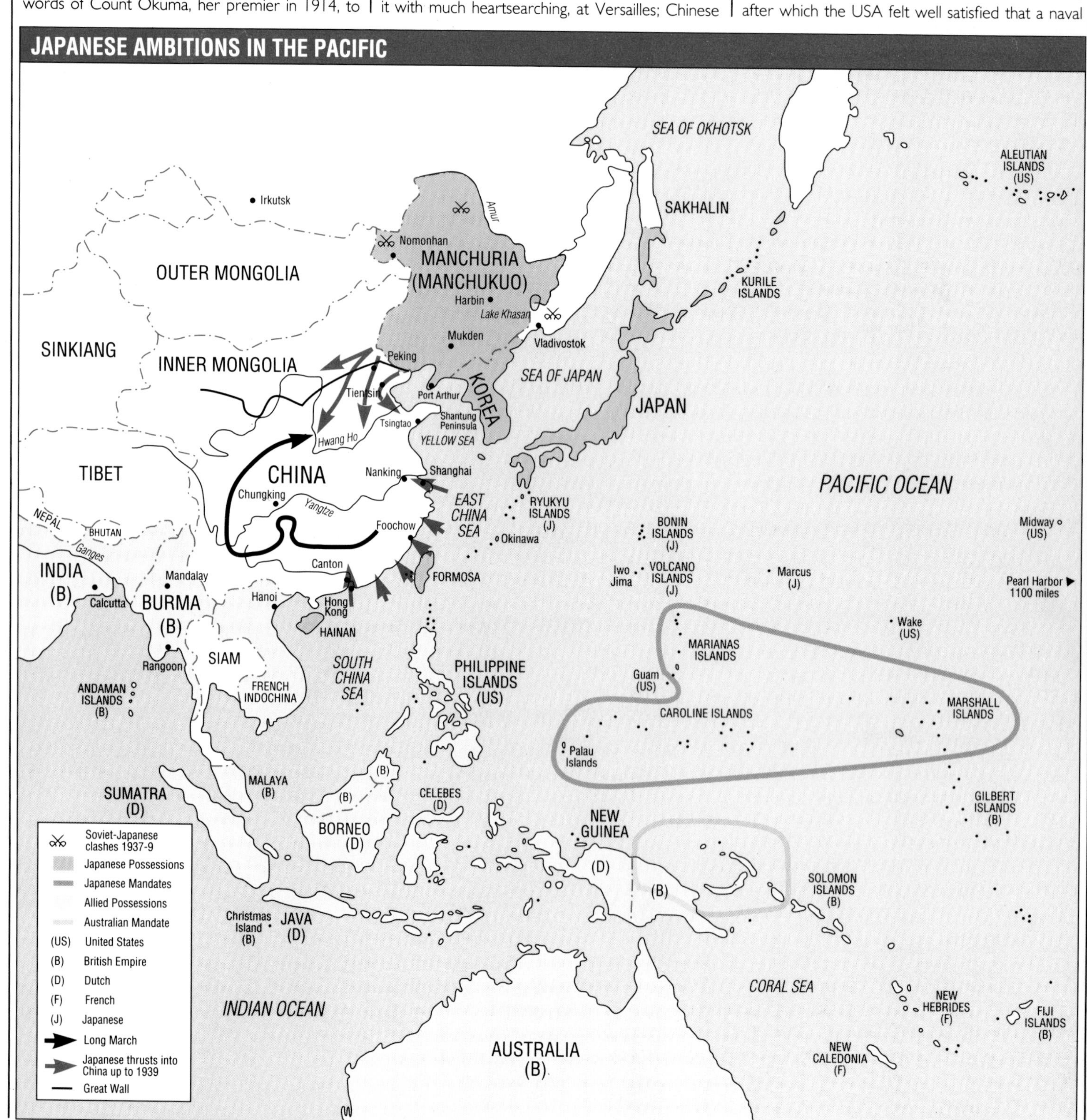

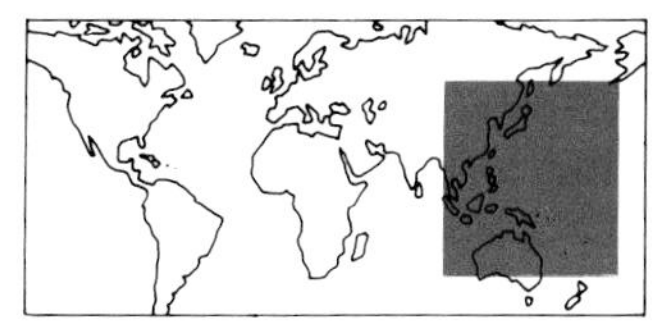

race with Japan seemed to have been prevented and that Japan had also agreed to recognize China's territorial integrity. Within Japan, however, the younger generation had been much impressed by the victory of the democracies over what they saw as the autocracies of the Central Powers. There was intense agitation to replace the corrupt feudal system of government, and in 1924 universal suffrage was introduced. It came too quickly. Corruption and *gekokujo* (political insubordination) were too deeply embedded, and political scandals quickly became commonplace. The upshot was to drive many Japanese to the extreme left or to right-wing nationalism.

One of Japan's growing problems was that the four main islands were undergoing a population explosion. This stretched the economy to the limit, creating unemployment and poverty, especially since Japan had few natural resources and was increasingly dependent on imports from abroad, particularly oil. To the young idealist nationalists, many of them junior army officers, the solution lay in Manchuria.

After Japan's 1904–5 war with Russia, influence over this northern region of China had been split between the two nations. It was rich in natural resources, and there had been some Japanese settlement in the southern half, which was garrisoned by the Japanese Kwantung Army. In her efforts to gain the respect of the Western democracies, Japan had been careful not to exploit her position there, and it was regarded as a virtual wilderness, dominated by a Chinese warlord, Marshal Chang.

4 June 1928 Marshal Chang killed.
His train was mined by a Kwantung Army staff officer. This had been organized by two Japanese colonels serving in the Kwantung Army, Kanji Ishihari and Seishiro Itagaki, who were determined to secure Manchuria for Japan and saw the removal of Chang as the first step.

19 September 1931 Japanese seized Mukden in Manchuria.
This marked the next step in Ishihari's and Itagaki's plan. A dynamite charge laid on the railway near a local Chinese Army barracks was the pretext that enabled Japanese troops to move in 'to restore law and order'. A Japanese general sent by the Tokyo government to bring the Kwantung Army under control was hoodwinked, but also supported the action. In spite of the Japanese Government's attempts to restrict the fighting, the Kwantung Army soon overran Manchuria.

17 October 1931 Arrest of members of the secret Cherry Society (*Sakurakai*).
The young Japanese army officers had formed a number of secret societies to further their nationalist cause. The Cherry Society planned to overthrow the Japanese Government, but its members were arrested before they could mount the *coup*. They had much public sympathy and were given only nominal sentences. There followed a number of assassinations of corrupt politicians and financiers, which culminated in the murder of Prime Minister Tsuyoshi Inukai on 15 May 1932. The assassins were brought to trial amid another wave of public sympathy for them, and they were given mild prison sentences.

27 March 1933 Japan left the League of Nations.
This showed up the weakness of the League. Only the USA and the Soviet Union were in a position to take action against the Japanese aggression in Manchuria, but neither was a member, although the USA did protest. Not until early 1933 did the League itself make a formal protest to Japan, and she promptly left it. By then Manchuria had been established as a puppet state under the name Manchukuo.

17 April 1934 Japan issued a statement that she alone was responsible for political relations and military security in the Far East.

29 December 1934 Japan threw off naval treaty restrictions.
The Japanese warned delegates at the London Naval Conference that after two more years Japan would no longer consider herself bound by naval treaty limitations.

26 February 1935 Another attempted military *coup* in Tokyo.
This involved a very much larger number of army officers than previous *coups*, and they killed or wounded a number of dignitaries. With the help of the navy, members of which were not involved, the *coup* was put down. The ringleaders were tried *in camera* and shot. Only the army could prevent further *coups*, but solely by supporting the demands of the nationalist junior officers. Thus the military influence on the government increased.

25 November 1936 Anti-Comintern Pact signed by Japan and Germany.
Having fallen out with the Western democracies and fearful of the Communist threat posed by Russia and Mao Tse-tung, whose Communists had been at war with Chiang Kai-shek's nationalist central Chinese government since 1927, Japan needed new allies. Italy joined the Pact on 6 November 1937.

7 July 1937 Beginning of Sino-Japanese War.
An exchange of fire at the Marco Polo Bridge, Peking, marked the outbreak of war. The Japanese had been allowed to station troops in Peking, as had other participant nations, since the 1900 Boxer Rebellion. It is possible that the first shots fired were accidental, but efforts to maintain a local cease-fire repeatedly failed. Kwantung Army units began to move into north China from Manchukuo, and Japan demanded that Chinese troops be withdrawn from the area. Chiang Kai-shek refused.

25 July 1937 First major clash between Japanese and Chinese forces at Langfang, south of Peking.
Next day Japan demanded the withdrawal of all Chinese troops from Peking. This was ignored, and Japanese reinforcements were sent there. Japanese troops began to overrun northern China.

August 1937 Sino-Soviet Non-Aggression Pact.
This reflected Soviet concern over the Anti-Comintern Pact and Japanese activities in China. On 22 September the Chinese Communists declared that they would support Chiang Kai-shek in his struggle against Japan.

9 November 1937 Japanese captured Shanghai.

12 December 1937 Japanese attacks on British and American ships.
Two British gunboats were fired on by Japanese shore batteries, and British merchant ships and other warships were attacked by Japanese aircraft, all near Nanking. The USS *Panay* was similarly attacked and sunk. President Roosevelt proposed to the British a joint naval blockade of Japan to cut off her supplies of raw materials, but the British feared that this would lead to war. In the event, the Japanese apologized to both governments, who accepted the apology.

14 December 1937 Nanking fell to the Japanese.
Six weeks of rape and pillage followed, which shocked the world at large.

August 1938 Chiang Kai-shek's government withdrew to Chungking.

October 1938 Japanese overran Canton.
They thereby isolated the British colony of Hong Kong. The British and French Governments sent protest notes, which were ignored.

December 1938 President Roosevelt made a loan of $25 million to Chiang Kai-shek, who continued to fight on.

May–September 1939 Russo-Japanese clashes.
Fighting broke out between the Japanese and Russians in the Nomonhan region of the Manchukuo–Outer Mongolia border. The Russians had signed a non-aggression pact with Outer Mongolia in 1936. In June 1937 there had been clashes with the Japanese on the River Amur, and the following year a more serious action in the Lake Khasan area. These new clashes were on an altogether wider scale and culminated in a massive armoured attack by the Russians led by General Georgi Zhukov on **20 August**, which resulted in a decisive defeat of the Japanese and a curtailment of their design to seize Mongolian territory.

Japan Threatens · P72

Dress Rehearsals – Abyssinia and Spain

ABYSSINIA

Italy, like other European nations, had tried to carve herself an empire in Africa in the late 19th century. She had, however, encountered a severe reversal in 1896 when her army had been defeated by the Abyssinians at Adowa. She was left with merely two small coastal colonies, Eritrea and Italian Somaliland. In 1911–12 she had waged a more successful war against Turkey and wrested what is now Libya from her. One of her disappointments at Versailles had been that she had not received any share of the ex-German territories in Africa, but once Mussolini had come to power he was determined that Italy should have her proper 'place in the sun'.

Mussolini planned to use his footholds in Africa to carve out an East African empire, and the key to this lay once more in Abyssinia. He hoped, however, to be able to exert Italian influence over that country through friendly overtures. Thus, he supported Abyssinia's application to join the League of Nations in 1923 and signed a treaty of friendship with her in 1928. Abyssinia's emperor, Haile Selassie, wanted, however, to open his country up not just to Italy, but to other nations as well, and this was increasingly resented by Mussolini, who now began to see war as his only option.

5 December 1934 **Italian and Abyssinian forces clashed at the oasis of Wal Wal inside Abyssinia.**
Italy demanded indemnity. On **30 December** Mussolini ordered his forces to begin preparing for an attack on Abyssinia which was to take place in autumn 1935, after the rainy season. Abyssinia first demanded arbitration and then, on **3 January 1935**, appealed to the League of Nations. Italy now agreed to arbitration, but reinforced her garrison in Eritrea. Further armed clashes ensued. Abyssinia once more appealed to the League (**17 March**), which was by now more concerned by German rearmament.

11–14 April 1935 **Stresa Conference.**
Attended by Britain, France and Italy, this was called in order to provide a united front against German rearmament – Abyssinia was not mentioned. France had earlier secretly indicated that she would not block Italian designs, and these factors led Mussolini to assume that he would be allowed a free hand.

24–26 June 1935 **British Foreign Secretary Anthony Eden, met Mussolini in Rome.**
The British Government had undergone a change of heart after Stresa and decided that Italy must not be allowed to break the League Covenant. Accordingly, Eden suggested that, in return for Abyssinia handing over the Ogaden region to Italy, Mussolini should cede the port of Zeila and a corridor from Abyssinia to it. This Mussolini dismissed out of hand.

11 September 1935 **British Foreign Secretary Sir Samuel Hoare declared in the League Assembly that his country would stand by the principle of collective resistance to aggression.**

3 October 1935 **Italian forces invaded Abyssinia.**

19 October 1935 **Limited economic sanctions against Italy.**
This was only agreed after some deliberation. Since the sanctions did not include coal or oil, two vital commodities for waging modern war, and Germany and the USA, not being members, were not bound by the sanctions, they had little effect but to drive Mussolini from Britain and France into Hitler's arms. The truth is that Britain and France considered themselves militarily too weak to be able to take tougher measures.

9 May 1936 **Mussolini proclaimed Italy's annexation of Abyssinia.**
The primitively armed Abyssinians had little chance against a modern European army, which employed tanks, aircraft, heavy artillery and even poison gas. On **2 May 1936** Haile Selassie and his family were forced to flee the country and sought exile in England. Three days later Italian troops entered his capital of Addis Ababa. Once again the League of Nations had failed to halt aggression.

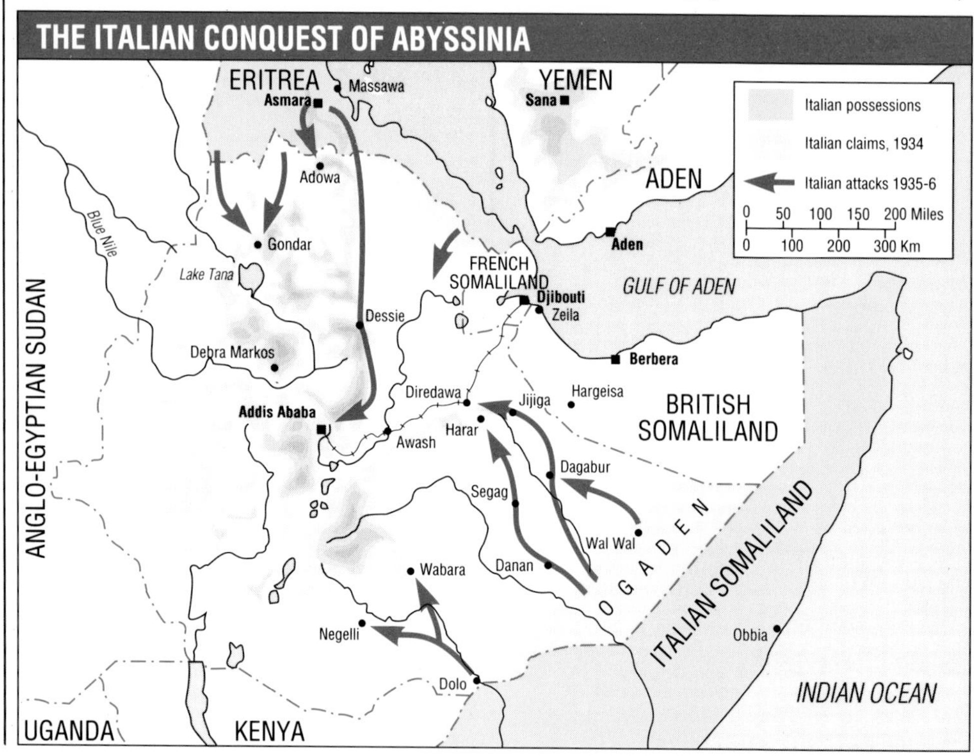

SPAIN

Although she had stayed out of the First World War, Spain was, like many other countries, beset by a series of weak governments at its conclusion. In September 1923, however, General Primo de Rivera had led a successful *coup* and became dictator of Spain. His rule lasted for seven years until increasing dissatisfaction with his absolute rule, which was aggravated by the Depression, forced his resignation in January 1930 and democracy returned to Spain. Then, in April 1931, left-wing election successes resulted in the abolition of the monarchy, King Alphonso XIII being forced into exile, and a republic was proclaimed.

During the next few years Spain was governed alternately by the left and the right, and there was growing unrest as political opinion became increasingly polarized. In February 1936 the parties of the left – Republicans, Socialists, Anarchists, Syndicalists and Communists – formed the Popular Front to fight the elections of that month. Ranged against them was the CEDA, a coalition of right-wing Catholic parties and the more extreme Falange, which had been founded by Primo de Rivera's son. The Popular Front achieved power, even though almost half the country voted for the Nationalist opposition, on a programme of previously agreed relatively moderate reform. One of the first steps that the new government took was to ban the Falange, and this provoked street fighting between left and right, left-inspired seizures of land and an increasing number of strikes. To the Nationalists, especially those in the army, it seemed as though the government were about to be hijacked by the Communists, and the only way to prevent this was armed rebellion.

17 July 1936 **Army garrisons in Spanish Morocco rebelled against the government.**
Within a week mainland garrisons had seized control of a number of cities, including Seville in the south, those in Galicia, Oviedo (capital of Asturias) and Saragossa (capital of Aragon). Some senior officers

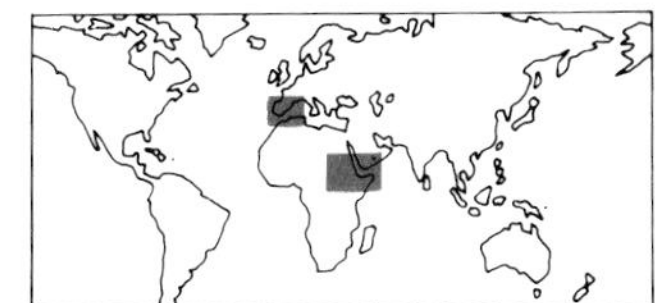

remained loyal to the government, however, and in Madrid and Barcelona the uprisings were quickly crushed. The Basque provinces in the north also remained firmly behind the government. Both sides quickly began to inflict atrocities on their opponents.

26 July 1936 Comintern agreed to furnish volunteers and money to support the Republic.

28 July 1936 German aircraft began to arrive in Morocco to airlift General Francisco Franco's Army of Africa to the Spanish mainland.
This had been the result of a written request from Franco to Hitler. Two days later Mussolini sent Italian aircraft to help as well.

2 August 1936 France announced a policy of non-intervention.
This was only after a split in Leon Blum's Popular Front cabinet, and it did not prevent French volunteers going to Spain to fight for the Republican cause.

15 August 1936 Britain announced an embargo on arms exports to Spain.

24 August 1936 Germany, Italy and Portugal agreed in principle to Anglo-French proposals for non-intervention.
A Non-Intervention Committee was set up and held its first meeting in London on 9 September. Germany and Italy, however, ignored the agreement and continued to supply *matériel* and men to support the Nationalists.

29 September 1936 Franco proclaimed Nationalist Head of State and Commander-in-Chief of the Nationalist armies.

6 October 1936 The Soviet Union warned that she would only be bound by non-intervention to the same extent as Germany and Italy.
She began to supply arms and military advisers to the Republicans.

6 November 1936 The Republican Government, withdrew to Valencia.
Madrid was now under direct threat from the Nationalist armies, but would hold out until almost the end of the war, its defenders being swelled at this time by the International Brigades made up of foreign volunteers.

18 November 1936 Germany and Italy recognized Franco's regime.

2 January 1937 Britain and Italy made a 'gentleman's agreement' not to upset the status quo in the Mediterranean.
No mention was made of Italian 'volunteers' being sent to Spain.

THE SPANISH CIVIL WAR

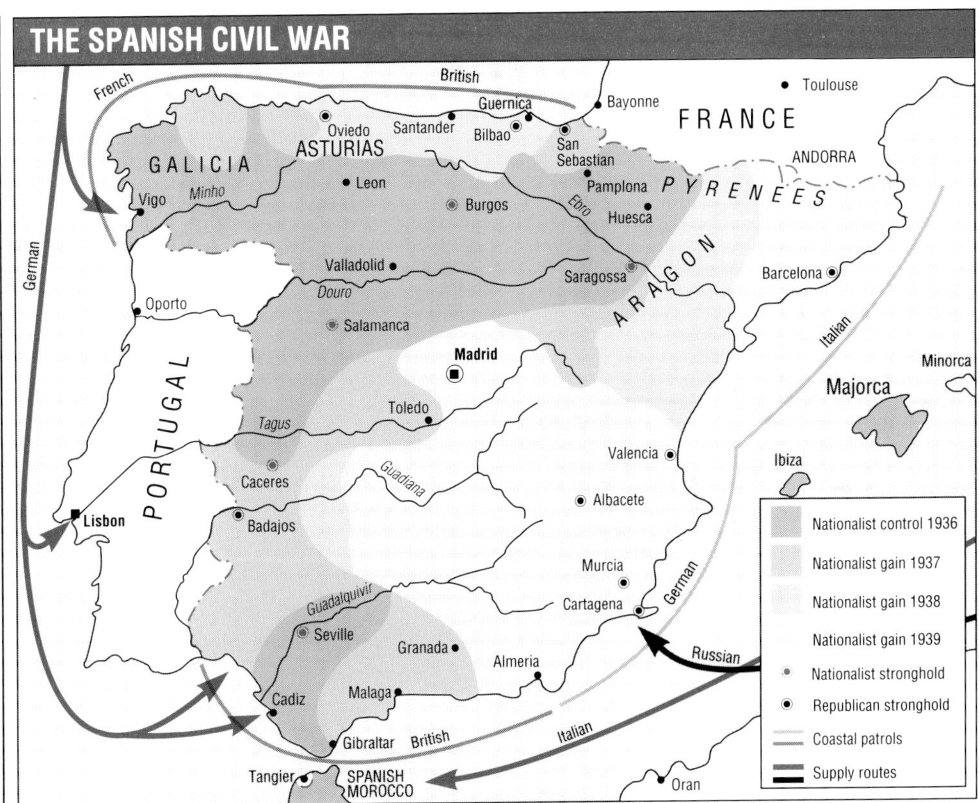

19 April 1937 New non-intervention measures were put into effect.
All foreign troops were to be withdrawn from Spain, the borders with Spain watched by international observers and Spain's coasts were to be patrolled, in the Mediterranean by the German and Italian navies, and the Atlantic by the British and French navies. Germany and Italy made it clear that they would not withdraw their troops until Franco's victory was assured. The measures ignored aircraft; there were attacks on ships, and external support for both sides was not halted. The Noyon Agreement between the Mediterranean powers in September did, however, reduce naval piracy.

26 April 1937 Bombing of Guernica.
German aircraft of the Kondor Legion bombed the Basque town of Guernica causing 6,000 deaths. This gave rise to revulsion in much of the world and inspired one of Picasso's most famous paintings.

1 July 1937 The Spanish bishops endorsed Franco's regime.
The Vatican made a similar move on 28 August.

29 October 1937 The Republican Government moved to Valencia.
By now the Nationalists had secured all but northern Spain and some parts of the south-east.

28 November 1937 Franco began to blockade the Spanish coast.

30 January 1938 Franco formed his first ministry.

5 July 1938 The Non-Intervention Committee approved a plan to withdraw volunteers from Spain.
This was accepted by the Republicans but not by Franco. On 4 October they withdrew their foreign volunteers from the front line, and shortly afterwards they left Spain. By this stage it could only be a matter of time before Franco had total control over the country.

5 February 1939 The Republican Government crossed the Pyrenees into France, accompanied by the beginning of a flood of refugees.

27 February 1939 British Prime Minister Neville Chamberlain recognized Franco's government.

28 March 1939 Madrid finally fell to the Nationalists.

31 March 1939 Last Republican resistance ceased.

1 April 1939 Franco declared the end of the Civil War.
His government was recognized by the USA.

Apart from being a tragedy for Spain, which still bears its scars, the Spanish Civil War finally showed that the League of Nations was no longer a world force. Germany, Italy and the Soviet Union had, as much as anything, used it as a laboratory for the testing of new weapons, and the failure of Britain and France to act more positively merely served to hasten Europe's descent into major war.

Lebensraum and the Path to War · P18

Lebensraum and the Path to War

EUROPE OF THE AGGRESSORS

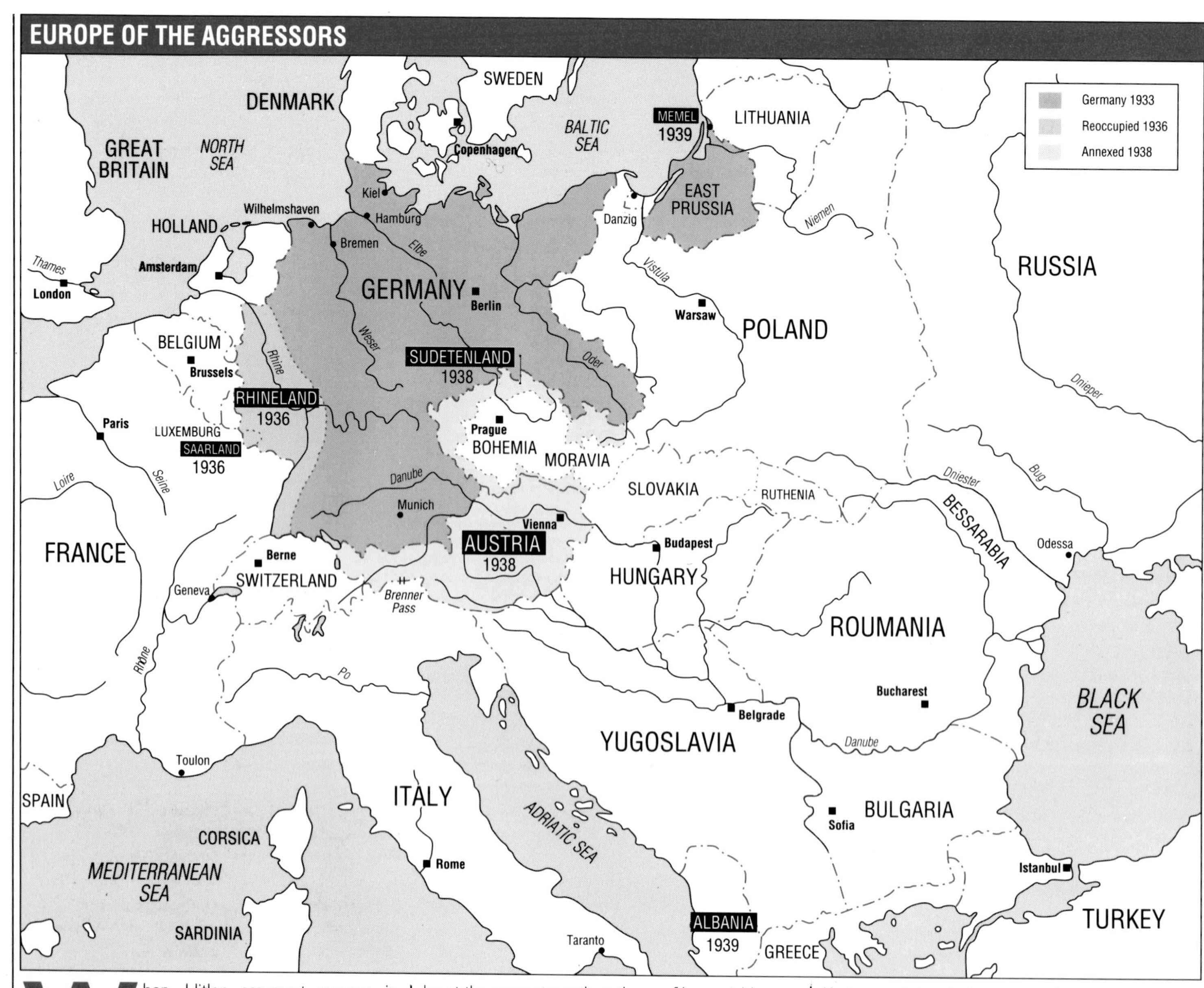

When Hitler assumed power in Germany in 1933 and made it clear that he would brook no opposition, the reaction of the world was generally muted. Indeed, there was a general feeling that Germany had suffered enough and that it was time for her to be allowed to attain at least something of her former status. Hitler, however, wanted more than this. He was still firmly wedded to the concept of a Greater Germany and provision of sufficient *Lebensraum* (living space), for the German people meant more than mere restoration of Germany's 1914 borders. He also appreciated that he would require strong armed forces to support his foreign policy.

14 October 1933 **Germany left the League of Nations.**
This was caused by Germany's failure to obtain agreement at Geneva that her armed forces should be at the same strength as those of her neighbours, especially France. Even though Hitler was still bound by Versailles it removed one brake on the increasing of his military strength.

26 January 1934 **Germany signed a ten-year non-aggression pact with Poland.**
Hitler had two motives for this: he wanted to disguise his aggressive intentions and also to draw Poland away from her alliance with France.

25 July 1934 **Chancellor Engelbert Dollfuss of Austria murdered by Nazis.**
This was a setback in Hitler's plans to unite Austria with Germany. Dollfuss, fearful of threats from both left and right, had ruled Austria without a parliament since 1932. In February 1934 he had, with much severity, put down a suspected workers' uprising in Vienna. Hitler had encouraged a Nazi *coup*, but in the event it was bungled, and government forces under Kurt von Schuschnigg retained control. Mussolini made clear his opposition to a Nazi takeover by deploying troops to the Brenner Pass, and Hitler was forced to back down.

13 January 1935 **Plebiscite held in the Saarland.**
The result was an overwhelming vote for return to Germany. On **1 March** Hitler sent his own 'household troops', the SS Leibstandarte Adolf Hitler, to the Saar to welcome it back into the fold.

9 March 1935 **Hitler notified the Western Powers of the existence of a German Air Force (Luftwaffe).**
It had been suspected for more than a year that Hitler was creating this in direct contravention of Versailles. On **16 March** Hitler announced that the army would be increased to 36 divisions. While the existence of the Luftwaffe caused Britain to begin to expand her air force, she did not see the increase in

P16 · Dress Rehearsals – Abyssinia and Spain

the army as such a threat. France did, but was not prepared to condemn it without British support.

18 June 1935 **Anglo-German Naval Agreement signed.**
By this Germany agreed to restrict her surface fleet to 35 per cent of that of the Royal Navy and to parity in submarines. This reassured Britain that there would be no naval race but angered France, who viewed this as another contravention of Versailles.

7 March 1936 **Germany reoccupied the Rhineland.**
Hitler took advantage of the fact that Britain and Italy, guarantors of Locarno, which confirmed that the Rhineland should remain demilitarized, and France were all preoccupied with the situation in Abyssinia. Even so, it was a military gamble since Hitler had few troops available, and if positive action had been taken against him he would have been forced to climb down. As it was, it merely served to boost his confidence.

1 November 1936 **Hitler and Mussolini signed the Berlin-Rome Axis.**
This marked the failure of Anglo-French efforts to keep Italy away from Germany. It was also the end of attempts to maintain Versailles. From now on the prime aim of the Western democracies would be to prevent – at almost any cost – war breaking out in Europe.

13 March 1938 **Anschluss (Union) between Austria and Germany proclaimed.**
Chancellor Kurt von Schuschnigg of Austria was determined, like Dollfuss before him, to keep his country out of Hitler's clutches. He had been somewhat reassured by the Austro-German agreement of 1936 when Hitler promised to respect Austria's independence and not interfere in her internal affairs, but Hitler had only done this to mollify Mussolini. In January 1938 the existence of a Nazi plot in Austria was discovered. Von Schuschnigg met Hitler on 12 February to complain, but was treated to a diatribe on his treatment of Austrian Nazis. Tension mounted and von Schuschnigg was forced to announce a plebiscite on whether his people wished Austria to remain independent. This was to be held on 13 March. Fearful that it might produce the wrong result, Hitler ordered his troops to cross the border on 12 March. His supporters welcomed him and Austria lost her independence.

20 May 1938 **In the face of German threats, Czechoslovakia mobilized her army.**
Hitler's next target was the Sudetenland, the most westerly region of Czechoslovakia, which contained a sizeable German minority. He used Konrad Henlein, the Sudetenland Germans' leader, as his tool, getting him to demand full autonomy for the region and a revision of Czech foreign policy. Hitler also pretended that he was prepared to take military action. President Hacha of Czechoslovakia refused to be intimidated, and hence the mobilization of his comparatively large army. Even though neither Britain nor France seemed prepared to go to war over Czechoslovakia, Hitler was sufficiently deterred not to take immediate action, although he made it plain to his generals that he was determined to resolve the problem by 1 October.

29 September 1938 **Munich Pact signed.**
Tension between Germany and Czechoslovakia had continued as the summer wore on. British Prime Minister Chamberlain, fearful that Hitler's continued demands would lead to general war, flew to Germany on **12 September** and obtained Hitler's assurance that provided he could have the Sudetenland he would make no more territorial demands. Chamberlain managed to sell this to the French, who told the reluctant Czechs that they would withdraw their support unless the German parts of the Sudetenland were surrendered to Germany. Hitler, however, wanted the whole region, and this was granted at Munich over the heads of the Czechs. Britain, France, Germany and Italy signed the agreement. Chamberlain flew back to London and declared 'peace in our time' to the joy of the British people. On 1 October German troops entered the Sudetenland.

28 October 1938 **German demands on Poland.**
Hitler demanded that the Poles restore Danzig to Germany and the right to construct road/rail links through the Polish Corridor to East Prussia. The Poles refused.

15 March 1939 **Dismemberment of Czechoslovakia.**
After Hitler had seized the Sudetenland, two other Czech provinces, Slovakia and Ruthenia, began to create difficulties for the Czech Government. President Hacha was eventually forced to sack their premiers. One of them, Monsignor Tiso of Slovakia, complained to Berlin, and Hitler demanded independence for Slovakia. This brought Hacha to Berlin, but he was browbeaten as von Schuschnigg had been and forced to place his country under German protection. Bohemia and Moravia were annexed by Germany; Slovakia was made a protectorate and Ruthenia was handed over to Hungary. This merely produced a weak British protest even though Hitler had gone back on his word at Munich.

21 March 1939 **Hitler reiterated his Polish demands.**
They were again turned down.

23 March 1939 **German troops occupied Memel.**
This lay on the border of East Prussia and Lithuania. Poland warned Hitler that any similar attempt to seize Danzig would mean war. This was reinforced on **31 March** when Britain and France declared that they would stand by Poland.

7 April 1939 **Mussolini, jealous of Hitler's successes, sent his troops into Albania.**
This country had been very much under Italian influence since the civil war of 1925, in which Italy had intervened.

15 April 1939 **President Roosevelt sought assurances from Germany and Italy that they would not attack other European countries.**
Such assurances were not forthcoming. Hitler and Mussolini knew that Roosevelt's hands were tied by the 1935–7 Neutrality Acts, which forbade the USA giving help to either side in the event of war.

18 April 1939 **USSR proposed a ten-year alliance with Britain and France.**
Negotiations on this continued throughout the summer, but the main stumbling-block was mutual Polish-Soviet suspicion.

28 April 1939 **Hitler denounced his 1934 non-aggression pact with Poland and repeated his demand for Danzig.**

22 May 1939 **Italy and Germany signed the Pact of Steel.**
This was a guarantee to support each other in any future war.

23 August 1939 **Germany and the USSR signed a non-aggression pact in Moscow.**
This was a crippling blow to the hopes of Britain and France and marked Poland's death-knell, since one of the clauses agreed a split of the country between Germany and the USSR. It also gave Russia a free hand in the Baltic states and Bessarabia, both of which she coveted. Hitler now gave orders for the invasion of Poland on **26 August**.

25 August 1939 **Britain signed a formal alliance with Poland.**
The British Government now accepted that Hitler could be appeased no longer. This treaty and Mussolini's complaint that he was not yet ready for war caused Hitler to cancel the invasion at the last minute.

27–29 August 1939 **Britain and France tried to persuade Poland to negotiate with Germany, but she was adamant.**

31 August 1939 **Hitler received the Polish Ambassador to Berlin.**
This was mainly to appease Mussolini, who was trying to establish a peace formula. The talks lasted no longer than a few minutes: Hitler had already made up his mind to invade next day.

Military Strengths · P20

2 JUST A EUROPEAN WAR, September 1939 to June 1940

SEPTEMBER 1939

Military Strengths

At the outbreak of war Hitler was in danger of finding himself involved in what the Germans had traditionally feared: war on two fronts. He was committed to attack Poland, but in the west were Poland's allies, Britain and France. Germany's ally, Mussolini, had made it plain that he was not yet ready for war and could not therefore be counted on for military support. This left Germany, on the surface at least, numerically inferior to the combined strengths of Poland and her allies. She did, however, enjoy a number of very significant advantages as the following survey will show.

GERMANY

Hitler had come to power in 1933 determined to break the shackles of Versailles and rearm Germany. In **February 1934** he had given orders that the armed forces were to be strong enough to defend Germany within five years and by 1942 capable of offensive action. The army was to be increased from 100,000 to 300,000 men.

16 March 1935 Conscription reintroduced.

By now the army had a strength of 27 divisions, made up of volunteers. With conscription it was to be increased to 36 divisions. At the outbreak of war the army could field a total of 106 divisions, of which 55 were first line, capable of mobilizing within 48 hours. The remainder were reliant on trained reservists. The standing army included six Panzer (armoured) divisions, and it was on these that the Germans had based their new form of warfare.

Blitzkrieg had its origins on the Western Front in 1916–18 in an endeavour to break the deadlock of trench warfare. While the Allies introduced the tank, the Germans developed the *Sturmtruppen* (storm troops), who relied on infiltration tactics. After the war a number of military theorists, led by the Britons Major-General J. F. C. Fuller and Captain B. H. Liddell Hart, conceived the idea of high-speed warfare based on the tank and other armoured vehicles. The Germans seized on these ideas and refined them. *Blitzkrieg* or 'Lightning War' was based on the concept of fighting a battle at such a pace that the enemy had no chance to seize the initiative and his command and control systems became paralyzed. The idea was for the Panzer divisions to break through weak points in the enemy lines and create huge pockets of enemy, which would then be reduced by the foot-marching infantry divisions following up behind. It must be stressed, however, that at no stage in the war was more than a proportion of the German Army mechanized and by far the larger part remained reliant on its feet and horse-drawn transport.

A crucial element of the *Blitzkrieg* doctrine was the German Air Force (Luftwaffe). Hitler had conceived grandiose plans for it from the start. By April 1936 he was demanding a strength of 12,300 aircraft. The emphasis was to be on medium bombers, which he saw as an instrument for threatening neighbouring countries. Spain was an ideal laboratory for testing Luftwaffe technical and tactical doctrine, and one of the weapons systems tested there was the Ju 87 dive-bomber, which was built into the *Blitzkrieg* doctrine as a form of aerial artillery to give close support to the tanks as they broke through the enemy positions. On 1 September 1939 the Luftwaffe had 4,093 frontline aircraft, of which 75 per cent were serviceable. The total included equal quantities of bombers and fighters (mainly the Me 109), some 1,170 each, and 400 dive-bombers.

The German Navy was slightly the 'poor relation'. Up until 1938 the assumption was that Germany would not find herself at war with Britain, the major naval power in Europe, and the 1935 Anglo-German Naval Treaty served to reinforce this. Consequently the emphasis was placed on surface units to give 'status'. In 1938, in the light of growing Anglo-French protests at Hitler's expansionist policies, there was a change of heart and a new plan was drawn up – Plan 'Z'. This called for further capital ships, but also a dramatic increase in U-boat (submarine) construction. The programme would not, however, be completed until 1948. Thus, by September 1939, it had hardly got under way. The total strength of the navy was five battleships, two heavy cruisers, six light cruisers, 34 destroyers/torpedo-boats and 57 U-boats. Significantly, it possessed no aircraft carriers and, indeed, no naval air arm, since all air operations were retained firmly in the hands of Hermann Goering's Luftwaffe.

POLAND

On its own, Poland stood little chance against the military power that Germany could range against her. She was not a rich country and could not afford much in the way of modern armaments.

The army had a standing force of 23 infantry divisions, which could be quickly increased to 30 on mobilization, the equivalent of an armoured brigade with some 300 mainly light tanks (10 per cent of what Germany possessed, although 90 per cent of these were also light tanks), and 37 horsed cavalry regiments. The artillery was entirely horse-drawn and of light calibre. In addition there was a frontier defence organization, which lacked any heavy weapons, and the National Defence, which was a pool of reservists and as yet unconscripted youths.

The air force was in an even more parlous state. It had only 420 operational aircraft, the majority obsolete or obsolescent types. The anti-aircraft defences were also meagre and badly deployed. The navy, with the Baltic as its only interest, was also small, with four destroyers, one minelayer, six minesweepers and five submarines.

FRANCE

Defence policy in France after 1918 had been dominated by the awful losses she had suffered in the First World War and the determination that this should never happen again. Accordingly, in 1927 it was decided to construct a line of fortifications along the Franco-German border. Work began in earnest two years later under the direction of the Minister of War, André Maginot, after whom the line was named. By 1936 the bulk of the work had been completed. In May 1938, in order to deter any French attack while they dealt with Czechoslovakia, the Germans began work on a similar fortified line, the *Westwall* or Siegfried Line.

The Maginot Line so dominated French strategy that it suffocated progressive military thinking. True, France had maintained an interest in tanks and could match the Germans in numbers at the outbreak of war, but when a junior officer, Charles de Gaulle, proposed in a book in 1937 that a professional armoured force be formed, his ideas were dismissed, although later there would be a gradual change of heart. Nevertheless, on paper at least, France's military strength on the eve of war looked impressive. She had 65 active divisions, including one armoured division then being formed, and two motorized. A further 25 divisions could be mobilized very quickly and an additional twenty in due course.

France's air force was also seemingly large, with 1,300 aircraft. However, a significant proportion were non-operational, and there were few modern types. The main problem was that the French aircraft industry had become hopelessly inefficient and, although it was nationalized in 1936, it was only producing 600 aircraft per year compared with the Luftwaffe's 3,000.

The navy, however, was in better shape, with five battleships, two battlecruisers, one aircraft carrier, eighteen cruisers, 28 destroyers, 71 submarines and a number of smaller craft. Most of the ships were modern and the crews well trained.

GREAT BRITAIN

Like France, Britain had no wish to repeat the experiences of 1914–18. Her defence policy throughout the 1920s had been based on the premise that there would be no major war in Europe for ten years, and this was renewed every year. Priority of defence lay with her empire. It was only at the end of 1935 that a cautious programme of rearmament was instituted, and then priority went overwhelmingly to the Royal Air Force.

The British Army, apart from the years 1916–18, had always been a volunteer force, and consequently was small compared to Continental armies. True, in April 1939, in view of the worsening situation in Europe, limited conscription had been introduced, but its effects had hardly made themselves felt by September. Leaving aside commitments in the Middle East, India and elsewhere, the core of the army was built around four Regular infantry divisions and an armoured division still in the early stages of formation (a second had been formed in Egypt). In February 1939 the government had decided that

P18 · Lebensraum and the Path to War

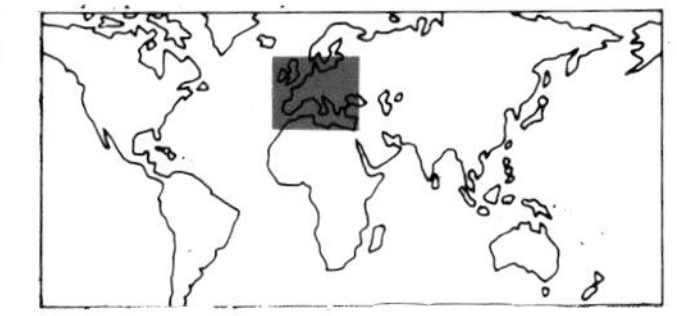

these, together with four Territorial Army (TA) divisions, should be committed to the Continent in the event of war. This was a marked improvement from earlier policy which, under the so-called Doctrine of Limited Liability, had permitted no more than two divisions to be sent because of fears of British lives being sacrificed in another European blood-bath. Even so, it was a relatively small contribution and, because the army had the lowest priority in terms of rearmament, this new British Expeditionary Force (BEF) was still in the process of re-equipping.

The RAF had been subjected to a series of expansion plans from 1935 onwards. Initially the emphasis had been on bombers on the supposition that 'the bomber will always get through' and that quantity was more important than quality in order to match the numerical strength of the Luftwaffe, but gradually the proportion of fighters had been increased. On 31 August 1939 the RAF had 920 bombers of various types, but all medium or light, with some 200 of these earmarked to accompany the BEF to France. Of the remainder, half were non-operational since they were being used for training. It had some 770 fighters, including an increasing number of Hurricanes and Spitfires, and some 800 other types (maritime patrol, reconnaissance, etc.). In total it was numerically two-thirds the strength of the Luftwaffe.

The Royal Navy traditionally had had pride of place and was still in 1939 the largest in the world. It had twelve battleships, three battlecruisers, seven aircraft carriers, fifteen heavy and 45 light cruisers, 58 submarines (following the terms of the Anglo-German Naval Agreement) and numerous smaller surface craft. There was also an impressive programme of new construction in progress. It must be remembered, though, that the Royal Navy had worldwide commitments, and in the event of a purely European war it looked to the French Navy to help contain the Germans.

Britain could also call upon her empire resources, but time was needed to mobilize these.

THE PRINCIPAL EUROPEAN ANTAGONISTS: September 1939

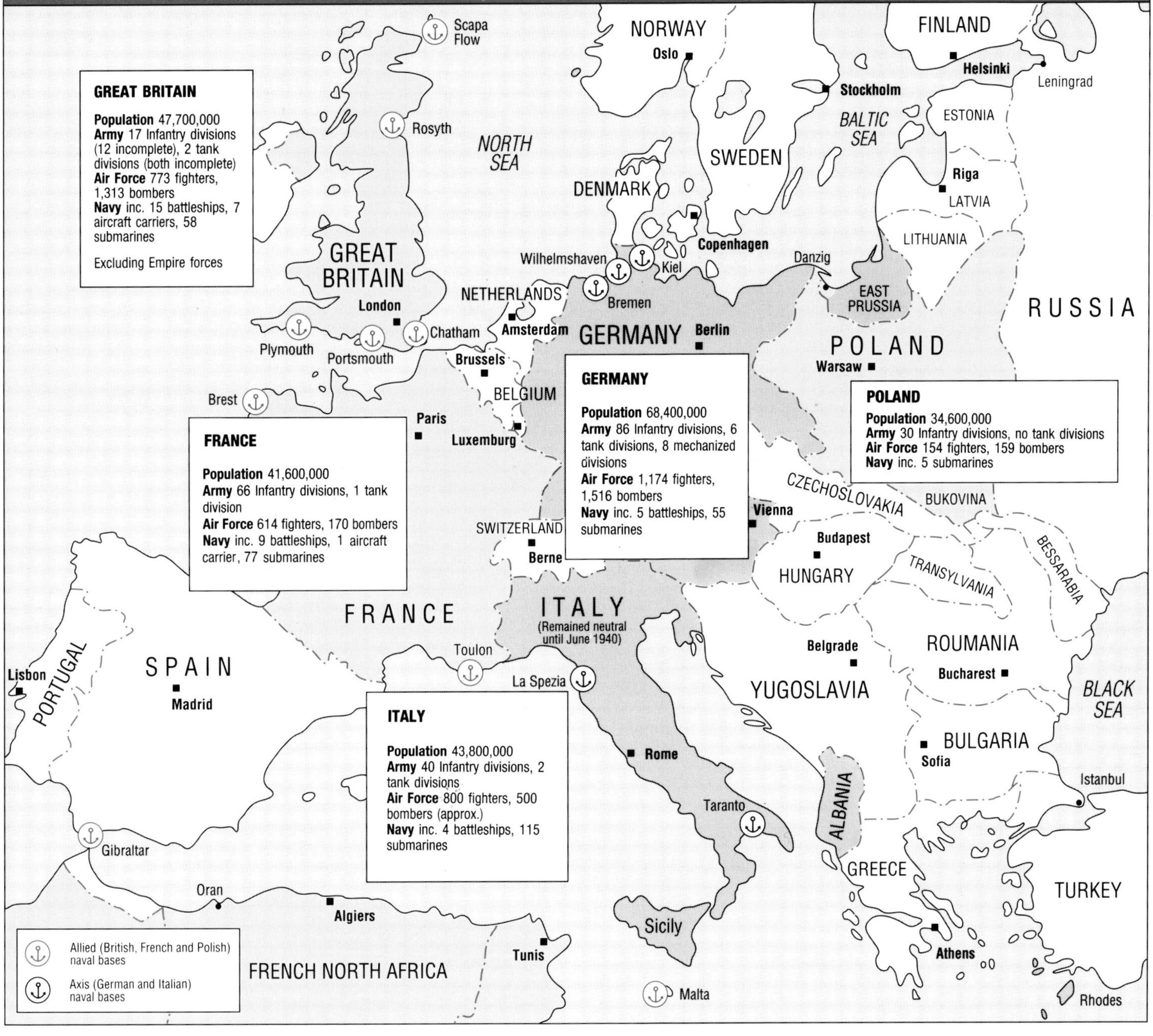

GREAT BRITAIN

Population 47,700,000
Army 17 Infantry divisions (12 incomplete), 2 tank divisions (both incomplete)
Air Force 773 fighters, 1,313 bombers
Navy inc. 15 battleships, 7 aircraft carriers, 58 submarines

Excluding Empire forces

FRANCE

Population 41,600,000
Army 66 Infantry divisions, 1 tank division
Air Force 614 fighters, 170 bombers
Navy inc. 9 battleships, 1 aircraft carrier, 77 submarines

GERMANY

Population 68,400,000
Army 86 Infantry divisions, 6 tank divisions, 8 mechanized divisions
Air Force 1,174 fighters, 1,516 bombers
Navy inc. 5 battleships, 55 submarines

POLAND

Population 34,600,000
Army 30 Infantry divisions, no tank divisions
Air Force 154 fighters, 159 bombers
Navy inc. 5 submarines

ITALY

Population 43,800,000
Army 40 Infantry divisions, 2 tank divisions
Air Force 800 fighters, 500 bombers (approx.)
Navy inc. 4 battleships, 115 submarines

ITALY (Remained neutral until June 1940)

Allied (British, French and Polish) naval bases
Axis (German and Italian) naval bases

Poland

Hitler's plan for the invasion of Poland, *Fall Weiss* (Plan 'White'), had been drawn up during the summer, once it was clear that Poland was not going to submit to his demands without a fight. It called for twin simultaneous thrusts. The first, mounted from Pomerania and East Prussia, was to clear the Polish Corridor and then turn south-east, while the other was launched from north of the Carpathian Mountains and was to link up with the northern thrust in the Warsaw area. Speed was crucial – Poland must be defeated before the Western Allies could react, for two-thirds of the German forces were committed to Poland, leaving the remainder to guard Germany's western frontier. Mobilization took place, mainly under the cover of manoeuvres, during August, and all was ready by 26 August, eve of Hitler's original start-date.

When, on that same day, Hitler ordered a postponement, some units only received the message a mere hour or so before they were due to go into action, and one small group with a special mission to seize a Polish railway station and nearby tunnel in south-west Poland before the main attack went in never got the order. They went ahead with their mission and shots were fired, arguably the first of the Second World War, and casualties were caused. A truce was arranged next day and they were returned to Germany. If the Poles had not already realized Hitler's intention to invade, this was the clearest possible indicator. The Polish dispositions played into the German hands. They had adopted a linear defence along the frontier, hoping to provide depth through the mobilization of the National Defence. This gave ideal prospects for the double envelopment tactics enshrined in the *Blitzkrieg* doctrine. The Poles, however, were very much relying on a promise made to them by the French that they would attack Germany within fifteen days of an attack on Poland.

THE CONQUEST OF POLAND: The German Strategic Plan

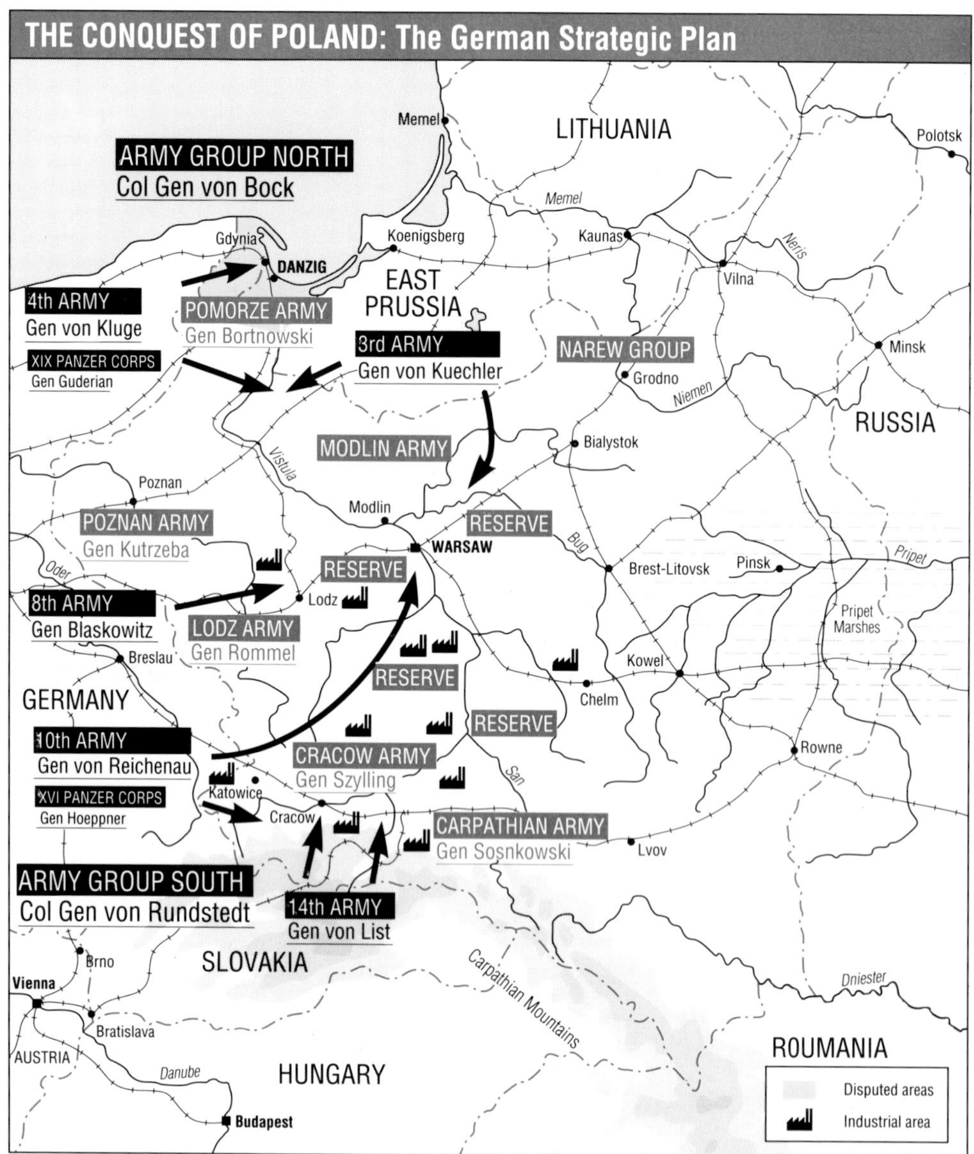

1 September 1939 At 0445 hours German troops crossed the frontier into Poland.
The invasion had been preceded the previous evening by attacks on German installations close to the border by men dressed in Polish uniforms. These men were actually concentration camp inmates, the operation having been organized by the SS to give Hitler a pretext to invade that he could show the world.

The prime task of the Luftwaffe was to destroy the Polish Air Force on the ground. The Poles had, however, deployed their aircraft to satellite airfields, which initially saved them, but their technical and numerical inferiority, together with Luftwaffe attacks on communications, which starved them of fuel, meant that the Germans quickly gained air supremacy.

The British and French governments, instead of immediately offering military support, looked to Mussolini who had proposed an international conference to revise the Versailles terms.

2 September Hitler indicated to the Western Allies that he would withdraw from Poland provided that he was allowed to retain Danzig and the Polish Corridor. This was dismissed and a joint ultimatum was given to Germany to withdraw her troops within twelve hours or find herself at war with Britain and France.

3 September Britain and France declared war on Germany.
This also brought in the British Empire, apart from Canada and South Africa, who wished to debate the issue in their parliaments. That evening the British liner SS *Athenia*, with several US citizens on board, was sunk in error by the German U-boat *U-30*.

4 September Japan declared her neutrality.
By now the Germans had cut off the Polish Corridor in the north and in the south had crossed the River Pilica, 50 miles into Poland. The Polish armies were becoming isolated from one another and the mounting of co-ordinated counter-attacks was becoming increasingly difficult.

5 September The USA declared its neutrality.
The sinking of *Athenia* had increased anti-German feeling, but isolationism was still strong.

6 September South Africa declared war on Germany.
The Polish forces began to withdraw to the line Narew–Vistula–San.

7 September French forces penetrated German territory in the Saarland.
Nine divisions were used, but their advance was very slow and no effort was made to attack the *Westwall* itself.

10 September Canada declared war on Germany.
This was after a formal parliamentary debate.

P20 · Military Strengths

12 September Desperate battle opened between the Germans and the Poznan Army, which was trying to break out of encirclement across the River Bzura. After six days it was forced to surrender and the Germans netted 170,000 prisoners.

15 September Converging German armies surrounded Warsaw.
Next day they demanded that Warsaw surrender. When it refused the city was subjected to a massive air and artillery bombardment.

17 September The Soviet Union invaded Poland.
At the same time they declared that Poland no longer existed as an independent state. The Polish Government fled across the border into Roumania. Next day its members were interned as a result of Soviet pressure.

19 September Soviet and German troops met at Brest-Litovsk.
Hitler entered Danzig in triumph and made a seemingly conciliatory speech directed at Britain and France.

22 September Soviet troops entered Lvov.
Polish troops began to fight their way into Roumania and Hungary, both still neutral countries.

27 September Warsaw surrendered.
On the same day Hitler summoned his generals to a meeting in Berlin. He informed them of his intention to invade France and asked them how long a preparation period was required.

28 September Ten Polish divisions, encircled in the Modlin area since the 10th, finally surrendered.

29 September The German-Soviet discussions began.
Foreign ministers von Ribbentrop and Molotov met in Moscow to modify the non-aggression pact between the two countries. It was agreed that the Soviet Union would be given a free hand in Lithuania and would retain Belorussia and Ukrainian Poland. In exchange, Germany was given the whole of ethnic Poland.

30 September General Wladyslaw Sikorski formed a Polish government-in-exile in Paris.
This was the first of a number of governments-in-exile to be formed as a result of German conquests. Sikorski went on to form an army of Polish expatriates and those who had managed to escape from Poland; this was placed under French command and was equipped by them.

1 October Fighting on the Polish coast ended.
Three Polish destroyers and two submarines managed to escape to the West. The Soviet Union signed a treaty of 'mutual assistance' with Estonia, which enabled her to occupy Estonian naval bases. The French began a voluntary withdrawal in the Saarland and by 4 October were back behind the security of the Maginot Line.

5 October Soviet-Latvian Mutual Assistance Treaty.
This enabled the Soviet Union to establish military bases in that country. A similar treaty was signed with Lithuania on 10 October and this marked the end of all three Baltic states' independence.

6 October The last Polish resistance ended.
The Polish campaign had been a devastating demonstration of the effectiveness of *Blitzkrieg*. Although the Poles had fought with great gallantry, they proved to be no match for the German Panzer columns and their accompanying Stukas. The casualties revealed the extent of the victory. The total German casualties – killed, wounded, missing – were 40,000. They captured no less than 700,000 Poles; no figures exist for the number of killed and wounded, which included many civilians, especially in the bombing of Warsaw. The Soviets captured a further 217,000 men.

The only way in which Poland could have been saved would have been if the Western Allies had made a determined attack across Germany's western border. Twenty years of purely defensive thinking had, however, left them ill equipped, not just materially but also psychologically, to do this. As it was, they did little to assimilate the lessons of the Polish campaign, and this was to prove fatal eight months later.

Poland herself now fell under the dark shadows of Nazi and Stalinist rule. The two regimes were equally determined that the country should never again enjoy total independence and embarked on wholesale purges of the ruling classes and intelligentsia. In German-occupied Poland another sinister policy was also quickly put into effect: this was the persecution of Poland's large Jewish population.

THE CONQUEST OF POLAND: The First Blitzkrieg

The Russo-Finnish War

As we shall see in the next spread, Hitler did not immediately turn on the West after his conquest of Poland. Apart from some sea and air activity, western Europe was to remain relatively quiet throughout the winter of 1939/40. This was not so in the east, where another conflict quickly erupted.

Finland, like Estonia, Latvia and Lithuania, was a Baltic neighbour of the Soviet Union with the same experience of being part of the Russian Empire until the 1917 Revolution, when it had gained its independence. In Soviet eyes, Finland was of significant strategic importance. The common border between the two countries ran within twenty miles (36km) of Leningrad, and the Finns possessed the northern shore of the Gulf of Finland, the maritime approach to Leningrad. Furthermore, in the extreme north the Finns possessed the Rybachiy Peninsula on the Barents Sea, and this dominated the approaches to the vital port of Murmansk. At the same time Finland maintained an open anti-Russian stance, and Stalin feared that if the country came under German influence it would place both Leningrad and Murmansk under threat.

12 October 1939 Soviet-Finnish negotiations opened.
The Russians proposed that the Finns cede territory on the shores of Lake Ladoga and the Gulf of Finland and a lease of Finnish ports, including Viipuri in the south and Petsamo in the north. In return, Finland was offered a chunk of the desolate terrain of Soviet Karelia. The Finns, observing how the Russians had taken over the Baltic states, and fearful that to agree would merely encourage them to make further demands, refused to countenance it. The negotiations dragged on through November.

30 November Soviet forces invaded Finland.
Stalin's patience had become exhausted and he decided that military force was the only answer.

On the surface Finland stood little chance. She could raise forces of no more than 150,000 men, many times fewer than those her giant neighbour had available. Her only significant defences were the Mannerheim Line (named after Field Marshal Baron Carl von Mannerheim, the Finnish Commander-in-Chief and a national hero) which lay across the Karelian isthmus between Lake Ladoga and the Gulf of Finland.

The Soviets were undoubtedly complacent and initially used only troops from the Leningrad Military District in an attack up the Karelian isthmus. The Finns, however, resisted fiercely and grave defects in the Red Army soon became apparent. At the root of these were Stalin's purges of the late 1930s. They had resulted in the removal of not just those whom Stalin saw as potential political rivals, but a large proportion of the military heirarchy, leaving, for the most part, the more incompetent. This had resulted in a wholesale lowering of morale within the armed forces. Yet, so certain were the Soviets of a quick victory that many of the troops had just their thin summer uniforms; they were to suffer dreadfully once the northern winter took hold.

1 December A Finnish puppet government was formed.
This was established in Moscow under the veteran Finnish Communist, Otto Kuusinen, who immediately acceded to the Soviet demands.

3 December The Finns withdrew in good order to the Mannerheim Line.

6 December The Soviets attacked the Mannerheim Line.
This was the first of several fruitless attacks.

7 December Denmark, Sweden and Norway declared their neutrality.
At the same time Britain and France decided to send arms to Finland, and later began to organize troops to be sent there. The neutrality of the other Scandinavian countries meant that neither men nor *matériel* could be transported across their territory. This made it impossible for the Western Allies to give Finland much in the way of support. On the same day the Soviet Ninth Army attacked on the central front.

14 December The League of Nations expelled Russia.
This was one of the few positive actions of the League, which also exhorted member nations to give all possible support to Finland. By this stage, however, the League had little standing in world affairs.

There was also a wave of sympathy for Finland in the USA, which remained a non-member of the League, and strong protests were made to Moscow.

29 December Successful Finnish counter-attack north of Lake Ladoga.

7 January 1940 General Semyon Timoshenko took command of the Soviet forces in Finland.
He began to build up the Soviet forces for a major offensive.

8 January Successful Finnish counter-attack on the central front.

29 January Russia reopened negotiations using Sweden as an intermediary.
The Russians indicated that they might withdraw their support from Kuusinen's puppet government.

1 February Timoshenko launched a major attack across the iced-up Viipuri Bay.
It was disrupted by some of the few remaining Finnish aircraft.

5 February Anglo-French plans to send an expeditionary force to Finland confirmed.
Serious consideration was given to disregarding Norwegian neutrality and landing the force in northern Norway. This was eventually agreed.

11 February The Russians finally breached the Mannerheim Line.
The Finns withdrew to a second line of defence.

23 February Russia announced final conditions for peace.
Finland must hand over the Karelian isthmus and the shores of Lake Ladoga and grant a thirty-year lease on the Hango peninsula. A mutual assistance treaty was to be signed guaranteeing the security of the Gulf of Finland against external threats. In return the Russians undertook to evacuate the Petsamo area.

On the same day Sweden announced that she would not permit the movement of Allied troops across her territory.

28–29 February Russian troops overran the second line of Finnish defences on Karelian isthmus.

1 March Russian peace ultimatum expired.

3 March Massive Russian offensive took place along the front.
Next day Viipuri came under direct attack. The Finns now realized that they could not resist for much longer in the face of overwhelming Russian strength.

6 March Finnish delegation arrived in Moscow.

8 March Viipuri taken.
The Finns sought an immediate armistice, which was refused. They therefore ordered the delegation in Moscow to sue for peace.

12 March Soviet-Finnish Peace Treaty signed in Moscow.
The terms were harsh on the Finns. They were forced to cede the whole of the Karelian isthmus, including Viipuri, which was renamed Vyborg, and parts of eastern Karelia, including Lake Ladoga, as well as the Rybachiy Peninsula and Petsamo area. The Russians were granted a thirty-year lease on the Hango peninsula. They did, however, drop their recognition of the Kuusinen puppet government. Next day hostilities ceased.

The Finns had suffered 25,000 killed and 45,000 wounded during the campaign. The Russians had lost 200,000 dead and an unknown number of wounded. Many had died of cold. The experience was a severe shock for the Red Army and resulted in a radical and wide-ranging overhaul of the Russian armed forces. The Western Allies had not learnt from the Polish experience of the difficulties of supporting a country situated at a distance. Their

P22 · Poland

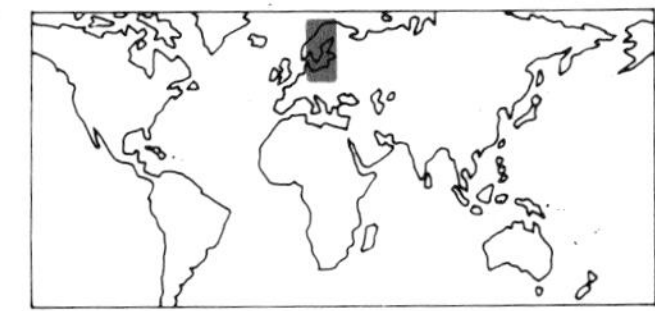

BALTIC FRONTIER: Russian Annexations to June 1941

23 Aug 1939 German–Russian Non-Aggression Pact gave Russia a free hand in the Baltic states and Bessarabia.
Sept–Oct 1939 Invasion and partition of Poland by Germany and Russia.
1-10 Oct 1939 Mutual Assistance Treaties between Russia and the Baltic states enabled Russia to occupy military bases in Estonia, Latvia and Lithuania.
28 June 1940 Russia claimed Bessarabia from Roumania.
21 July 1940 Estonia, Latvia and Lithuania became autonomous republics within USSR.
3 Sept 1940 By the Vienna Award, Roumania was forced to cede Bessarabia to Russia

Helsinki
Leningrad
BALTIC SEA
ESTONIA
Riga
LATVIA
LITHUANIA
Danzig
EAST PRUSSIA
Warsaw
POLAND
BUKOVINA
Budapest
HUNGARY
TRANSYLVANIA
BESSARABIA
ROUMANIA
Ploesti
Belgrade
Bucharest
YUGOSLAVIA
BULGARIA
Sofia
BLACK SEA
Istanbul
Ankara
GREECE
TURKEY

THE RUSSO-FINNISH WAR: 30 November 1939 to 12 March 1940

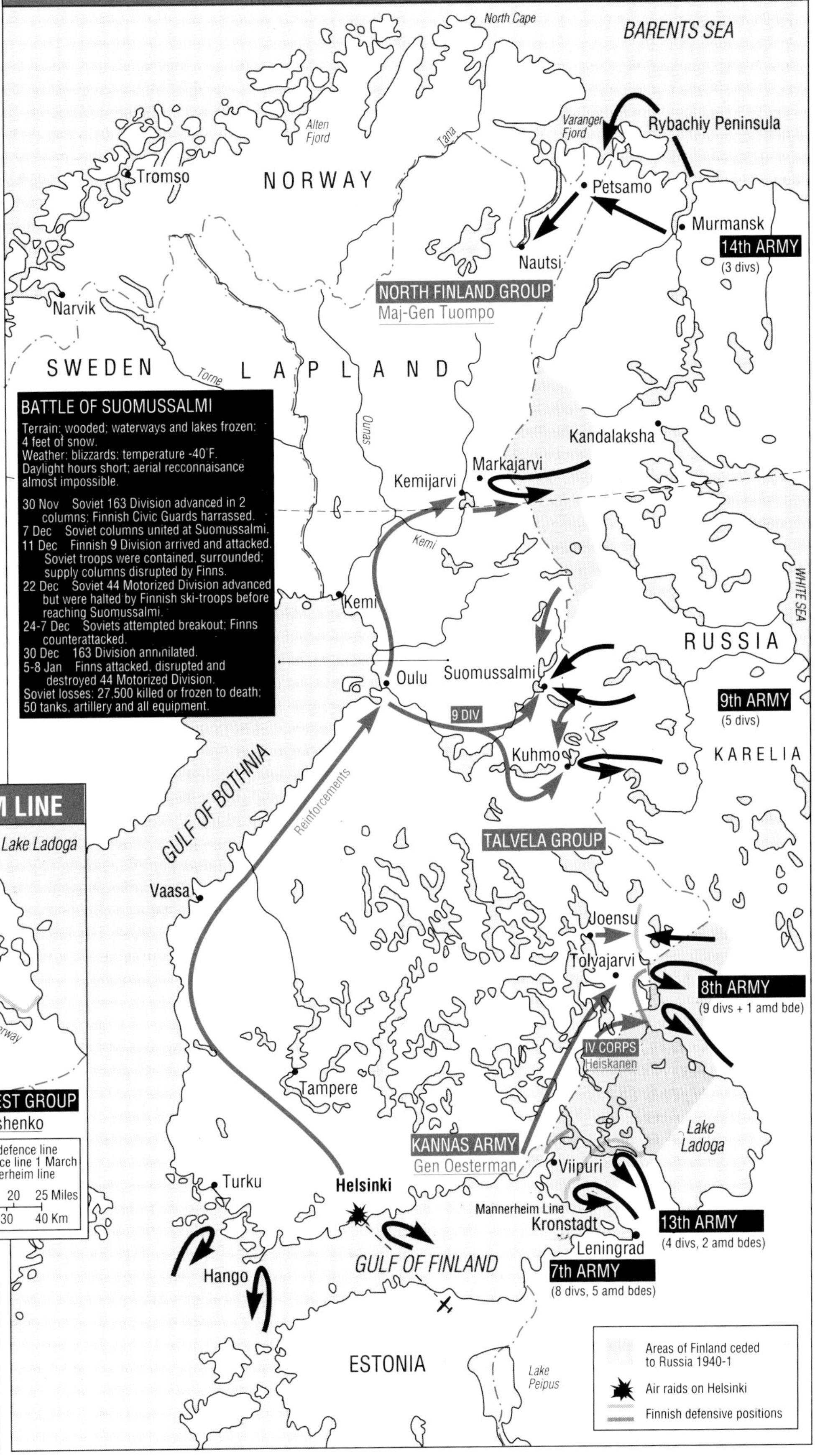

BATTLE OF SUOMUSSALMI

Terrain: wooded; waterways and lakes frozen; 4 feet of snow.
Weather: blizzards; temperature -40°F.
Daylight hours short; aerial recconaisance almost impossible.

30 Nov Soviet 163 Division advanced in 2 columns; Finnish Civic Guards harrassed.
7 Dec Soviet columns united at Suomussalmi.
11 Dec Finnish 9 Division arrived and attacked. Soviet troops were contained, surrounded; supply columns disrupted by Finns.
22 Dec Soviet 44 Motorized Division advanced but were halted by Finnish ski-troops before reaching Suomussalmi.
24-7 Dec Soviets attempted breakout; Finns counterattacked.
30 Dec 163 Division annihilated.
5-8 Jan Finns attacked, disrupted and destroyed 44 Motorized Division.
Soviet losses: 27,500 killed or frozen to death; 50 tanks, artillery and all equipment.

North Cape
BARENTS SEA
Alten Fjord
Tana
Varanger Fjord
Rybachiy Peninsula
Tromso
NORWAY
Petsamo
Murmansk
14th ARMY (3 divs)
Nautsi
NORTH FINLAND GROUP
Maj-Gen Tuompo
Narvik
SWEDEN
Torne
LAPLAND
Ounas
Kandalaksha
Markajarvi
Kemijarvi
Kemi
WHITE SEA
RUSSIA
Oulu
Suomussalmi
9 DIV
9th ARMY (5 divs)
Kuhmo
KARELIA
GULF OF BOTHNIA
Reinforcements
TALVELA GROUP
Vaasa
Joensu
Tolvajarvi
8th ARMY (9 divs + 1 amd bde)
IV CORPS
Heiskanen
Tampere
Lake Ladoga
KANNAS ARMY
Gen Oesterman
Viipuri
Turku
Helsinki
Mannerheim Line
Kronstadt
Leningrad
13th ARMY (4 divs, 2 amd bdes)
7th ARMY (8 divs, 5 amd bdes)
Hango
GULF OF FINLAND
ESTONIA
Lake Peipus

Areas of Finland ceded to Russia 1940-1
Air raids on Helsinki
Finnish defensive positions

THE BREAKING OF THE MANNERHEIM LINE

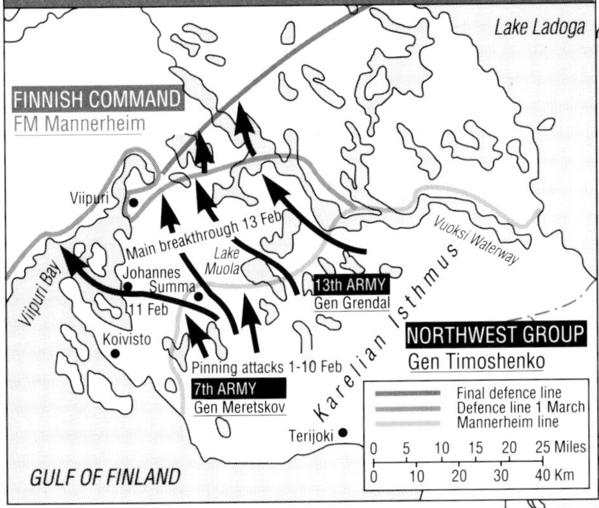

Lake Ladoga
FINNISH COMMAND
FM Mannerheim
Viipuri
Vuoksi Waterway
Main breakthrough 13 Feb
Lake Muola
Viipuri Bay
Johannes
Summa
11 Feb
13th ARMY
Gen Grendal
Karelian Isthmus
NORTHWEST GROUP
Gen Timoshenko
Koivisto
Pinning attacks 1-10 Feb
7th ARMY
Gen Meretskov
Terijoki
GULF OF FINLAND

Final defence line
Defence line 1 March
Mannerheim line

0 5 10 15 20 25 Miles
0 10 20 30 40 Km

strategy was unreal and born of their frustration at the stagnant situation then prevailing, together with their seeming inability to make positive progress towards achieving any form of victory.

As for Finland, she now sat back to lick her wounds. The opportunity for revenge against Russia would not be long in coming.

The Invasion of Russia · P62

3 SEPTEMBER 1939 TO 5 APRIL 1940

The Phoney War

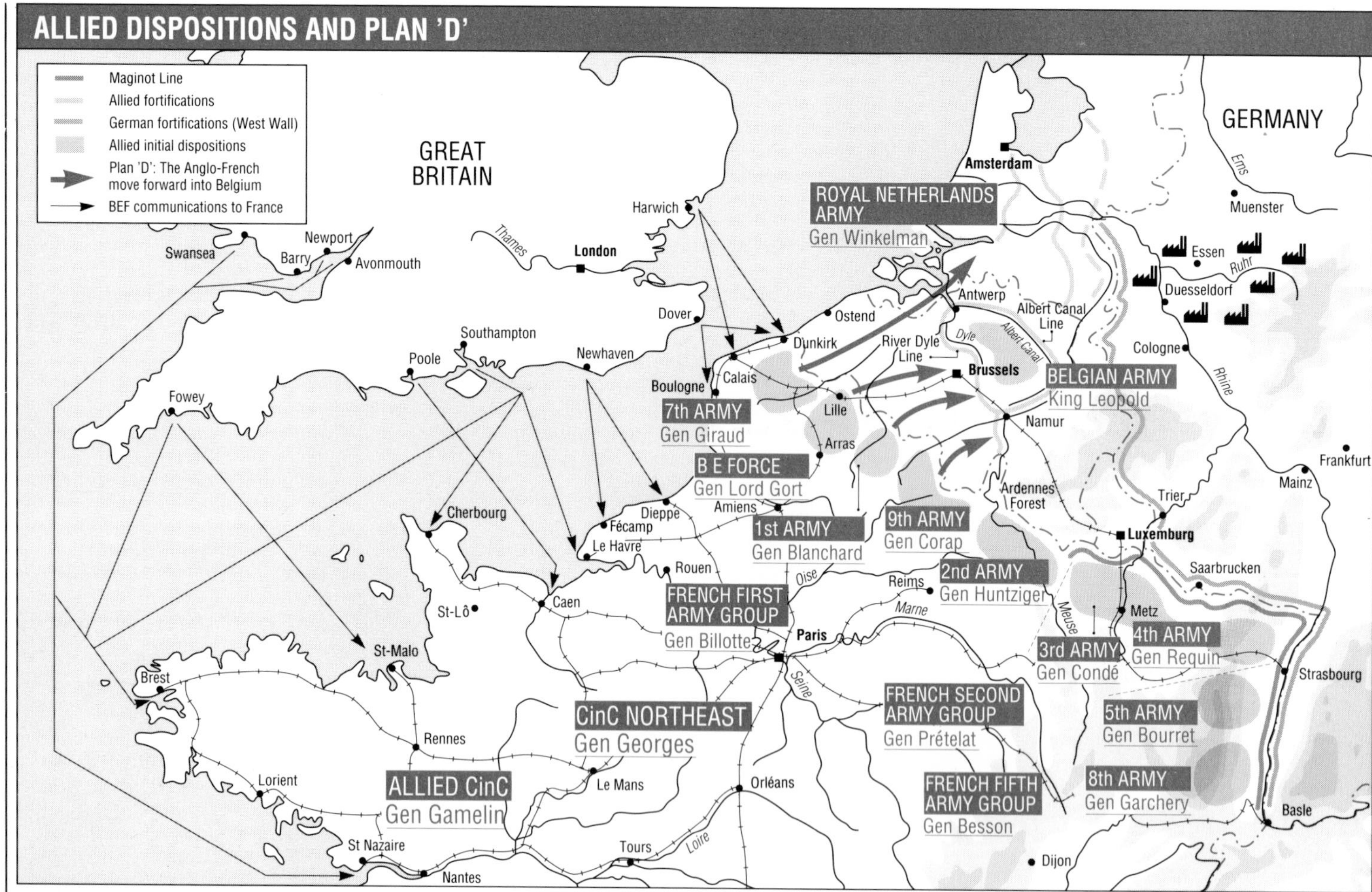

The opening months of the war in the west were in stark contrast to the violent clashes of arms that had taken place 25 years before. Then, the Anglo-French forces had had to combat an immediate German invasion. The only similarity was that both in August 1914 and September 1939 the French had attempted to attack Germany. In 1914 they had done so with great *élan*, but had been repulsed with heavy casualties, while in 1939 they had closed cautiously up to the *Westwall* and then withdrawn to the safety of the Maginot Line. There followed months of relative inactivity, a period dubbed by a US journalist as the 'phoney war' and by the Germans as the *Sitzkrieg*.

The French defensive-mindedness, engendered by Maginot, meant that this time the Allies were to wait for the Germans to attack. The main problem was that, for political reasons, the Maginot Line itself only extended as far as the Belgian border. Along this frontier up to the North Sea coast the Allies had to build defences from scratch, and it was this that was to keep them mainly occupied during the autumn and winter.

There was, however, a weapon with which the Allies could strike directly at Germany – the bomber. Popular pre-war opinion had believed that the war would open with massed bomber attacks on the cities of the combatants, but this did not happen. The truth was that both sides had made a conscious policy to attack only strictly military targets from the air. (The one exception early in the war, Warsaw, had been so attacked because it refused to surrender.) To avoid inflicting civilian casualties and the resultant danger of enemy retaliation in kind, the British Air Ministry concluded that only naval targets – ports and ships – were safe to attack.

3 September 1939 On the day Britain declared war an RAF Blenheim bomber of 139 Squadron flew over to check on shipping in the Schillig Roads. This was the RAF's first operational sortie of the war. With a frozen radio it was unable to transmit any information back to base and by the time it landed it was too late to mount an attack that day. That night Whitley bombers dropped propaganda leaflets over Germany, the only other type of operational sortie allowed to RAF Bomber Command.

4 September First RAF bombing attacks of the war.
Three separate attacks were made on German shipping in the Schillig Roads and entrance to the Kiel Canal. Seven out of 30 aircraft were shot down by anti-aircraft (AA) guns and only one ship was slightly damaged.

9 September Advanced parties of the BEF crossed to France.
The four Regular divisions were deployed opposite the Belgian border by mid-October.

6 October Hitler proposed peace.
In a speech, he proposed peace with Britain and France in return for recognition of the status quo in Eastern Europe. Both countries rejected this.

9 October Hitler issued written orders for the attack in the west.
The plan was for a wheel through the Low Countries – as in 1914, and just what the Allies expected – but this time Holland would be overrun as well as Belgium. Only the start-date was not specified, although Hitler was thinking of November. Bad weather would, however, cause frequent postponements, as well as demands by the generals for more preparation time.

16 October First German air attack on British territory.
German bombers damaged the cruisers *Southampton* and *Edinburgh* and a destroyer in the Firth of Forth, Scotland.

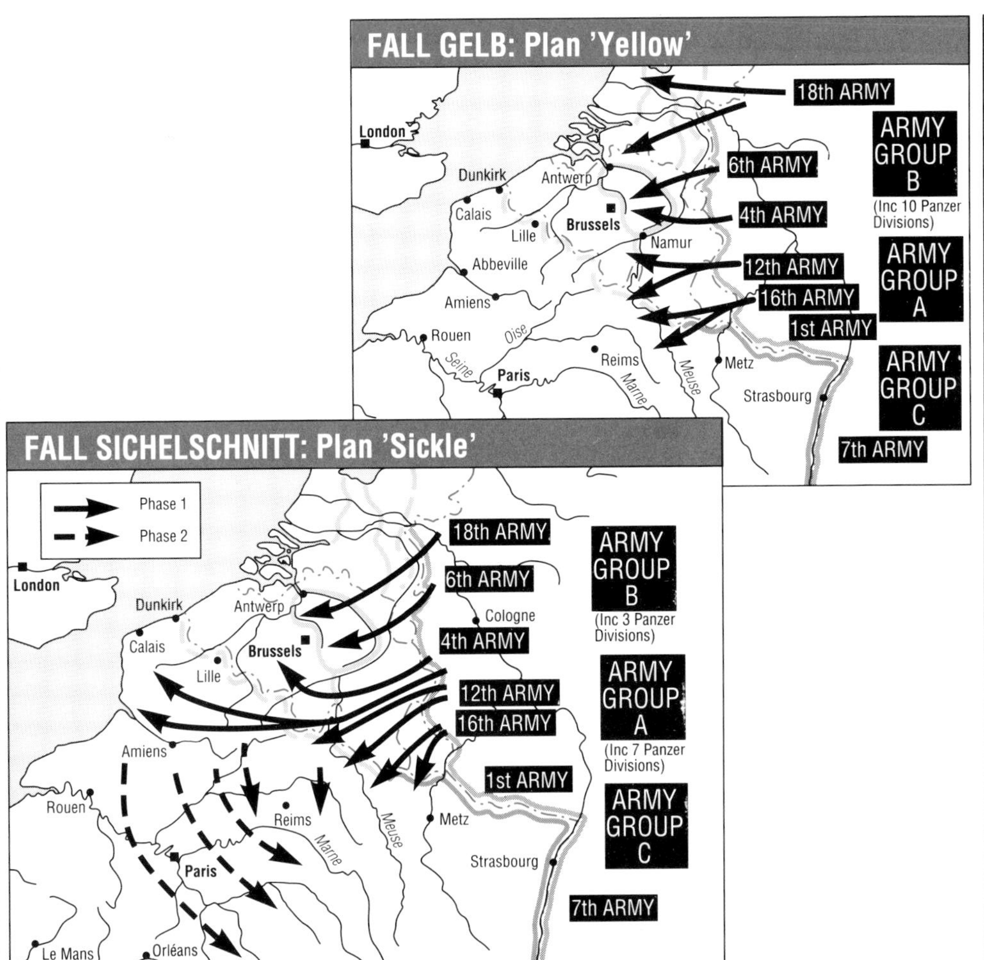

7 November **The Belgian and Dutch monarchs offered to act as mediators in peace negotiations.**
Both their countries emphasized their neutrality in the conflict. Hitler turned down the offer, as did the Western Allies. A similar offer made by King Carol of Roumania was also rejected by both sides.

8 November **Assassination attempt on Hitler.**
He was in Munich for the anniversary of the 1923 *putsch*. A bomb went off in a beer hall, but Hitler was not present at the time.

17 November **The Allies decided to move forward into Belgium to meet the German attack.**
The Albert Canal and the Rivers Dyle and Meuse provided significant natural obstacles which north-east France did not have. The problem was that Belgium, careful to preserve her neutrality, would not even allow reconnaissance parties into her territory before she had actually been invaded by Germany.

7 December **Italy reaffirmed her neutrality.**

15 December **A fifth, Regular, division joined the BEF in France.**

18 December **Twelve out of 24 RAF bombers were lost in a daylight attack on shipping in the Schillig Roads.**
This was the culmination of a series of RAF day-light raids which had cost an increasing number of aircraft. This eventually resulted in a switch to bombing attacks by night, but at a cost in bombing accuracy.

24 December **Pope Pius XII made a Christmas appeal for peace.**

10 January 1940 **Hitler informed his commanders that the attack in the west would begin on 17 January.**
On that same day a German light aircraft made a forced landing at Malines in Belgium, near the German frontier. Its occupants were carrying details of the German plans, which alerted Belgium and Holland to Hitler's intentions. On 16 January Hitler postponed his attack until the spring. The reasons for this were the likely compromise of *Fall Gelb* (Plan 'Yellow') and increasing criticism from some commanders that it was too predictable. Led by Gerd von Rundstedt they proposed instead that the main blow should come through the wooded Ardennes region in southern Belgium, something the Allies would not expect.

During January and February the first three British TA divisions crossed to France. Preparations for the coming battle continued, and British units had the opportunity to spend brief tours in the Maginot Line, where they were able to blood themselves in patrol actions against the Germans. The French also began forming a second and third armoured divisions.

11 February **Germany and the Soviet Union signed an economics agreement.**
The Soviets would export raw materials, especially oil and grain, to Germany in return for manufactured goods.

1 March **US Secretary of State Sumner Wells arrived in Berlin at the start of a tour of the belligerent countries.**
His mission, to search for ways to peace, was doomed to failure.

6 March **Hitler changed his plans for the invasion of the west.**
At a military conference in Berlin, he decided to adopt the plan put forward by von Rundstedt and his former chief of staff, Erich von Manstein, for the Ardennes option. Code-named *Fall Sichelschnitt* (Plan 'Sickle'), it called for the attack against the Low Countries to go ahead, but with slightly fewer forces, in order to draw the Allies forward, while the decisive thrust would be mounted through the Ardennes. The Maginot Line would be masked.

16 March **The first British civilian was killed in a German bombing attack.**
This was during a Luftwaffe raid on the British Grand Fleet anchorage at Scapa Flow in the Orkney Islands. Three nights later the RAF retaliated when 50 bombers attacked a seaplane base at Hornum on the Island of Sylt off the west coast of Schleswig-Holstein. Later photographic reconnaissance revealed little damage to the target.

18 March **Hitler and Mussolini met at the Brenner Pass on the Austro-Italian border.**
Mussolini promised that Italy would join in the war against Britain and France.

20 March **A new French government was formed.**
That of Edouard Daladier, who had a reputation as an appeaser, was replaced by one under the more positive Paul Reynaud. One of his first acts was to agree with the British that neither nation would make a separate peace with Germany.

5 April **British Prime Minister Chamberlain told the British people that Hitler had 'missed the bus'.**
What he meant was that the German invasion of the west was now unlikely to succeed, because they had delayed too long. The truth of the matter was that both sides' attentions were focused elsewhere – on Scandinavia.

Norway · P30

The War at Sea

Being an island, Britain had been traditionally reliant on maritime communications. It was for this reason that she had always maintained a large navy. In early 1917 the German U-boats had mounted an all-out offensive on Britain's trade and had come close to throttling it – at one point the country had only three weeks' reserve stocks of food left. The institution of convoying and the development in 1918 of a means of detecting submarines underwater (ASDIC, or sonar) had averted the peril and led to the defeat of the U-boat.

The various naval agreements between the wars had restricted submarine warfare, both in the manner in which it was carried out and its extent in terms of numbers of submarines permitted to navies. Consequently, the Royal Navy did not regard the U-boat as a major threat in 1939 and was much more concerned about Germany's growing surface navy. Plan 'Z', the German switch of emphasis to U-boat construction, which signified the tearing up of the Anglo-German Naval Treaty, came too late for it to have much influence on the situation at the outbreak of war. Thus, on 3 September 1939, the Germans had a strength of only 57 U-boats, of which seventeen were at sea. The German naval C-in-C, Admiral Erich Raeder, wanted to launch a major offensive against Allied shipping before they could adopt effective counter-measures, but Hitler refused since he was hoping to be able to come to terms with Britain and France. Nor was he prepared to draw the Royal Navy into a general fleet action, since the German surface strength was numerically very inferior. The sinking of *Athenia* convinced the British that Hitler had launched a campaign of unrestricted submarine warfare, and they immediately reinstituted convoying. This, however, took time to put into effect, both for organizational reasons and also because of a grave shortage of convoy escort vessels. At the same time Britain announced a naval blockade of Germany.

17 September 1939 ***U-29*** **sank the British aircraft carrier** ***Courageous*** **off south-west Ireland.**
In order to hunt down the U-boats the Admiralty initially adopted 'search and destroy' tactics based on carrier battle groups. Three days earlier a torpedo from *U-39* had just missed the carrier *Ark Royal*. (*U-39* herself was immediately sunk by three escorting destroyers, the first U-boat of the war to be destroyed.) The Royal Navy concluded that the risk was too great and withdrew the carriers from this task.

27 September **German pocket battleships were ordered to begin attacking British shipping in the Atlantic.**
Deutschland and *Graf Spee* had sailed from Germany in August, before the war had started, but had been held in waiting areas until now.

CRUISES OF DEUTSCHLAND AND GRAF SPEE

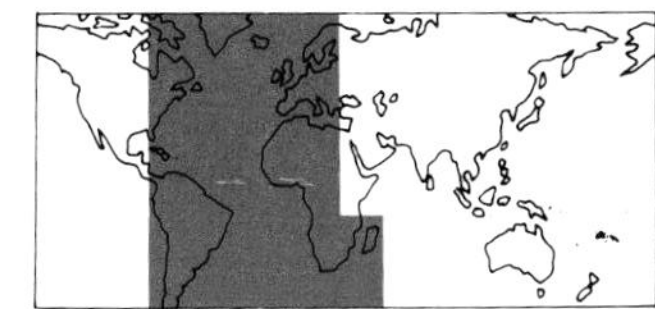

30 September *Graf Spee* sank the British steamship *Clement* off Pernambuco, Brazil.

During the next three weeks she sank four more vessels in the South Atlantic and then moved into the Indian Ocean. The Admiralty began to organize task forces to hunt down *Graf Spee*. *Deutschland* sank two ships in the North Atlantic, but engine trouble forced her to return home in early November.

14 October *U-47* (Lt Guenther Prien) penetrated the Home Fleet anchorage at Scapa Flow and sank the battleship *Royal Oak*.

A total of 883 members of the crew were lost. It was a heavy blow to British morale, and Prien himself became a hero overnight in Germany.

15 November *Graf Spee* sank the merchantman *Africa Shell* off Mozambique.

Next day she stopped another merchantman and then decided to return to the South Atlantic, where the pickings were richer. In the meantime no less than six Allied naval tasks forces had been formed to hunt down *Graf Spee*, which was now posing a serious threat to trade routes.

21 November Battlecruisers *Scharnhorst* and *Gneisenau* set off to harry the sea routes in the North Atlantic.

Two days later they intercepted a convoy escorted by the armed merchant cruiser *Rawalpindi*. She was sunk by *Scharnhorst* after engaging her to enable the convoy to escape, but managed to give a radio warning. The Home Fleet put to sea, but failed to make contact and the two battlecruisers returned to port. Such was the British shortage of convoy escorts that merchant vessels had had to be hastily converted to fulfill this role.

23 November The first German magnetic mine was recovered intact by the British.

This type of mine, normally laid by aircraft, had been causing an increasing number of casualties to shipping. The antidote was degaussing, the passing of an electric current through a cable round a ship's hull to cancel out its inherent magnetic field, and an urgent programme was instituted for all warships and merchantmen.

24 November Germany warned neutral merchant shipping to stay away from British and French coasts or risk being sunk.

A number of neutral vessels had already fallen victim to U-boats, especially by night when identification was difficult. The restrictions on U-boat operations had gradually been lifted; now they were permitted to attack any vessel not showing lights.

3 December *Graf Spee* sank another merchant vessel, this time off the west coast of South Africa.

She now decided to concentrate on the South America routes and sank another ship on the 7th.

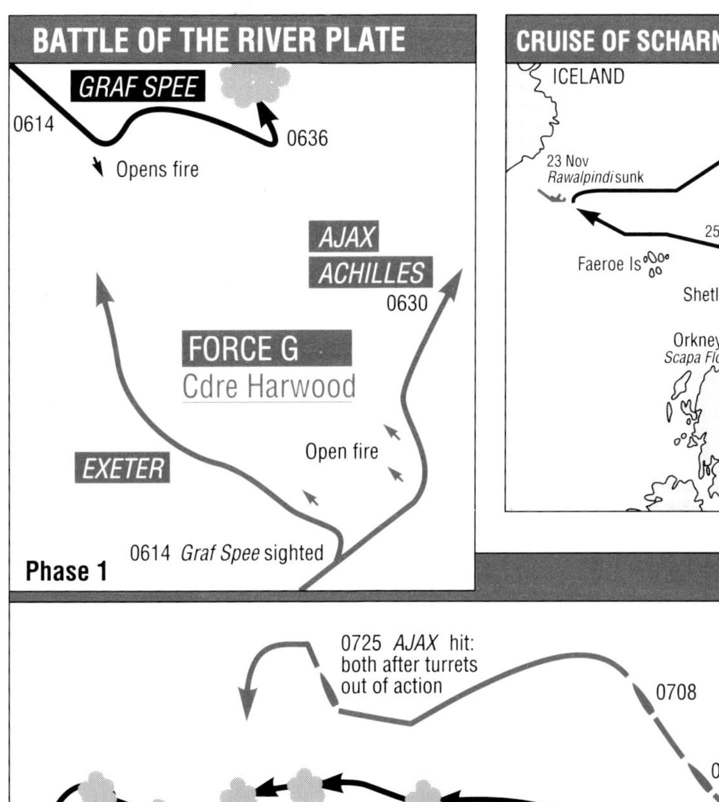

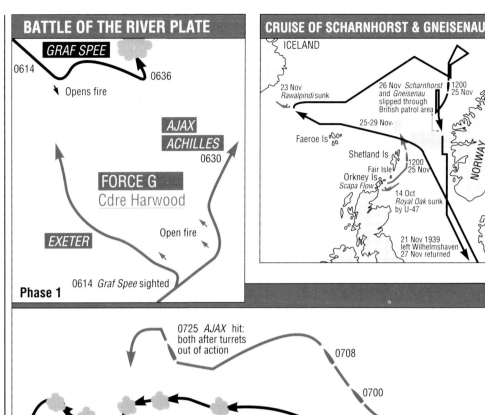

12 December Two German cruisers were damaged by torpedoes from the British submarine *Salmon* in the North Sea.

They had been accompanying five destroyers on a minelaying mission off the north-east coast of England.

13 December The Battle of the River Plate.

Graf Spee was finally brought to bay. Force G, consisting of four cruisers and based on the Falkland Islands, was one of the Allied groups hunting *Graf Spee*. Commodore Harwood decided to concentrate his force, less one cruiser in urgent need of a refit, off the River Plate, in response to radio messages from the German raider's victims. Langsdorff, *Graf Spee*'s captain, spotted their smoke and decided to attack, thinking that they were merely destroyers escorting a convoy. After some two hours' firing, *Exeter* and *Ajax* were badly damaged by *Graf Spee*'s heavier armament; *Achilles* was virtually unscathed. But *Graf Spee* had also been hit, and Langsdorff decided to put into the neutral port of Montevideo to carry out repairs before starting back to Germany. Using bluff, the British managed to convince him that Harwood had been reinforced. Langsdorff, fearing that he was trapped, scuttled his ship on 17 December. He himself committed suicide, probably because he had disobeyed his orders not to engage enemy warships.

The Battle of the River Plate meant that 1939 ended on a high note for the Allies. They could be reasonably satisfied that, so far, the multiple threats to their trade routes had been contained. In all, German surface raiders had sunk fifteen vessels, U-boats 114, of which only twelve had been in convoy, while mines had accounted for 79. Yet only nine U-boats had been sunk and many more merchant ships might have been sunk if the Germans had not experienced technical problems with torpedoes. Within the next year the situation was to change dramatically.

The Battle of the Atlantic: The First 'Happy Time' · P44

Norway

Norway had first begun to assume importance in the war when the Allies attempted to give direct support to Finland in her struggle against the Soviet Union. But even before this, as early as 19 September 1939, the British Government had begun to worry about Sweden's supplies of iron-ore to Germany, which in the winter months went through the Norwegian northern port of Narvik. The Germans, too, were beginning to realize the importance of Norway and on 3 October 1939 Admiral Raeder had proposed to Hitler that bases be obtained in the country.

By early January 1940, the British and French were drawing up operational plans for halting the flow of Swedish iron-ore to Germany. If this proved successful, it was thought that Germany could not continue to fight for more than a year. Simultaneously the Germans were preparing to seize Norwegian bases.

27 January 1940 **Hitler personally took over the planning of Plan 'Weser', as the Norwegian operation was called.**

16 February **The British destroyer *Cossack* entered Jossing Fiord in Norwegian waters and rescued British prisoners from the German vessel *Altmark*.**
These prisoners came from ships sunk by *Graf Spee*. Norway complained of this violation of her neutrality, but Britain replied that Germany was the guilty party and accused the Norwegians of failing to take action against Germany. The Germans considered the incident as evidence that Norway would not resist British force.

20 February **General von Falkenhorst appointed to command German expedition to Norway.**

12 March **British plans for expedition to Norway finalized.**
The pretext was to support Finland. Landings would be made at Narvik and Trondheim, the railway line to Sweden secured and the iron-ore fields occupied. The Finnish surrender that same day meant that Britain had lost her excuse.

28 March **The French and British agreed to begin mining Norwegian waters from 8 April.**
Troops would be embarked and held ready in Allied ports in case the Germans invaded Norway.

2 April **Hitler gave orders for the invasion of Norway and Denmark to take place on the 9th.**

5 April **Norway and Sweden were informed of the Allied intention to mine Norwegian waters, and the minelaying forces sailed.**

7 April **RAF aircraft spotted German ships steaming north to Narvik and Trondheim.**
That evening the Home Fleet sailed to intercept these forces. A gale blew up.

8 April **The British destroyer *Glowworm* was sunk by the cruiser *Hipper* after attempting to ram her.**
Because of the gale, this and the sinking of a German transport by a Polish submarine were the only intercepts.

9 April **The Germans invaded Denmark and Norway.**
There was little resistance among the surprised Danes, and Copenhagen, the capital, was occupied within twelve hours. Next day the Danes surrendered. The Germans made six landings in Norway: sea-borne troops landed at Oslo, Kristiansand, Bergen, Trondheim and Narvik, while airborne troops seized the airfield at Stavanger. A Norwegian coastal battery sank the heavy cruiser *Bluecher* in Oslo Fiord. British submarines damaged two German cruisers, one fatally.

10 April **Six British destroyers surprised ten German destroyers in Narvik Fiord.**
They sank two of the Germans but lost two themselves. Captain Warburton-Lee, the flotilla commander, was killed. He was awarded a posthumous VC.

11 April **The first British military contingent sailed for Norway.**
Many of the troops had been disembarked on naval orders. The hurried re-embarkation created confusion and meant that they sailed without much of their heavy equipment.

12 April **British naval forces re-entered Narvik Fiord.**
Destroyers, supported by the battleship *Warspite*, sank seven German destroyers.

15 April **British troops landed at Harstad in the Lofoten Islands opposite Narvik.**
By this time the Germans had consolidated their landings, cleared the Oslo area and were advancing inland. Hitler, however, was deeply worried about the Narvik force and wanted it to escape into Sweden. The German High Command managed to persuade him to allow it to remain where it was.

16 April **Second British landing, at Namsos.**
French troops were also sent there.

18 April **More British troops landed at Aandalesnes.**
The plan was for these two forces, in co-operation with Norwegian troops, to link up in a combined attack to retake Trondheim. The Aandalesnes force was, however, persuaded by the Norwegian commander, General Ruge, to move south in order to give support to his troops still holding out at Lillehammer. They were taken there by truck, but were quickly forced back by the superior firepower of the Germans. French reinforcements arrived at Aandalesnes on 24 April, but these were unable to halt the retreat. The Namsos force set out for Trondheim, which the Germans hastily reinforced. Lacking artillery and with no air support available, little progress was made by the Allies.

24 April **Norwegian troops attacked the Germans south of Narvik but were beaten back.**
The Allied force at Harstad was being considerably reinforced, and during the last week of April three battalions of French mountain troops arrived. These were followed by six further battalions, including four Polish, in early May. The Allied commander, General Mackesy, planned to encircle the Germans and close in on them until they were forced to surrender.

26 April **The British decided to evacuate southern Norway.**
This stunned both the French and the Norwegians.

29 April **King Haakon and his government were evacuated from Molde by the Royal Navy.**
They were taken to Tromsö in northern Norway to continue the fight from there.

30 April **Remnant of the Aandalesnes force was evacuated.**

2 May **Namsos force was evacuated.**
By now the Germans had secured the whole of southern Norway up to Namsos and were beginning to advance north.

21 May **The Germans at Narvik were exhausted and could not hold on much longer.**
Allied operations had, however, been much hampered by deep snow and movement was slow.

28 May **Final Allied assault on Narvik.**
The town was captured, but the German garrison managed to slip out along the railway to Sweden. By this time, because of the grave situation in France, British Prime Minister Winston Churchill decided that the remaining troops must be evacuated from Norway.

3–8 June **Evacuation of Allied troops from Narvik.**
Almost the last to leave were King Haakon and his government, who formed a government-in-exile in London.

In terms of human loss of life the Norwegian campaign was not severe: Germans 2,700; Allies 7,000 (British 4,400; Norwegians 1,335 and French and Poles 530). In ships, however, the material losses were more serious. The Royal Navy's carrier *Glorious* was sunk during the last few days, and they lost

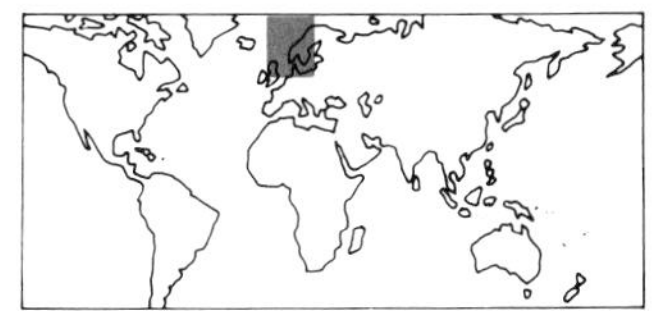

two cruisers, nine destroyers and four submarines. The bill would have been even higher if the U-boats had not continued to have problems with their torpedoes. The German losses were just as severe: one heavy cruiser, two light cruisers, ten destroyers, six U-boats and sixteen smaller craft. Furthermore, three German capital ships had been damaged and two more were damaged in June. Germany was left with one heavy and two light cruisers fit for action.

Yet the Germans could take enormous satisfaction at the way the campaign had gone. The seizure of Norway would certainly prove itself worth the sacrifice made. The Allied expedition had been poorly thought out, organized and equipped and once again revealed the lack of reality that so dominated this first phase of the war. But from 10 May onwards Norway had been relegated to no more than a minor side-show.

THE INVASIONS OF NORWAY AND DENMARK

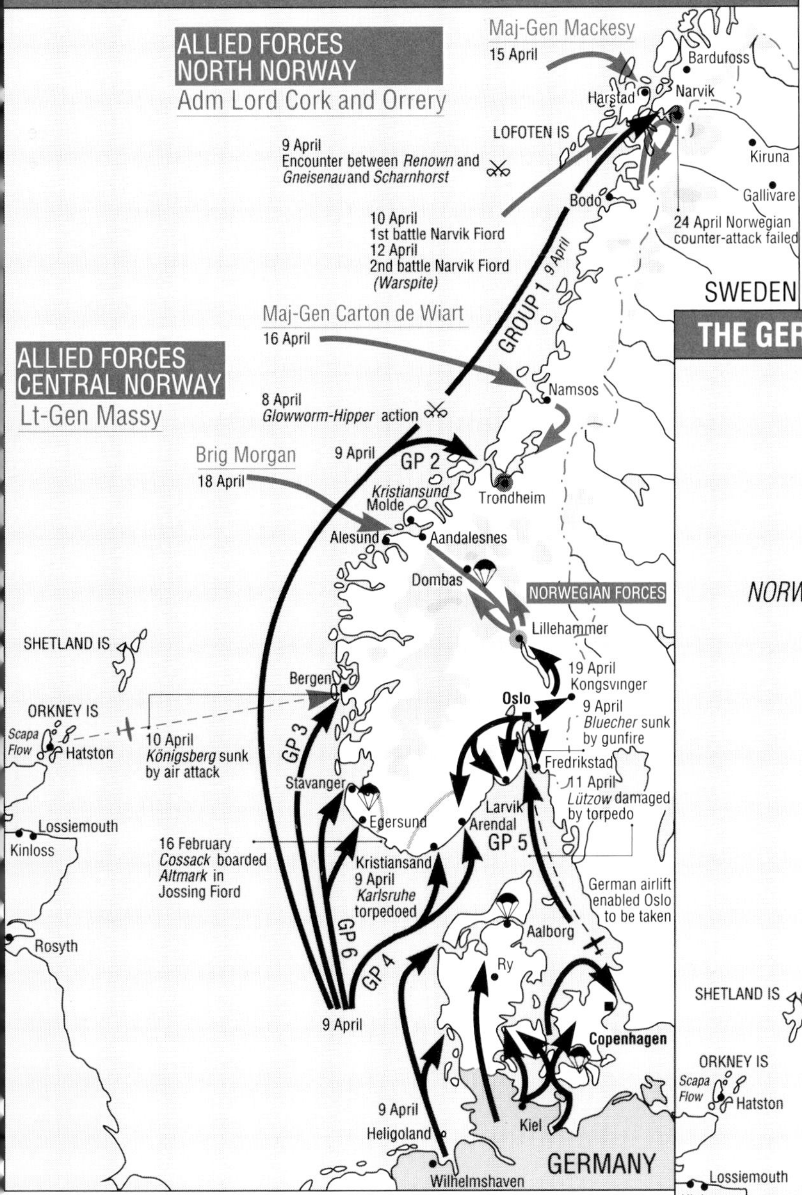

ALLIED FORCES NORTH NORWAY
Adm Lord Cork and Orrery

Maj-Gen Mackesy
15 April

Bardufoss
Harstad
Narvik
LOFOTEN IS
Kiruna
Gallivare
Bodo

9 April
Encounter between *Renown* and *Gneisenau* and *Scharnhorst*

10 April
1st battle Narvik Fiord
12 April
2nd battle Narvik Fiord
(Warspite)

24 April Norwegian counter-attack failed

SWEDEN

GROUP 1 9 April

Maj-Gen Carton de Wiart
16 April

ALLIED FORCES CENTRAL NORWAY
Lt-Gen Massy

8 April
Glowworm-Hipper action

Namsos

Brig Morgan
18 April

9 April
GP 2
Kristiansund
Molde
Trondheim
Alesund
Aandalesnes
Dombas
NORWEGIAN FORCES
Lillehammer

SHETLAND IS
Bergen
19 April
Kongsvinger
Oslo
9 April
Bluecher sunk by gunfire

ORKNEY IS
Scapa Flow
Hatston
10 April
Königsberg sunk by air attack
GP 3
Stavanger
Fredrikstad
11 April
Lützow damaged by torpedo

Lossiemouth
Kinloss
Egersund
Larvik
Arendal
GP 5

16 February
Cossack boarded *Altmark* in Jossing Fiord

Kristiansand
9 April
Karlsruhe torpedoed

German airlift enabled Oslo to be taken

Rosyth
GP 6
GP 4
Aalborg
Ry
9 April
Copenhagen

9 April
Heligoland
Kiel
Wilhelmshaven
GERMANY

THE GERMAN CONQUEST OF NORWAY

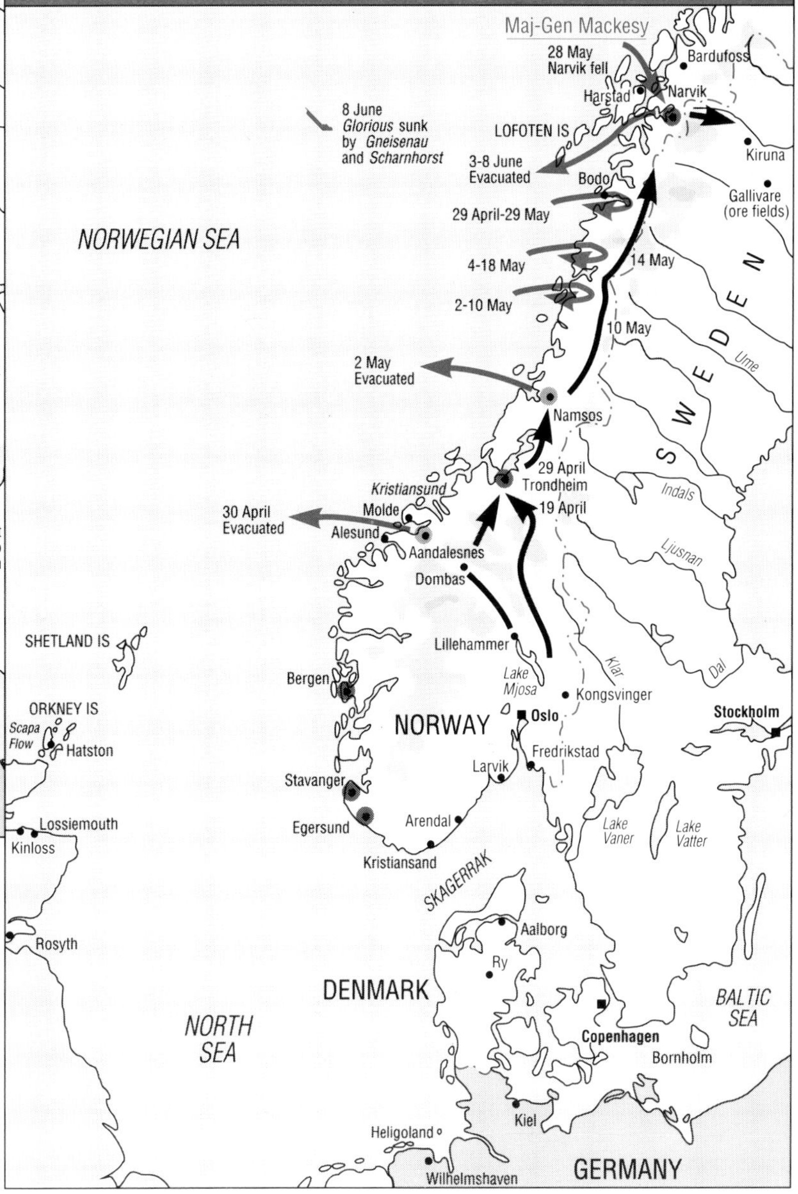

Maj-Gen Mackesy
28 May
Narvik fell
Bardufoss
Harstad
Narvik
8 June
Glorious sunk by *Gneisenau* and *Scharnhorst*
LOFOTEN IS
Kiruna
3-8 June
Evacuated
Bodo
Gallivare (ore fields)
29 April-29 May

NORWEGIAN SEA

4-18 May
14 May
2-10 May
10 May

SWEDEN

2 May
Evacuated
Namsos
Ume

29 April
Trondheim
19 April
Kristiansund
Molde
30 April
Evacuated
Alesund
Aandalesnes
Indals
Dombas
Ljusnan

SHETLAND IS
Lillehammer
Klar
Bergen
Lake Mjosa
Kongsvinger
ORKNEY IS
Scapa Flow
Hatston
NORWAY
Oslo
Dal
Stockholm
Fredrikstad
Larvik
Stavanger
Lossiemouth
Kinloss
Egersund
Arendal
Lake Vaner
Lake Vatter
Kristiansand
SKAGERRAK
Aalborg
Rosyth
Ry
DENMARK
BALTIC SEA
NORTH SEA
Copenhagen
Bornholm
Kiel
Heligoland
Wilhelmshaven
GERMANY

Hitler Attacks West

British Prime Minister Chamberlain's remark of 5 April 1940 that Hitler had 'missed the bus' was unfortunate and reflected a complacency the Allies were soon to regret. The truth was that Hitler had not dropped his intention to invade France and the Low Countries; he had merely postponed it a little longer while he dealt with Scandinavia. On 1 May 1940, satisfied that the situation in Norway was now in hand, he decided to attack on 5 May.

The final German plan called for the decisive effort to be made by von Rundstedt's Army Group A. Consisting of seven Panzer, three motorized and 34 infantry divisions, it was to cross the border south of Aachen, pass through Luxemburg and cross into France between Namur and Sedan. The Allies north of the River Somme were then to be cut off by an advance on the axis Amiens–Abbeville. Further north, Fedor von Bock, with Army Group B (which in the original plan was to strike the main blow) had been allocated three Panzer, one motorized and 24 infantry divisions. His task was to overrun Belgium and Holland, and by doing so draw the Franco-British troops forward into Belgium. Finally, Wilhelm von Leeb's Army Group C would mask the Maginot Line with seventeen infantry divisions. In reserve were a further 44 infantry and one motorized divisions. To support the attack there were 2,700 combat aircraft from Luftflotten (Air Fleets) 2 and 3.

Numerically the Allies appeared to have the advantage. The French had 78 divisions deployed, although more than half of these were in or behind the Maginot Line, and a further 22 in reserve, including their three armoured divisions. The BEF now had nine divisions, but three of these were ill-trained and poorly equipped and were detailed to lines-of-communication roles. A tenth division was doing duty in the Maginot Line. The Belgians had 22 divisions and extensive fortifications, especially around Liège, and the Dutch ten divisions. The Allies had an equal number of tanks to the Germans, 2,600 in all, but fewer aircraft, only some 2,100.

Beneath the surface, however, there were grave defects. The Belgians, and more especially the Dutch, were poorly equipped and had, because of their neutrality, done little to modernize their forces. The French command structure, under which the BEF had been placed, was very cumbersome. There had been no chance to reconnoitre the ground in Belgium to which the northern armies, which fielded the best-quality troops, were initially to deploy. The tanks, apart from the armoured divisions, were scattered rather than concentrated, and the aircraft, apart from a few, were inferior to their Luftwaffe counterparts. More serious was the fact that in the French armies, especially those opposite the main German axis, morale was low. The long months of the Phoney War had sapped spirits and many men had lost interest.

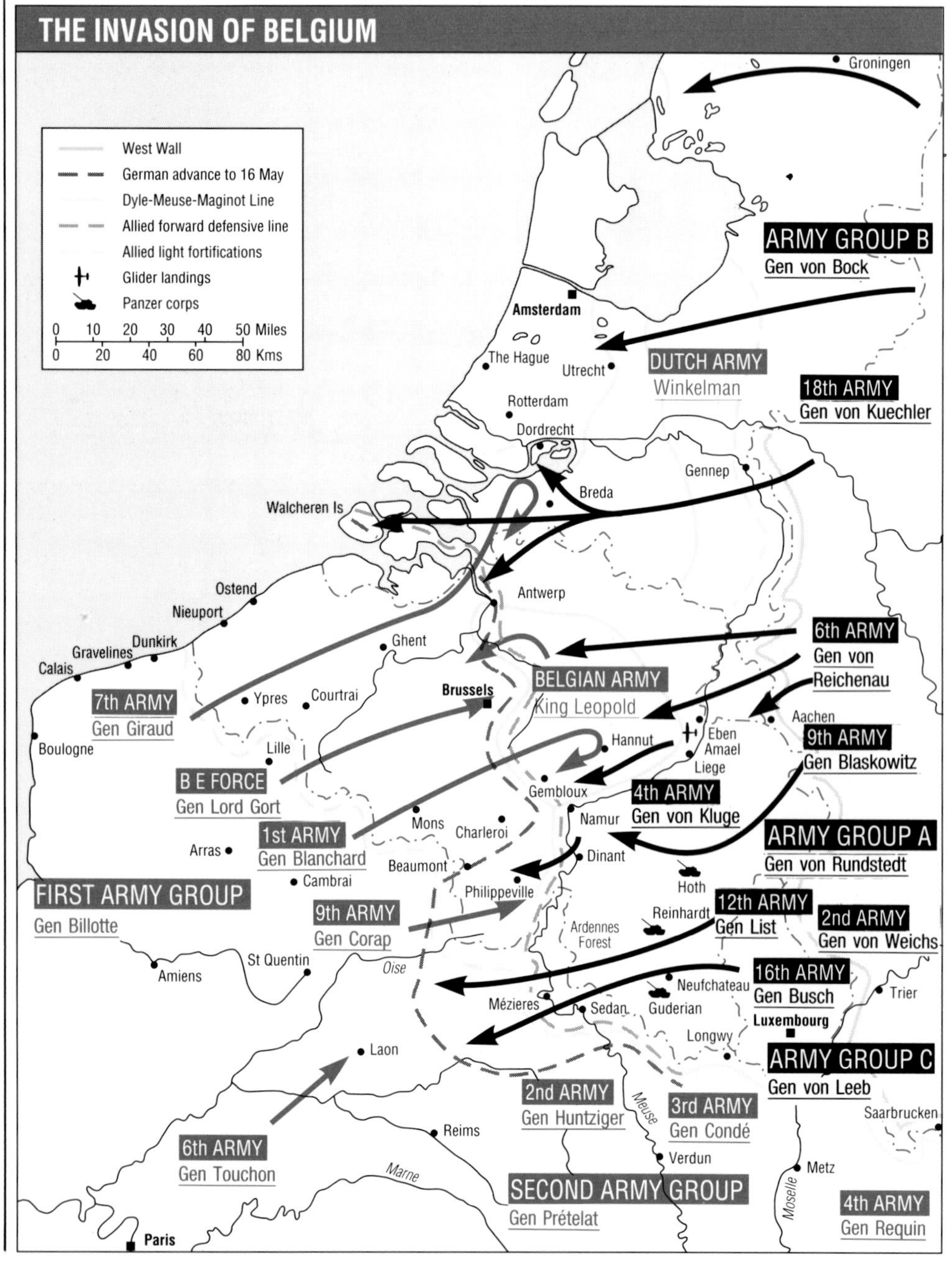

3 May 1940 Hitler postponed X-Day to the 6th. During the next few days, mainly because of the weather but also because he was looking for a suitable excuse to violate Belgian neutrality, he postponed it further, a day at a time. By the 8th, however, both the Belgians and the Dutch had sensed what was in the wind and had begun to mobilize. On this day Hitler firmly decided to attack on the 10th.

10 May Germany invaded Belgium and Holland. At 0545 hours the Luftwaffe began attacks on Allied airfields, and paratroops dropped to seize vital bridges over the Dutch rivers. A small force of glider-borne troops seized the supposedly impregnable fortress of Eben Emael, key to the Liège defences. Ground forces crossed the Dutch and Belgian borders. Two hours later the Allies put their Plan 'D' into effect: the BEF and the three northern French armies moved into Belgium to take up positions along the line of the Rivers Dyle and Meuse.

That evening Neville Chamberlain resigned and Winston Churchill formed a national coalition government. RAF Bomber Command was ordered to attack targets west of the Rhine to hamper the German advance.

11 May **President Roosevelt expressed to King Leopold of the Belgians the dismay of the US people at the German invasion.**

12 May **The leading Panzer elements of Army Group A crossed into France and secured the north bank of the Meuse.**

The Allies were deployed on the Dyle-Meuse line in Belgium, but the French Seventh Army, which had moved into Holland, was ordered back to the line of the River Scheldt. The Germans were advancing rapidly in Holland in the face of only light resistance.

13 May The Germans crossed the Meuse on each side of Sedan.
The Dutch troops were ordered to fall back to the Amsterdam–Rotterdam–Utrecht area for a last-ditch stand. Queen Wilhelmina and her government left for London.

14 May Rotterdam bombed.
Much of the city was devastated just after it had surrendered. The cause was a communications fault that prevented an order getting through for the German bombers to turn back.

The French failed to prevent the German build-up in the bridgehead at Sedan and several Allied aircraft were lost in attempts to destroy the bridges over the Meuse.

15 May The Netherlands surrendered.
The Germans penetrated the Allied positions between Namur and Louvain and began to break out of the Sedan bridgehead.

16 May The Allied armies, realizing the threat to their south, began to withdraw from Belgium.
German armour, from both Army Groups A and B, was beginning to cut a swathe westwards, 50-miles broad. The French Ninth Army, which was in its path, disintegrated.

Churchill urged Mussolini not to become involved in the war and Roosevelt asked Congress for considerable funds to strengthen the US Armed Forces.

17 May The Germans entered Brussels.
Charles de Gaulle's newly raised 4th Armoured Division tried to attack the Panzers on their southern flank, in the Laon area, but made little impression.

18 May Erwin Rommel's 7th Panzer Division reached Cambrai.
The German armour was now ordered to halt since it was feared that it was getting too far ahead of the follow-up infantry and might be cut off.

19 May General Gamelin, commanding the French land forces, was replaced by Maxime Weygand.
At the same time Marshal Henri Pétain, the elderly hero of the First World War, was made Deputy Prime Minister. These changes came too late to affect the Allies' misfortunes.

20 May German armour reached Noyelles at the mouth of the River Somme, thus splitting the Allied armies in two.
The northern armies had now fallen back to the River Escaut.

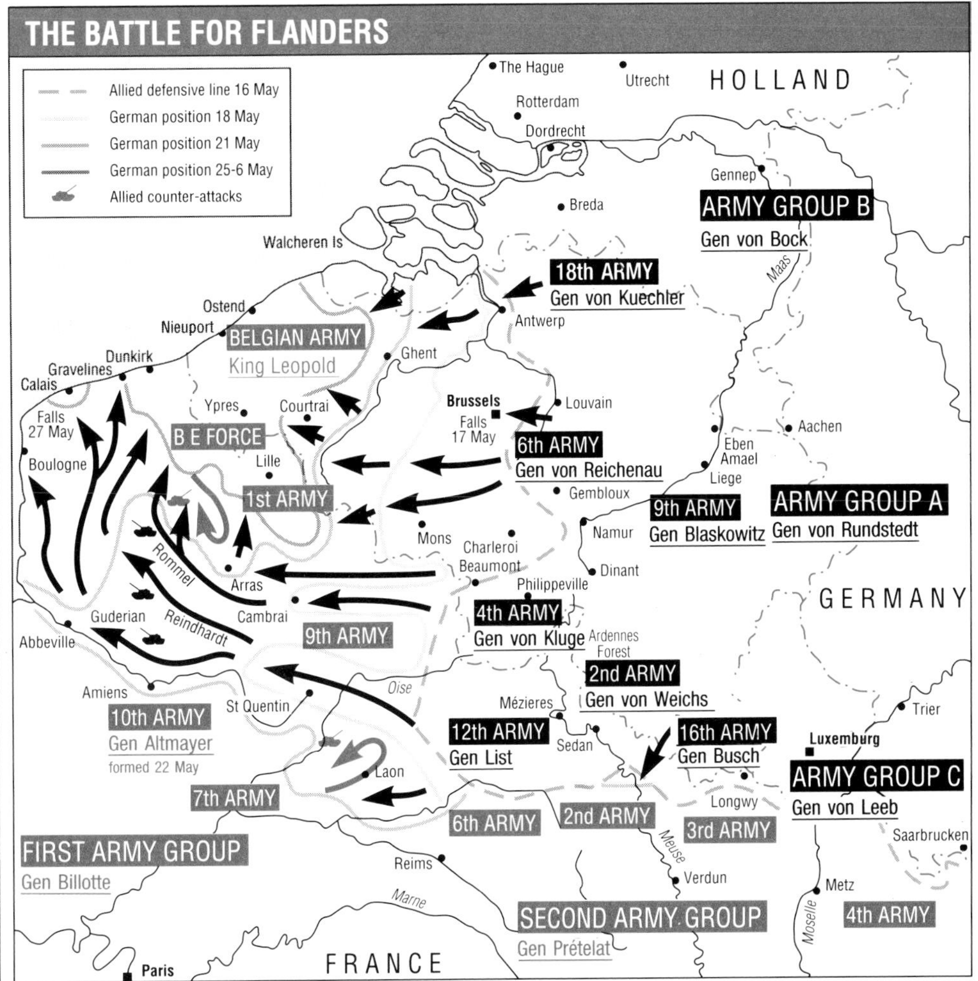

21 May British counter-attacked at Arras.
This was made by two battalions of tanks with infantry support, and struck Rommel's 7th Panzer Division, momentarily throwing it off balance. The French made a simultaneous counter-move south of the Panzer axis of advance, but made little progress. If co-ordination had been better and more tanks available, this counter-stroke might have caused the Germans a serious setback.

22 May German armour now turned north towards the Channel ports of Boulogne and Calais.
Boulogne fell on the 25th and Calais, after a desperate defence by the British, on the 27th.

Weygand now proposed a major counter-stroke. The BEF and the French First Army would attack from the north, while the French Seventh and Tenth Armies would attack in the south to cut off the German armour. However, heavy German pressure and poor communications made it impossible to carry this out.

23 May Von Rundstedt ordered his Panzers to halt.
By this stage he had isolated the BEF, Belgian and First French Armies but was concerned that his Panzer divisions were beginning to suffer from the hard motoring of the past two weeks and needed time to repair their tanks, especially since some formations were down to 30 per cent of their established tank strength. Next day Hitler visited his HQ and approved his decision.

25 May The Belgian High Command warned the French and British that its situation was very grave. Lord Gort, commanding the BEF, decided that his duty lay in saving as much of his army as possible so that it could fight another day, rather than take part in Weygand's planned offensive. The BEF began to withdraw towards Dunkirk.

On this same day Hitler confirmed the halt order originally initiaited by von Rundstedt. His Panzers were to hold a line Gravelines–Lens and allow the Allied troops being driven back by the remainder of Army Group B to attack them. At the same time Hermann Goering stepped in and said that the Luftwaffe could destroy the trapped Allied forces. This suited Hitler's plans, bearing in mind that most of France was yet to be overrun and that he needed his armoured forces to be as strong as possible in order to achieve this. This decision was to have far-reaching consequences.

The Fall of France · P34

The Fall of France

Lord Gort's decision to withdraw the BEF to the coast took not just his French and Belgian allies by surprise, but also the British Government. Yet, the last-named quickly realized that the time had come to put national ahead of Allied interests. This did not mean that they viewed the battle for France as having ended. Rather it was merely a phase that had gone badly, and time was needed to regroup in order to continue the fight elsewhere in France. Indeed, on 23 May the British 1st Armoured Division had finally begun landing at Cherbourg, although still not fully equipped and missing its infantry, which had been sent to defend Calais.

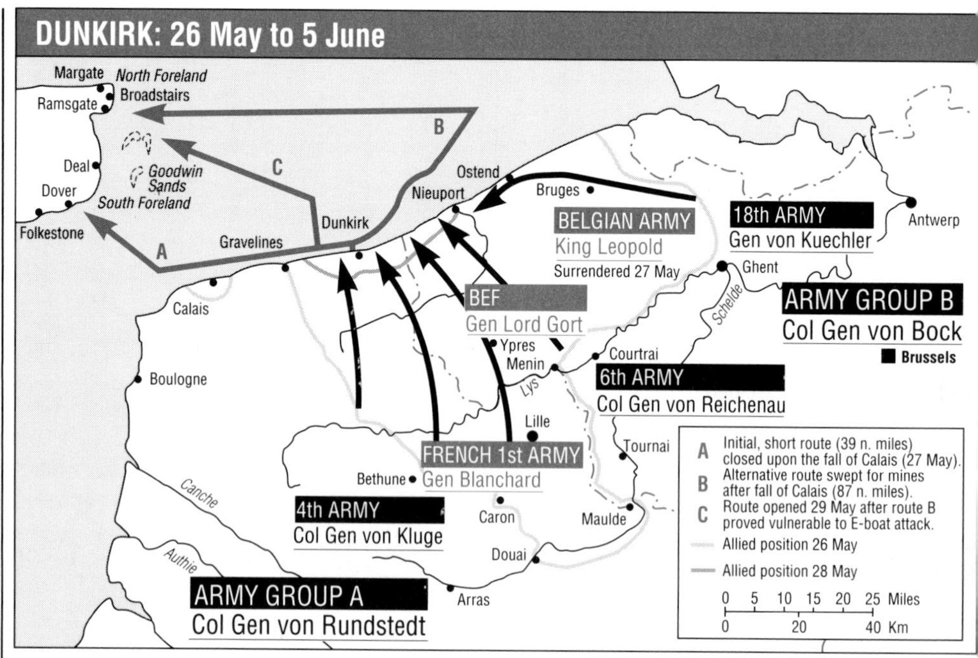

26 May Operation 'Dynamo', the evacuation of the BEF, was set in motion.
In overall command of this was Admiral Bertram Ramsay, Flag Officer, Dover. As early as 20 May he had been ordered to make preparations in the event that elements of the BEF might have to be rescued, and he had by now collected a number of vessels for this purpose. By the time 'Dynamo' was put into effect it was reckoned that no more than a small proportion of the BEF could be saved.

27 May King Leopold of the Belgians offered to surrender to the Germans.
He did not inform his allies beforehand of his intention, which angered the British. Yet Gort had not told him of his decision to withdraw to Dunkirk, which meant that the remnants of Leopold's army had been left isolated, and he wished to save his people from further suffering. Belgium formally surrendered next day. The Belgian Government had already escaped to England.

The evacuation of Dunkirk began in the early hours of this day. The first vessel to arrive was the Isle of Man packet *Mona's Isle*, which embarked 1,420 troops. During this and the next day 25,000 troops were successfully taken off.

29 May Hitler ordered the main offensive to be switched southwards.
Luftwaffe activity over the contracting Dunkirk beachhead increased and Allied craft were being hit. Nevertheless, 47,300 men were taken off.

30 May Nearly 54,000 men were evacuated from Dunkirk.
The toll of Allied ships sunk, both warships and merchant vessels, was rising. The Luftwaffe accounted for three sunk and six badly damaged in destroyers alone. A number of 'little ships', which ranged from cross-Channel ferries to small pleasure craft, were sunk as well. The RAF, flying combat patrols from southern England, was doing its best to protect the evacuation, but was having to husband its strength for the worst case – French surrender and Britain left to face a German invasion.

31 May 68,000 Allied troops were evacuated from Dunkirk.
The French, too, were being given room on the ships. The French First Army was fighting with especial gallantry to aid its ally, as were the French marines and sailors under Admiral Jean Abrial, commanding the Dunkirk area. German pressure on the perimeter was increasing all the time.

Churchill flew to Paris, his second visit since 10 May, for a meeting of the Allied Supreme War Council. He declared that Britain would fight until the end.

1 June Almost 65,000 Allied troops were evacuated from Dunkirk.
The toll of sunk and damaged Allied vessels continued to rise, and the evacuation was restricted to the hours of darkness.

2 June 24,000 men were evacuated.
The BEF had now been almost completely saved, and the French had taken over the perimeter defences.

3 June Last night of the evacuation; 26,700 men, mainly French, were taken off the beaches.
In all, 220,000 British and 120,000 French and Belgian troops were rescued. The majority of the French troops returned to France, however, to continue the fight. Some 200 ships of all types were lost and 177 aircraft (against the Luftwaffe losses of 140). The BEF had been forced to leave all its heavy weapons and equipment behind. Two British divisions were left in France: 51st Highland, which had been in the Maginot Line on 10 May, and 1st Armoured. There were also some 120,000 men on the lines of communication. Both divisions were in action south of the Somme.

4 June The Germans entered Dunkirk.
Churchill made his famous speech of defiance: 'We shall fight on the beaches, we shall fight in the fields . . . we shall never surrender.'

5 June The Germans began offensive against the French armies in the south.
De Gaulle was appointed French Under-Secretary of State for War.

6 June The Germans broke through on the lower Somme and reached the River Aisne.

9 June The French were routed on the Somme.
Part of the French Tenth Army, including the British 51st Highland Division, withdrew to the coast at St-Valéry hoping to be evacuated.

10 June Italy announced that she would be at war with Britain and France with effect from the 11th.
The French Government left Paris for Tours. President Roosevelt condemned Germany and Italy and promised material help to the Allies.

11 June Paris declared an open city.
The French pleaded for RAF support, but Churchill refused as he wanted to husband its slender strength for the battle for Britain, which now seemed increasingly likely. Nevertheless a second 'BEF' of two divisions, including 1st Canadian Division, which had been in Britain since December 1939, was sent to Cherbourg to bolster the French, the idea being to form a 'redoubt' in Brittany.

12 June The British 51st Highland Division and four French divisions forced to surrender at St-Valéry.

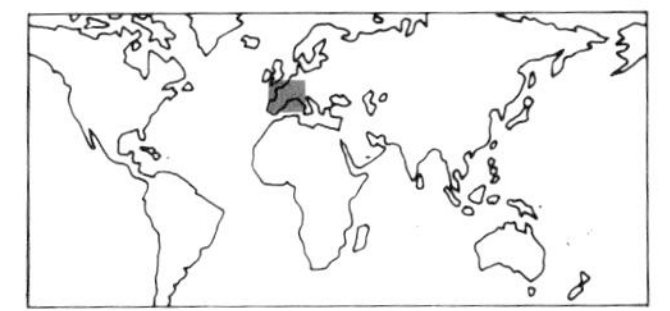

Weygand and Pétain pressed for an armistice, but French Prime Minister Reynaud was determined to fight on.

13 June **The first US ship, *Eastern Prince*, sailed for Britain with arms.**

14 June **The Germans entered Paris.**
The Maginot Line was breached near Saarbrücken and the Germans began operations to cut off the French forces withdrawing towards Bordeaux, and to thrust towards Dijon and Lyons.

16 June **The French decided to seek an armistice.**
Prime Minister Reynaud resigned and a new government was formed by Pétain. Orders were given for the remaining British troops to leave France. Their evacuation was completed on the 18th.

18 June **General de Gaulle broadcast to the French people from London.**
He declared that the war was not over merely because France was about to surrender, and called for volunteers to join in continuing the struggle.

19 June **French ships sought refuge in British and North African ports.**
The Germans invited the French to send representatives to discuss armistice terms.

20 June **Italian troops invaded France.**
The Germans continued their drive south.

22 June **France signed an armistice.**
This took place at Rethondes in the very same railway coach in which the November 1918 Armistice had been signed.

24 June **France signed an armistice with Italy.**

25 June **Hostilities ceased in France.**
So ended the battle for France. In just six weeks Germany had overrun the west. She had lost 45,000 killed and missing while the Allies had suffered more than 100,000 fatal casualties with many more taken prisoner. Three-fifths of France were now to be under German occupation, leaving just the southern part of the country under French control. Under the leadership of Marshal Pétain, this part was to have its seat of government at Vichy and would become known as 'Vichy France'. It had been a devastating defeat and represented the fruits of twenty locust years.

Britain now stood alone. Few outside her shores gave her much chance of surviving unless she came to terms with Hitler.

THE CONQUEST OF FRANCE: 5 to 25 June

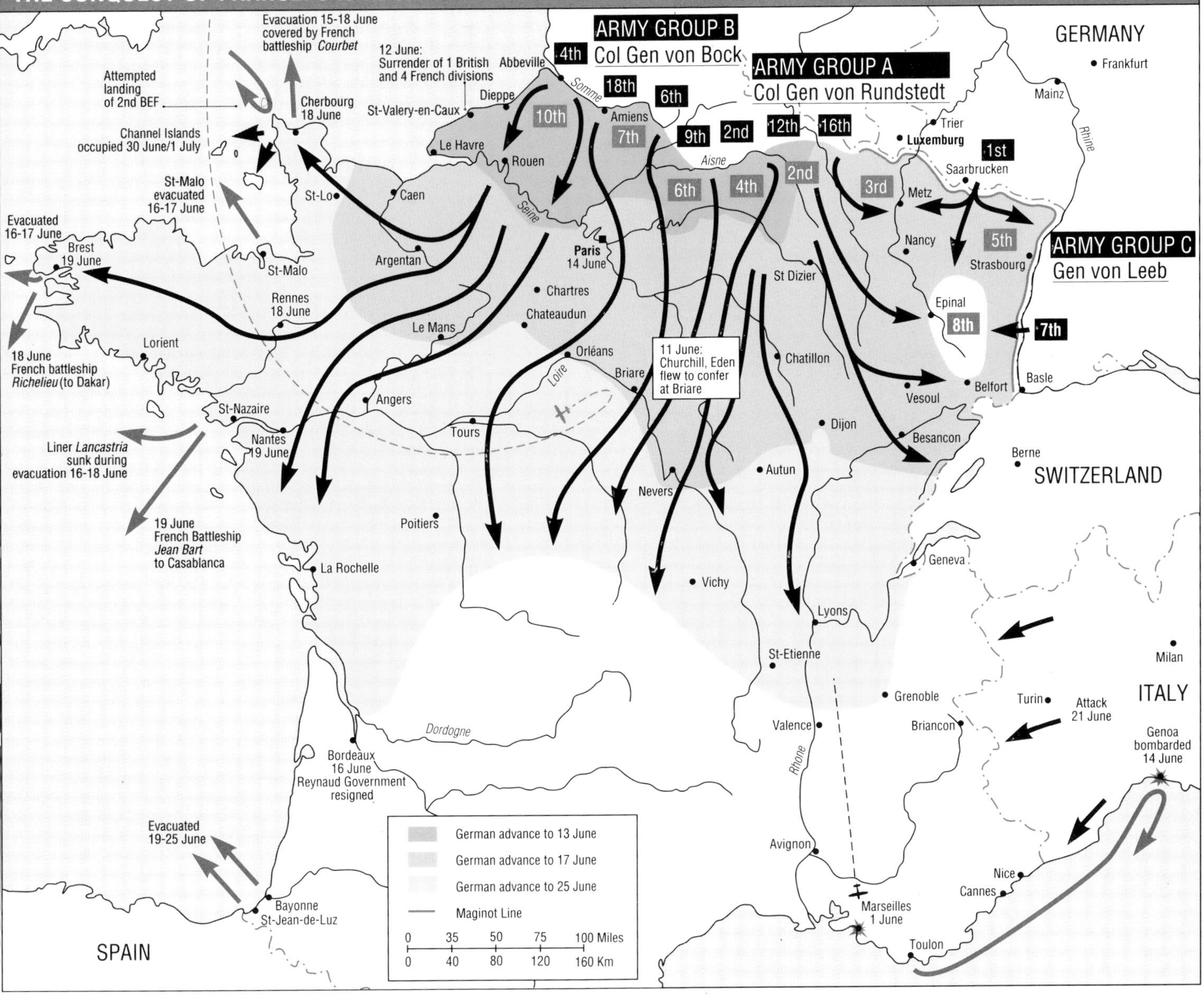

ARMY GROUP B
Col Gen von Bock
ARMY GROUP A
Col Gen von Rundstedt
ARMY GROUP C
Gen von Leeb
Evacuation 15-18 June covered by French battleship *Courbet*
12 June: Surrender of 1 British and 4 French divisions
Attempted landing of 2nd BEF
Cherbourg 18 June
Channel Islands occupied 30 June/1 July
St-Malo evacuated 16-17 June
Evacuated 16-17 June
Brest 19 June
Rennes 18 June
Paris 14 June
18 June French battleship *Richelieu* (to Dakar)
Liner *Lancastria* sunk during evacuation 16-18 June
Nantes 19 June
19 June French Battleship *Jean Bart* to Casablanca
11 June: Churchill, Eden flew to confer at Briare
Bordeaux 16 June Reynaud Government resigned
Evacuated 19-25 June
Marseilles 1 June
Attack 21 June
Genoa bombarded 14 June
GERMANY
SWITZERLAND
ITALY
SPAIN

German advance to 13 June
German advance to 17 June
German advance to 25 June
Maginot Line
0 35 50 75 100 Miles
0 40 80 120 160 Km

Britain's Plight · P36

3 BRITAIN ALONE, July 1940 to June 1941

3 JUNE 1940 TO 27 SEPTEMBER 1940

Britain's Plight

With the surrender of France, Britain stood alone, together with her Empire, against an ebullient Germany and Italy, now Hitler's ally. At home Britain now faced the threat of cross-Channel invasion, while Mussolini's entry into the war meant that her position in the Mediterranean and the Middle East was in jeopardy.

3 June 1940 Churchill ordered the setting up of raiding forces.
His aim was to keep German troops tied down in the occupied countries. This was the origin of the Commandos, who would eventually play a leading part in all theatres of war in which British troops were engaged.

Night of 24/25 June First British Commando raid against the French coast.
No casualties or damage were inflicted and the raid was abortive. It was followed on the night of 14/15 July by an equally unsuccessful operation against German-occupied Guernsey in the Channel Islands. After this, official policy changed to one of preparing for large-scale raids once the threat of invasion of Britain had receded.

26 June Turkey announced that she would stay out of the war.

27 June All French ships in British ports seized by the Royal Navy.

28 June Britain officially recognised General Charles de Gaulle as leader of the Free French.

28 June The Pope offered to mediate.
He sent messages to Churchill, Hitler and Mussolini offering to mediate for peace; the King of Sweden made a similar offer.

28 June Stalin demanded Roumania cede the provinces of Bessarabia and northern Bucovina to her.
Stalin was taking advantage of the German preoccupation in the west to consolidate his position in eastern Europe. Not wanting a rift with the Soviets at this stage, the Germans advised Roumania to hand over these territories: they were occupied by Soviet troops next day.

30 June Germany occupied the Channel Islands.
Since their close proximity to enemy-held France rendered them indefensible, the British had demilitarized the islands a few days earlier. They would remain in German hands for the rest of the war and be the site of the only concentration camp on British soil, on Alderney.

3 July Anglo-French naval clashes at Oran and Mers-el-Kebir.
The Royal Navy bombarded the French fleet in these North African ports (Operation 'Catapult').

The British were very concerned that the French fleet might fall into German hands and thus drastically increase the threat to the Royal Navy.

5 July Vichy France broke off diplomatic relations with Britain.
The casualties caused by 'Catapult' angered the French and even upset French people living in Britain. In retaliation, Vichy France aircraft raided Gibraltar from North Africa but caused little damage.

11 July Marshal Philippe Pétain formally proclaimed Head of State in France.

19 July In a speech in the Reichstag, Hitler made his last plea for Britain to make peace.
By this time he had already drawn up plans for the invasion of Britain. The British Government immediately rejected his offer.

20 July President Roosevelt signed the Two-Ocean Navy Expansion Act.
This was Roosevelt's first positive step to prepare his country for war, although at this time only 8 per cent of the American people declared themselves willing to enter the war. It provided for a large shipbuilding programme. On **27 August** Congress authorized the President to call the National Guard and other reserves to active duty for one year. Three weeks later, on **16 September,** the Burke-Wadsworth Bill was passed providing for limited conscription. Both measures confined the employment of troops raised under them to the Western Hemisphere and US possessions.

21 July Estonia, Latvia and Lithuania became autonomous republics within the USSR.
A week earlier in general elections all three had voted overwhelmingly for union with the USSR.

22 July Special Operations Executive (SOE) was founded.
This was designed to support and encourage Resistance movements in German-occupied Europe.

23 July Provisional Czech government formed.
In Britain, Eduard Beneš, the former Czech President, established a government in exile.

1 August Soviet Foreign Minister Molotov confirmed USSR neutrality in the continuing war.

13 August Lend–lease agreement.
Roosevelt agreed to supply Britain with fifty First World War destroyers in return for the lease of naval bases in the Caribbean. Churchill had been pleading with Roosevelt for some weeks to supply Britain with these ships (to make good losses during the evacuation from Dunkirk) and other war *matériel*. Churchill saw this deal as 'a long step towards [USA] coming into the war on our side'.

3 September The Vienna Award, whereby Roumania was forced to cede territory to Hungary.
Moscow's seizure of Roumanian territory had alarmed Hitler, especially since Germany was heavily dependent on the Roumanian oilfields. When Hungary and Bulgaria made territorial demands the threat to German access to this oil increased. Italy and Germany therefore awarded Hungary Transylvania, which had been taken from her after the First World War, and guaranteed the integrity of the remaining Roumanian territory.

This quickly brought about the downfall of the Roumanian Government and the abdication of King Carol II. General Ion Antonescu, a friend of Hitler's, assumed power as a dictator, thus ensuring that Roumania was now firmly in the Axis camp.

23–25 September Abortive British/Free French attack on Dakar in French West Africa.
De Gaulle hoped to win French West Africa over to his cause, but the garrison of Dakar remained firmly loyal to Vichy France and, after refusing demands to surrender, damaged two British battleships, *Barham* and *Resolution*. Deciding that a landing would cost too much in men and *matériel* the British naval force withdrew. Instead de Gaulle raised his flag in the French Cameroons.

27 September Germany, Italy and Japan signed a tripartite pact in Berlin.
This obliged them to give military assistance to one another should they be attacked by a country not already at war. Furthermore, Japan recognized the Axis right to establish a 'new order' in Europe in return for recognition of Japan's right to impose her 'new order' in Asia.

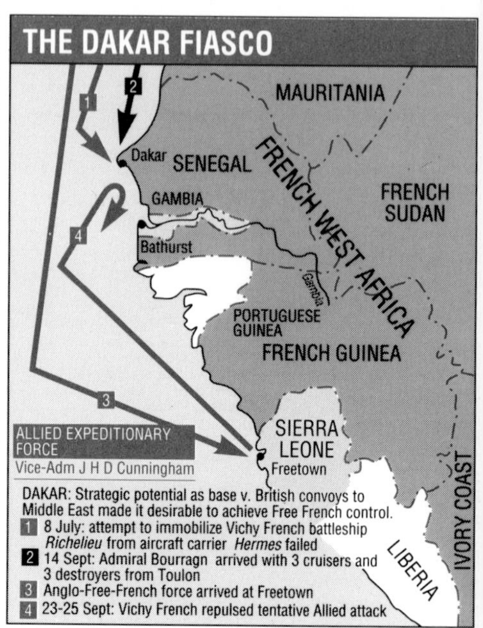
THE DAKAR FIASCO
MAURITANIA
Dakar
SENEGAL
FRENCH WEST AFRICA
FRENCH SUDAN
GAMBIA
Bathurst
Gambia
PORTUGUESE GUINEA
FRENCH GUINEA
SIERRA LEONE
Freetown
LIBERIA
IVORY COAST
ALLIED EXPEDITIONARY FORCE
Vice-Adm J H D Cunningham
DAKAR: Strategic potential as base v. British convoys to Middle East made it desirable to achieve Free French control.
1 8 July: attempt to immobilize Vichy French battleship Richelieu from aircraft carrier Hermes failed
2 14 Sept: Admiral Bourragn arrived with 3 cruisers and 3 destroyers from Toulon
3 Anglo-Free-French force arrived at Freetown
4 23-25 Sept: Vichy French repulsed tentative Allied attack

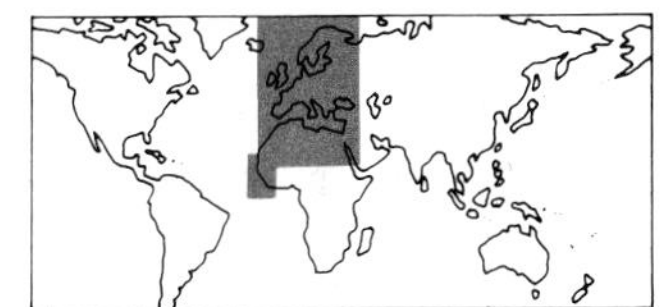

BRITAIN ALONE: EUROPE UNDER THE NAZIS

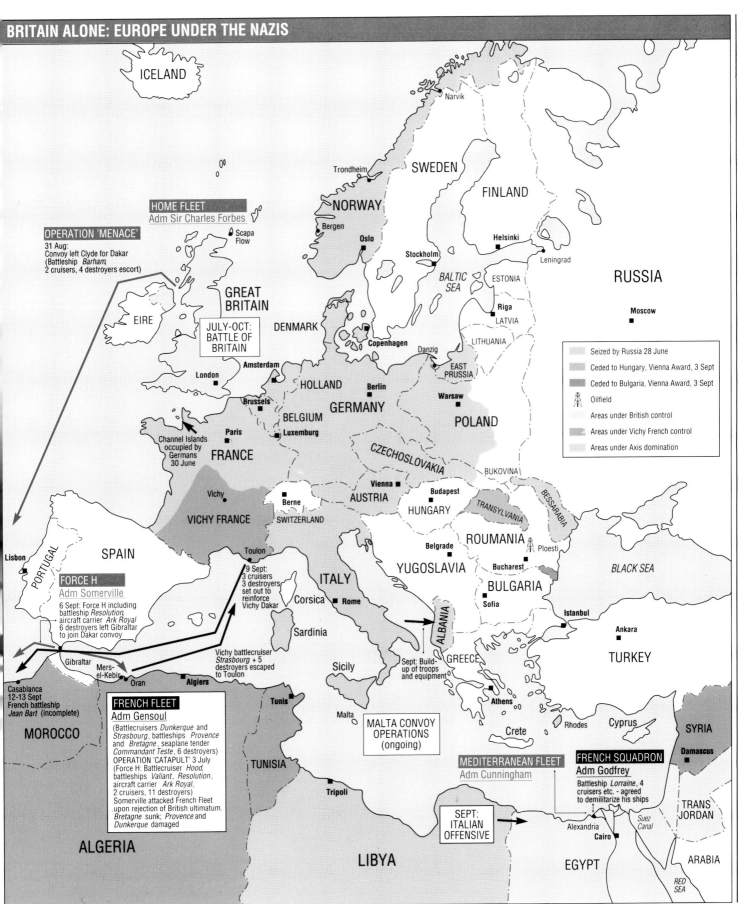

HOME FLEET
Adm Sir Charles Forbes

OPERATION 'MENACE'
31 Aug:
Convoy left Clyde for Dakar
(Battleship *Barham*,
2 cruisers, 4 destroyers escort)

JULY-OCT:
BATTLE OF
BRITAIN

Channel Islands
occupied by
Germans
30 June

FORCE H
Adm Somerville
6 Sept: Force H including
battleship *Resolution*,
aircraft carrier *Ark Royal*,
6 destroyers left Gibraltar
to join Dakar convoy

9 Sept:
3 cruisers
3 destroyers
set out to
reinforce
Vichy Dakar

Vichy battlecruiser
Strasbourg + 5
destroyers escaped
to Toulon

Casablanca
12-13 Sept
French battleship
Jean Bart (incomplete)

FRENCH FLEET
Adm Gensoul
(Battlecruisers *Dunkerque* and
Strasbourg, battleships *Provence*
and *Bretagne*, seaplane tender
Commandant Teste, 6 destroyers)
OPERATION 'CATAPULT' 3 July
(Force H: Battlecruiser *Hood*,
battleships *Valiant*, *Resolution*,
aircraft carrier *Ark Royal*,
2 cruisers, 11 destroyers)
Somerville attacked French Fleet
upon rejection of British ultimatum.
Bretagne sunk; *Provence* and
Dunkerque damaged

MALTA CONVOY
OPERATIONS
(ongoing)

Sept: Build-
up of troops
and equipment

MEDITERRANEAN FLEET
Adm Cunningham

FRENCH SQUADRON
Adm Godfrey
Battleship *Lorraine*, 4
cruisers etc. - agreed
to demilitarize his ships

SEPT:
ITALIAN
OFFENSIVE

Seized by Russia 28 June
Ceded to Hungary, Vienna Award, 3 Sept
Ceded to Bulgaria, Vienna Award, 3 Sept
Oilfield
Areas under British control
Areas under Vichy French control
Areas under Axis domination

ICELAND
Narvik
Trondheim
SWEDEN
FINLAND
NORWAY
Bergen
Oslo
Scapa Flow
Helsinki
Leningrad
Stockholm
BALTIC SEA
ESTONIA
RUSSIA
GREAT BRITAIN
EIRE
Riga
LATVIA
Moscow
DENMARK
Copenhagen
LITHUANIA
Danzig
EAST PRUSSIA
Amsterdam
London
HOLLAND
Berlin
Warsaw
Brussels
BELGIUM
GERMANY
POLAND
Paris
Luxemburg
FRANCE
CZECHOSLOVAKIA
BUKOVINA
Vienna
AUSTRIA
Budapest
HUNGARY
TRANSYLVANIA
BESSARABIA
Vichy
Berne
SWITZERLAND
VICHY FRANCE
ROUMANIA
Ploesti
Belgrade
Bucharest
YUGOSLAVIA
BLACK SEA
Lisbon
PORTUGAL
SPAIN
Toulon
ITALY
BULGARIA
Sofia
Corsica
Rome
ALBANIA
Istanbul
Ankara
Sardinia
TURKEY
Gibraltar
Mers-el-Kebir
Oran
Algiers
Sicily
GREECE
Tunis
Athens
Malta
Rhodes
Cyprus
Crete
MOROCCO
SYRIA
Damascus
TUNISIA
Tripoli
TRANS JORDAN
Alexandria
Suez Canal
Cairo
ALGERIA
LIBYA
EGYPT
ARABIA
RED SEA

Operation 'Sealion'

Hitler had hoped that after France had fallen and Britain was on her own she would realize that to continue fighting would be self-destructive and that she would make peace. Thus, when he launched his attack in the west he had made no contingency plan to deal with a Britain determined to fight on. By the end of June, however, Churchill had repeatedly made it clear that there could be no question of peace while Germany remained in occupation of so many countries. Britain's main problem was not manpower, but lack of weapons, especially since so much *matériel* had been left behind in France.

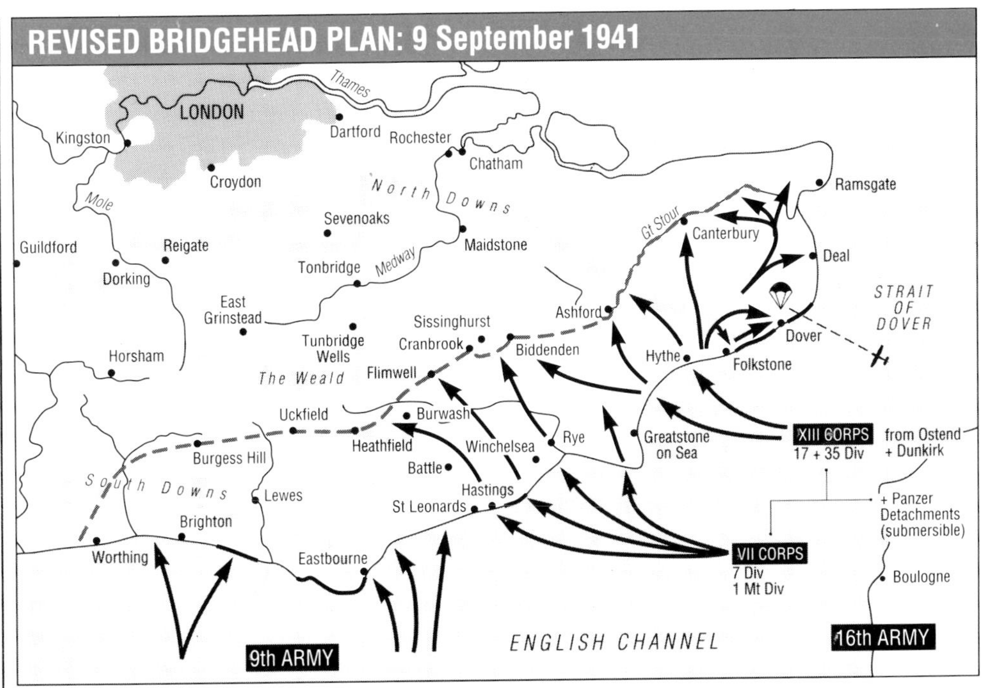

REVISED BRIDGEHEAD PLAN: 9 September 1941

14 May 1940 **Britain established a part-time defence force.**
British Secretary of State for War Anthony Eden called for volunteers to form the Local Defence Volunteers (LDV). They were to provide an invaluable addition to Britain's defences. Within 24 hours 250,000 volunteers had enrolled and by the end of July the figure had risen to 1,250,000. On 23 July, on Churchill's prompting, the LDV was retitled the Home Guard.

12 June **Plan for defence of Britain completed.**
This was drawn up under the direction of General Sir Edmund Ironside, CinC, Home Forces. The main defensive line was the GHQ Line, which ran south from Edinburgh to the Medway, covering the east coast, and south of London to south of Bristol, facing the south coast. In front of this were a series of 'stop lines'. The defences themselves largely comprised anti-tank ditches and small concrete strong points known as 'pillboxes'. A massive construction programme was immediately put in hand (and more than 5,000 pillboxes survive in Britain to this day).

2 July **First German military directive on the invasion of Britain issued.**
While this laid down that preparations for an invasion must begin immediately, it made it clear that Hitler was still undecided. No date was given for the invasion, and it was stressed that as yet it was only a plan. It was recognized that the attainment of air superiority was an essential prerequisite.

11 July **Admiral Raeder expressed his reservations to Hitler about the invasion.**
Raeder, CinC Navy, saw it only as a last resort to make Britain sue for peace, believing that the strangling of her maritime trade and air attacks on her cities would be a more effective method.

13 July **Hitler declined an Italian offer to participate in the invasion.**

16 July **Hitler issued Directive No. 16 for Operation 'Sealion', the invasion of Britain.**
Twenty divisions would take part, but the Luftwaffe had to gain absolute air superiority over the English Channel first. The aim was 'to eliminate the English homeland as a base for the carrying on of the war against Germany, and, should it become necessary, to occupy it completely'. But even now, Hitler had still not finally made up his mind to proceed.

17 July **The German Army presented its invasion plan.**
The landings would be carried out by von Rundstedt's Army Group A. Six divisions would land between Ramsgate and Bexhill in the south-east corner of England, four would land between Brighton and the Isle of Wight and three on the Dorset coast. Two airborne divisions would also be deployed, and the follow-up forces would include six Panzer and three motorized divisions. Once ashore the troops would advance north, sealing off Devon, Cornwall and Wales; they would surround and reduce London and then continue northwards.

19 July **General Sir Alan Brooke became CinC, Home Forces.**
Brooke's views differed from Ironside's on how best to defend Britain against invasion. He considered that the German landings must be defeated on the beaches; accordingly, he deployed his mobile reserves much farther forward.

31 July **Hitler appraised the Army plan at a conference of his military chiefs.**
Raeder criticized the Army's plan as being on a front far too broad for the German Navy to be able to secure, especially in view of the might of the Royal Navy. Furthermore, some 2,500 barges and other craft were needed to transport the invading force and, because of the time needed to collect and concentrate these, the invasion could not be mounted before 15 September at the earliest. Moreover, conditions in the Channel were beginning to worsen, and he recommended that the invasion be postponed to May 1941. The Army refuted Raeder's criticisms, arguing that to land on a narrow front would enable the British to concentrate their limited forces and that the longer the invasion was delayed the more time they would have to rebuild their forces.

1 August **Hitler issued further directives.**
Directive No. 17 was addressed primarily to the Luftwaffe, but also to the Navy. The Luftwaffe was to commence operations to gain air supremacy beginning on or after 6 August. Once local or temporary superiority had been attained, attacks were to be made on ports and food supply sources. No 'terror attacks' were to be launched without Hitler's express order – and then only 'as a means of reprisal'. The Navy was to begin 'intensified' warfare at the same time as the air offensive was started.

Another directive was signed by Field Marshal Wilhelm Keitel, Chief of Staff of the German Armed Forces. All preparations were to be completed by 15 September, and Hitler would decide 8–14 days after the commencement of the air offensive whether the invasion would be mounted immediately or postponed until 1941. The broad-front plan was to be maintained, despite the Navy's objections.

While the German Navy struggled to collect the necessary craft, and the troops taking part underwent rigorous training in amphibious warfare, the Luftwaffe made its final preparations for the assault that Goering was certain would sweep the RAF from the skies. On the other side of the Channel the British waited, grim and expectant.

The Battle of Britain · P40

The Battle of Britain

To fight the Battle of Britain, Goering intended to use two *Luftflotten* (Air Fleets), Albert Kesselring's Luftflotte 2 and Hugo Sperrle's Luftflotte 3, which were based in Belgium and north-west France. This represented a strength of some 2,500 combat aircraft of all types. He could also call on Luftflotte 5 (Hans-Juergen Stumpff) based in Norway and Denmark. This had an additional 160 aircraft. The Luftwaffe believed at the beginning of July that RAF Fighter Command had some 600 aircraft and that British fighter production was running at 180–300 per month.

RAF Fighter Command was organized into four groups, each covering a part of the United Kingdom. Throughout the forthcoming battle it would be No 11 Group that would bear the brunt, but with continuous reinforcement from its northern neighbour, No 12. No 10 Group would be kept quite busy, but after mid-August No 13 Group would have a relatively quiet time.

The battle itself had, in fact, begun much earlier than Hitler's Directive No. 17 laid down. Indeed, the Luftwaffe had been overflying the Channel from the fall of France onwards.

THE LUFTWAFFE AND THE RAF

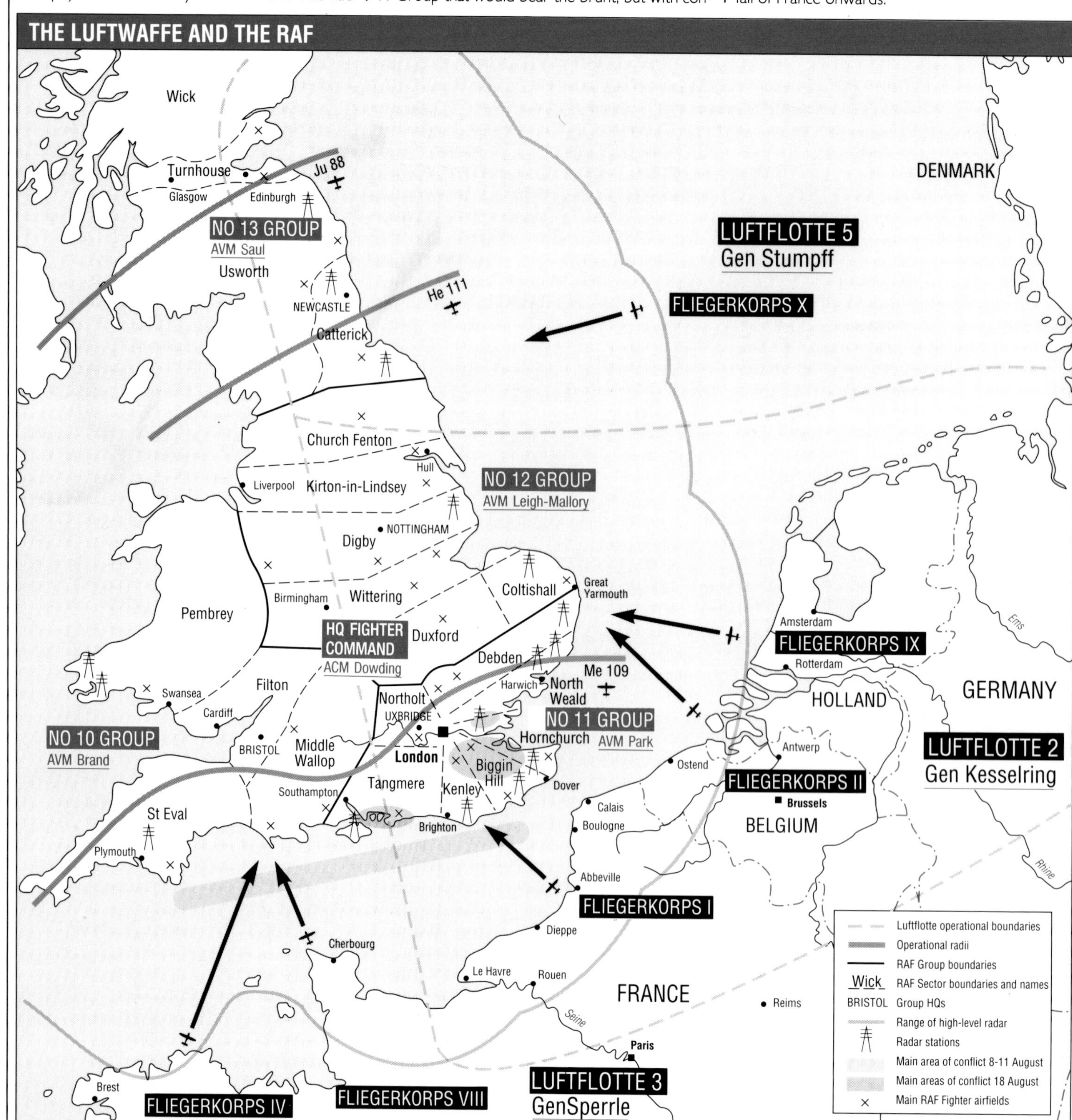

P38 · Operation 'Sealion'

10 July 1940 **Luftwaffe raided South Wales docks.**
This 70-aircraft raid marked the beginning of the first or 'contact' phase of the battle. Goering hoped to tempt the RAF into battle by attacks on convoys in the Channel and ports. Hugh Dowding, CinC, RAF Fighter Command, saw as his priority the rebuilding of his command after its losses in France and hence refused to be drawn. By the end of the month he had just under 600 fighters, of which one-third were unserviceable. Aircraft production, however, dramatically outstripped German estimates. This was largely thanks to the dynamism of Lord Beaverbrook, a newspaper magnate whom Churchill had appointed as Minister of Aircraft Production on **11 May**. Monthly production of fighters rose from 256 in April to 496 in July.

30 July **Beginning of a lull in the Luftwaffe's attacks.**
This, to all intents and purposes, marked the end of the first phase of the battle.

6 August **Goering set 10 August as opening day of the main offensive.**
Poor weather prospects on the next day caused a postponement and a new start date was eventually fixed for **13 August**. A vital intelligence tool possessed by the British was their ability to decipher the Luftwaffe's coded messages passed through their Enigma cipher machines. Dowding was therefore well-aware of the German plans.

8 August **Luftwaffe renewed its attacks in the Channel.**
On this day the Luftwaffe caused serious losses to a convoy and its escorts, but lost 31 aircraft against 16 RAF fighters shot down. This marked the beginning of the next phase. Three days later, in further battles over the Channel the losses were 35 German and 29 British aircraft.

12 August **Luftwaffe switched its attacks to airfields and radar stations.**
This was in preparation for the launch of the main attack next day. Three forward airfields were badly damaged and one out of six radar stations were put out of action. These radar stations were crucial, since it was through them that the RAF received timely warnings of raids so that fighters could be 'scrambled' to intercept them. The air losses were Luftwaffe 26, RAF 22.

13 August **Luftwaffe's largest attacks to date.**
They flew 1,485 sorties, but because of confusion and delays the main attacks were not mounted until the afternoon. Some airfields were attacked and damaged, but significantly they were not primarily fighter bases. Losses were RAF 15, Luftwaffe 39, including a large proportion of Ju 87 Stukas, which were, after further heavy losses, withdrawn from the battle a few days later.

15 August *Adlertag* **('Eagle Day').**
Because of the disappointments of the 13th, Goering decreed that the 15th would now be 'Eagle Day' or the opening of the decisive phase of the battle. A total of 1,786 sorties were flown, attacks being concentrated on airfields. The Luftwaffe lost 76 aircraft, many from Luftflotte 5, which made two attacks on north-east England, designed to draw fighters away from the south, and it took no further part in the battle. The RAF lost 35 fighters.

18 August **Crisis day for the British.**
The Germans inflicted severe damage on Fighter Command airfields, doing much to upset the command and control system. Losses: Luftwaffe 67, Fighter Command 33. More serious than the loss of aircraft, however, was RAF fighter pilot casualties. During the past two weeks 106 had been killed and the survivors were very tired. The rate of supply of replacement pilots was not keeping up with wastage. Luckily for the RAF, there was now a four-day lull caused partly by the weather and partly by a fighter reorganization within the Luftwaffe.

20 August **'Never in the field of human conflict was so much owed by so many to so few.'**
Churchill's famous tribute to the RAF Battle of Britain fighter pilots.

24 August **The third phase of the battle began.**
The Luftwaffe was now sending over an increased proportion of fighters and fewer bombers. It continued to concentrate on airfields, especially in south-east England. That night the first bombs – dropped in error – fell on central London.

Night of 25/26 August **RAF bombers attacked Berlin for the first time.**
This was in retaliation for the bombs on London the previous night. Some 50 bombers were involved, but the damage to the capital of the Third Reich was slight. Meanwhile, Luftwaffe attacks on airfields and fighter sector HQs continued day in, day out.

6 September **End of third phase of the battle.**
During this phase the Luftwaffe had lost 308 aircraft and the RAF 273 fighters. The margin was significantly closer than in earlier phases and the rate of aircraft production was falling behind the RAF's loss rate. Furthermore, the continual attacks were now seriously disrupting command and control. The Luftwaffe had also attacked a number of towns and cities by night. On the night of **5/6 September** London was intentionally bombed for the first time, thus marking the beginning of the London Blitz.

7 September **In the late afternoon London was subjected to a massive air attack, marking the start of the fourth phase.**
Following a speech in Berlin on the 4th, when Hitler vowed to raze British cities in retaliation for RAF raids on German cities, the Luftwaffe switched to a concentrated and prolonged assault on London, by day and by night, to break the morale of the British people. This switch from attacks on airfields gave RAF Fighter Command a valuable breathing space.

That night the code-word 'Cromwell' was issued to all defending forces in southern England. It meant that invasion was probable within the next 24 hours.

10 September **Hitler decided to postpone 'Sealion' to 24 September.**
Four days later it was further postponed to the 27th, the last day of the month on which the tides would be suitable.

15 September **Climax of the Battle of Britain.**
Goering believed that the RAF had now been broken, and planned a final decisive assault on London. In the event 1,300 sorties were flown against the capital, while the RAF was able to put 170 fighters into the air; 58 German aircraft were shot down for the loss of 26 British fighters. The realization that air superiority had not been achieved caused a severe dent in the Luftwaffe's morale.

17 September **Hitler postponed 'Sealion' indefinitely.**
Although the Battle of Britain did not officially end until **31 October**, and indeed there were still some fierce clashes to come, it was effectively over after 15 September. That it was one of the decisive battles of the war there is no doubt. While the Luftwaffe lost some 1,880 aircraft, and 2,660 aircrew as opposed to RAF Fighter Command's 1,020 aircraft and 537 pilots killed, it was not mere numbers that marked the victory. The significance was that the RAF had *prevented* the Germans from achieving their aim rather than inflicting a wholesale defeat on the Luftwaffe. If the RAF had failed it would have marked Britain's death knell.

While there was little to choose between the quality of the Luftwaffe's main fighter, the Me109, the RAF's Spitfire and Hurricane or their aircrews, there were clear-cut reasons why the Luftwaffe failed. Because of the distance involved, the German fighters had only limited loiter time over England compared with their RAF counterparts. The RAF tactic of concentrating on the German bombers rather than their fighter escorts also paid off, and the German bombers themselves had only a limited bomb-load. The German conduct of the battle was also fatally flawed in two respects. The first was their failure to maintain their attacks on the radar stations, which were Fighter Command's 'eyes'; and the second, the switch from attacks on airfields to an offensive against London.

Yet, while the threat of invasion had receded and, indeed, on **12 October** Hitler abandoned all preparations for it, the British people still had to endure the bombing of their cities, which would continue night after night throughout the winter.

The Blitz · P42

7 SEPTEMBER 1940 TO 11 MAY 1941

The Blitz

As we have seen, the Blitz on London and Britain's other cities began on **7 September 1940** and was in retaliation for the RAF raid on Berlin two weeks before. It must, however, be pointed out that both the RAF and the Luftwaffe had been attacking each other's towns and cities for some time before this. The Luftwaffe had been bombing ports and aircraft factories, while RAF Bomber Command had been attacking industrial and communications targets in Germany. In both cases civilian casualties had been caused because of the inaccuracy of the bombing and navigation techniques of the day. RAF Bomber Command had also played its part in the Battle of Britain by mounting attacks on concentrations of invasion craft and German airfields in France and the Low Countries.

Like the RAF, the Luftwaffe, eventually recognizing the problems of protecting its bombers, switched to night bombing and there would be few nights during the winter of 1940–1 when Londoners would not be disturbed by the sounding of air raid sirens. Bombing by night further reduced accuracy and hence increased civilian casualties.

In the years leading up to the outbreak of war the British Government had instituted measures to protect the people from air attack. Shelters had been built and the Air Raid Precautions (ARP) services had been set up. In September 1939 there had been a mass evacuation of children and mothers from the cities to the rural areas, but when the expected air onslaught did not materialize they drifted back home. Now that the bombing had started there was another evacuation.

Night of 23/24 September 1940 129 RAF bombers raided Berlin.
They attacked a number of industrial targets. Throughout most of the month, however, RAF Bomber Command's main target was the concentrations of invasion barges in the Channel ports.

27 September In daylight raids the Luftwaffe lost 52 aircraft shot down and the RAF 28.

30 September Last Luftwaffe major daylight attack on England.
One thousand figher and 173 bomber sorties were flown, the main targets being London and the Westland aircraft factory at Yeovil. 43 aircraft were lost against the RAF's 16. This finally convinced the Germans that they must switch to night attacks.

WAR IN THE AIR: Autumn 1940 to spring 1941

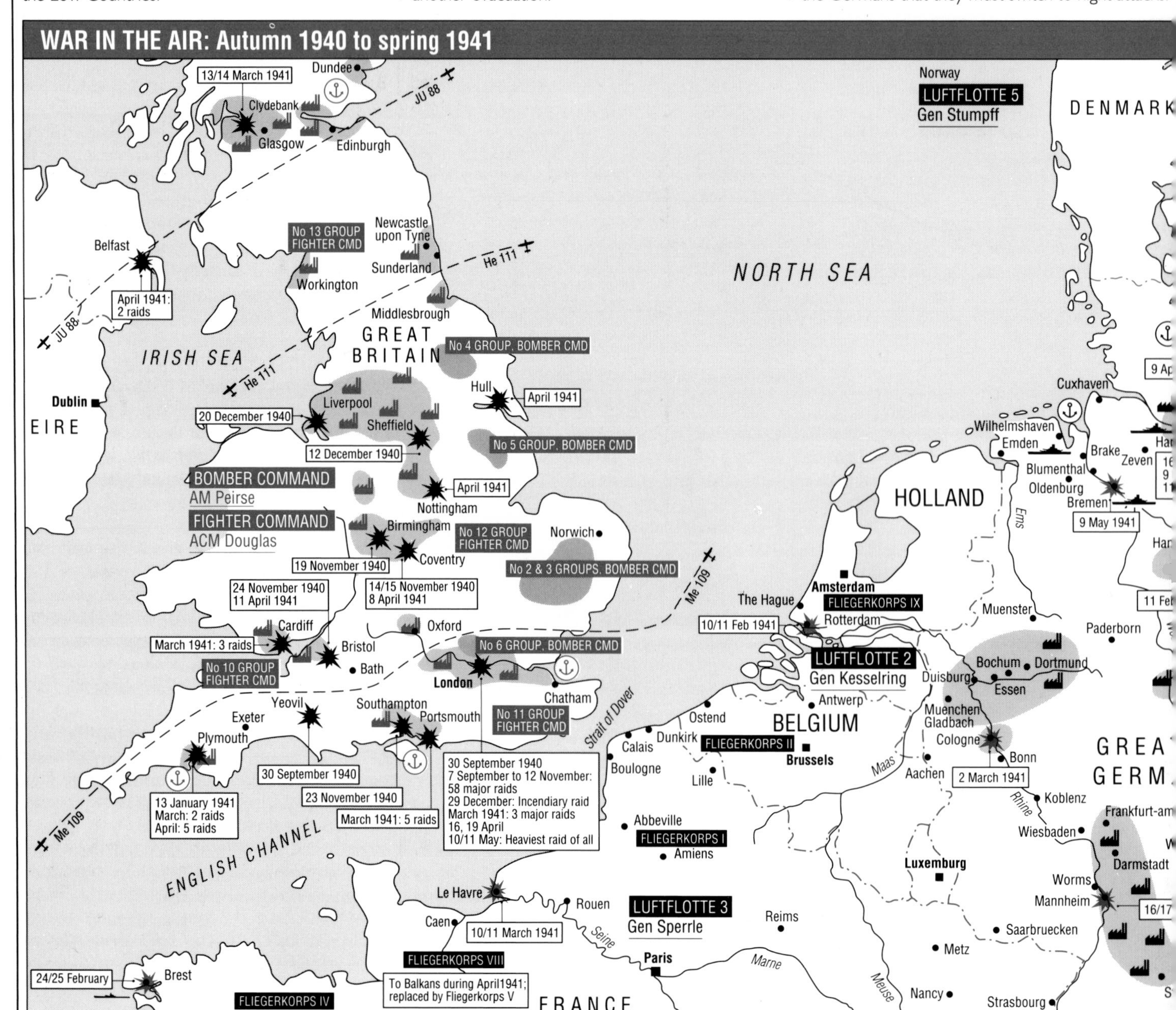

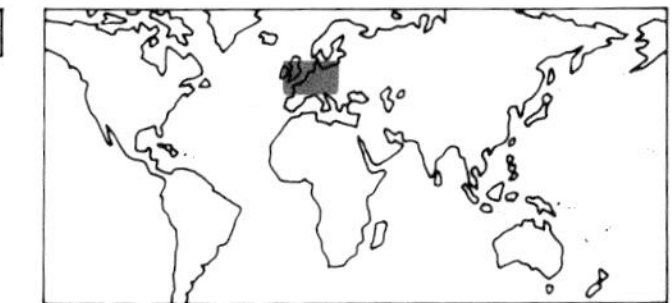

They had, however, been developing a navigation system, *Knickebein* (Crooked Leg), based on a stream of radio signals, aimed at the target, down which aircraft would fly. The British were aware of this and had developed counter-measures, but the Germans then refined the system with a device called *X-Geraet*. The aircraft flew down a fine beam of signals within a wide, coarse band and picked up three intersecting beams, the last of which was the signal to bomb.

During the period **7 September to 12 November** the Luftwaffe flew 58 major raids against London – there was only one night when German bombers were not over the capital. Some 15,000 Londoners were killed and many more injured. The destruction of buildings was serious, especially homes. Indeed, more than 250,000 people had been made homeless. Nevertheless the resilience of the British people disproved the pre-war theorists.

A major problem for the British at this time was air defence. Despite a massive expansion in anti-aircraft artillery just before the war, the guns to defend London were few, and radar-equipped night fighters were in their infancy.

During this time the RAF continued to attack targets, mainly oil and communications, in Germany.

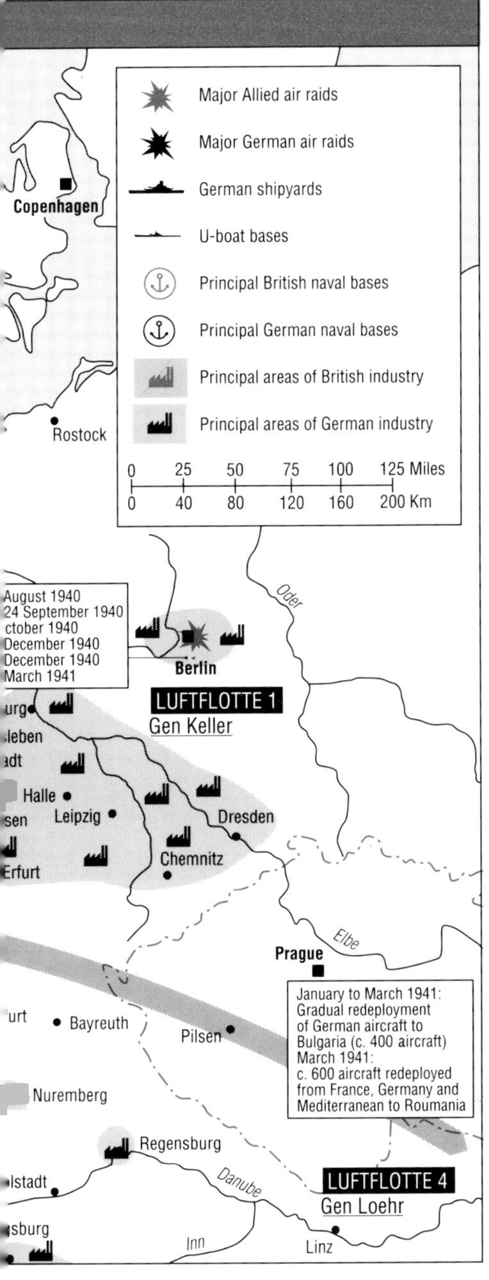

Night of 14/15 November **The Coventry raid.**

This marked a new Luftwaffe strategy. The pressure was taken off London and attacks were made on other industrial cities. A total of 449 bombers were involved and destroyed much of the heart of Coventry, making almost one-third of the houses uninhabitable and causing some 1,100 casualties, as well as destroying 21 factories. Because of the relatively small size of Coventry the shock of the raid was that much greater. But if the Germans wanted to destroy Coventry completely they made the mistake of not returning immediately; thus its vital war industry was able to recover. This raid produced a new word in the English and German languages – 'Conventrate' or '*Coventrieren*', meaning the physical and psychological destruction of a city.

This was followed by heavy raids on Birmingham **(19 November)**, Southampton **(23 November)**, Bristol **(24 November)**, Sheffield **(12 December)** and Liverpool **(20 December)**. Casualties to British civilians for November were 4,588 killed and 6,202 injured.

Night of 16/17 December **134 RAF bombers, the largest number to attack a single target so far, raided Mannheim.**

This was in retaliation for recent attacks on British cities and marked a new departure in that for the first time the bombers were ordered to attack the centre of the city rather than specific industrial targets. It thus marked the beginning of RAF Bomber Command's 'area bombing' strategy. Total civilian casualties were 115, and 1,266 were made homeless.

29 December **Heavy incendiary raid on London.**

Many historic buildings were destroyed or badly damaged.

British civilian casualties for December were 3,793 killed and 5,244 injured.

13 January 1941 **Heavy raid on Plymouth.**

Bad weather restricted Luftwaffe operations during January and February.

Night of 10/11 February **Operational début of the RAF's 4-engine Stirling bomber.**

The Stirling was the first of the 'heavies' and this operation was an attack on oil storage tanks at Rotterdam in The Netherlands.

Night of 24/25 February **The RAF's Manchester bomber made its first raid, against Brest.**

This was a 2-engine heavy bomber, but was to prove mechanically unsatisfactory. From it would develop the famous Lancaster bomber. Another 'heavy', the Halifax, first saw action in a raid on Le Havre on the night of **10/11 March**, but one of the six taking part was unfortunately shot down by an RAF night fighter during its return flight.

13 and 14 March **Heavy raids on Clydebank, near Glasgow.**

35,000 out of its 47,000 inhabitants were made homeless. During March, London suffered three major raids, Cardiff three, Portsmouth five, Plymouth two. Much of the Luftwaffe bombing effort was directed against west coast ports from which the Atlantic convoys set out and at which they arrived.

8 April **Heavy raid on Coventry marked the end of a temporary lull.**

This new phase was designed as much as anything to disguise German preparations for the invasion of Russia. Bristol was struck on the 11th and Belfast on the 15th. On **16** and **19 April** London was hit. There were more than 2,000 fatal casualties and 148,000 houses were damaged or destroyed. Five more raids on Plymouth followed, which almost destroyed the city, and there were attacks on Belfast, Hull and Nottingham.

Night of 10/11 May **The last night of the Blitz and the heaviest attack of all on London.**

Casualties numbered 1,436 killed and 1,792 seriously injured. One-third of the streets in Greater London were rendered impassable and 155,000 families found themselves without gas, water or electricity.

The Blitz ended because all available Luftwaffe strength was now needed for the invasion of Russia. What the Blitz had shown, however, was that pre-war theories that bombing alone could destroy the will of a people to fight were apparently untrue – although if the attacks on London had continued after 10 May it is likely that cracks in morale might have appeared.

The RAF had now also found itself drawn to adopt the same strategy, partly because it lacked accurate bombing aids and partly in retaliation. From now on attacks on the morale of the German people were to receive ever greater priority as the size of RAF Bomber Command began to grow. It must be remembered, however, that at this stage of the war bombing was the only means by which Britain could strike directly at Germany. This would assume even greater significance once Hitler invaded Russias as the only direct way in which the British could take some of the appalling pressure off their new and hard-pressed ally.

Enter 'Bomber' Harris · P100

The Battle of the Atlantic: The First 'Happy Time'

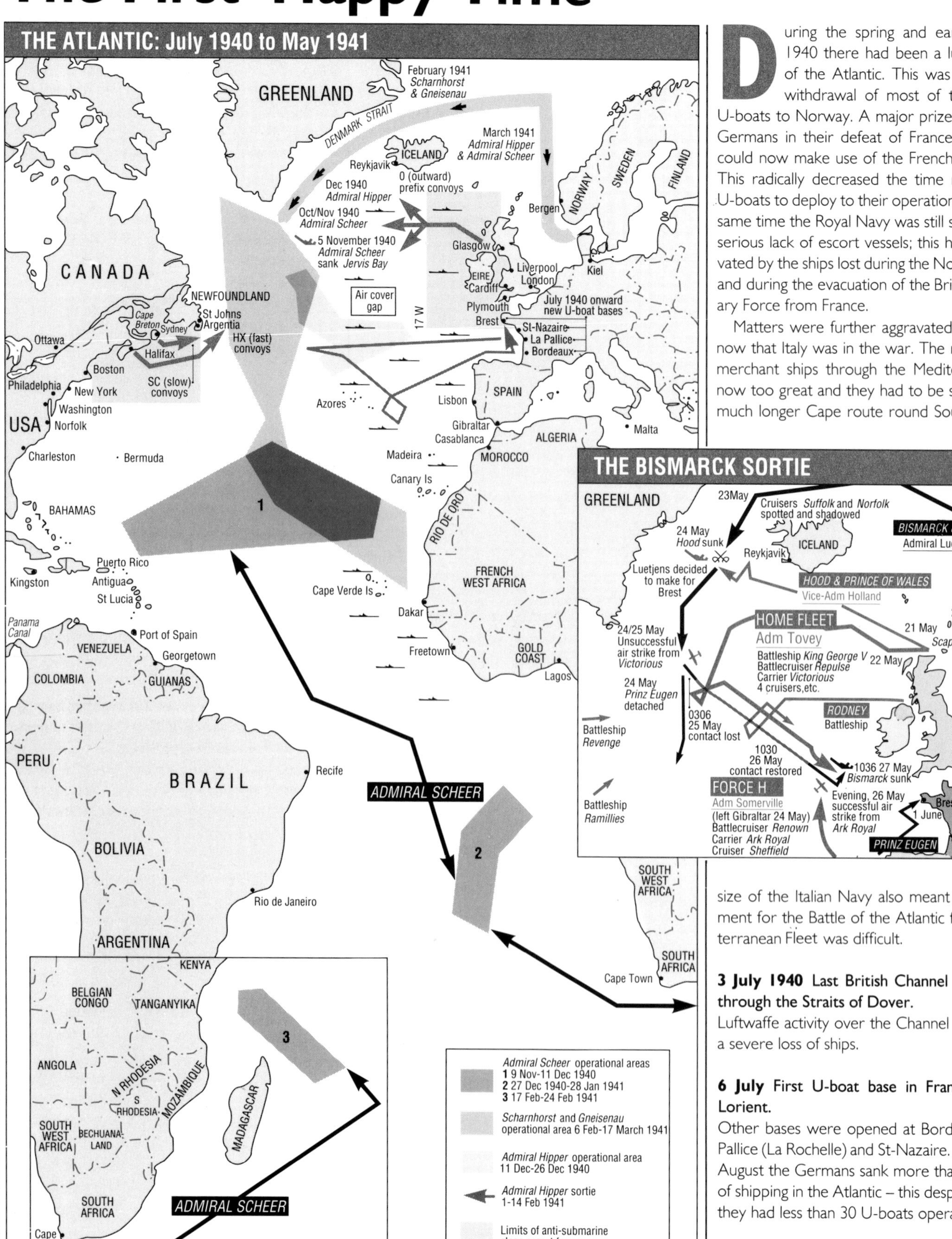

During the spring and early summer of 1940 there had been a lull in the Battle of the Atlantic. This was caused by the withdrawal of most of the operational U-boats to Norway. A major prize reaped by the Germans in their defeat of France was that they could now make use of the French Atlantic ports. This radically decreased the time needed by the U-boats to deploy to their operational areas. At the same time the Royal Navy was still suffering from a serious lack of escort vessels; this had been aggravated by the ships lost during the Norway campaign and during the evacuation of the British Expeditionary Force from France.

Matters were further aggravated for the British now that Italy was in the war. The risks of sending merchant ships through the Mediterranean were now too great and they had to be switched to the much longer Cape route round South Africa. The size of the Italian Navy also meant that reinforcement for the Battle of the Atlantic from the Mediterranean Fleet was difficult.

3 July 1940 Last British Channel convoy passed through the Straits of Dover.
Luftwaffe activity over the Channel had resulted in a severe loss of ships.

6 July First U-boat base in France opened, at Lorient.
Other bases were opened at Bordeaux, Brest, La Pallice (La Rochelle) and St-Nazaire. During July and August the Germans sank more than 700,000 tons of shipping in the Atlantic – this despite the fact that they had less than 30 U-boats operational.

17 August Hitler announced a total maritime blockade of Britain.
Neutral ships would be sunk without warning.

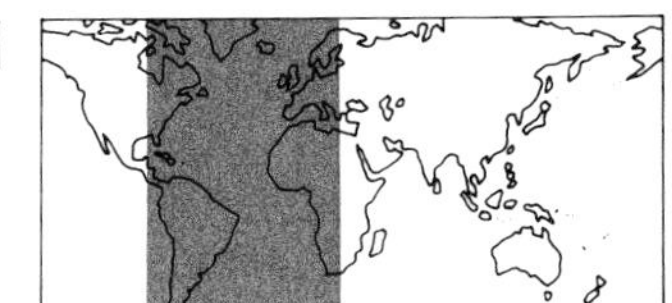

2 September **US Congress finally agreed to the handing over of 50 obsolete destroyers to Britain.**
This was in return for 99-year leases on naval bases in Antigua, St Lucia, Trinidad, British Guiana, the Bahamas, Jamaica and Argentia. The first eight destroyers were taken over on **6 September**. The deal had been drawn up by Churchill and Roosevelt.

By the late summer convoys had been organized into 'fast' (9–14.9 knots) and 'slow' (7.5–9 knots). Inward fast convoys had the prefix 'HX' followed by the convoy number and assembled at Halifax, Nova Scotia. Slow inward ('SC') assembled at Sydney, Cape Breton, while outward convoys were prefixed 'OA' (British east coast assembly) and 'OB' (remainder). The shortage of escort vessels meant that often only one warship was available to protect the convoy in mid-Atlantic; only east of the 17°W meridian were additional escorts provided. The U-boats were also helped by the basing of a Focke-Wulf Fw 200 Kondor long-range maritime reconnaissance aircraft squadron at Bordeaux, which were used to locate the convoy and guide the U-boats on to it. They themselves accounted for 30 ships (110,000 tons) during July and August. Furthermore the Germans were able to read the signals code used by Allied merchant shipping.

17–20 October **Eight U-boats attacked Convoys SC7 and HX79, sinking 32 ships totalling 152,000 tons.**
A further four ships were damaged. The total number of merchant ships in the two convoys was 91. Losses in the Atlantic for September and October were 403,000 and 418,000 tons respectively.

5 November **German pocket battleship *Admiral Scheer* sank the armed merchant cruiser *Jervis Bay* in the Atlantic.**
This marked a resurgence of the surface threat to the convoys. *Jervis Bay* managed to hold *Admiral Scheer* long enough for the convoy to scatter, and only five ships were lost. *Admiral Scheer* continued down to the South Atlantic and subsequently returned to Germany having sunk a total of 17 ships.

Bad weather continuing into December restricted U-boat operations. This was reflected in merchant shipping losses, which fell to 294,000 tons in November and were 322,000 in December.

7 December ***Admiral Hipper* left Kiel on an anti-convoy cruise.**
On Christmas Day she intercepted a troop convoy bound for the Middle East, but was seen off by the three cruisers providing the escort. She was forced to put into Brest for repairs.

January 1941 **Shipping losses in the Atlantic totalled 310,000 tons.**

1 February ***Hipper* slipped out of Brest.**
On the 12th she sank seven out of nineteen ships in an unescorted homeward bound convoy from Freetown in West Africa and then returned to Brest.

4 February ***Scharnhorst* and *Gneisenau* slipped out of the Baltic.**
They had been foiled once by the British Home Fleet, but managed to get into the Atlantic when the latter had to return to port to refuel. They arrived at Brest on **22 March**, having caused havoc on the Atlantic shipping routes, sinking 115,000 tons and disrupting the entire convoy system.

Total shipping losses in the Atlantic for February rose to almost 370,000 tons.

7 March ***U-47* sunk by HMS *Wolverine*.**
This was in attacks on convoy OB293 south of Iceland and reflected improved training and stronger escorts. The U-boat was still commanded by Prien, hero of the sinking of *Royal Oak* in Scapa Flow. Another U-boat was sunk and one damaged, while the convoy suffered only two ships sunk and two damaged.

17 March ***U-99* and *U-100* sunk by British escorts while attacking homeward bound convoy HX112.**
U-99 was commanded by Otto Kretschmer, top-scoring U-boat skipper with 263,682 tons to his credit, and was forced to surrender to *Walker* and *Vanoc*. *Vanoc* also accounted for *U-100*, commanded by another ace, Joachim Schepke. The convoy lost five ships.

The British successes were also attributable to Type 286M radar, with which an increasing number of escorts were now equipped; it enabled U-boats to be located at a range of three miles (5km) on the surface.

19 March **Churchill formed the Battle of the Atlantic Committee.**
This afforded co-ordination at the highest level. For the first time since the previous September the Germans had 30 U-boats operational, and despite the increased strength of the escorts, shipping losses in the Atlantic rose to a staggering 517,000 tons.

Escort groups were now based in Iceland to increase escort coverage of the convoys, and RAF Coastal Command also deployed aircraft there. This, and the increase in strength of the Royal Canadian Navy (RCN) meant that an escort, although weak, could be provided by the RCN from Canada to 35°W. Iceland-based escorts then took over until 18°W.

8 May ***U-110* (Julius Lemp) forced to surrender to HMS *Bulldog*.**
She had been attacking convoy OB318 south of Greenland. This was critical to Allied fortunes in the Battle of the Atlantic at this stage. Forced to the surface, Lemp ordered his men to abandon ship and then set off charges to destroy the U-boat. But the detonators did not work, and a boarding party was able to seize the Enigma cipher machine and code-books. Lemp committed suicide by allowing himself to drown and *U-110* later broke her tow and sank; but the British now had the means to decipher the coded signals between the U-boats and their HQ and were able to steer convoys around U-boat concentrations.

18 May **The battleship *Bismarck* and heavy cruiser *Prinz Eugen* left the Polish port of Gydnia bound for the Atlantic.**

21 May **RAF reconnaissance aircraft sighted the two ships in harbour at Bergen, Norway.**
The Home Fleet was alerted and sailed for the Denmark Strait in the early hours of the next day.

23 May **That evening the cruiser *Suffolk* sighted the two German ships in the Denmark Strait.**
The Home Fleet planned to intercept them at dawn next day.

24 May ***Bismarck* sank HMS *Hood*.**
Hood had long been the pride of the Royal Navy. Only three men from her crew of more than 1,400 were saved. *Prince of Wales*, in company, was also hit and forced to break off the action. The Admiralty now called up reinforcements from Force H at Gibraltar, while the two German ships separated.

26 May **After contact with *Bismarck* had been lost she was sighted again by an RAF Coastal Command Catalina 700 miles west of Brest.**
That evening torpedo-carrying Swordfish aircraft from *Ark Royal* attacked *Bismarck*. They eventually managed to damage her steering gear, which slowed her considerably.

27 May ***Bismarck* was sunk by the battleships *King George V* and *Rodney*, supported by two cruisers.**
Of her 2,300-man crew only 110 were saved. *Prinz Eugen*, meanwhile, managed to avoid the Royal Navy and arrived at Brest on **1 June**.

27 May **First convoy to have continuous escort protection across the Atlantic, HX129, sailed from Canada.**
The most immediate of the early Ultra successes was the sinking of six supply ships and one tanker which had been deployed to support *Bismarck* during her projected Atlantic cruise. The Admiralty's ability to steer the convoys around U-boat concentrations soon brought results. Shipping losses, which had totalled 381,000 tons in April, 436,500 in May and 415,000 in June, plummetted to 113,000 in July, and this in spite of the fact that Doenitz now had 60 operational boats. The first 'happy time' for the U-boats was over.

The Battle of the Atlantic: The Second 'Happy Time' · P86

Early Italian Successes in North and East Africa

Italy's entry into the war on **11 June 1940** posed a serious threat to Britain's position in the Mediterranean and in Egypt and Palestine. It also jeopardized her oil supplies in the Middle East and her vital line of communication with India and the Far East through the Suez Canal. At sea the Italians had a modern fleet, which included six battleships, 21 cruisers and 50 destroyers. The Royal Navy presence, which was represented by Force H at Gibraltar and the Mediterranean Fleet based at Alexandria, Egypt, was six battleships, one battlecruiser, two aircraft carriers, eight cruisers and 37 destroyers. In the air and on the ground the picture was very different. The Italian air force, the *Regia Aeronautica*, had 330 aircraft in Libya and the Dodecanese, 150 in East Africa and some 1,200 in Italy itself. The RAF could muster no more than 205 serviceable aircraft in Egypt and Palestine and 163 in East Africa; most of the British aircraft types were obsolete or obsolescent.

The disparity in the numbers of troops on each side was even more marked. In Egypt and Palestine the Commander, Middle East Forces, General Sir Archibald Wavell, had some 63,000 troops opposing 250,000 Italian and native troops in Libya. Furthermore, the British troops had the additional responsibility of policing Iraq and Palestine, where there had been an Arab rebellion during 1936–9, and after June 1940 to watch the Vichy French in Syria. In Italian Eritrea and Abyssinia a further 300,000 Italians and native troops were opposed by little more than 10,000 British, who were based in scattered garrisons in the Sudan, British Somaliland and Kenya. The picture was indeed bleak.

11 June 1940 **Italian aircraft raided Malta nine times and bombed Aden and Port Sudan.**
British aircraft attacked targets in Eritrea, and Libyan airfields. RAF Bomber Command sent 36 Whitleys to attack industrial targets in Turin and Genoa that night. Adverse weather over the Alps meant that only thirteen aircraft reached Italy. Further intermittent attacks were made against northern Italy during the next few months.

11 June **British armoured cars crossed from Egypt into Libya and ambushed Italian trucks near Fort Capuzzo.**
These were the opening shots of the North African campaign, which would last just under three years. It was notable, both in the air and on the ground, that the Italian forces in Libya had not been prepared for Mussolini's declaration of war.

14 June **The British captured Forts Capuzzo and Maddalena.**
Because of overwhelming Italian numerical superiority, the forts were evacuated after their guns had been destroyed.

Throughout the next few weeks the British continued to patrol aggressively on the Italian side of the Egyptian-Libyan border and prepared a defensive line at Mersa Matruh, 300 miles west of the Suez Canal. The RAF continued to attack airfields and other targets in Libya, but the losses it suffered could not be replaced: priority lay with the defence of Britain.

28 June **Marshal Balbo, Governor-General of Libya killed.**
This distinguished airman's aircraft was shot down by one of his own side. His place was taken by General Rodolfo Graziani.

4 July **Italians attacked in the Sudan.**
The Italians attacked and captured the British posts at Kassala and Gallabat on the Sudan borders with Eritrea and Abyssinia. The Italians made no attempt to drive deeper into the Sudan.

4 August **25,000 Italians invaded British Somaliland from Abyssinia.**
The small British garrison could do little but fight a delaying action.

17 August **The overruning of British Somaliland was completed.**
The British garrison was successfully evacuated from the port of Berbera by the Royal Navy. The Italians were now in a position to threaten the southern entrance to the Red Sea.

The British now began to deploy the newly arrived 5th Indian Division to defend the Sudan. The organization of a revolt by Abyssinians loyal to the Emperor Haile Selassie also got under way.

19 August **Mussolini ordered Graziani to invade Egypt on the day that the invasion of Britain was mounted.**

22 August **A heavily escorted convoy carrying 150 tanks and other units sailed from England bound for the Middle East.**
Despite the threat of invasion to Britain, Churchill had made the decision on the 15th to send this valuable reinforcement to Wavell. Rather than risk Italian attack in the Mediterranean the convoy was sent around the Cape of Good Hope and docked at Port Said on **24 September**.

13 September **The long-awaited Italian invasion of Egypt began.**
Mussolini could no longer wait for Operation 'Sealion'. Five divisions with 200 tanks crossed the frontier and occupied Sollum. The British Western Desert Force, consisting of 7th Armoured and 4th Indian Divisions, began to withdraw. Its plan was to fight a delaying action back to Mersa Matruh and stand and fight there.

16 September **Italian forces occupied Sidi Barrani, 60 miles from the Libyan border.**
The Italians now halted and built a series of fortified camps. Casualties during the North African campaign to date made a total of 3,500 Italians and 150 British.

21 September **Wavell ordered planning to begin for a counter-attack.**
It was to drive the Italians out of Libya and to capture the port of Tobruk. He took this step since, with the reinforcements that had just arrived from Britain, he outnumbered the Italian forces in Egypt in tanks. Graziani also became aware of this and refused, despite constant prodding from Mussolini, to advance farther into Egypt. Mussolini therefore turned his attention elsewhere.

28 October **Italian troops invaded Greece from Albania.**
Although Greece had been firm in maintaining her strict neutrality, Mussolini was determined that the Balkans were to come under his heel, just as Hitler had achieved in western and northern Europe. Two days before, he had sent the Greeks an ultimatum, complaining of their non-neutral attitude towards Italy.

On that same day, the 28th, Mussolini met Hitler in the Brenner Pass. He had informed him only the day before of his intention to invade Greece. Hitler concealed his anger and offered Mussolini troops, which the latter declined.

Churchill offered direct military support to Greece, which her premier, General Joannis Metaxas, refused; but he did agree that the British could help garrison Crete. Consequently, in early November, Wavell had to send an infantry brigade there. Wavell, concerned at this dilution of his forces, confided his plan for an attack against the Italians in the Western Desert to Minister of War Anthony Eden, who strongly supported it, as did the British Cabinet.

4 November **The Greeks mounted a counter-attack against the Italian invaders.**
So successful was this that within a few days the Italians were forced to retreat and were driven back into Albania.

Mussolini's generals had warned him of the dangers of launching an attack in this mountainous terrain so late in the year. Exasperated, his Chief of Staff, Marshal Pietro Badoglio, resigned. Matters for Mussolini were made worse when, on **4 December**, his Under Secretary of State for War, General Ubaldo Soddu, recommended an armistice with the Greeks.

The facts that Italian attention was turned towards the Balkans and that there were still no signs of further Italian advances in either Egypt or the Sudan made Wavell's idea of a counter-stroke in Egypt that much more promising. Detailed preparation for it was now under way.

P34 · The Fall of France

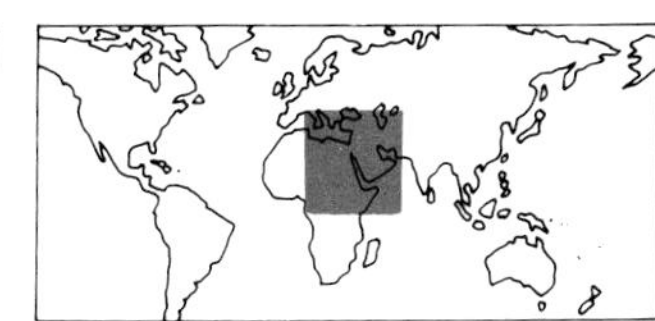

MUSSOLINI'S EMPIRE

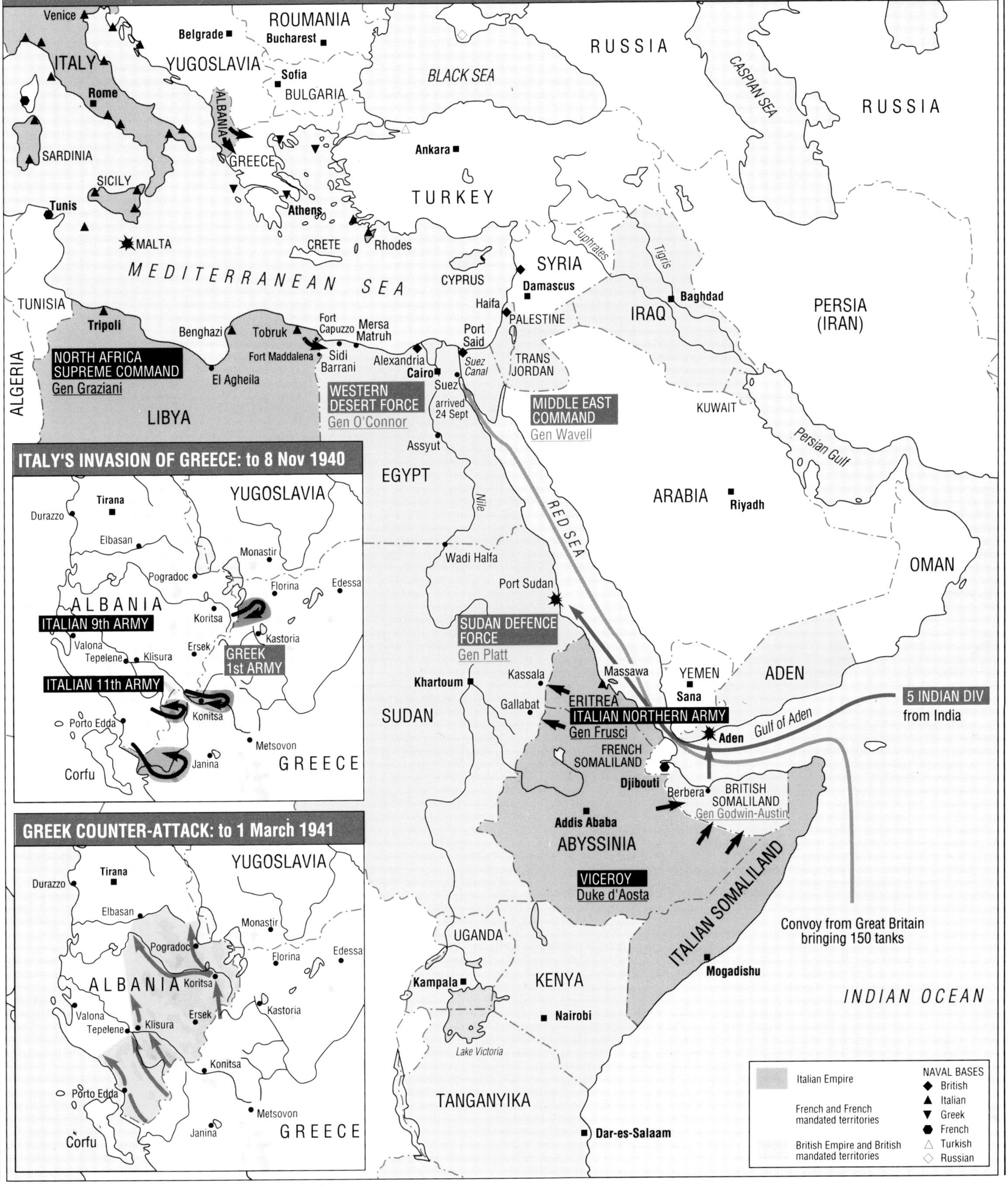

Venice
Belgrade
ROUMANIA
Bucharest
RUSSIA
ITALY
YUGOSLAVIA
Sofia
BLACK SEA
CASPIAN SEA
Rome
ALBANIA
BULGARIA
RUSSIA
SARDINIA
GREECE
Ankara
SICILY
TURKEY
Tunis
Athens
MALTA
CRETE
Rhodes
Euphrates
Tigris
SYRIA
MEDITERRANEAN SEA
CYPRUS
Damascus
Baghdad
TUNISIA
Haifa
PALESTINE
IRAQ
PERSIA (IRAN)
Tripoli
Fort Capuzzo
Mersa Matruh
Benghazi
Tobruk
Port Said
Fort Maddalena
Sidi Barrani
TRANS JORDAN
NORTH AFRICA SUPREME COMMAND
Gen Graziani
Alexandria
Cairo
Suez Canal
ALGERIA
El Agheila
Suez
WESTERN DESERT FORCE
Gen O'Connor
arrived 24 Sept
MIDDLE EAST COMMAND
Gen Wavell
KUWAIT
LIBYA
Assyut
Persian Gulf
EGYPT
Nile
RED SEA
ARABIA
Riyadh
Wadi Halfa
OMAN
Port Sudan
SUDAN DEFENCE FORCE
Gen Platt
Massawa
YEMEN
ADEN
Kassala
Khartoum
Sana
5 INDIAN DIV from India
ERITREA
Gallabat
ITALIAN NORTHERN ARMY
Gen Frusci
SUDAN
Gulf of Aden
Aden
FRENCH SOMALILAND
Djibouti
Berbera
BRITISH SOMALILAND
Gen Godwin-Austin
Addis Ababa
ABYSSINIA
ITALIAN SOMALILAND
VICEROY
Duke d'Aosta
Convoy from Great Britain bringing 150 tanks
UGANDA
Mogadishu
Kampala
KENYA
INDIAN OCEAN
Nairobi
Lake Victoria
TANGANYIKA
Dar-es-Salaam

Italian Empire
French and French mandated territories
British Empire and British mandated territories

NAVAL BASES
British
Italian
Greek
French
Turkish
Russian

ITALY'S INVASION OF GREECE: to 8 Nov 1940

Tirana
YUGOSLAVIA
Durazzo
Elbasan
Monastir
Pogradoc
Florina
Edessa
ALBANIA
ITALIAN 9th ARMY
Koritsa
Valona
Kastoria
Tepelene
Klisura
Ersek
GREEK 1st ARMY
ITALIAN 11th ARMY
Konitsa
Porto Edda
Metsovon
Janina
Corfu
GREECE

GREEK COUNTER-ATTACK: to 1 March 1941

Tirana
YUGOSLAVIA
Durazzo
Elbasan
Monastir
Pogradoc
Florina
Edessa
ALBANIA
Koritsa
Valona
Kastoria
Tepelene
Klisura
Ersek
Konitsa
Porto Edda
Metsovon
Janina
Corfu
GREECE

British Counter-Stroke in North Africa · P48

British Counter-Stroke in North Africa

While Wavell was naturally encouraged by the support given to him by the British Government for his proposal to deal with the Italian Tenth Army in Egypt, he still had a difficult 'juggling act' to perform. He could not blind himself to the Italian threat from East Africa and realized that this had to be dealt with as well. Furthermore, the prospect remained that he might be ordered to send part of his slender resources to help the Greeks. Operation 'Compass', as it was code-named, therefore had to have built-in flexibility.

Thus, rather than make Tobruk the ultimate objective, as Wavell had originally envisaged, he decided that initially 'Compass' would be no more than a five-day 'raid' designed to destroy the Italian fortified camps in Egypt. After this, 4th Indian Division would be redeployed to the Sudan in order to attack the Italians in Eritrea. If 'Compass' went well he would continue into Libya with the remainder of his forces, which were built around 7th Armoured Division. In time, he could expect to reinforce these with a division *en route* from Australia.

The Italian camps in Egypt numbered ten: six were west and south of Sidi Barrani, and the other four in depth in the Sofafi-Rabia area. They had one major weakness, which the British had spotted; they were too far apart to be mutually supporting.

26 November 1940 **The British began Training Exercise No. 1.**

This involved General Dick O'Connor's Western Desert Force which was to carry out 'Compass', and was a dress rehearsal for it. Surprise, and hence secrecy, was vital – the troops themselves had no idea that it was more than an exercise.

6 December **The Western Desert Force began Training Exercise No. 2.**

This initially consisted of a 60-mile approach march to a point called Piccadilly, which lay some twenty miles south of Maktila. The WDF concentrated here by the late afternoon of the 8th.

9 December **4th Indian Division captured the camps at Nibeiwa and Tummar East and West.**

7th Armoured Division drove south of the camps at Sofafi and Rabia and then turned north towards Buq Buq on the coast road. A small force also advanced along this road from Mersa Matruh to Maktila. British warships bombarded Sidi Barrani and Maktila.

10 December **Sidi Barrani surrounded.**

Italian troops fled west from the camps at Sofafi and Rabia. The thrust by 71st Armoured Division had by now virtually cut these camps off.

11 December **Wavell ordered 4th Indian Division to the Sudan.**

Its place was to be taken by the newly arrived 6th Australian Division, but this would not be ready for operations for some days. Sidi Barrani and Maktila fell. By now the 30,000 men of the WDF had captured 38,000 prisoners, 237 guns and 73 tanks. By the end of the following day the Italians had only three toe-holds left in Egypt – Sollum, Fort Capuzzo, Sidi Omar. Wavell now resolved to continue to attack and the raid therefore became an all-out offensive.

20 December **No Italian troops left on Egyptian soil.**

The Italians were now determined to hold on to the port of Bardia; but next day 6th Australian Division arrived and began to prepare its capture. It was well fortified, and it would take some days for the attack on it to be prepared.

1 January 1941 **Western Desert Force was renamed XIII Corps.**

5 January **Bardia fell to the Australians.**

It had taken two days' hard fighting to capture, with support being given by the guns of the Mediterranean Fleet. Another 38,000 prisoners and much

OPERATION 'COMPASS'

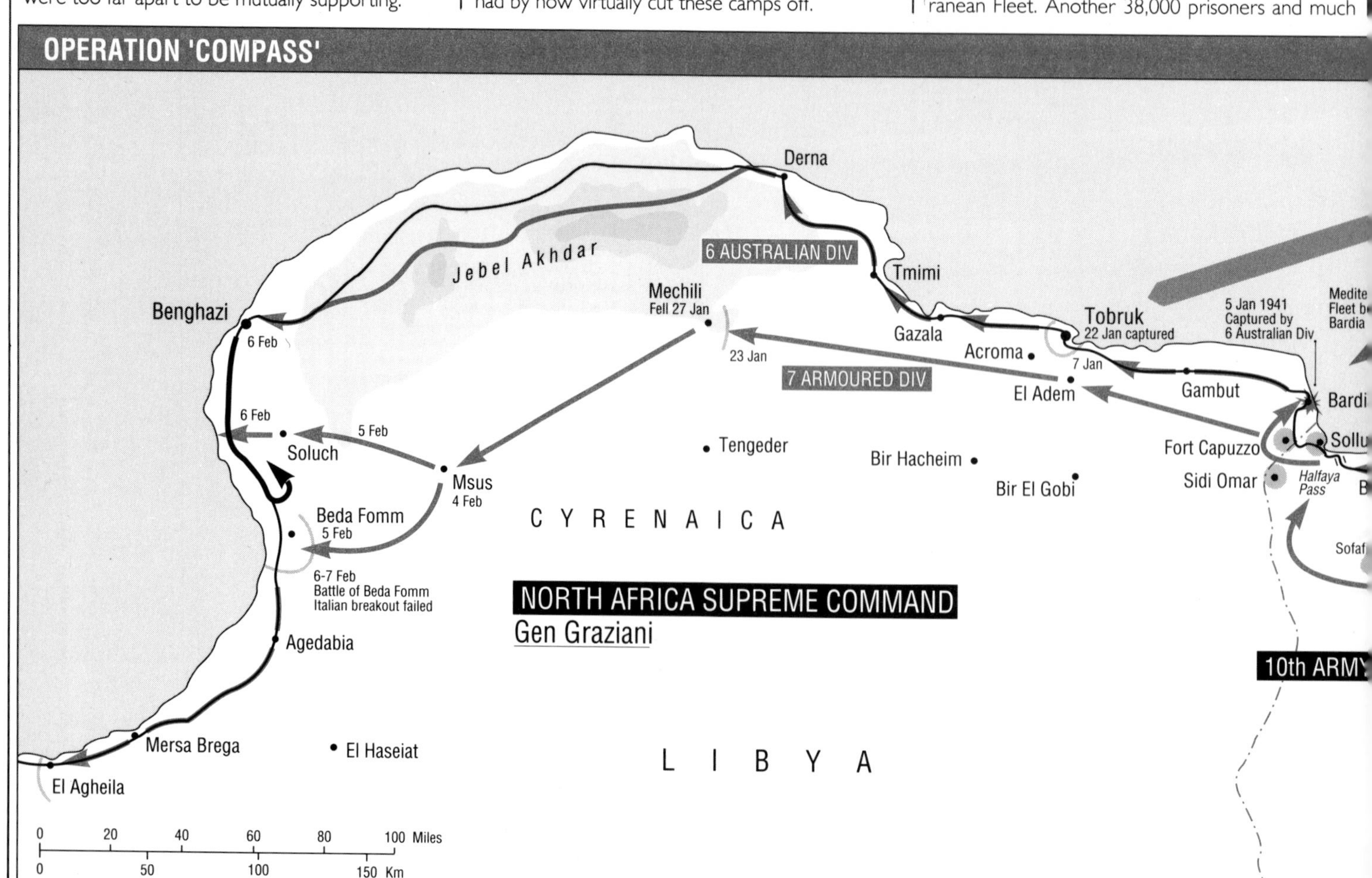

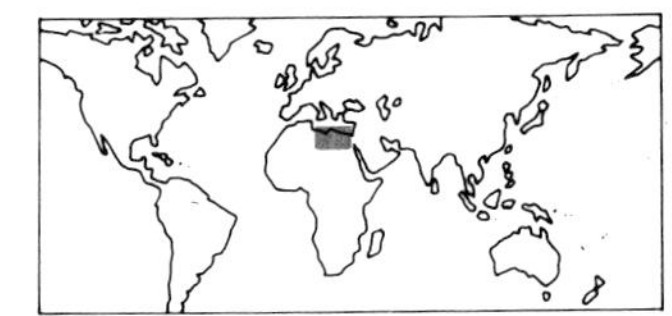

equipment were captured at a cost of 500 Commonwealth casualties.

6 January **Churchill decreed reinforcement to Greece as priority.**
Churchill was determined that the Greeks, who had now driven the Italians back deep into Albania, should remain in the war, and was prepared to sacrifice further advances in North Africa to achieve this. General Metaxas was, however, still adamant that he needed no British help.

7 January **Tobruk was invested.**
This was, like Bardia, heavily defended, and more supplies needed to be brought up for XIII Corps' ever-lengthening supply lines.

22 January **Tobruk fell after 24 hours of fighting.**
Once again XIII Corps had a large bag of prisoners – 25,000 – together with 208 guns and 87 tanks. Commonwealth casualties were 400. In spite of Italian efforts, the port was opened to shipping within 48 hours and did much to alleviate the supply problem.

The British Government now ordered Wavell to push on and capture Benghazi. Accordingly, O'Connor decided to send his tanks round the base of the mountainous Jebel Akhdar in the Cyrenaican 'bulge', and 4th Armoured Brigade set out that evening. The Australians, meanwhile, would continue to advance along the coast road.

23 January **4th Armoured Brigade reached Mechili.**
This fort, astride the track running along the base of the Jebel Akhdar, was more strongly garrisoned than expected. There was now a pause while O'Connor brought up the rest of 7th Armoured Division.

27 January **Mechili occupied.**
The Italians had evacuated it the previous night. The Australians meanwhile had come up against a strong position beyond Derna. O'Connor therefore decided to use 7th Armoured Division to make an outflanking move against it. First, however, its dwindling tank strength needed to be reinforced, and he decided not to start this operation until 12 February.

4 February **RAF reconnaissance reported that the Italians were beginning to evacuate Benghazi.**
Their plan was to set up a blocking position at El Agheila to stop the British advancing into Tripolitania. O'Connor therefore gave orders to 7th Armoured Division to move immediately in order to cut off these withdrawing forces.

5 February **Advanced elements of 7th Armoured Division reached the coast road 70 miles south of Benghazi.**
This consisted merely of armoured cars, which blocked the road and trapped a convoy of artillery and civilians. In the early evening the armoured cars were reinforced by 4th Armoured Brigade, whose tanks had travelled 150 miles in 33 hours. Part of this brigade was sent 10 miles north to Beda Fomm and was immediately in action.

6 February **The Australians entered Benghazi.**

6–7 February **Battle of Beda Fomm.**
The Italians made repeated attempts to break through the weakly held British block, but failed because they did not make a concentrated attack against it. Eventually 20,000 men, 200 guns and 120 tanks fell into the hands of a force of no more than 3,000 men. Anthony Eden parodied Churchill's famous battle of Britain tribute: 'Never has so much been surrendered by so many to so few.' Agedabia also fell. The Italians had now been cleared from Cyrenaica.

This was the first real British victory on land and had been achieved in spectacular fashion. The resultant euphoria was, however, to be very short-lived.

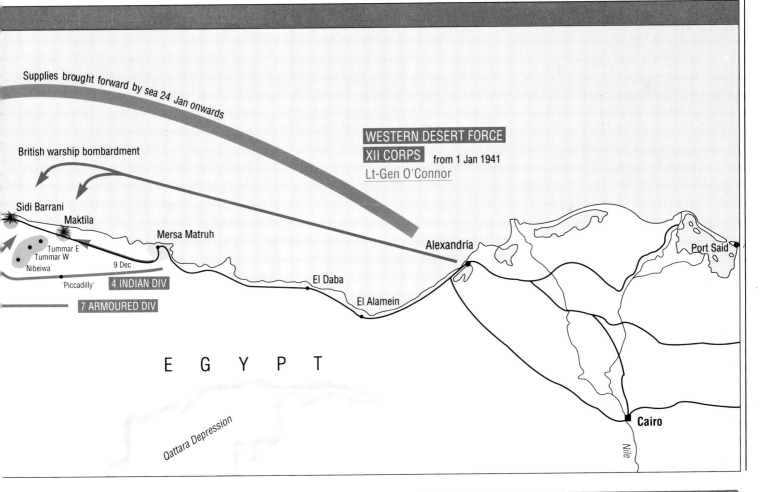

Enter Rommel · P54

The Conquest of Italian East Africa

Wavell's plan for driving the Italians out of East Africa called for twin pincers to attack, from north and south. In the north, General William Platt's 4th and 5th Indian Divisions were to strike Eritrea from the Sudan. From Kenya, General Alan Cunningham with a force of East, South and West Africans was to overrun Italian Somaliland and move into Abyssinia. The two pincers were to meet at the Italian stronghold of Amba Alagi.

In addition, another force, from Aden, was to land at Berbera and recapture British Somaliland, and rebellion was fomented within Abyssinia itself. The Emperor Haile Selassie himself had arrived in Khartoum from England on **3 July 1940** and began to rally the chieftains in western Abyssinia as well as gather together an army from the numerous Abyssinian refugees in the Middle East.

Time was needed to prepare for these operations, and it was not until January 1941 that all was ready. By now, the disasters suffered by the Italians

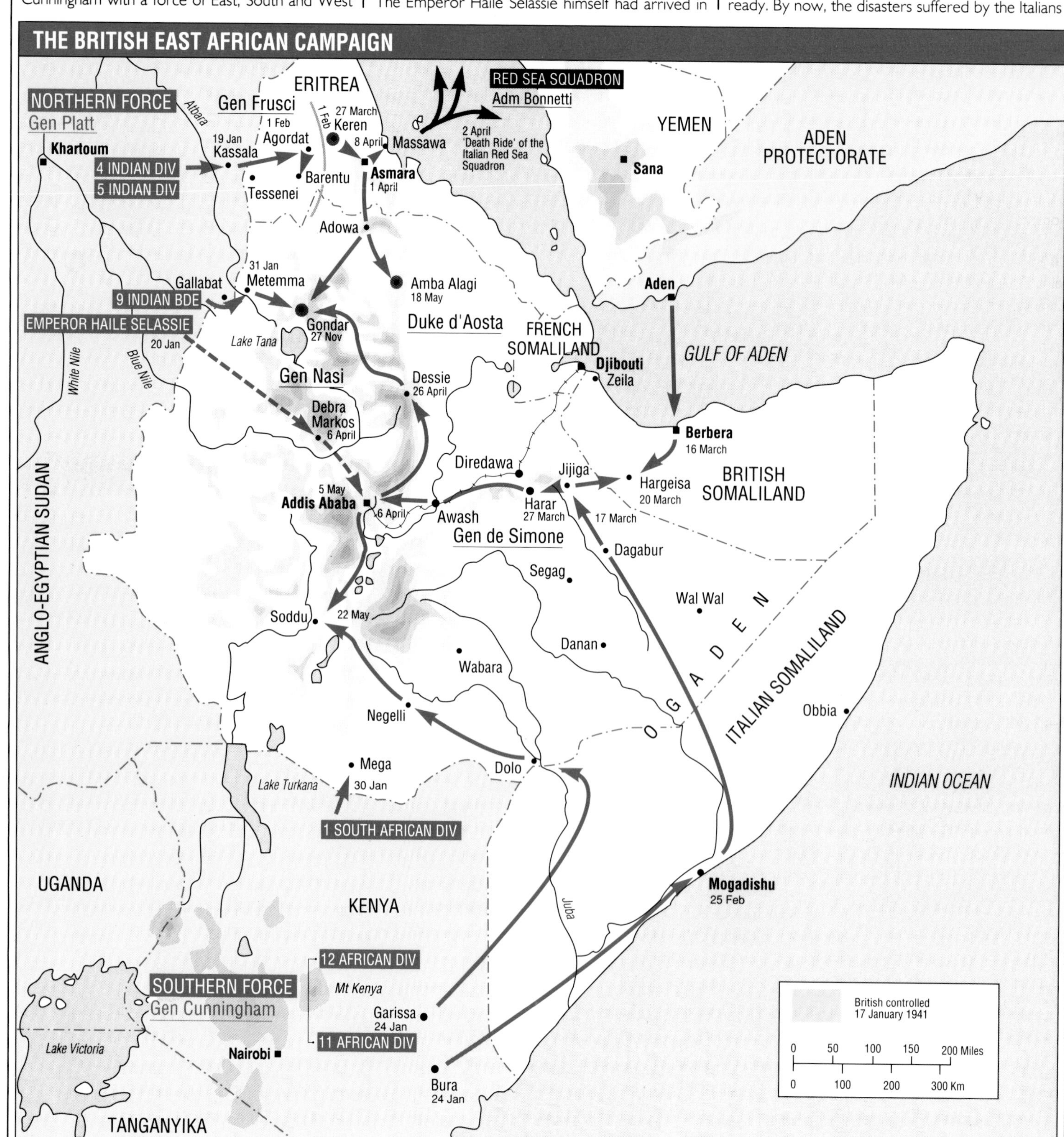

P46 · Early Italian Successes in North and East Africa

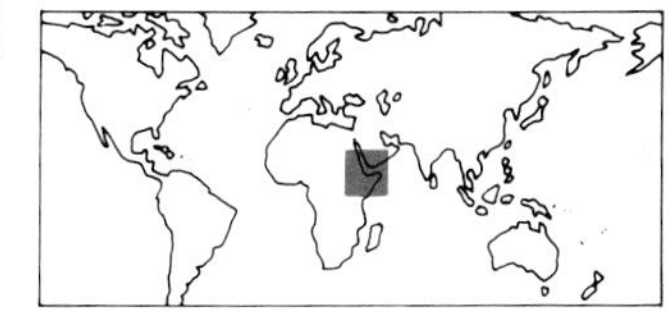

in Libya meant that any thoughts they might have had of resuming their advance into the Sudan were dispelled. All they could do was to go on to the defensive, and orders were given for withdrawal from their outposts in the Sudan.

17 January 1941 **The Italians evacuated Kassala and Gallalabat during the night.**

19 January **Platt's troops occupied Kassala and drove eastwards into Eritrea.**

20 January **Haile Selassie crossed the Abyssinian border at Um Idla.**

24 January **Cunningham's forces invaded Italian Somaliland from Garissa and Bura in Kenya.**

30 January **1st South African Division launched a feint attack in the Mega area of southern Abyssinia.**
They had already overrun Italian outposts just inside Kenya. Their objective was to encourage an insurrection in the area and prevent the Italians from sending reinforcements to Somaliland.

31 January **9th Indian Brigade occupied Metemma.**
The Italian garrison had been under increasing pressure for the past three weeks and now withdrew towards Gondar. The Indians followed up, but were considerably impeded by mines. Eventually, in March, they were transferred to the Keren front before Gondar could be taken.

1 February **Agordat fell to 5th Indian Division.**
This was after two days' fighting. Barentu was captured next day and the Italian forces withdrew towards Keren, a mountain fortress in which the Eritrean army planned to make a final stand.

3–12 February **First battles for Keren.**
Keren was guarded by a series of peaks and razor-like ridges. Initial attempts to secure these were unsuccessful, and Platt decided that he must build up his strength before trying again.

25 February **11th African Division occupied Mogadishu, having advanced up the Red Sea coast.**
12th African Division was driving north along the line of the River Juba.

1 March **11th African Division began a lightning pursuit of the Italian forces north to the Ogaden Plateau.**

15–27 March **Final battles for Keren,**
A series of attacks by 4th and 5th Indian Divisions eventually secured the high ground overlooking Keren and the Italians were forced to withdraw. The fighting cost the British 4,000 and the Italians 3,000 casualties.

16 March **British troops landed at Berbera, British Somaliland.**

17 March **11th African Division occupied Jijiga.**
Making use of the Italian-built *Strada Imperiale*, it had advanced 744 miles in seventeen days.

20 March **The Berbera force and elements of 11th African Division met at Hargeisa.**
Both British and Italian Somaliland were now in British hands.

27 March **11th African Division occupied Harar.**
The Italians had declared it an 'open' town a few days earlier.

1 April **Asmara, capital of Eritrea, surrendered to Platt.**

2 April **Rear-Admiral Bonnetti, Commander, Italian Red Sea Squadron, ordered his destroyers out on 'do or die' missions.**
Of the seven destroyers, one was sunk outside Massawa by the Royal Navy, two were sunk by the Fleet Air Arm, two ran aground near Jedda, Saudi Arabia, but were seized by the British, and the remaining two were sunk by the Royal Navy *en route* for Suez. The other target had been fuel storage tanks at Port Sudan.

6 April **Haile Selassie's troops occupied the forts at Debra Markos.**
His force, with its British advisers, had carried out an epic march through the hinterland, relying on camels to carry their supplies.

6 April **Addis Ababa, capital of Abyssinia, surrendered to 11th African Division.**

8 April **Massawa captured.**
This was the last Italian stronghold in Eritrea and its capture meant that the threat to the British sea routes through the Red Sea was now removed. The Italian forces in Eritrea had now been totally destroyed: Platt had captured 40,000 prisoners, 300 guns and vast amounts of *matériel*.

In view of the worsening situation in North Africa, Wavell now ordered that 4th Indian Division must return to the Western Desert.

5 May **Emperor Haile Selassie returned to his capital in triumph.**
It was five years to the day since Marshal Badoglio had entered it at the head of the Italian forces. The restoration of Haile Selassie to his throne did not mean that the campaign in Abyssinia was at an end. Significant Italian forces still remained at large, both in the north of the country, especially in the fortresses of Amba Alagi and Gondar, as well as in the south. The first objective of the British and Commonwealth forces was to seize Amba Alagi, which was commanded in person by the Governor of Abyssinia, the Duke d'Aosta. Once again the pincer strategy was to be used, with Cunningham's South Africans moving north from Addis Ababa and 5th Indian Division south from Asmara.

26 April **The fortress of Dessie, south of Amba Alagi, fell to the South Africans.**

18 May **5th Indian Division captured Amba Alagi.**
It had taken eighteen days to reduce the defences in the hills and mountains surrounding the fortress. On its surrender the last man to leave Amba Alagi was the Duke d'Aosta himself.

22 May **Fall of Soddu marked the end of the campaign in the south.**
Once again the pincer strategy had been adopted, an East African brigade of 11th African Division advancing south from Addis Ababa while West Africans from 12th African Division moved north. The Italians resisted stoutly. This and the difficult terrain meant that it took seven weeks to crush Italian resistance.

Only Gondar in the north now remained to be taken. Three forces had been sent against Gondar: one along the route from Metemma, one south-west from Adowa and the third north-west from Dessie. All three, however, were halted well short of their objective by the rains that arrived in early July. Little progress was therefore possible before the end of September. The task of capturing Gondar was assigned to 12th African Division.

27 September **Wolchefit Pass captured.**
This was the gateway to Gondar from the north-east and had resisted British efforts to seize it for more than three months.

23 October **Decision made that the approach from Adowa should be the main thrust.**
This was because the road was in better shape than on the other two routes.

27 November **Gondar finally fell, marking the end of the campaign in East Africa.**
Italian resistance was strong until the very end and much use was made of deception and feint attacks in order to overcome it. General Nasi, the commander at Gondar, eventually surrendered 23,500 men; total British casualties were 500.

The campaign in Abyssinia and Eritrea had been a spectacular success for British arms and marked the end of Mussolini's dreams of an African empire. However, the high point, May 1941, came at a time when the British were suffering worsening crises in North Africa and the Mediterranean, and these overshadowed the achievements of their forces fighting further south. Indeed, Wavell had constantly had to draw troops off from East Africa.

Enter Rommel · P54

Italo-British Naval War

At the outbreak of war the British and Italian naval forces in the Mediterranean were, as we have seen, fairly evenly matched. True, the Italian Navy possessed no aircraft carriers, but aircraft from Italy, Sicily, the Dodecanese and Libya could dominate most of the Mediterranean all the same. Both the British and the Italians recognized from the start that the island of Malta played a crucial role in Mediterranean strategy. If the Italians could seize the island the eastern Mediterranean would be denied to the Royal Navy and the ability to attack the sea lanes between Italy and North Africa lost, as well as the capability to reinforce Greece or Turkey should they be drawn into the war. The CinC, Mediterranean Fleet, Admiral Sir Andrew Cunningham, therefore had a difficult task ahead of him.

9 July 1940 First major clash between the British and Italian fleets.
A British force, including one aircraft carrier and three battleships, was in action against an Italian squadron under Admiral Campioni, which consisted of two battleships, six heavy and twelve light cruisers off the Calabrian coast. Campioni broke off the action after his flagship *Giulio Cesare* was hit by the guns of HMS *Warspite* and retired to Messina. The result was that the Italian fleet now stayed in port for the next few weeks.

30 August Reinforcements for the British Mediterranean Fleet.
The battleship *Valiant*, aircraft carrier *Illustrious* and two cruisers left Gibraltar to reinforce Cunningham, who planned to use this operation both to resupply Malta and to 'trail his coat' in order to tempt the Italian fleet to put to sea. Although the Italians did so, they soon turned back to their main base at Taranto. An attack by Swordfish aircraft was made on targets in the Italian Dodecanese, but four were shot down. One Italian motor torpedo-boat was sunk and a convoy of British merchant ships was escorted from the Aegean to Alexandria.

29 September Cunningham took a convoy to Malta from Alexandria under strong escort.
Once again he hoped to provoke a fleet action and again the Italians put to sea only to return prematurely once more to Taranto.

8 October Another Malta resupply convoy set out from Alexandria.
Bad weather prevented the Italian fleet leaving port, but on the escort's return voyage it was attacked by torpedo-boats and destroyers. Two of the former and two of the latter were sunk and a further destroyer damaged.

Night of 11/12 November Swordfish aircraft from HMS *Illustrious* attacked the Italian fleet in Taranto harbour.
Cunningham had been planning such an attack for some time and had originally wanted it to take place on 21 October, the anniversary of the Battle of Trafalgar (1805), but a fire aboard the carrier *Illustrious* had forced a postponement. The operation was combined with the dispatch of more reinforcements and supplies to Malta. Twelve Swordfish took part, of which two were shot down. They severely damaged three Italian battleships, one of which, *Conte di Cavour*, was never put back in service. This marked a significant reduction in Italian naval strength and was hailed as a great victory in Britain – the first for almost a year. The Italian fleet now temporarily withdrew to ports on the west coast of Italy, putting it farther from the vital operational areas in the Mediterranean.

27 November Fleet action off Sardinia.
The British Admiralty had ordered the battleship *Ramillies* and two cruisers to leave the Mediterranean and reinforce the Atlantic Fleet. This was made possible by the reduction in Italian naval strength caused by the Taranto attack. Cunningham planned for his ships to escort another convoy to Malta and rendezvous with Force H so that *Ramillies* could sail back with them. Just when the two forces were about to meet, *Ramillies*, the two cruisers, ten destroyers and the carrier *Ark Royal* were intercepted by Campioni's squadron of two battleships, seven cruisers and sixteen destroyers. The battlecruiser *Renown* now joined and Campioni withdrew with one cruiser and two destroyers damaged. Admiral Somerville, the British commander, was mildly censured for not having pursued the Italians.

21 December Battleship *Malaya* transferred from the Mediterranean Fleet to Force H.
This was also made possible by the Taranto attack and involved the sending of another convoy to Malta. One British destroyer was lost to a mine.

10 January 1941 First Luftwaffe attacks on British ships in the Mediterranean.
The Mediterranean Fleet was escorting three merchant ships to Greece when 40 Stukas attacked. *Illustrious* was hit by six 1,000lb bombs and severely damaged, but managed to limp into Malta next day; *Warspite* was slightly damaged. Next day the Luftwaffe attacked the cruisers *Gloucester* and *Southampton*, slightly damaging the former, but sinking the latter. Meanwhile British submarines began to harry the German convoys crossing to Libya.

8 February Force H bombarded Genoa.
The Italian fleet and air force failed to take any action because of poor air reconnaissance and lack of co-ordination.

23 February German Stukas sank the British monitor *Terror* and a destroyer off Tobruk.

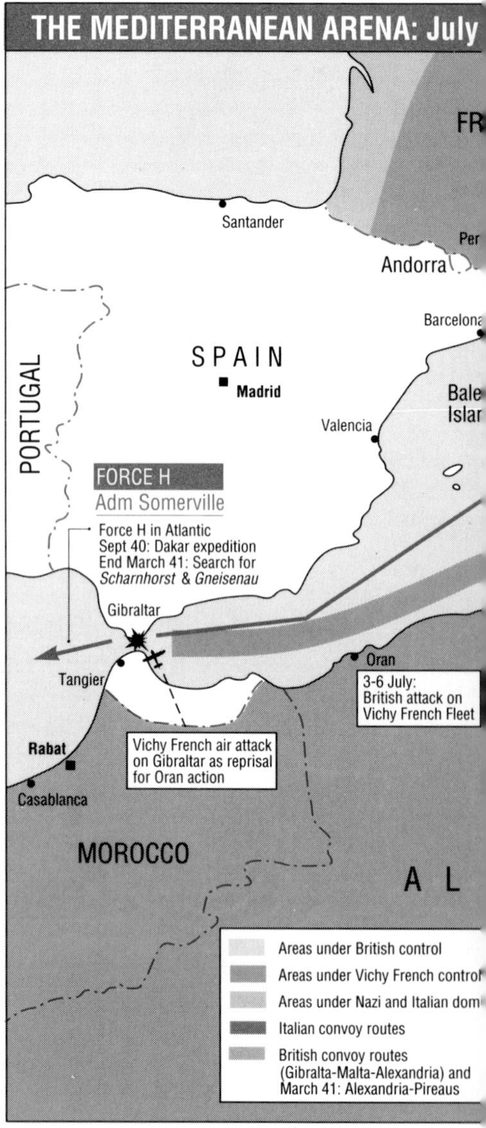

25 February British submarine *Upholder* sank the Italian cruiser *Armando Diaz*.

25–28 February Abortive British attempt to capture Castelorizzo in the Italian Dodecanese.
Cunningham wanted this island as a motor torpedo-boat base and a possible stepping-stone for the capture of Rhodes. British Commandos from Crete successfully captured the island, but were left to hold it without naval support. The arrival of reinforcements was delayed, allowing time for the Italians to land again on the island. The Commandos were evacuated.

5 March The Royal Navy began to escort British and Commonwealth troops from Egypt to Greece.

6 March German aircraft laid mines in the Suez Canal, blocking it for three weeks.
The mines were a mix of magnetic and acoustic and there were problems clearing them. One result was that the carrier *Formidable*, which was joining the

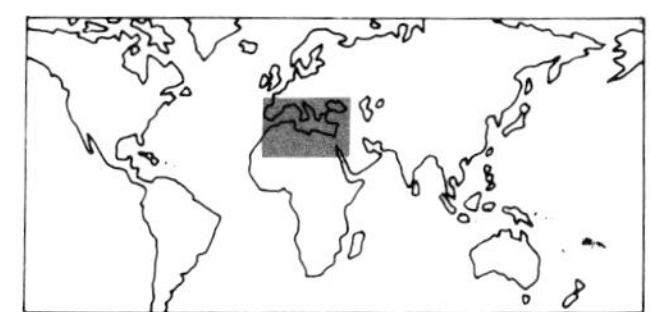

arch 1941

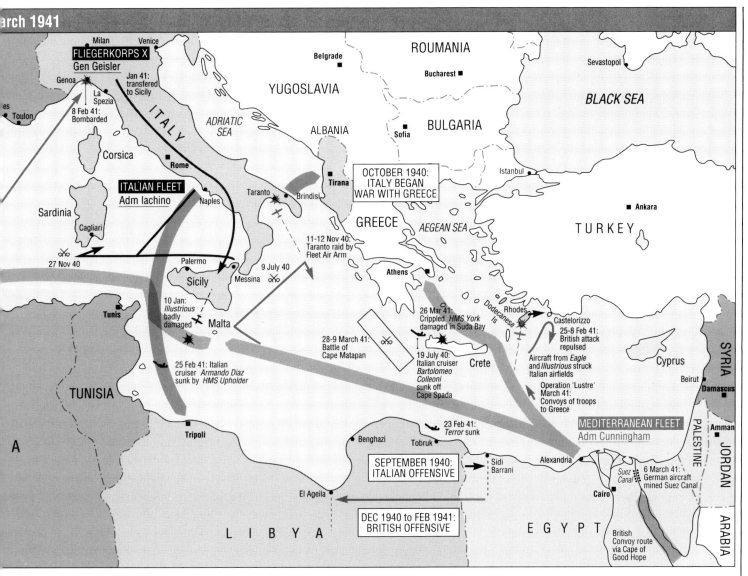

Mediterranean Fleet as a replacement for *Illustrious*, was held up at the southern end of the Canal. Only when she arrived in Alexandria could convoys to Malta be resumed.

19 March The German naval staff complained to the Italians over their lack of effort to intercept the convoys to Greece.
This stirred the Italians into action.

26 March The British cruiser *York* was severely damaged by an Italian motor-boat loaded with explosives in Suda Bay, Crete.
This was the first successful use of this weapon, which the Italians called *Mezzi Navali d'Assalto* (naval assault machines). *York* was beached and later destroyed by bombing during the battle for Crete.

28 March Battle of Cape Matapan.
Stung by the German complaint over their inactivity, Admiral Iachino, the Italian naval CinC, planned two easterly sweeps by cruisers north and south of Crete to intercept British Greece-bound convoys. He was promised air cover by the Germans. He gathered eight cruisers, nine destroyers and the battleship *Vittorio Veneto*, and these sailed secretly from their Italian west coast bases. They began the sweeps on the 27th, but the promised air cover did not appear. An RAF flying-boat did, however, spot two of the cruisers and alerted Cunningham. That night the Mediterranean Fleet slipped anchor at Alexandria. In view of the lack of air cover the Italians decided to cancel their northern sweep and the force earmarked for this was ordered to rendezvous with the southern element south of Crete.

Next morning the Italians sighted a force of four British cruisers and four destroyers, which had been covering the Greek convoys. The latter drew the Italians towards the British main body, which included three battleships and *Formidable*. After some manoeuvring, aircraft from *Formidable* hit *Vittorio Veneto* with a torpedo, but she was able to get back to Taranto. Later they hit the cruiser *Pola*, which was eventually sunk. Cunningham, realizing that this was the first proper fleet action in which the Royal Navy had been engaged since Jutland (1916), continued the battle until well into the night. The Italians had, however, fled for home after the air attacks, but had detached two cruisers and four destroyers to assist the stricken *Pola*. Cunningham intercepted these with his battleships and sank two cruisers and two destroyers.

Although the British were disappointed that *Vittorio Veneto* had got away, they had won a significant victory, which kept the Italian fleet in port for the next few months. Mussolini now ordered the conversion of two ships to aircraft carriers, but these would not be completed by the time of the Italian armistice in September 1943.

The spring of 1941 marked a high tide for British naval fortunes in the Mediterranean. But while they dominated the surface of the sea, the skies over the Mediterranean were shortly to be a different matter. It was to prove a costly summer for the Royal Navy.

Wavell Under Pressure · P60

Enter Rommel

Hitler had always regarded Mussolini's plans for seizing Egypt and the Suez Canal as a very secondary strategy. He did, however, recognize the threat that the Royal Navy posed in the Mediterranean, but believed that this could be removed by capturing Gibraltar. Accordingly he had directed that plans be drawn up in autumn 1940 for Operation 'Felix', which envisaged not just the seizure of Gibraltar, but the occupation of the Spanish Canary Islands and Portuguese Cape Verde Islands. A subsidiary plan, 'Isabella', called for the occupation of Portugal. In order to ensure success, however, it was essential that Spain join the war on the Axis side. The Spanish dictator, General Francisco Franco, however, kept Hitler at arm's length through vague promises but no firm commitment.

By the end of 1940 the continuing Italian reverses in both the Balkans and North Africa made it clear to Hitler that he would have to give direct military assistance to his ally. Otherwise there was the danger that Italy might leave the war.

8–9 January 1941 **Hitler announced his plans for direct military support of Italy.**
Anti-tank units and aircraft were to be sent to Libya and two and a half divisions were to reinforce the Italians in Albania.

11 January **Hitler confirmed his intentions in his Directive No. 22.**
The code-name for the German reinforcement of Libya was Operation 'Sunflower'; that for Albania was 'Alpine Violets'.

6 February **Hitler made one last appeal to Franco to enter the war.**
Franco replied on the 26th that, while he supported the Axis, he was not prepared to declare war. The truth was that Spain was still suffering from the aftermath of her Civil War. This put an end to any further serious thought of capturing Gibraltar. Franco remained neutral, but did send volunteers, the Spanish Blue Division, to the Eastern Front.

6 February **General Erwin Rommel appointed to command the German Libya contingent.**
Rommel had made his name as a young infantry officer in the First World War and then as commander of the 7th Panzer Division in France in May 1940. He was to be given two divisions, one light and one Panzer, and his command was to be called the *Deutsches Afrika Korps* (DAK).

12 February **Rommel landed at Tripoli.**
He reported to General Gariboldi who had taken over command from Marshal Graziani and was to be Rommel's superior. At this time the Italians had five divisions in Tripolitania, of which one, the *Ariete*, was motorized; this was to be placed under Rommel's command.

14 February **German 5th Light Division began to arrive at Tripoli.**
It was immediately sent forward to Sirte.

23 February **Greece formally accepted the offer of British troops.**
General Metaxas had died and his successor, Alexandros Korizis, lacked the same will to resist the continuing British pressure. The troops could only come from Wavell's command. At the same time, units that had taken part in the conquest of Cyrenaica were desperately in need of rest and refitting. The first effect of this was that it was no longer possible for Wavell to continue his victorious advance into Tripolitania. Instead, 6th Australian and 7th Armoured Divisions were withdrawn and their places taken by the newly arrived 2nd Armoured and 9th Australian Divisions. However, one of the former's two armoured brigades was earmarked for Greece. Such was the shortage of equipment that it had to be partially equipped with inferior, captured Italian tanks. The RAF in the theatre suffered in a similar way.

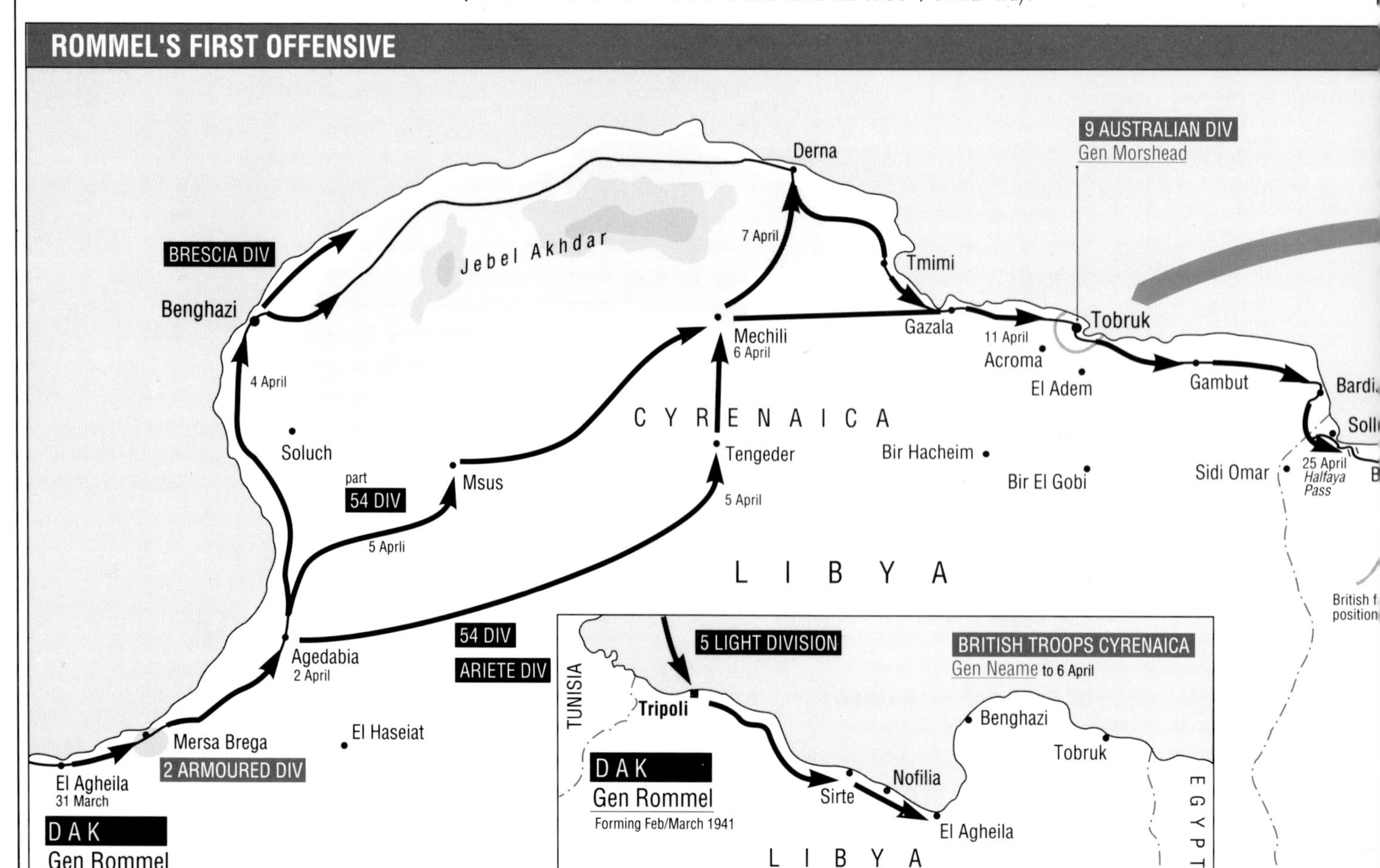

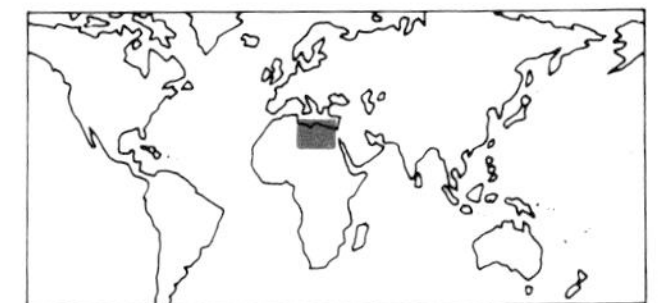

24 February First clash between British and German troops in Libya.
This was between reconnaissance elements and took place at Nofilia on the coast road between Sirte and El Agheila.

4 March The British contingent destined for Greece began to leave Egypt.
Commanded by General Maitland Wilson, it consisted of four divisions and represented a sizeable slice of Wavell's stretched forces.

11 March The German 5th Light Division was now complete in Tripolitania.
Rommel had in the meantime flown back to Germany for further orders and been told that when 15th Panzer Division arrived, at the end of May, he was to destroy the British around Agedabia and perhaps recapture Benghazi. He left orders for 5th Light Division to prepare an attack on El Agheila.

24 March Rommel drove the British out of El Agheila.
The seeming ease with which he managed to do this encouraged him to press deeper into Cyrenaica.

31 March Rommel attacked 2nd Armoured Division at Mersa Brega.
The battle went on all day, but by evening the British had been driven out. Two days later Rommel had reached Agedabia. The British, surprised and caught off balance, decided to withdraw. Wavell himself came up to visit and ordered General O'Connor to take over from General Philip Neame, VC, commanding the British troops in Cyrenaica. Rommel now decided to clear Cyrenaica, advancing on three routes: the coast road to Benghazi, north-east to Mechili and east and then north to Tengeder.

4 April The Germans entered Benghazi unopposed.

6 April Rommel occupied Mechili.
The British forces were now in danger of being cut off, especially the Australians withdrawing along the coast road after Derna was seized by the Germans on the 7th. That night Generals Neame and O'Connor were captured. The remnants of the defence of Cyrenaica retreated to Tobruk, from where they would be taken back to Egypt by sea. In the meantime an Australian infantry brigade and some tanks had been sent by sea from Alexandria to reinforce Tobruk. Further reinforcements were hurried to the Egyptian frontier.

11 April Rommel began to attack Tobruk.
His initial attempts were foiled, but by now his men and vehicles were becoming very tired after three weeks of continuous action.

13 April Rommel received orders from Berlin.
He was ordered to consolidate on the Egyptian border and to concentrate on capturing Tobruk. He himself was prepared to ignore Tobruk and drive on towards the Suez Canal. He decided not to make another major attack on Tobruk until 15th Panzer Division had arrived.

25 April British driven out of Halfaya Pass.
They fell back to the line Buq Buq–Sofafi, and once again attention turned to creating a main defensive position at Mersa Matruh.

Thus, by the end of April the British found themselves back where they were five months ago. The only difference was that they had managed to cling on to Tobruk, which would continue to act as a thorn in Rommel's side. Rommel's début in North Africa had been little short of sensational. Numerically inferior to his enemies, he had routed them through sheer pace and his own personal energy.

For Wavell, the fact that he had lost almost all his gains of the winter was but one of the setbacks and worries that faced him at this time.

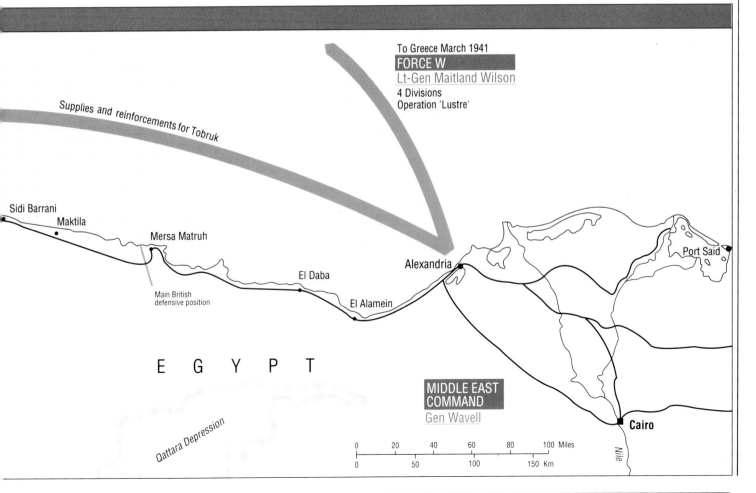

To Greece March 1941
FORCE W
Lt-Gen Maitland Wilson
4 Divisions
Operation 'Lustre'
Supplies and reinforcements for Tobruk
Sidi Barrani
Maktila
Mersa Matruh
Main British defensive position
El Daba
El Alamein
Alexandria
Port Said
Cairo
Nile
EGYPT
Qattara Depression
MIDDLE EAST COMMAND
Gen Wavell
0 20 40 60 80 100 Miles
0 50 100 150 Km

Hitler Looks East

The 1939 German-Soviet Non-Aggression Pact had been a 'marriage of convenience' for both countries. It had enabled the Soviet Union to grab the Baltic states and begin to build a buffer to protect her borders. For Germany it had made the conquest of Poland easier, and it meant she could turn on the Western democracies without having to worry too much about her 'back'.

It was inevitable, however, that there would be conflict between two so diametrically opposed creeds as Nazism and Communism, and by autumn 1940 splits were beginning to appear. Mutual suspicion had been generated over Roumania – the Soviet claim on Bessarabia and German concern to protect their sources of oil there – and was heightened on the Soviet side by the signing of the Tripartite Pact by Germany, Italy and Japan on **27 September 1940** in spite of German reassurances that it was not directed towards the USSR. Soviet concern was further raised by the German plan to reinforce their troops in northern Norway by sending them through Finland.

But these were merely surface disagreements. Hitler had already made up his mind to invade Russia. As early as October 1939 he had laid down that Poland should be regarded as an 'assembly area for future German operations' and the following month he had told his generals that he would turn on Russia once he had finished in the west. In July 1940 he began to elaborate on his plan and at one point called for an attack that autumn.

31 July 1940 Hitler formally announced to his military commanders that he intended to attack Russia.
He argued that if Russia were smashed, Britain's last hope for salvation would be removed. The attack was to take place in spring 1941. He intended to use 120 divisions organized in two groups. One would drive south to Kiev and the River Dneiper while the other overran the Baltic states and then headed for Moscow. He believed that he could complete this in five months.

26 August Hitler ordered two Panzer and ten infantry divisions from the west to Poland.
While this was the first stage of the build-up for the invasion, their immediate task was to stand by for a move into Roumania to secure the oilfields there.

12–13 November Soviet Foreign Minister **Molotov visited Berlin.**
Molotov tried without success to discuss the presence of German troops in Finland. Hitler, on the other hand, invited the Soviet Union to join the Tripartite Pact. Stalin, however, would only join if German troops were removed from Finland, and if Bulgaria, the Dardanelles and the Persian Gulf came into his sphere of influence. These demands Hitler could not accept.

20 November Hungary joined the Tripartite Pact.

23 November Roumania joined the Tripartite Pact.
This secured Hitler's interests in the oilfields.

24 November Slovakia joined the Tripartite Pact.

5 December Hitler's staff presented their plan for Operation 'Otto', the invasion of Russia.
Hitler emphasized that Moscow was not important as an objective. The purpose was to surround and annihilate the Red Army north and south of the Pripet Marshes.

13 December Hitler issued a directive for Operation 'Marita', the occupation of the Balkans.
He recognized that the securing of his southern flank was crucial if his invasion of Russia was to succeed. Twenty-four divisions were to be sent through Hungary to Roumania. If necessary, an attack on Greece was to be mounted, especially if British troops were sent there.

18 December Hitler issued Directive No. 18 confirming his plan for what was now called Operation 'Barbarossa'.
All preparations were to be completed by **15 May 1941.** Finland and Roumania would provide additional jump-off positions. While the immediate aim was to destroy the Red armies in western Russia, Hitler now laid down that Moscow would be taken after this had been achieved. Three axes of advance were now envisaged: directed on Leningrad, White Russia and then to link up with the northerly thrust, and through the Ukraine to Kiev.

1 January 1941 Negotiations for the passage of German troops through Bulgaria began.
Hitler wanted to use Bulgaria as one of his springboards for an attack on Greece.

10 January Germany and the Soviet Union signed a fresh treaty.
This recognized the existing spheres of influence and reaffirmed existing trade agreements.

13 January Hitler demanded that Bulgaria join the Tripartite Pact.
The Bulgarians tried to play for time.

19 January Hitler and Mussolini met at Berchtesgaden.
Mussolini accepted Hitler's offer of military help in North Africa, but not in Albania since he was fearful that Hitler was trying to bring this country under his sphere of influence. In Albania the Italians had managed to halt the Greek advance in the Klisura area and on **24 January** launched a counter-attack.

3 February Hitler reviewed the plans for 'Barbarossa'.
It was estimated that the Red Army would have some 155 divisions available as against 116 German and allied divisions. The disparity in numbers would be more than compensated by German technical and tactical superiority. The starting-date still stood as 15 May.

9 February In a radio broadcast Churchill warned Bulgaria not to join the Axis.

12 February The British Foreign Secretary toured the Balkans.
Eden and General Sir John Dill, Chief of the Imperial General Staff, left London for tour of Balkan capitals with the objective of establishing an anti-Axis pact. Yugoslavia refused to see them, Turkey would not go along with their proposal and only Greece showed positive interest.

14 February Hitler began to apply pressure on Yugoslavia to join the Tripartite Pact.

15 February Britain broke off diplomatic relations with Roumania.
It was clear that Roumania was now firmly wedded to the Axis.

1 March Bulgaria finally signed the Tripartite Pact.
The discovery of a plot for a pro-British *coup* helped to drive Bulgaria into the Axis camp. Next day the German Twelfth Army moved into Bulgaria, despite Soviet protests. On the 5th, Bulgaria broke off diplomatic relations with Bulgaria. Now, apart from Greece, the only Balkan country not firmly under Axis influence was Yugoslavia.

4 March Hitler began to pressure Yugoslavia to join the Tripartite Pact.
He invited Prince Paul, the Regent, to Berchtesgaden and demanded that he allow German troops to pass through his territory for an attack on Greece. In exchange, Yugoslavia would be given the port of Salonika and part of Macedonia.

7 March British and Commonwealth troops began to land in Greece.

25 March Yugoslavia finally signed the Tripartite Pact.
Virtually surrounded by Axis-influenced countries, there seemed to be little else that the Yugoslavs could do. Nevertheless, many sections of the population voiced their disapproval.

Hitler had now achieved almost all he had set out to do in the Balkans, and it seemed a simple matter to overrun a now isolated Greece. The path appeared clear for the launching of 'Barbarossa' on 15 May.

1939 | 1940 | 1941 | 1942 | 1943 | 1944 | 1945

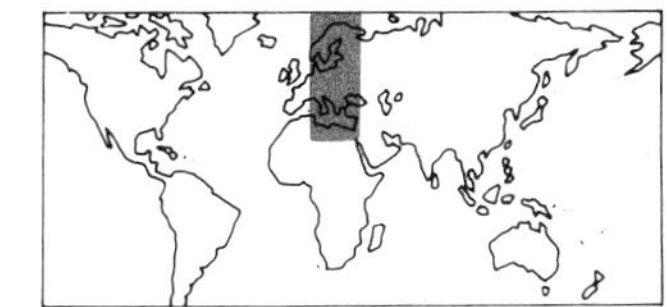

GERMAN INITIAL PLAN FOR INVASION OF RUSSIA

Leningrad
BALTIC SEA
ESTONIA
LATVIA
Riga
Moscow
Danzig
LITHUANIA
Smolensk
RUSSIA
EAST PRUSSIA
Warsaw
Pripet Marshes
GREATER GERMANY
Kiev
Kharkov
Lvov
HUNGARY
Odessa
Belgrade
ROUMANIA
Black Sea

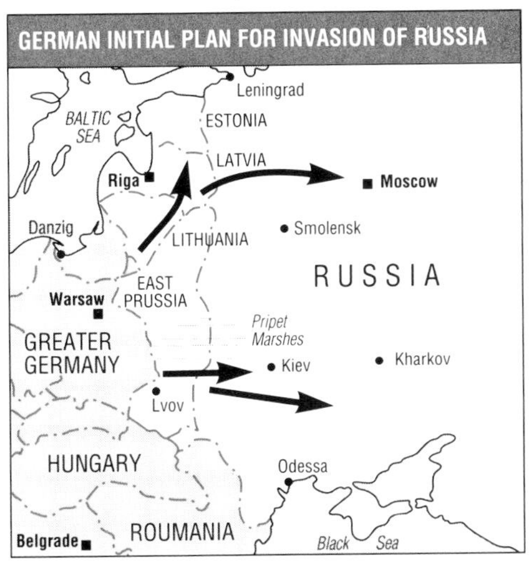

OPPOSING STRENGTHS, June 1941

AXIS	RUSSIAN
Finland 24 divisions (inc. 8 German)	**Leningrad Military District** 18 divisions approx.
Army Group North 29 divisions (inc. 3 Panzer and 3 motorized divisions)	**Baltic Military District** 25 divisions (inc. 4 tank and 2 motorized divisions)
Army Group Centre 50 divisions (inc. 9 Panzer and 5 motorized divisions)	**Western Military District** 44 divisions (inc. 12 tank and 6 motorized divisions)
Army Group South 55 divisions (inc. 5 Panzer, 3 motorized 14 Roumanian divisions)	**Kiev Military District** 59 divisions (inc. 16 tank and 8 motorized divisions)
Theatre Reserve 26 divisions (inc. 2 Panzer divisions)	**Odessa Military District** 22 divisions (inc. 4 tank and 2 motorized divisions)

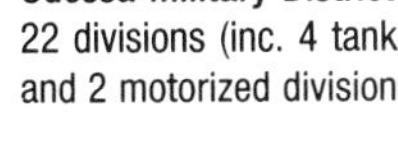

HITLER'S DIRECTIVE OF 18 DECEMBER 1941

Leningrad (Baltic closure)
BALTIC SEA
ESTONIA
LATVIA
Moscow (Political/military/ communications target)
ARMY GROUP NORTH
EAST PRUSSIA
RUSSIA
ARMY GROUP CENTRE
Pripet Marshes
Kharkov
Kiev
Donets (industrial area)
ARMY GROUP SOUTH
Lvov
Ukraine (wheat/oil)
HUNGARY
Odessa
Caucasus (oilfields)
Belgrade
ROUMANIA
Black Sea

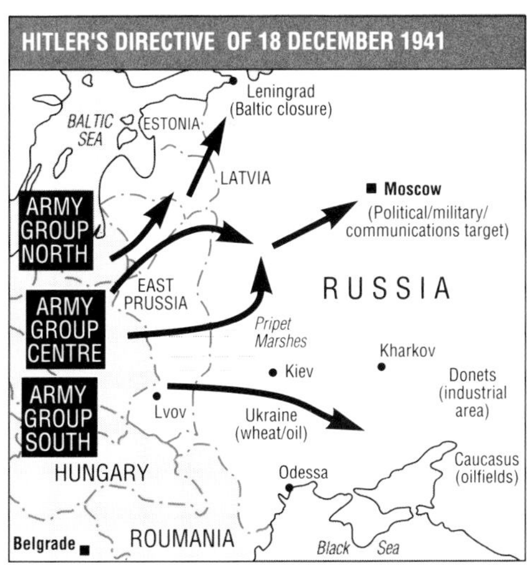

PREPARATIONS FOR THE EASTERN OFFENSIVES

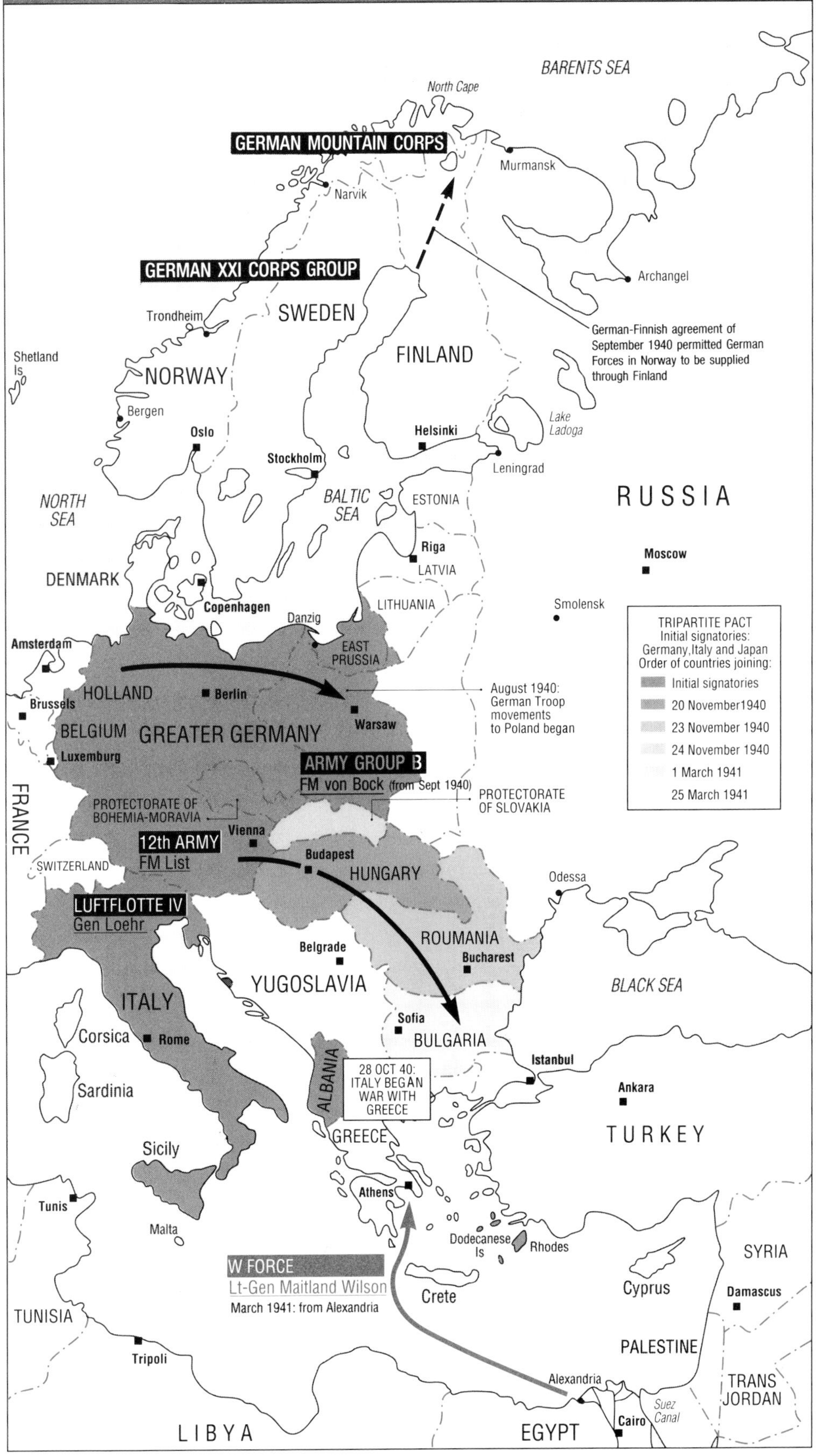

BARENTS SEA
North Cape
GERMAN MOUNTAIN CORPS
Murmansk
Narvik
GERMAN XXI CORPS GROUP
Archangel
Trondheim
SWEDEN
German-Finnish agreement of September 1940 permitted German Forces in Norway to be supplied through Finland
Shetland Is
NORWAY
FINLAND
Bergen
Lake Ladoga
Oslo
Helsinki
Stockholm
Leningrad
NORTH SEA
BALTIC SEA
ESTONIA
RUSSIA
Riga
LATVIA
Moscow
DENMARK
Copenhagen
LITHUANIA
Smolensk
Danzig
Amsterdam
EAST PRUSSIA
TRIPARTITE PACT
Initial signatories: Germany, Italy and Japan
Order of countries joining:
Initial signatories
20 November 1940
23 November 1940
24 November 1940
1 March 1941
25 March 1941
HOLLAND
Berlin
Brussels
August 1940: German Troop movements to Poland began
Warsaw
BELGIUM
GREATER GERMANY
Luxemburg
ARMY GROUP B
FM von Bock (from Sept 1940)
FRANCE
PROTECTORATE OF BOHEMIA-MORAVIA
PROTECTORATE OF SLOVAKIA
Vienna
12th ARMY
FM List
Budapest
SWITZERLAND
HUNGARY
Odessa
LUFTFLOTTE IV
Gen Loehr
ROUMANIA
Belgrade
Bucharest
YUGOSLAVIA
BLACK SEA
ITALY
Sofia
Corsica
Rome
BULGARIA
ALBANIA
28 OCT 40: ITALY BEGAN WAR WITH GREECE
Istanbul
Sardinia
Ankara
GREECE
TURKEY
Sicily
Tunis
Athens
Malta
Dodecanese Is
Rhodes
SYRIA
W FORCE
Lt-Gen Maitland Wilson
March 1941: from Alexandria
Crete
Cyprus
Damascus
TUNISIA
Tripoli
PALESTINE
Alexandria
TRANS JORDAN
LIBYA
EGYPT
Cairo
Suez Canal

Balkan Interlude · P58

Balkan Interlude

Just when the way ahead seemed to be clear for Hitler there took place on **27 March 1941** a bloodless *coup d'état* in Yugoslavia. It was carried out by a group of air force officers opposed to the Tripartite Pact. They dissolved the Regency of Prince Paul and set up a government of national unity under General Dusan Simovic. Prince Paul was exiled, and in his place the 17-year-old Prince Peter, heir to the throne, became King. One of the government's first acts was to sign a non-aggression pact with the Soviet Union and to indicate its willingness to discuss an anti-Axis Balkan coalition with the British.

Hitler was furious and immediately decreed that Yugoslavia must be crushed. Operation 'Marita' was to be hurriedly recast and 'Barbarossa' postponed, if necessary, by four weeks. Within three days a fresh plan had been approved by him.

This called for simultaneous attacks on Yugoslavia and Greece by German forces in Bulgaria, Roumania and Austria, and by the Hungarians, and the Italian forces in north-east Italy and Albania. In all, the Axis forces available totalled some 50 divisions with strong air support. To face this the Yugoslavs had 28 divisions, many poorly equipped, and they had made little preparation for defence. Worse, they dispersed their forces along their 1,000-mile border, holding back little as a central reserve. There was also inadequate effort to co-ordinate defence plans with the Greeks.

The Greek defences were based on two fortified lines, the Metaxas Line guarding Macedonia and the Aliakmon Line designed to prevent a thrust westwards through Macedonia into the main part of Greece. Most of the Greek Army was committed in Albania, and the Greek commander, General Papagos, refused to countenance any withdrawal. Consequently, the eastern part of the country, where the main threat seemed to lie, was held by just the four divisions of the British expeditionary force, W Force, whose equipment was still arriving, and little more than four weak Greek divisions.

6 April 1941 **Axis forces invaded Yugoslavia and Greece.**
There was a heavy air attack on Belgrade, and much of the Yugoslav air force was destroyed on the ground. Luftwaffe aircraft flying from Bulgaria also hit a British ammunition ship, *Clan Fraser*, in Piraeus harbour, the BEF's main supply port. The resultant explosion closed the port.

8 April **Skopje and Nis in Yugoslavia fell.**
By now the Yugoslav forces were beginning to disintegrate. To the east, German forces had now closed on the Metaxas Line.

9 April **Germans captured Salonika.**
They had crossed the Yugoslav border the previous night. The Greek Second Army defending the Metaxas Line was now trapped and forced to surrender. At the same time Monastir was captured, and a threat began to develop to the rear of the Aliakmon Line.

10 April **British forces began to withdraw from the Aliakmon Line.**
General Wilson's intention was to take up a new position in the area of Mount Olympus. Zagreb fell and the Yugoslav state of Croatia declared its independence. Its sympathies lay with Italy.

11 April **Italian forces began to clear the Yugoslav coast.**

13 April **The Germans occupied Belgrade.**
Italian forces in Albania began to drive the Greeks back.

MILITARY STRENGTH OF THE BALTIC STATES

Figures are taken from Whitaker's Almanack (1942 edition) and are as at 3 September 1939. They should be looked at in terms of comparative strength rather than actual strength in spring 1941.

BULGARIA
Army 650,000 men, Air Force 100 aircraft, Navy nil.

GREECE
Army 500,000 men, Air Force 120 aircraft, Navy 2 cruisers, 2 coastal defence vessels, 21 destroyers.

HUNGARY
Army 700,000 men, Air Force 1,000 aircraft, Navy nil.

ROUMANIA
Army 1,700,000 men, Air Force 1,000 aircraft, Navy nil.

YUGOSLAVIA
Army 1,400,000 men, Air Force 800 aircraft, Navy 2 cruisers, 2 destroyers.

16 April **Sarajevo captured.**

17 April **Yugoslavia surrendered to the Axis.**
The Axis forces took 334,000 prisoners. The RAF flew King Peter to Athens and thence to London, where he set up another government-in-exile.

18 April **The Germans penetrated the Aliakmon Line.**
Having established a crossing over the River Aliakmon, they created a gap between the Greek First Army and the BEF. They were quick to exploit this, and Wilson's troops were forced to withdraw. The Greek Premier Alexandros Korizis meanwhile committed suicide.

19 April **The Greeks agreed that W Force should be evacuated.**
Wilson planned to maintain a strong rearguard at Thermopylae, the scene of the epic defence by Leonidas's 300 Spartans in 480BC, to cover the withdrawal of his troops to ports in the Peloponnese.

20 April **Greek First Army surrendered.**
The surrender was accepted by Sepp Dietrich, commander of the SS Leibstandarte Adolf Hitler, Hitler's own personal bodyguard. He did this without referring to his superior commander, List, and the terms were generous: all Greeks were allowed to return to their own homes, and officers were permitted to retain their sidearms. Mussolini was furious when he heard of this, and next day the Greeks were forced to sign another surrender document with much harsher terms.

22 April **Evacuation of W Force began.**

23 April **RAF flew King George of Greece and his government to Crete.**

24 April **British rearguard was finally driven from Thermopylae.**
German paratroops occupied Greek islands in the north-east Aegean.

25 April **German paratroops seized Corinth.**
German troops also crossed the Corinth Canal to the Peloponnese.

27 April **Germans entered Athens.**

28 April **Evacuation of W Force completed.**
The Royal Navy had provided six cruisers and nineteen destroyers, together with numerous transports. Two destroyers and four transports were sunk. The evacuated troops were taken to Crete.

Thus ended the campaign in the Balkans. The Greeks lost 15,700 killed and missing and 300,000 were made prisoner. British and Commonwealth forces suffered 12,000 casualties, of whom almost 10,000 were made prisoner. Although the evacuation had been surprisingly successful, W Force had been compelled to leave all its heavy equipment behind. It was a sorry end to Churchill's Balkans gamble.

As for the Axis, Italian losses during their six months' fighting in Albania and Greece totalled 100,000, including more than 12,300 cases of severe frost-bite. The Germans, on the other hand, in three weeks had suffered 1,684 killed, 3,752 wounded and 548 missing. It was a relatively small price to pay for their territorial gains.

There was just one drawback. On **30 April** Hitler decreed that the start-date for 'Barbarossa' had been put back to **22 June**. Most of the German forces involved in 'Marita' were needed for the invasion of Russia, but required time to re-equip and redeploy. Bearing in mind the German General Staff estimates that it would take five months to accomplish the overrunning of western Russia, this meant that the campaign would not be completed before the onset of the Russian winter. This was to prove fatal.

1939	1940	1941	1942	1943	1944	1945

THE CONQUEST OF THE BALKANS

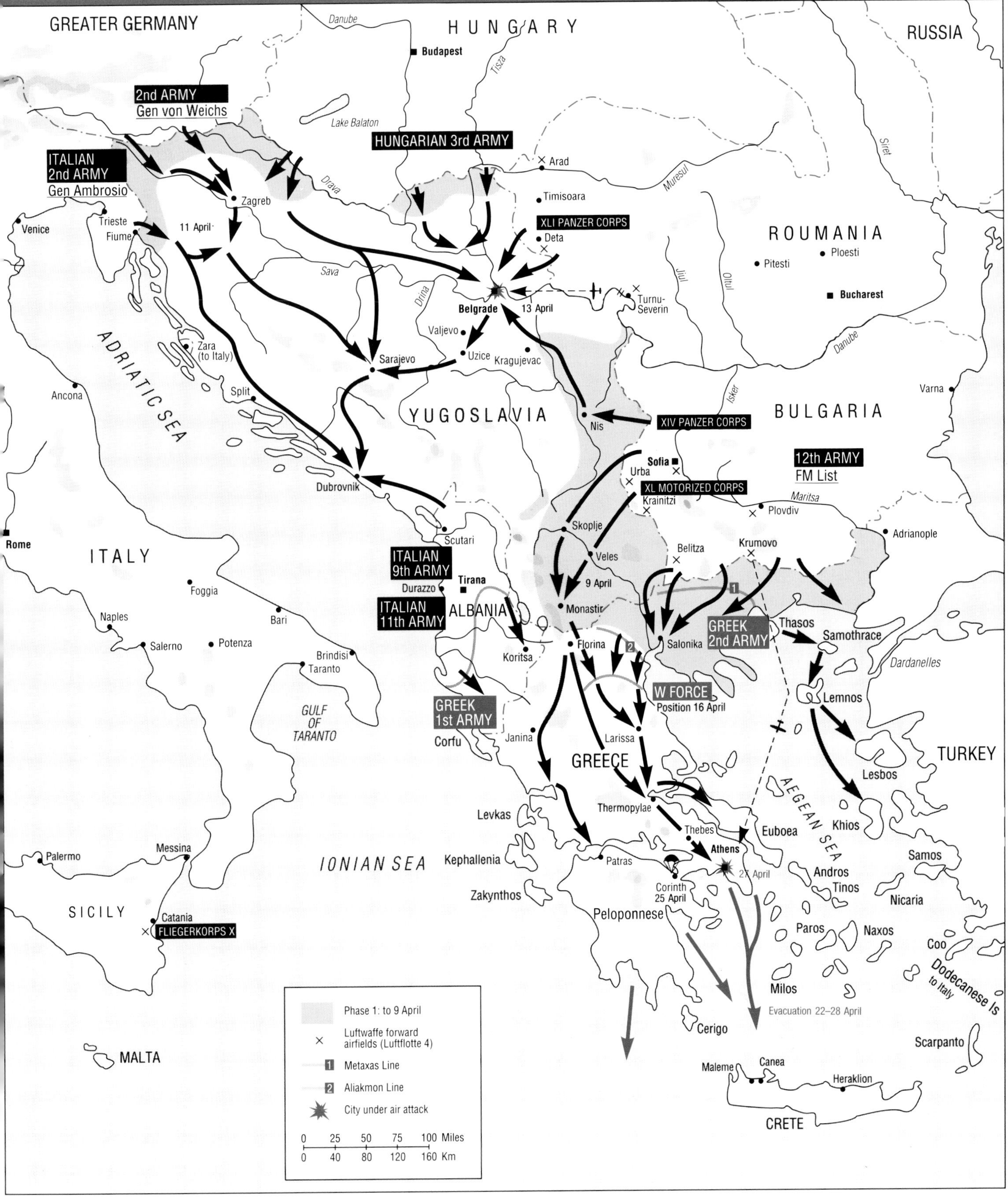

GREATER GERMANY
HUNGARY
RUSSIA
ROUMANIA
BULGARIA
YUGOSLAVIA
ALBANIA
ITALY
GREECE
TURKEY
SICILY
MALTA
CRETE

ADRIATIC SEA
IONIAN SEA
AEGEAN SEA
GULF OF TARANTO

Danube
Tisza
Lake Balaton
Drava
Sava
Drina
Muresul
Siret
Jiul
Oltul
Isker
Maritsa
Dardanelles

2nd ARMY
Gen von Weichs
ITALIAN 2nd ARMY
Gen Ambrosio
HUNGARIAN 3rd ARMY
XLI PANZER CORPS
XIV PANZER CORPS
12th ARMY
FM List
XL MOTORIZED CORPS
ITALIAN 9th ARMY
ITALIAN 11th ARMY
GREEK 1st ARMY
GREEK 2nd ARMY
W FORCE
Position 16 April
FLIEGERKORPS X

Budapest
Arad
Timisoara
Deta
Zagreb
11 April
Trieste
Fiume
Venice
Belgrade
13 April
Turnu-Severin
Pitesti
Ploesti
Bucharest
Valjevo
Uzice
Kragujevac
Sarajevo
Zara (to Italy)
Split
Ancona
Nis
Varna
Sofia
Urba
Krainitzi
Plovdiv
Adrianople
Dubrovnik
Scutari
Skoplje
Veles
9 April
Belitza
Krumovo
Tirana
Durazzo
Monastir
Thasos
Samothrace
Salonika
Florina
Koritsa
Lemnos
Rome
Foggia
Naples
Bari
Salerno
Potenza
Brindisi
Taranto
Corfu
Janina
Larissa
Lesbos
Levkas
Thermopylae
Thebes
Euboea
Khios
Athens
27 April
Kephallenia
Patras
Corinth
25 April
Andros
Tinos
Samos
Nicaria
Zakynthos
Peloponnese
Paros
Naxos
Coo
Dodecanese Is
to Italy
Milos
Evacuation 22–28 April
Cerigo
Scarpanto
Palermo
Messina
Catania
Maleme
Canea
Heraklion

Phase 1: to 9 April
Luftwaffe forward airfields (Luftflotte 4)
1 Metaxas Line
2 Aliakmon Line
City under air attack

0 25 50 75 100 Miles
0 40 80 120 160 Km

The Invasion of Russia · P62

Wavell Under Pressure

At the end of April 1941, British fortunes in the Middle East and Mediterranean were at a low ebb. Driven out of Libya and the Balkans, with much of the Mediterranean now under Axis air domination, the picture looked bleak. But Wavell was about to be beset by numerous other problems that would further stretch his limited forces.

1 April 1941 Raschid Ali seized power in Iraq.
He was in the pay of the Germans who hoped that he might allow their aircraft to be based in Iraq. The British had two air bases in the area, at Shaibah near Basra and at Habbaniyah. They also had the right to pass troops through Iraq to Palestine. The first step they took was to divert an Indian brigade, about to sail for Malaya, to Basra, and they demanded right of passage through Iraq. Raschid Ali acceded to this, aware at the time that the Germans could not give him immediate support. This brigade began to land on **18 April** and moved to protect Basra itself and the RAF base at Shaibah. Further reinforcements were due to arrive at Basra on **29 April**. This time, Raschid Ali, aware that the Germans now held Greece, refused permission for them to land.

25 April Hitler issued Directive No. 28, Operation 'Mercury' – the capture of Crete.
The basic plan called for the employment of 22,750 paratroops: 750 to be landed by glider, 10,000 by parachute, 5,000 by Ju 52 transports and the remainder by sea. Supporting them would be 650 combat aircraft. The first objectives would be the airfields of Maleme, Canea, Retimo and Heraklion. 'Mercury' was to have been launched on 18 May, but this was later put back to the 20th.

29 April Raschid Ali laid siege to RAF Habbaniyah.
The RAF retaliated by flying air strikes against the Iraqi forces. A second Indian brigade now landed at Basra.

29 April Ultra intercepts gave the British firm intelligence that the Germans were planning to attack Crete.

5 May Wavell appointed Major-General Bernard Freyberg, VC, as commander of the British forces in Crete.
Freyberg had commanded the New Zealand Division in Greece. Although aware of the German plans, he faced a difficult task. Most of the 30,000 Australian, British and New Zealand troops under his command, having just been evacuated from Greece, retained little more than their small-arms, and the 10,000 Greek troops on the island were also poorly equipped. What few guns and tanks Wavell had been able to spare him were worn, and he had very few aircraft. Supply by sea was also difficult now that the Luftwaffe could operate from Greek airfields.

6 May A third Indian brigade landed at Basra.
This meant that the whole of 10th Indian Division, which was about to be commanded by Major-General Bill Slim, was present. The War Office ordered the conduct of operations to be handed over to Wavell by GHQ, India, since Habbaniyah could only be relieved from the west. In the meantime Axis aircraft began to land at Mosul.

9 May A British brigade-sized 'flying-column' (Habforce) crossed into Iraq from Palestine.

12 May A convoy, code-named 'Tiger', arrived at Alexandria with urgently needed tanks and aircraft.
This had been authorized by Churchill in response to a plea by Wavell and had been sent through the Mediterranean. Wavell now prepared an operation, 'Brevity', designed to drive Rommel across the border and back into Libya.

14 May British aircraft attacked Syrian airfields.
These airfields had been put at Axis disposal by the Vichy French authorities. Churchill demanded that the Vichy French presence be removed from Syria, but Wavell could not do anything immediately because of his commitments to Crete, Iraq and 'Brevity'.

15 May Operation 'Brevity' launched.
The British regained Halfaya Pass and captured Sollum and Capuzzo. Rommel, believing that the attack was designed to relieve Tobruk, counter-attacked next day and drove the British back to their start-line, apart from the Halfaya Pass, which they retained.

15 May The Luftwaffe began preparatory attacks on Crete.

16 May Rommel was ordered by Berlin to leave Tobruk to the Italians and concentrate the DAK on the Egyptian frontier.

18 May In Iraq, Habforce arrived at Habbaniyah.

19 May Fallujah captured.
The Iraqis launched fierce counter-attacks during the next few days, but were repulsed.

19 May In Crete, Freyberg ordered his remaining aircraft to fly to Egypt.
In view of the Luftwaffe's overwhelming superiority, he considered that to retain them would be a needless sacrifice of pilots' lives. He promised Wavell that the airfields would be made unusable.

20 May The German attack on Crete began.
After air attacks, paratroops dropped on the four airfields, but suffered heavy losses. By evening they had managed to capture only Maleme. That night the Royal Navy intercepted troop convoys sailing for Crete. One convoy suffered heavy losses, one was forced to turn back, but the others sailed on.

21 May The Royal Navy suffered its first casualties in the battle for Crete.

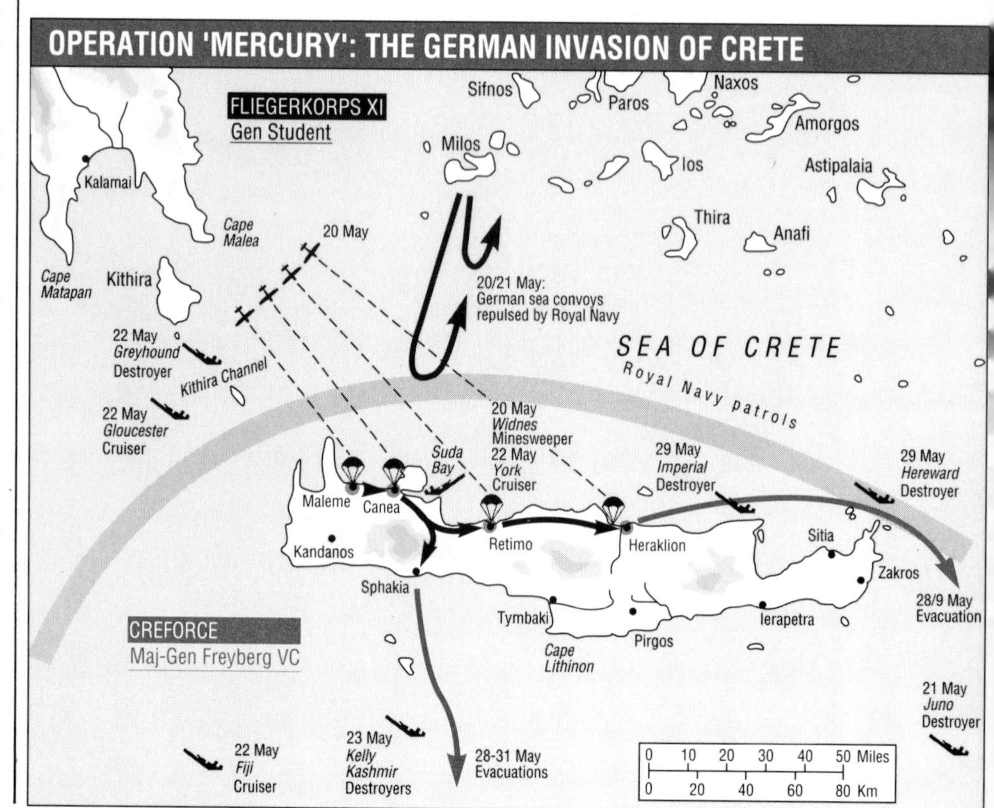

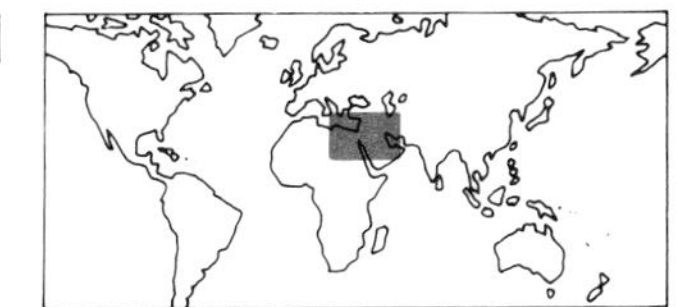

At dawn German aircraft sank a destroyer and damaged the cruiser *Ajax* (which had fought the *Graf Spee* in December 1939). Fighting around the airfields continued. Next day the Royal Navy suffered further losses – two cruisers and four destroyers, while four other ships were damaged. A counter-attack on Maleme airfield failed.

22 May **That evening Freyberg decided to withdraw towards the port of Suda.**
He believed that he must safeguard the main entry point for supplies and reinforcements and pause for breath before launching another counter-attack on Maleme.

25 May **The Germans went on to the offensive.**
They had begun to land reinforcements at Maleme.

27 May **Freyburg decided that the battle for Crete had been lost.**
An evacuation of his forces was organized. Retimo, Heraklion and Canea were still holding out, but the last-named fell by the end of the day and the Germans were able to seize Suda Bay. The British evacuation was to take place from the small port of Sphakia on the south of the island. The withdrawal of the British forces was covered by the newly arrived Layforce, made up of two Commando battalions. The garrisons of Retimo and Heraklion were to be taken off separately by the Royal Navy.

27 May **British advanced in Iraq.**
10th Indian Division, having secured the Basra area, began to advance north towards Baghdad, as did Habforce.

27 May **Rommel recaptured Halfaya Pass.**
He had now been reinforced by 15th Panzer Division.

28 May to 1 June **British evacuated Crete.**
Some 16,000 men were taken off the island, but the cost to the Royal Navy was high. During the battle it had lost three cruisers and six destroyers sunk; three battleships, one carrier, six cruisers, and seven destroyers had been damaged. All were victims of the Luftwaffe. The land forces lost 16,500 killed, wounded and captured, while the German casualties were 6,200. The Axis now dominated the eastern Mediterranean.

30 May **The Iraqi leader, Raschid Ali, fled into Persia.**
Next day British forces entered Baghdad and an armistice was agreed. This provided for the internment of all Axis personnel in the country and for Iraqi support against the Axis.

8 June **British, Commonwealth and Free French forces invaded Syria and Lebanon.**
It was hoped that the Vichy French might offer only token resistance, but this was not to be, and their 45,000 men fought fiercely.

15 June **Wavell launched an attack, 'Battleaxe', in the Western Desert.**
He had been under constant pressure from Churchill to mount such an operation in order to relieve Tobruk. The plan was to break through the Axis defences on the Egyptian-Libyan border, drive on to Tobruk and then exploit to Derna and Mechili. But the offensive was a disaster. Although the British managed to take Capuzzo, their tanks proved very vulnerable, especially to the German 88mm anti-tank guns. By the evening of the 17th, Rommel had driven them back to their start-line at a cost of 91 tanks destroyed against only twelve of his own.

The failure of 'Battleaxe' cost Wavell his command; on **5 July** he was relieved by General Sir Claude Auchinleck.

21 June **Free French forces occupied Damascus in Syria.**
In spite of the fall of the capital, the Vichy French continued to fight on, and forces from Iraq were now also deployed to help crush the last resistance.

15 July **Convention of Acre marked the end of the fighting in Syria.**
All French *matériel* was handed over to the British, and the Vichy French were given the choice of joining the Free French or repatriation to France. Most chose the latter. The Allied forces suffered 2,400 killed and wounded and the Vichy French 3,350.

There was now a lull in operations in the Middle East. Attention turned to the north – and the unleashing of Hitler's mighty assault on Russia.

PRESSURES AND DIVERSIONS IN THE MIDDLE EAST

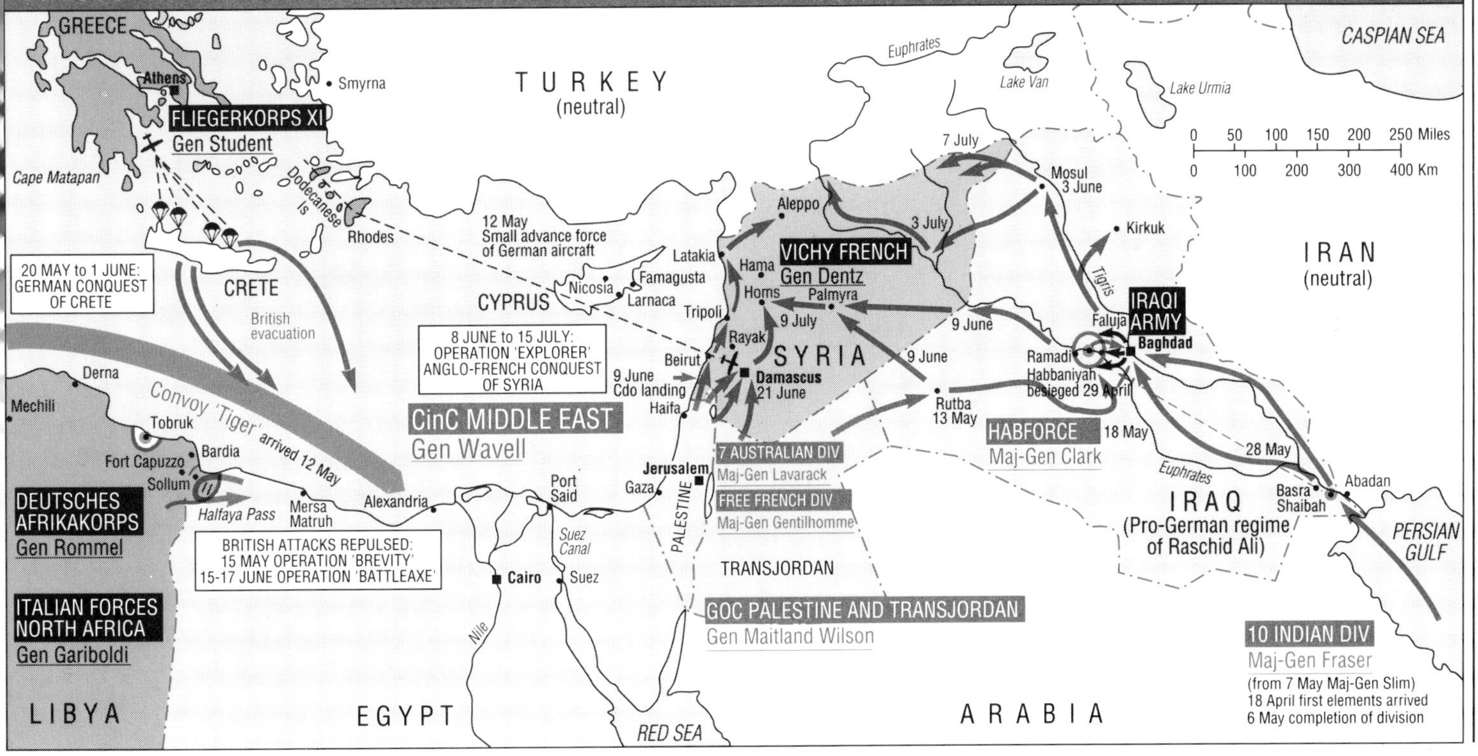

British Offensive in North Africa · P68

13 APRIL 1941 TO 4 SEPTEMBER 1941

The Invasion of Russia

Since January 1941, Stalin had received increasing indications of Hitler's intentions to invade. Reports from British and US intelligence sources arrived in increasing quantities. There were continuous reconnaissance flights by German aircraft over Soviet territory. The Soviets themselves had two prime intelligence sources: a spy in Tokyo, Richard Sorge, and the 'Lucy' spy ring in Switzerland. The latter was built around a spy highly placed in Berlin, code-named 'Lucy', whose identity has not been revealed to this day. Stalin regarded the information received from the Americans and British as merely a means of trying to provoke a war between him and Hitler, so he discounted it. Nevertheless, some organization for the defence of the Soviet Union's western borders was initiated. The *Blitzkrieg* campaign in the Balkans gave Stalin a nasty jolt. He did not believe that Russia was yet in a state to resist the Germans and adopted a very placatory attitude to Hitler.

13 April 1941 Japan–Soviet Neutrality Pact signed in Moscow.
It was designed to last for five years.

23 April The Germans had 59 divisions deployed in the east.
Five weeks earlier the total had been 34.

6 May Stalin made himself Chairman of the Council of People's Commissars.
Stalin was now seen to be openly declaring himself leader of the Russian people rather than hiding behind the anonymity of the title 'Secretary-General of the Communist Party'. The Germans saw this as an indication of Stalin's determination to improve relations with them.

10 May Rudolf Hess, Hitler's deputy, flew to Scotland.
Hess did this on his own initiative, believing that he could persuade Britain to make peace. He was imprisoned there for the remainder of the war. Hitler was furious and considered him a traitor; Stalin viewed it as part of the British plot to persuade Hitler to attack the USSR.

5 June 100 German divisions were now deployed in the east.
Many of these were deployed on the frontier with Russian-occupied Poland. The Soviets were well aware of these increasing concentrations, and in early May they had produced a plan for the defence of their frontiers. But this assumed that the Germans would make a formal declaration of war and would initially commit only limited forces, thereby enabling the troops on the frontier to buy time while the bulk of the Red Army was mobilized. The troops available in western Russia were therefore committed to the frontiers, with few reserves to counter German penetrations. Some effort had

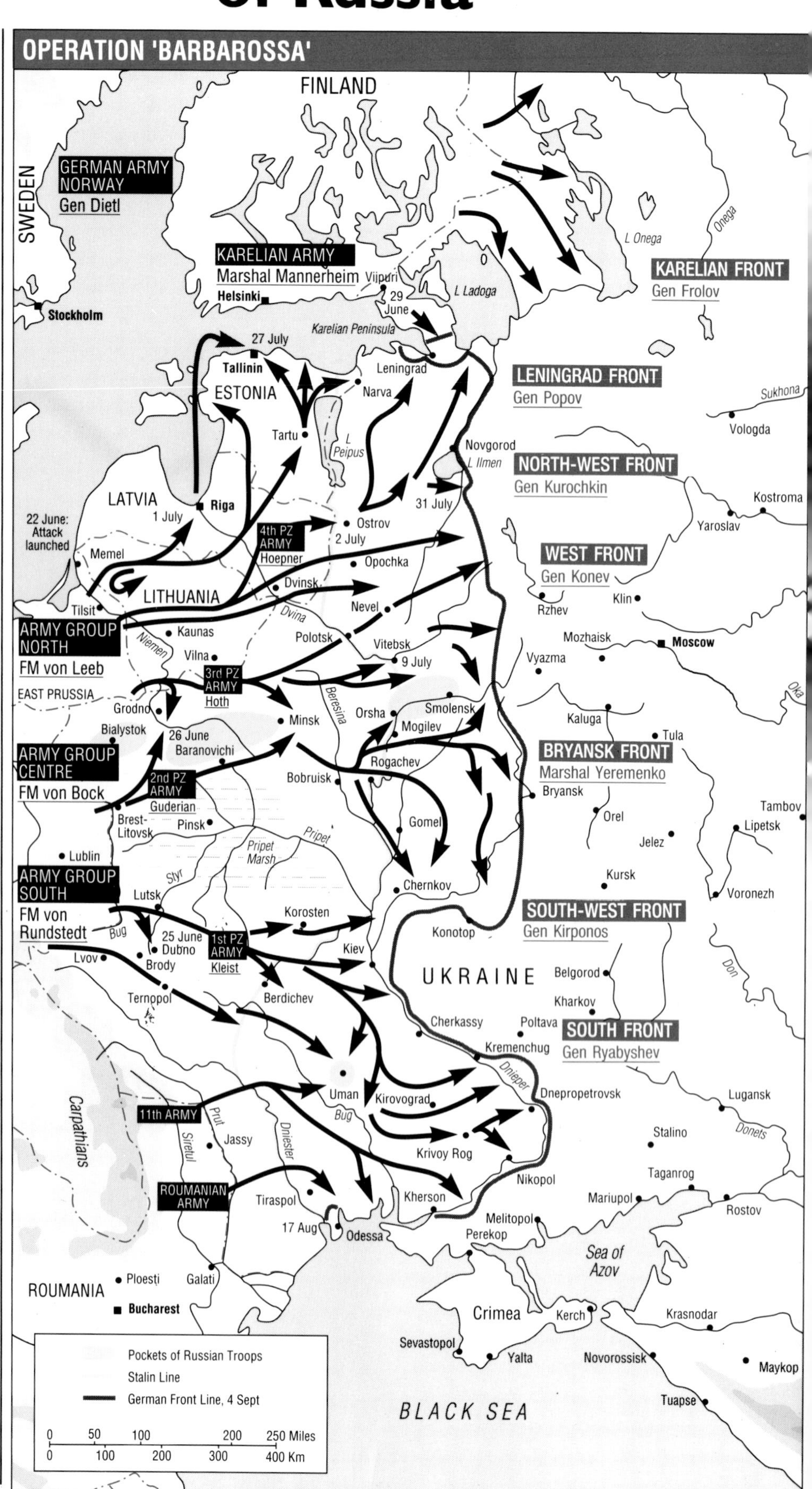

P58 · Balkan Interlude

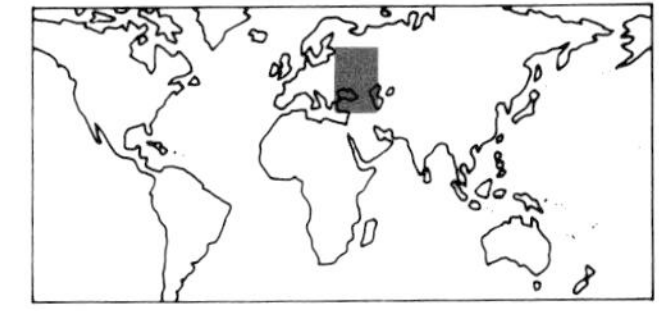

been made to resurrect the old pre-September 1939 border defences, which had fallen into a bad state of repair, and were to become known as the 'Stalin Line'. The Soviet forces were also in the midst of a major reorganization as a result of lessons learnt from the war against Finland. Stalin himself still, at least on the surface, discounted an imminent attack.

13 June The Soviets began to arrest those in the Baltic states who might support a German occupation.
In all, 50,000 were imprisoned.

14 June Soviet newspapers denied that Germany was about to attack.
At about this time the 'Lucy' spy ring passed the date set for the invasion, 22 June, to Moscow.

15 June German higher formation commanders received confirmation of date and time of the attack.
It was to be 0330 hours on the 22nd. Armoured units began to move up by night to their jump-off positions.

17 June Finland began secret mobilization.
The Germans had been wooing the Finns since October 1940 and supplying them with arms since that summer. The Finns had agreed to co-operate with the Germans by sealing off Murmansk and attacking south-east in the Lake Ladoga area, near Leningrad.

19 June Moscow ordered a black-out of major cities and towns near the border.
Troops, however, had been forbidden to deploy to their battle positions – this in spite of the information given by one or two deserters who had crossed the lines.

Night of 21/22 June Soviet forces alerted.
Just after midnight Moscow issued orders for the western military districts to be brought to combat readiness. The order did not call for deployment to battle positions and was vague as to whether the troops were to prepare for mere 'provocations' or a full-blown attack.

22 June 0330 hours 'Barbarossa' was launched.
Just 90 minutes before the last Soviet grain train had passed over the River Bug at Brest-Litovsk, at 0315 hours the German artillery opened fire and then the Luftwaffe took off to attack Soviet airfields. At the end of the day they claimed 800 aircraft destroyed on the ground and a further 400 in the air. From the outset, the Soviet command and control systems were thrown into complete confusion. Most bridges over the Bug were captured intact; some were even unguarded. Italy and Roumania declared war against the USSR. Churchill stated: 'Any state which fights Nazism will have our aid.'

23 June German spearheads had penetrated 50 miles inside Russian Poland.
Brest-Litovsk, which had been bypassed to the north and south, continued to hold out. The Red Army launched furious counter-attacks with tanks north-east of Tilsit, Lithuania. They were beaten back with heavy losses.

24 June Slovakia declared war on the Soviet Union.

25 June Von Rundstedt's Army Group South captured Dubno.
A large Soviet force was in danger of being cut off by Army Group Centre in the Bialystok area. In the north the Russians began to attack Finnish positions.

26 June Finland declared war on the Soviet Union.
Army Group North entered Lithuania while Army Group Centre closed the Bialystok pocket.

27 June Hungary declared war on the Soviet Union.
Hungarian troops came under von Rundstedt's command from **3 July**.

28 June Albania declared war on the Soviet Union.
The Germans meanwhile began to threaten Minsk. In the south, however, Soviet resistance was proving tougher than expected.

29 June The Finns launched an assault in the Karelian Peninsula.
This was planned to join eventually the thrust by Army Group North. Brest-Litovsk fell. (Soviet historians later tried to assert that it held out for six weeks, but this was not so.)

30 June Reduction of the Bialystok pocket.
When it finally surrendered on **3 July** 290,000 prisoners, 2,500 tanks and 1,500 guns fell into German hands. Bridgeheads were also established across the River Beresina.

1 July Riga fell.

2 July The Germans broke through the Stalin Line on the Latvian border.

3 July Stalin spoke to the Russian people for the first time since the invasion had begun.
'A grave threat hangs over our country.' He exhorted the Russian people to defend to the last.

9 July The Germans captured Vitebsk.

12 July Britain and the USSR signed a mutual assistance pact.
They undertook not to sign a separate peace with the Axis.

15 July The Germans encircled a large pocket of Russians around Smolensk.

16 July Von Rundstedt's Army Group South created a large pocket at Uman between Kiev and Odessa.

19 July Hitler issued Directive No. 33.
During the past few weeks Hitler had been increasingly interfering with the conduct of operations, and his generals were becoming confused as to where their priorities lay. Hitler now laid down that Moscow was no longer the primary objective. Instead, once the Smolensk pocket had been reduced, Army Group Centre was to hand its armour over to its neighbours, north and south, so that Leningrad could be captured and the fertile Ukraine overrun. He did, however, order the bombing of Moscow.

20 July Stalin became People's Commissar for Defence.
This meant that he was personally taking over conduct of operations.

27 July Tallinin, capital of Estonia, captured by the Germans.

31 July Army Group North reached Lake Ilmen.
The drive on Leningrad had slowed down, partly because of the heavily wooded terrain, but also because of the growing exhaustion of the troops.

5 August Smolensk pocket surrendered.
310,000 Soviet prisoners were captured.

8 August Uman pocket surrendered.
100,000 Soviet prisoners were captured. Von Rundstedt now set about creating another pocket around Kiev, which Stalin ordered to be defended to the last.

17 August Odessa put under siege.

4 September Leningrad besieged.
To the north of the city the Finns had closed up to their pre-1941 border with the USSR, but were unwilling to cross it for political reasons. The only link Leningrad now had with the rest of the USSR was by water, across the southern part of Lake Ladoga.

By this stage the German armies had captured well over one million men and vast quantities of weapons and equipment. It seemed that it could only be a matter of time before the Russians were totally broken. Once again, the effectiveness of Blitzkrieg was being demonstrated.

Ever Deeper East · P64

Ever Deeper East

On **5 September 1941**, Hitler changed his mind yet again. Having spread his forces across the whole breadth of western Russia to secure Leningrad and the Ukraine rather than concentrating on Moscow, he now decided that Moscow after all would be the primary objective. Leningrad, even though it had not been captured, was to become merely a secondary front. Army Group North was ordered to hand over the bulk of its armour and air support to Army Group Centre; likewise, the forces the latter had lent to Army Group South had now to be returned. This was easier said than done because they were at that moment engaged in creating an enormous pocket around Kiev. So the drive on Moscow would not be able to start until the end of the month and, with the autumn rains due in mid-October, to be followed by snow, it would be a race against time.

The Russians, who had always believed that their capital would be the primary objective, were desperately building defences to protect Moscow and bringing in reinforcements from east of the Urals. At the same time they were moving their industry to the east to get it out of range of the German bombers, which had been attacking Moscow. Yet these attacks could not be compared to the London *Blitz* or to those the RAF was beginning to develop against Germany. Range and the demands of the ground forces for close support meant that, although the first attack on Moscow on **22 July** involved 127 aircraft, of the remaining 75 attacks mounted during 1941, 59 comprised ten aircraft or less.

19 September 1941 Kiev fell to the Germans.
600,000 prisoners, 2,500 tanks and 1,000 guns were netted. Heinz Guderian's Second Panzer Army was now freed to rejoin Army Group Centre and would approach Moscow from the south-west.

25 September Army Group South began to drive into the Crimea.

27 September The first of the autumn rains fell.
They quickly turned the ground to mud.

30 September Operation 'Typhoon', the drive on Moscow, was launched.
Large pockets were quickly created around Vyazma and Bryansk.

3 October Hitler told the German people that Russia, 'has already been broken and will never rise again'.

10 October Soviet General Georgi Zhukov took over command of the West Front formed for the defence of Moscow.

14 October The Bryansk pocket surrendered.
But many of the trapped Soviet troops managed to break out eastwards and only 50,000 prisoners were netted. Rain and mud were becoming increasing obstacles to the German advance. Hitler now decided that instead of attacking Moscow directly it was to be enveloped.

16 October Mass exodus from Moscow.
Panic gripped the city and there was widespread looting. Much of the machinery of government, including the foreign embassies, was moved back behind the River Volga. Stalin remained in Moscow. Meanwhile Odessa fell after a two-month siege.

17 October Taganrog on the Sea of Azov fell to Army Group South.

18 October The Germans penetrated the Mozhaisk defence line 80 miles west of Moscow.

19 October Vyazma pocket finally reduced.
The yield here was 670,000 Soviet prisoners, 1,000 tanks and 4,000 guns.

24 October Army Group South captured Kharkov.

27 October The Crimea fell.
The whole of the Crimea, apart from Sevastapol and Kerch, had now been overrun by the Germans.

30 October The mud and weather had now forced the German attack to a virtual halt.
On that day Second Panzer Army failed to take Orel and was almost out of fuel – indeed, the supply system had virtually broken down. Worse, most of the German troops were still in their summer uniforms and were beginning to suffer dreadfully from the cold. Units were now reduced to half their established strength, and the replacement system had not been able to keep up with demand. So now there was a pause while the Germans 'gathered breath'; this reduced pressure on the Soviets, who were able to take the opportunity to reinforce the troops in front of Moscow.

3 November Kursk captured.

7 November Decision to resume the advance on Moscow.
The snows and frosts had now arrived and rendered the ground firm once more. But by now it was estimated that 80 Soviet divisions stood in front of Moscow.

15 November Drive on Moscow resumed.

16 November Kerch in the Crimea captured.
Sevastapol, although besieged, continued to hold out and would do so for eight months.

17 November The Germans established *Reichskommissariat Ostland*.
This was set up under Alfred Rosenberg to administer the territories of the east, including the Baltic States and Belorussia (White Russia). Many of the inhabitants of the occupied territories had initially welcomed the Germans, in the hope of being liberated from Stalin's Communism. They were soon to be sadly disillusioned. Hitler regarded the peoples of the East as *Untermenschen* (sub-humans), and the treatment meted out to them by the Germans became brutal. As a result many fled to join the increasing number of partisan groups operating behind the German lines. These would become ever more of a thorn in the flesh of the German supply lines.

20 November Rostov-on-Don, gateway to the Caucasus, captured.

23 November German troops were now only thirty miles north-west of Moscow.
In the south the closest point reached was Kashira on the River Ugra, some sixty miles from the capital.

29 November The Soviets launched a counter-attack on Rostov.
Von Rundstedt recognized that his forces were over-extended here and wanted to withdraw, but Hitler forbade this. Once the Soviet attack began von Rundstedt on his own initiative pulled his men back and evacuated Mariupol and Taganrog as well, taking up a new line on the River Mius. Hitler was furious and sacked von Rundstedt.

5 December The German offensive came to a halt, nineteen miles from Moscow.
In the north the Germans had reached the Volga Canal, but nowhere had they closed up to the three lines of fortifications protecting the capital. A sudden drop in temperature to –35°C the previous night meant that tank engines would not start, weapons would not operate and there were many cases of frost-bite. Hitler reluctantly agreed to local withdrawals to more defensible terrain.

5 December Britain declared war on Finland, Hungary and Roumania.

There is no doubt that 'General Winter' had played the main part in bringing the German onslaught to a halt. Hitler's decision to go into the Balkans and put back the launch-date for 'Barbarossa' had now come home to roost. The Germans had, it is true, captured almost two million prisoners and crushed the Red Armies in the west. Yet they themselves had suffered 250,000 dead and twice this number wounded. In spite of reinforcements, the German armies on the Eastern Front were 340,000 men under establishment, and already divisions were having to be transferred from France in order to make good the shortfall. The German lines of communication were over-stretched and the harshness of the Russian winter was upon them.

1939	1940	1941	1942	1943	1944	1945

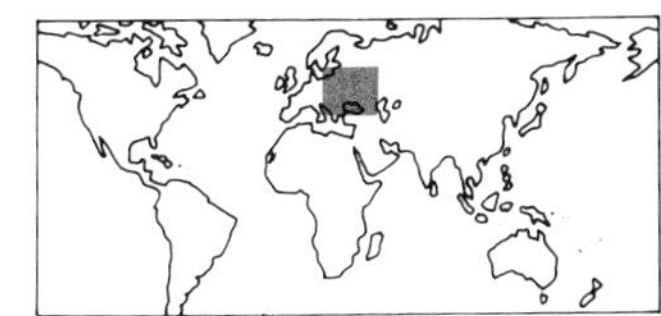

THE DRIVE FOR MOSCOW

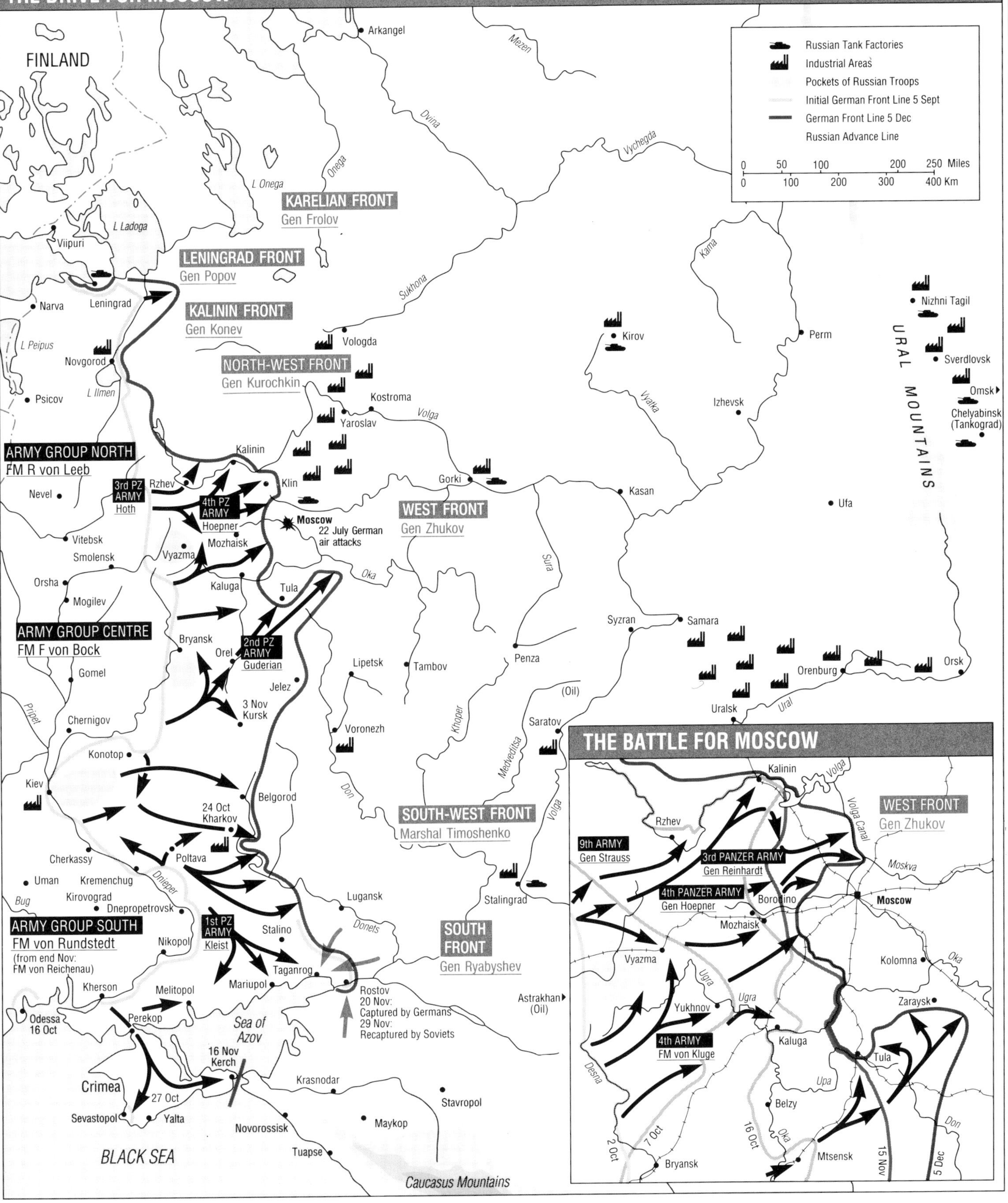

Russian Tank Factories
Industrial Areas
Pockets of Russian Troops
Initial German Front Line 5 Sept
German Front Line 5 Dec
Russian Advance Line

0 50 100 200 250 Miles
0 100 200 300 400 Km

FINLAND
Arkangel
Mezen
Dvina
Vychegda
Onega
L Onega
KARELIAN FRONT
Gen Frolov
L Ladoga
Viipuri
LENINGRAD FRONT
Gen Popov
Leningrad
Narva
KALININ FRONT
Gen Konev
Sukhona
Kama
Nizhni Tagil
Kirov
Perm
Vologda
L Peipus
Novgorod
NORTH-WEST FRONT
Gen Kurochkin
Sverdlovsk
URAL MOUNTAINS
Psicov
L Ilmen
Kostroma
Volga
Vyatka
Izhevsk
Omsk
Chelyabinsk (Tankograd)
Yaroslav
ARMY GROUP NORTH
FM R von Leeb
Kalinin
Rzhev
3rd PZ ARMY
Hoth
4th PZ ARMY
Hoepner
Klin
Gorki
Kasan
Nevel
WEST FRONT
Gen Zhukov
Ufa
Moscow
22 July German air attacks
Vitebsk
Mozhaisk
Smolensk
Vyazma
Sura
Oka
Orsha
Kaluga
Tula
Mogilev
ARMY GROUP CENTRE
FM F von Bock
Syzran
Samara
Bryansk
2nd PZ ARMY
Guderian
Orel
Penza
Gomel
Lipetsk
Tambov
Orenburg
Orsk
Jelez
(Oil)
Pripet
3 Nov
Kursk
Khoper
Uralsk
Ural
Chernigov
Voronezh
Saratov
Medveditsa
Konotop
Kiev
Belgorod
Don
Volga
24 Oct
Kharkov
SOUTH-WEST FRONT
Marshal Timoshenko
Cherkassy
Poltava
Uman
Kremenchug
Dnieper
Bug
Kirovograd
Dnepropetrovsk
Lugansk
Stalingrad
ARMY GROUP SOUTH
FM von Rundstedt
(from end Nov: FM von Reichenau)
1st PZ ARMY
Kleist
Stalino
Donets
SOUTH FRONT
Gen Ryabyshev
Nikopol
Taganrog
Mariupol
Kherson
Melitopol
Rostov
20 Nov: Captured by Germans
29 Nov: Recaptured by Soviets
Astrakhan (Oil)
Odessa
16 Oct
Perekop
Sea of Azov
16 Nov
Kerch
Crimea
27 Oct
Krasnodar
Stavropol
Sevastopol
Yalta
Novorossisk
Maykop
BLACK SEA
Tuapse
Caucasus Mountains

THE BATTLE FOR MOSCOW

Kalinin
Volga
WEST FRONT
Gen Zhukov
Rzhev
Volga Canal
9th ARMY
Gen Strauss
3rd PANZER ARMY
Gen Reinhardt
Moskva
4th PANZER ARMY
Gen Hoepner
Borodino
Moscow
Mozhaisk
Vyazma
Kolomna
Oka
Ugra
Yukhnov
Zaraysk
4th ARMY
FM von Kluge
Kaluga
Tula
Desna
Upa
Belzy
Don
2 Oct
7 Oct
16 Oct
Oka
Bryansk
Mtsensk
15 Nov
5 Dec

Before the Gates of Moscow · P70

Deepening US Involvement

The discreet help that President Roosevelt was giving Britain had been put to the test in the presidential election of **November 1940**. His vote held up, and on **29 December 1940** in his close of year speech he spoke of the four essential freedoms at stake in the war – of speech and religion, and from want and fear. To uphold these, America must become 'the arsenal of the democracies'. Even so, he recognized that the American people, despite their admiration for the way in which Britain was standing up to the Axis powers, were still not prepared to enter the war. Indeed, as late as **May 1941** a Gallup poll revealed that 79 per cent of Americans were of this mind; nevertheless an increasing number were beginning to realize that sooner or later the USA would be drawn in.

10 January 1941 **Roosevelt introduced his Lend-Lease bill to Congress.**
Recognizing the fact that neither Britain nor China were able to pay *ad infinitum* for *matériel* supplied to them, Roosevelt proposed that repayment be in kind, but not until after the end of the war. He likened this to lending a neighbour a garden hose in order to put out a fire.

1 February **The US Navy was reorganized into three fleets: Asiatic, Atlantic and Pacific.**
Roosevelt had also ordered that the crews of warships gradually be brought up to war establishment.

8 March **Lend-Lease became law.**
Initial priority was given to Britain and Greece.

29 March **Conclusion of US–British Staff Conference.**
By the end of 1940, US planners had concluded that if war became inevitable they would find themselves allied to the British. It was therefore important to agree a common strategy so that plans could be further developed. Encouraged by both Roosevelt and Churchill, these talks began on **29 January** and comprised fourteen separate sessions. The result was Plan 'ABC-1'. The main elements of this were: Germany must be defeated first, so the USA would exert its main military effort in the Atlantic and Europe; Allied positions in the Mediterranean were to be maintained; the strategic defence of the Far East was also important, and the US Navy would be employed there offensively. These conclusions were not politically binding on either nation, but they did at least provide US planners with an operating framework.

31 March **A US scientific/military team arrived in Greenland to consider the establishment of military bases there.**
Greenland (a Danish colony) was to become an important platform for US aircraft engaged in the Battle of the Atlantic.

11 April **Roosevelt extended the Pan-American security zone in the Atlantic from 60°W to 26°W.**
This was the limit within which US warships would protect their merchant vessels. Hitler gave express orders that U-boats were not to sink US ships.

12 April **US troops landed in Greenland.**

14 June **Roosevelt ordered the freezing of all German and Italian assets in the USA.**
In retaliation Germany and Italy demanded that all US consulates be closed in their countries.

4 July **Roosevelt voiced a warning to the American people.**
In an Independence Day broadcast he warned that the US 'will never survive as a happy and prosperous oasis in the middle of a desert of dictatorship'. This was part of his programme for preparing the American people for war.

7 July **US Marines began to relieve the British garrison in Iceland.**
This gave Roosevelt the excuse to provide US escorts for convoys from North America to and from Iceland.

15 July **US air base set up at Argentia, Newfoundland.**

2 August **US Lend-Lease aid began to be sent to the USSR.**

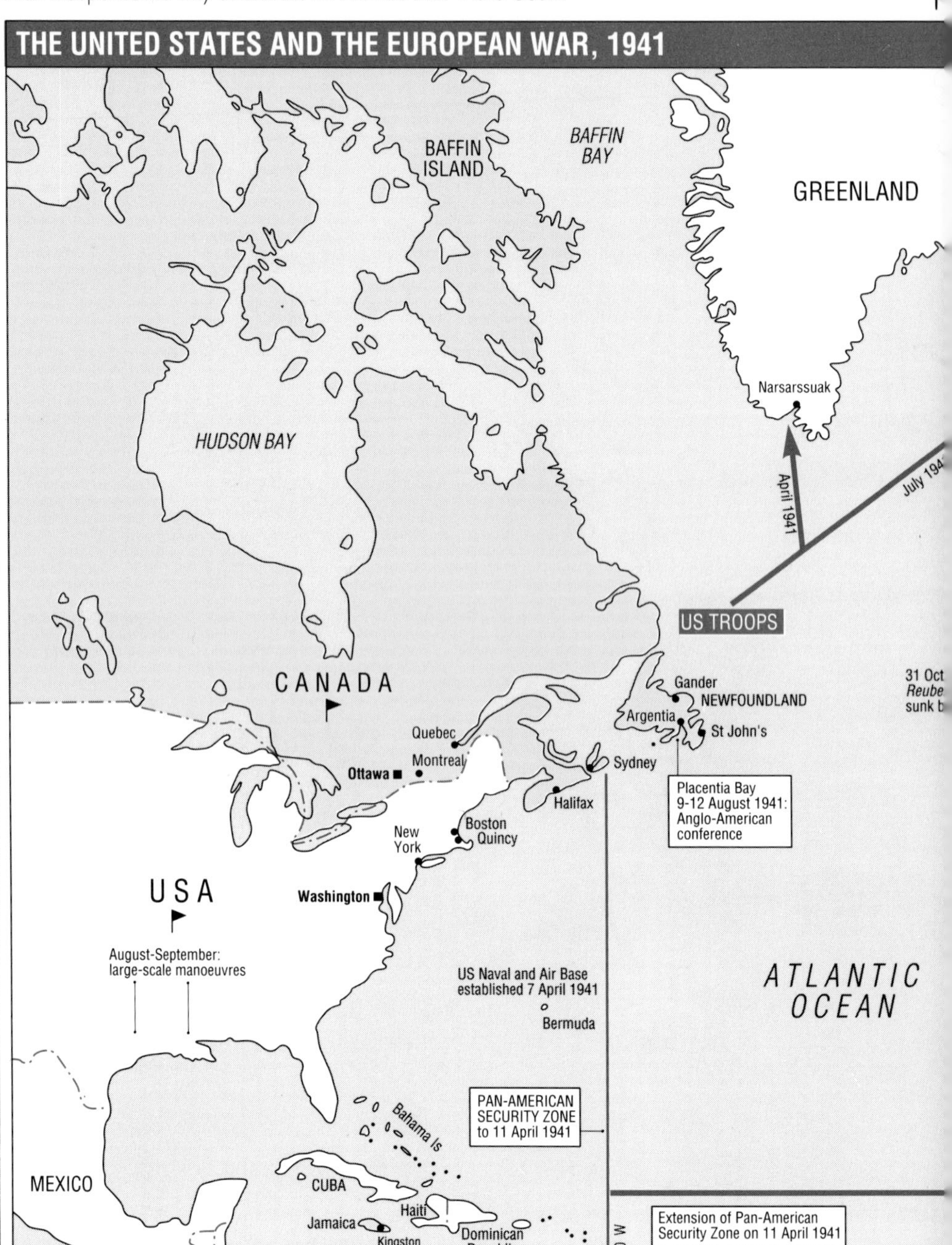

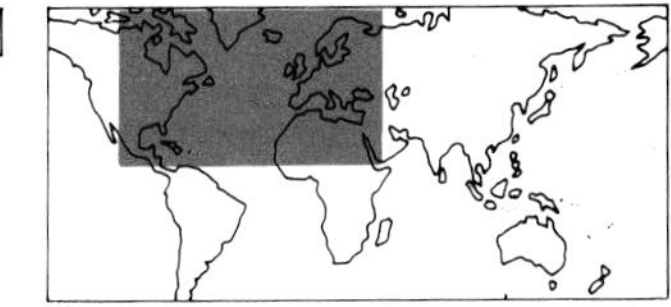

August to September **Louisiana–Texas manoeuvres.**
400,000 US troops took part in these exercises, which were designed to prepare the US Army for modern *Blitzkrieg* warfare.

9–12 August **Roosevelt and Churchill met in Placentia Bay, Newfoundland.**
Churchill had sailed across the Atlantic in the battleship *Prince of Wales* and Roosevelt was aboard the cruiser *Augusta*. Churchill hoped to be able to persuade Roosevelt to join in the war, but was unsuccessful. All he received was an undertaking that the USA would do so if Japan attacked British possessions in the Far East. Nevertheless, a major result of the meeting was the formulation of the Atlantic Charter. This defined the war aims of the democracies and laid down the foundations of what was to become the United Nations.

4 September **US destroyer *Greer* had an inconclusive brush with a U-boat in the North Atlantic.**
As a result Roosevelt warned that, 'from now on if any German or Italian vessels of war' entered the Pan-American Security Zone they would do so 'at their own risk'.

16 September **US announcement that it would provide escorts for ships carrying Lend-Lease material up to 26°W.**
This meant that clashes with U-boats would become highly likely.

29 Sept-1 Oct:
Soviet-US-British conference

British and Empire territories and mandated territories
Axis and Axis-allied territories at start 1941
Axis and Axis-allied territories at start December 1941
Vichy France
Axis aggression 1941
Atlantic Charter signatories, 24 September 1941

24 September **First fifteen nations signed the Atlantic Charter.**
The signatories, which included governments-in-exile, were: Australia, Belgium, Canada, Czechoslovakia, France, Great Britain, Greece, Luxemburg, Netherlands, New Zealand, Norway, Poland, USA, USSR and Yugoslavia. Many neutral countries would also sign.

27 September **First 'Liberty' ship launched.**
With merchant shipping losses beginning to exceed the production of new ships, it was important to speed up production methods. Liberty ships were assembled from prefabricated sections, often made by different factories well away from the coast. Since the shipyard merely had to put them together, more efficient use was made of capacity. The first Liberty ship was *Patrick Henry*, launched at Baltimore naval dockyard.

29 September to 1 October **Soviet–US–British conference in Moscow to discuss aid to Russia.**

17 October **US destroyer *Kearney* torpedoed by a U-boat north-west of Iceland.**
She was badly damaged, but managed to struggle into port.

31 October **US destroyer *Reuben James* was sunk by a U-boat west of Iceland.**
More than 100 of her crew were lost.

6 November **The German blockade-runner *Odenwald* was captured by the US cruiser *Omaha* and destroyer *Somers*.**
She was disguised as a US merchant vessel.

13 November **1939 Neutrality Act repealed.**
This loosened the legal constraints on Roosevelt's entering the war, but the majorities in both Congress and Senate were very narrow.

Throughout 1941, President Roosevelt had increased his country's involvement in the war. Yet he was still conscious that a significant proportion of the American people would not follow him if he made a voluntary declaration of war. Many still hoped that the USA would be able to stay out of it. In spring 1941, US Congress renewed his 1940 Selective Service Act by the narrowest of margins – 203 votes against 202. That summer there began to appear on walls throughout the country the initials 'OHIO' – 'Over the hill in October' – an exhortation to draftees to refuse to report for service. Even Roosevelt himself had agreed plans to start deactivating the National Guard divisions, and this was due to begin in February 1942.

Before 1941 ended, however, the American people were to receive a devastating shock. Churchill's prayers of the past two years were about to be answered.

Day of Infamy · P74

British Offensive in North Africa

On **1 July 1941**, just after General Sir Claude Auchinleck had arrived from India to take over command of the Middle East from Wavell, Churchill sent him a signal. It was a veiled order to take the offensive as soon as possible and relieve Tobruk. Auchinleck, however, realized that his forces would not be in a fit state to attack Rommel for some time. They had suffered losses in Greece and Crete, the Syrian and Abyssinian campaigns were continuing and the forces in Egypt were recovering from their recent setbacks during 'Brevity' and 'Battleaxe'. He was also very conscious of the spectacular German successes in Russia and the possibility that the Germans might threaten Syria and/or Iraq from the Caucasus. His fears were heightened by the seemingly anti-Allied attitude of Reza Shah Pahlavi in Persia (Iran), through which the Germans would have to pass to reach the Middle East. Iran's armed forces had German advisers even though the country had declared its neutrality. Auchinleck replied to Churchill along these lines, but the immediate response was a promise of 500 new tanks, including US models, by the end of July and further exhortations to relieve Tobruk.

26 July 1941 **Auchinleck flew to London for talks.**
These followed a continued exchange of signals culminating in one from Auchinleck stating that he would not be ready to attack Rommel until mid-November. Reassured by the promise of further reinforcements, Auchinleck had decided by mid-August that he could launch a full-blown offensive in mid-November rather than merely a limited operation to relieve Tobruk.

19–29 August **An Australian brigade in Tobruk was relieved by Poles.**

25 August **British and Soviet troops invaded Iran.**
The Russians were as aware as the British of Iran's strategic importance. The two allies' ambassadors had made demands for their countries to be invited into Iran; when these were rejected, there was no alternative but invasion. Soviet troops moved south from both sides of the Caspian Sea, and the British east from Iraq and north from the head of the Persian Gulf. Opposition was slight.

26 August **British troops completed the occupation of the vital Abadan oilfields in Iran.**

27 August **Iran asked for a cease-fire.**
A government more sympathetic to the Allies had been formed and the cease-fire came into effect two days later.

28 August **Robert Menzies replaced by his deputy, F. W. Fadden, as prime minister of Australia.**
Fadden had a very narrow majority and, under pressure from the political opposition, demanded that the remainder of the Australians in Tobruk be relieved. After much protest the British agreed to this and a further Australian brigade was relieved by British troops during the period **19–27 September** and the remainder, after Fadden's government had fallen, during the period **12–25 October**. John Curtin took over from Fadden.

2 September **Auchinleck issued his first directive on the forthcoming offensive.**
General Sir Alan Cunningham, who had commanded the Kenya-based drive into Italian East Africa, had been appointed to command what used to be called the Western Desert Force, which was to carry out the operation, code-named 'Crusader'. Auchinleck charged him with the task of producing a plan for the relief of Tobruk and the re-conquest of Cyrenaica.

10 September **The Allies demanded that Iran expel all Axis nationals within 48 hours.**
This was impossible to fulfill, and on **17 September** Soviet and British troops occupied Tehran, out of

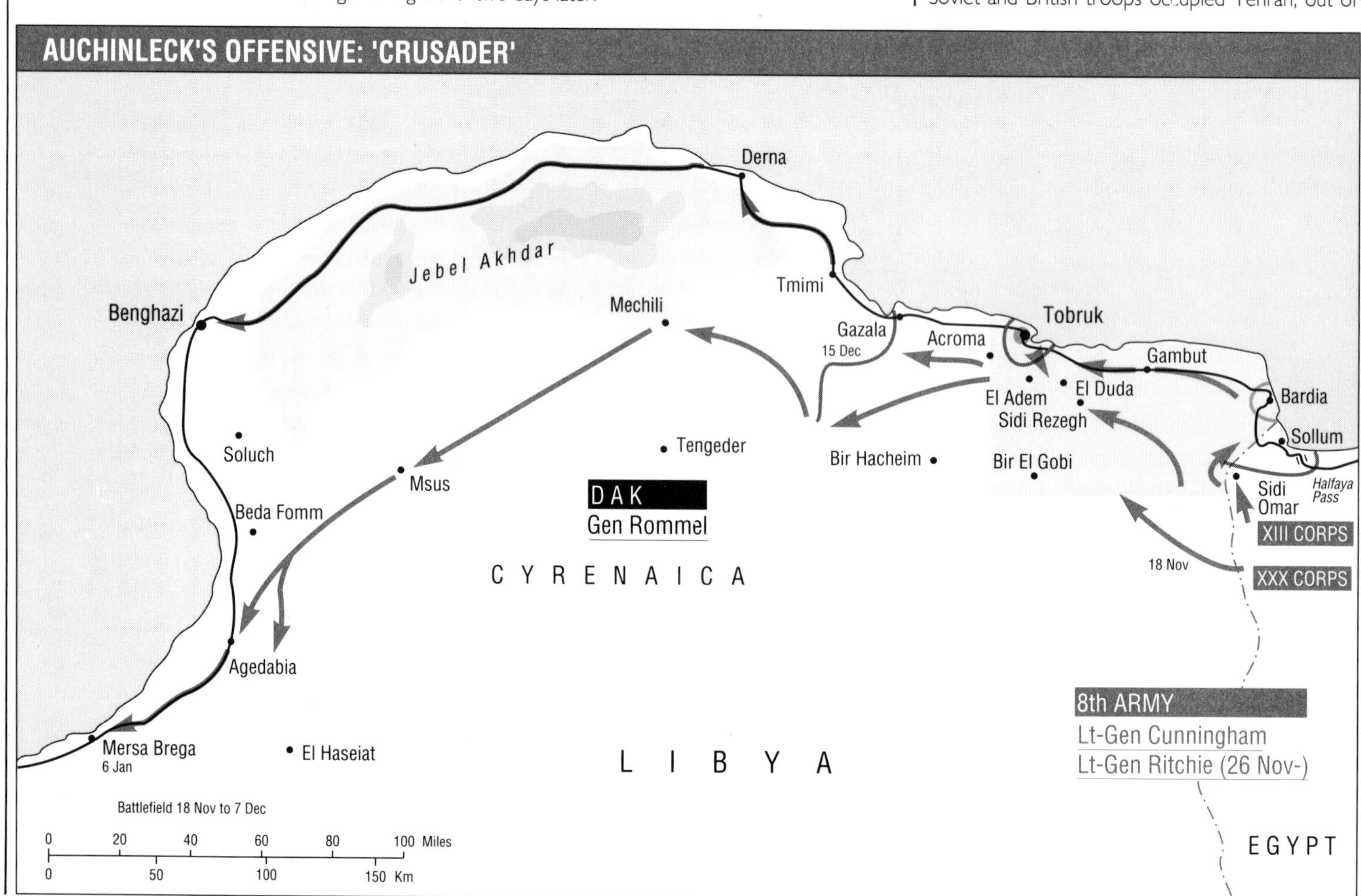

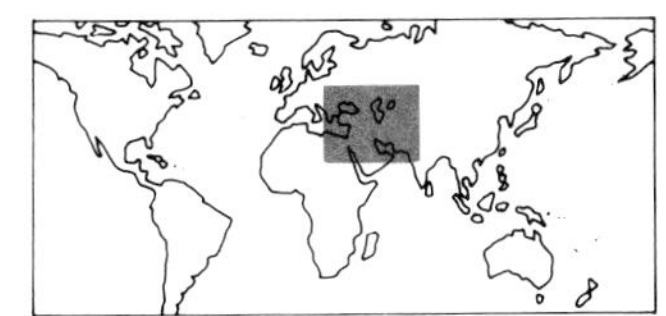

which they had previously agreed to stay. The Shah abdicated in favour of his son, Mohammad Reza Pahlavi.

14–25 September **Probing operation by 21st Panzer Division towards Sidi Barrani.**
Rommel mistakenly believed that the British had a fuel dump here. The British forces fell back, as ordered. Rommel then withdrew his troops believing that Auchinleck had adopted a strictly defensive posture. 21st Panzer Division had been created from 5th Light Division, and a third German division, 90th Light, had also arrived in North Africa. 15th and 21st Panzer Divisions now formed the DAK and Rommel commanded this, 90th Light and XXI Italian Corps.

26 September **Formation of the Eighth Army.**
By now the British had two complete corps, XIII and XXX, in the Western Desert under Cunningham, and his command was given army status, It now contained, in addition to British troops, Australian, Indian, New Zealand, South African, Free French and Polish elements. At much the same time two other British armies were formed in the Middle East: Ninth in Palestine and Tenth in Iraq and Persia.

3 October **Cunningham's plan for 'Crusader' approved.**
XXX Corps, which incorporated the bulk of the armour, was to draw the DAK into battle and destroy its tanks, while XIII Corps, having contained the Axis defences on the frontier and then enveloped them from the south, would advance on Tobruk, whose garrison would break out when the time was ripe. A third, but smaller element, Oasis Force, would advance westwards deep into the Libyan desert to deceive Rommel into thinking that the main effort would be made there. Two Special Forces operations were to be mounted: one by the newly formed 'L' Detachment, Special Air Service (SAS), on enemy airfields to destroy aircraft on the ground; the other by submarine-landed Commandos on what was thought to be Rommel's HQ at Beda Littoria in the Jebel Akhdar. 'Crusader' was to be launched on 11 November.

3 November **Auchinleck was forced to postpone 'Crusader' by one week.**
This was to enable 1st South African Division, newly arrived from East Africa, to undergo more training. In the meantime Rommel had been planning an assault on Tobruk during the period 15–21 November.

Night of 17/18 November **Special Forces operations launched.**
The Commando operation was a failure in that the suspected HQ was merely a logistics one and, in any event, Rommel had gone to Rome for consultations. Likewise, the SAS failed to achieve their aim when

the aircraft from which they were to be inserted behind the enemy lines were blown off course by a severe sandstorm.

18 November **At 0600 hours 'Crusader' was launched.**
Rommel, who returned that day, was initially caught by surprise, and XXX Corps made good progress. The airfield at Sidi Rezegh, ten miles south-east of Tobruk was captured. The DAK, believing that Bardia was about to be enveloped, was sent on a 'wild-goose chase' in this direction.

20 November **The Tobruk garrison was ordered to break out.**
Rommel, now realizing the threat, sent the DAK to attack at Sidi Rezegh. During the next two days the picture was confused, but Eighth Army was stopped in its advance, with the loss of many tanks, and the break-out from Tobruk was halted. On the XIII Corps front, progress was better, with Sidi Omar and Capuzzo captured.

24 November **Rommel gave orders for his tanks to thrust eastwards to cut off the Eighth Army from its supply routes.**
There now followed Rommel's famous 'dash to the Wire' (nickname for the Egyptian-Libyan frontier). By the end of the day he had reached the frontier, causing complete confusion in the Eighth Army. Cunningham now wanted to halt the offensive and fall back to the frontier. Auchinleck overrode him and replaced him by his Deputy Chief of Staff, General Neil Ritchie. By this time, the 26th, Rommel was running out of fuel and being ceaselessly pounded by the Desert Air Force. Furthermore, the Tobruk garrison and the New Zealand Division had linked up at El Duda. Rommel was now forced to turn in his tracks to deal with this development, but failed after repeated attacks to reinvest Tobruk.

5 December **Rommel ordered the evacuation of the eastern part of the Tobruk perimeter.**
He did this in order to mount a final attack on the British forces around Bir el Gobi, which failed.

7 December **Rommel withdrew to Gazala and Tobruk was relieved.**

15 December **Eighth Army attacked the Gazala position.**
Fearful of being outflanked, Rommel now ordered a further withdrawal which entailed giving up Cyrenaica.

6 January 1942 **Rommel was back once more on the Tripolitanian frontier.**
Efforts by the British to cut him off during his withdrawal had failed.

17 January **Bardia finally recaptured by the British.**
The Axis garrison had held out here since the start of 'Crusader'.

By now both sides were exhausted after the hectic fighting of the past two months. The Axis had suffered some 30,000 casualties and the Eighth Army 18,000; each side had lost some 300 tanks. Auchinleck had won because he had kept his nerve the longer.

The success of 'Crusader' was matched by the fact that events on the other side of the world had brought Britain a new ally.

Rommel Attacks Once More · P88

Before the Gates of Moscow

When the German offensive against Moscow literally froze to a halt on **5 December 1941** the Russians had little idea of the predicament in which their enemy now found himself. To them the threat to their capital was very great, and almost in desperation they launched a series of counter-attacks. In terms of forces available, the three Soviet 'fronts' defending Moscow numbered 718,800 men, 7,985 guns and 720 tanks (many obsolete) – against 800,000 Germans with 14,000 guns and 1,000 tanks.

5 December 1941 **First major Soviet counter-attack.**
Launched by Konev's Kalinin Front across the frozen upper Volga, this began in the early hours of the morning and took place north-west of Moscow. Despite the severe cold, German resistance was so fierce that only one of Konev's three armies, Yushkevich's Thirty-First, enjoyed success, and by the end of the 6th had penetrated twenty miles and recaptured Turginovo.

6 December **Zhukov's West Front attacked.**
This was intended to prevent 3rd and 4th Panzer Groups outflanking Moscow to the north-east. It was initially undertaken by the three most northerly of Zhukov's armies, but progress was initially slow, even after a fourth army (Sixteenth) joined the following day. On the 9th Zhukov issued an order forbidding further frontal attacks, which had merely enabled the Germans to withdraw in good order, in favour of envelopments and outflanking moves. The key was the town of Klin on the Moscow-Leningrad railway route. If Zhukov could capture this quickly 3rd Panzer Group would be cut off and the left flank of Army Group Centre unhinged.

7 December **Zhukov's left-flank armies began to attack south of Moscow.**
Their initial target was Guderian's Second Panzer Army, which had already begun to withdraw. The aim was to cut if off in the area of Stalinogorsk.

On this same day von Brauchitsch, Commander-in-Chief of the German Army, tendered his resignation to Hitler. He had recently suffered a heart attack. Hitler did not immediately accept his resignation.

Fierce fighting continued for the next week in the Klin and Stalinogorsk areas as the Germans strove to contain increasing Soviet pressure.

13 December **Timoshenko's South-West Front began to attack north-westwards between Yelets and Livny.**
This attack by the Soviet Thirteenth Army struck the right flank of the German Second Army to Guderian's immediate south. Second Army was severely mauled, and Guderian, his right flank in the air, was forced to make a hurried withdrawal.

On this day the Soviet Press issued triumphant statements on the repulse of the German armies before Moscow.

Von Brauchitsch travelled to Russia to meet von Bock, CinC of Army Group Centre. As a result, von Brauchitsch decided that Army Group Centre should withdraw to a 'winter line' some ninety miles to the rear. Secret orders were passed to this effect.

14 December **Hitler countermanded von Brauchitsch's withdrawal order.**
Hitler was furious at what he considered to be weakness on the part of his generals. Wholesale sackings followed. Von Bock, who was a sick man, was replaced by von Kluge on 18 December; Guderian was removed on Christmas Day; Hoepner, commanding 4th Panzer Group, and another leading exponent of armoured warfare, was also dismissed. Finally, Hitler accepted von Brauchitsch's resignation and announced on **19 December** that he himself was taking personal command of the Germany Army.

15 December **Organs of the Soviet Government were ordered to return to Moscow.**
This reflected Stalin's confidence that the threat to the capital had been removed. Further, he now ordered a general counter-offensive. Army Group Centre was to be destroyed by double envelopment from the north and south. Also on this day, Klin was recaptured.

18 December **Stalin created a new Front.**
This, the Bryansk Front, was to operate between the West and South-West Fronts and lend added weight to the southern prong of the double envelopment of Army Group Centre.

20 December **The German Propaganda Minister Josef Goebbels broadcast an appeal for winter clothing for the troops on the Eastern Front.**
For the first time the German leadership admitted that the soldiers were ill-equipped to face the Russian winter.

29 December **Soviet troops made an amphibious landing at Feodosiya on the south coast of the Crimea.**
This was designed to relieve pressure on Sevastapol and clear the Germans from the Crimea. It succeeded in its first aim, and also caused the German corps commander in the Kerch area to make a hurried withdrawal. He was dismissed and later, in 1944, shot. Fierce fighting continued in the Crimea for the next three months, but the Soviets failed to dislodge the Germans.

7 January 1942 **The Soviet North-West Front attacked south of Lake Ilmen.**
Simultaneously, the newly created Volkhov Front attacked south of Leningrad.

12 January **Von Leeb, CinC, Army Group North, requested permission to withdraw his forces south of Lake Ilmen to behind the River Lovat.**
His troops in the Demyansk area were in danger of being cut off. Hitler refused this and von Leeb voluntarily relinquished his command. His place was taken by von Kuechler.

18 January **Von Bock assumed command of Army Group South.**
Von Reichenau, who had relieved von Rundstedt, had died of a heart attack.

On the same day the Soviet South-West Front launched an attack across the River Donets south of Kharkov, designed to cut off the German forces north of the Sea of Azov. It reached the River Orel and cut the Kharkov-Lozovaya railway, but by early March had been halted.

1 February **Zhukov promoted to command the West Theatre.**
This command included the West, Kalinin and Bryansk Fronts. By this time the Soviets were trying to create a huge pocket based on Vyazma, which contained the German Fourth and Ninth Panzer Armies. Partisans and airborne troops were also being used, but then found themselves cut off and were gradually reduced. The Soviet counter-offensive was beginning to run out of steam.

8 February **The Soviets created their first sizeable pocket at Demyansk south of Lake Ilmen.**
90,000 German troops were cut off and had to be resupplied by air.

19 March **Soviet Second Shock Army cut off between Novgorod and Gruzino.**
Since January the progress of this thrust north-west to relieve Leningrad had been slow, partly because of the extensive forests in the area, but also because of the resilience of the Germans. Eventually the Germans counter-attacked at the 'neck' of the Soviet advance, on both flanks. Second Shock Army, commanded by General Vlasov, was doomed: all the subsequent efforts to relieve him failed.

By the end of March the Soviet counter-offensives had largely ground to a halt. They had failed in their objectives of relieving Leningrad, destroying Army Group Centre and liberating the Crimea. The truth is that, while the Soviets had done well to deny Hitler the ultimate prize of Moscow, their forces, as a result of the earlier disasters in 1941, were not ready successfully to carry out major counter-strokes. They had also under-estimated the German capacity to fight in the Russian winter. This was in spite of the German reverses in front of Moscow and 900,000 casualties which could be ill afforded.

Hitler remained undeterred. The spring of 1942 would see a return to the offensive.

P64 · Ever Deeper East

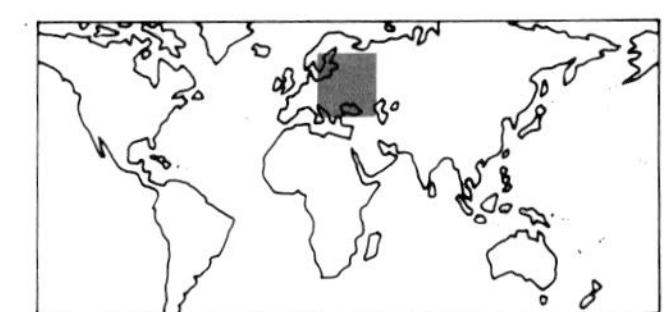

THE SOVIET COUNTER-ATTACK

Front Line on 5 Dec 1941

0 50 100 200 250 Miles
0 100 200 300 400 Km

FINLAND
SWEDEN
KARELIAN FRONT
Gen Frolov
FINNISH KARELIA ARMY
Marshal Mannerheim
Helsinki
Stockholm
Viipuri
L Ladoga
L Onega
Dvina
Onega
Vychegda
Kama
Sukhona
Marshal Voroshilov
VOLKHOV FRONT
Gen Meretskov
Offensive opened 7 January 1942
Vologda
Tallinin
Narva
Leningrad
19 March
ESTONIA
Tartu
L Peipus
Novgorod
2nd SHOCK ARMY
L Ilmen
Kirov
NORTH-WEST FRONT
Gen Korotchin
Offensive opened 7 January 1942
Kostroma
Volga
Yaroslav
Demyansk
Lovat
Vyatka
Izhevsk
Jelgava
Riga
LATVIA
Memel
ARMY GROUP NORTH
FM von Leeb
From mid January FM von Kuechler
Dvina
KALININ FRONT
Gen Konev
Offensive opened 5 December 1941
Kalinin
Gorki
Kazan
LITHUANIA
Tilsit
Koenigsberg
Kaunas
Dvinsk
Polotsk
Rzhev
Klin
Moscow
WEST FRONT
Offensive opened 6 December 1941
WEST THEATRE
Gen Zhukov
EAST PRUSSIA
Niemen
Vilna
Vitebsk
Mozhaisk
Smolensk
Vyazma
Beresina
Kaluga
Oka
Sura
Grodno
Minsk
Orsha
Tula
Bialystok
Mogilev
From 1 December
BRYANSK FRONT
Gen Cherevichenko
Baranovichi
ARMY GROUP CENTRE
FM von Bock
From 18 December FM von Kluge
Syzran
Samara
Warsaw
Brest-Litovsk
Bobruisk
Pripet Marsh
Bryansk
Siedlce
Pinsk
Pripet
Orel
Lipetsk
Tambov
Penza
Yelets
Gomel
Livny
Lublin
Bug
Styr
Chernkov
Kursk
13 Dec 1941
Khoper
Uralsk
Voronezh
Saratov
Lutsk
Korosten
SOUTH-WEST FRONT
Marshal Timoshenko
Medveditsa
Konotop
Dubno
Lvov
Brody
Kiev
ARMY GROUP SOUTH
FM von Reichenau
From 18 January FM von Bock
Belgorod
Don
Berdichev
Ternopol
Kharkov
Poltava
Cherkassy
SOUTHERN FRONT
Gen Malinovsky
Uman
Kremenchug
Dnieper
Stalingrad
Carpathians
Bug
Kirovograd
Dnepropetrovsk
Lugansk
Prut
Donets
Volga
Siretul
Jassy
Dniester
Krivoy Rog
Nikopol
Stalino
Taganrog
Tiraspol
Kherson
Melitopol
Mariupol
Rostov
Astrakhan
Odessa
Perekop
Sea of Azov
TRANSCAUCASUS FRONT
Gen Kozlov
Ploesti
Galati
ROUMANIA
Bucharest
Kerch
CASPIAN SEA
Crimea
Krasnodar
Danube
Sevastopol
Stavropol
Constanta
Yalta
Novorossisk
Maykop
BULGARIA
29 Dec
Tuapse
Varna
BLACK SEA
Caucasus Mountains

Kharkov and the Crimea · P94

Japan Threatens

Japan's ambitions to carve herself an empire in the Far East had been encouraged greatly during 1940 and the first half of 1941. She had seen two of her colonial rivals, France and Holland, vanquished; a third, Britain, was under intense pressure in Europe and the Middle East. The time was becoming ripe, at least in the view of the Japanese Army, and on **16 July 1940** it had brought down the moderate government of Admiral Yonai and replaced it with one under Prince Konoye.

Earlier, on **12 July,** Britain had been forced to close the Burma Road to China, the one route through which Chiang Kai-shek could receive aid from the Western powers. Britain, now fighting alone, was not ready for war against Japan. Neither was the USA, who refused to support Britain in resisting this Japanese demand. Britain also withdrew her garrisons from Shanghai and Tientsin. All Roosevelt was prepared to do was to announce a limited embargo on the export of scrap iron, steel and certain grades of aviation fuel to Japan. He did this on **26 July** to encourage Chiang Kai-shek, but dared go no farther for fear of driving Japan into the Axis camp.

27 July 1940 **Proclamation of the Greater East Asia Co-Prosperity Sphere.**
This was formulated by the Liaison Conference – a policy-making council of Japanese naval and military officers and politicians. It recognized that Japan was currently very heavily dependent on the Western powers for raw materials, especially oil, of which she produced none. Consequently the Japanese planned to incorporate the material-rich Dutch East Indies, Malaya, Thailand, Burma and the Philippines in their empire. The risk was war against Britain and the USA; hence they began to prepare for this eventuality. They hoped, however, to be able to achieve their aims through peaceful means.

29 August **The Vichy French acceded to demands that the Japanese station forces in northern Indo-China.**
The French were in a very weak position and did not want a conflict with Japan.

25 September **A US cryptanalyst, Harry L. Clark, discovered the key to the Japanese top secret codes.**
From now on the Americans were able to read the Japanese diplomatic, naval and military top secret coded traffic. The code-name for this operation was 'Magic' and was directly equivalent to 'Ultra', the reading of the German codes.

27 September **Signing of the Tripartite Pact by Japan, Germany and Italy.**
Japan took this step because she hoped to deter the USA. It had, however, the opposite effect – to Americans, Japan appeared to be siding with the aggressor nations. There was increased determination to resist, and this was first manifested in US support for the Dutch refusal to enter into a long-term contract to supply Japan with oil from the Dutch East Indies. A $25 million loan was approved for China and this was followed by a further $50 million in November.

18 October **Britain reopened the Burma Road.**
The closure had been conditional for three months on progress towards peace between Japan and China. This had not happened. At the end of the month, Britain, the Netherlands and Australia entered into talks on mutual defence of their possessions in the Far East.

16 January 1941 **French forces in Indo-China launched attacks on Thai military and naval forces.**
There had been a number of border provocations by the Thais, who wanted to regain territories lost to the French some forty years earlier. This was the French response. Although repulsed on land, the French won a naval victory at Koh-Chang. The Japanese now intervened and imposed an armistice on **31 January.** In a peace treaty signed on 9 May much of the disputed territory was handed over to Thailand. French forces were too weak to resist the Japanese demands.

8 March **US Lend-Lease Act enacted.**
China stood to benefit by this, but priority was given to Britain. In April, 100 P-40 fighters were earmarked for China and an executive order was passed allowing US military pilots to be recruited to fly them. They were to form the American Volunteer Group (AVG) under Colonel Claire Chennault, Chiang Kai-shek's air adviser.

13 April **Japanese-Soviet Non-Aggression Pact signed.**
This was a significant Japanese diplomatic victory in that it removed a potential threat from the north.

11 May **Japan made proposals to the USA for improving relations.**
Japan demanded a cessation of US aid to China and restoration of normal Japanese-US trade links. The USA did not accept these, but was prepared to continue negotiations rather than give Japan an excuse to go to war. Likewise, Japan, not yet ready for war, was also happy to continue talking.

29 June **Germany demanded that Japan launch an attack on Russia.**
This was considered at a meeting of the Liaison Conference, held in the presence of the Emperor, on **2 July.** The Japanese expected the Germans quickly to subdue Russia, but decided to reinforce their army in Manchukuo (Manchuria) as a precaution against a Russian attack. Their rear guarded, they resolved to strike southward and seize French bases in Indo-China in preparation for this. They would continue to use diplomatic means, but if war became inevitable they would accept the fact.

18 July **The belligerent Japanese foreign minister, Yosuke Matsuoka, was replaced.**
Matsuoka had consistently ruffled US feathers and had strongly advocated an attack on the USSR. His replacement by a moderate was designed to appease the US.

23 July **Vichy France acceded to Japanese demands to send troops into southern Indo-China.**
Japan had presented the French with an ultimatum.

26 July **The USA froze all Japanese assets.**
Roosevelt had, thanks to 'Magic', read all communications between Tokyo and the Japanese Ambassador to Vichy and was in no doubt that the move into southern Indo-China was an aggressive act. Britain and the Netherlands quickly followed suit, and the immediate result was that Japan was now cut off from 90 per cent of her oil supplies. Her only option seemed to be the seizure of the oil-rich Dutch East Indies. As the Japanese Naval Chief of Staff said, Japan was like 'a fish in a pond from which the water is gradually being drained away'.

6 August **Japanese Foreign Minister Admiral Nomura proposed a meeting between Roosevelt and Prime Minister Konoye.**
Prince Konoye did this to try and forestall the aggressive intentions of the Japanese Navy and Army. The US reply on **17 August** was that this would be acceptable only if outstanding differences between the two countries were settled first.

6 September **Japanese decision to be fully prepared for war by the end of October.**
Prince Konoye was permitted to continue his negotiations with the USA in the meantime.

10–13 September **War-games held at the Naval War College, Tokyo, to develop Japanese military strategy in the Pacific.**

16 October **Prince Konoye resigned as Prime Minister.**
He had failed to make any headway in his negotiations, and pressures on him from the military heirarchy were too strong. His place was taken by the belligerent General Hideki Tojo, the war minister.

This was not quite the end of activity on the diplomatic front in the Far East. During the next three weeks there was a last flurry when Japan made modified proposals, giving an undertaking to withdraw from French Indo-China and from parts of China. In return the USA was not to interfere in peace negotiations between Japan and Chiang Kai-

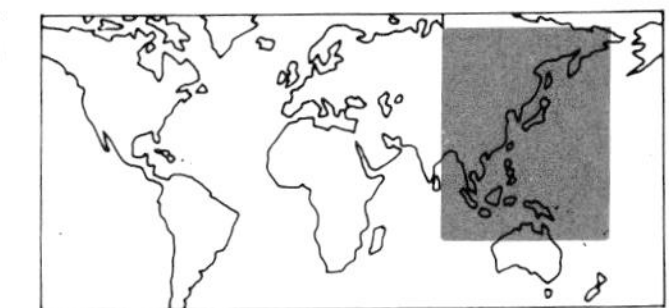

ENCROACHMENT IN INDO-CHINA

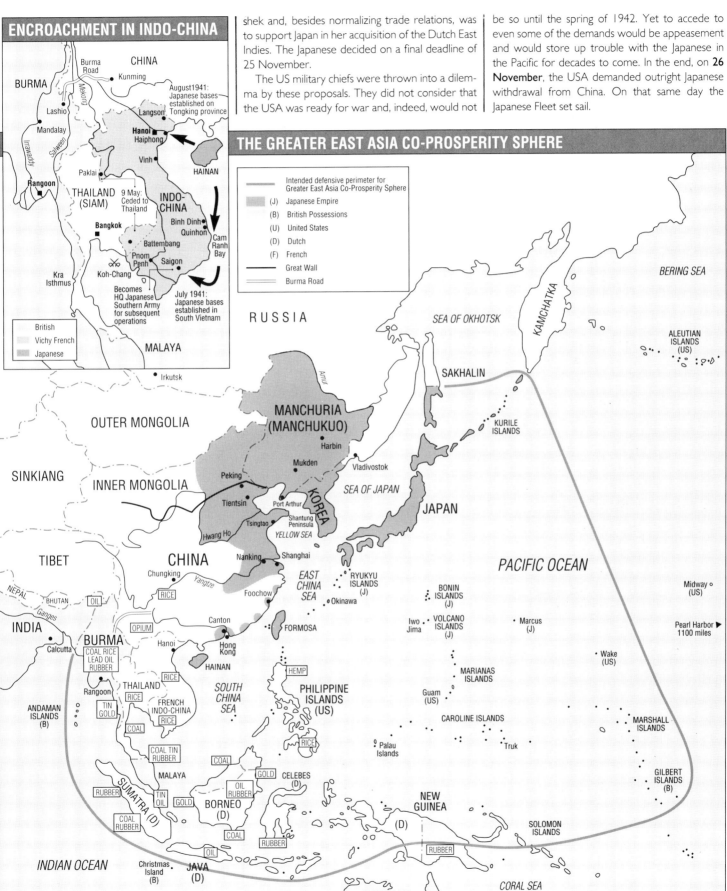

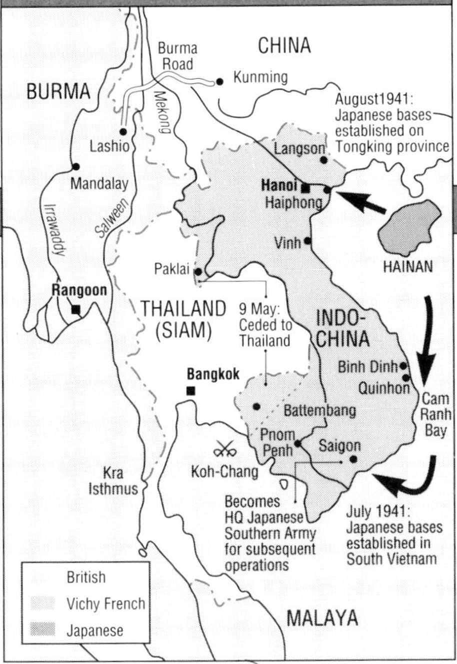

shek and, besides normalizing trade relations, was to support Japan in her acquisition of the Dutch East Indies. The Japanese decided on a final deadline of 25 November.

The US military chiefs were thrown into a dilemma by these proposals. They did not consider that the USA was ready for war and, indeed, would not be so until the spring of 1942. Yet to accede to even some of the demands would be appeasement and would store up trouble with the Japanese in the Pacific for decades to come. In the end, on **26 November**, the USA demanded outright Japanese withdrawal from China. On that same day the Japanese Fleet set sail.

THE GREATER EAST ASIA CO-PROSPERITY SPHERE

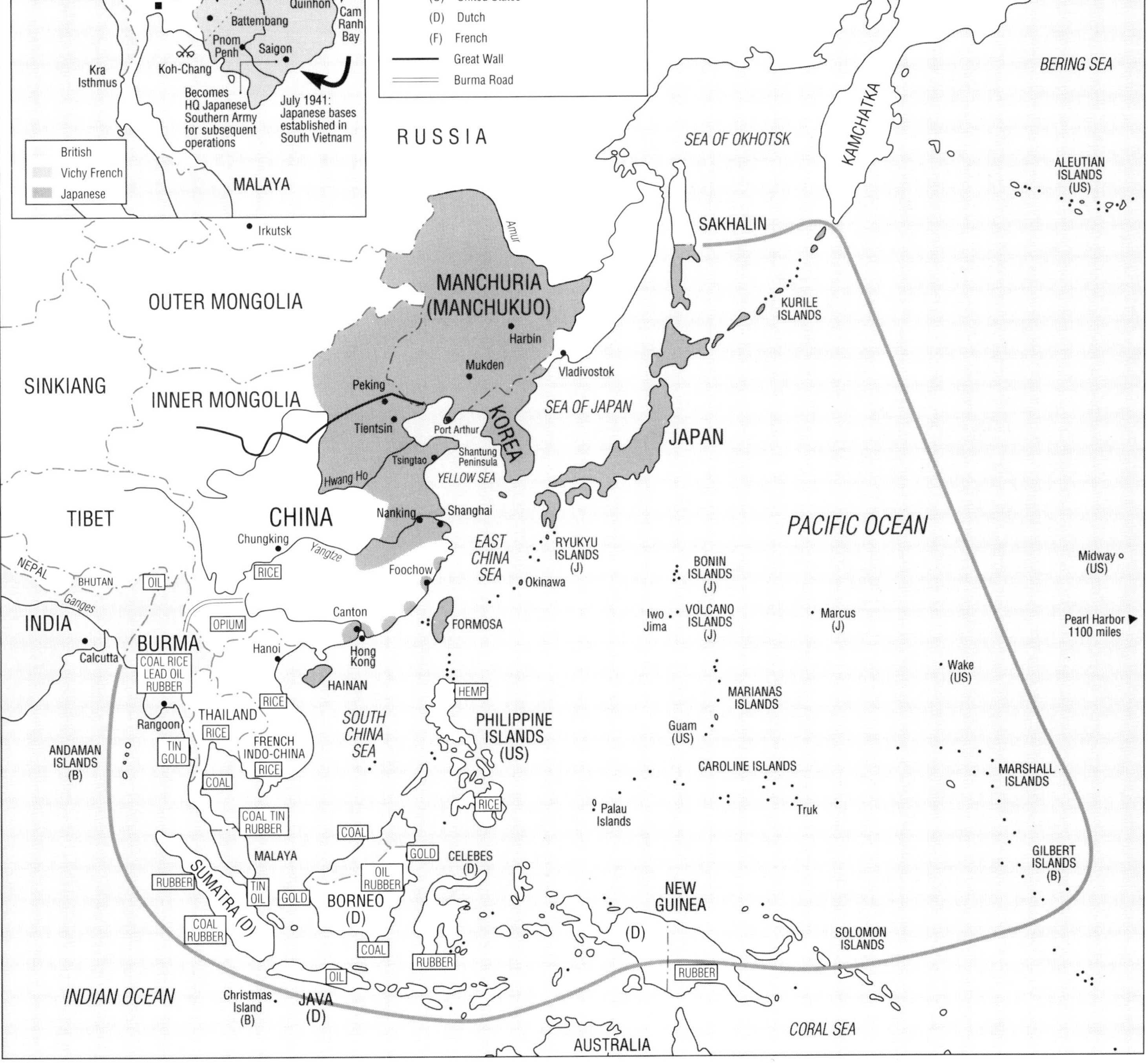

Day of Infamy

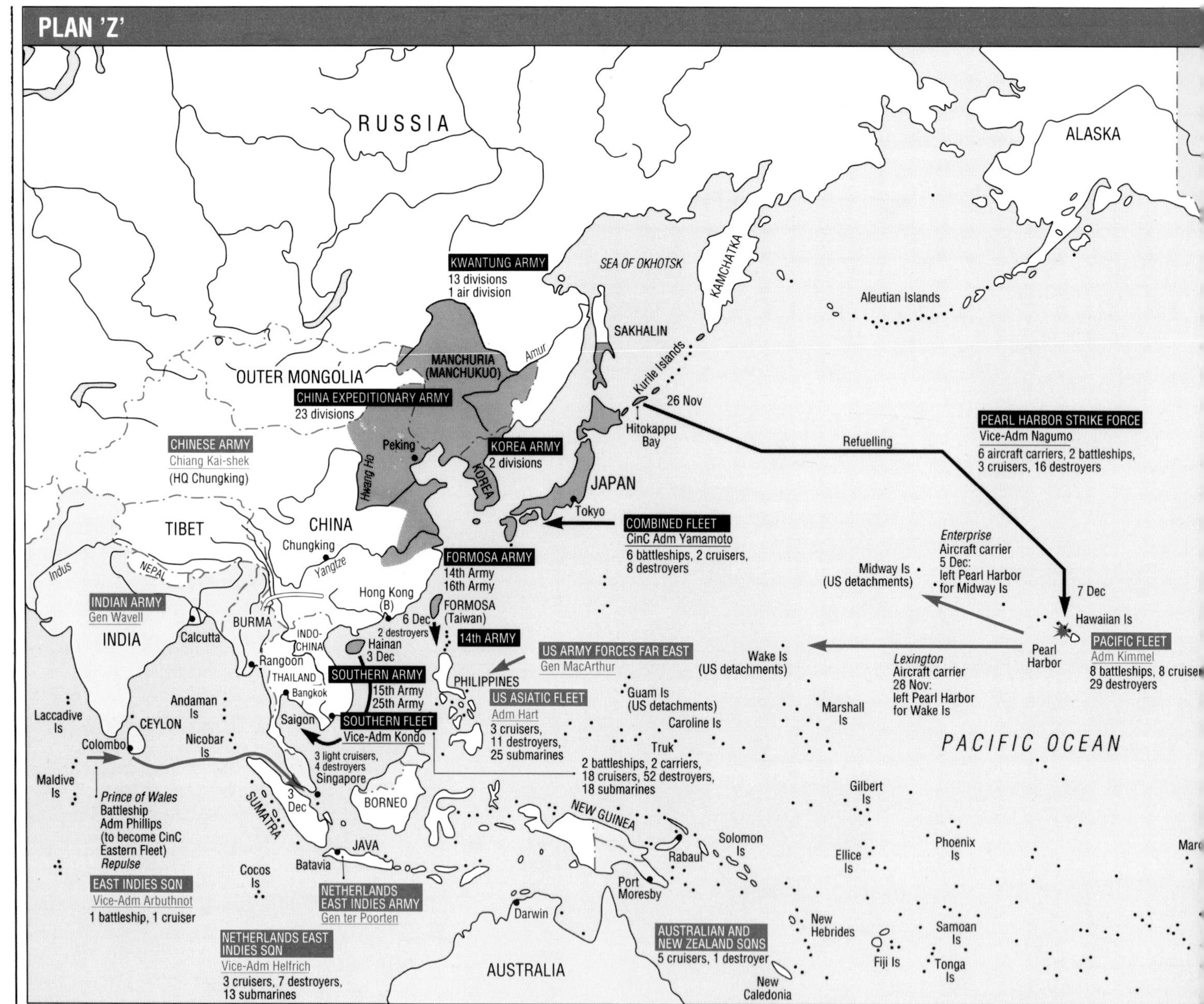

The original Japanese plan for overrunning the Pacific called for simultaneous attacks on Thailand, Malaya, the Philippines and the Dutch East Indies. It was assumed that the US Pacific Fleet would immediately sail to help defend the Philippines. After being harried from Japanese bases in the Marshall and Caroline islands, it would be brought to battle by the Japanese Fleet. This was a realistic scenario in that the Japanese were quite right in thinking that the main US effort in the Pacific would be defence of the Philippines. The plan, however, did have a flaw, which was recognized by the CinC of the Japanese Fleet, Admiral Isoroku Yamamoto.

He recognized the enormous US superiority over Japan in natural resources and that the only way Japan could hold on to her newly won empire would be to become so well established in it that the Western powers would consider the cost too great to try and wrest it from her. For this to happen Japan needed time, and the only way this could be achieved was to knock out the US Pacific Fleet at the outset of war. To allow it to leave its anchorage at Pearl Harbor in Hawaii would reduce the chances of achieving this.

The British success against the Italian Fleet at Taranto in November 1940 had made a deep impression on Yamamoto. Pearl Harbor was much the same size as Taranto and, provided that surprise could be achieved, the Japanese Navy, with its six fleet carriers, could achieve the knock-out blow.

Throughout the first half of 1941, Yamamoto and his staff worked to perfect what became known as Plan 'Z'. There was, however, even within the Navy, a strong body of opposition. The Chief of the Naval Staff himself, Admiral Nagano Osami, did not like the idea. The carriers were needed to support the land operations, and the chances of achieving surprise at the end of a 3,400-mile voyage seemed slim. Yamamoto remained undeterred. Eventually, after further doubts had been raised at the Tokyo War College war-game in September, Yamamoto threatened to resign. But such was his prestige that within a month the opposition to Plan 'Z' had collapsed and it was built into the overall plan.

This had as its immediate objective the seizure of the Dutch East Indies, Malaya and Singapore. The US Pacific Fleet would be destroyed through Plan 'Z', and US forces in the Philippines threatening the flank of the Japanese would be destroyed and the islands later captured. Finally, in order to cut US communications across the Pacific, the islands of Wake and Guam would be seized. Once these

P72 · Japan Threatens

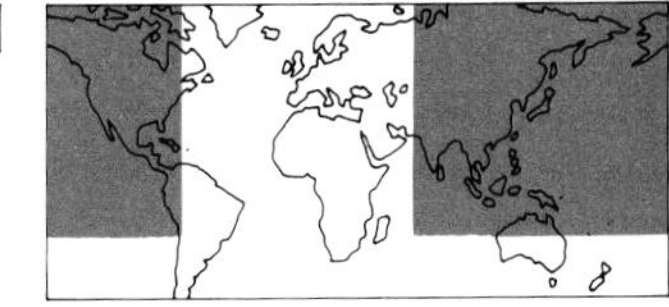

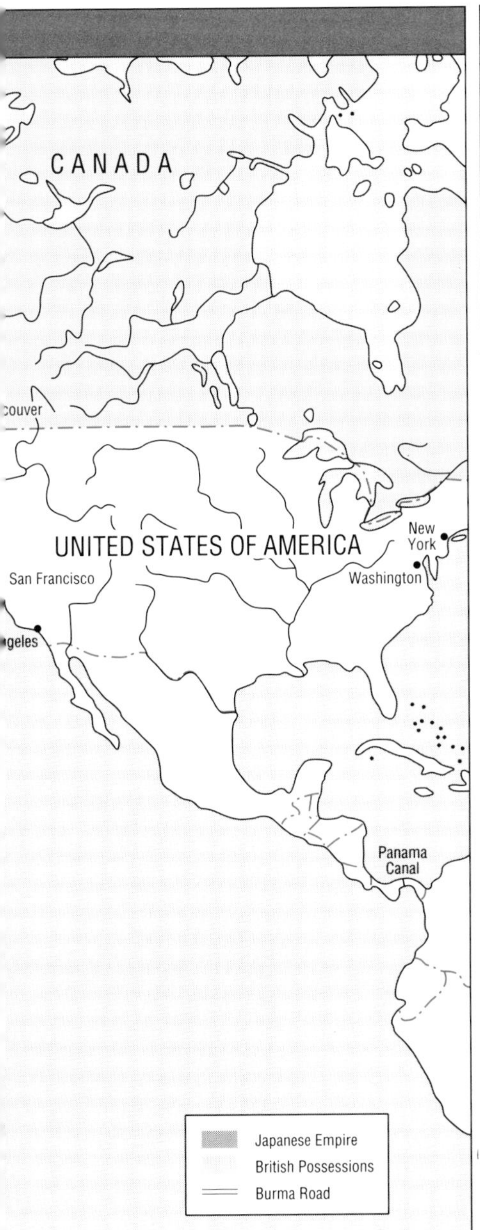

aims had been achieved the priority would be fortification of their newly won territory. Because of fears of a Soviet attack through Manchukuo and the continuing fighting in China, less than a quarter of the Japanese Army could be made available. Likewise, the Navy, faced with a number of simultaneous objectives, would be compelled to split its forces.

16 October 1941 Admiral Harold R. Stark, US Chief of Naval Operations, warned of the coming hostilities.
The Pacific and Asiatic Fleet commanders were advised of the strong possibility of war between the USSR and Japan. Stark also said that there might be war between Japan and the USA as well, and ordered the commanders to take necessary precautions. The message to the US Army, however, was that no 'abrupt change' in Japanese foreign policy was expected. On this same day, Prince Konoye resigned as prime minister of Japan.

3 November US Ambassador to Tokyo, Joseph C. Grew, warned that war might come very suddenly.
He noted that recent Japanese troop movements placed Japan in a position to attack either Siberia or the South-West Pacific – or both. As early as **27 January** he had also reported talk in Tokyo of a surprise attack on Pearl Harbor.

6 November The Japanese Southern Army was ordered to prepare detailed operational plans.
Four days later, naval and military staffs began to work out the details of their joint operations.

20 November Japanese attack orders issued.
Operations, however, were not to begin until the results of the diplomatic negotiations were known.

24 November US Army commanders warned that the possibility of diplomatic agreement being reached was slight.
Attacks on the Philippines and Guam were a possibility. This warning was quickly followed by one to the garrisons of Hawaii, the Philippines, Panama and San Francisco on the imminence of war. The US Navy issued a further warning on **27 November**, which was a more clear-cut, final alert. But none of these warnings mentioned the possibility of an attack on Pearl Harbor.

26 November The Pearl Harbor strike force left its anchorage in the Kurile Islands, north of the Japanese mainland, bound for Hawaii.
Commanded by Admiral Chuichi Nagumo, it consisted of six aircraft carriers, two battleships, three cruisers, nine destroyers and eight oil tankers. It sailed under strict radio silence.

27 November Japan rejected the US demand for outright withdrawal from China.
They decided, however, to try and keep talking to the Americans in order to gain a few days.

30 November Japan finally decided to attack.
Up to the last moment, members of the government expressed doubts over going to war with the USA.

1 December Date of attack fixed for 7 December (8th according to Japanese standard time).
Tokyo time is 13 hours ahead of Washington time. Apart from vague hints, the Japanese did not inform Berlin or Rome of their intentions.

4 December Japanese Embassy to Washington began to leave.
'Magic' intercepts revealed the destruction of code-books. By now the Japanese 25th Army was embarking for Malaya from the ports of Hainan in China; the Philippines task force was about to leave Formosa and the Pescadores; the Guam invasion force was *en route*; that for Wake was preparing at Kwajalein.

6 December Roosevelt sent a last-minute plea for peace to the Emperor of Japan.
That night Tokyo began to transmit a long message to the Japanese Ambassador to Washington, to be handed to the US State Department next day, 30 minutes after the strike on Pearl Harbor. Thirteen of the fourteen parts of the message were in US hands through 'Magic', as well as reports of Japanese convoys. Next morning the final part of the message made it clear that Japan was bent on war, but when and where were not clear. Further warnings were sent to US Pacific garrisons, but that to Hawaii was delayed through inefficient communication handling.

Sunday 7 December Japanese attacked Pearl Harbor.
The US Pacific Fleet had been excercising at sea during the week, but had returned to port for the weekend. All units were in harbour apart from the carriers *Lexington* and *Enterprise*, which were transporting additional aircraft to Wake and Midway respectively.

At 0615 hours (local time) the first wave of Japanese aircraft took off from their carriers positioned some 200 miles north of Hawaii. Fifteen minutes later the US destroyer *Ward* spotted a midget submarine at the port entrance to Pearl Harbor. It was one of five that the Japanese had planned to send into Pearl Harbor, and *Ward* quickly engaged and sank her.

At 0750 hours the first wave of Japanese aircraft (43 fighters, 51 dive-bomber, 70 torpedo-bombers and 50 ordinary bombers) appeared over Hawaii. They attacked the airfields at Wheeler, Kaneohe, Ewa and Hickham and launched torpedoes at the serried ranks of warships anchored in 'Battleship Row'. Surprise was complete. Within a few minutes five battleships, two light cruisers and an old target battleship had been destroyed, and almost all the US aircraft on the ground were wiped out.

A second wave of aircraft (36 fighters, 80 dive-bombers, 54 bombers) appeared an hour later, but this time the US air defences were a little better prepared. Nevertheless, the aircraft damaged another battleship and wrecked three destroyers. By 1000 hours it was all over.

Plan 'Z' appeared to have succeeded beyond Yamamoto's wildest dreams and at a cost of only 29 aircraft and the five midget submarines. It was, said President Roosevelt, a day of 'infamy'. Yet, the Japanese had missed two vital targets: the two carriers and the oil tanks on Hawaii. These were omissions they would regret in the months to come.

Japanese Onrush · P78

5 THE DARK BEFORE THE DAWN, December 1941 to June 1942

11 DECEMBER 1941 TO 26 JANUARY 1942

Germany First

The surprise attack on the US Pacific base at Pearl Harbor meant that the war was no longer a strictly European affair but had become global overnight. On **8 December 1941** the USA and Britain both formally declared war on Japan. Roosevelt was now faced with a dilemma: the USA was not at war with Germany and there were many Americans who wanted to concentrate on punishing Japan without getting involved in the war in Europe. The problem was, however, quickly resolved.

11 December 1941 **Germany and Italy declared war on the USA.**
Under the terms of the Tripartite Pact, Germany and Italy were bound to join Japan in war only if Japan were attacked, but at the end of November the Germans had reassured the Japanese that they would declare war on the USA if Japan became engaged in war against her. A signal reflecting this, from the Japanese Ambassador in Berlin to Tokyo, had been intercepted by the USA; this was another reason why Roosevelt did not automatically declare war on Germany and Italy. Hitler hoped that Japan would also declare war on the Soviet Union, but this did not suit the Japanese purpose. Likewise, Stalin was in no position to become engaged in a two-front war and was also content to uphold his non-aggression pact with Japan.

12 December **The US requisitioned all Vichy French ships in US ports.**

13 December **Churchill set sail in the battleship *Duke of York* to meet Roosevelt.**
The idea of a meeting was Churchill's. He wanted to discuss the Allied war plan and production and distribution of *matériel*.

22 December 1941–13 January 1942 **Anglo-US conference in Washington, DC, code-named 'Arcadia'.**
The global situation at this time can be summed up as improved in Europe and the Middle East, but disastrous in the Far East and Pacific.

In Europe the Soviets had reduced the pressure on Moscow and were recapturing territory recently lost to the Germans. East Africa had been cleared of the Italian presence, and the British had once more captured the Libyan province of Cyrenaica. Malta, however, remained under constant Axis air attack. In the Battle of the Atlantic losses were still high and were about to undergo a sharp rise. The British strategic bombing offensive had slackened because of high losses of aircraft. Life in the occupied countries of Europe was becoming increasingly grim, especially for the Jews whose extermination was about to become official Nazi policy. The flames of resistance were being fanned among the peoples of Occupied Europe, but as yet they were weak.

In the Pacific the picture grew darker by the day as one Allied territory after another fell to the Japanese. The prospect of bombing attacks and – at worst – invasion of the west coast of the USA became increasingly real. Indeed, this area was declared an operational zone from the onset of war, and agitation grew for the internment of the 112,000 Japanese Americans who lived on the west coast.

It was against this background that Roosevelt and Churchill, and their respective staffs, had to formulate a general policy for prosecuting the war and achieving ultimate victory. They did, however, have Plan ABC-1, which they had agreed a year before, to guide them.

The primary decision to be made was where the priority should lie: defeat of the Axis powers in Europe or that of Japan? ABC-1 had decreed that it should be 'Germany first', and this remained the British view, since this threat lay closer to home. The US view was not so clear-cut; the Japanese threat appeared more immediate, especially in the eyes of the US Navy, but Roosevelt overruled his Admirals and confirmed that Germany must be defeated first.

To achieve this, both sides agreed that the continent of Europe would have to be invaded and that Britain would be the spring-board for this. Thus there had to be a build-up of US forces in Britain. It was also agreed that a strategy of encirclement of Germany must be followed, and to this end it was essential to keep the Soviet Union in the war. This could only be done by keeping her supplied with weapons. The strategic bombing campaign and naval blockade of Germany would be maintained.

More difficult to resolve were the strategic priorities in the Mediterranean. The British were very keen to clear the coast of North Africa, including French territories, before foot was set in Europe. The Americans considered this to be an unnecessary diversion from the business of invading Europe and thought that the British were motivated by self-

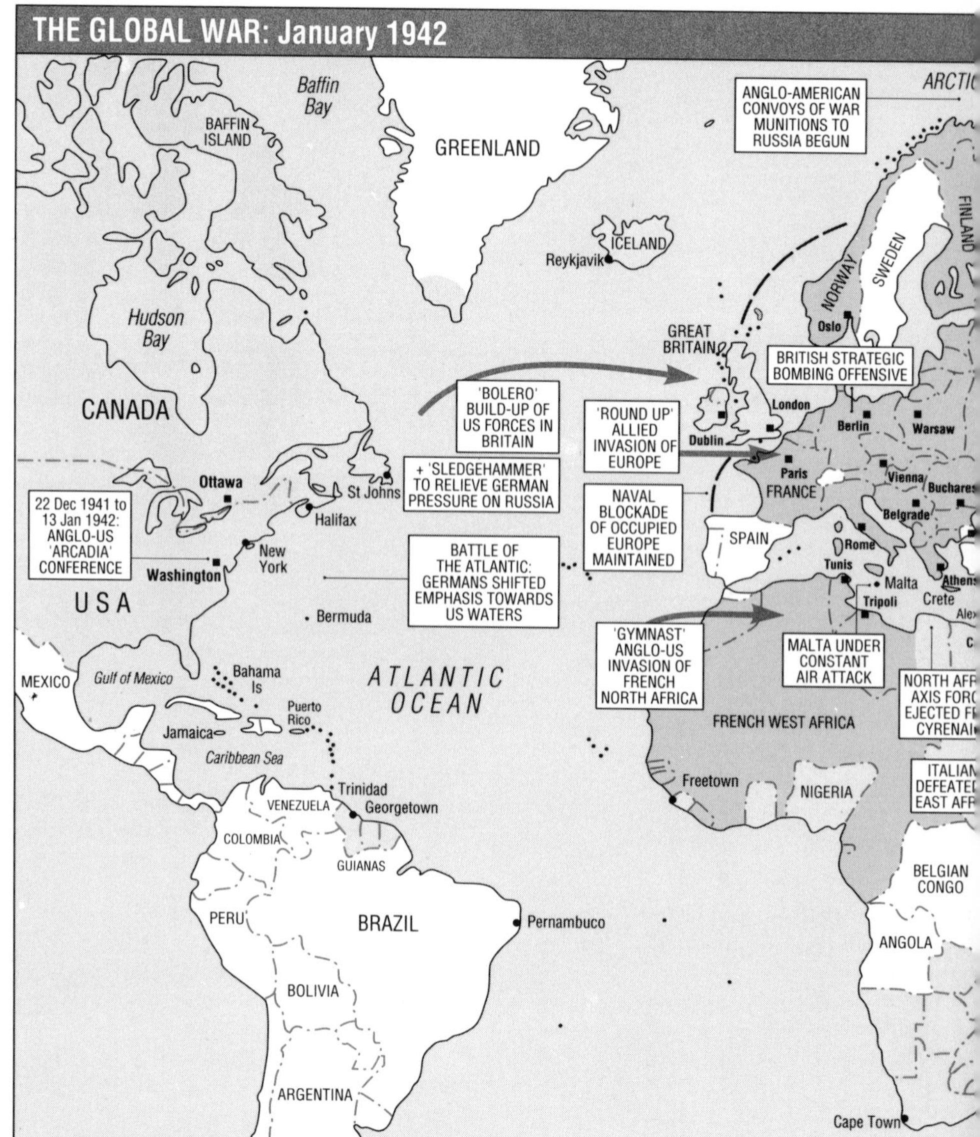

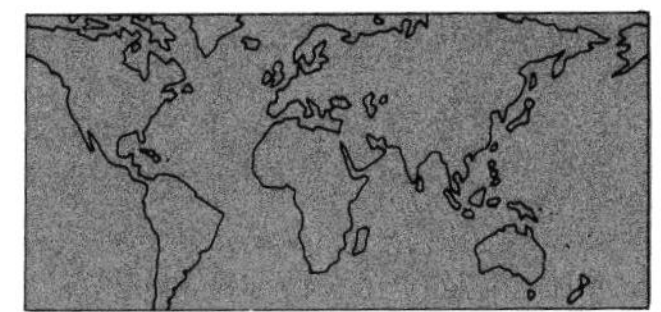

interest, to re-establish communications through the Mediterranean to their empire in the Far East. Eventually it was agreed that plans should be drawn up for a joint invasion of French North Africa. It was accepted that this could not take place before May 1942 at the earliest.

As far as the Pacific was concerned, little clear-cut policy was evolved – events were moving too quickly for a coherent plan to be formulated. All that was agreed was that an Allied supreme command be set up. This was called ABDA (American, British, Dutch, Australian) and General Sir Archibald Wavell, now Commander-in-Chief, India, was appointed to command it. Geographically his command was very large, ranging from the Philippines to the Dutch East Indies, Malaya and Burma.

One final point agreed at 'Arcadia' was the setting up of the Combined Chiefs of Staff. This group was drawn from the Chiefs of Staff of Britain and the USA and was to be responsible for the co-ordination of higher strategy. Their initial task was to resolve a number of conflicting strategic necessities which had arisen out of 'Arcadia'. These were:

a. The mounting of a major operation (code-named 'Sledgehammer') somewhere in continental western Europe in 1942 in order to relieve pressure on the Russians.

b. An invasion of Europe across the English Channel in 1943 ('Round Up').

c. An Anglo-US invasion of French North Africa ('Gymnast').

d. A build-up of US forces in Britain for operations in western Europe as a whole ('Bolero').

6 January 1942 Roosevelt asked Congress to approve additional spending on war production.
He wanted sufficient money to be able to produce 125,000 aircraft, 75,000 tanks, 35,000 guns and 8 million tons of shipping by the end of 1943. This was not merely to equip the US armed forces, but also America's allies, thus living up to the President's vow that his country was to become the 'Arsenal of Democracy'.

26 January First US troops arrived in Northern Ireland.
This was the beginning of 'Bolero'. The Republic of Ireland's premier, Eamon De Valera, protested since he feared that British and US troops might invade his country in order to occupy bases there, which De Valera had refused to allow the British use of, being determined that Eire should remain neutral.

With the USA's massive resources and huge industrial base now committed to the war, eventual victory for the Allies became much more than just a dream. It would, however, despite Roosevelt's efforts to prepare his country for war, be some time yet before the USA was fully mobilized and the Allies could go on to the offensive. In the meantime, especially in the Pacific and Far East, the clouds were to grow darker.

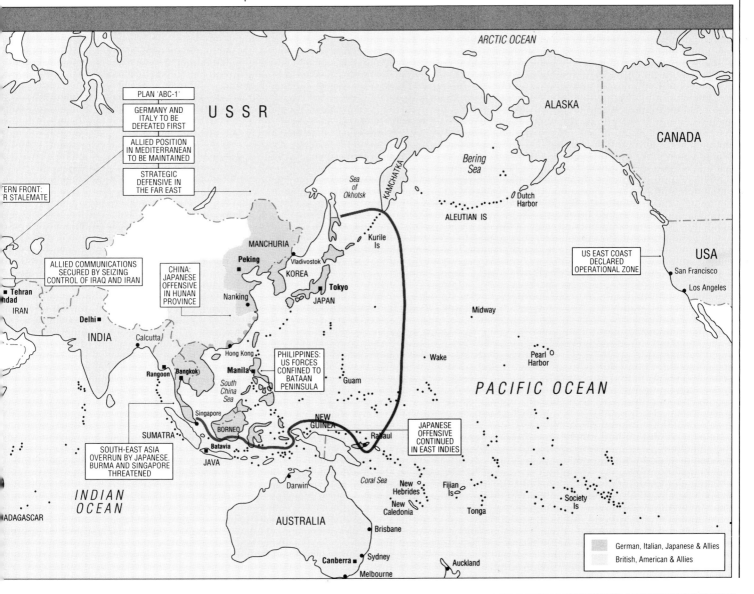

Japanese Onrush

The strike on Pearl Harbor was not the sole Japanese operation on **7 December 1941**, but the major blow of many. The islands of Guam and Wake were bombed, and two Japanese destroyers shelled Midway. The Japanese Second Fleet was escorting General Tomoyuko Yamashita's Twenty-Fifth Army to the north-east coast of Malaya, and three divisions were preparing to invade the British colony of Hong Kong. During the next few months Western views of Japanese military capabilities were to be severely dented.

8 December 1941 Japanese aircraft bombed Singapore.
This happened in the early hours of the morning, and the task of the bombers was made easier because there was no black-out. Some 200 casualties, largely civilian Chinese, were inflicted.

Two newly arrived British capital ships, *Prince of Wales* and *Repulse*, set sail from Singapore to intercept Japanese landings already taking place at Kota Bharu on the Malayan north-east coast and other locations just inside Thailand.

Japanese aircraft based on Formosa (now Taiwan) bombed Luzon and the Mindanao Islands in the Philippines.

In Shanghai and Tientsin the US garrisons were overrun, and aircraft bombed Wake and Guam.

Japanese forces invaded the New Territories, part of the British colony of Hong Kong. Hong Kong was defended by a weak division's worth of British, Canadian and Indian troops, augmented by local volunteers.

9 December Japanese troops landed on Tarawa and Makin in the Gilbert Islands.
The Japanese also occupied Bangkok and continued to land troops on the north-eastern coast of Malaya and across the border in Thailand.

10 December Japanese aircraft sank *Prince of Wales* and *Repulse*.
This robbed the Royal Navy of its main striking power in the Far East and demonstrated once again the superiority of aircraft over ships. The commander of this strike force, Force Z, Admiral Tom Phillips, went down with his ship, *Prince of Wales*.

The Japanese seized Guam and landed on the northern tip of Luzon and on the island of Camiguin in the Philippines.

11 December The US garrison in Peking (now Beijing) was taken prisoner.
The Americans had maintained a small garrison here ever since the 1900 Boxer Rebellion.

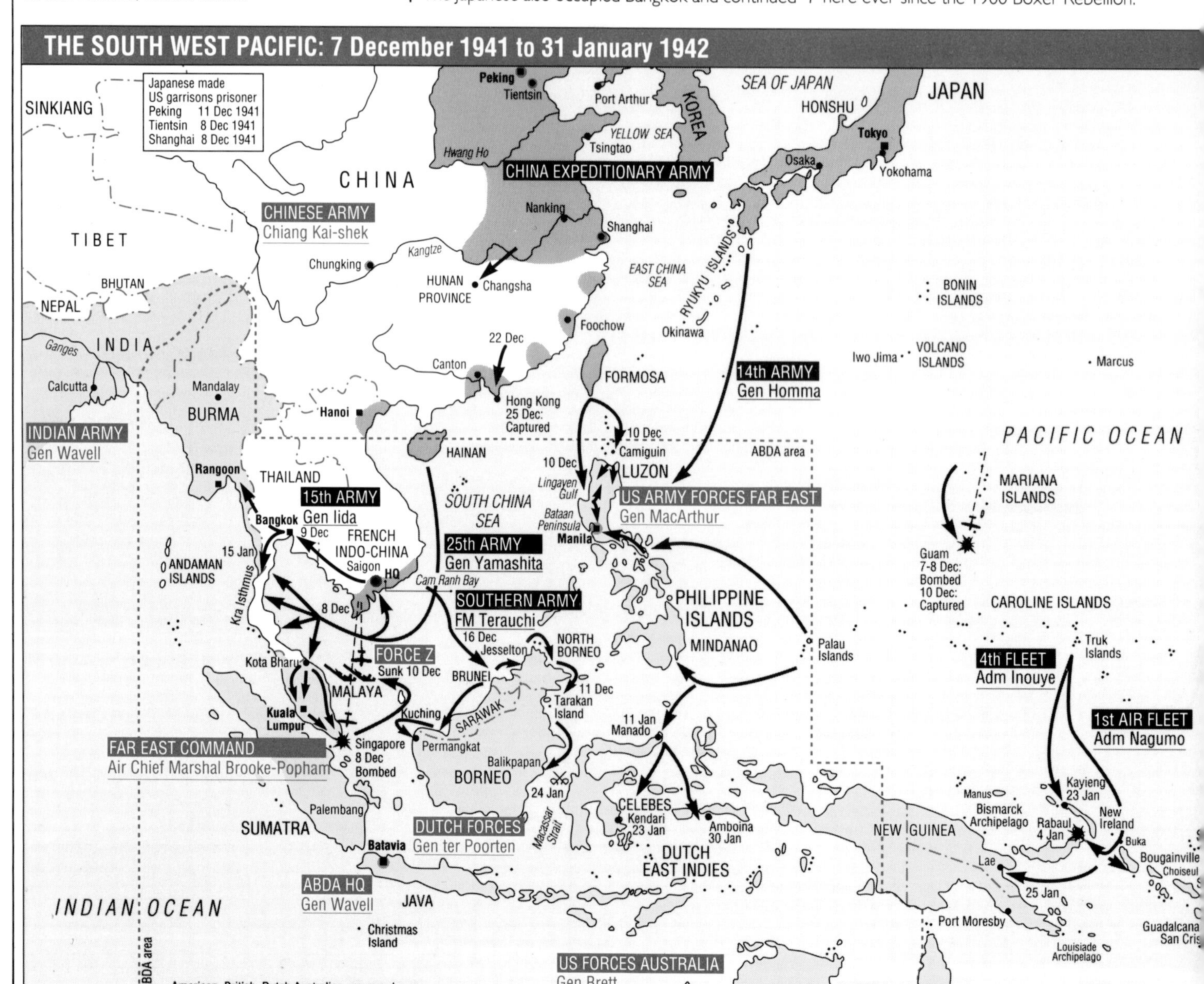

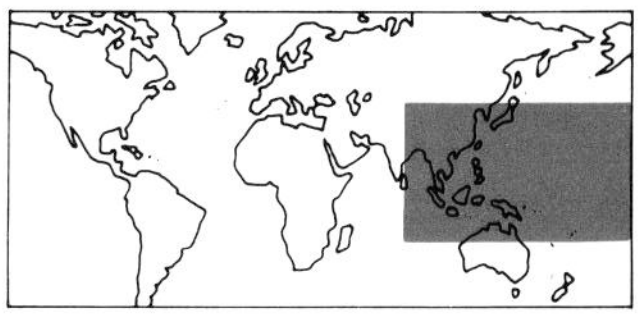

In Hong Kong the British garrison began to withdraw from the mainland to the island of Hong Kong.

The Japanese attempted to land on Wake, but were repulsed by the US garrison with the loss of two destroyers. Further landings meanwhile took place in the Philippines.

3 December Japanese surrender demand rejected by the Governor of Hong Kong.

Throughout the theatre the Japanese had gained air supremacy, mainly by constant attacks on Allied airfields.

Japanese forces on the Thai side of the Kra Isthmus caused the British to evacuate Victoria Point in the extreme south of Burma and withdraw towards the north.

A US naval task force under Rear-Admiral Frank Fletcher set sail from Pearl Harbor to relieve Wake Island.

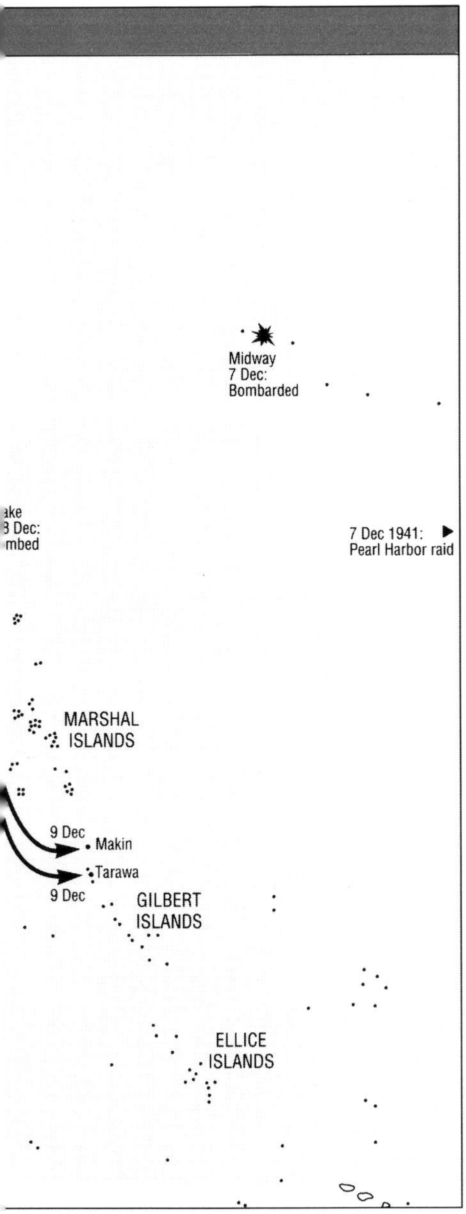

14 December Thailand formally allied herself with Japan.

Further Japanese landings took place in the Philippines.

15 December Japanese forces entered Burmese territory in the Kra Isthmus.

The main attack on Burma would not begin for another month.

16 December Japanese forces landed in Sarawak and Brunei in Borneo.

18 December Japanese troops landed on Hong Kong Island.

22 December The main Japanese landings took place on Luzon, Philippines.

These were 43,000 troops of General Masaharu Homma's Fourteenth Army. They landed in Lingayen Gulf, 150 miles north-north-west of Manila, and quickly linked up with the earlier landings in the north of the island. Further landings south of Manila on **24 December** cut off the US and Filipino garrison.

23 December The Japanese captured Wake.

The small US garrison had been constantly attacked from the air and was in no position to resist a second Japanese landing. The Japanese renamed the island Bird Island. Admiral Fletcher's task force was still more than 400 miles away and was diverted to Midway.

The Allied forces on Luzon began to withdraw to the Bataan peninsula.

25 December Hong Kong fell.

The Allied casualties were 1,000 killed, 1,000 missing and 2,300 wounded. The remainder were to suffer awful privations as prisoners of war, as did the many British civilians trapped in Hong Kong.

28 December General Wavell took command of the defence of Burma.

31 December Admiral Chester W. Nimitz appointed to command the US Asiatic Fleet.

On the same day Lieutenant-General George H. Brett took command of the US Forces in Australia, which was now to be used as a concentration area for US forces in the south-west Pacific.

3 January 1942 The Allies set up the South-West Pacific Command.

This followed directly from the 'Arcadia' decision to form ABDA. Wavell was appointed to command with Brett as his deputy.

4 January Chiang Kai-shek appointed Supreme Allied Commander, China.

At the same time he was resisting a Japanese offensive in the Changsha area of Hunan province.

Japanese aircraft now began to attack Rabaul in the Bismarck Archipelago. They would maintain these attacks on this important strategic base for the next few weeks.

7 January The Japanese completed the capture of Sarawak.

Next day the Japanese captured Jesselton in British North Borneo.

11 January Japanese landings at Manado in the extreme north of Celebes Island.

Simultaneous landings were made on the island of Tarakan off the east coast of Borneo. Both places were quickly made air bases.

12 January Japan formally declared war on the Dutch East Indies.

14 January Wavell arrived at Batavia, Java, to set up his ABDA HQ.

15 January Japanese invasion of Burma began.

19 January British North Borneo secured by the Japanese.

21 January General Joseph W. Stilwell appointed Chief of Staff to Chiang Kai-shek.

The Japanese began air attacks on New Guinea.

23 January Japanese landings at Rabaul and Kavieng on New Ireland.

Simultaneous landings took place on Bougainville in the Solomons and Kendari, south of Celebes.

24 January Japanese landings at Balikpapan on the east coast of Dutch Borneo.

These were followed on **27 January** by further landings at Pemangkat on the west coast.

Also on the 24th there were further landings at Kendari. The Allied forces in Malaya and Borneo were now being encircled.

24 January Naval action in the Macassar Strait between Borneo and Celebes.

Four US destroyers and some submarines attacked a Japanese convoy and sank one destroyer and four transports. One US destroyer was damaged. This delayed the Japanese invasion of Java.

25 January Japanese landing at Lae, New Guinea.

Thailand declared war on Britain and the USA.

30 January The Japanese seized the important naval base of Amboina between Celebes and New Guinea.

31 January The British and Commonwealth forces completed the evacuation of Malaya, crossing The Causeway to Singapore Island.

The Fall of Malaya, Singapore and Java · P80

The Fall of Malaya, Singapore and Java

The economic and strategic importance of Malaya and Singapore had been recognized by the British long before the outbreak of war. Shortly after the end of the First World War the decision had been made to construct a large naval base at Singapore and to make this the epicentre of Britain's defence of her possessions in the Far East. (Malaya was rich in rubber and tin, which was a good reason for locating a naval base at Singapore.) Shortly afterwards it was decided that coastal batteries should be built to protect the base from attack by sea.

During the 1930s Army planners began to recognize that Singapore might not necessarily be attacked from the sea – an invasion from Thailand into Malaya was equally possible. Troops and aircraft were therefore needed, but when it came to defence commitments as a whole, Singapore had a low priority. This became even more pronounced when war came in 1939. Britain's military resources were committed to Europe and the Mediterranean, and there was little available for the Far East. The fact that for the first two years, Japan was not at war with Britain did little to help Singapore's cause; besides which, Japan's military capabilities were drastically under-estimated.

True, a number of airfields were constructed in Malaya, and exercises were conducted in its defence; but little effort was made to train for jungle warfare. There was, too, conflict between the civil and military authorities. The military wanted to construct defences in Malaya, but the civil administration objected to this since it would interfere with the enormous economic contribution that Malaya was making to Britain's war effort.

The Japanese, of course, had long coveted Malaya's tin and rubber, and during 1940 and 1941 a plan for seizing it gradually evolved. It was to be carried out by General Tomoyuki Yamashita's Twenty-Fifth Army of three divisions, with a fourth standing by in Japan should he need it. Yamashita would strike across the border from Thailand and also land by sea. Initially he would be supported by Thailand-based aircraft, but he aimed to capture airfields in northern Malaya swiftly and to make a two-pronged thrust down the east and west coasts.

The British plan for the defence of Malaya was built round three divisions: two Indian and one Australian, plus four independent brigades. Their quality was variable. Recognizing the threat of coastal invasion, the two Indian divisions were deployed to northern Malaya to cover the coasts, with the 8th Australian Division defending Johore. There was also a plan ('Matador') for advancing into southern Thailand to deny to the Japanese the airfields and the ports of Patani and Singora.

On **20 October 1941** the Admiralty, which had resisted sending capital ships to Singapore because of threats nearer to home, agreed that *Repulse, Prince of Wales* and the aircraft carrier *Indomitable* should be sent there, but the last-named, which was in the Caribbean at the time, ran aground, so that only the battleship and battlecruiser were sent. There were, however, neither the troops nor the aircraft to spare to reinforce Malaya in autumn 1941.

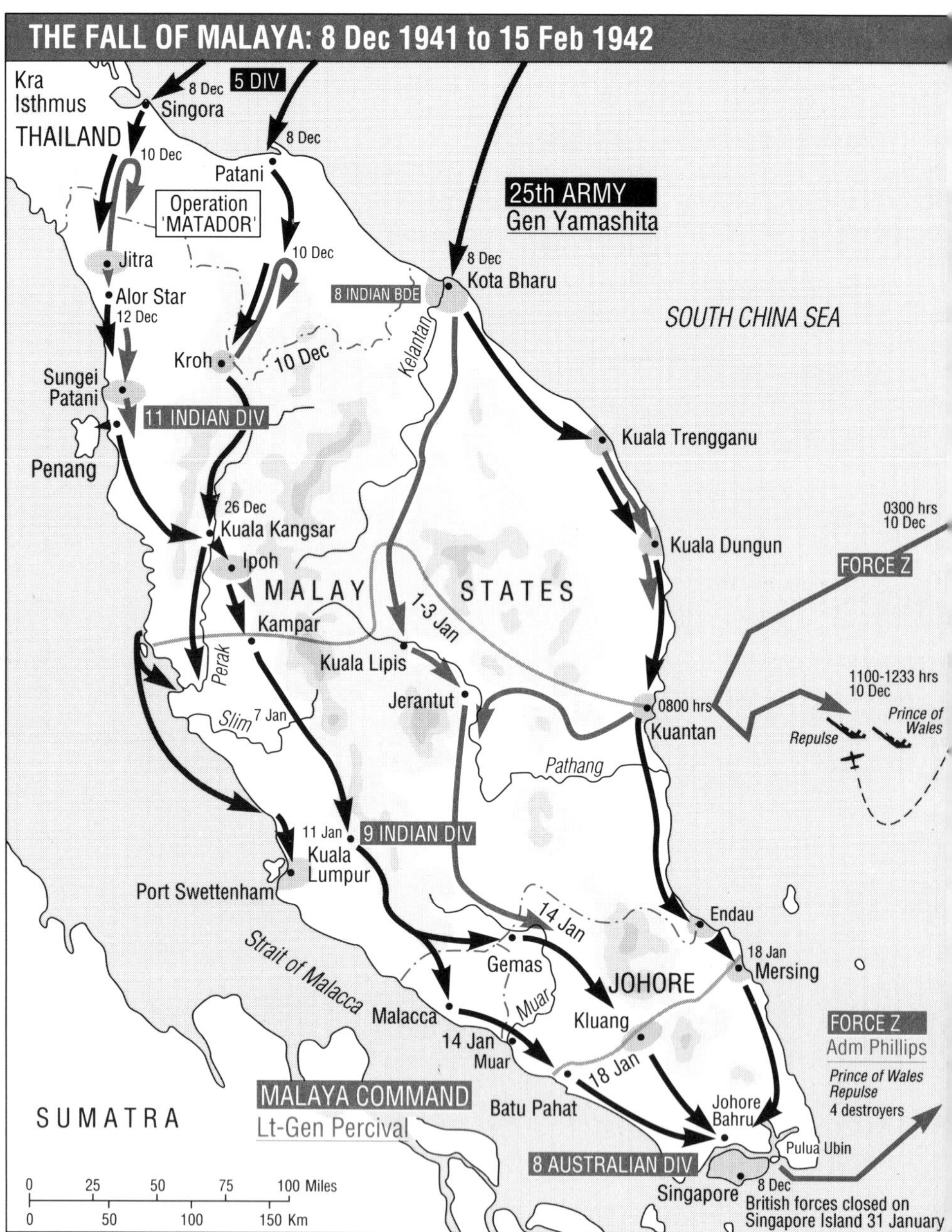

6 December 1941 An RAF Hudson aircraft spotted Japanese transports steaming west off Cape Cambodia.

Fear of the implications of violating Thai neutrality, especially with regard to US reactions, dissuaded the British from launching 'Matador', which was dependent on having 24 hours' warning of a Japanese attack.

8 December First Japanese landings at Khota Bharu, northern Malaya.

These took place just after midnight. Resistance by 8th Indian Brigade was fierce, and air attacks damaged three Japanese transports, two seriously. Nevertheless the Japanese were able to establish a beachhead, and rumours that they had broken through the defences caused the RAF to evacuate Kota Bharu airfield. That night 8th Indian Brigade began to withdraw. Meanwhile, that afternoon, Air Chief Marshal Sir Robert Brooke-Popham, CinC, Far East, had decided to launch a limited version of 'Matador' designed to seize a prominent feature inside Thailand known as The Ledge and to delay the Japanese who had landed unopposed at Singora and Patani.

10 December Sinking of *Prince of Wales* and *Repulse*.

By this stage the RAF had lost most of its aircraft in northern Malaya, mainly as a result of Japanese air attacks on airfields. The remainder were withdrawn to Singapore. The troops that had advanced

ıto Thailand were halted by the Japanese and next ay were forced to withdraw. A major problem was ıe lack of suitable weapons to combat the Japanese anks. For the past few days there had been constant eavy rain.

2 December 11th Indian Division withdrew rom Jitra to Alor Star.
'he Japanese facing them were inferior in numbers, ut rumours, command and control problems, and oor training resulted in many surrenders and nnecessary casualties among the Indian troops. 1any were persuaded into surrendering by memɔers of what was to become the Indian National Army, dedicated to giving India her independence rom the British.

6 December Penang Island evacuated.

7 December The British and Commonwealth orces began to fall back to the River Perak.
Next the British authorities made an urgent request o London for more troops and aircraft.

26 December The Japanese crossed the River Perak.
'amashita now sensed that resistance was weakenng and determined not to allow his enemy time to eorganize. His tactics were simple: advance down he roads until reaching a defensive position and hen outflank it through the jungle.

2 January 1942 Outflanked at Kampar, the British and Empire forces withdrew to the River Slim.

7 January The Japanese crossed the River Slim.
General Arthur E. Percival, the British land forces commander, now hoped to be able to hold Johore, at least until mid-February. Wavell, who flew to Singapore on the 8th, agreed with him.

11 January Japanese 5th Division entered Kuala Lumpur.
This was the main supply base for III Indian Corps. By this time the Japanese were engaging Major-General H. G. Gordon Bennett's 8th Australian Division for the first time. The Australians had some initial success by mounting a series of ambushes, but further amphibious landings threatened Bennett's communications, and he was forced to withdraw. This put paid to hopes of a protracted defence of Johore.

19 January Wavell warned Churchill that Singapore could not be held.
Little had been done to prepare the landward defences. Churchill replied that Singapore *must* be defended and that 'no question of surrender be entertained until after protracted fighting among the ruins of Singapore city'. Wavell now ordered Percival to prepare the island for a siege.

22 January At last reinforcements began to reach Singapore.
First to land was an Indian brigade, followed two days later by the British 18th Division and Australian troops.

31 January Withdrawal of troops from Malaya to Singapore completed.
Singapore now had the equivalent of four divisions to defend it, but morale was low and there were grave shortages of weapons.

7 February Feint Japanese landing on Pulua Ubin Island.

8 February Main Japanese landings on the west coast of Singapore.
By dawn on the 9th the Japanese 5th and 18th Divisions were firmly established on the island and began to advance south-east towards Singapore city.

10 February Wavell's last visit to Singapore.
By now there was nothing he could do to alter the situation.

14 February Japanese airborne landing at Palembang, Sumatra.
Sumatra and Java were the next Japanese targets after Singapore.

15 February Singapore surrendered.
The decision to do so was prompted as much as anything by the plight of the one million civilian inhabitants of the island. The Allies lost 9,000 killed and wounded and 130,000 captured, many of whom would find themselves working as slaves on construction of the notorious Burma-Thai Railway. The Japanese casualties were 9,000. In Britain, the fall of Singapore, which the public had long thought of as impregnable, came as a severe shock.
On this same day the Japanese landed at Muntok, Sumatra.

19 February Battle of Lumbok Strait, off Bali.
An Allied naval squadron tried to prevent the Japanese landing on Bali. It was driven off, with one Dutch destroyer sunk and two Dutch cruisers and one US destroyer damaged. Japanese carrier-based aircraft meanwhile raided Darwin in northern Australia, causing extensive damage to the port.

20 February Japanese landings on Portuguese Timor.

23 February Wavell's HQ began to leave Java for Australia.
Wavell himself left on the 25th, and ABDA was broken up.

27 February Battle of Java Sea.
An Allied naval squadron under the Dutch Admiral, Karel Doorman, was destroyed while trying to intercept the Japanese invasion of Java, which took place the following day.

1 March Battle of the Sunda Strait.
The remnant of the Allied naval force in the Dutch East Indies tried to flee to Australia, but was caught by the Japanese, who sank one Australian and one US cruiser, and one British, one Dutch and two US destroyers.

7 March The Dutch Government fled Java for Australia.
Two days later resistance ceased, and the Dutch East Indies were totally under Japanese control.

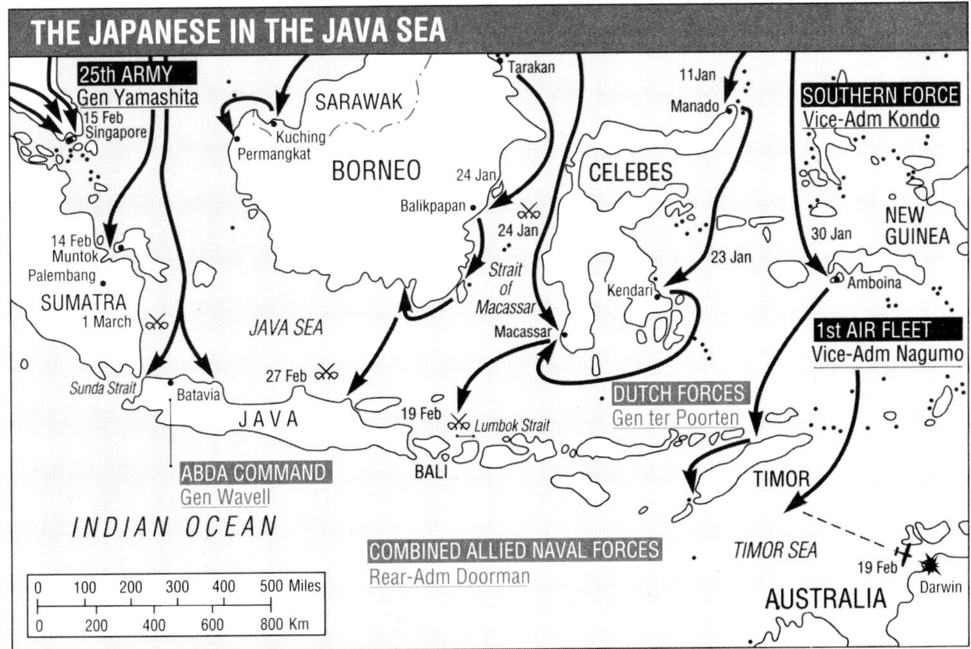

Australia Under Threat · P102

Bataan and Corregidor

It had long been recognized by US planners that the Philippines would be a likely Japanese target in the event of war, and much thought had gone into their defence. They realized, however, that it would be difficult to send reinforcements if the Japanese did attack the Philippines. Thus plan WPO-3 of April 1941 saw a three-stage defence – first to prevent enemy landings on the main island of Luzon, followed by a delaying action and then the defence of Manila Bay so that it was denied to the Japanese fleet. It was expected that the garrison could hold out for six months, but it might take as long as two years for the US fleet to fight its way across the Pacific and reach the islands.

On **26 July 1941,** in response to the Japanese occupation of bases in Indo-China, a new American command was formed, US Army Forces in the Far East (USAFFE). Appointed to head it was General Douglas C. MacArthur, former US Army Chief of Staff and from 1935 to 1937 military adviser to the Filipino Government. He disagreed with the pessimistic nature of the plans for the defence of the Philippines and wanted to concentrate on defeating the Japanese on the beaches. In mid-October Washington agreed to this.

MacArthur had available ten divisions for the defence of the Philippines, but only one of these was US, the Philippine Division. Apart from this and the Filipino Scouts, the standard of training was poor. MacArthur divided his troops into four – North Luzon Forces (the largest), South Luzon Forces, the Reserve Area around Manila and the Visayan–Mindanao Force, since MacArthur believed that all the Philippines, not just Luzon, should be defended. While receiving no further ground reinforcements in the weeks before the Japanese attack, MacArthur did have 35 B-17 Flying Fortress bombers sent to him, together with some 100 modern fighters. These were deployed to six airfields around Manila, but only the largest, Clark Field, could take the B-17s. The naval forces available to him consisted of one old cruiser, two light cruisers, thirteen old destroyers, 29 submarines and some smaller craft.

The Japanese, whose intelligence about the Philippines was detailed and accurate, were so confident of their ability to overrun the islands in 50 days that General Homma's Fourteenth Army was allotted little more than two divisions for the attack. Like the other Japanese operations, the first objective was to gain air supremacy.

On **7 December 1941** Japanese aircraft struck the airfields around Manila. Within a few hours they had destroyed 17 B-17s, 56 fighters and 30 other aircraft, damaging many more. The US Far East Air Force ceased to be a serious threat. These attacks continued for the next few days and prompted the evacuation of much of the available naval power and the remaining B-17s.

MacArthur refused to be drawn by the early Japanese landings on the Batan Islands **(8 December)** and in the extreme north (**10 December)** and extreme south **(12 December)** of Luzon. He rightly recognized that these were merely to seize airfields, but he did warn President Manuel Quezon on **12 December** to be prepared to move to Corregidor at four hours' notice, while denying that he had changed his plans.

22 December 1941 **Main Japanese landings in Lingayen Gulf, Luzon.**
The Filipino troops here failed to prevent a beach-head from being established and the Filipino Scouts sent forward to hold the defiles barring the way to the south were also unsuccessful. By the end of the next day North Luzon Force was withdrawing to the River Agno.

24 December **Japanese landing in Lamon Bay south-east of Manila.**
This was the 16th Division, which began to drive towards Manila.

On this day MacArthur announced his decision to withdraw his forces to Bataan. A supply base was set up on Corregidor with sufficient stocks to carry on the fight for six months.

26 December **Manila declared an open city.**
Thanks to the skill of the withdrawal, the Japanese did not enter Manila until **2 January**.

5 January 1942 **Withdrawal to Bataan successfully completed.**
One US and seven Filipino divisions, totalling 80,000 men, now held Bataan. 26,000 civilians had also fled here, but the food stocks were only sufficient to feed 43,000 men for six months.

The Japanese quickly closed up to the first main defence line, which was based on Mounts Santa Rosa and Natib.

9 January **Japanese attacked the east side of the Santa Rosa–Natib defence line.**
Initially they made some gains, but counter-attacks forced them virtually back to their start-line.

13 January **A Japanese attack just east of Mount Natib began to pose a threat to the left flank of II Corps.**

14 January **The Japanese began to attack I Corps on the west side of Bataan.**

22 January **MacArthur ordered the withdrawal of all troops to the final defence line in Bataan.**
This was the Bagac–Orion Line. Despite repeated counter-attacks, the Japanese had continued to make progress, and there was a danger that they would destroy the integrity of the US-Filipino defences.

That night the Japanese attempted two battalion-size landings at Quinauan Point and Longoskawayan Point in the south of Bataan. Allied reserves first contained and then, after three weeks' fighting, destroyed both these incursions.

26 January **Withdrawal to the Bagac–Orion Line successfully completed.**
The Japanese quickly followed up the withdrawal and made several penetrations, but these were contained and destroyed. Bitter fighting continued for the next few weeks, but little progress was made by either side.

8 February **President Quezon proposed to Roosevelt that his country be granted total independence.**
The Philippines would declare itself neutral, and Japanese and US forces would leave the country. MacArthur also warned that the garrison had suffered almost 50 per cent casualties and it was 'near done'. Roosevelt dismissed Quezon's proposal, but said that MacArthur could surrender Filipino, but not US troops, who were to fight until the end.

20 February **President Quezon left for Australia in a US submarine.**
The Japanese, who had suffered heavy casualties during the past few weeks, from disease as well as from battle began to slacken their pressure in Bataan. Disease was also rife among the Allied troops.

11 March **MacArthur left the Philippines for Australia.**
He had been ordered by Roosevelt to assume command of the new South-West Pacific area. In effect, this meant command of all Allied forces in the Pacific. His last words on leaving were: 'I shall return!' General Jonathan M. Wainwright took over command of the Philippines.

24 March **The Japanese began an intensive bombing campaign of Bataan and Corregidor.**
Homma had been reinforced by a fresh division, the 4th, from Shanghai. For the Allies on Bataan, however, food was becoming very short, and the meagre diet encouraged disease.

3 April **Final Japanese offensive in Bataan opened.**
It was preceded by five hours of artillery and air bombardment. After four days' desperate fighting the Japanese had penetrated four miles and Wainwright's forces were beginning to disintegrate.

9 April **The Allied forces on Bataan surrendered.**
Some 78,000 men surrendered. They were subjected to a march of 65 miles from Mariveles to San Fernando under the hot sun, with hardly any water or food. In what became known as the 'Bataan Death March' many thousands died. Of the 12,000 Americans captured at Bataan only one third were to survive the war.

The Japanese were still fighting on Mindanao, and the Allies still held the islands between Luzon and

P78 · Japanese Onrush

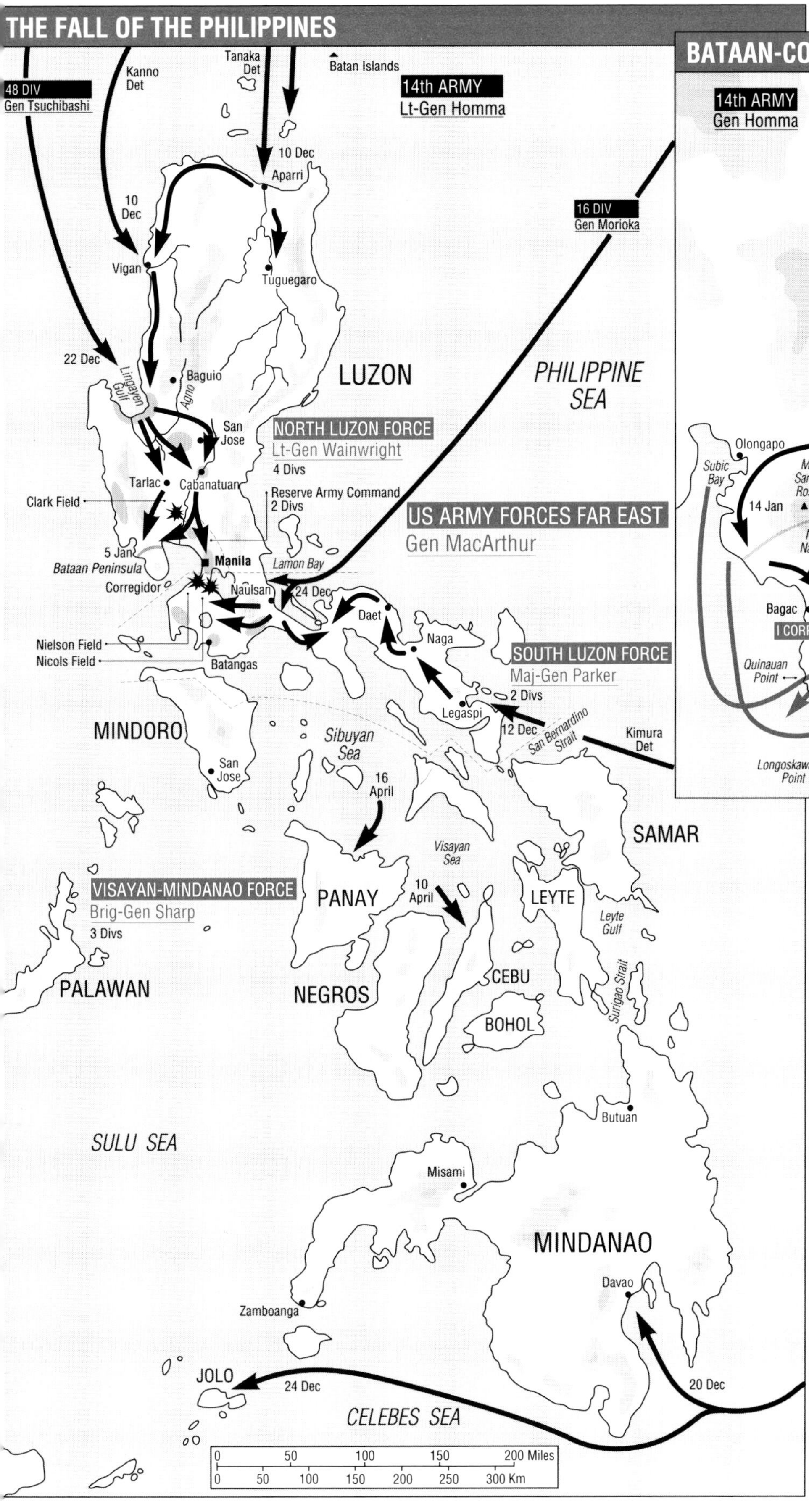

THE FALL OF THE PHILIPPINES

48 DIV
Gen Tsuchibashi
Kanno Det
Tanaka Det
Batan Islands
14th ARMY
Lt-Gen Homma
10 Dec
Aparri
10 Dec
Vigan
Tuguegaro
16 DIV
Gen Morioka
22 Dec
Lingayen Gulf
Baguio
Agno
LUZON
PHILIPPINE SEA
San Jose
NORTH LUZON FORCE
Lt-Gen Wainwright
4 Divs
Tarlac
Cabanatuan
Clark Field
Reserve Army Command
2 Divs
US ARMY FORCES FAR EAST
Gen MacArthur
5 Jan
Bataan Peninsula
Manila
Lamon Bay
Corregidor
Naulsan
24 Dec
Daet
Nielson Field
Nicols Field
Batangas
Naga
SOUTH LUZON FORCE
Maj-Gen Parker
2 Divs
Legaspi
12 Dec
San Bernardino Strait
Kimura Det
MINDORO
Sibuyan Sea
San Jose
16 April
SAMAR
Visayan Sea
VISAYAN-MINDANAO FORCE
Brig-Gen Sharp
3 Divs
PANAY
10 April
LEYTE
Leyte Gulf
PALAWAN
NEGROS
CEBU
Surigao Strait
BOHOL
Butuan
SULU SEA
Misami
MINDANAO
Davao
Zamboanga
JOLO
24 Dec
20 Dec
CELEBES SEA
0 50 100 150 200 Miles
0 50 100 150 200 250 300 Km

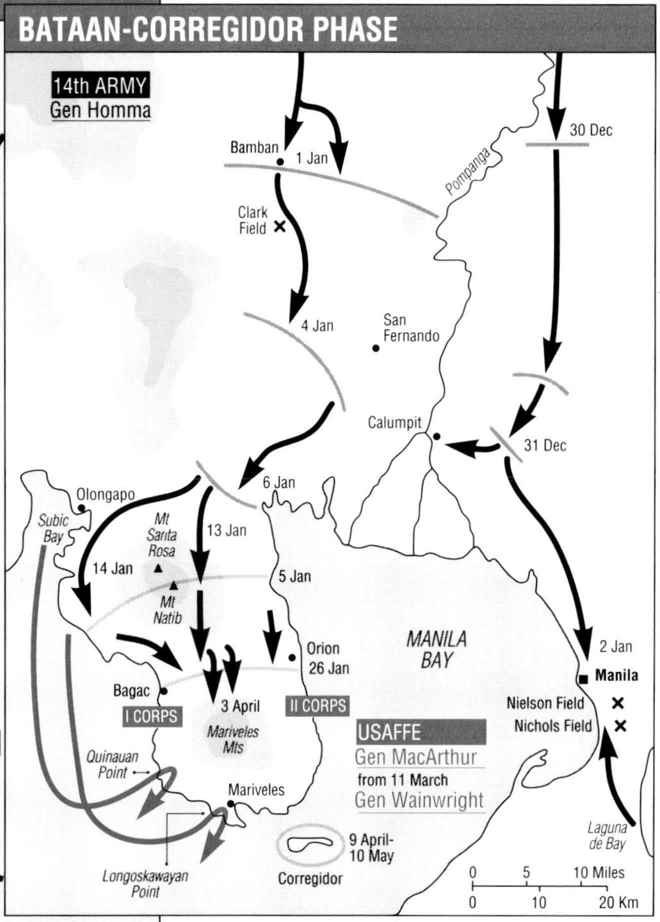

BATAAN-CORREGIDOR PHASE

14th ARMY
Gen Homma
Bamban
1 Jan
30 Dec
Clark Field
Pampanga
4 Jan
San Fernando
Calumpit
31 Dec
6 Jan
Olongapo
Subic Bay
Mt Santa Rosa
13 Jan
14 Jan
Mt Natib
5 Jan
MANILA BAY
2 Jan
Orion
26 Jan
Manila
Bagac
3 April
I CORPS
II CORPS
Mariveles Mts
Nielson Field
Nichols Field
USAFFE
Gen MacArthur
from 11 March
Gen Wainwright
Quinauan Point
Mariveles
Laguna de Bay
9 April-
10 May
Longoskawayan Point
Corregidor
0 5 10 Miles
0 10 20 Km

Mindanao and the fortress of Corregidor, which continued to deny the Japanese the use of Manila Bay.

10 April Japanese landings on Cebu Island.
After three days' fighting the remainder of the 4,500 US-Filipino garrison withdrew to the hills. By the 19th the Japanese hold on the island was secure.

16 April Japanese landings on Panay Island.

29 April Japanese reinforcements landed on Mindanao.
Attacks against the Filipino garrison increased in intensity. Meanwhile, shelling of Corrigedor increased.

5 May Japanese landing on Corregidor.
General Wainwright, with no hope of relief, surrendered his 15,000-man garrison two days later.

10 May General William Sharp, commanding Central Philippines, ordered the surrender of the remaining Allied forces.
Thus ended the campaign for the Philippines, which had held out for twice as long as the Japanese expected – but not the six months forecast by the US planners.

Australia Under Threat · P102

Burma and the Indian Ocean

The original Japanese expansion plans did not include the capture of Burma. True, they accepted that the British might well use the country as a base from which to launch a counter-attack in Malaya. Thus, in order to secure their flank they decided that the port of Rangoon, Tenasserim and the airfields on the Kra Isthmus would need to be seized; but that was all. What made them change their minds was the continued irritation of the Allied supply route running from Rangoon into China, which was doing much to help Chiang Kai-shek keep the Japanese at bay. There was also a significant independence movement among the Burmese population.

The task of seizing Burma was assigned to General Shojiro Iida's Fifteenth Army. Initially it consisted of the 33rd and 55th Divisions, and its first task on the outbreak of war had been the securing of Thailand, which it would then use as a spring-board for its entry into Burma. Its first task would be to seize the Kra Isthmus and then, once the Japanese High Command was satisfied that the invasion of Malaya was going to plan, make a three-pronged attack on Burma. One prong would move up the Kra Isthmus to Rangoon while the other two would use the Rivers Salween and Sittang as their axes.

In autumn 1941 there had been much chopping and changing over responsibility for the British defence of Burma. Initially it came under Far Eastern Command in Singapore, but on **12 December 1941** reverted to India. Eighteen days later, however, it was handed over to ABDA. The defence of Burma itself was entrusted to Lieutenant-General Tom Hutton's Burma Army which was an army in name only, consisting of little more than a division of recently raised Burmese units stiffened by two British battalions and an Indian brigade. There were only 37 aircraft available, including one of Chennault's P-40 squadrons, which Chiang Kai-shek had agreed could be retained in Burma. The Japanese initially had 100 aircraft in the area of operations.

15 December Japanese troops crossed from Thailand and seized Victoria Point in the extreme south of Burma.

23 December First Japanese air raid on Rangoon.
A significant number of Japanese aircraft were destroyed, but Allied aircraft could not prevent damage to the docks.

During the first part of January, reinforcements in the shape of 17th Indian Division began to arrive in Burma and were deployed east of Rangoon.

15 January 1942 Japanese attack up the Kra Isthmus began.
The airfields around Tenasserim were quickly captured, enabling Japanese fighters to operate from there against Rangoon. By **19 January** the Japanese had reached Tavoy.

20 January Japanese 55th Division invaded Burma from Raheng.
It quickly threatened Moulmein, using the same tactics as in Malaya of outflanking through the jungle.

30 January Moulmein and its airfield fell to the Japanese.
The garrison withdrew across the River Salween.

31 January An additional Indian brigade landed at Rangoon and was sent to join 17th Division.

11 February The Japanese crossed the Salween.
The commander of 17th Division, Lieutenant-General John Smyth, was now concerned that his troops would be cut off and urged Hutton to allow him to withdraw across the Sittang. He was initially ordered to hold on the River Bilin, and not until the 19th did Hutton relent; by then Smyth was in real danger of being outflanked.

23 February The bridge over the River Sittang blown.
The Japanese tried to seize it while more than half of 17th Division were on the far bank; nevertheless, Smyth decided to blow it. The remnant of the Division withdrew to Pegu, where they were joined by 7th Armoured Brigade, which had come as a reinforcement from the Middle East. Wavell removed Smyth from his command. The Japanese, having managed to get across the Sittang, now began to infiltrate between 17th Division and 1st Burma Division to the north.

5 March General Sir Harold Alexander arrived at Rangoon to take over from Hutton.
Wavell had given him orders to hold Rangoon at all costs. Alexander, in turn, ordered 1st Burma Division to counter-attack from the north and 17th Division, which had been reinforced by another brigade, to the east of Pegu. Both attacks failed, and Alexander realized that Rangoon could not be held. He therefore ordered the evacuation of the capital and for his troops to regroup in the Irrawaddy valley to the north.

8 March The Japanese entered Rangoon.
17th Indian Division was now holding the Irrawaddy area and 1st Burma Division the upper Sittang Valley. Farther north, guarding the approaches to China were two Chinese 'armies' – Fifth at Mandalay, and Sixth in the Shan States with a division at Toungoo. They were commanded by the American General Joseph Stilwell.

12 March British garrison in the Andaman Islands evacuated.
They were occupied by the Japanese on **23 March**.

19 March General Bill Slim appointed to command I Burma Corps (Burcorps).
This covered all Burmese, British and Indian troops in Burma, leaving Alexander to concentrate on co-ordination with the Chinese. By now the Japanese were attacking the Chinese at Toungoo and had been reinforced by the 18th and 56th Divisions, which had arrived by sea at Rangoon.

28 March Alexander ordered Burcorps to attack at Paungde and Prome in the Irrawaddy valley.
This was in response to a request by Stilwell to relieve the increasing pressure on Toungoo.

30 March The Chinese abandoned Toungoo.
The Chinese failed to destroy the bridge over the Sittang at Toungoo, and this left the way to the Chinese border wide open to the Japanese. The abandonment of Toungoo meant that Burcorps, whose attacks in the Prome area had been forced back, was left exposed; it therefore began to withdraw to the Yenangyaung oilfields.

3 April Heavy Japanese air attacks on Mandalay.
By this time the remaining British aircraft had been withdrawn to India.

5 April Japanese aircraft attacked Colombo, Ceylon, and sank two British cruisers in the Indian Ocean.
They came from a strong Japanese naval squadron under Admiral Nobutake Kondo, which had been tasked with destroying the British Indian Ocean squadron based at Colombo. The latter, however, had received prior warning and had sailed to a secret anchorage in the Maldive Islands. Later it withdrew temporarily to the Persian Gulf.

12 April The Japanese captured Migyaungye.
This exposed the west flank of Burcorps and put the oilfields under threat.

15 April Burcorps began to destroy the Yenangyaung oil wells.
By this stage 1st Burma Division was being cut off by the Japanese south of Yenangyaung. It was eventually extricated with the help of the Chinese 38th Division, which had been sent down by Chiang Kai-shek from Mandalay. The British and Chinese forces now withdrew under increasing Japanese pressure.

29 April The Japanese seized Lashio, thus cutting the Burma Road.

30 April Burcorps withdrew across the River Irrawaddy.

1 May The Japanese captured Monywa and Mandalay.
The fall of Monywa threatened to cut off the Allied withdrawal and converted it to a disorganized retreat.

1939	1940	1941	1942	1943	1944	1945

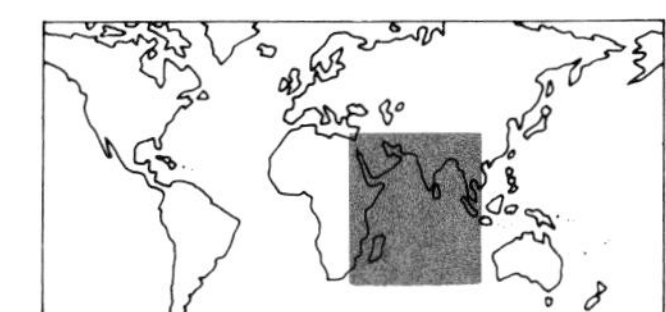

THE JAPANESE CONQUEST OF BURMA

THE INDIAN OCEAN: April-May 1942

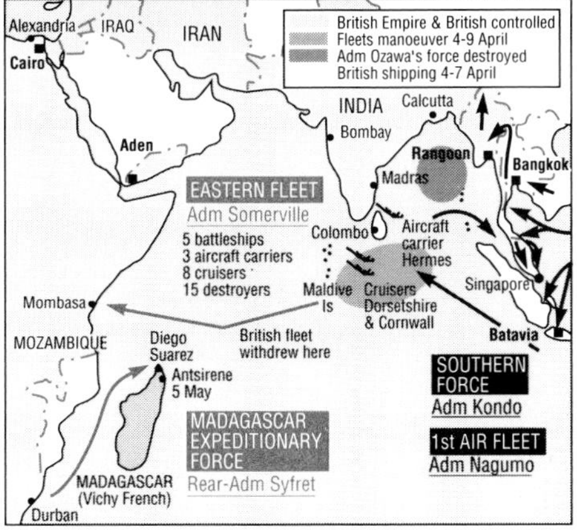

4 May The British abandoned Akyab on the Burmese coast.

5 May British troops landed on Vichy French Madagascar.
The aim was to prevent the Japanese from using it as a base. The ports of Diego Suarez and Antsirene were quickly captured, but Madagascar would not be entirely secured until **5 November.**

8 May The Japanese captured Myitkyina.

15 May Stilwell crossed the border into Assam after a gruelling march on foot.

20 May Burcorps crossed the border into India and was disbanded.

As was the case elsewhere, the Allies in Burma had been completely outfought by the Japanese. Apart from losing the country, the British and Commonwealth forces alone suffered 13,500 casualties (no figure are available for the Chinese losses) as opposed to less than 5,000 Japanese. There was now a widespread belief that the Japanese soldier was superior to his Allied counterpart, at least in the jungle, and there seemed to be little reason why the Japanese should not immediately continue their drive into India itself.

Burma – First Steps Back · P140

9 DECEMBER 1941 TO 1 AUGUST 1942

The Battle of the Atlantic: The Second 'Happy Time'

The second half of 1941 had marked an upsurge in British fortunes in the Atlantic. Indeed, apart from one month, September, the tonnage of merchant shipping lost never rose above 200,000 tons. There were several reasons for this. An increasing number of escorts were available, and they were becoming more efficient at anti-submarine warfare, both in terms of tactics and technical aids. With the loss of a number of the 'aces' during the first half of the year, U-boat commanders were less experienced, and for much of the time the Admiralty had warning of U-boat concentrations through Ultra. Finally, there was the increasing role being played by the US Navy. With America's entry into the war, it would have been reasonable to expect the situation to improve still further, but this did not happen – rather the reverse.

9 December 1941 Hitler lifted his ban on U-boats operating in US territorial waters.
This was two days before his formal declaration of war on the USA. Doenitz wanted immediately to deploy twelve U-boats to the eastern seaboard of the USA, but was only allowed to send five, since priority lay with the Mediterranean.

20 December **Admiral Ernest J. King appointed Commander, US Navy.**
He had been commanding the Atlantic Fleet and handed this over to Admiral Royal E. Ingersoll, who, as such, was to be responsible for anti-submarine operations in the Atlantic. Ingersoll, however, was beset by a number of problems.

There was a very large amount of maritime traffic passing up and down the eastern seaboard of the USA, and on **1 July 1941** the coast had been split into a number of 'sea frontiers' to allocate responsibility for providing air and sea protection for shipping up to 200 miles from the coast. There were few suitable aircraft or vessels available for this task in December 1941, and this in spite of the fact that on **1 November 1941** the US Navy had taken over the US Coast Guard and its cutters. Many of these vessels were totally ill equipped to combat the U-boats.

Since there were few escort vessels available, it was decided not to implement convoying for coastal traffic. Instead, on **7 December 1941** all merchant vessels were ordered to follow designated coast-hugging routes. Unfortunately, no effort was made to institute any form of black-out on the eastern seaboard, and lights continued to burn as in peacetime.

Conditions could not have been better for the first wave of U-boats that were now on their way across the Atlantic.

12 January 1942 ***U-123*** **sank the British steamer** ***Cyclops*** **300 miles east of Cape Cod.**
This marked the beginning of what Doenitz called Operation 'Paukenschlag' ('Drum Roll'). By the end

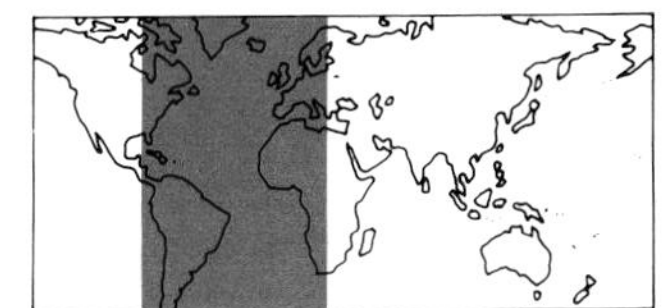

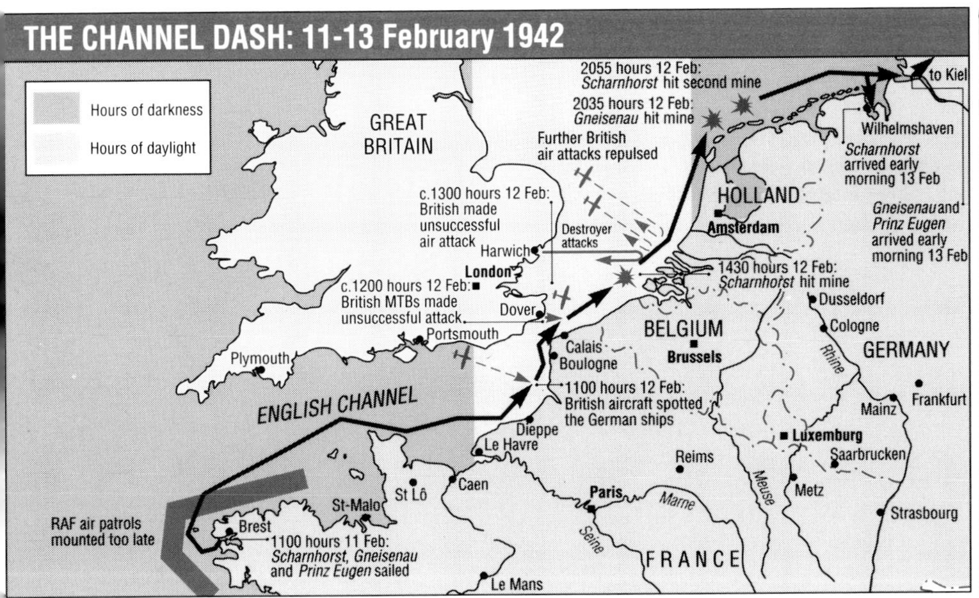

THE CHANNEL DASH: 11-13 February 1942

of the month, out of 46 ships sunk, all but six had been sunk off the US eastern seaboard. Most of these were attributable to the five Type IX ocean-going boats and three additional ones that arrived later in the month. Doenitz now wanted to deploy all available Type IXs to the western Atlantic, but Hitler had become convinced that the Allies were planning to invade Norway and ordered eight Type IXs to be stationed there. Doenitz was forced to make use of his more limited range Type VIIs, but this was not before a further five Type IXs had already sailed for the Caribbean; these would be in position in mid-February.

1 February **The U-boats adopted a new Enigma cipher.**
Code-named 'Triton', the new cipher had an additional rotor in the Enigma machine to that of the previous cipher, 'Hydra'. This meant that Bletchley Park was unable to read the U-boat coded communications traffic until the end of the year. This made the task of the Admiralty's Submarine Tracking Room very difficult, although it was still able to obtain some intelligence from the use of 'Hydra' by the German naval commands.

In the meantime, Hitler, still worried about the threat to Norway and the fact that three major units of his surface fleet – *Scharnhorst, Gneisenau* and *Prinz Eugen* – had been shut in Brest and at the mercy of RAF Bomber Command since spring 1941, decided on **12 January** that they must return to Germany. Admiral Otto Ciliax, commanding the three battlecruisers, decided that their best chance of avoiding the British Home Fleet was to take the most direct route up the English Channel.

11 February **After dark, Ciliax's squadron slipped anchor.**
This was not detected by the British until 1100 hours next day. They had, however, received indications that the squadron was intending to leave port, and had deployed attack aircraft along the south coast of England. By this time the squadron was entering the Straits of Dover. Motor Torpedo-Boats (MTBs) from Dover attempted a torpedo attack, but were forced to do so at extreme range and missed. Six Swordfish aircraft then tried a torpedo attack, but five were shot down and all torpedoes again missed. That afternoon *Scharnhorst* was slightly damaged by a mine. Destroyers from Harwich, aircraft from Bomber Command and Beauforts of RAF Coastal Command all then attacked, but without success. Late that evening both *Scharnhorst* and *Gneisenau* were damaged by mines.

13 February **Ciliax's squadron reached the ports of Wilhelmshaven and Kiel.**
The fact that Ciliax had managed to slip through the Channel with such apparent ease was yet another setback for Britain during this very dark part of the war. Some consolation was gained when the submarine HMS *Trident* torpedoed and put out of action *Prinz Eugen* as she sailed north to Norway ten days later, and on the **night of 26/27 February** RAF bombers hit *Gneisenau* in a floating dock at Kiel: the battlecruiser was never put to sea again under her own power.

16 February **Doenitz ordered a mass attack by the U-boats off the US eastern seaboard.**
The U-boats sank 71 merchant vessels in February, again all but six in US waters.

1 March **First US successes against U-boats.**
An Argentia-based Hudson of Squadron VP-82 sank *U-656* off Cape Race, Newfoundland, and on **15 March** an aircraft of the same squadron sank *U-503* near the Grand Banks of Newfoundland. These two successes did not prevent the U-boats from sinking a further 86 vessels in US waters during March. More than half of these were tankers – such was the lack of defence that the U-boats were able to pick their targets at leisure.

1 April **Partial convoying instituted along the US eastern seaboard.**
At last the US authorities were beginning to realize that more stringent defensive measures must be taken. Known as the 'Bucket Brigade', merchant ships steamed in convoy during daylight hours as close inshore as possible and anchored for the night in protected harbours. Escorts were still too few to make continuous convoying possible, and the Bucket system did not apply to the Caribbean or Gulf of Mexico.

Night of 13/14 April **First US warship success against a U-boat.**
The US destroyer *Roper* sank *U-85* south of Norfolk, Virginia. (During the first six months of 1942 US forces accounted for six U-boats only out of a total of 21 sunk.)

18 April **Eastern Sea Frontier ordered a black-out of lights on the coast.**
Up until now the civilian authorities had rejected this because they feared it would ruin the tourist trade. This and the other steps taken reduced the sinkings in US waters to 69 for the month of April; meanwhile the U-boats began to concentrate on the Caribbean.

21 April ***U-459*, the first U-boat tanker, set sail.**
Hitherto the only way in which the U-boats could prolong their stay in US waters was by refuelling from disguised merchant vessels, but this was risky. U-boat tankers, or 'milch cows', carried some 600 tons of fuel, together with torpedoes and other supplies. As a result, Doenitz was able to deploy 32 U-boats to the eastern seaboard and Caribbean in May. This represented half of the operational strength at that time.

The switch of emphasis to the Caribbean reaped speedy dividends. In May sinkings here and off the eastern seabord rose to 111 and in June reached 121 ships.

1 August **Interlocking convoy system instituted.**
During the past few months local convoys had been introduced in the Caribbean and Gulf of Mexico, but the Interlocking system marked the beginning of comprehensive convoying throughout the region. Sinkings fell dramatically.

Doenitz had, however, recognized that the Americans would eventually introduce proper convoying, and when they did so the Second 'Happy Time' would be at an end. He therefore decided to switch his effort once more to the North Atlantic – especially to the gap south-west of Iceland in which the Allies still lacked the means to provide air cover.

Atlantic Victory · P136

Rommel Attacks Once More

No sooner had Rommel withdrawn back into Tripolitania in January 1942 than he was thinking of taking the offensive again. As so often happened in the ebb and flow of the desert campaigns, his lines of communication were now considerably shortened, while those of his enemy were now stretched, especially since the Luftwaffe had denied the British the use of the harbour at Benghazi by sowing mines in it. Lax British radio security revealed that the British were suffering from tank unserviceability. Furthermore, on **19 January** two German transports, *Mongevino* and *Ankara*, landed a total of 45 replacement tanks at Tripoli and at Benghazi (just before Rommel had evacuated the town). They were survivors of a convoy that had been intercepted largely thanks to Ultra. To Rommel, who was careful to conceal his plans from the Italians and his superior in Rome, the German CinC, South, Albert Kesselring, it made sense to strike immediately rather than wait for the British to 'recover their breath'.

His command, which on **22 January** would be designated Panzerarmee Afrika, consisted of the three divisions of the DAK and seven Italian divisions (one armoured, one motorized, five infantry). He had 139 serviceable German and 89 Italian tanks.

Facing him in Cyrenaica was the inexperienced 1st Armoured Division with 150 tanks, but widely dispersed; 4th Indian Division holding Benghazi and Barce; and, farther east, 7th Armoured Division, which was refitting in the Tobruk area. Beginning, as they were, to prepare for a continuation of offensive operations into Tripolitania, the last thing that Auchinleck and Ritchie expected was for Rommel to attack.

21 January 1942 Rommel attacked into Cyrenaica.

21st Panzer Division quickly seized Mersa Brega while 15th Panzer to its south advanced to Wadi Faregh and swung north to Agedabia. The British, taken totally by surprise, were quickly brushed aside.

22 January Agedabia fell to Rommel.

He went on to trap part of 1st Armoured Division in the Antelat – Sannu area, destroying 70 of its tanks.

23 January The Italian High Command remonstrated with Rommel over his independent action.

They wanted him to withdraw to his original start-line and consider his attack as merely a raid – which was what the British, initially, thought it was. Rommel remained adamant. The Italians refused to allow their troops any farther east. Undeterred, Rommel pressed on with the DAK.

25 January Rommel captured Msus.

1st Armoured Division lost more tanks. The capture of Msus now threatened 4th Indian Division in Benghazi. Ritchie ordered it to withdraw to the Derna–Mechili line, but this was countermanded by Auchinleck, who had flown up from Cairo. Instead, Auchinleck ordered a counter-stroke to be mounted, but the Eighth Army was too dispersed and Rommel was moving too quickly for this to be practicable. Rommel now decided to seize Benghazi, but feinted first towards Mechili. This successfully deceived Ritchie into drawing forces here and leaving 4th Indian Division unsupported.

29 January Rommel captured Benghazi.

He also seized a large quantity of supplies and 4th Indian Division was lucky to get out of the trap. Rommel now quickly cleared Eighth Army from the Jebel Akhdar.

2 February Godwin-Austen, commanding British XIII Corps, resigned.

He had been commanding in western Cyrenaica, but had objected to Ritchie bypassing him and

ROMMEL'S SECOND OFFENSIVE

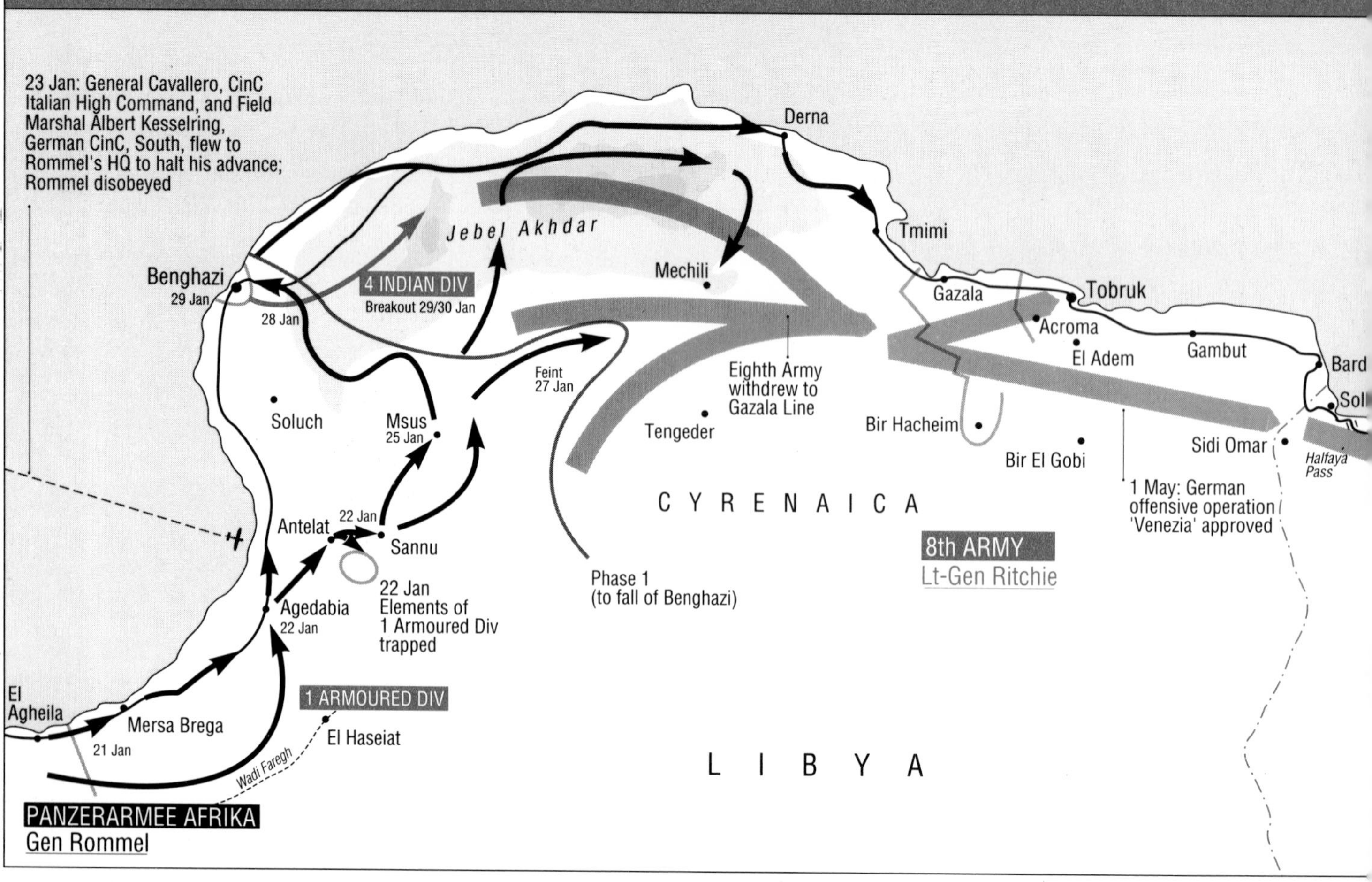

23 Jan: General Cavallero, CinC Italian High Command, and Field Marshal Albert Kesselring, German CinC, South, flew to Rommel's HQ to halt his advance; Rommel disobeyed

Derna
Jebel Akhdar
Tmimi
Benghazi 29 Jan
28 Jan
4 INDIAN DIV
Breakout 29/30 Jan
Mechili
Gazala
Tobruk
Acroma
El Adem
Gambut
Bard
Sol
Feint 27 Jan
Eighth Army withdrew to Gazala Line
Soluch
Msus 25 Jan
Tengeder
Bir Hacheim
Bir El Gobi
Sidi Omar
Halfaya Pass
1 May: German offensive operation 'Venezia' approved
CYRENAICA
Antelat
22 Jan
Sannu
8th ARMY
Lt-Gen Ritchie
Agedabia 22 Jan
22 Jan Elements of 1 Armoured Div trapped
Phase 1 (to fall of Benghazi)
El Agheila
Mersa Brega
21 Jan
1 ARMOURED DIV
El Haseiat
Wadi Faregh
LIBYA
PANZERARMEE AFRIKA
Gen Rommel

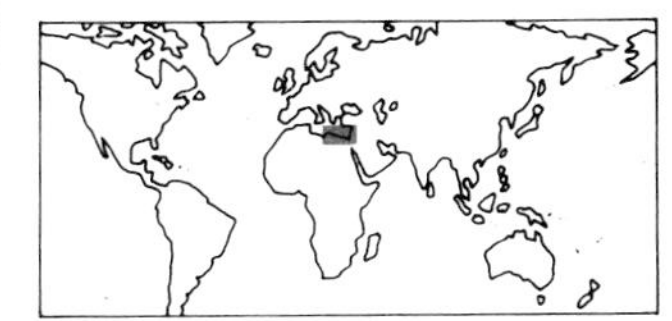

dealing direct with his divisional commanders – which is indicative of the confusion in Eighth Army's command and control that Rommel had caused.

4 February **Rommel's offensive came to a halt in front of the Gazala – Bir Hacheim Line.**
By this stage he was virtually out of fuel and not strong enough to take on the remainder of Eighth Army, which had deployed to this line and begun to fortify it. Thus ended what the horse-racing fraternity in the Eighth Army referred to as the 'Second Benghazi Handicap', the first having taken place just a year before. Although the British casualties were only some 1,400 men, more than 100 tanks had been lost, and they had been totally outfought. Rommel was now convinced that the British would not be ready for further offensive operations for some time to come. Both sides now contemplated their next move.

26 February **Churchill exhorted Auchinleck to attack once more.**
He was especially concerned over the predicament of Malta now that the airfields in western Cyrenaica had been lost. Churchill also pointed out that the longer Auchinleck delayed the more time Rommel would have to build up his strength. Auchinleck replied that his intentions were to build up an armoured striking force as quickly as possible and strengthen the Gazala Line. He wanted to improve his lines of communication by pushing the railway from Egypt towards Tobruk and to build up his supplies in the forward area. He would look for the opportunity to mount a limited operation to retake the landing grounds in the Derna–Mechili area, but not if this jeopardized the main offensive or the security of the port of Tobruk. He did not consider that he would be ready to mount a major attack before 1 June. Churchill was not pleased by this: he considered that Auchinleck was much too defensive minded and did not recognize the prime strategic importance of Malta, now under renewed Axis air attack.

The argument between the two rumbled on for the next two months. Finally, Churchill threatened to move part of the Desert Air Force to India, now coming under threat from the Japanese in Burma. Auchinleck now agreed to bring forward the date of his attack to mid-May, but then changed his mind and put it back to mid-June.

At this time there was also dissension in the Axis camp over future strategy in the Middle East. Both Rome and Berlin, unlike London, were trying to restrain their local commander. By the end of March 1942 it was decided that Malta must be seized in order to safeguard the Axis supply lines to North Africa. A plan for an Italo-German airborne and seaborne assault in the island was drawn up (Operation 'Herakles'), and the air offensive on the island was intensified. Rommel, on the other hand, believed that he had the British in Libya on the run and pleaded for reinforcements so that he could quickly drive on into Egypt and seize the Suez Canal. Hitler, however, with his eye once more on a fresh offensive in Russia, continued to regard North Africa as a low priority and would not countenance this.

Eventually, on **1 May**, Rommel received permission for a limited offensive designed to capture Tobruk. If this were a quick success he would be allowed to advance to the Egyptian frontier, where he would have to halt since all available aircraft would be needed to support 'Herakles', which was to be mounted at any time from mid-June onwards. The code-name for Rommel's attack was 'Venezia'. At some future date, though, Rommel would be allowed to continue to the Delta (Operation 'Aida').

Thus, as the Libyan spring moved into summer, both sides prepared to attack, and it was a question of who would strike first. In the meantime, the battle for Malta reached a climax.

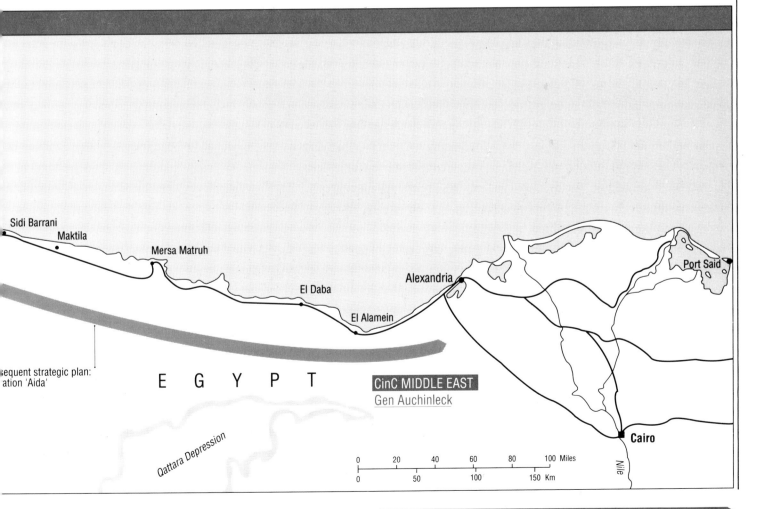

Malta Beseiged

Malta had been under virtual siege since spring 1941 and subjected to continuous air attack. Nevertheless, it had been possible in the early months to keep the island supplied through slipping merchant ships in, covered by movements of Force H and the Mediterranean Fleet. At the same time, submarines and aircraft operating from the island had caused increasing havoc among the Axis supply convoys to North Africa. Matters reached such a pitch that in the autumn Hitler, against Doenitz's advice, ordered six more U-boats to the Mediterranean and ordered the Luftwaffe in Sicily and Crete to make convoy protection rather than offensive action its prime role. This relieved the pressure on Malta, and on **21 October** the Admiralty felt confident enough to detach two cruisers from the Home Fleet and two destroyers from Force H to form Force K based at Malta.

This and the Malta-based submarines and aircraft continued to decimate the Axis convoys, and in November losses rose to a staggering 63 per cent. This loss of supplies had an influence on the outcome of Auchinleck's offensive 'Crusader' that month. However, the German U-boats suddenly had two notable successes. On **13 November** *U-81* sank the carrier *Ark Royal*. This was a devastating blow in that it left Force H with no integral air cover, and hence it could no longer escort convoys to Malta. Twelve days later *U-331* sank the battleship *Barham* of the Mediterranean Fleet. Further Axis successes followed.

2 December 1941 **Hitler issued Directive No. 38.**
This tasked Kesselring, as CinC, South, with the gaining of sea and air supremacy of the area between southern Italy and Libya and the denial of supplies to Malta and Libya. In order to do this Hitler gave him an additional air formation, Fleigerkorps II, transferred from Russia. This, together with the existing Fleigerkorps X (already in theatre), was to form Luftflotte 2. This gave the Axis a significant numerical superiority in aircraft.

Night of 13/14 December **British destroyers sank two Italian light cruisers off Cape Bon.**
Both were carrying much-needed fuel for Panzerarmee Afrika. Also on the 13th an Italian convoy had been forced to turn back when the British deceived it into believing that it was under threat from the Mediterranean Fleet. On the following day *U-557* sank the cruiser *Galatea* outside Alexandria.

Night of 18/19 December **Successful attack by Italian frogmen on warships in Alexandria harbour.**
They crippled the battleships *Valiant* and *Queen Elizabeth*, as well as a tanker and a destroyer. This meant that Cunningham had now lost all his battleships and could no longer muster a force strong enough to take on the Italian fleet. So long as the British retained the airfields in eastern Cyrenaica it was possible to infiltrate supply ships through to Malta from Egypt, but Rommel's offensive put paid to this. It meant, too, that more supplies were able to reach him across the Mediterranean.

21 December **Renewed Axis air offensive on Malta began.**
This increased in intensity as the months wore on. The Hurricanes on the island, which were the cornerstone of the defence, were gradually reduced to almost zero.

2 February 1942 **Supply convoy set out from Alexandria for Malta.**
It consisted of three fast freighters escorted by two cruisers, eight destroyers and an anti-aircraft ship. In spite of this protection, the Luftwaffe operating from Cyrenaica destroyed all three merchantmen before they could reach the island.

7 March **Force H sailed from Gibraltar with replacement aircraft for Malta.**
These were Spitfires carried on the old cruisers *Argus* and *Eagle*. Fifteen were successfully flown off and landed on the island. Sixteen more followed on **21 March** and sixteen again on **29 March**.

20 March **Kesselring launched an intensified air offensive against Malta.**
During March the Luftwaffe flew 4,927 sorties against Malta as against 2,497 in February.

22 March **Second Battle of Sirte Gulf.**
On the 20th a further four freighters had left Alexandria for Malta, escorted by three cruisers, one anti-aircraft cruiser and seventeen destroyers. This force would later be strengthened by the cruiser *Penelope* and a destroyer from Force K. The Axis were alerted, and the following night the Italian Admiral Iachino sailed from Taranto in the battleship *Littorio* with four destroyers, and Admiral Parona left Messina with three cruisers and a further four destroyers. In the late afternoon of the 22nd, after an Italian torpedo-aircraft attack had failed, Iachino's squadron engaged the convoy. This protected itself with a smokescreen, but the cruiser *Cleopatra* was damaged.

Admiral Philip Vian, commanding the escort, now sent his destroyers in a torpedo attack on *Littorio*. By now it was getting dark, and Iachino turned away and sailed for home. Next day the convoy came under concentrated air attack when approaching Malta. One freighter was sunk and one disabled, but the other two made port at Valletta, only to be sunk there on the 26th. Of the 26,000 tons of supplies sent from Egypt only 5,000 were eventually unloaded in Malta.

Attacks on the Malta docks meant that all surface warships had to be evacuated, leaving just two damaged destroyers and the cruiser *Penelope*. The former were totally destroyed, but on **8 April** the bomb-pocked *Penelope* managed to limp to Gibraltar.

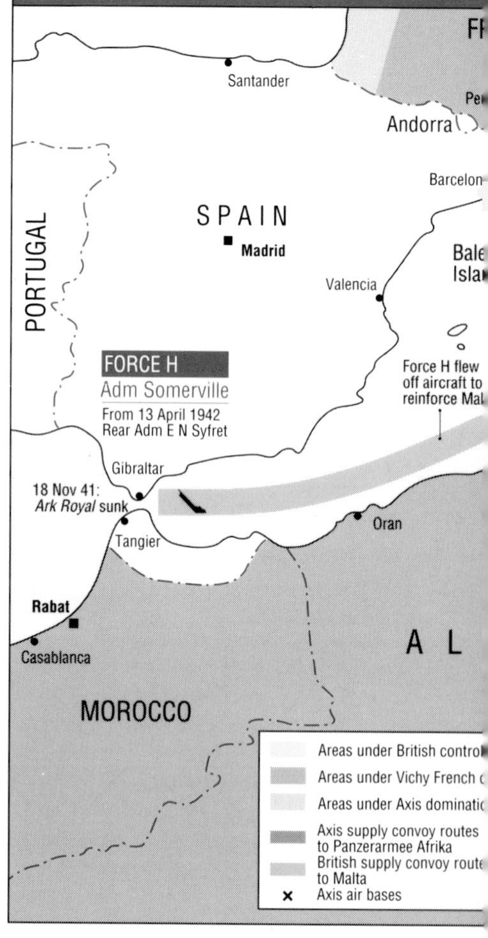

16 April **King George VI awarded Malta the George Cross.**
This was in recognition of the manner in which the Maltese people had stood up to the incessant bombing and constant shortages of the past twelve months.

20 April **The US carrier *Wasp* flew in 46 Spitfires to Malta.**
Such, however, was the intensity of the Axis air effort (9,599 sorties were flown against the island in April) that almost all had been destroyed on the ground within three days.

26 April **Cunningham ordered the withdrawal of the 10th Submarine Flotilla from Malta.**
This was forced by the bombing and mines laid both from the air and by German E-boats. By this time Kesselring believed that Malta had been neutralized. He had also been pressured to release some of his aircraft to Russia. The Italians took a more pessimistic view.

P60 · Wavell Under Pressure

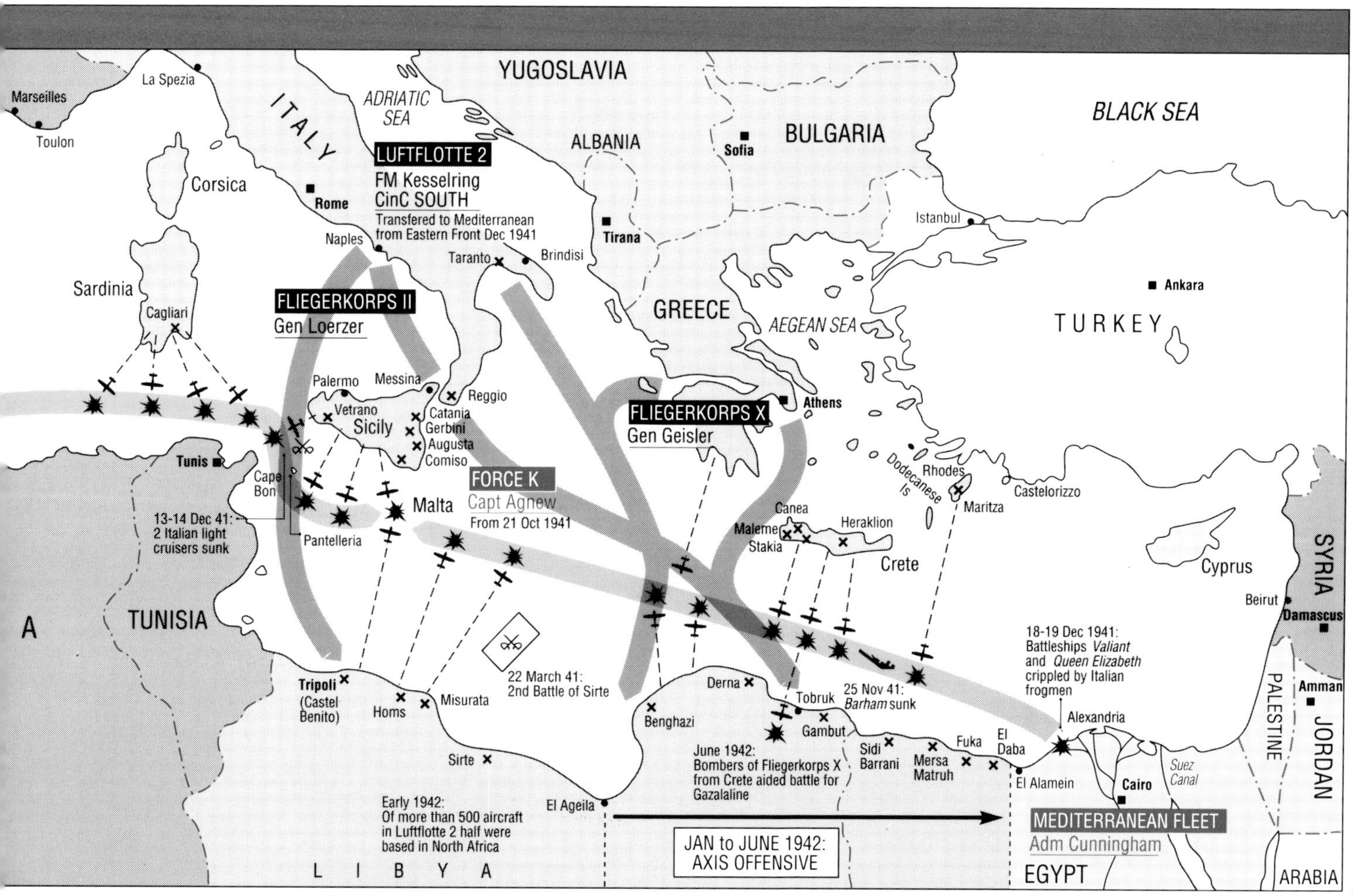

Marseilles
Toulon
La Spezia
Corsica
Sardinia
Cagliari
ITALY
Rome
Naples
ADRIATIC SEA
YUGOSLAVIA
LUFTFLOTTE 2
FM Kesselring
CinC SOUTH
Transfered to Mediterranean from Eastern Front Dec 1941
Taranto
Brindisi
ALBANIA
Tirana
Sofia
BULGARIA
BLACK SEA
Istanbul
Ankara
TURKEY
GREECE
AEGEAN SEA
FLIEGERKORPS II
Gen Loerzer
Palermo
Messina
Reggio
Vetrano
Sicily
Catania
Gerbini
Augusta
Comiso
FLIEGERKORPS X
Gen Geisler
Athens
Tunis
Cape Bon
13-14 Dec 41: 2 Italian light cruisers sunk
Pantelleria
Malta
FORCE K
Capt Agnew
From 21 Oct 1941
Dodecanese Is
Rhodes
Castelorizzo
Maritza
Canea
Maleme
Stakia
Heraklion
Crete
Cyprus
SYRIA
Beirut
Damascus
A
TUNISIA
22 March 41: 2nd Battle of Sirte
Tripoli (Castel Benito)
Homs
Misurata
Derna
Benghazi
Tobruk
25 Nov 41: *Barham* sunk
Gambut
18-19 Dec 1941: Battleships *Valiant* and *Queen Elizabeth* crippled by Italian frogmen
Alexandria
PALESTINE
Amman
JORDAN
Sirte
June 1942: Bombers of Fliegerkorps X from Crete aided battle for Gazalaline
Sidi Barrani
Mersa Matruh
Fuka
El Daba
El Alamein
Cairo
Suez Canal
Early 1942: Of more than 500 aircraft in Luftflotte 2 half were based in North Africa
El Ageila
JAN to JUNE 1942: AXIS OFFENSIVE
MEDITERRANEAN FLEET
Adm Cunningham
EGYPT
ARABIA
L I B Y A

30 April **Hitler and Mussolini agreed that the capture of Malta ('Herakles') should take place on 10 July.**

This was to be after Rommel had recaptured Tobruk.

9 May **Sixty Spitfires landed in Malta from *Wasp* and *Eagle*.**

10 May **Kesselring declared that Malta's neutralization was complete.**

But that same day the Axis air forces found themselves outnumbered for the first time in the skies above Malta. They lost twelve aircraft as against three Spitfires. This marked a definite turning-point in the fortunes of Malta. Enemy air activity noticeably slackened, but the desperate shortage of fuel and food remained, as did the Axis intention to invade the island.

Attention now turned to Libya, where on **26 May** Rommel attacked again. By this time British aircraft strength on Malta had increased sufficiently for the risk of sending in further supplies by sea to be worthwhile once more.

11 June **Simultaneous convoys set out for Malta from Gibraltar and Alexandria.**

The Gibraltar convoy (code-name 'Harpoon') consisted of five freighters and a US tanker. It was escorted initially by a battleship, two carriers, three cruisers and eight destroyers and then, for the final and most vulnerable stage, by an anti-aircraft cruiser and nine destroyers. The Alexandria convoy ('Vigorous') had eleven freighters escorted by seven light cruisers and 26 destroyers.

14 June **First Axis attacks on 'Harpoon' and 'Vigorous'.**

'Harpoon' lost one freighter and a cruiser damaged to Axis aircraft off the Tunisian coast. The carriers turned back to Gibraltar as planned. 'Vigorous' passed out of air cover range in the late afternoon and lost two freighters. Another had been sent back to Alexandria as she was too slow.

15 June **Repeated air and sea attacks on 'Harpoon' and 'Vigorous'.**

An Italian naval squadron intercepted 'Harpoon' and disabled two destroyers, as well as damaging the anti-aircraft cruiser *Cairo*. One Italian destroyer was lost. Aircraft then attacked and sank two freighters, the tanker *Kentucky* and one destroyer. Another Italian squadron had sailed from Taranto to intercept 'Vigorous'. As a result the latter reversed course in the early hours. While it was doing so, German E-boats sank a destroyer and damaged a cruiser with torpedoes. Torpedo-aircraft from Malta attacked the Italian ships and disabled a cruiser, which was later sunk by a submarine. In the meantime, 'Vigorous' turned towards Malta once more, but reports that the Italians were continuing to steam south caused another course reversal. German Stukas now damaged another cruiser and sank a destroyer. The Italian squadron turned north to cover Malta, but Vian, commanding 'Vigorous', decided that he did not have enough ammunition left to turn west once more and continued back to Alexandria. In the process *U-205* sank the cruiser *Hermione* and Stukas accounted for another destroyer. Malta-based aircraft did, however, torpedo the battleship *Littorio*; she was under repair for two months.

The failure of these two convoys was a severe reverse for the British, and matters were to become worse for Malta when on **26 June** Cavallero directed that additional aircraft be returned from Libya to Sicily to step up attacks on the island. Furthermore, on **30 June** the submarine depot ship *Medway* was sunk by *U-372*; the loss of the torpedo stocks she carried put a severe brake on British submarine operations in the Mediterranean.

Rommel Repulsed · P116

Rommel's Third Offensive

Ritchie's Gazala Line consisted of a number of wired-in, brigade-size defensive 'boxes' stretching 40 miles southwards from Gazala to Bir Hacheim, which was held by the Free French. Extensive minefields covered the flanks and front of each box. There was, however, a weakness in this layout in that neighbouring boxes were not near enough to one another to be able to provide mutually supporting direct fire. Responsibility for holding the Gazala Line was given to XIII Corps, now commanded by General 'Strafer' Gott, a distinguished desert veteran.

Apart from the infantry tanks, which were under XIII Corps, the bulk of the armour was with XXX Corps (General Willoughby Norrie). Auchinleck had wanted this kept concentrated, but Ritchie, worried about his supply dumps (which were forward, since Eighth Army was itself preparing to attack), insisted that Norrie keep his armoured formations dispersed to cover them. This was to prove another weakness.

Rommel had had plenty of time to reconnoitre the Gazala Line. Rather than try to break through it frontally, he decided to take his armour round the southern flank at Bir Hacheim while the Italian infantry masked the Line itself. By the last week in May he considered that he had built up his supplies sufficiently and that the time to launch 'Venezia' had arrived. In terms of strength he had 560 tanks, with a further 77 in reserve, as against the Eighth Army with 563 cruiser tanks and, with XIII Corps, 276 infantry tanks. Axis air power, thanks to the reinforcements received during the winter and poor serviceability in the Desert Air Force, was significantly superior – 497 aircraft against 190.

26 May 1942 Rommel began his approach march.
In the evening he set out for the south and was soon spotted. Ritchie believed this move was a feint and was convinced that Rommel would make his main attack in the centre of the Gazala Line.

27–28 May Rommel pushed north-east of the Gazala Line.
This period was marked by much tank fighting as the DAK engaged elements of 7th Armoured and then 1st Armoured Divisions. Tank losses were high on both sides, but the British armour became increasingly scattered. The Italian Ariete Armoured Division met stiff resistance from the Free French at Bir Hacheim, while the Trieste Motorized Division, because of a navigation error, found itself grinding through minefields, not covered by fire, further north. Rommel, however, was beginning to run out of fuel, and his tanks were likewise becoming scattered. In order to get his supply lines working he decided to punch through the Gazala Line.

31 May Opening of the Battle of the 'Cauldron'.
Rommel's target was the box held by 150 Brigade (British 50th Division). The Italians attacked from the west and elements of the DAK from the east. The remainder of DAK had, in the meantime, taken up defensive positions and were repulsing armoured counter-attacks. Ritchie, was hampered by his inability to concentrate his tanks, and was unable to relieve 150 Brigade because of Rommel's anti-tank guns.

2 June Rommel overran the Cauldron.
This enabled him to get his supplies flowing and he now turned his attention to reducing Bir Hacheim with 90th Light and the Trieste divisions. He also distracted Ritchie by sending 21st Panzer Division to operate in the Acroma area.

5 June Ritchie launched counter-attack 'Aberdeen' against the Cauldron.
His plan was to destroy Rommel's armour here and cut his supply lines. It went disastrously wrong. An infantry tank brigade was destroyed in minefields, and an Indian Infantry Brigade attacked the wrong positions, leaving the third element of the counter-attack force, 22 Armoured Brigade, to be repulsed easily by the untouched defences.

Auchinleck and Ritchie, with the remainder of 50th Division and 1st South African Division still firm in the northern part of the Line, decided to wait for Rommel to attack once more. Their remaining forces were now facing south along the line from the Knightsbridge Box to El Adem.

11 June Bir Hacheim finally fell.
The resistance of the Free French, totally cut off since the opening of 'Venezia', had been especially gallant.

11–13 June Battle of Knightsbridge.
Rommel, having brought up reserve tanks, could now muster 124 against 248 British, and attacked between Knightsbridge and El Adem. He trapped much of the remaining British armour in Knightsbridge and destroyed it.

This threatened the main British supply route along the Trigh Capuzzo and 50th and 1st South African Divisions, still in the Gazala Line. Without informing Auchinleck, who wanted him to hold west

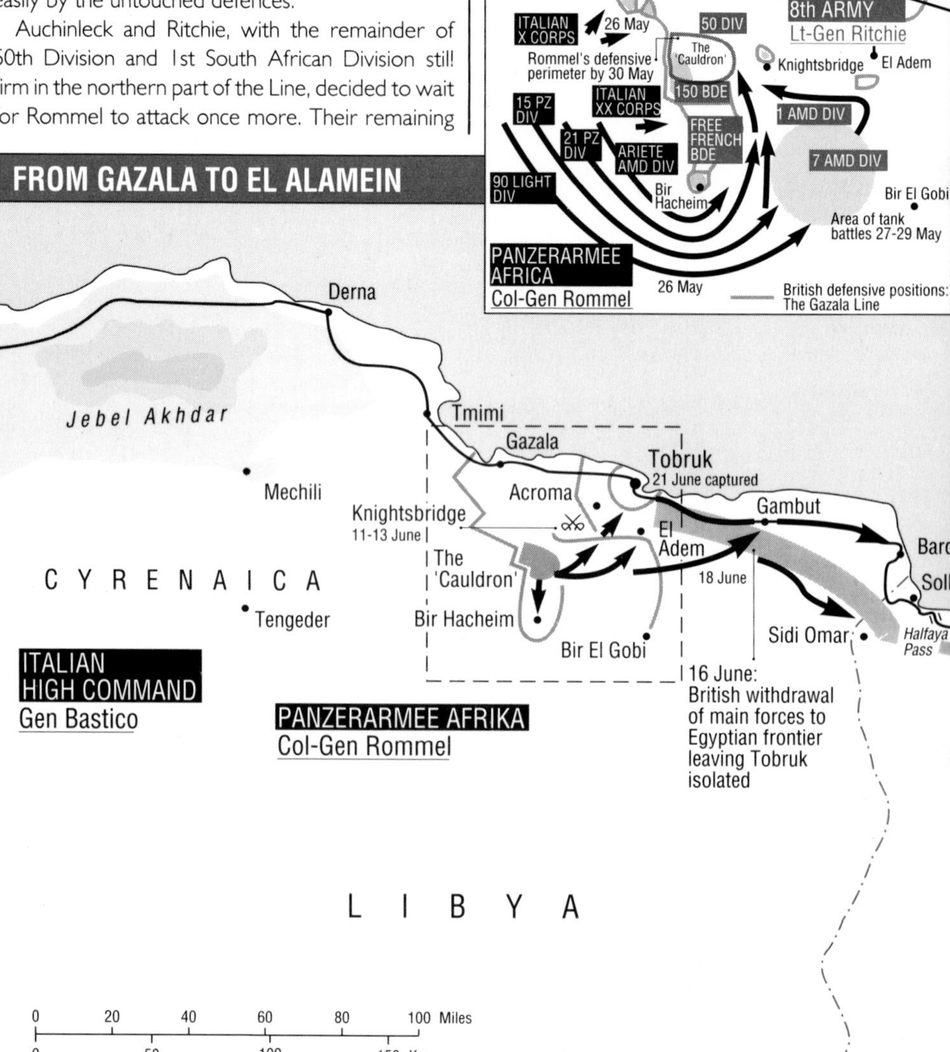

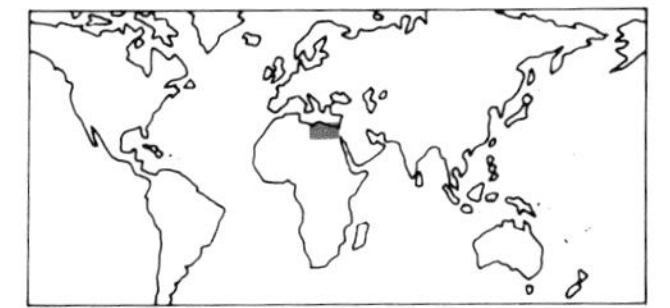

of Tobruk, Ritchie ordered these two divisions back to the Egyptian frontier.

14 June Auchinleck told Ritchie that Tobruk must be held.
Churchill reiterated this to Auchinleck. Eighth Army now held the line Acroma – El Adem – Bir El Gobi. Rommel attacked it the following day, but was repulsed. However, Norrie, who was holding it, feared that he lacked sufficient tanks to keep Rommel at bay for more than a short time.

16 June Ritchie allowed Norrie to withdraw.
This had the effect of peeling back the outer defences of Tobruk, whose defences had been allowed to deteriorate during the winter. Norrie withdrew to Mersa Matruh to re-equip, leaving Gott to hold the frontier.

18 June Rommel isolated Tobruk.
This was effected by cutting the coast road at Gambut. The speed of his advance took the garrison of Tobruk, which was built round 2nd South African Division, by surprise. Its predicament was made worse because the loss of forward landing grounds meant that the Desert Air Force could give little support. Rommel then launched a surprise attack from the south-east – an unexpected quarter.

21 June Rommel captured Tobruk.
Churchill later referred to this as 'one of the heaviest blows I can recall during the war' and had to ward off a censure motion in the House of Commons.

23 June Rommel resumed his advance eastwards.
On the same day he signalled Kesselring requesting permission not to halt on the frontier but to continue into Egypt, pointing out that he had captured large stocks of *matériel* in Tobruk.

25 June Auchinleck relieved Ritchie and took charge of the Eighth Army himself.
Ritchie's intention had been to stage a 'do or die' defence at Mersa Matruh. Auchinleck saw the priority as keeping the Eighth Army in being whatever happened. He therefore intended to hold Rommel on the El Alamein Line and, if this failed, to fight on the Suez Canal and then in Palestine.

26 June Rommel began to attack at Mersa Matruh.
Kesselring, Cavallero (Italian Chief of Staff in Rome) and Bastico (Italian CinC in Libya) arrived at Rommel's HQ and gave him grudging permission to continue into Egypt.

27 June Rommel began to outflank the Mersa Matruh position.
The British began to withdraw, as radio intercepts had indicated to Rommel that they would.

28 June Rommel captured Fuqa.
By now there was increasing confusion in the Eighth Army.

29 June Rommel secured Mersa Matruh.
Further large quantities of supplies fell into his hands. Meanwhile, Mussolini arrived in Libya to prepare for his triumphant entry into Cairo, while confusion increased as British and Axis columns intermingled with one another in a mad dash eastwards.

30 June The Eighth Army was back on the El Alamein line.
Such was the perceived threat to the Suez Canal that on this day the Mediterranean Fleet left Alexandria (where the port facilities were prepared for demolition) for Haifa, Port Said and Beirut. In Cairo, in what became known as 'Ash Wednesday', British HQs began to destroy classified papers and prepared for evacuation to Palestine.

The Eighth Army, 'brave but baffled' and in desperate need of reorganization, now prepared for Rommel's next attack, which Ultra had told them would come the following day.

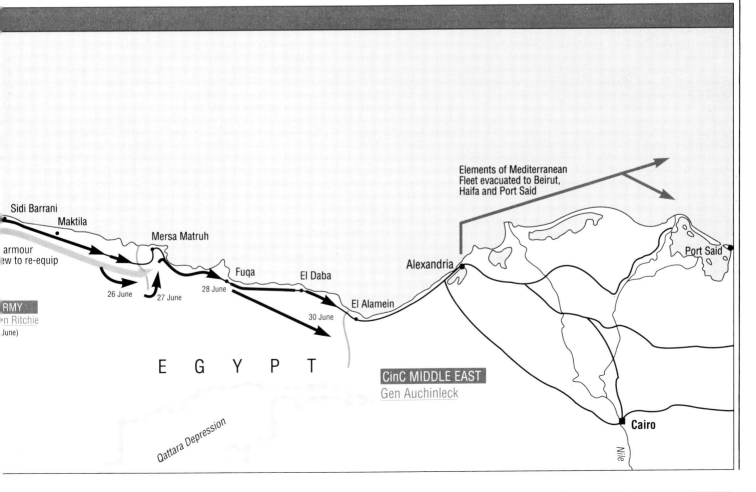

Kharkov and the Crimea

PREPARATIONS FOR THE CAUCASUS OFFENSIVE

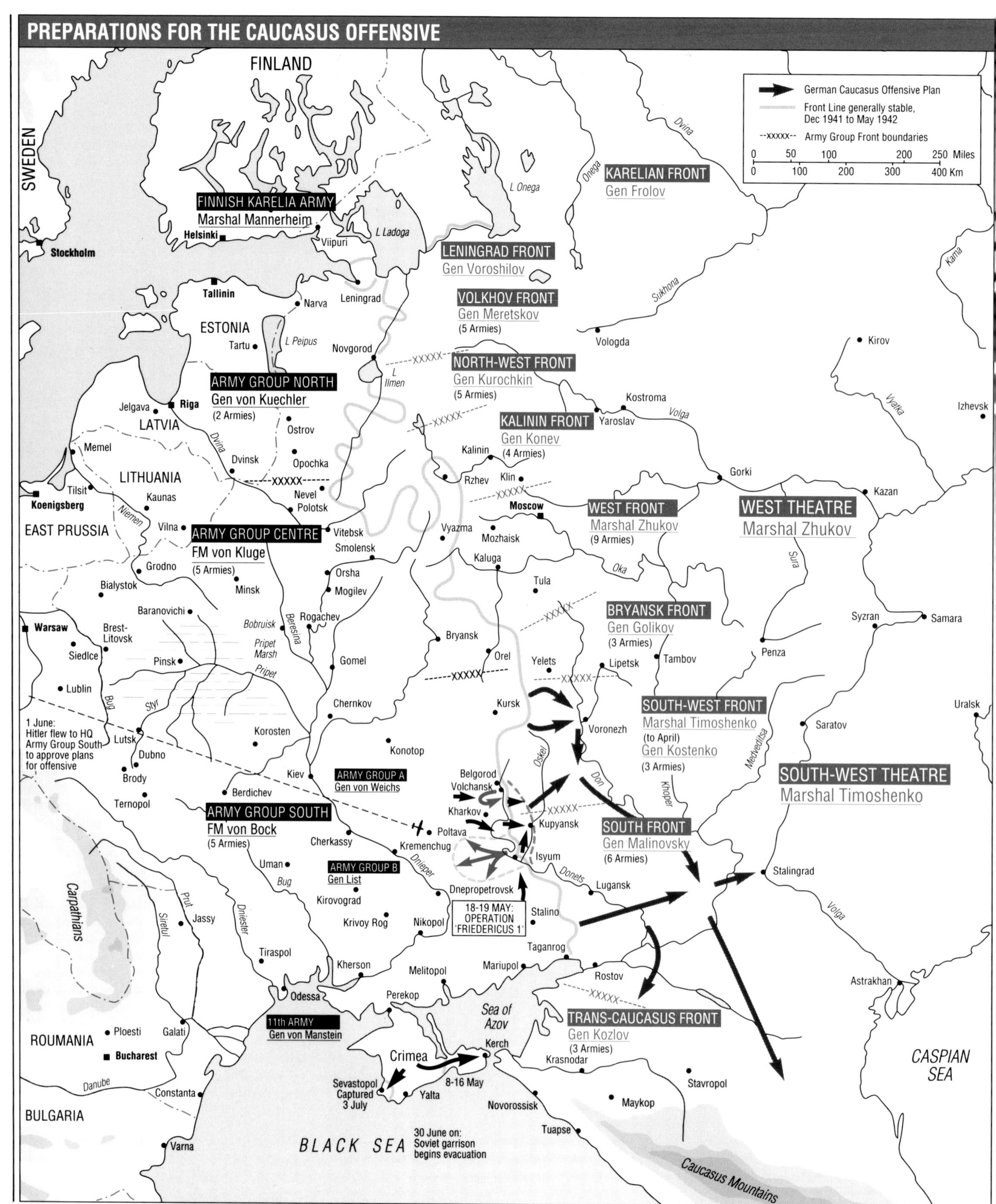
German Caucasus Offensive Plan
Front Line generally stable, Dec 1941 to May 1942
--xxxxx-- Army Group Front boundaries
0 50 100 200 250 Miles
0 100 200 300 400 Km
FINLAND
SWEDEN
FINNISH KARELIA ARMY
Marshal Mannerheim
Helsinki
Stockholm
Viipuri
L Ladoga
L Onega
KARELIAN FRONT
Gen Frolov
LENINGRAD FRONT
Gen Voroshilov
VOLKHOV FRONT
Gen Meretskov
(5 Armies)
Tallinin
Narva
Leningrad
ESTONIA
Tartu
L Peipus
Novgorod
L Ilmen
NORTH-WEST FRONT
Gen Kurochkin
(5 Armies)
ARMY GROUP NORTH
Gen von Kuechler
(2 Armies)
Jelgava
Riga
LATVIA
Ostrov
Opochka
Dvinsk
Memel
LITHUANIA
Tilsit
Koenigsberg
Kaunas
Nevel
Polotsk
EAST PRUSSIA
Vilna
ARMY GROUP CENTRE
FM von Kluge
(5 Armies)
Vitebsk
Smolensk
Orsha
Mogilev
Grodno
Minsk
Bialystok
Baranovichi
Rogachev
Bobruisk
Beresina
Warsaw
Brest-Litovsk
Siedlce
Pinsk
Pripet Marsh
Pripet
Lublin
Bug
Styr
Gomel
Chernkov
1 June: Hitler flew to HQ Army Group South to approve plans for offensive
Lutsk
Dubno
Brody
Ternopol
Korosten
Kiev
Berdichev
ARMY GROUP SOUTH
FM von Bock
(5 Armies)
ARMY GROUP A
Gen von Weichs
ARMY GROUP B
Gen List
Konotop
Cherkassy
Uman
Bug
Kirovograd
Krivoy Rog
Nikopol
Kremenchug
Dnieper
Poltava
Kharkov
Belgorod
Volchansk
Kupyansk
Isyum
Dnepropetrovsk
18-19 MAY: OPERATION 'FRIEDERICUS 1'
Stalino
Taganrog
Mariupol
Melitopol
Kherson
Tiraspol
Odessa
Perekop
Carpathians
Prut
Siretul
Dniester
Jassy
ROUMANIA
Ploesti
Galati
Bucharest
Danube
Constanta
BULGARIA
Varna
11th ARMY
Gen von Manstein
Crimea
Sevastopol Captured 3 July
Yalta
8-16 May
Kerch
Sea of Azov
BLACK SEA
30 June on: Soviet garrison begins evacuation
Novorossisk
Tuapse
Krasnodar
Maykop
Stavropol
Caucasus Mountains
CASPIAN SEA
Astrakhan
Rostov
TRANS-CAUCASUS FRONT
Gen Kozlov
(3 Armies)
Lugansk
Donets
SOUTH FRONT
Gen Malinovsky
(6 Armies)
Stalingrad
Volga
Don
Khoper
Medveditsa
Oskel
Voronezh
SOUTH-WEST FRONT
Marshal Timoshenko
(to April)
Gen Kostenko
(3 Armies)
SOUTH-WEST THEATRE
Marshal Timoshenko
Saratov
Uralsk
Kursk
Yelets
Lipetsk
Tambov
Penza
Syzran
Samara
Orel
Bryansk
BRYANSK FRONT
Gen Golikov
(3 Armies)
Tula
Kaluga
Oka
Vyazma
Mozhaisk
Moscow
WEST FRONT
Marshal Zhukov
(9 Armies)
WEST THEATRE
Marshal Zhukov
Sura
Rzhev
Klin
Kalinin
KALININ FRONT
Gen Konev
(4 Armies)
Yaroslav
Kostroma
Volga
Gorki
Kazan
Vologda
Sukhona
Onega
Dvina
Kama
Kirov
Vyatka
Izhevsk

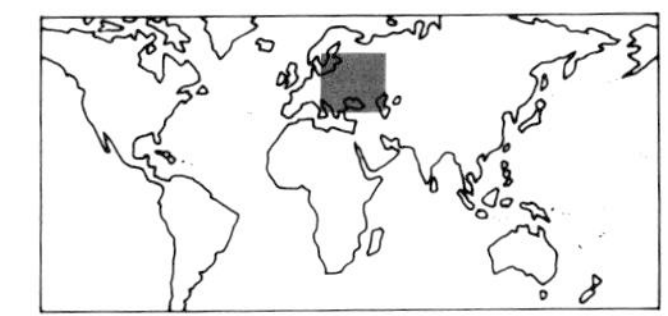

In spite of the reverse in front of Moscow the previous December and the hard fighting to hold off the Soviet counter-offensives during the first few months of 1942, Hitler remained determined to bring Russia to her knees. Thus there would be another major German offensive in summer 1942. This time, however, instead of attacking Moscow once more, as some of his generals recommended, Hitler decided to seize the cornerstone of the Soviet economy – the rich industrial area between the Rivers Donets and Volga in the Ukraine, and the Caucasian oilfields.

5 April 1942 Hitler issued Directive No. 41 for the summer offensive in Russia.
Conduct of the main offensive was given to von Bock, commanding Army Group South. An attack launched north of Kharkov was to proceed south-east between the Donets and the Don. This would link-up with a second thrust towards the junction of the Donets and Don, whereupon the axis of advance would turn southwards into the Caucasus, which would be overrun. A subsidiary thrust would also drive east to Stalingrad, whose capture would provide flank protection for the drive into the Caucasus. In order to simplify von Bock's command and control, two new commands were formed under him: Army Group A (Maximilian von Weichs) and Army Group B (Siegmund List).

The other main objectives for 1942 were to be the capture of Leningrad and linking-up with the Finns. The central part of the front was to remain on the defensive. Before the main attack in the Caucasus, however, two preliminaries had to be achieved. The Crimea was to be cleared and the salient created by the Russians during their attack south of Kharkov had to be eradicated.

8 May Von Manstein's Eleventh Army attacked in the Crimea.
The primary object was to clear the Kerch Peninsula so that it could be used eventually as a spring-board into the Caucasus. This was achieved on **16 May** and von Manstein now turned his attention to seizing Sevastapol, which had been under siege since the previous October.

12 May Soviet offensive south of Kharkov.
Stalin and his commanders had been convinced that the Germans would strike again at Moscow, but he himself wanted to maintain the active defence of constant attacks along the whole front to keep the Germans off balance. Thus, when Semyon Timoshenko, commanding the South-West Theatre, proposed in March to mount an offensive from the salient he had earlier gained south of Kharkov, Stalin did not object. Two fronts were to be used, South and South-West, but Stalin would not allow Timoshenko to use the Bryansk Front as well, since he wanted it as a reserve to cover the approaches to Moscow from the south.

Timoshenko's attack took the Germans by surprise while they were preparing for their own blow to remove the Isyum salient. This was to be launched by Friedrich Paulus's Sixth Army on **18 May** under the code-name 'Fridericus I'. Consequently, Timoshenko was initially very successful and drove Sixth Army back across the River Orel. Hitler's answer was to bring 'Fridericus I' forward. This was helped by the fact that the Soviet offensive, instead of increasing in momentum, began to falter because of faulty intelligence as to the location of the German Panzer reserves.

18 May German counter-stroke into the Isyum salient.
Group von Kleist, with fifteen divisions (including two Panzer and one motorized) attacked from the south. By this stage Kostenko's South-West Front, which was leading the Soviet attack, had become detached from Malinovsky's South Front.

AXIS GROUND FORCES, June 1942

EASTERN FRONT	
German 167 divisions	Italian 6 divisions
Roumanian 12 divisions	Spanish 1 division
Hungarian 10 divisions	Slovak 1 division
FINLAND	
Finnish 17 divisions	German 5 divisions
NORWAY	
German 12 divisions	
FRANCE AND LOW COUNTRIES	
German 26 divisions	
BALKANS	
Italian 12 divisions	German 5 divisions
NORTH AFRICA	
Italian 8 divisions	German 3 divisions

The German attack fell on the South Front, sweeping it aside and capturing Izyum and Barvenkova the following day. Counter-attacks organized by Timoshenko failed. Stalin nevertheless ordered Kostenko to continue his attack on Paulus. By the 19th, now virtually isolated, he was forced to halt. Paulus now began to attack from the north.

22 May Paulus and von Kleist linked up.
Kostenko was now trapped.

29 May 'Fridericus I' completed.
German casualties in the fighting around Kharkov were some 20,000 while the Soviets lost in prisoners alone 214,000 men as well as 1,200 tanks and 2,000 guns.

1 June Hitler flew to HQ Army Group South at Poltava and approved von Bock's plan for the main offensive.
A high-level deception plan had been prepared to make the Russians believe that Moscow was still the objective. Goebbels organized leakages to this effect to the foreign press while von Kluge, still commanding Army Group Centre, made overt preparations for an offensive under the cover-name of 'Kremlin'.

Two more preliminary operations were agreed before the main offensive got under way. A small salient at Volchansk, north of Kharkov, was to be cleared, as was the area south-east of Kharkov to Kupyansk on the River Oskel.

2 June Von Manstein opened his attack on Sevastapol.
It began with a massive five-day bombardment, which included super-heavy siege artillery, and the infantry assault began on **7 June.** The Russian troops defended tenaciously.

10–15 June Paulus successfully cleared the Volchansk pocket.

19 June Plans for the Caucasus offensive fell into Soviet hands.
They were being carried, against orders, by a staff officer of 23rd Panzer Division in a light aircraft, which was shot down. The corps commander, General Stumme (XL Corps), and his chief of staff were immediately sacked and imprisoned on Hitler's orders. Stumme was later released and died at the Second Battle of El Alamein. Hitler did not, however, order any changes to the plan. The Russians considered the captured plan authentic, but believed that it was only a subsidiary thrust and that Moscow was still the main objective.

22–26 June German advance to and capture of Kupyansk.
By this time the South-West Theatre was in ruins and quite inadequate to face the German offensive.

30 June The Soviet garrison began to leave Sevastapol by sea.
Such had been the ferocity of the Russian resistance that von Manstein had had to call for reinforcements from Seventeenth Army to help him. He lost some 24,000 men and in the end relied on bombing and artillery fire to achieve final victory. By the time the port was totally secured on **3 July** 90,000 Russian prisoners had been captured.

So impressed was Hitler with von Manstein that, besides promoting him, he ordered his army north to undertake the reduction of Leningrad, thus cancelling the plan to move it across the Kerch Strait into the Caucasus.

By the time that Sevastapol fell, von Bock's main offensive was already under way. With Rommel's continuing success in North Africa, Hitler now believed that he could wrest the entire Middle East from the British by double envelopment through the Caucasus and across the Suez Canal. Overall victory seemed within his grasp.

German Drive into the Caucasus · P110

The Holocaust

The darkest shadow that lies over the history of Hitler's Germany is undoubtedly the Nazi treatment of the Jews. Even today, more than forty years after the end of the Second World War, the effects are still felt.

Hitler himself always said that he developed his personal hatred for the Jewish race when he was in Vienna before the First World War. The Jews were also a convenient scapegoat for the 'stab in the back' of 1918 and this view became a major plank in the Nazi Party platform.

On 1 April 1933, within a month of coming to power, Hitler made his first move against the Jews, proclaiming a national boycott of Jewish shops. By the end of that year the Jews had been banned from holding public office and from the civil service, teaching, farming and the arts. From then on life for the German Jews became more and more difficult and an increasing number began to leave the country.

20 March 1933 First Concentration Camp opened.

This was Dachau, which was set up to house Hitler's political opponents, especially the Communists, but quickly began to include Jews among its inmates. By August 1937 it had been joined by Sachsenhausen, Buchenwald and, for women, Lichtenburg. A year later, in order to cater for Austrian prisoners, another camp was opened at Mauthausen.

15 September 1935 Institution of the Nuremberg Laws.

Gradually persecution of the Jews increased. In 1934 the stock exchanges were prohibited to them and the following year came the promulgation of the Nuremberg Laws. These deprived the Jews of full German citizenship – from henceforth they merely had the status of 'subjects' – and forbade marriage and sexual relations between Jews and Aryans. Later the medical and legal professions would also be banned to the Jews.

9–10 November 1938 Crystal Night.

As a result of the murder of a German diplomat by a Polish Jew in Paris there was officially sanctioned and widespread looting of Jewish property, burning of synagogues and even murder of Jews in what became known as Crystal Night. Thereafter all Jews left in Germany – half the 600,000 Jewish population emigrated during the 1930s – were forced to wear a prominent yellow star on their breast, something which would soon apply to all Jews in Occupied Europe.

After the Germans overran Poland in September 1939 they found themselves with an additional three million Jews on their hands. As yet they had no formal extermination policy and began to move the Jews eastwards, at the same time driving them into ghettoes, the largest of which was in Warsaw. In their place they planned to move in ethnic Germans from the Russian-occupied Baltic states.

Victory in the west resulted in many more Jews coming under Nazi rule and at one time there was a plan to settle 500,000 on the island of Madagascar.

Very quickly the Nazi hierarchy realized that the Jews, whom they had always considered expendable, were an ideal source of slave labour. The number of concentration camps rapidly increased, not just in Germany and Poland but also in other countries. Deaths from malnutrition, disease and indiscriminate shootings began to rise steeply. Within the occupied countries some Gentiles risked their lives to shelter Jews and hide them from the Germans. Others sided with the occupying forces to both betray and help round up Jews for transportation to the east.

17 July 1941 Heydrich's *Einsatzgruppen* order.

The invasion of Russia in June 1941 served to increase radically the Jewish problem for the Nazis. The Jewish population here was five million. There were also the Russian Communists with which to contend. Accordingly Himmler formed SS *Einsatzgruppen* (Action Squads) in early 1941. The orders for their activities in occupied Russia were signed by Reinhard Heydrich, head of the secret police, four weeks after the invasion of Russia had begun. They were to kill all Jews, Communists and agitators.

NON-EUROPEAN COUNTRIES ACCEPTING JEWISH REFUGEES

Country	Number
USA	170,000
Palestine	100,000
Argentina	28,000
Brazil	23,000
China (Shanghai)	18,000
Paraguay	17,000
Chile	12,000
Uruguay	11,000
Australia	9,000
Canada	8,000
South Africa	6,000

15 September 1941 First use of gas as an extermination weapon.

The *Einsatzgruppen* carried out murder by shooting and it soon became clear that the numbers were too great to achieve the mass extermination of the Jews in the East by this means. As a more 'efficient' alternative it was decided to experiment with poison gas. The first such atrocity took place at Auschwitz, in Poland, the most notorious camp of all, using Zyklon B, which had been supplied for disinfectant purposes and was in fact Hydrogen Cyanide.

20 January Wannsee Conference.

The formal adoption of the mass extermination policy or 'Final Solution of the Jewish Problem', as it was euphemistically called, did not become fact until a conference was convened by Heydrich in the Wannsee suburb of Berlin to co-ordinate the efforts of all the relevant departments. In essence, all Jews in Occupied Europe were to be transported to the East. The able-bodied were to be worked until they died, while the remainder were to be put to death.

The direct result of the Wannsee Conference was that a new type of concentration camp was introduced, the extermination camp. Beginning with Auschwitz, these were set up in Poland and occupied Russia and their sole purpose was mass slaughter of Jews. Gas chambers were built and crematoria for disposing of the corpses. The gas chambers themselves were disguised as shower rooms, with the gas being piped through the shower nozzles. It was only after they had stripped and the outer doors had been locked shut that the victims realized what was happening. Death seldom took more than a minute. All valuables, including even gold teeth, were extracted from the victims and sent to swell the Nazi coffers.

Some Jews, and Russian prisoners of war, were also subjected to bizarre medical experiments before they died. These included sterilization, high altitude and extreme cold tests.

As the war went on so the daily rate of extermination increased. By the beginning of 1944 6,000 Jews a day were being murdered at Auschwitz alone. By this time the Allies were well aware of what was going on and, indeed, had been so since mid-1942. Yet, in many cases the information was sketchy and in others it was hard to believe the enormity of the crime that was being committed.

The Nazis themselves did everything possible to keep the mechanics of the Final Solution secret, but, in order to counter Allied accusations, they also began a propaganda campaign. This was based on the ghetto at Theresienstadt in northern Czechoslovakia. Here the Jewish inmates lived a seemingly idyllic existence with reasonable food and their own local government. Indeed, the Nazis tried to create a holiday camp atmosphere. At the beginning of 1944 the German Propaganda Ministry even made a film of it. For the inmates, however, their stay was only temporary before they were forced to board the transports bound for the extermination camps in the East.

The camps elsewhere remained straightforward concentration camps. They housed not just Jews, but opponents of the Nazi regime, gypsies, Allied agents, members of the Resistance and common criminals. The SS camp authorities often used the last-named category as warders and they were as brutal as the SS guards. There was no deliberate attempt to murder the inmates of these camps, but lack of attention, disease, especially typhus, and general maltreatment all contributed to an ever sharply rising death toll.

At the beginning of 1945, when it became clear that the war was lost, Himmler ordered the evacua-

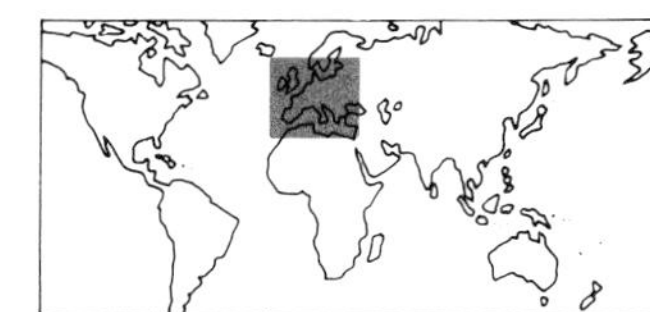

CONCENTRATION CAMPS IN EUROPE

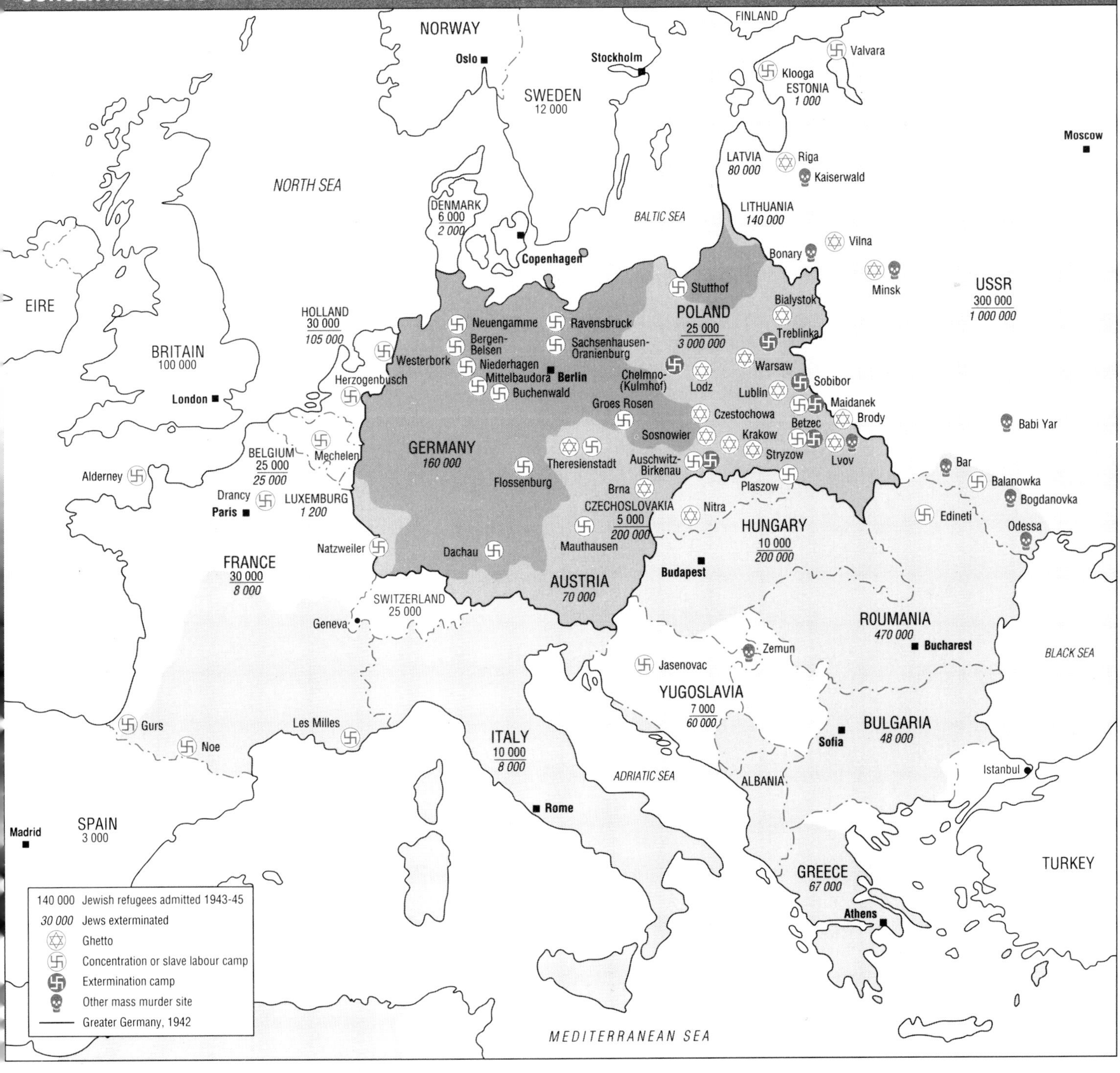

140 000 Jewish refugees admitted 1943-45
30 000 Jews exterminated
Ghetto
Concentration or slave labour camp
Extermination camp
Other mass murder site
Greater Germany, 1942

tion of the extermination camps in the East and their destruction. Many of the inmates were force-marched westwards and a considerable number of these died *en route*, either murdered by their guards, or being too weak to face the rigours of the winter. Those who did arrive at concentration camps in the western part of Germany merely added to the overcrowded conditions and accelerated the death rate, often because the camp administration simply could not cope. Some, however, did survive to be liberated by the Allies. It was their testimony coupled with the fact that the SS bureaucracy dictated that only a small portion of the written records could be destroyed, that enabled the Allies to establish precisely what had taken place during the Nazi occupation of Europe.

In spite of awareness of the existence of the concentration camps, the Allied troops who liberated the camps were horrified and deeply shocked by what they saw, which surpassed their wildest imaginings. Those who were responsible and who ran the camps became the prime targets of the Allied war crimes jurisdiction.

No one knows for sure how many perished in the Nazi concentration camps. Figures for Jews alone range between five and six million, or just about half the pre-war Jewish population of Europe. To these must be added many hundreds of thousands of Gentiles. What is clear, though, is that the Holocaust, as it has been dubbed, was one of the greatest crimes that the world has ever known. There has never been a starker example of man's inhumanity to man.

War Crimes Trials · P119

Resistance in Occupied Europe

The degree of resistance to occupation by Axis forces and the forms that it took varied very much from country to country. For it to blossom there were two essential prerequisites. The resisters had to believe in eventual victory, which could only be achieved through liberation by the forces of the Free World; and they had to have outside support from the same source.

This latter requirement had been recognized very early on by the British when they created the Special Operations Executive (SOE) in July 1940. In May 1942 the Americans formed a similar organization, the Office of Strategic Services (OSS), under William J. Donovan. The resistance they planned to engender had two roles – sabotaging the Axis war effort and intelligence gathering.

Albania The Italian occupation had produced two distinctly different resistance factions. In the north were the fiercely independent and very tribal mountain peoples whose loyalties lay with the exiled King Zog. In the south, on the other hand, by the end of 1941 it was the Communists under the leadership of Enver Hoxha who made the running. There was little love between the two movements and much fighting between them before they really began to concentrate on the common enemy. The Communists were, however, better organized, and they eventually took the lead; they preferred to deal with the Russians rather than SOE and OSS, who had a generally difficult time.

Belgium Matters here were complicated by the position of King Leopold. While there was a government-in-exile in London, the King had remained in Belgium and considered himself a prisoner of war of the Germans. The British thought ill of him because of his surrender. The most influential resistance group was the Légion Belge, but this was more concerned with restoring the King to his throne than fighting the Germans. For this reason they were vehemently opposed by the Communist-organized Front de l'Indépendance. Eventually, in **July 1943**, the government-in-exile took control of matters and ordered the Légion to form the Armée Secrète of 50,000 men which would operate under Allied orders.

Czechoslovakia Czech resistance was constantly beset by schisms. The first group formed was in 1939 by Czech Army officers and was called Defence of the Nation. Other groupings also appeared, including OSVO (Falcon Organization of Resistance based on the nationwide gymnastics clubs of that name). The government-in-exile did its best to try and co-ordinate resistance on a national scale, but was seldom successful. Agents flown in from London did, however, assassinate Reinhard Heydrich, German Protector of Bohemia and Moravia, in a grenade attack on **27 May 1942**. The German reprisal was the eradication of the village of Lidice and its inhabitants.

Denmark Resistance cells were set up very quickly after the German invasion of April 1940 and thrived under the initially relaxed way Germans ran the country. They were formed by the Army and supported by SOE and a cell in Sweden. Not until 1943, however, were civilians brought in on a wide scale when the Danish Freedom Council was set up to co-ordinate Russian and London-based arms deliveries. Danish countryside provided little cover, and sabotage was always sporadic.

France As the most likely place at which the Western Allies would re-enter the continent of Europe, France was always given most attention by SOE and OSS. Matters, however, were complicated by a number of factors. First, there was the loyalty dilemma, especially in Vichy France, where Pétain and his government were firmly against resistance. In London, de Gaulle was jealous of what he saw as Allied interference and preferred to operate exclusively through his Bureau Central de Renseignements et d'Action (BCRA). Even so, the Gaullists had a tough time since they were generally distrusted by their fellow countrymen. SOE's French Section also initially found it hard going to set up a comprehensive network, not helped by the wide range of political opinions reflected in the various groups. The breakthrough really came in the summer of 1942 when the Germans began forcibly to recruit French workers to be sent to Germany. More and more young men began literally to 'take to the hills', especially the *maquis* (scrub) area centred on the River Rhône, from which an ever-growing secret army took its name.

Greece Greece too was bedevilled by political in-fighting among the various resistance groups. There were four main factions: the National Union, which supported the Greek monarchy, the pro-republican EDES and EKKA, and the Communist EAM. Each had its own secret army, of which the best organized was the Communist ELAS. Friction among them increased as the war went on and much of the successful sabotage of Axis communications there was achieved by SOE agents acting on their own.

Netherlands The Dutch, apart from a few extreme right-wing elements, were hostile to the German occupation from the start, but early attempts at sabotage were quickly crushed by the Germans. In autumn 1940 the Order Service was formed with the object of maintaining order in the country once the Germans left; but it did little to foster resistance while they were still there. This was left to the politically left-of-centre, who supported the government-in-exile in London rather than the more right-wing Order Service.

On **6 March 1942** the Germans arrested an SOE radio-operator with his set and for the next eighteen months used him without SOE being aware of it. Known by the Germans as the *Englandspiel* (England Game) this was the most successful penetration of resistance groups by the Germans during the war, with much of the Dutch resistance network being destroyed or compromised.

Norway From 1942 onwards Hitler was convinced that the Allies intended to invade Norway, and he therefore maintained a sizeable garrison there. The Allies themselves were concerned about Norway because of its use as a naval base for capital ships, notably *Tirpitz*, and the presence of the hydro-electric plant at Vermork, which was capable of producing heavy water, an essential ingredient of atomic weapons. The Norwegians themselves formed a large underground army, Milorg, but this did little for much of the war, and resistance was passive rather than active. What activity took place was mainly by Norwegians sent from Britain. Notable among them was the network of radio spies that monitored the Norwegian coast and the highly successful raid on Vermork on **28 February 1943** after an earlier British attempt had failed in the previous November.

Poland In spite of mass deportations of almost all the potential partisan leaders, resistance began from the moment the country was overrun in September 1939. After some debate, it was decided to concentrate against the Germans rather than the Russians, and a secret army, the Polish Home Army, was raised. This began a campaign of sabotage and guerrilla activity, but, after the fall of France, Sikorski ordered it to cease active operations – he believed that they were causing too much suffering in the form of reprisals to the Polish people as a whole. Nevertheless, SOE did manage to fly agents in to foster resistance, but for much of the war it was intelligence gathering that was important. In the meantime, the Home Army gathered weapons and waited for orders to strike.

Yugoslavia The mountainous terrain favoured guerrilla operations, more perhaps than in any other occupied country. Resistance was quickly polarized under two leaders, Colonel Drava Mihailovic and his Cetniks, who were strongly royalist, and the Communists under Josip Broz, better known by his cover-name of Tito. The Cetniks initially followed the policy of the government-in-exile in London and were supported in this by SOE, who wanted them to build up strength and not to strike until the time was right. Tito, on the other hand, received orders from Moscow to begin offensive operations on the day the Germans invaded Russia. The Cetniks, for ideological reasons, refused to operate with Tito and turned more and more to the Germans. The British and Americans were slow to realize that Tito's was the most effective force, but gradually began to switch their allegiance, although their motives were viewed with suspicion by Tito.

P36 · Britain's Plight

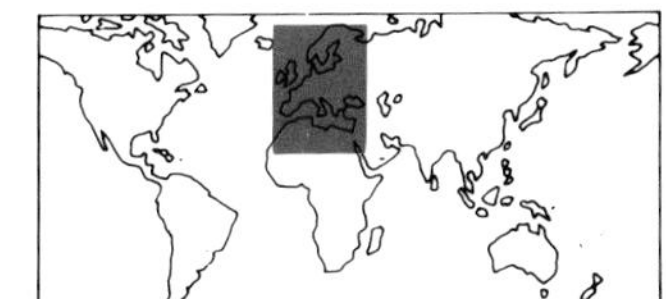

OCCUPIED EUROPE: 1942

ICELAND
Narvik
Trondheim
SWEDEN
FINLAND
Ryti
Reichskommissar Terboven
Scapa Flow
Bergen
NORWAY
Oslo
Vermork
Helsinki
Leningrad
Stockholm
BALTIC SEA
RUSSIA
GREAT BRITAIN
German Plenipotentary Best
Riga
Moscow
EIRE
DENMARK
Gauleiter Forster
Copenhagen
OSTLAND
Governor Seyss-Inquart
Danzig
EAST PRUSSIA
Reichskommissar Lohse
Military Governor Von Falkenhausen
HOLLAND
Berlin
GREATER GERMAN REICH
Governor Greisler
BELGIUM
POLAND
Governor Frank
Military Governor Von Stuelphagel
Luxemburg
Lidice
PROTECTORATE OF BOHEMIA & MORAVIA
UKRAINE
Reichskommissar Koch
FRANCE
Gauleiter Buerckel
Tiso
SLOVAK REPUBLIC
Reichsprotector Heydrich/Daluege
Vichy
SWITZERLAND
HUNGARY
Horthy
TRANSYLVANIA
BESSARABIA
Vichy France: Petain
Rhone
CROAT REPUBLIC
ROUMANIA
Antonescu
Toulon
Pavelic
PORTUGAL
SPAIN
ITALY
Nedic
SERBIA
BULGARIA
King Boris
BLACK SEA
Corsica
Rome
ALBANIA
Kruja
Istanbul
Ankara
Sardinia
Tsolakoglov
TURKEY
Gibraltar
Mers-el-Kebir
Oran
Algiers
Sicily
GREECE
Casablanca
Tunis
Athens
Malta
Rhodes
Cyprus
SYRIA
Vichy French North Africa Governor Darlan
Crete
MOROCCO
ALGERIA
MEDITERRANEAN SEA
Damascus
TUNISIA
Tripoli
TRANS JORDAN
Alexandria
Suez Canal
Cairo
Military Governor Bastico
EGYPT
SAUDI ARABIA
LIBYA
RED SEA

Axis Powers and Allies
Governed by German Reichskommissariat
German Military Government
Italian Military Government
Vichy France
British Government and Allies
Annexed territories

Tito and Yugoslavia · P172

7 NOVEMBER 1941 TO 4 JULY 1942

Enter 'Bomber' Harris

The German attack on Russia in June 1941 had brought RAF Bomber Command into even greater prominence, for it was the only means by which Britain could ease the appalling pressure on her new ally. By the end of that summer it had been widely recognized that Bomber Command could best achieve this by attacks designed to destroy German economic life and morale. The Air Ministry had accordingly drawn up a list of 43 German cities and believed that if these could be attacked and destroyed in the same way as Coventry had been in November 1940 Germany could be brought to her knees. They calculated that to do the job they needed a force of 4,000 bombers. At the time, they had only a fraction of this number.

Churchill, who had originally been a strong supporter of bombing, expressed his doubts that bombing on its own could be decisive. In order to convince him, the Chief of the Air Staff, Air Chief Marshal Sir Peter Portal, decided to organize a large raid on a number of targets in Germany. This took place on the **night of 7/8 November 1941** and was a disaster: 21 out of 169 aircraft failed to return from Berlin, 7 out of 55 from Mannheim and 9 out of 43 from the Ruhr. This marked the culmination of a trend of increasing losses, and the upshot was that a new conservation policy was introduced by Churchill. Operations would be concentrated on easier targets with minimum risk, while all effort was to be put into building up a strong force by spring 1942.

Much of the reason for RAF Bomber Command's increasing losses had been the improvement in German air defences. During 1941 the Germans had set up a defence belt of radars, searchlights and anti-aircraft guns, with nightfighters co-operating through Germany and the Low Countries and into France. This was called the Kammhuber Line after Luftwaffe General Josef Kammhuber who set it up.

As it happened, much of Bomber Command's effort during the period from December 1941 to February 1942 went into trying to destroy the three German capital ships in the port of Brest.

14 February 1942 Bomber Command received Directive No. 22.
This marked the end of the period of conservation, although attacks were still not to be pressed in the face of bad weather or 'extreme hazard'. The reasons for this change were primarily two. First, a new heavy bomber, the Lancaster, was just beginning to come into service; it was to prove the outstanding bomber of the war. Second, Bomber Command was now equipped with a new navigation device, GEE, which it was hoped would make locating targets easier; it did, however, have a maximum range of only 400 miles and could be jammed.

23 February Air Marshal Arthur Harris took over Bomber Command.
He already had the reputation of being a determined and forceful character and was convinced that the bombing of Germany could bring her to her knees and be decisive in winning the war.

24–25 February Two-day debate in the House of Commons on the conduct of the war.
Many of the speakers were sharply critical of government policy, and that on bombing was called particularly into question.

Night of 3/4 March Successful bombing attack on the Renault factory at Billancourt near Paris.
235 aircraft took part and only one failed to return. GEE was not used, but the target was marked with flares for the first time and extensive damage was done. This provided a much-needed morale boost for the crews. On the same night the Lancaster made its operational début, minelaying off Brest.

Night of 8/9 March First use of GEE in target marking in a raid on Essen.
GEE-equipped aircraft marked the target with flares – a technique known as 'Shaker'. Results were disappointing and were the same on the following night when Essen was once more the target. Essen, because of the constant industrial haze over it and the lack of clear landmarks, was a notoriously difficult target to find.

Night of 28/29 March Devastating attack on Luebeck.
234 bombers took part and destroyed much of this old city on the north German coast. Thirteen aircraft were lost, and from one of these the Germans obtained their first specimen of the GEE equipment. In retaliation, Hitler ordered the Luftwaffe to bomb historic British cities and towns.

16 April An official inquiry into British bombing policy set up under Mr. Justice Singleton.
This was the result of a debate between Churchill's two top scientific advisers, Lord Cherwell and Sir Henry Tizard. Cherwell, supported by the Air Ministry, drew up a list of 58 German cities and towns whose destruction would knock Germany out of the war. Tizard argued that less emphasis should be put on the bombing of Germany and more on using aircraft in the Battle of the Atlantic.

17 April Daylight raid by Lancasters on Augsburg in southern Germany.
The attack was pressed home with great gallantry, the raid leader, Squadron Leader J. D. Nettleton, being awarded the VC. But seven out of fourteen aircraft were lost, and this convinced Harris that daylight raids by heavy bombers were too costly.

23–28 April Four major attacks against Rostok on the Baltic coast.
142, 91, 128 and 107 aircraft respectively were sent against this target, with the results improving each night.

24 April The Luftwaffe bombed Exeter.
This was the first of Hitler's retaliatory attacks for Luebeck. They became known as the Baedeker raids after the famous guidebook series of that name. Bath was bombed on the 25th and 26th and Norwich on the 27th. The raids continued.

17 May Harris gained Churchill's support for a raid by 1,000 bombers.
Harris was convinced that the only way to get a strong bomber force would be to demonstrate what could be achieved with one. Although his own operational strength was less than 500 aircraft, by calling on RAF Coastal Command and his own training organization he was convinced that he could field 1,000 bombers. He planned to launch the operation, called 'Millenium', before the month was out.

20 May Singleton Report published.
This concluded that GEE was disappointing, but

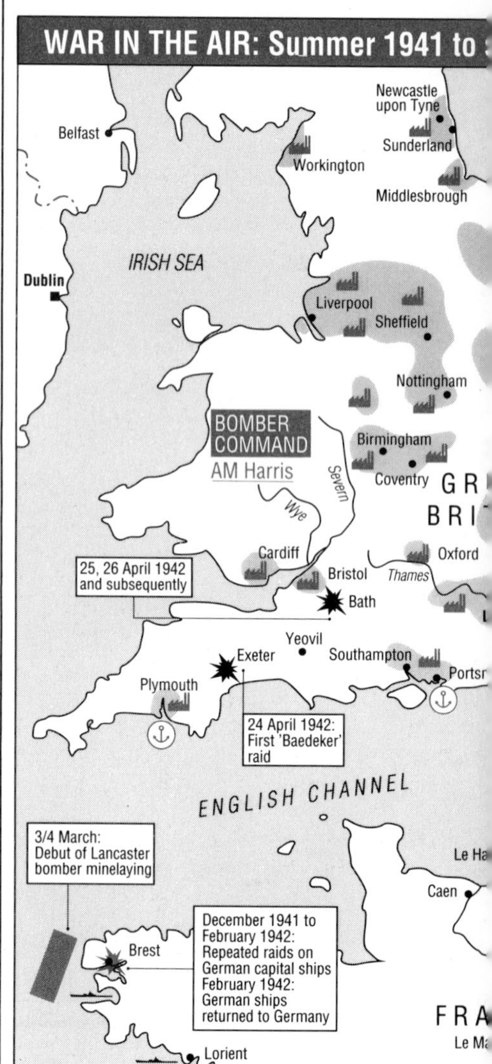

that more accurate bombing might result when a new aid, H2S, being developed, came into service. Provided greater accuracy could be achieved, bombing could prove a 'turning-point', but only after sustained effort. The report was so hedged about by 'ifs' and 'buts' that it was hardly conclusive.

23 May **Harris issued his orders for 'Millenium'.**
The target was to be Hamburg, with Cologne as the alternative. The raid was to take place on the night of 28/29 May or the first suitable night thereafter. Two days later the Admiralty refused to allow Coastal Command to take part, which made a shortfall of 250 aircraft. However, by scraping of resources within his own command Harris still managed to find more than 1,000 bombers. During this period normal operations continued.

Night of 30/31 May **First 1,000 bomber raid against Cologne.**
Bad weather brought about postponements, and on the night conditions over Hamburg were still poor, so Cologne, easily identifiable being on the Rhine, was selected. No less than 1,050 bombers took off, and 890 claimed to have attacked the correct target. The vast majority attacked over a period of just 75 minutes, which marked a new departure from the past when aircraft were given much latitude over when they attacked. Forty aircraft failed to return and a further nineteen crashed for one reason or another. The damage done to Cologne was considerable, although bad weather meant that it was a couple of days before post-raid photographs could be obtained.

Night of 1/2 June **956 aircraft took off to bomb Essen.**
Harris was determined to ram home the message while he still had such a large number of bombers available. They were, however, defeated by the Essen haze once more, and the results were disappointing. Nevertheless, Churchill was highly impressed and sanctioned further raids on this scale. Harris's achievement was recognized by a knighthood on **14 June**.

Night of 25/26 June **1,006 bombers took off to bomb Bremen.**
This time Churchill had insisted that Coastal Command, which provided 102 Hudsons, take part. As with the earlier 1,000 bomber raids, a full moon had been selected to make target-finding easier. None the less, the results were disappointing, and 49 aircraft failed to return, a high proportion of which were manned by trainee crews.

The Bremen raid marked the end of the 1,000 bomber raids for two years. The main problem was that the Bomber Command training programme of replacement crews was being seriously disrupted. Although the British public were generally pleased, one or two voices raised doubts as to the morality of this 'city busting', among them the military theorist Captain Basil Liddell Hart.

On 4 July six Bostons of the US Army Air Force (USAAF) 15th Bombardment Squadron (Separate) combined with six Bostons from the RAF's 226 Squadron for a raid on Dutch airfields. Two US and one RAF aircraft failed to return. This marked the USAAF's entry into the war in Europe and the beginning of what was to become the Combined Bombing Offensive against Germany.

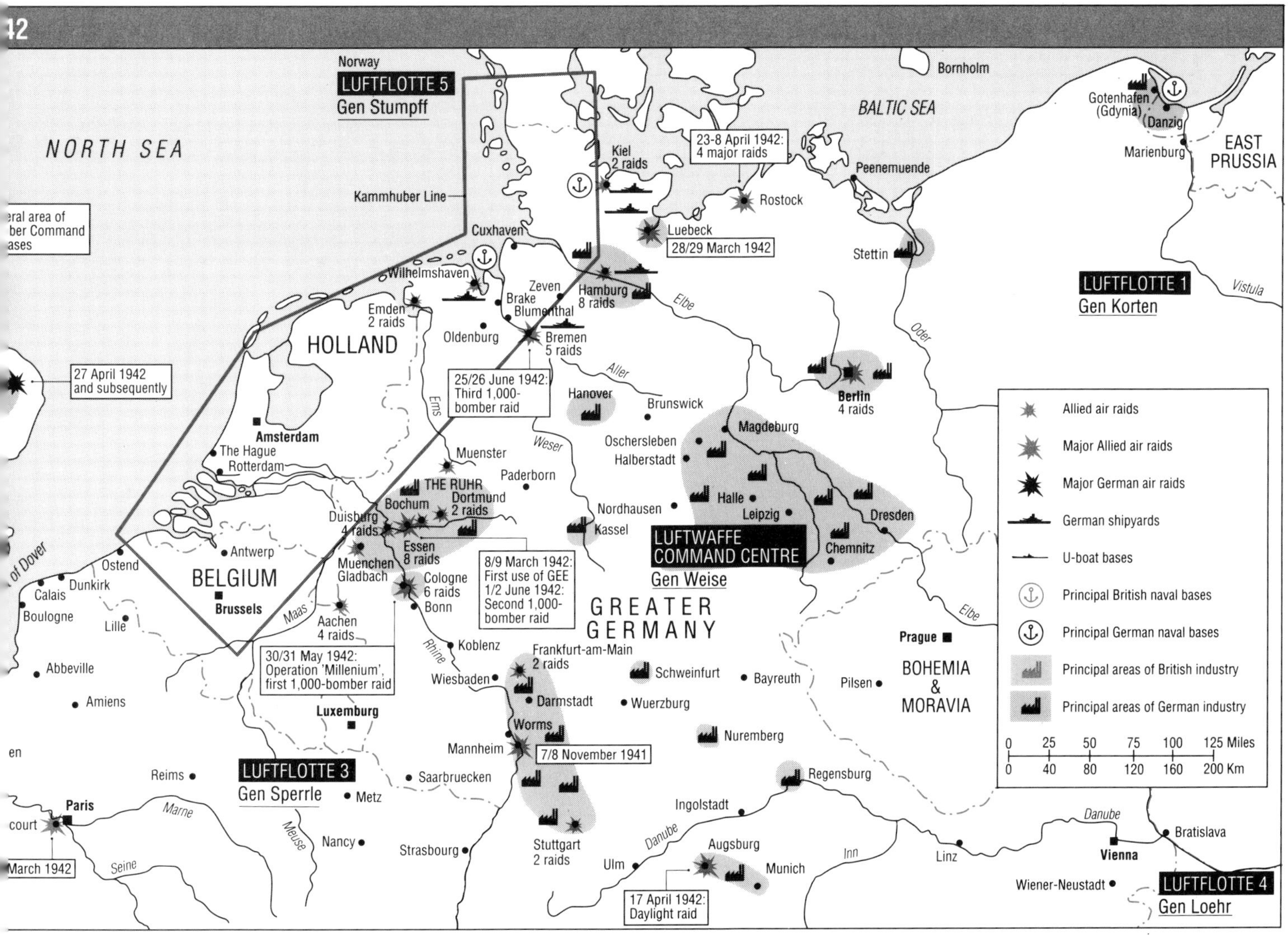

42

Norway
LUFTFLOTTE 5
Gen Stumpff
NORTH SEA
Kammhuber Line
...eral area of ...ber Command ...ases
BALTIC SEA
Bornholm
Kiel 2 raids
23-8 April 1942: 4 major raids
Rostock
Peenemuende
Gotenhafen (Gdynia)
Danzig
Marienburg
EAST PRUSSIA
Cuxhaven
Luebeck 28/29 March 1942
Stettin
Wilhelmshaven
Zeven
Brake
Blumenthal
Hamburg 8 raids
Elbe
LUFTFLOTTE 1
Gen Korten
Vistula
Emden 2 raids
Oldenburg
Bremen 5 raids
Oder
HOLLAND
27 April 1942 and subsequently
25/26 June 1942: Third 1,000-bomber raid
Ems
Aller
Hanover
Brunswick
Berlin 4 raids
Amsterdam
The Hague
Rotterdam
Muenster
Weser
Oschersleben
Halberstadt
Magdeburg
Paderborn
THE RUHR
Bochum
Dortmund 2 raids
Duisburg 4 raids
Essen 8 raids
Nordhausen
Kassel
Halle
Leipzig
Dresden
Chemnitz
LUFTWAFFE COMMAND CENTRE
Gen Weise
Antwerp
Ostend
Dunkirk
Calais
Boulogne
Lille
Straits of Dover
BELGIUM
Brussels
Muenchen Gladbach
Cologne 6 raids
Bonn
8/9 March 1942: First use of GEE 1/2 June 1942: Second 1,000-bomber raid
Maas
Aachen 4 raids
GREATER GERMANY
Koblenz
Rhine
Frankfurt-am-Main 2 raids
Wiesbaden
30/31 May 1942: Operation 'Millenium', first 1,000-bomber raid
Abbeville
Amiens
Luxemburg
Darmstadt
Schweinfurt
Bayreuth
Wuerzburg
Prague
Pilsen
BOHEMIA & MORAVIA
Worms
Nuremberg
Mannheim
7/8 November 1941
Reims
LUFTFLOTTE 3
Gen Sperrle
Metz
Saarbruecken
Regensburg
Paris
Marne
Meuse
Nancy
Strasbourg
Stuttgart 2 raids
Ingolstadt
Danube
Augsburg
Munich
Ulm
Inn
Linz
Vienna
Bratislava
Wiener-Neustadt
...March 1942
Seine
17 April 1942: Daylight raid
LUFTFLOTTE 4
Gen Loehr

Allied air raids
Major Allied air raids
Major German air raids
German shipyards
U-boat bases
Principal British naval bases
Principal German naval bases
Principal areas of British industry
Principal areas of German industry
0 25 50 75 100 125 Miles
0 40 80 120 160 200 Km

Australia Under Threat

The surrender of the Dutch East Indies on **9 March 1942** meant that the Japanese had now secured almost all the planned southern reaches of their Greater East Asia Co-Prosperity Sphere. Ever since the fall of Singapore and the first Japanese bombing of Darwin on **19 February** Australians had increasingly believed that the Japanese intended to invade. They had little with which to stop them. Of their four field divisions, one had been lost at Singapore and the other three were in the Middle East, although two were on their way home. Their navy was scattered about the world, and what aircraft they had were obsolete and no match for Japanese air power.

8 March 1942 **Japanese landings on Australian New Guinea.**
The landings at Lae and Salamaua were unopposed.

10 March **Japanese landing at Finschhafen in Dutch New Guinea.**
US aircraft from the carriers *Lexington* and *Yorktown* attacked the Japanese at Lae and Salamaua while Japanese aircraft attacked Port Moresby in Papua. The presence of the US carriers caused the Japanese to decide to postpone their occupation of Port Moresby until May, by which time their carriers presently *en route* to Japan from the Indian Ocean would be available once more. The Japanese occupied Buka in the Solomons.

12 March **US troops occupied New Caledonia.**

18 March **US forces occupied the New Hebrides.**
These were to guard Australia's west coast.

General Douglas MacArthur had now arrived at Darwin from where he made his way to Melbourne. The situation facing him was grim. Almost the whole of his South-West Pacific Command area was in Japanese hands. Although some 25,000 Americans were already in Australia, they were mainly specialists and, because of the 'Germany first' policy, he had only been earmarked two US field divisions, the first of which was not due to arrive until mid-April. Otherwise all he had to call on were some 250,000 ill-equipped and partially trained Australian militiamen.

22 March **Further Japanese air attacks on Darwin.**
Next day Japanese aircraft attacked Port Moresby once more.

25 March **US troops occupied the Society Islands.**

29 March **Australian War Cabinet implemented a 'total denial' policy in northern Australia.**
The plan was to conduct a fighting withdrawal in the event of a Japanese invasion, ensuring that nothing of value was left for the enemy. A vast migration of sheep and cattle southwards was already under way; those who took part were nicknamed the 'Overlanders'.

30 March **The Allies formally divided the Pacific theatre into two commands.**
MacArthur's South-West Pacific Command, based in Australia, covered the Philippines, New Guinea, the Bismarck Archipelago and Dutch East Indies; the remainder of the Pacific came under the command of Admiral Chester W. Nimitz, based at Pearl Harbor. His Pacific Ocean Zone was further sub-divided into three: North Pacific Area, which he himself commanded, Central Pacific Area (Admiral Thomas Kinkaid) and South Pacific Area (Admiral Robert L. Ghormley). At the same time, a Pacific War Council was set up in Washington with representatives from Australia, Britain, Canada, China, New Zealand, Netherlands, Philippines and the USA.

1–20 April **Further Japanese landings on Dutch New Guinea.**

6 April **Japanese landing on Manus Island in the Bismarck Archipelago.**

18 April **First US air raid on Japan.**
Sixteen B-25 bombers commanded by Lieutenant-Colonel James H. Doolittle, took off from the carrier *Hornet* 750 miles east of Tokyo. Escort fighters were provided by the carrier *Enterprise*. Bombs were dropped on Tokyo, Kobe, Yokohama, Nagoya and Yokusuka. Only one aircraft was slightly damaged over Japan, but all sixteen were lost in crash-landings in China. Most crews were rescued by the Chinese and Doolittle was awarded the Congressional Medal of Honor. The raid had little material effect and would be the last on Japan for many months to come, but it did give the Allies a psychological boost at a time when their fortunes in the Pacific were at their lowest.

By this time the US cryptanalysts through Magic intercepts were beginning to obtain a very clear idea of the next Japanese objective. Under the code-name 'Mo' the Japanese were now preparing to seize Port Moresby. Forces under the overall command of Admiral Shigeyoshi Inouye would seize Tulagi and the Louisiades and establish seaplane bases there while the Port Moresby force sailed from Rabaul around the south-east of Papua and approached the target from the south. A carrier-force would also sail south from Truk to prevent interference from the US Pacific Fleet.

30 April **The US carriers *Hornet* and *Enterprise* sailed from Pearl Harbor for the Coral Sea.**
They had only just returned from the Doolittle raid on Japan and were under the command of Admiral William 'Bull' Halsey.

Of the other two US carriers in the Pacific, *Lexington* and *Yorktown*, the former had left Pearl Harbor on **16 April** after reprovisioning and was ordered by Nimitz to link-up with *Yorktown*, which was in the Tonga Islands. Admiral Frank J. Fletcher, who was flying his flag in the latter, was ordered by Nimitz on **29 April** to rendezvous with *Lexington*, which he was to take under command, and to operate in the Coral Sea from **1 May**.

1 May ***Lexington*** **and** ***Yorktown*** **met 250 miles south-west of Espiritu Santo.**
Both elements of the task force now began to refuel.

2 May **The Australian garrison of Tulagi was evacuated.**
Fletcher left *Lexington* and her escorts to continue refuelling while he steamed north towards Tulagi.

3 May **Japanese landed on Tulagi.**
The Japanese escort, which included the carrier *Shohu*, immediately left to cover the Port Moresby landings.

4 May **The Port Moresby invasion force left Rabaul.**
Yorktown launched air strikes against the Japanese invasion fleet off Tulagi. One destroyer was disabled, three minesweepers and four landing barges were sunk for the loss of three US aircraft. Fletcher now doubled back to the Coral Sea.

5 May **The main Japanese striking force entered the Coral Sea.**
It was built round the carriers *Shokaku* and *Zuikaku*, whose aircraft bombed Port Moresby.

6 May **Fletcher organized his forces for the battle he was now certain would come.**
Neither side's reconnaissance aircraft were able to spot the other's on this day, apart from Australia-based B-17s, which located and attacked the carrier *Shoho* south of Bougainville, but missed her. Fletcher, however, was convinced that the main Japanese force would make for the Jomard Passage.

7 May **The Battle of the Coral Sea began.**
First strike was made by the Japanese, who attacked the oiler *Neosho* and the destroyer escorting her on their way to the next rendezvous with Fletcher's task force. The oiler was badly damaged and eventually had to be scuttled. Fletcher ordered a cruiser squadron to attack the Port Moresby invasion force, but this soon came under Japanese air attack. This diverted Japanese attention from Fletcher's carriers. At the same time, Inouye ordered the invasion force to turn away from the Jomard Passage until he had dealt with Fletcher.

Fletcher now launched a strike from *Yorktown* against a Japanese task force that proved to be nothing more than two light cruisers and two gunboats. *Lexington's* aircraft, however, spotted *Shoho* and sank her. Later that afternoon the

P80 · The Fall of Malaya, Singapore and Java

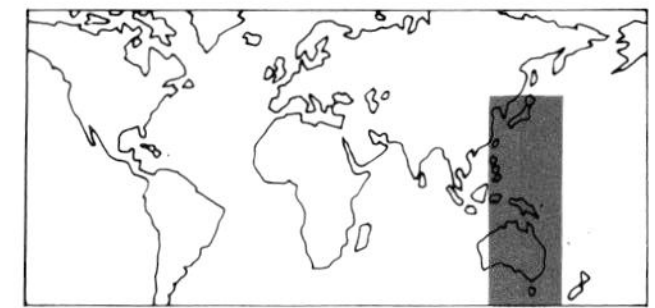

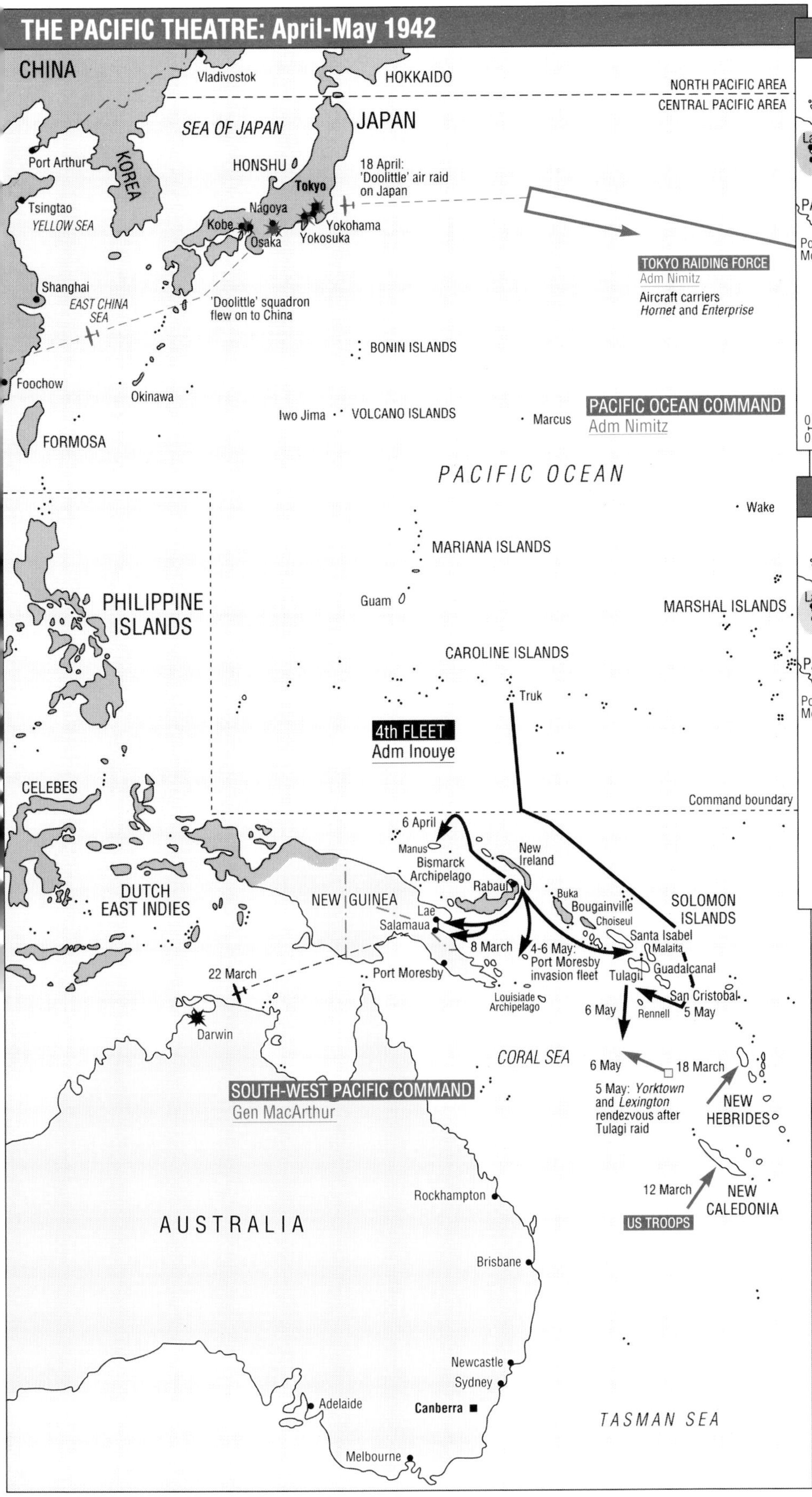

THE PACIFIC THEATRE: April-May 1942

18 April: 'Doolittle' air raid on Japan

'Doolittle' squadron flew on to China

TOKYO RAIDING FORCE
Adm Nimitz
Aircraft carriers *Hornet* and *Enterprise*

PACIFIC OCEAN COMMAND
Adm Nimitz

4th FLEET
Adm Inouye

SOUTH-WEST PACIFIC COMMAND
Gen MacArthur

US TROOPS

6 April

8 March

4-6 May: Port Moresby invasion fleet

22 March

6 May

5 May

18 March

5 May: *Yorktown* and *Lexington* rendezvous after Tulagi raid

12 March

Command boundary

NORTH PACIFIC AREA
CENTRAL PACIFIC AREA

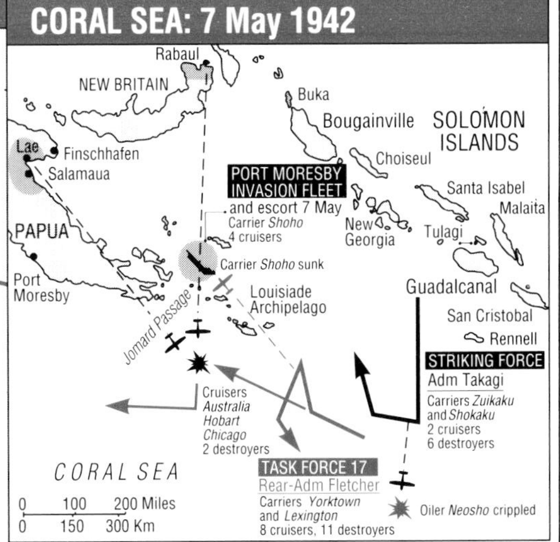

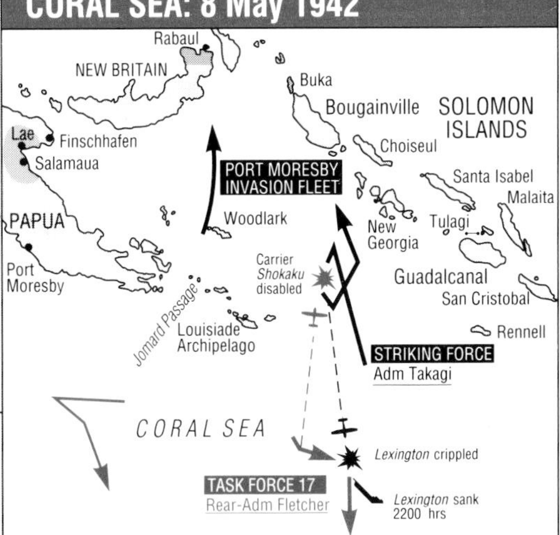

Japanese launched 27 aircraft against the US carriers, but they failed to locate their targets and only six returned safely.

At midnight Inouye decided to postpone the invasion for two days.

8 May End of Battle of the Coral Sea.
Each carrier force located the other shortly after 0800 hours and sent out attack aircraft. *Lexington* was torpedoed and later abandoned, while *Shokaku* was disabled and retired to Truk. The Japanese then launched further strikes to try and destroy the remainder of Fletcher's force, but this had now withdrawn out of range.

The Battle of the Coral Sea had seemingly left the Japanese as victors, since they had forced Fletcher to retire. But, for the first time, the Allies had frustrated Japanese designs – the Port Moresby invasion was now postponed indefinitely. The battle also marked the beginning of a new form of naval warfare, where carriers took over from battleships and the opposing surface fleets never directly sighted each other.

Midway · P104

Midway

Operation 'Mo', the Port Moresby landings, was not the only attack that the Japanese had planned for May 1942. Doolittle's audacious raid on the Japanese mainland had made a deep impression, and to prevent such a thing happening again two attacks were planned. The first was an offensive in the Chekiang province of China, the nearest to the Japanese mainland not already in their hands, in order to deny the Allies use of airfields there. This opened on **11 May**. The second step they planned to take was Operation 'Mi', the seizure of Midway, which Admiral Nagumo himself described as Pearl Harbor's 'sentry'.

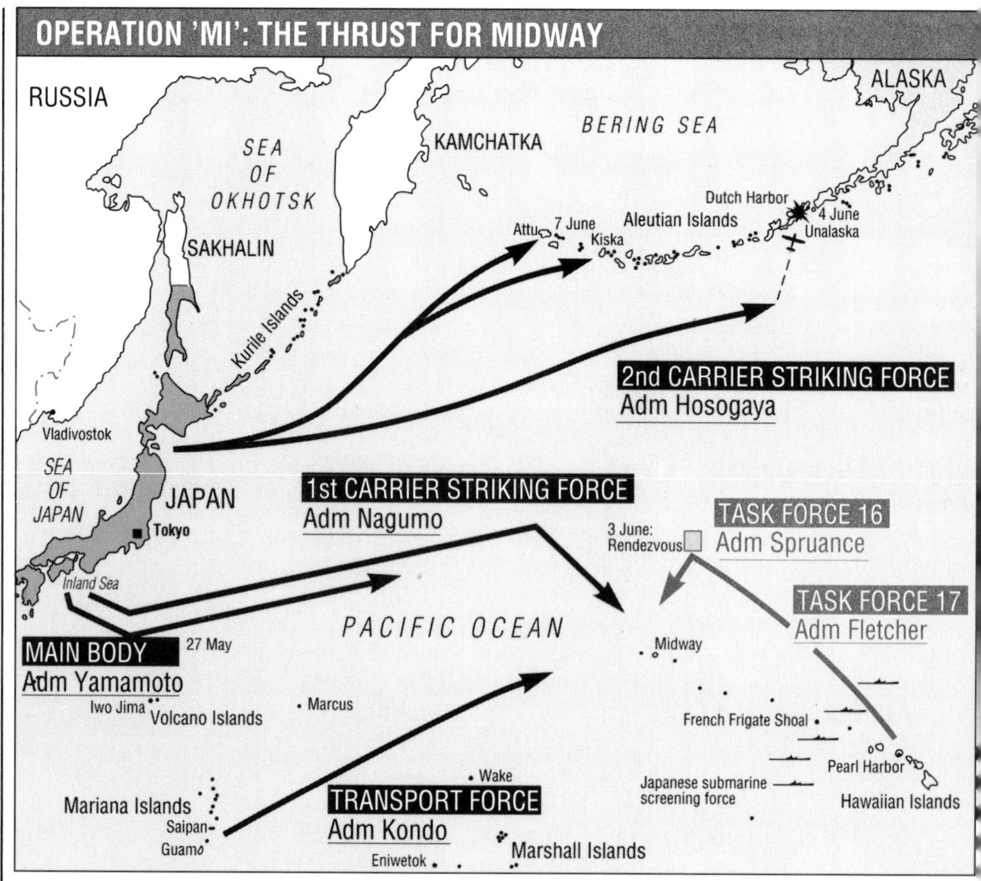

16 April 1942 Imperial GHQ Naval Order No. 18 issued for Operation 'Mi'.
This ordered Admiral Yamamoto, CinC, Combined Fleet, to draw up plans for both the capture of Midway and the Aleutians well to the north. In fact, the original proposal to attack Midway had come from Yamamoto in March, but it had not found favour because of the difficulty of keeping the atoll supplied. Eventually, Yamamoto threatened to resign and the opposition caved in. At this time, however, with the Japanese more interested in Papua-New Guinea, no date for the mounting of 'Mi' was given.

20 April The Japanese decided that 'MI' must be undertaken as soon as possible.
While 'Mo' would continue, plans to seize Samoa, Fiji and New Caledonia were to be postponed. This was as a result of the Doolittle raid.

20 May Yamamoto issued his orders for 'Mi'.
The plan was complicated, wherein lay its downfall.

The Northern Force would sail for the Aleutians during **25–27 May**. First to leave would be the 2nd Carrier Striking Force (two small carriers, two cruisers, three destroyers), which would mount an air strike on Dutch Harbor on **3 June**. This was designed to force Nimitz to send part of his force northwards. When he did so, it would be met by the Guard Force (four battleships, two cruisers, twelve destroyers), which would position itself between the Aleutians and Pearl Harbor. The third part would be the transports carrying the force to be landed on the islands of Attu and Kiska on **5 June**.

Meanwhile the 1st Carrier Striking Force (four carriers) under Nagumo would sail from the Inland Sea bound for Midway. This would carry out preparatory strikes on Midway on **4 June**. Following it would be the Transport Force with the invasion troops on board, with three cruisers from Guam to provide additional protection.

Finally, the Main Body, with Yamamoto flying his flag in the biggest battleship in the world, *Yamato*, and two other battleships and their escorting destroyers, would sail with the Main Support Force (two battleships, four heavy cruisers and destroyers).

In order to ensure that the US Fleet's whereabouts was known at all times, two flying-boats were based at French Frigate Shoal, 500 miles north-west of Hawaii, to check on the anchorage at Pearl Harbor during the period **31 May to 3 June**, and three cordons of submarines were positioned north and west of Hawaii.

27 May The Japanese Combined Fleet weighed anchor.
On this same day, Nimitz issued orders to the US Pacific Fleet. For more than a month his cyptanalysts under Commander Joseph Rochefort had been intercepting Japanese naval signals, and slowly the jigsaw had taken shape. The Japanese were intending to attack Midway. This intelligence was of enormous value. But with only three carriers, eight cruisers and nineteen destroyers (there were still no battleships in the Pacific after the December 1941 attack on Pearl Harbor), Nimitz was at a grave numerical disadvantage.

He therefore ordered Task Force 16 (the carriers *Enterprise* and *Hornet*, six cruisers, eleven destroyers, two tankers and nineteen submarines) under Admiral Raymond A. Spruance (who had recently relieved Halsey, who was sick) to sail for Midway on the following day. Also in Pearl Harbor, refitting after the Coral Sea operations, was Fletcher's Task Force 17 (*Yorktown*, two cruisers, six destroyers). This would sail on **30 May** for Midway and meet Spruance there. On no account was Nimitz prepared to split his forces by being drawn north to the Aleutians.

3 June Spruance and Fletcher met 350 miles north-east of Midway.
Fletcher assumed overall command of the joint task force, although the two would act separately. US reconnaissance aircraft now spotted two carriers 400 miles from Kiska in the Aleutians.

3 June Midway-based aircraft sighted and attacked Yamamoto's transports.
The armada was now some 600 miles from Midway, but suffered no losses.

4 June Opening of the Battle of Midway.
Nagumo's aircraft made the first move with an attack on Midway, but the garrison had received warning from a spotter aircraft. Although Japanese losses were less than the Americans', they failed to neutralize US air power on the island. Nagumo now ordered a second attack, but his aircraft had first to replace their torpedoes with bombs. In the meantime, US carrier-borne aircraft attacked the Japanese, initially with no success. The Americans then launched another wave and this hit three out of four Japanese carriers, *Akagi*, *Soryu* and *Kaga*. The damage to all three was intensified by the fact that they had aircraft on deck still rearming.

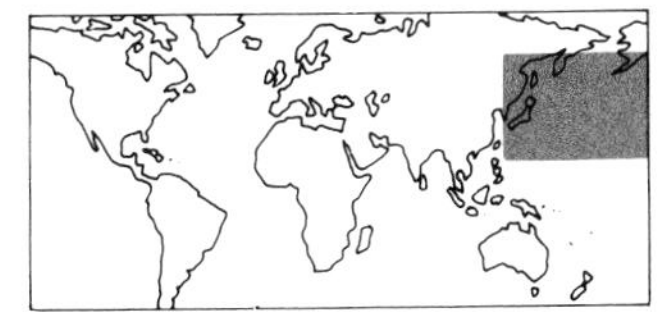

Farther north, Japanese aircraft attacked Dutch Harbor on Unalaska Island in the Aleutians as planned. They damaged a US ship and fuel tanks. US efforts to locate the Japanese task force were unsuccessful.

5 June The Battle continued.
There was no contact in the morning or late afternoon. At 1530 hours the blazing *Akagi* was torpedoed on Yamamoto's orders. In the early evening Fletcher located the Japanese fleet once more and sank Yamamoto's remaining carrier, *Hiryu*. Just after this the casualties of the previous day, *Soryu* and *Kaga*, sank.

6 June In the early hours, Yamamoto ordered a withdrawal.
Just before this, two of his cruisers collided and one was later sunk by a US submarine. A Japanese submarine sank the US destroyer *Hammam*. The US fleet lost contact with the withdrawing Japanese.

7 June Japanese landings on Attu and Kiska in the Aleutians.

7 June A Japanese submarine sank the carrier *Yorktown*.
She had been attacked and damaged on **4 June**. This marked the end of the Battle of Midway.

While both sides had claimed the Battle of the Coral Sea as a victory, there was no doubt about Midway. The Japanese had lost four carriers, a heavy cruiser, 322 aircraft and 5,000 officers and men, while the American casualties were one carrier, a destroyer, 150 aircraft and 300 men. The only gain for the Japanese had been the two islands in the Aleutians, but these were so peripheral as to be of little consequence, and the Americans made no immediate effort to regain them. The Japanese, while they would not admit a catastrophic defeat, were no longer prepared to risk a major fleet-versus-fleet action and were forced on to the defensive. Midway marked a major turning-point.

THE CLIMAX AT MIDWAY: 4 June 1942

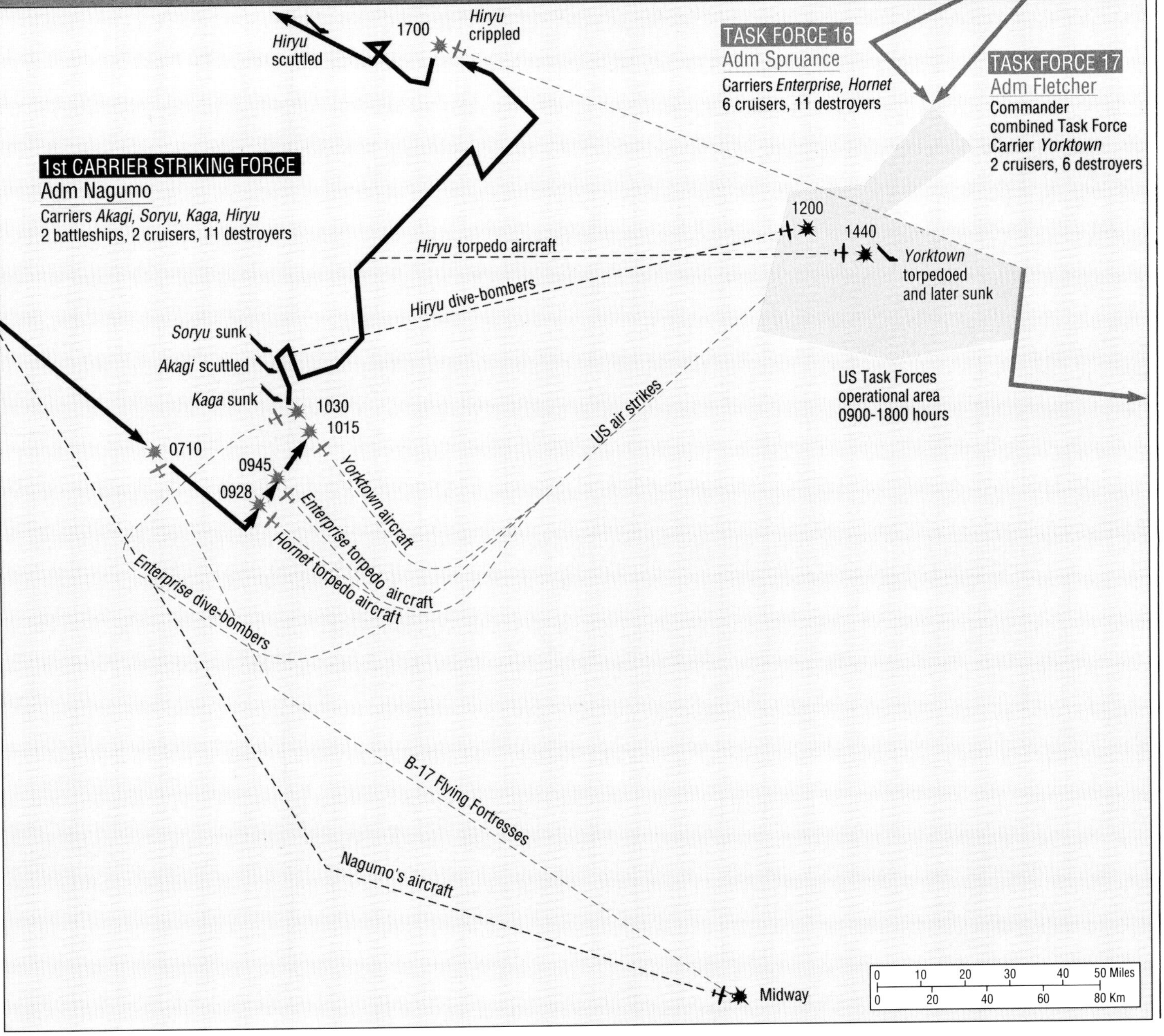

The Landings on Guadalcanal · P112

8 APRIL 1942 TO 19 AUGUST 1942

Second Front Now!

At the beginning of July 1942 the Allied fortunes were as mixed as they had been at the time of the 'Arcadia' conference six months earlier. Yet now, in terms of theatres of war, the situation had been reversed. Whereas in North Africa the British had been in the ascendant six months before, Rommel was now knocking at the gates of Cairo. The Battle of the Atlantic had, as a result of the Second Happy Time, reflected a sharp increase in Allied shipping losses, and on the Eastern front the Germans seemed once more to be sweeping all before them. The situation in South East Asia remained gloomy, with the British and Chinese still licking their wounds after being bundled out of Burma; but in the Pacific, the Battles of the Coral Sea and Midway had presented more than just a glimmer of light, and it would not be long before the Allies turned from the defensive to the offensive.

In the meantime, the main debate in the Allied camp, and one that had been growing in intensity, was the question of the invasion of Europe. On **22 June 1941,** the day that the Germans invaded Russia, Churchill had pledged that, 'we shall give whatever help we can to Russia and the Russian people'. He had followed this up on **7 July** with a personal message to 'Monsieur Stalin'. The latter eventually replied on **18 July**. The best way that Britain could help her ally would be to establish a second front in France, with a subsidiary front in Norway and Scandinavia specifically to relieve the pressure on Leningrad. The Russians continued to agitate for this during the remainder of 1941, but it was clearly beyond Britain's means at the time. All she could do to help her ally was to continue bombing Germany (although the resources to do this effectively were still lacking) and to supply Russia with what *matériel* she could spare.

The US entry into the war, and the 'Arcadia' decision that the defeat of Germany must take precedence over that of Japan, renewed Russian hopes for the early establishment of a second front on the continent of Europe. Indeed, as we have seen, the US Chiefs of Staff, suspicious of Britain's Mediterranean strategy, which they viewed as far too indirect and solely in Britain's interest, themselves wanted to open a second front in Europe in 1942 under the code-name 'Round Up'. In Britain, too, the political left, especially the Communists, who had been opposed to the war until 22 June 1941, were agitating for the same, and 'Second Front Now!' slogans were increasingly chalked on walls. Churchill publicly rebuked these agitators in January 1942, but as winter turned to spring demands for a second front intensified.

In the meantime the British had gained some experience of amphibious operations through the employment of their Commando forces. Notable raids had been on the Lofoten Islands off northern Norway (**4 March 1941**), Vaagso, south-west Norway (**27 December 1941**) and the destruction of the dry dock at St-Nazaire (**night of 27/28 March 1942**).

8 April 1942 US delegation arrived in Britain to discuss second front strategy.
This was led by special presidential adviser Harry L. Hopkins and Joint Chiefs of Staff Chairman General George C. Marshall. The proposal they brought from Roosevelt was for major landings on the French coast in summer 1943, with Antwerp as the initial objective, and for a similar but smaller operation in 1942 to take advantage of sudden German disintegration or to stave off an imminent Russian collapse. The British expressed general agreement, but were anxious to have US support to remove the Japanese threat to the Indian Ocean.

10 April Soviet Ambassador to USA demanded immediate second front.
This was in a speech given in Philadelphia.

23 April Churchill declared that the liberation of Europe was 'the main war plan' of Britain and the USA.
This was in a speech delivered at a secret session of the House of Commons.

13 May Major raid against Dieppe approved by British Chiefs of Staff.
This had been under consideration since March, especially by Admiral Lord Louis Mountbatten, Chief of Combined Operations, who wanted to explore the problems of an opposed landing on the French coast. This was code-named 'Rutter'.

26 May Anglo-Soviet Treaty signed in London.
Each country pledged itself to fight Germany until final victory and not to make separate peace with her. They also agreed a 20-year alliance, not to join any coalition or treaty directed against one of them, and not to interfere in the internal affairs of other states.

Molotov, who signed on behalf of the Soviet Union, continued to press for the second front to be opened in 1942, and did so again in Washington.

11–12 June First rehearsal for the Dieppe raid.
General Bernard Montgomery's South-Eastern Army had been tasked with mounting 'Rutter', and he had selected the 2nd Canadian Division for the job. It was to make a frontal assault on the town with airborne troops neutralizing the batteries on the headlands at each side of the port. This first

THE GLOBAL WAR: Summer 1942

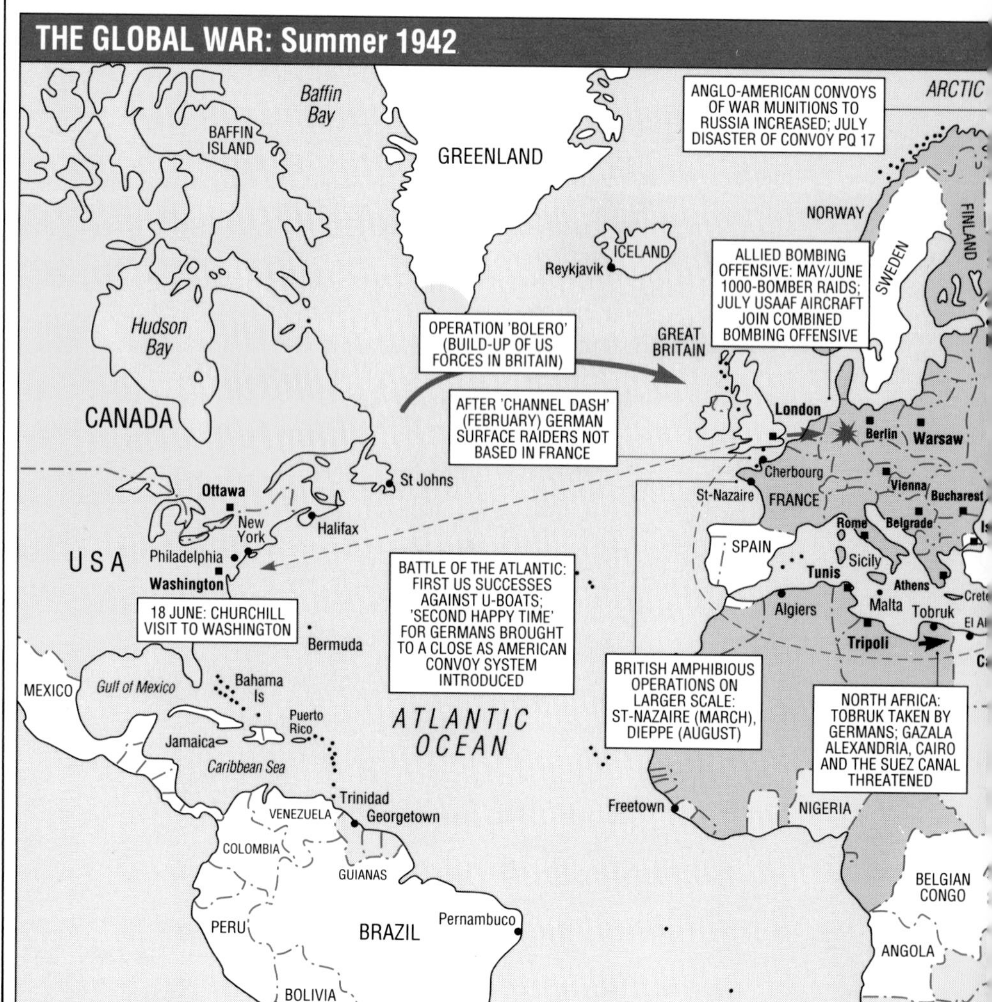
Baffin Bay
BAFFIN ISLAND
GREENLAND
ANGLO-AMERICAN CONVOYS OF WAR MUNITIONS TO RUSSIA INCREASED; JULY DISASTER OF CONVOY PQ 17
ARCTIC
NORWAY
FINLAND
SWEDEN
ICELAND
Reykjavik
ALLIED BOMBING OFFENSIVE: MAY/JUNE 1000-BOMBER RAIDS; JULY USAAF AIRCRAFT JOIN COMBINED BOMBING OFFENSIVE
Hudson Bay
OPERATION 'BOLERO' (BUILD-UP OF US FORCES IN BRITAIN)
GREAT BRITAIN
CANADA
AFTER 'CHANNEL DASH' (FEBRUARY) GERMAN SURFACE RAIDERS NOT BASED IN FRANCE
London
Berlin
Warsaw
St Johns
Cherbourg
Ottawa
St-Nazaire
FRANCE
Vienna
Bucharest
New York
Halifax
Rome
Belgrade
SPAIN
USA
Philadelphia
Washington
Sicily
Tunis
Athens
Crete
BATTLE OF THE ATLANTIC: FIRST US SUCCESSES AGAINST U-BOATS; 'SECOND HAPPY TIME' FOR GERMANS BROUGHT TO A CLOSE AS AMERICAN CONVOY SYSTEM INTRODUCED
Algiers
Malta
Tobruk
18 JUNE: CHURCHILL VISIT TO WASHINGTON
Bermuda
Tripoli
MEXICO
Gulf of Mexico
Bahama Is
BRITISH AMPHIBIOUS OPERATIONS ON LARGER SCALE: ST-NAZAIRE (MARCH), DIEPPE (AUGUST)
NORTH AFRICA: TOBRUK TAKEN BY GERMANS; GAZALA ALEXANDRIA, CAIRO AND THE SUEZ CANAL THREATENED
Puerto Rico
ATLANTIC OCEAN
Jamaica
Caribbean Sea
Trinidad
Freetown
NIGERIA
VENEZUELA
Georgetown
COLOMBIA
GUIANAS
BELGIAN CONGO
PERU
BRAZIL
Pernambuco
ANGOLA
BOLIVIA

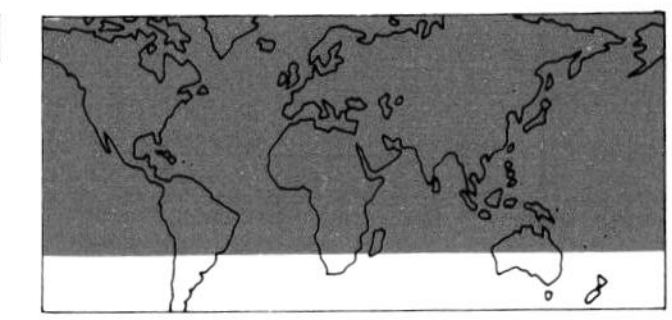

rehearsal did not go well, but a second one held ten days later was better.

18 June Churchill arrived in Washington for further discussions with Roosevelt.

The main purpose of his visit was to consider a number of conflicting plans for taking the offensive against Germany in 1942. The main ones were: 'Rutter', a 24-hour cross-Channel raid on Dieppe; 'Sledgehammer', using six divisions to establish a lodgement on the French coast at Cherbourg in autumn 1942; and 'Jupiter', the establishment of a lodgement in northern Norway. In addition, there was the main cross-Channel attack, 'Round Up', which was scheduled to take place in early summer 1943. There was also 'Gymnast', the proposed landing in French North Africa in autumn 1942.

Churchill and Roosevelt agreed that 'Bolero' (the build-up of US forces in Britain) was to press ahead with all speed and that operations against France and the Low Countries were preferable for 1942. If these were found impracticable, 'Gymnast', 'Jupiter' or a landing on the Iberian Peninsula would be considered as alternatives. One major problem that was recognized was the drastic shortage of landing craft.

25 June General Dwight D. Eisenhower appointed to command US Forces in the European Theatre (USFET).

1 July Montgomery informed General Bernard Paget, CinC Home Forces, that 'Rutter' would be mounted on 4 July.

Bad weather intervened, and on **7 July** it was postponed. Montgomery wanted it cancelled because too many people knew about it, but Mountbatten and Paget insisted that it go ahead in August.

1–2 July No Confidence motion debated in the House of Commons.

This attack on Churchill was defeated by 475 votes to 25.

8 July Churchill urged Roosevelt to agree to 'Gymnast' as the best 1942 offensive option.

The British had concluded that 'Sledgehammer' would merely detract from 'Round Up' and that 'Jupiter' was not feasible, although Churchill himself still hankered after it.

24 July Roosevelt agreed to 'Gymnast' and the cancellation of 'Sledgehammer'.

This was after Marshall and Hopkins had visited London once more in order to press the case for 'Sledgehammer'. The main problem now was how to placate Stalin.

12 August Churchill arrived in Moscow.

He had come from Cairo, where he had been investigating the problems in the Middle East. In the course of four days of often acrimonious talks, Stalin was eventually forced to accept that there would be no second front in 1942.

19 August The Dieppe raid.

Now code-named 'Jubilee', it was a disaster. Fifty per cent of the Canadian troops taking part were killed or captured on the beaches, and only on the flanks, where Commandos had been substituted for airborne troops, was there any success. A number of landing craft and one destroyer were lost. In air battles overhead, the RAF claimed to have shot down 170 aircraft at a cost of 106 of their own.

The controversy over Dieppe continues to this day. What it did prove, if nothing else, was how ill-prepared the Western Allies were for major cross-Channel operations in 1942; the lessons learnt would bear fruit 22 months later.

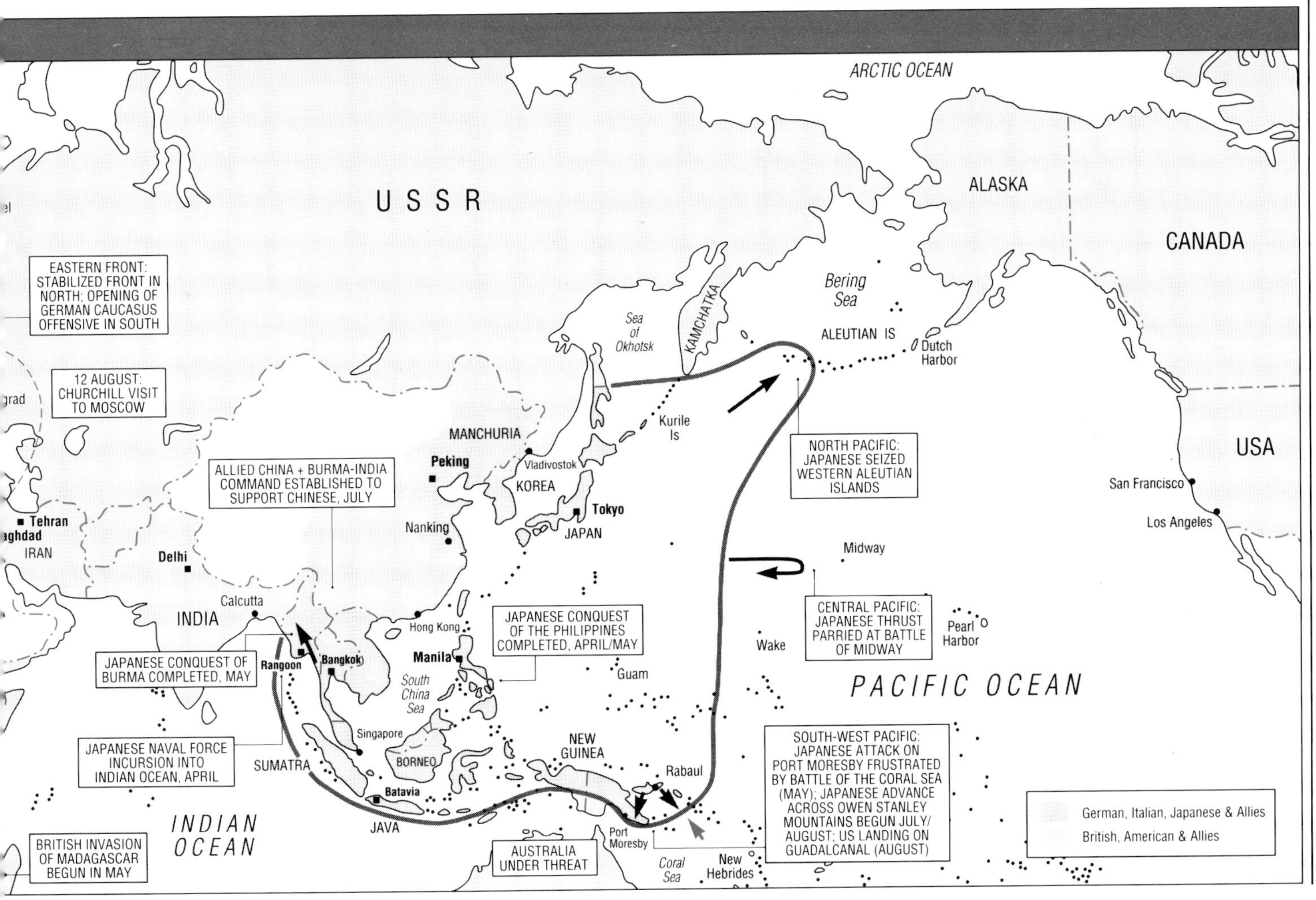

ARCTIC OCEAN
USSR
ALASKA
CANADA
USA
Bering Sea
Sea of Okhotsk
KAMCHATKA
ALEUTIAN IS
Dutch Harbor
Kurile Is
MANCHURIA
Peking
Vladivostok
KOREA
Tokyo
JAPAN
Nanking
Tehran
Baghdad
IRAN
Delhi
INDIA
Calcutta
Rangoon
Bangkok
Hong Kong
Manila
South China Sea
Guam
Wake
Midway
Pearl Harbor
San Francisco
Los Angeles
PACIFIC OCEAN
Singapore
BORNEO
SUMATRA
Batavia
JAVA
NEW GUINEA
Rabaul
Port Moresby
Coral Sea
New Hebrides
INDIAN OCEAN

EASTERN FRONT: STABILIZED FRONT IN NORTH; OPENING OF GERMAN CAUCASUS OFFENSIVE IN SOUTH

12 AUGUST: CHURCHILL VISIT TO MOSCOW

ALLIED CHINA + BURMA-INDIA COMMAND ESTABLISHED TO SUPPORT CHINESE, JULY

NORTH PACIFIC: JAPANESE SEIZED WESTERN ALEUTIAN ISLANDS

CENTRAL PACIFIC: JAPANESE THRUST PARRIED AT BATTLE OF MIDWAY

JAPANESE CONQUEST OF THE PHILIPPINES COMPLETED, APRIL/MAY

JAPANESE CONQUEST OF BURMA COMPLETED, MAY

JAPANESE NAVAL FORCE INCURSION INTO INDIAN OCEAN, APRIL

SOUTH-WEST PACIFIC: JAPANESE ATTACK ON PORT MORESBY FRUSTRATED BY BATTLE OF THE CORAL SEA (MAY); JAPANESE ADVANCE ACROSS OWEN STANLEY MOUNTAINS BEGUN JULY/AUGUST; US LANDING ON GUADALCANAL (AUGUST)

AUSTRALIA UNDER THREAT

BRITISH INVASION OF MADAGASCAR BEGUN IN MAY

German, Italian, Japanese & Allies
British, American & Allies

Allied Aid to Russia

Very soon after the German invasion of Russia in June 1941, Churchill realized that in order to keep her in the war it was imperative to offer the Russians material aid. With the signing of the mutual assistance pact on **12 July 1941** Churchill immediately dispatched some Hurricanes and anti-aircraft defences to the northern port of Murmansk and 10,000 tons of rubber to the other major Soviet port in northern waters, Archangel. Earlier, on **26 June**, the Americans had declared that the 1939 Neutrality Act would not apply to the Soviet Union and on **8 July**, in response to this, the Soviet Ambassador to Washington submitted a massive list of material needs, including no less than 3,000 bombers and 3,000 fighters. Because there was considerable doubt as to how long the Russians would survive the German onslaught, Roosevelt decided to send Harry Hopkins (his personal representative in Britain) to Moscow to obtain a clearer idea of Soviet prospects. Hopkins met Stalin during **29–30 July**, but could gain no information on Soviet plans, only that they wanted the USA to enter the war quickly and would welcome any economic aid that she could give. Accordingly, US Lend-Lease was extended to the Soviet Union on **2 August**.

26 September 1941 The first Arctic convoy to Russia left Britain.
It consisted of ten merchantmen with escorts and was designated PQ1. It arrived at Archangel with no casualties.

28 September to 1 October Allied conference in Moscow to decide on what aid the Russians needed.
Lord Beaverbrook represented Britain and Averell Harriman the USA. A protocol was signed by which Britain and the USA undertook to supply the Russians with 400 aircraft immediately and 500 aircraft per month until 30 June 1942. Thereafter the protocol would be renewable annually. Furthermore, both countries undertook to deliver 41,000 tons of aluminium immediately, and 6,000 tons of rubber and 1,500 tons of tin per month. Food and medical supplies were also included.

The routes by which these were to be delivered were three. Aircraft would fly from Alaska to Siberia, and some supplies would be sent through Iran, using the rail link from Basra through Tehran to the Caspian Sea. Initially this route had only very limited capacity, and it was delivery by sea from Britain to Murmansk and Archangel that provided the main transport route.

6 October Churchill gave a personal undertaking to Stalin to send a convoy every ten days to Russia's northern ports.
By the end of 1941, however, only seven convoys totalling 53 merchant vessels had been sent. 750 tanks, 800 fighters, 1,400 other vehicles and 100,000 tons of stores were delivered. The main problems were the need to repair weather damage to escorts between voyages – there were insufficient ships to provide immediate replacements – and that the unloading facilities at Murmansk and Archangel were limited. Ice meant that from mid-December only Murmansk could be used.

Not until mid-November did the Germans begin to take counter-measures when Raeder, as CinC, German Navy, ordered Doenitz to increase his U-boat strength in Norwegian waters and also sent five destroyers to northern Norway. Even so, no merchantmen were lost until the end of 1941.

12 January 1942 German battleship *Tirpitz* ordered to Norway.
She arrived at Trondheim two days later, but not until 23 January did the British locate her. In February the heavy cruisers *Scheer* and *Prinz Eugen*, which had just escaped from Brest, were also ordered to Norway, but the latter was torpedoed *en route*.

In the meantime four more convoys had steamed to Murmansk with the loss of just one destroyer and one merchantman torpedoed, but towed into port.

Night of 29/30 January First RAF Bomber Command attack on *Tirpitz* in Trondheim.
It was unsuccessful.

2 March Churchill declared *Tirpitz* 'the most important naval vessel in the situation today'.
He believed her destruction would 'profoundly affect the course of the war'.

6 March Hitler approved the interception of Convoy PQ12 by *Tirpitz*.
German reconnaissance aircraft had located PQ12 the previous day. *Tirpitz* set sail accompanied by three destroyers, but was spotted by a British submarine. Bad weather resulted in failure to locate the convoy and she returned to Trondheim, but not before aircraft from the carrier *Victorious* had made an unsuccessful attack on her. As a result, Hitler ordered Goering to reinforce the Luftwaffe in Norway, something the latter had so far resisted doing. It was this, rather than the threat of *Tirpitz*, which was to result in PQ12 being the last convoy to reach Russia unscathed. PQ13 sent in March, PQ14 (April) and PQ15 (May) suffered from increasing German pressure and lost a total of two cruisers and fifteen merchant vessels. Matters were not helped by the onset of the Arctic summer, which brought perpetual daylight.

Night of 30/31 March Second unsuccessful RAF attack on *Tirpitz*.
A further attempt was made on the night of **27/28 April**. Wing Commander Donald Bennett, who led the raid, crashed in his Halifax, but was able to escape to Sweden and thence back to England, where he was to raise the RAF's Pathfinder Force.

18 May Despite increasing losses, Churchill was determined that the Arctic convoys continue.
This was in spite of the fact that they would be within range of Norway-based enemy aircraft for seven days; because of the ice the northern route to Archangel, which permitted the convoys to keep mainly out of range of land-based aircraft, could not be used until July. It was vital that all possible help for Russia, now once again under German attack, should continue. That night PQ16 set sail and reached Murmansk with the loss of six ships.

27 June Convoy PQ17 set sail from Iceland.
Iceland was the assembly point for the Arctic convoys. Because of the backlog of ships waiting to sail to Russia, this convoy was twice the size of previous ones and eventually sailed with 33 merchant vessels and a tanker. The escort consisted of six destroyers, two anti-aircraft ships, four corvettes, three minesweepers, four trawlers and two submarines. Further support was available in the shape of two battleships, one carrier, six cruisers and seventeen destroyers.

1 July German aircraft sighted PQ17.
U-boats began to trail the convoy.

4 July PQ17 ordered to scatter.
The convoy had been under Luftwaffe attack all day and had lost two merchantmen sunk and two damaged. The previous day the Admiralty had learnt that *Tirpitz*, *Hipper* and *Scheer* had left Trondheim and the threat to the supporting cruiser squadron was considered too serious, with the battleships and carrier not able to arrive in time to save the convoy.

5 July Luftwaffe attacks on the scattered convoy.
Twelve ships were sunk in the first 24 hours, and only ten finally reached Archangel. The German capital ships failed to contact the convoy and returned to port on the 5th after a Russian submarine had made an unsuccessful torpedo attack on *Tirpitz*.

The switch of priority to maintaining supplies to Malta and the high casualties to PQ17 meant that no further convoys were sent to Russia until September.

2 September PQ18 sailed from Loch Ewe, Scotland.
By this time there had been a radical overhaul of escort policy, and the 40 merchant ships were accompanied by sixteen destroyers and an escort carrier. In spite of intense Luftwaffe attacks the convoy got through, with the loss of one destroyer and one minesweeper plus 13 merchant ships in return for 3 U-boats sunk and five damaged, and 41 Luftwaffe aircraft were shot down.

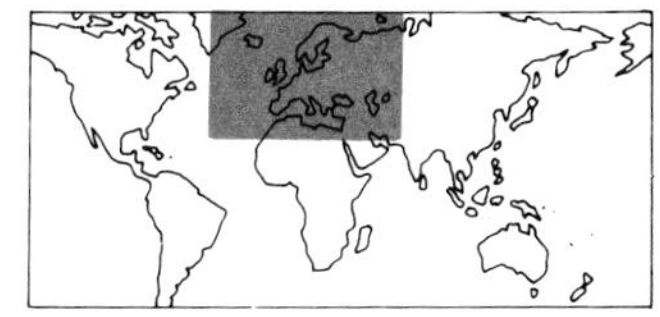

RUSSIAN RESUPPLY: 1941-1942

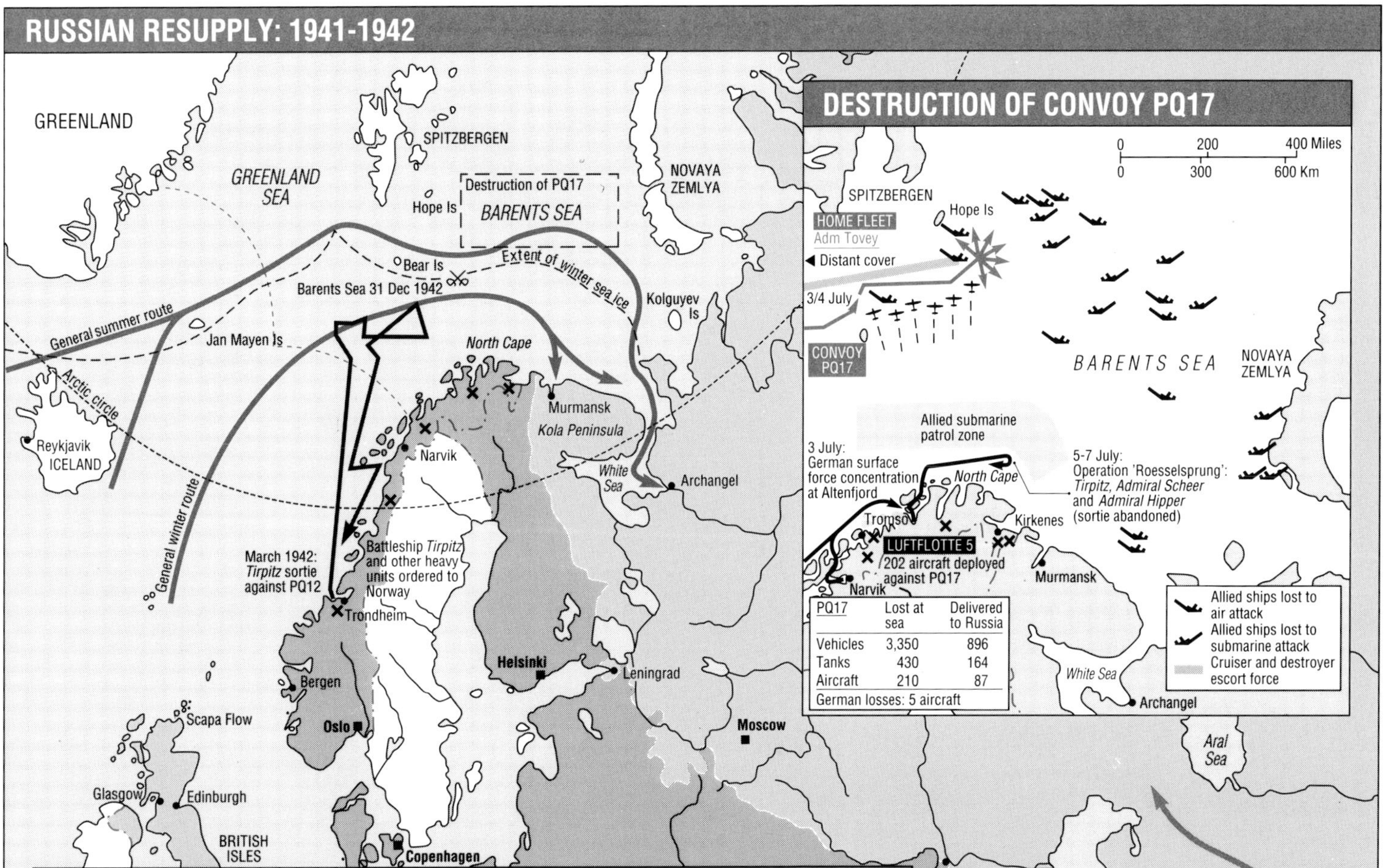

DESTRUCTION OF CONVOY PQ17

PQ17	Lost at sea	Delivered to Russia
Vehicles	3,350	896
Tanks	430	164
Aircraft	210	87

German losses: 5 aircraft

Areas of German control, end 1942
Areas of Allied control, end 1942
Allied supply routes to Russia
General location of German air bases
Limit of Allied land-based air cover

BATTLE OF THE BARENTS SEA

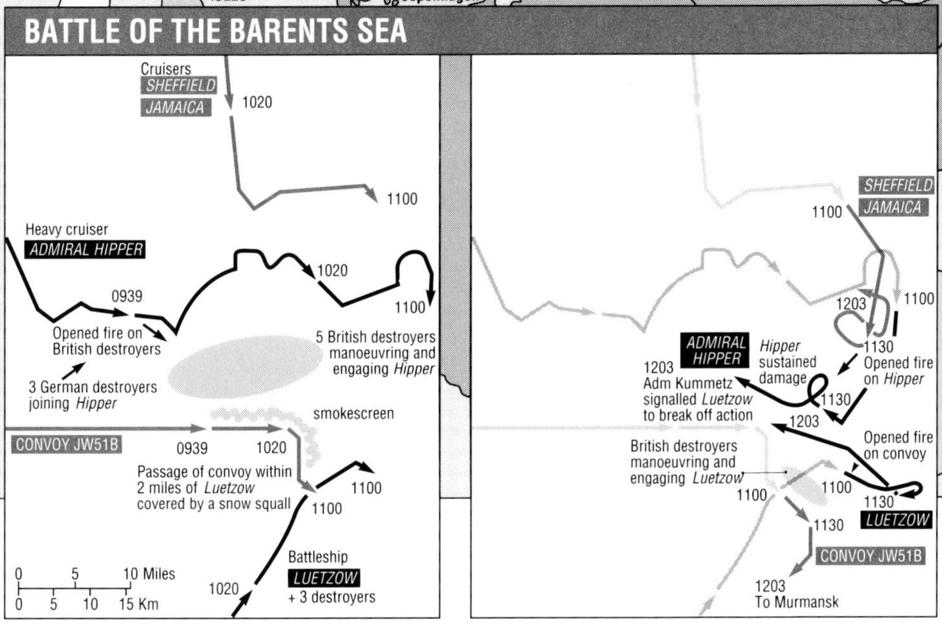

There was now another lull while priority was switched to the Allied landings in French North Africa, but the Arctic convoys were resumed once more in December with the new prefix of 'JW'.

In the meantime, on **23 October**, *Tirpitz* had been sent south for a refit, and Luftwaffe strength in Norway was reduced because of demands from the Mediterranean.

15 December Convoy JW51A set sail. Convoys were now split in two in order to stretch German resources. JW51B sailed five days later.

25 December JW51A arrived at Murmansk unscathed.

31 December Battle of the Barents Sea.

Hipper and *Luetzow* were seen off by the destroyer and cruiser escort of Convoy JW51B, which arrived at Murmansk on **3 January 1943** without casualties. The result was that Hitler demanded the scrapping of his surface ships. Raeder resigned and was replaced by Doenitz.

The Arctic convoys were now getting through to Russia, but only with excessively large escorts. In the meantime, throughout 1942 the British had been working hard to increase the capacity of the Iran supply route to Russia.

Securing the Arctic Convoy Route · P186

German Drive into the Caucasus

In the aftermath of the defeat of the Soviet forces at Kharkov, Stalin initiated another reorganization of the command structure in the Ukraine. The South-West Theatre HQ was abolished and Timoshenko was left with merely the South-West Front, the Bryansk and South Fronts being placed directly under control of the High Command (Stavka). With the Crimea Front now destroyed, a new front, the North Caucasus Front, under Marshal Semion Budenny was formed. Stavka, although well aware of the German intentions, remained convinced that von Bock's thrust into the Caucasus was merely a preliminary to a much larger operation designed to encircle Moscow. Consequently when von Weichs launched his attack in the Kursk area in the early hours of **28 June** the Russian defenders were caught unprepared and off balance.

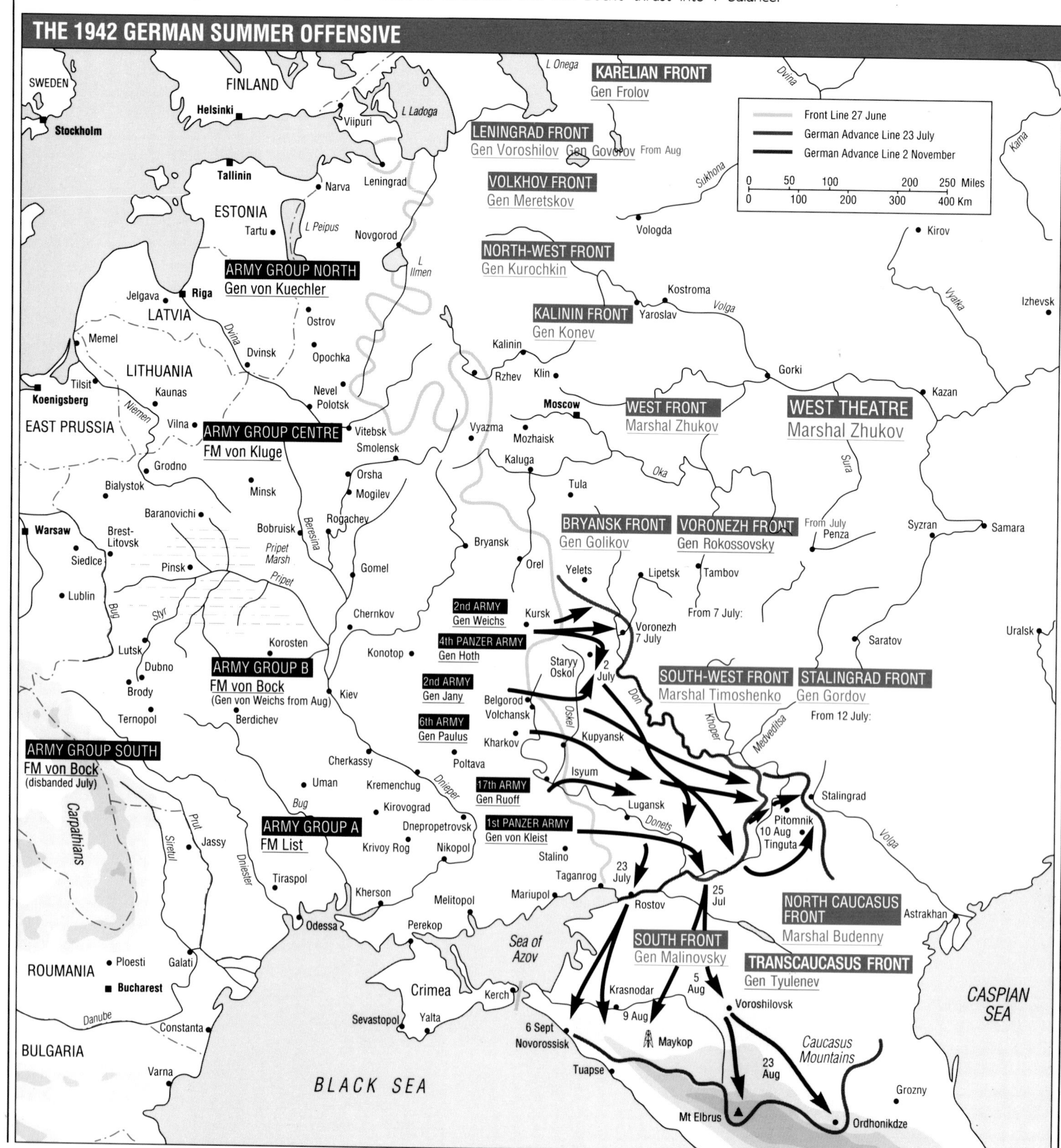

P94 · Kharkov and the Crimea

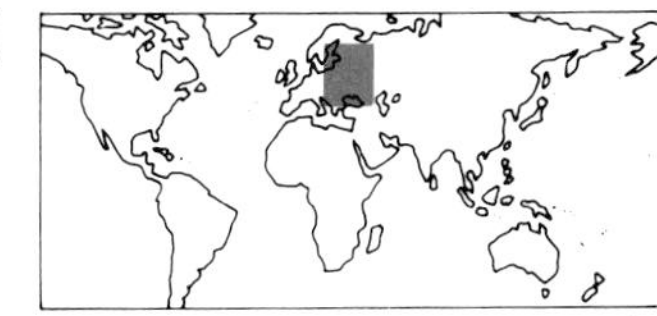

30 June 1942 **Paulus's Sixth Army attacked the Soviet South-West Front.**

2 July **Paulus and von Weichs linked up near Staryy Oskol.**
This created a small pocket, but the bulk of the Soviet forces were able to escape across the Don.

July **Army Group B reached the Don north and south of Voronezh.**
The Russians evacuated Voronezh, which was entered by the Germans two days later.

7 July **Army Group A began to attack into the Donets Basin.**
Next day First Panzer Army crossed the Donets. In the meantime von Bock began to switch Panzer formations from the Voronezh area to the south, but only slowly because he was worried that his flank on the Don was not yet secure. Lack of fuel and heavy rain slowed the move southwards, enabling the Soviet armies to withdraw intact.

13 July **Hitler switched forces from the drive on Stalingrad to the Donets Basin.**
He was convinced that sizeable Soviet forces remained west of the Don (which was in fact not so) and was determined to trap them in the Rostov area. Army Group B was now tasked with flank protection for Army Group A.

18 July **Hitler ordered Army Group B to resume the advance on Stalingrad.**
This revealed a change of mind from his orders of five days earlier. But because almost all the armour had been sent to Army Group A, the advance on Stalingrad was left to Paulus reinforced by just two corps, one of them Panzer. The remaining Panzer formations were ordered to thrust south over the lower Don on a broad front.

23 July **Von Bock dismissed from command.**
Hitler had been dissatisfied by what he viewed as his tardiness since the beginning of the offensive. Von Bock's HQ was dissolved and von Weichs took command of Army Group B.

On that same day Hitler issued Directive 45 for Operation 'Brunswick', the overrunning of the Caucasus. Army Group A, having destroyed the enemy in the Rostov area, was to secure the entire eastern coastline of the Black Sea, simultaneously capturing Maikop and Grozny, and then advance to Baku. Army Group B would continue east to seize Stalingrad and then advance down the Volga to Astrakhan. This meant that the two would advance on diverging axes and a large gap would develop between them. This was aggravated by the return of Hoth's Fourth Panzer Army to Army Group B.

The Russians in the meantime had formed new fronts: Voronezh from elements of the Bryansk Front (**7 July**) and Stalingrad from the South-West Front (**12 July**). Timoshenko, however, was removed from command of the latter on **23 July** and replaced by Gordov.

On this same day Rostov fell once more to the Germans.

25 July **Army Group A broke out of its bridgeheads on the lower Don.**
Fourth Panzer Army, which had been holding the most easterly bridgehead, drove east and then north-east to link up with Army Group B. Malinovsky's South Front was quickly shattered and the remnants absorbed by the North Caucasus Front. In spite of constant resupply problems and the heat, the German advance was surprisingly rapid.

Paulus also attempted to bounce the Don just west of Stalingrad, but was repulsed. He decided to wait until Hoth had fought his way up to join him before trying again.

5 August **Voroshilovsk (now Stavropol) fell.**

9 August **The Germans occupied the Maikop oilfields.**
Much of the installations had been destroyed and little refined oil was found.

10 August **Paulus crossed the Don and reached the outskirts of Stalingrad.**
He now had the support of von Richthofen's Fourth Air Fleet, which had been switched from Army Group A.

15 August **Troops of Army Group A reached the foothills of the Caucasus Mountains.**

19 August **Paulus began to attack Stalingrad itself.**
He had still not yet been joined by Hoth.

23 August **The German Swastika hoisted on Mount Elbrus, highest peak in the Caucasus Mountains.**
The Russian defence was stiffening, however, much helped by the terrain. This feat marked the 'high water' mark in the German attempts to secure the Black Sea coastline. Matters for Army Group A were not helped by the increased priority given to Army Group B in its fight for Stalingrad, where the civilian population was being hastily evacuated. On this same day Paulus reached the Volga just north of Stalingrad. The city itself was heavily bombed by the Luftwaffe. Hoth was held up in the area north of Tinguta.

24 August **Stalin ordered that Stalingrad be held.**
Zhukov was sent by Stalin to supervise its defence.

3 September **Hoth finally linked up with Paulus near Pitomnik.**
The Germans now tried to break into the city from the west, but were unable to do so because the Russians launched limited counter-attacks on the flanks, which diverted a significant proportion of Paulus's forces.

6 September **The port of Novorossisk fell to the Germans.**

9 September **List dismissed.**
Hitler assumed personal responsibility for Army Group A which, foiled in the west, was now meeting increasingly fierce resistance in its drive on Astrakhan and Baku.

14 September **Paulus renewed his attacks on Stalingrad.**
By this time the Soviet garrison was hemmed into a narrow strip along the west bank of the Volga not more than ten miles at its widest and four miles at its narrowest. Shortage of troops, however, meant that Paulus could only attack on very narrow frontages, and the fact that he was fighting in built-up areas meant that progress was slow and costly.

20 September **Paulus declared that he could attack no longer without substantial reinforcements.**
There was now a short comparative lull at Stalingrad. Von Weichs and Paulus were also becoming increasingly concerned over the flanks of the Stalingrad salient, which were held by Hungarian, Italian and Roumanian troops. Hitler was determined, though, to secure Stalingrad before tackling the problem of the flanks.

28 September **German pressure in Stalingrad stepped up once more.**
From now until the end of October Paulus's men struggled desperately with their equally exhausted enemies but made little progress. Stalemate had been reached.

2 November **Von Kleist's Panzers in Army Group A were finally halted five miles west of Ordhonikidze.**
This marked the southernmost extent of the thrust into the Caucasus. Increasing supply problems, growing Soviet resistance and now the onset of winter had finally brought the German offensive to a halt.

The 1942 German offensive had failed largely because, in the course of it, Hitler had switched objectives. Increasingly mesmerised by Stalingrad, he allowed the offensive to devolve into two independent thrusts which could not support one another. Stalin too had become determined that Stalingrad be held at whatever cost, but increasingly he realized that the Germans were at their most vulnerable on their flanks. He now resolved to attack these. The consequences for Paulus would be fatal.

The Landings on Guadalcanal

COUNTER-ATTACK IN THE SOLOMONS

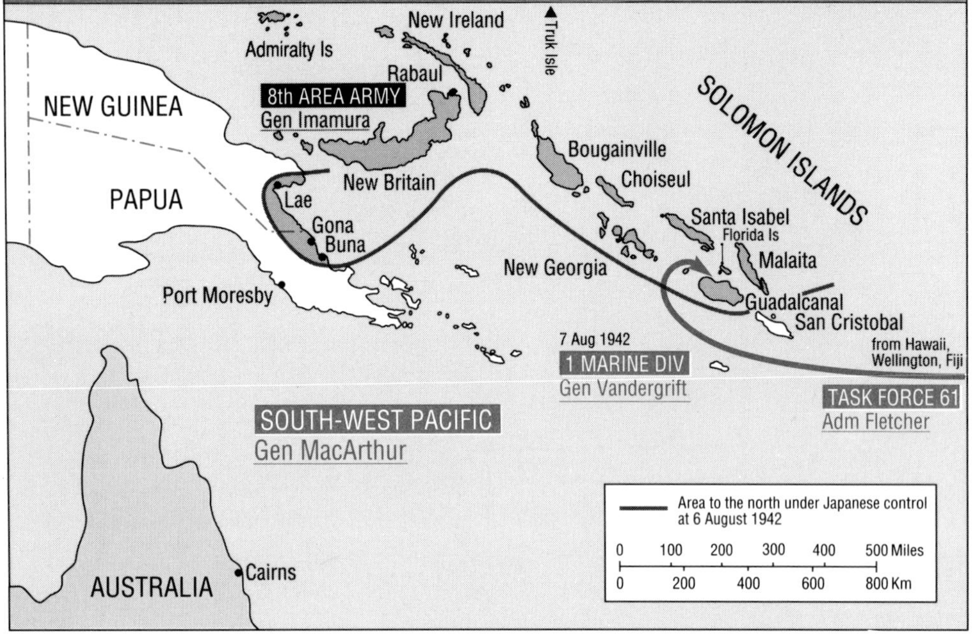

After the US naval victory over the Japanese fleet at Midway, the Americans were keen to exploit their success as quickly as possible. The key to the Japanese dominance of the South-West Pacific was their base at Rabaul on the north-east corner of the island of New Britain. General Douglas MacArthur wanted to attack it directly, but the Chiefs of Staff considered that this had little chance of success in view of the limited Allied forces available.

2 July 1942 Directive for recapture of the Solomons issued

Accordingly the US Chiefs of Staff ordered a three-phase operation. First, Admiral Chester Nimitz was to capture the Santa Cruz islands and eastern Solomons, in particular Tulagi and Guadalcanal. Next, MacArthur was to clear the Japanese from Lae and the rest of the Solomon Islands. Finally MacArthur was to go on to capture Rabaul. The start-date was set as **1 August.**

On **5 July** it was reported that the Japanese were building an airstrip on Guadalcanal and reinforcing the island. It was now decided that this should be the initial primary objective and, to allow a little more time for preparation, the landings were postponed to **7 August.**

Selected to carry out the landings was the US 1st Marine Division (Maj-Gen Alexander A. Vandergrift which was in Australia. Tactical command was given to Frank Fletcher, who had played such a major part in Coral Sea and Midway, with Vice-Admiral Robert L. Ghormley having overall control.

Even with the putting back of the landings to 7 August the Americans were hard pressed to get their forces organized in time for what had been codenamed 'Operation Watchtower'. So short were the numbers of men, supplies and shops available for it that it quickly became known as 'Operation Shoestring' and was a planner's nightmare.

It was clear that the success at Midway had taken the Americans by surprise in that the necessary base organization to mount major amphibious landings was not yet in place. As it was, the 1st Marine Division set sail with only ten days' worth of ammunition and less than half its vehicles. Even then it was forced to put into Wellington, New Zealand, in order to reorganize its stores to make more room on the ships.

It was decided that the complete force, amphibious shipping, escorts and Fletcher's Task Force 61 of three carriers – the only air support available for the landing – should all rendezvous at Fiji since part had had to come from Hawaii. This was achieved on **26 July** but there was only the opportunity to carry out one practice landing before the force set sail for Guadalcanal on the 31st.

The force hove to off Guadalcanal on the night of **6/7 August** having successfully evaded the Japanese naval patrols in the area. Little was known of the Japanese strength on the island, and it was a tense time for all.

7 August US Landing on Guadalcanal

Recognizing the threat of land-based Japanese aircraft and the fact the Marines could rely only on the aircraft of Fletcher's carriers, the planners had decided that the airstrip must be the primary objective on Guadalcanal. Soon to become known as Henderson Field, this was situated on the north coast and the landing was to be made at Lunga Point just near it. The Marines went ashore shortly after dawn and quickly established themselves on the beach. The Japanese on the island numbered some 2,200 only mostly construction workers employed on the airfield. They had been taken by surprise and put up little resistance, quickly withdrawing to the mountainous terrain further inland. Next day the airstrip was secured and it seemed as if 'Watchtower' was going to be a walkover.

One regiment of 1st Marine Division had made simultaneous landings on Tulagi and Gavutu-Tanambogo, which lay off Florida Island, 20 miles north of Guadalcanal. This had been an added complication to the planning, but was as the insistence of the US Navy, who wanted protected anchorages for the ships supporting Vandergift. Here it was a different story, with the Japanese resisting fiercely and it took three days to secure the islands. In the meantime there was a sudden change in the US fortunes.

Night of 8/9 August Battle of Savo Island

The Japanese reaction to the US landings came less than 48 hours after they had taken place. On the night of **8/9 August** they sent a naval task force in from the north-west to destroy the US transports standing off the beaches. Penetrating the US destroyer screen, the Japanese cruisers attacked five US cruisers, leaving four of them sinking. Japanese naval night fighting techniques were markedly superior to those of the US Navy at this stage of the war, and subsequent night actions around Guadalcanal would serve to confirm this.

This defeat gave the Americans a fright, and they withdrew the transports and Fletcher's carriers, leaving the Marines on Guadalcanal totally unsupported both in terms of resupply and air cover. Soon they found themselves on short rations and this, together with the debilitating climate, quickly led to sickness and later disease.

Luckily, the Japanese were slow to reap the benefits of their Savo Island success and it was not until **18 August** that the first Japanese reinforcements were landed on Guadalcanal, at Taivu, 20 miles east of the US beachhead. This was a regiment of 900 men commanded by Colonel Ichiki. Two days later Henderson Field was opened to combat aircraft and the Marines once more had air support, but only just in time. It did not, however, ease the resupply problem.

21 August First Japanese counter-attack

Ichiki's regiment attacked the Marines in their beachhead the day after Henderson Field had been opened to aircraft. In what became known as the Battle of Tenaru River, Ichiki's men were bloodily repulsed and then annihilated at a cost of 35 US dead and 75 wounded. Ichiki himself committed *hara-kiri*.

23-25 August Battle of the Eastern Solomons

Three Japanese carriers supporting efforts to resupply the Japanese force on Guadalcanal clashed

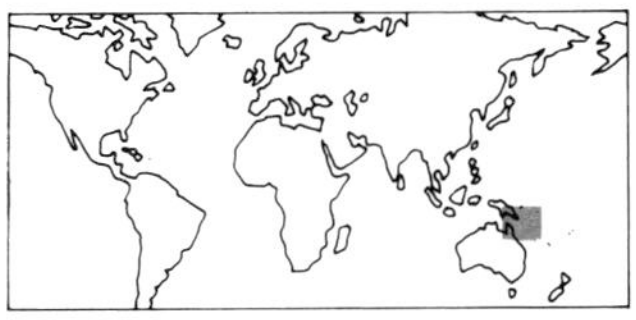

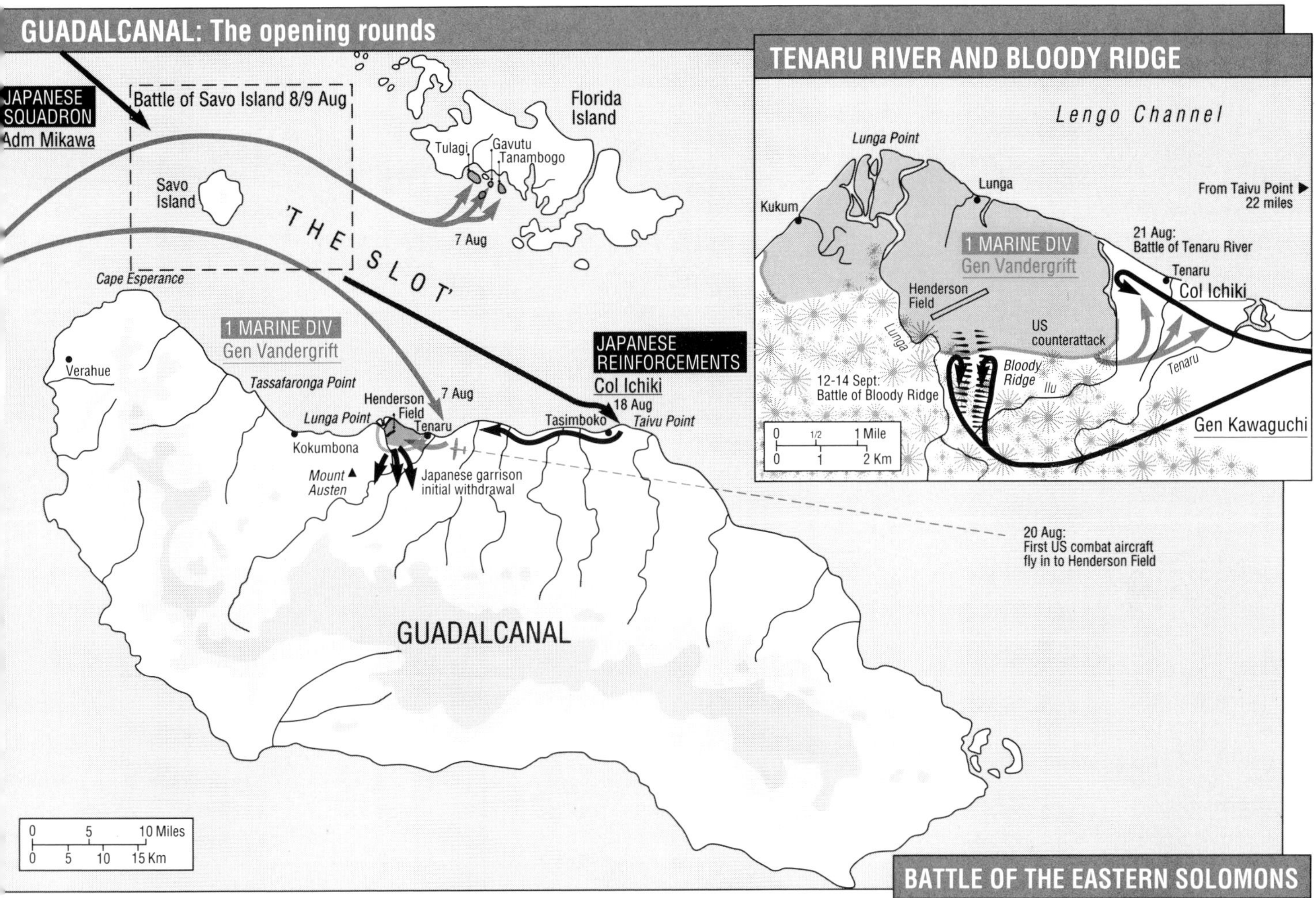
GUADALCANAL: The opening rounds
JAPANESE SQUADRON
Adm Mikawa
Battle of Savo Island 8/9 Aug
Florida Island
Tulagi
Gavutu
Tanambogo
Savo Island
'THE SLOT'
7 Aug
Cape Esperance
1 MARINE DIV
Gen Vandergrift
Verahue
Tassafaronga Point
Henderson Field
7 Aug
Lunga Point
Tenaru
JAPANESE REINFORCEMENTS
Col Ichiki
18 Aug
Tasimboko
Taivu Point
Kokumbona
Mount Austen
Japanese garrison initial withdrawal
20 Aug:
First US combat aircraft fly in to Henderson Field
GUADALCANAL
0 5 10 Miles
0 5 10 15 Km
TENARU RIVER AND BLOODY RIDGE
Lengo Channel
Lunga Point
Kukum
Lunga
From Taivu Point ▶ 22 miles
21 Aug:
Battle of Tenaru River
1 MARINE DIV
Gen Vandergrift
Henderson Field
Tenaru
Col Ichiki
US counterattack
Lunga
Bloody Ridge
Ilu
Tenaru
12-14 Sept:
Battle of Bloody Ridge
0 1/2 1 Mile
0 1 2 Km
Gen Kawaguchi

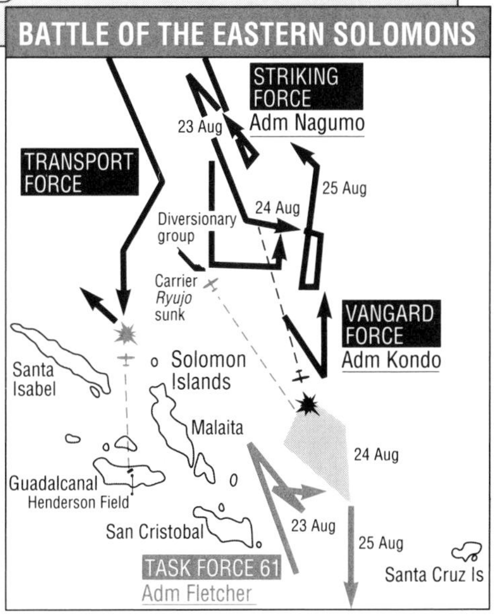
BATTLE OF THE EASTERN SOLOMONS
STRIKING FORCE
Adm Nagumo
23 Aug
TRANSPORT FORCE
25 Aug
24 Aug
Diversionary group
Carrier Ryujo sunk
VANGARD FORCE
Adm Kondo
Santa Isabel
Solomon Islands
Malaita
24 Aug
Guadalcanal
Henderson Field
San Cristobal
23 Aug
25 Aug
TASK FORCE 61
Adm Fletcher
Santa Cruz Is

with Fletcher's task force east of Santa Isabel. This time the Americans fared better. Spotting the Japanese carriers, Fletcher launched an air strike, but the Japanese had hurriedly reversed course and it was unsuccessful. Later that same day, 23rd, Fletcher spotted one of the Japanese carriers again and this time his aircraft sank it. A Japanese counter-strike did, however, succeed in disabling the US carrier *Esperance*. Both carrier forces now withdrew. but the Japanese transports continued on towards Guadalcanal. Two days later they were forced to turn back when aircraft based on Henderson Field sank two of them and a destroyer. As a result of this action the Japanese surrendered daytime control of the waters around Guadalcanal to the Americans. From now on they carried out reinforcement and resupply of Guadalcanal only by night from Bougainville in what became known as the Tokyo Night Express, which made frequent runs down the Slot, as the channel between Guadalcanal and Florida Island was nicknamed.

7 September Raid on Taivu

Aware that most Japanese reinforcements were being landed at Taivu, the Marines made a successful amphibious raid on it. Besides destroying stores and equipment, they also gained intelligence that another Japanese attack was pending.

12-14 September Battle of Bloody Ridge

In spite of the warning, the now exhausted Marines were hard pressed to repel the Japanese attack which came along the axis of Bloody Ridge. This posed a direct threat to Henderson Field. The Japanese under General Kawaguchi managed to infiltrate the US lines, but were eventually driven back in bitter and desperate fighting. The Japanese suffered 600 killed, while the Americans lost 150.

The Marines now extended their line to the summit of Bloody Ridge and reinforcements began to arrive. Henderson Field had, in spite of intermittent artillery fire on it, been developed to the extent that transport aircraft could use it by **28 September**. By this time Vandergrift had some 23,000 men and felt strong enough to be able to take to the offensive. On **27 September** he launched his first attack, which was designed to widen his beachhead to the west. Little progress was made and it was clear that the Japanese were not going to be driven off Guadalcanal easily. Indeed, the Imperial Japanese Headquarters had decreed that the recapture of the island must be given top priority. As a result Lieutenant-General Hyakutake decided to leave Rabaul with his Seventeenth Army and take control of operations personally.

Much bitter fighting on both sea and land was to take place before Guadalcanal was finally secure in US hands. The initial stages of the campaign had, however, demonstrated that the US Marine could better his Japanese counterpart in jungle combat.

Guadalcanal Secured · P124

7 JULY 1942 TO 22 JANUARY 1943

Papua – New Guinea: Allied Counter-Offensive

The Japanese attempt to land troops at Port Moresby had been frustrated by the Battle of the Coral Sea, but the Allies had little doubt that they would try again. At the same time, General Douglas MacArthur, having been given his directive for the regaining of the Solomons and the eventual capture of Rabaul, decided that he needed an airfield on Papua in order to support his operations in the Solomons. He selected the Buna Government Station north of Milne Bay, where a small landing strip already existed. He also recognized that Buna was a likely Japanese landing place, since it gave them an approach to Port Moresby through the Owen Stanley Mountains by a steep and tortuous track called the Kokoda Trail. To cover this approach the small Maroubra Force was formed at Port Moresby in June; it consisted of two infantry battalions: one Australian and one Papuan.

7 July 1942 **Maroubra Force began to move to Kokoda via the Kokoda Trail.**

15 July **Maroubra Force arrived at Kokoda.**
The men were exhausted. On the same day MacArthur issued orders for the occupation of Buna under the code-name 'Providence'. This was planned to begin on **31 July**.

21 July **Japanese landed at Gona on the coast above Buna.**
This was a 2,000-man force under Colonel Yosuke Yokoyama. His was an advanced detachment with orders to make the Kokoda Trail fit for motor traffic prior to the landing of the main force, General Tomitaro Horii's South Seas Detachment. On this day MacArthur set out from Melbourne by train to establish his HQ at Brisbane.

23 July **First clashes between Maroubra Force and the Japanese.**
Maroubra Force withdrew, evacuating Kokoda.

8 August **Maroubra Force recaptured Kokoda.**
Now short of food and ammunition, they were quickly forced to evacuate it once more. In the meantime MacArthur had ordered 7th Australian Division, newly returned from the Middle East, to Papua. Two brigades were sent to Port Moresby and one to Milne Bay.

16 August **One brigade of 7th Australian Division began to move out on the Kokoda Trail.**
Its orders were to hold the Owen Stanleys and retake Buna.

18 August **Main Japanese force landed at Buna.**
By the 21st the Japanese had landed 11,500 men.

21 August **7th Australian Division linked up with Maroubra Force near Myola.**
In the meantime Japanese air raids on Port Moresby had destroyed much of the supplies for 7th Australian Division.

26 August **Japanese landings at Milne Bay.**
At the same time they launched an offensive on the Kokoda Trail, which was initially held.

28 August **The Australians began to counter-attack at Milne Bay.**
Further Japanese reinforcements were landed next day, but they were outnumbered two to one by the Australians. By **6 September** they were forced to evacuate their troops, who returned to Rabaul.

29 August **On the Kokoda Trail, after fierce fighting the Australians were forced back.**
They withdrew to Alola and then to their advanced base at Myola, arriving there on **3 September**. Next day they pulled back further to Efogi.

8 September **The Japanese infiltrated the Efogi position.**
This forced further withdrawals, and by the 11th the Australian remnants were close to the Imita Ridge, the last natural obstacle before Port Moresby. By this time 7th Division's second brigade, the 25th, was ready for action.

14 September **25th Brigade began a counter-attack to recover Kokoda.**
It was initially repulsed. The Japanese counter-attacked and forced the Australians back to Imita Ridge, where they stood firm on the 17th.

15 September **US troops began to land at Port Moresby.**
MacArthur planned to use a regiment from 32nd Infantry Division, one of the two US divisions in Australia under General Robert L. Eichelberger, to make a wide turning movement through the mountains south of the Kokoda Trail.

24 September **The Japanese facing Imita Ridge received orders to withdraw to Buna.**
There were a number of reasons for this. The original Japanese plan had been for a two-pronged assault by land and sea on Port Moresby, but the failure at Milne Bay had upset the timings. The Japanese had therefore been ordered to halt until the amphibious landings could be organized. Conscious of the arrival of US troops at Port Moresby and the success of the US landings on Guadalcanal, the Japanese feared that MacArthur intended to make an amphibious landing at Buna, thus cutting their supply route from Rabaul.

27 September **The Australians began to advance once more along the Kokoda Trail.**

1 October **MacArthur issued fresh orders.**
Simultaneous thrusts were to be made along the Kokoda Trail and the Kapa Kapa Track to its south with the object of cutting off the Japanese beyond Kokoda. The Milne Bay–Cape Nelson coastline was to be secured and Buna recaptured.

6 October **US troops set off along the Kapa Kapa Track.**
The going was hard, and not until **20 October** did the leading elements reach Jaure; it was a further eight days before the main body was concentrated here.

In the meantime a second US infantry regiment had been flown into Port Moresby, and this was transported by air and sea to Pongani, 30 miles south of Buna. Here they were ordered to wait until the Australians were well across the River Kumusi.

21–28 October **Battle for Eora Creek.**
The Japanese had left a strongly defended rearguard position at this point on the Kokoda Trail, which held up the Australians and caused MacArthur to replace the 7th Division commander. Their forces on the Trail had now been joined by another brigade. Renewing the advance, Alola was reached on **30 October**. Here one brigade went north to capture Kokoda (entered **2 November**) and the other continued eastward to capture Oivi.

5–10 November **Battle for Oivi.**
Once more the Japanese had dug in and resisted strongly. During their subsequent withdrawal General Horii was drowned while crossing the River Kumusi.

6 November **MacArthur flew into Port Moresby and set up his HQ there.**

14 November **US advance on Buna began.**

15 November **The Australians crossed the Kumusi.**

17 November **1,000 Japanese reinforcements landed at Buna.**

18 November **The Australians reached the main Japanese defensive position in the Gona–Buna area.**
The Americans did the same next day, on which the annual rains began. The Japanese had been preparing their defences since September, and they were strong.

1 December **The US commander was replaced by Eichelberger.**
This unusual step of appointing a corps commander to take over a force equal to less than a full division reflected MacArthur's frustration in the lack of progress against Buna. Slowly the Americans inched forward, but ten days later Buna was still in Japanese hands.

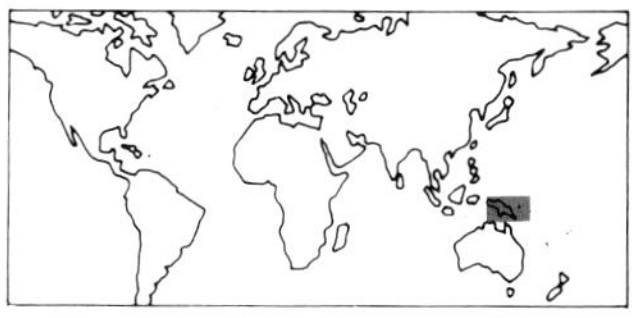

2 December Further Japanese reinforcements from Rabaul landed at the mouth of the Kumusi. Allied aircraft had earlier forced them back to Rabaul. Another attempt was made on **7 December** but was again forced back to Rabaul for the same reason. A final attempt eventually succeeded on **14 December**; after being harried by aircraft, 800 men were landed in Mambare Bay.

10 December The Australians captured Gona. This was after 12 days' desperate fighting, which cost them nearly half their strength.

14 December Eichelberger launched another attack on Buna village. The Japanese had, however, evacuated it, withdrawing to Buna Station and Sananada.

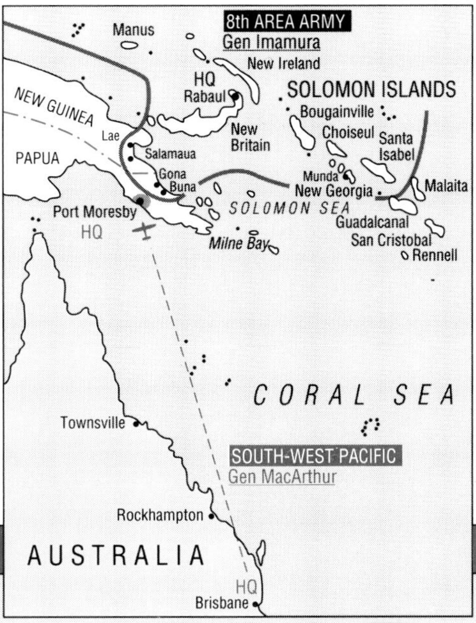

Manus
8th AREA ARMY
Gen Imamura
New Ireland
HQ
Rabaul
SOLOMON ISLANDS
Bougainville
Choiseul
Santa Isabel
New Britain
NEW GUINEA
Lae
Salamaua
PAPUA
Gona
Buna
Munda
New Georgia
Malaita
SOLOMON SEA
Port Moresby
HQ
Milne Bay
Guadalcanal
San Cristobal
Rennell
CORAL SEA
Townsville
SOUTH-WEST PACIFIC
Gen MacArthur
Rockhampton
AUSTRALIA
HQ
Brisbane

18 December Final Allied attacks began. Japanese resistance remained fierce.

2 January 1943 Buna Station finally captured.

22 January Last Japanese resistance around Sananda eradicated.

The fighting in Papua had cost the Allies 8,500 battle casualties and the Japanese almost 12,000. Many others from both sides were suffering from disease. Few campaigns during the war were fought under such terrible conditions, in terms of both terrain and weather, something MacArthur did not appreciate as much as he might have done. For the Allies the fighting in Papua–New Guinea marked the first successful land campaign against the Japanese.

THE BUNA-GONA CAMPAIGN

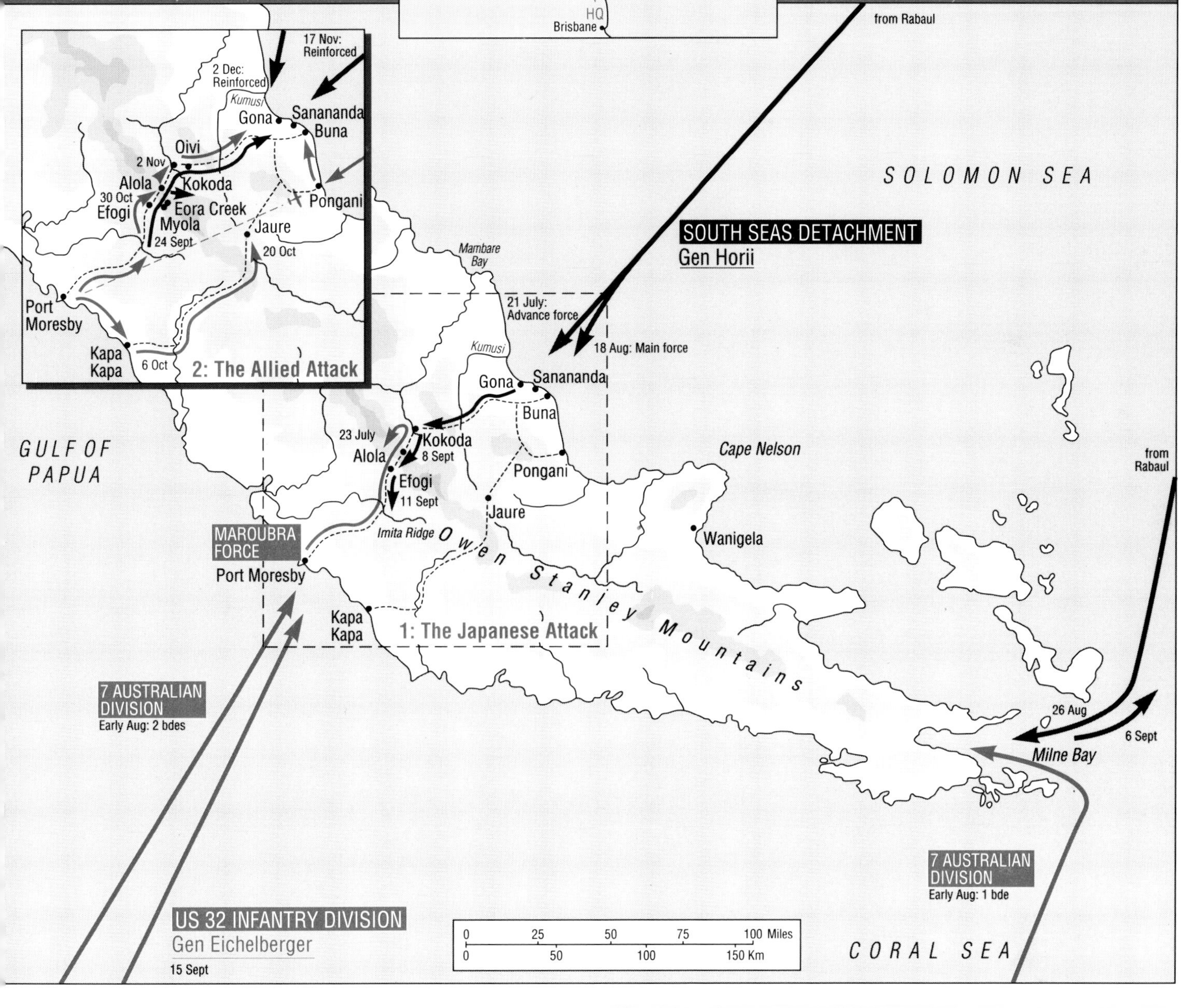

17 Nov: Reinforced
2 Dec: Reinforced
Kumusi
Gona
Sananda
Buna
Oivi
2 Nov
Alola
Kokoda
30 Oct
Efogi
Eora Creek
Pongani
Myola
Jaure
24 Sept
20 Oct
Port Moresby
Kapa Kapa
6 Oct
2: The Allied Attack
from Rabaul
SOLOMON SEA
SOUTH SEAS DETACHMENT
Gen Horii
Mambare Bay
21 July: Advance force
18 Aug: Main force
Kumusi
Gona
Sananda
Buna
23 July
Alola
Kokoda
8 Sept
Cape Nelson
GULF OF PAPUA
Efogi
11 Sept
Pongani
Jaure
MAROUBRA FORCE
Imita Ridge
Owen Stanley Mountains
Wanigela
Port Moresby
from Rabaul
Kapa Kapa
1: The Japanese Attack
7 AUSTRALIAN DIVISION
Early Aug: 2 bdes
26 Aug
6 Sept
Milne Bay
7 AUSTRALIAN DIVISION
Early Aug: 1 bde
US 32 INFANTRY DIVISION
Gen Eichelberger
15 Sept
0 25 50 75 100 Miles
0 50 100 150 Km
CORAL SEA

The Aleutians and New Georgia · P144

Rommel Repulsed

Rommel stood before the El Alamein line with four immediate objectives. He aimed to defeat the British Eighth Army; seize the Suez Canal between Ismailia and Port Said, making it inoperable for the passage of further Allied reinforcements; occupy Cairo; and eradicate any threat from Alexandria. After the fierce fighting of the previous six weeks his troops were understrength and exhausted, but he realized that he could only break through if he gave the British no time to recover from their recent reverses.

1 July 1942 Rommel launched his first attacks. Heavy artillery fire, a violent sandstorm and the Desert Air Force all contributed to denying Rommel the knock-out blow that he sought, although he did overrun an Indian infantry brigade at Deir el Shein.

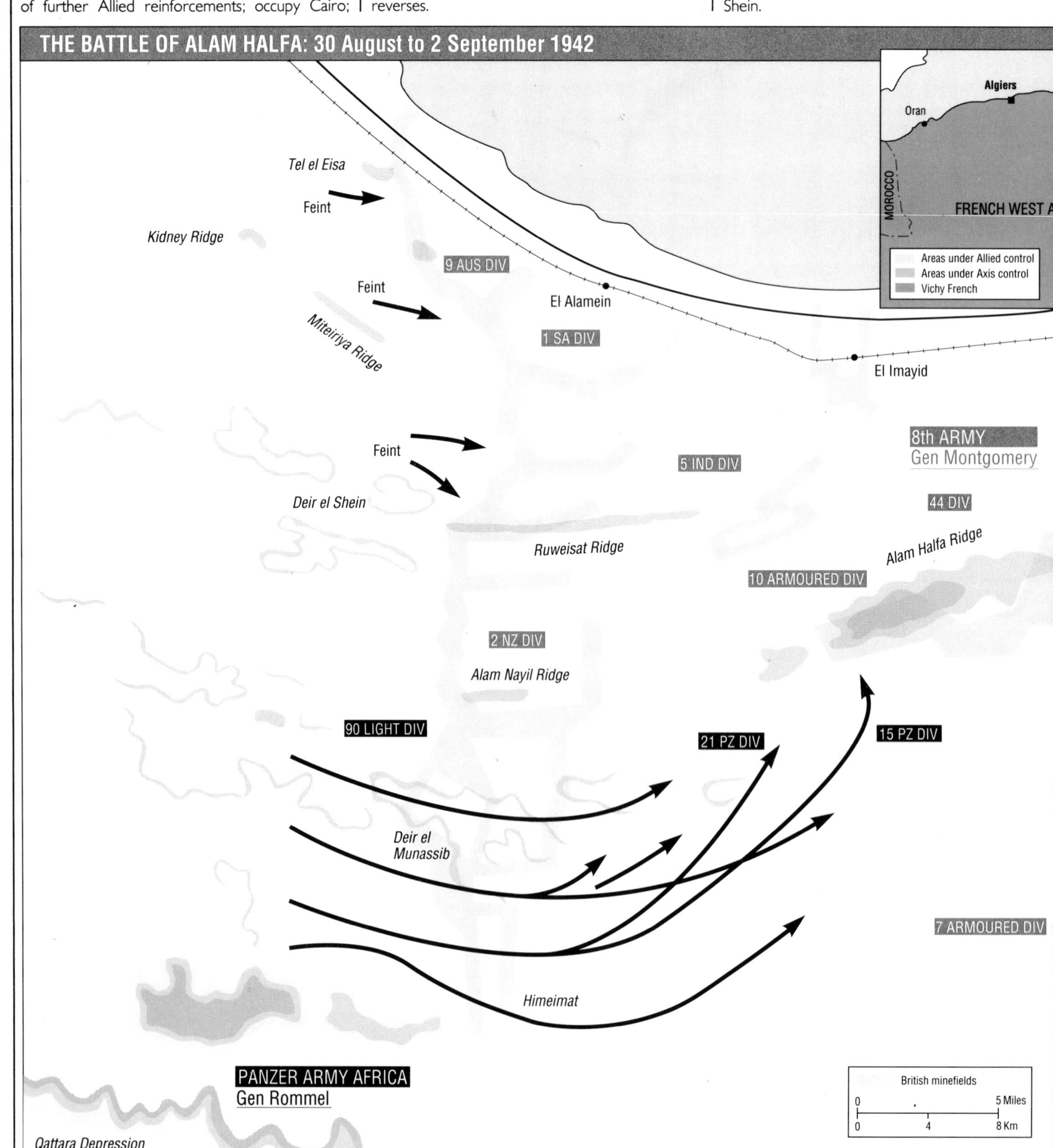

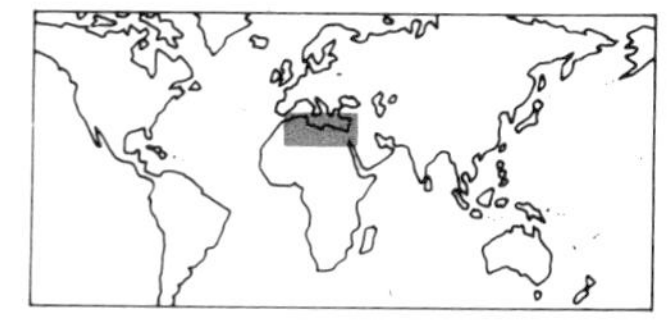
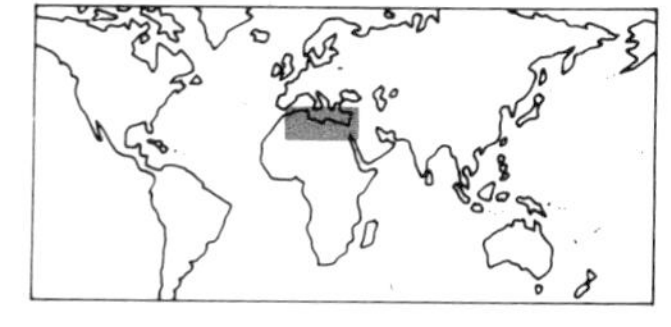

2 July **Rommel mounted further attacks between El Alamein and Ruweisat Ridge.**
Auchinleck, gauging Rommel's intentions from Ultra, attempted a counter-stroke from the south, but hit the Germans in the nose rather than the flank. Confused tank battles went on until dark, with the British being kept at bay by 88mm anti-tank guns.

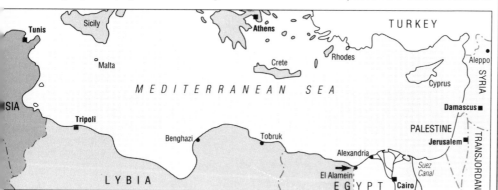

3 July **Rommel attacked once more along Ruweisat Ridge.**
He advanced nine miles, but by nightfall had been forced to a halt. He now realized that he had 'shot his bolt' for the time being and ordered his troops on to the defensive.

4 July **Auchinleck, believing his enemy was beaten, attacked with armour.**
Rommel's radio intercept service gave him forewarning, and there was hesitancy among British subordinate commanders. The British attacks were repulsed, and Rommel continued to withdraw his tanks from the front line and replace them with Italian infantry.

5–7 July **Auchinleck continued his attempts to get behind Rommel's defences from the south.**
Much of the fighting was centered on Deir el Shein, but the British attacks were piecemeal. Both sides received some reinforcements.

9 July **Rommel attacked the New Zealanders at Deir el Munassib.**
Again Auchinleck had been forewarned and pulled the New Zealand Division back, so that Rommel's blow hit thin air. This helped Auchinleck's new plan, which was to break through the Italians in the north.

10 July **The South Africans and Australians attacked from the El Alamein Box.**
They were initially successful in breaking through the Italian positions. Rommel, who was in the south with his armour, had to dash northwards, but managed to contain the damage by repeated counter-attacks next day.

12–13 July **Rommel attacked the El Alamein Box in the north once more.**
His progress was initially promising, but unusual lack of co-ordination between armour, infantry and engineers, and effective British artillery, brought the attack to a halt. This was the last major attack attempted by Rommel and marked a major turning-point in the battle.

Auchinleck now planned to break through the centre of the Axis position and then turn north to destroy Rommel's forces. First he had to recover the whole of the Ruweisat Ridge, which he saw as the key.

15 July **The New Zealanders attacked at Ruweisat.**
They did so from the south-east and were soon off the ridge, but the British armour did not move to support them, and the DAK was able to overrun the brigade occupying the western end of the ridge. During the next two days both sides put in local attacks, but little progress was made. Rommel was now becoming increasingly concerned about his situation, especially since the DAF had destroyed much of his fuel and ammunition stocks at Mersa Matruh.

22 July **Auchinleck launched another major attack.**
His plan was to use XXX Corps to contain the Axis forces in the north through local attacks, while XIII Corps broke through in the Ruweisat area and pursued the beaten enemy. Once again he failed to make much progress and lost a complete armoured brigade, which fell victim to a minefield and German tanks and 88s. Undeterred, Auchinleck turned once more to the north, where the Italians were.

27 July **The Australians attacked along the Miteirya Ridge.**
Once again lack of co-ordination between infantry and armour led to little success. Auchinleck, his reserves now exhausted, called a halt.

Thus ended the First Battle of El Alamein. The opposing armies had fought themselves to a standstill, but while Auchinleck had stopped Rommel, his troops had shown that they were not yet capable of going on to the offensive with any guarantee of success.

30 July **Auchinleck informed London that his forces would not attack again before mid-September.**

3 August **Churchill arrived in Cairo.**
He was disappointed that Auchinleck had failed to drive Rommel back and concerned that he had lost the confidence of his troops. He decided to split the existing command into two – Middle East (Persia and Iraq) and Near East (Egypt, Palestine, Syria). Auchinleck was offered the former while Alexander was to be brought in to command the latter. Gott was appointed to command the Eighth Army.

7 August **Gott killed in an air crash.**
Montgomery was appointed in his place, and the idea of splitting Middle East Command into two was dropped. Auchinleck now became CinC India, and Alexander took overall command in the Middle East.

13 August **Montgomery assumed command of the Eighth Army.**
His arrival provided an instant tonic to the troops. Knowing from Ultra that Rommel intended to attack again at the end of the month, he told his men that there was to be no question of any withdrawal from the El Alamein position. Rommel, meanwhile, had fallen ill on **2 August** and had asked to be relieved. This was refused. Now depending heavily on the arrival of six fuel and ammunition ships from Italy, he planned his next attack. On this day a vital convoy ('Pedestal') reached Malta from Gibraltar.

30 August **Late that night Rommel began his attack.**
The supply ships had not arrived: four out of six had been located by the British through Ultra and sunk. To get through to Cairo, Rommel would have to rely on capturing British stocks of fuel. His plan was to feint in the north and make his main thrust in the south against XIII Corps. The key was the Alam Halfa Ridge, from which the battle took its name. Rommel was repulsed here both on 31 August and 1 September.

2 September **Frustrated by his failure to take the Alam Halfa Ridge, Rommel fell back to his start-line.**
This marked the end of his efforts to reach the Suez Canal.

Night of 3/4 September **2nd New Zealand Division made a limited counter-attack.**
This was to close the gaps opened by Rommel in the minefields in front of the British position. The New Zealanders succeeded but were then withdrawn, as they were too exposed.

The British success at Alam Halfa reinforced Montgomery's standing both with his troops and with Churchill. The next task was to drive Rommel back, but Montgomery considered that the Eighth Army was in no fit shape to do this immediately and required much training before it could do so.

Desert Victory · P118

Desert Victory

No sooner had the Battle of Alam Halfa ended than Montgomery set about preparing the Eighth Army for the decisive blow against Rommel's Axis forces. First he replaced a number of subordinate commanders and then laid down strict guidelines for training, with emphasis on speed, flexibility and thoroughly understood, standard battle drills. He also received substantial reinforcements.

Rommel, on the other hand, even though on **8 September** he finally received the two surviving supply ships of the six promised him before his attack at Alam Halfa, was still very short of supplies. He made constant pleas to Rome and Berlin for an uninterrupted flow, but this never materialized. The truth was that in Hitler's eyes the campaign in North Africa was never more than a side-show when compared with the Eastern Front. Rommel did his best to prepare his defences for the attack he knew was bound to come.

Night of 13/14 September 1942 Abortive British raid on Tobruk.
Operation 'Agreement' was designed to destroy the harbour installations, thereby denying Rommel a reception point for supplies. The plan, involving several different units and land- and sea-based attacks, was over-complicated, and the result was a disaster; many men were lost and three destroyers were sunk. Simultaneous raids were mounted against Barce and Benghazi. A number of aircraft were destroyed during the former by the Long Range Desert Group, while that on Benghazi by the Special Air Service (SAS) was repulsed.

14 September Montgomery issued his plan for the attack on the Axis forces at El Alamein.
Code-named Operation 'Lightfoot', it called for simultaneous attacks in the north and south. That in the south by XIII Corps, which had one armoured division and infantry, was designed to draw Rommel's tanks away from the north, while XXX Corps in the north conducted the main break-in operation. X Corps, with two armoured divisions would then pass through the minefield gaps created by XXX Corps and establish itself in a position to threaten the Axis supply lines. After that the plan would depend on how the battle had gone. The attack would be launched during the October full moon period.

17 September Churchill cabled Alexander demanding that 'Lightfoot' be launched before the end of September.
Mounting criticism in parliament of the way in which the war was being conducted made Churchill impatient for an early victory. Alexander, prompted by Montgomery, replied that the Eighth Army would be insufficiently trained, whereas delaying 'Lightfoot' until October would ensure victory. On **23 September** Churchill grudgingly accepted this. The attack was to be launched on **23 October**.

23 September Rommel flew to Europe for a cure.
He had been suffering from liver problems and high blood pressure. He pleaded in person with both Mussolini and Hitler for more supplies. The latter assured him that the situation would be improved, but this turned out to be an empty promise. Rommel had left his deputy, General Georg Stumme, in charge in North Africa.

30 September Abortive attack to test Rommel's defences.
This was carried out by two brigades of 44th Division in the Munassib Depression. They were repulsed with heavy casualties by German and Italian paratroops.

5 October Eighth Army intelligence report emphasized the strength of the Axis minefields.
This caused some disquiet among Montgomery's subordinate commanders, and he decided to change his plan. X Corps would now fight with XXX Corps, using its armour to protect the infantry as they carried out the break-in operation.

Night of 23/24 October Opening of the Second Battle of El Alamein.
After a short, sharp bombardment by 900 guns, the infantry of XXX Corps advanced through the minefields. The Axis forces were initially caught by surprise. The southern thrust was the more successful, with the New Zealanders quickly securing the Miteiriya Ridge. 10th Armoured Division supporting them hesitated to pass through. Likewise the Australians in the north had difficulty in getting through the minefield, and 1st Armoured Division behind them became jammed in the partially opened lane. That day Stumme was killed by a mine.

25 October Rommel returned to North Africa.
He had been forced to cut short his cure. The break-in operation continued, but little progress was made. Likewise XIII Corps in the extreme south also became stuck. Montgomery's plans were in danger of coming to naught.

26 October Montgomery ordered the attacks to be halted temporarily.
This was in order to regroup and 'pause for breath'. He now planned that XIII Corps should attack north and north-westwards towards the coast.

27 October Axis counter-attacks.
Rommel used his armour to try and knock the British off Miteiriya and Kidney Ridges. These attacks were beaten off.

28 October Churchill expressed concern over Montgomery's slow progress.
This was especially in view of the fact that the planned Allied landings in French North Africa were imminent.

29 October Montgomery changed his plans once more.
By now it was clear that the Germans were concentrated in the coastal sector, and he decided to attack further inland. The new plan, code-named 'Supercharge', called for the infantry of XIII Corps to attack westwards while the X Corps armour operated north-westwards in order to ward off Rommel's Panzers. In the meantime, 9th Australian Division was to continue the spoiling attacks it had begun towards the coast on that day.

2 November 'Supercharge' began.
This was in the early hours of the morning. Rommel's troops were soon under pressure and, with fuel now desperately short, he began to withdraw his forces. An order from Hitler sent that night told him to stand and fight to the last, but it was too late. By the end of the next day the Eighth Army was poised to break out.

4 November Montgomery's armour began to pursue Rommel.
It first attempted to cut Rommel off at Fuqa, but failed. Montgomery now wanted to pin Rommel down here and use his armour to get to Mersa Matruh well behind the Axis forces. Heavy rain on **6–7 November** frustrated this. Rommel continued to pull back.

13 November The British recaptured Tobruk.

15 November Derna regained.

17 November Msus reached.

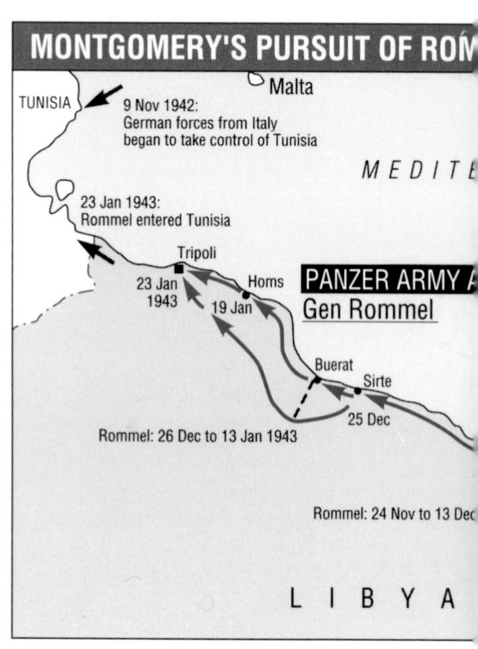

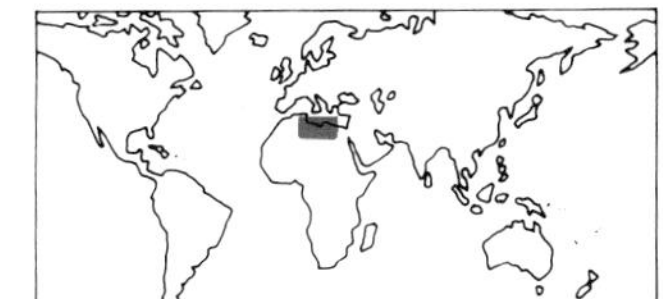

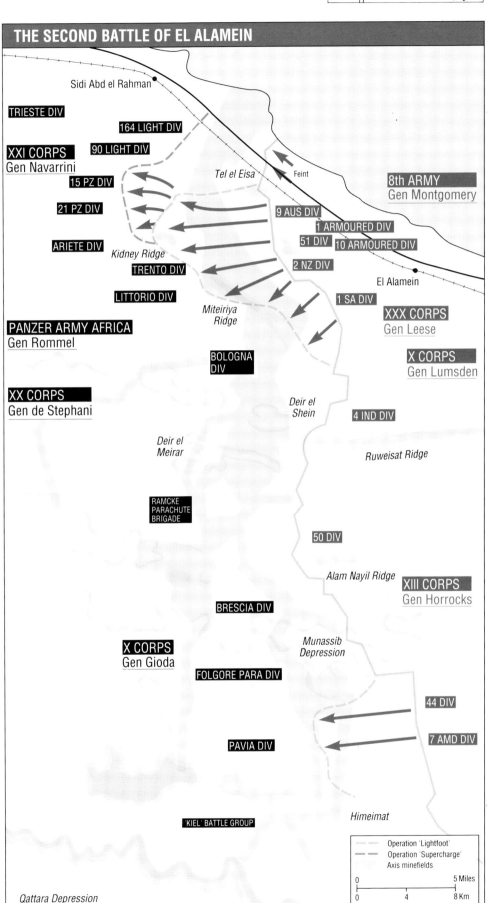

20 November Benghazi reoccupied.

24 November Rommel halted at El Agheila.
Both Hitler and Mussolini demanded that Rommel hold here, and Mussolini even expected him to launch a counter-offensive. Rommel himself wanted to evacuate his forces to Europe. Montgomery, his supply lines now very stretched, paused in order to open the port of Benghazi before turning Rommel out of his new position.

13 December Rommel began to withdraw from El Agheila.
He considered that the only way something could be salvaged from the wreckage of defeat would be to join with the Axis forces in Tunisia.

26 December Rommel halted at Buerat.
Mussolini ordered him to hold this to the last. Montgomery paused once more to allow his supplies to catch up.

13 January 1943 Rommel evacuated the Buerat position.
Again, this was just before Montgomery was about to attack.

23 January Eighth Army entered Tripoli.
Rommel crossed into Tunisia.

Montgomery's victory at El Alamein and his subsequent pursuit of Rommel was the last victory of the war achieved by British and Commonwealth arms alone. From now on, all fighting in North Africa and Europe would be conducted alongside the Americans. Montgomery's achievement marked, in Churchill's words, 'the end of the beginning' – there was still much fighting to be done before North Africa would be cleared of the Axis presence.

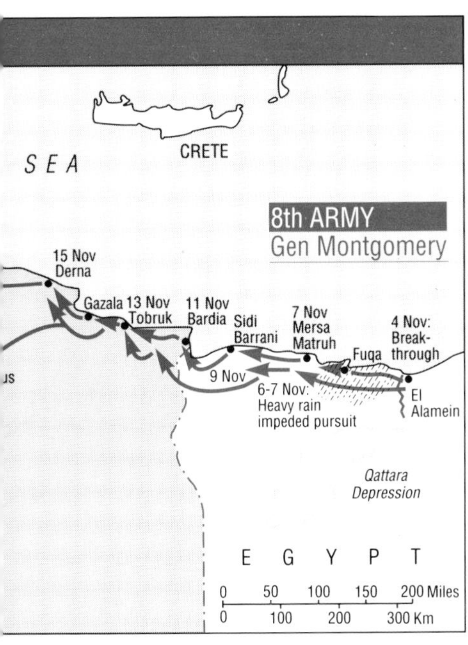

THE SECOND BATTLE OF EL ALAMEIN

Sidi Abd el Rahman
TRIESTE DIV
164 LIGHT DIV
90 LIGHT DIV
XXI CORPS
Gen Navarrini
15 PZ DIV
21 PZ DIV
ARIETE DIV
Tel el Eisa
Feint
8th ARMY
Gen Montgomery
9 AUS DIV
1 ARMOURED DIV
51 DIV
10 ARMOURED DIV
Kidney Ridge
TRENTO DIV
2 NZ DIV
El Alamein
LITTORIO DIV
1 SA DIV
Miteiriya
Ridge
XXX CORPS
Gen Leese
PANZER ARMY AFRICA
Gen Rommel
BOLOGNA
DIV
X CORPS
Gen Lumsden
XX CORPS
Gen de Stephani
Deir el
Shein
4 IND DIV
Deir el
Meirar
Ruweisat Ridge
RAMCKE
PARACHUTE
BRIGADE
50 DIV
Alam Nayil Ridge
XIII CORPS
Gen Horrocks
BRESCIA DIV
Munassib
Depression
X CORPS
Gen Gioda
FOLGORE PARA DIV
44 DIV
7 AMD DIV
PAVIA DIV
Himeimat
'KIEL' BATTLE GROUP
Operation 'Lightfoot'
Operation 'Supercharge'
Axis minefields
0 5 Miles
0 4 8 Km
Qattara Depression

Operation 'Torch'

The Allied decision to invade French North Africa before the end of 1942 had not been reached without difficulty. While Roosevelt and Churchill were agreed on it from early on, the majority of US military leaders and strategic planners believed that it was detrimental to the prospects of the invasion of Europe ('Round Up') in 1943. Nevertheless, the opponents of 'Gymnast' accepted that some form of offensive action by the Western Allies would be essential before the end of 1942 in order to satisfy Stalin and keep Russia fighting.

The original plan was drawn up immediately after the 'Arcadia' Conference. This envisaged a solely US invasion of French Morocco. A revised version ('Super-Gymnast'), incorporating a British proposal to invade Tunisia, had been approved by the Combined Chiefs of Staff on **19 February 1942.** Reverses at the hands of the Germans and Japanese had then caused 'Super-Gymnast' to recede into the background.

24 July 1942 **US Chief of Staff General Marshall issued CCS 94.**
This document stated that no final decision on the invasion of French North Africa (now code-named 'Torch') would be made until **15 September,** the earliest date on which it was considered that the outcome of the Axis offensive on the Eastern Front would be known. If by then it was clear that the Russians had suffered sufficiently for the Germans to transfer enough troops to the west to make 'Round Up' impracticable in 1943, 'Torch' would be mounted by 1 December.

25 July **Roosevelt declared that 'Torch' must go ahead by 30 October.**
This ignored CCS 94, and in doing so Roosevelt implicitly accepted that 'Round Up' was not possible in 1943. On **31 July** his decision was passed to Eisenhower and the British Chiefs of Staff.

9 August **Eisenhower, appointed to command 'Torch', drew up his first plan for it.**
There was a debate among the US and British planners as to whether merely to land on the Atlantic coast as a precaution against the Axis closing the Strait of Gibraltar or to take the bolder approach of landing deep inside the Mediterranean and, in conjunction with the British Eighth Army, secure Tunisia before the Axis could react. Eisenhower's plan favoured the second course, with just a weak landing on the French Moroccan coast.

Because of the lack of aircraft carriers and assault transports, the US Navy now believed that it would not be ready until 7 November at the earliest. The British, however, were prepared to skimp on training and rehearsals in favour of an earlier date. Consequently, Roosevelt told Marshall to aim for 7 October.

21 August **Eisenhower's second outline plan.**
This proposed a single landing at Oran in Algeria, with the forces employed then moving into Tunisia and Algeria. The start-date would be 15 October. The plan was not favourably received, mainly because of the inherent logistic problems, so there was further debate as to where the landing should take place.

Roosevelt himself wanted invasion on a broad front. Because of the anti-British sentiments still harboured by the Vichy French on account of the clashes between the two in 1940–41 (Roosevelt having gained excellent intelligence through the US Consul-General in Algiers, Robert C. Murphy), Roosevelt laid down that the initial assaults must be carried out by US troops only.

5 September **Churchill and Roosevelt reached agreement over the basic plan.**
Three landings would be made: at Casablanca (29,000 men plus 24,000 in the immediate follow-up); Oran (30,000 plus 20,000); Algiers (10,000 plus 15,000). The Casablanca landing would be mounted

THE ALLIED INVASION OF NORTH AFRICA: 8 November 1942

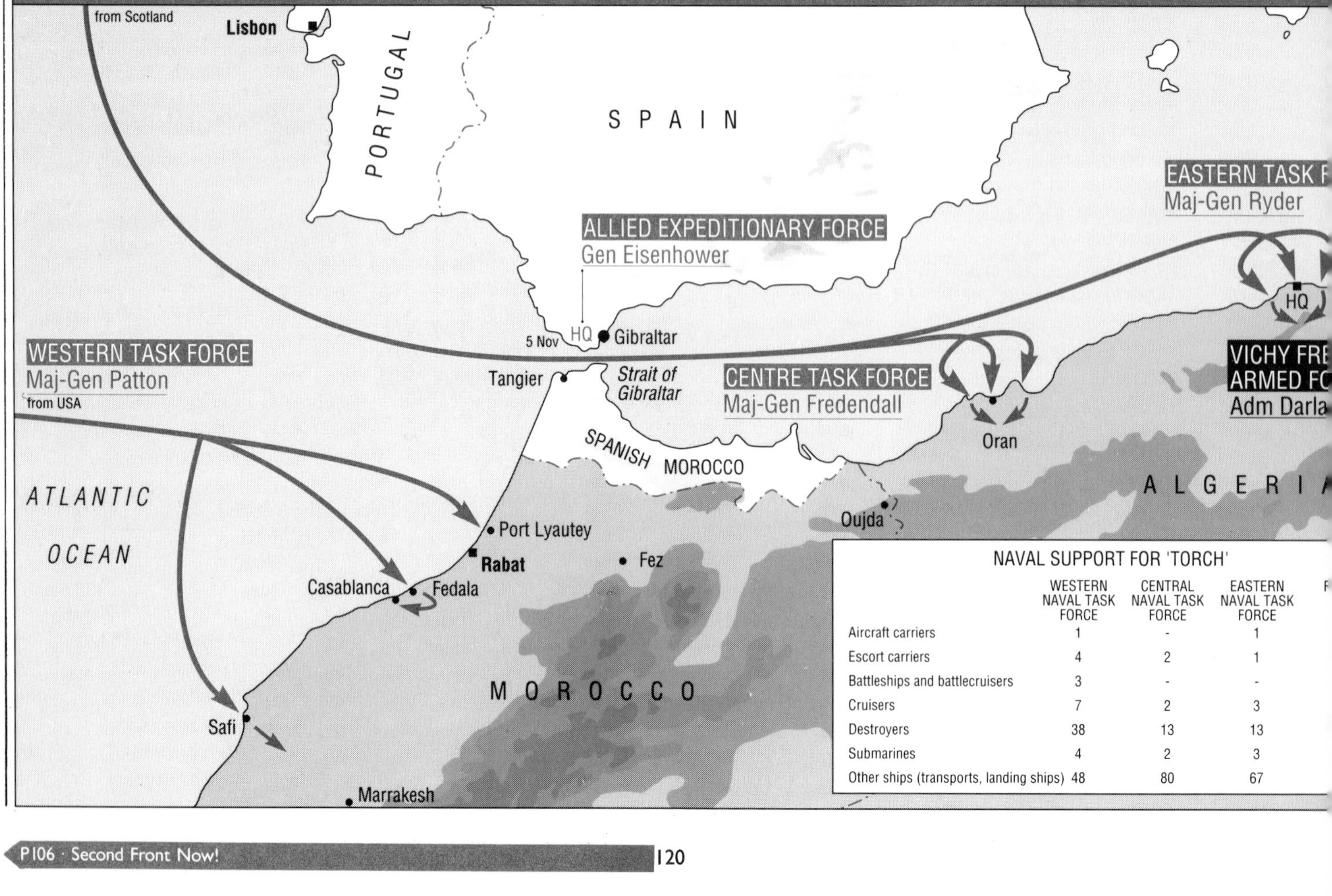

NAVAL SUPPORT FOR 'TORCH'

	WESTERN NAVAL TASK FORCE	CENTRAL NAVAL TASK FORCE	EASTERN NAVAL TASK FORCE	F
Aircraft carriers	1	-	1	
Escort carriers	4	2	1	
Battleships and battlecruisers	3	-	-	
Cruisers	7	2	3	
Destroyers	38	13	13	
Submarines	4	2	3	
Other ships (transports, landing ships)	48	80	67	

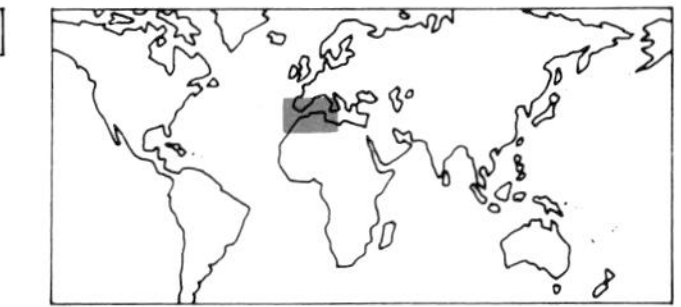

from the USA, with transports ready by 20 October, while the other two would come from Britain. All troops would be US apart from the follow-up force at Algiers, which would be entirely British. All that now remained to be agreed was the date for the operation.

20 September **Date for 'Torch' set as 8 November.**

Crucial to the success of 'Torch' was the degree of French resistance to the landings. Murphy had been working hard to sound out the French military leaders in North Africa. What was clearly needed was a figure around whom they could rally and who would keep resistance to a token minimum. Eventually he established that the one man whom they all respected was General Henri Giraud, a First World War hero who had made a spectacular escape from German imprisonment in April 1942. He was now living in Vichy France and was in contact with the leaders in North Africa.

22 October **General Mark Clark, deputy commander for 'Torch', secretly met General Charles Mast, commanding the French Algerian Division.**

Mark Clark was secretly landed on the Algerian coast from the British submarine *Seraph*, the meeting having been arranged by Murphy. Mast assured Clark that the French Army would follow the orders of Giraud and himself, although he was doubtful about the Navy. He would do everything to facilitate the landings, provided that there were an Anglo-US agreement to restore France's pre-1939 boundaries, to accept France as an ally and to rearm her forces in North Africa, and that the French should, at the 'appropriate time', be given supreme command in North Africa.

23 October **The first elements of the Casablanca landing force set sail from the USA.**

This force was named the Western Task Force and was under the command of General George C. Patton.

26 October **First elements for Oran and Algiers set sail from the Clyde, Scotland.**

The Oran landings were to be carried out by the Centre Task Force under General Lloyd Fredendall and those at Algiers by the Eastern Task Force (General Charles Ryder).

The Axis differed on their appreciations of what was about to happen. While both the Germans and the Italians sensed that the Allies were about to do something, the Germans believed that the strengthening of Malta or a landing at Dakar were the most likely options. The Italians, on the other hand, believed that landings in French North Africa were a very real possibility. Both agreed, however, that nothing should be done to provoke the French from immediately casting in their lot with the Allies.

During the period **26 October to 3 November** Axis submarines and aircraft made a number of sightings of 'Torch' convoys, but these were viewed as nothing untoward. A Freetown–UK convoy diverted many of the U-boats covering the Gibraltar approaches.

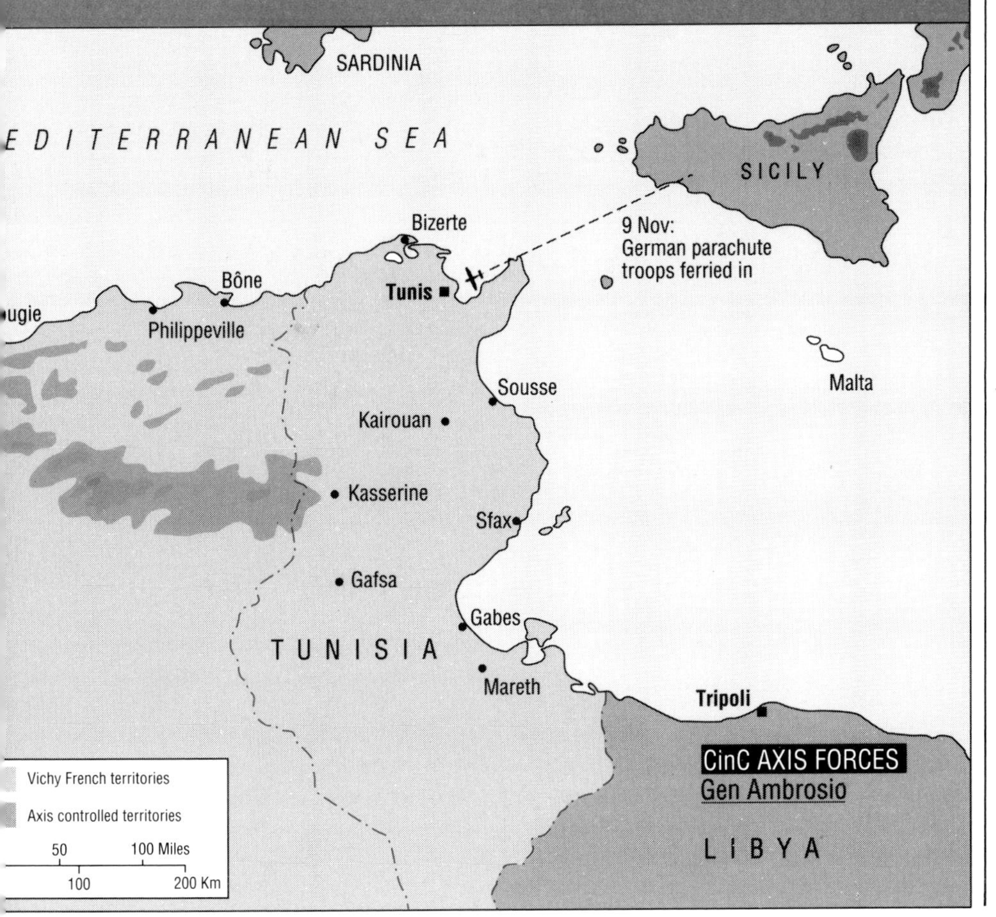

5 November **The 'Torch' convoys began to pass into the Mediterranean.**

Ahead of them was a screen of British submarines and aircraft patrols.

The Axis, still convinced that the Atlantic coast was the target, and their attention diverted by the fate of Rommel, whose position at El Alamein was now crumbling, took no action.

Night of 5/6 November **The British submarine *Seraph* embarked Giraud near Toulon.**

His demand to assume overall command of 'Torch' was turned down by Eisenhower.

8 November **The 'Torch' landings took place.**

The French resisted at all three landings and inflicted casualties on the Allies. Meanwhile a personal letter from Roosevelt was handed to Pétain informing him of the landings. Publicly, Pétain declared that his forces would resist, but he passed a secret message to the High Commissioner in Algiers, Admiral François Darlan, which gave him freedom to negotiate with the Allies. Pétain, however, was not prepared to join the Allies.

9 November **German paratroops landed at El Aouina airport, near Tunis.**

Vichy Prime Minister Pierre Laval had given the Germans permission to send troops from Italy and Sicily to Tunisia. Axis aircraft and submarines attacked and damaged a number of Allied ships off Algiers. On land, fighting continued around Algiers, Oran and Casablanca.

10 November **Darlan ordered the cessation of all resistance to the Allies.**

Oran was secured.

11 November **The French in Algeria and Morocco signed an armistice with the Allies.**

German troops now entered Unoccupied France, thus tearing up the armistice terms of June 1940.

Although French resistance to 'Torch' had proved tougher than expected, the landings had been remarkably successful and had provided an encouraging start to Anglo-US co-operation on the field of battle. The main question now was whether the Allies could seize Tunis before the Axis forces arriving daily there became too strong.

The Dash to Tunis · P122

The Dash to Tunis

The task of securing Tunisia for the Allies was given to General Kenneth Anderson's First British Army, but the troops made available to him hardly constituted an army. Initially they consisted of two infantry brigades and two Commandos, one of which, equipped with US weapons and wearing US helmets, had taken part in the 'Torch' landings at Algiers. He had little intelligence on Tunisia, and the available maps were out of date; nor could he expect much in the way of air support at the outset.

The attitude of the French in Tunisia was ambivalent. The Resident-General and naval commander decided on passive resistance to both sides and demonstrated this by blocking the ports. The army commander, General Georges Barré, was more positively anti-Axis, but recognized that his ill-equipped troops could do little against the Germans and therefore concentrated on keeping them out of harm's way.

9 November 1942 General Anderson arrived at Algiers.
His plan was to make a series of landings on the Tunisian coast and link up with them by means of other forces advancing from Algeria.

Night of 10/11 November 36 Brigade set sail for Bougie.
They landed here unopposed on the 11th. That afternoon their transports were attacked by the Luftwaffe, and two ships were crippled.

A small mobile column from 11 Brigade, Hart Force, set out by road from Algiers for Tunisia. Kesselring was given overall responsibility for Axis operations in Tunisia. By this day 1,000 German troops had landed at Tunis.

12 November British combined amphibious/airborne landing at Bône.
These were carried out by No. 6 Commando and 3rd Parachute Battalion. They were reinforced by an infantry battalion next day.

Two more transports were sunk by the Luftwaffe at Bougie, and the remaining ships returned to Algiers without having completed unloading. Having unblocked Bizerte harbour, the Axis began landing troops here. Tunis would be similarly opened on the 15th.

14 November General Walther Nehring arrived at Tunis.
He became the Axis commander on the ground, his forces being grouped as XC Corps. He ordered his troops to move westwards in order to block the British advance.

15 November Hart Force crossed into Tunisia at Tabarka.
A complete battalion from 36 Brigade set out from Algiers by road. The US 509th Para Battalion dropped at Youks les Bains and seized the airport there.

16 November British 1st Parachute Battalion dropped at Souk el Arba.
This secured another forward airfield at Souk el Khemis for the Allies and opened up another approach to Tunis. They exploited to Sidi Nisr and made contact with Barré's troops, who were holding a series of roadblocks designed to hinder the Germans in their move west.

17 November In the north the British were forced back to Djebel Abiod.
Their opponents were an all-arms battle group, which included fifteen tanks, led by Major Rudolph Witzig, who had led the airborne assault on the Belgian fortress of Eben Emael on 10 May 1940.

18 November German ultimatum to the French troops in Tunisia.
Nehring ordered Barré to remove all obstacles barring the way to the Algerian border. Barré refused and next morning found himself at war with the Axis.

20 November The French withdrew from Medjez el Bab.
German pressure on their flanks proved too much. The British 11 Brigade linked up with 1st Parachute Battalion at Beja.

21 November Anderson imposed a delay on further advances into Tunisia.
He was very short of supplies and reliant on a single antiquated railway line running east from Algiers. Recent heavy rain turned the Allied advanced landing grounds into mud, but the Axis, operating from concrete runways, did not have the same problem and enjoyed air superiority at this time. The longer the Allies delayed, however, the greater the Axis strength would be.

24 November The Allies began to advance once more.
The plan was to cut off the Axis forces in the north and then seize Bizerta and Tunis. German paratroops rebuffed 11 Brigade, supported by US tanks, at Medjez, while 36 Brigade's advance in the north from Djebel Abiod to Mateur was delayed. In the centre an armoured force made up of a British and a US tank battalion (Black Force) advanced towards Sidi Nisr.

This renewed pressure caused Nehring to pull his troops back closer to Tunis, and 11 Brigade secured Medjez unopposed next day.

27 November 11 Brigade, supported by Blade Force, reached Tebourba.
They were now up against the new Axis defence line.

THE INVASION OF TUNISIA

1st ARMY
Gen Anderson
Algiers

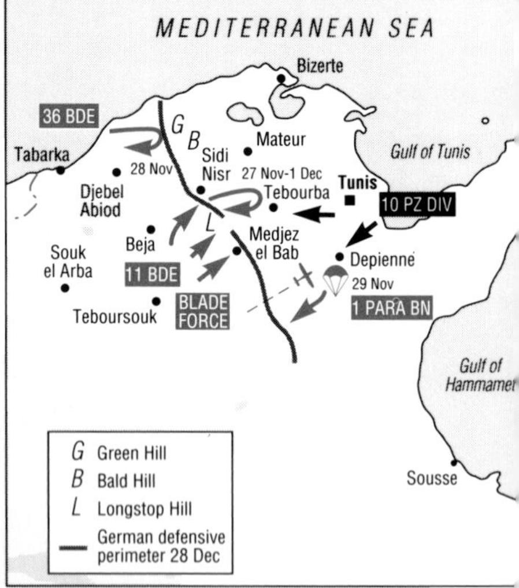

27 November French Fleet scuttled at Toulon.
The Germans had, when they originally entered Vichy France, undertaken not to seize the French Fleet. They changed their minds, however, and the French CinC, Admiral Jean de Laborde, ordered it to be scuttled. No less than two battleships, one battlecruiser, seven cruisers, 29 destroyers, two submarines and other craft were lost. Four submarines escaped to join the Allies.

28 November 36 Brigade rebuffed at Bald and Green Hills.
Kesselring ordered Nehring, now reinforced by part of 10th Panzer Division, to attack.

29 November Amphibious and airborne landings behind the Axis lines.

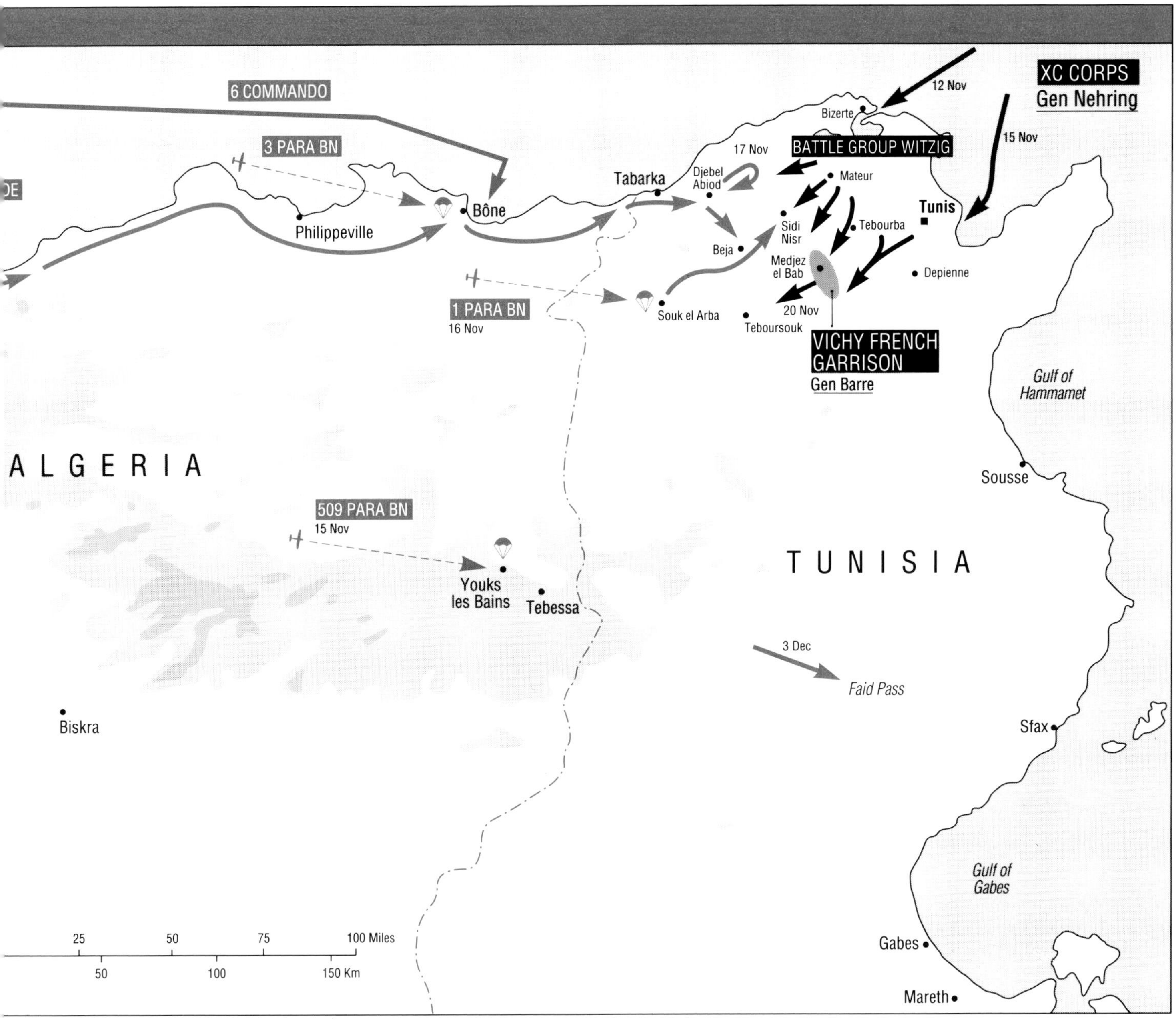

1939 | 1940 | 1941 | 1942 | 1943 | 1944 | 1945

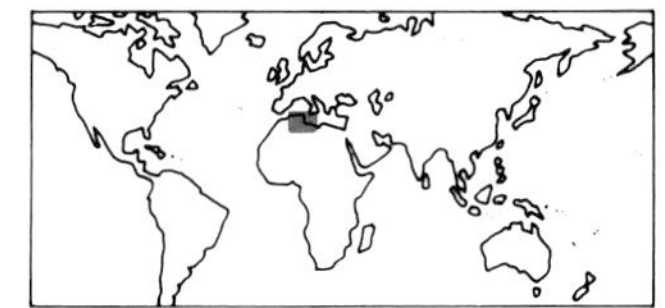

6 COMMANDO
3 PARA BN
Philippeville
Bône
Tabarka
Djebel Abiod
17 Nov
Bizerte
12 Nov
XC CORPS
Gen Nehring
15 Nov
BATTLE GROUP WITZIG
Mateur
Sidi Nisr
Tebourba
Tunis
Beja
Medjez el Bab
Depienne
1 PARA BN
16 Nov
Souk el Arba
Teboursouk
20 Nov
VICHY FRENCH GARRISON
Gen Barre
Gulf of Hammamet
ALGERIA
Sousse
509 PARA BN
15 Nov
TUNISIA
Youks les Bains
Tebessa
3 Dec
Faid Pass
Biskra
Sfax
Gulf of Gabes
25 50 75 100 Miles
50 100 150 Km
Gabes
Mareth

No. 1 Commando landed at Sidi el Moudjad and 1st Parachute Battalion at Depienne in an effort to regain the initiative. Both forces had to fight their way back to their own lines.

1 December **10th Panzer Division attacked the Chouigi Pass.**
This threatened Tebourba, which was evacuated next day. The Allies were forced to withdraw to Medjez, which they were determined to hold as a spring-board for another attempt on Tunis.

3 December **US and French troops seized Faid Pass.**

10 December **A German attack on Medjez el Bab was repulsed.**

20 December **An emissary from de Gaulle arrived in Algiers to persuade Darlan to join forces.**
Darlan, like most of the French in North Africa, distrusted de Gaulle, and turned down the proposal.

22–25 December **The battles for Longstop Hill.**
Pressured by Eisenhower, Anderson resumed his efforts to advance to Tunis. The first task was to seize Longstop Hill, which was achieved by a battalion of the newly arrived 1 Guards Brigade. This was relieved by a US infantry battalion, which was then beaten back by a German counter-attack. The Guards recovered the hill, but were forced off it in turn by another German counter-attack.

24 December **Darlan assassinated at Algiers.**
His killer was a French Royalist acting on his own. Giraud took over as High Commissioner, and de Gaulle renewed his approaches.

28 December **Further British attempts to seize Green and Bald Hills failed.**

This marked the final attempt by the Allies to break through, and they decided now to pause and consolidate before attacking once more. The dash to Tunis had been a gamble that had failed because the troops available were too few and the distances too long.

As for the Axis, they found themselves committed to an unexpected campaign. Hitler was now determined that Tunisia should not only be held but used as a base for counter-offensive operations against both First Army and, in the east, Eighth Army.

Tunisia · P134

Guadalcanal Secured

By mid-September 1942 the US Marines on Guadalcanal were exhausted after the hard fighting of the previous seven weeks. The Japanese, on the other hand, were now determined to drive them off the island and were prepared to concentrate all their efforts in the south-west Pacific to this end, even to the extent of reducing the pressure against Port Moresby.

During the second half of September and early October the Japanese transferred General Hyakutake's Seventeenth Army HQ to Guadalcanal, together with the 2nd Division. All this was done through the 'Tokyo Express', and the reinforcements were landed at Cape Esperance in the north-west of the island. By mid-October the Japanese had built up a force of some 20,000 men.

The Americans too received some reinforcements, notably another Marine regiment and an infantry regiment, to make up their strength to 23,000. Their air strength at Henderson Field was also increased.

Throughout this period there were constant naval clashes as both sides strove to hinder each other's reinforcement routes to the island. The US Navy had the carrier *Saratoga* damaged by a submarine on **31 August** near Santa Cruz, and on **15 September** they lost the carrier *Wasp* and a destroyer, while the battleship *North Carolina* was damaged again by submarines. It was these clashes that led to the next major naval action.

11–12 October 1942 Battle of Cape Esperance. A US supply convoy had set sail for Guadalcanal, escorted by a cruiser squadron that intended to ambush Japanese shipping in 'the Slot'. It intercepted a Japanese convoy, escorted by three heavy cruisers, two seaplane carriers and eight destroyers under Admiral Aritomo Goto, on the night of the 11th. When daylight came, Japanese and US aircraft from Rabaul and Henderson Field joined in. The Japanese were driven off, although some 800 men were landed, with the loss of one cruiser and three destroyers. Goto was killed. The Americans lost one destroyer and had two cruisers and two destroyers damaged. Henderson Field was badly damaged by Japanese aircraft, and naval gunfire during the next few nights almost put it out of action.

23 October Japanese attacked across the River Matanikau.

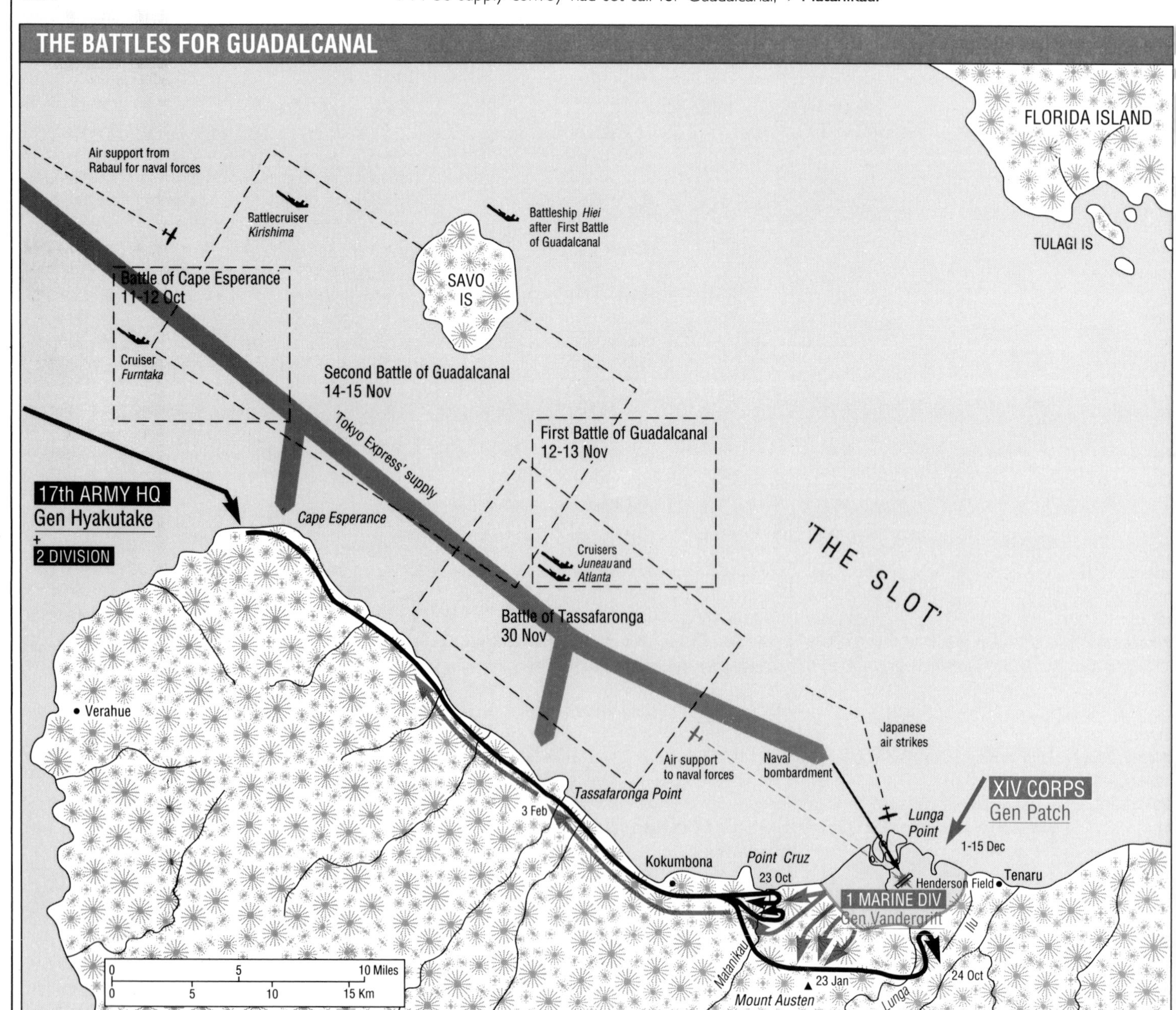

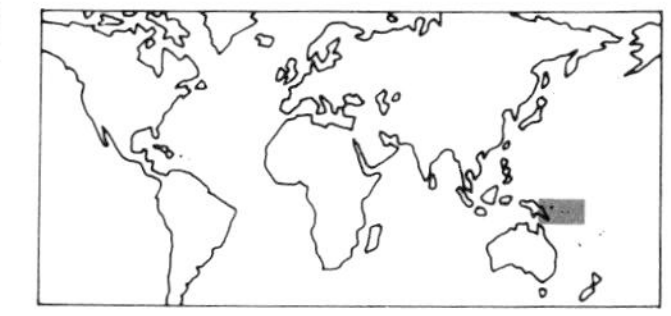

This was repulsed after 24 hours of savage fighting, but another attack was then made against the ridges south of Henderson Field. This too was thrown back.

24–26 October Battle of Santa Cruz.
The Japanese Combined Fleet moved to the north of Guadalcanal ready to fly aircraft on to Henderson Field, which the Japanese hoped to capture in their land assault. This was detected through Magic, and Admiral William 'Bull' Halsey, who had recently replaced Ghormley as Commander South Pacific, deployed two task forces built round the carriers *Enterprise* and *Hornet*. The Japanese fleet was sighted on the 25th, but an air strike failed to locate it. During the 26th both sides exchanged air strikes. The Japanese carriers *Zuiho* and *Shokaku* were damaged, but *Hornet* was sunk. This was a tactical victory for the Japanese; but they lost more than 100 naval aircraft, which it would be difficult to replace.

12–13 November First Battle of Guadalcanal.
In spite of the failure in October to drive the Americans into the sea, the Japanese were determined to try again and began planning an offensive to be launched in mid-January. They accordingly began a further programme of extensive reinforcement. A US cruiser squadron surprised a Japanese squadron by night in 'the Slot', and at daybreak the aircraft of both sides joined in. The result was a US defeat, with two light cruisers and seven destroyers sunk, and a battleship, three cruisers and four destroyers damaged. The Japanese lost; the battleship *Hiei*, a heavy cruiser and two destroyers, together with seven out of eleven transports was so badly damaged that she had to be scuttled.

Night of 14–15 November Second Battle of Guadalcanal.
The Japanese bombarded Henderson Field from the sea on the night of **13th/14th**, losing a cruiser to US aircraft during the return passage. US aircraft also struck at a Japanese convoy on the 14th, sinking much of it. That night the Japanese ships steamed to attack Henderson Field once more, but were intercepted by US ships. Once again US night fighting inferiority was revealed, and four destroyers were quickly put out of action. The battleship *South Dakota*, whose radar was inoperative, was also damaged, and it was only the guns of the battleship *Washington* that saw the Japanese off, sinking the battleship *Kirishima*. One Japanese destroyer was also lost. This was the last Japanese major attempt to reinforce Guadalcanal. From now on they relied on high-speed destroyers runs. Buoyant drums full of supplies were released in the hope that they would reach the shore. Few did.

30 November Battle of Tassafaronga.
The Americans received warning from coast-watchers that eight Japanese destroyers were heading for 'the Slot' and intercepted them. In the

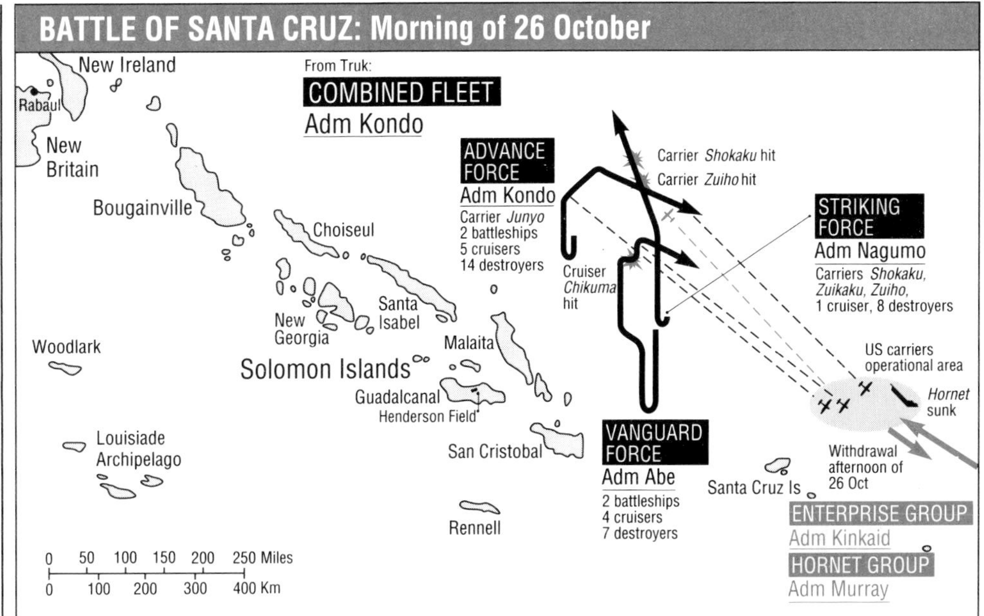

subsequent action the Japanese lost one destroyer sunk and one disabled, while the US Navy lost the cruiser *Northampton* and three others were damaged. Materially, it was a Japanese victory, but it did nothing to help the now-starving Japanese garrison on Guadalcanal.

1–15 December 1st US Marine Division relieved.
During the previous six weeks the US troops on the island had been concentrating on securing their perimeter and winkling out Japanese positions that threatened it. Now, however, the Marines were understrength and wasted by disease and incapable of going over to the offensive. They were relieved by the US XIV Corps under General Alexander Patch, consisting of 23rd, 25th and 2nd Marine Divisions. Patch began to prepare for a major offensive in January.

17 December US attack on Mount Austen began.
Patch saw the seizure of this feature dominating the River Lunga as a vital preliminary to his main attack. Japanese resistance was fierce, and Austin would not fall until well into January.

4 January 1943 Japanese ordered to evacuate Guadalcanal.
They finally realized that their position on the island was now hopeless, but the withdrawal was to be gradual and would be reliant on the 'Tokyo Express'. The Japanese troops were to be taken to New Guinea.

10 January Patch's offensive opened.
Mount Austin had still not been cleared, and progress was slow despite heavy air and artillery support.

23 January Mount Austen finally secured.

By now the Japanese were showing signs of weakening all along the front, but had not yet begun to evacuate their troops. The main US effort was directed towards Cape Esperance.

29–30 January 1943 Japanese air attacks on a Guadalcanal-bound supply convoy.
The cruiser *Chicago* was sunk and a destroyer damaged near Rennell Island.

Night of 1/2 February Japanese evacuation began.
This took place at Cape Esperance and involved twenty destroyers, of which one was lost to a mine. One US destroyer also was sunk by Japanese dive-bombers.

3 February US patrols probed close to Cape Esperance.
The main US advance had reached Tassafaronga.

Night of 8/9 February Final evacuation of the remaining Japanese troops on Guadalcanal.
A total of 11,000 men were successfully taken off by the 'Tokyo Express'.

9 February Guadalcanal secured by US forces.
Patch signalled Halsey: 'Tokyo Express no longer has terminus on Guadalcanal.'

Thus ended the long and arduous struggle for the island. It had cost the US ground forces 1,600 killed and 4,700 wounded as against nearly 24,000 Japanese killed or dead from disease. Both sides had lost a high tonnage in ships. More serious for the Japanese was that they had lost some 600 valuable airmen during the campaign. Guadalcanal and Papua–New Guinea marked the beginning of the long Allied reconquest of the Pacific.

The Aleutians and New Georgia · P144

Stalingrad – Phase One

The idea of a counter-stroke to cut off Paulus's Sixth German Army in Stalingrad was born as early as **12 September** in Stalin's office. While Stalin himself remained convinced that the ultimate German objective was an advance up the Volga to Moscow, the fact was that Paulus was out on a limb with his flanks guarded by lesser-quality Roumanian formations, and the idea grew in attraction, especially since it would nip a German offensive northwards in the bud. Reserves were not available to carry out the counter-stroke at an early date, and Soviet attention was diverted by abortive attacks to relieve Leningrad. These began on **19 August** and came to an end at the close of September. While they had not achieved their aim, they did forestall a major German assault on the city, one of Hitler's main plans for 1942, and kept German troops tied down who could have been better employed elsewhere. There was also the continued German pressure in the Caucasus and above all, at least in Stalin's eyes, on Stalingrad. The first priority was to prevent that city falling into German hands. Nevertheless, Zhukov and Vasilievsky commenced planning.

During the next month, Chuikov in Stalingrad desperately fought off fierce German attacks. As he did so, the plan for Operation 'Uranus' began to take shape. It would consist of a deep double envelopment. From the north, Nikolai Vatutin's South-West Front would attack the Third Roumanian Army and then drive on to Kalach. South of Stalingrad, Andrei Yeremenko's Stalingrad Front would destroy VI Roumanian Corps and then meet Vatutin in the Kalach area. A further attack would be launched by Konstantin Rokossovsky's Don Front and was designed to keep Paulus pinned down. The movement of troops and other preparations did not go unnoticed by the Germans, but they were not certain what was about to unfold, even after, at the end of October, a Russian propaganda campaign began to speak of 'large-scale operations against the Hitlerites'. At the end of October the start-date was fixed as **9 November**.

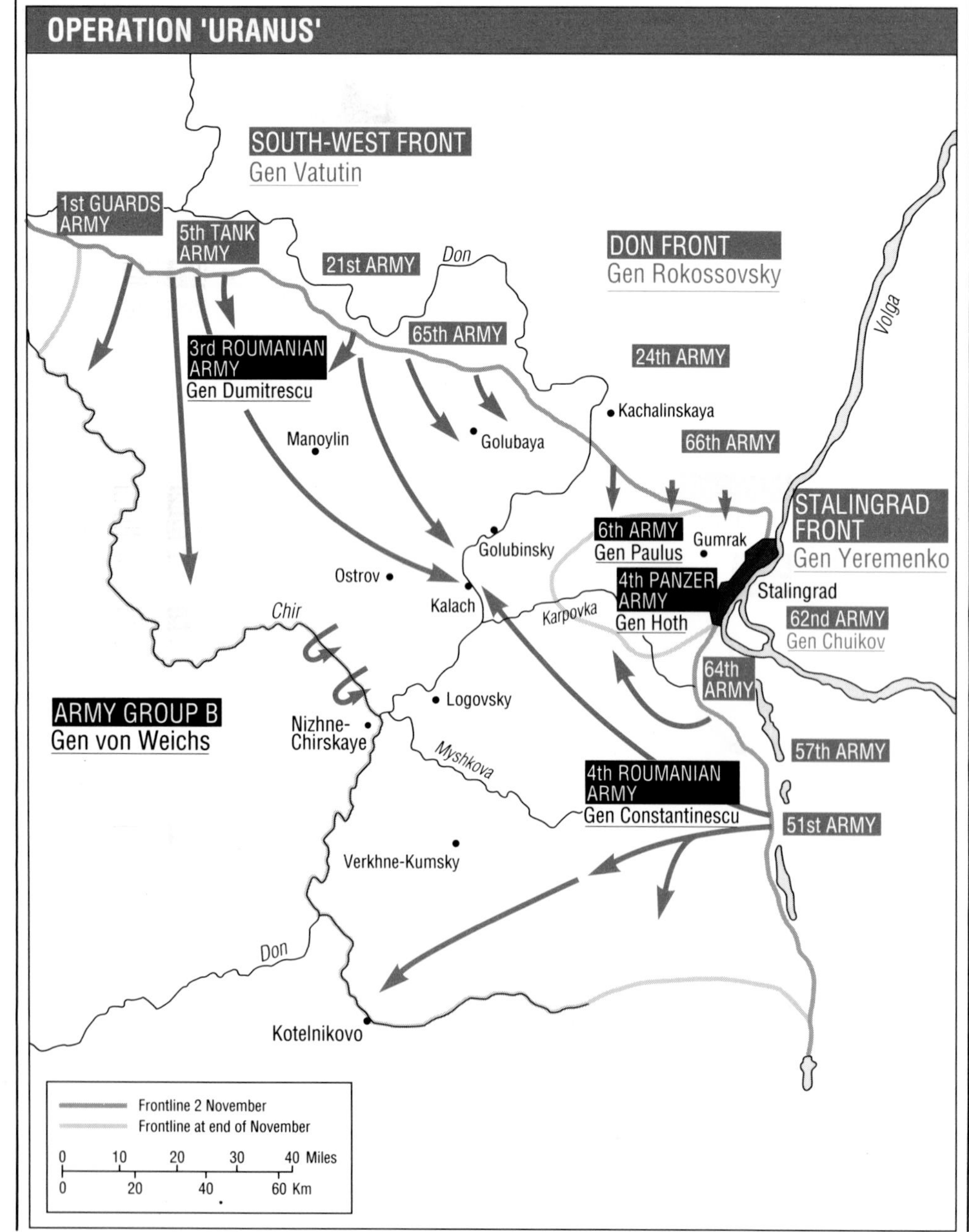

8 November 1942 Attack orders finally issued.
That night, however, the start-date was put back by one week because of delays in shifting troops and supplies.

11 November German attacks on Stalingrad renewed.
Chuikov's Sixty-Second Army was soon in a desperate situation, but managed to cling on. In the meantime it was decided that 'Uranus' should be launched on the 19th.

19 November The South-Western and Don Fronts began their attack.
It was preceded by a short, sharp, but massive bombardment. The Roumanians initially resisted strongly, and progress was slow.

20 November The Stalingrad Front attached.
Vatutin's attacks were now gaining momentum, and by the end of this day he had penetrated up to 25 miles.

21 November Paulus's HQ, now under threat, moved to Nizhne-Chirskaye on the River Chir.
Next day Hitler ordered Paulus to move his HQ east again to Gumrak, close to Stalingrad itself.

22 November Vatutin captured the vital bridge over the Don at Kalach.
It was the only intact bridge over the Don and was on Sixth Army's main communications to the rear.

23 November The South-West and Stalingrad Fronts linked up.
Sixth and part of Fourth Panzer Armies, comprising 22 divisions and some 330,000 men, were now trapped. The Roumanian Third Army had been destroyed and the Fourth badly battered. The next task was to destroy the trapped German forces, but the Soviet forces were too weak to do this immediately.

24 November Goering declared that he could keep Paulus supplied by air.
Paulus estimated that he required 750 tons per day. The Luftwaffe, however, simply did not have the number of transport aircraft needed to maintain this, and only one of the seven airstrips around Stalingrad had a night landing capability. Goering's

P110 · German Drive into the Caucasus

boast was therefore totally unrealistic. Nevertheless this decided Hitler that Paulus must remain where he was rather than break out to the west.

26 November Hitler ordered Sixth Army to stand fast.

27 November Army Group Don came into being.
Hitler appointed von Manstein to command it, and he was tasked with the relief of Paulus. He had one Luftwaffe, four Panzer and six infantry divisions, together with the remnants of a number of Roumanian formations. These forces were still concentrating, but von Manstein proposed to attack before they all arrived in order to achieve surprise and prevent a Soviet build-up. Rather than take the shortest route to Stalingrad, which ran initially along the River Don from its junction with the Chir, von Manstein chose the axis of the Kotelnikovo-Stalingrad railway instead. His reasons were reported concentrations of Soviet troops astride the former and the problem of crossing the Don and the Chir. He decided to launch 'Winter Storm', as it was code-named, on **3 December**.

30 November Soviet attacks to clear the Germans from the lower Chir launched.
A week's heavy fighting followed, during which von Manstein was forced to deploy formations earmarked for 'Winter Storm', which resulted in a postponement of that operation. The Soviets, however, failed to break through.

2 December Soviet attempt to split the German pocket at Stalingrad began.
This was carried out by the Don and Stalingrad Fronts with the object of linking up at Gumrak. After five days' heavy fighting virtually no progress had been made, and the attacks were called off. Stalin ordered a new attack to be prepared. This, code-named 'Ring', was to be a two-phase operation: (1) to liquidate the south and west parts of the pocket; (2) a general assault against the remainder of the pocket. Once again the Don and Stalingrad Fronts were to carry it out, and it was to begin on 16 December.

12 December Von Manstein unleashed 'Winter Storm'.
The attack was carried out by Group Hoth (General Hermann Hoth). Initially progress was good, but fierce resistance by 5th Shock Army brought time for Russian troops from the Stalingrad area to be deployed in defensive positions along the River Myshkova.

16 December Soviet attack launched against Italian Eighth Army.
Code-named 'Little Saturn', this was aimed at cutting across von Manstein's lines of communication and was carried out by elements of the Voronezh and South-West Fronts. The Italians were quickly annihilated, and Tatsinskaya, the main German-held airfield for resupplying Stalingrad, was overrun.

19 December Hoth's troops reached the Myshkova.
They were now within sixteen miles of Stalingrad. Since they could not break through the Soviet defence line (although they continued trying until the 23rd), von Manstein proposed that Paulus break out and link up with Hoth. Paulus was only prepared to release some tanks unsupported by infantry, since he still had to hold on in Stalingrad.

That day the Luftwaffe flew-in 250 tons to Paulus, which was a record and never again achieved, daily deliveries being only 90 tons on average.

24 December The Soviet counter-offensive broadened.
In the south the Stalingrad Front broke through the Fourth Roumanian Army and struck for the lower Don. Von Manstein, now threatened both from the north and from south, was forced to pull back Group Hoth.

28 December Hitler sanctioned a withdrawal by Army Groups Don and A to the line Konstantinovsk–Salsk–Armavir.
This put the army groups 125 miles away from Stalingrad and aggravated the resupply of Paulus still further. Even so, Hitler declared that he still intended to relieve the Sixth Army. Meanwhile the Russians could now prepare and execute the final reduction of the Stalingrad pocket.

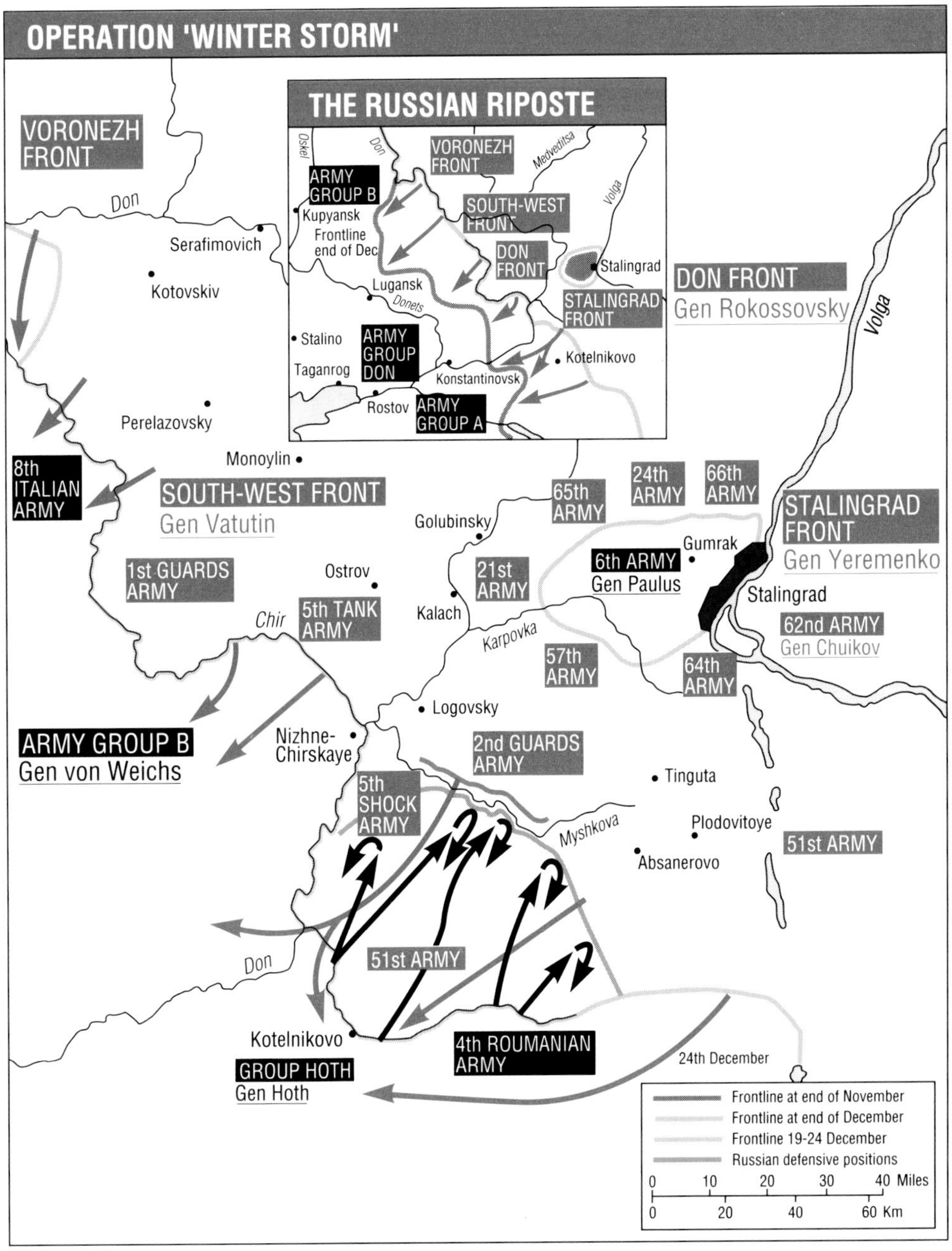

OPERATION 'WINTER STORM'

THE RUSSIAN RIPOSTE

VORONEZH FRONT
ARMY GROUP B
SOUTH-WEST FRONT
DON FRONT
STALINGRAD FRONT
ARMY GROUP DON
ARMY GROUP A
Kupyansk
Frontline end of Dec
Lugansk
Stalino
Taganrog
Rostov
Konstantinovsk
Kotelnikovo
Stalingrad

VORONEZH FRONT
Don
Serafimovich
Kotovskiv
Perelazovsky
Monoylin
8th ITALIAN ARMY
SOUTH-WEST FRONT Gen Vatutin
1st GUARDS ARMY
5th TANK ARMY
Chir
ARMY GROUP B Gen von Weichs
DON FRONT Gen Rokossovsky
65th ARMY
24th ARMY
66th ARMY
STALINGRAD FRONT Gen Yeremenko
Golubinsky
Ostrov
Kalach
21st ARMY
6th ARMY Gen Paulus
Gumrak
Stalingrad
62nd ARMY Gen Chuikov
Karpovka
57th ARMY
64th ARMY
Logovsky
Nizhne-Chirskaye
2nd GUARDS ARMY
5th SHOCK ARMY
Tinguta
Plodovitoye
Myshkova
Absanerovo
51st ARMY
Volga
Don
51st ARMY
Kotelnikovo
GROUP HOTH Gen Hoth
4th ROUMANIAN ARMY
24th December

Frontline at end of November
Frontline at end of December
Frontline 19-24 December
Russian defensive positions
0 10 20 30 40 Miles
0 20 40 60 Km

7 SLOWLY BUT SURELY, January to August 1943

26 NOVEMBER 1942 TO 31 JANUARY 1943

Blueprint for Victory

New Year's Day 1943 presented the Allies with a very different situation from that of 12 months previously. Then the Axis were exerting pressure on all fronts. Now the tide was on the turn. In the Far East, Papua–New Guinea and Guadalcanal had been virtually wrested from the Japanese, and the first hesitant steps towards going on to the offensive had been taken in Burma. On the Eastern Front the stage was set for the first major Axis reverse – Stalingrad. Rommel had been almost swept out of Libya, and French North Africa, apart from Tunisia, had been brought on to the Allied side. With the USAAF in Britain and RAF Bomber Command growing larger by the day, the strategic bombing offensive of Germany was gathering strength. In Occupied Europe the flames of resistance were being successfully fanned. The Bletchley Park cryptanalysts were once again able to read the Enigma cipher, and sinkings in the Atlantic, which had risen to a staggering 720,000 tons in November, had fallen off dramatically, although the winter gales were playing their part.

THE BELLIGERENT NATIONS, January 1943

AXIS

Albania	Italy
Bulgaria	Japan*
Finland	Roumania
Germany	Thailand
Hungary	

ALLIED

Abyssinia	Honduras
Australia	India
Brazil	Iraq
Britain	Mexico
Canada	New Zealand
China	Nicaragua
Costa Rica	Panama
Cuba	Salvador
Dominican Republic	South Africa
Dutch East Indies	USA
Guatemala	USSR*
Haiti	

* Not against each other

Given the developments of the previous few months, it was obviously vital that the Western Allies at least agree a common strategy for 1943.

On the day after the 'Torch' landings Churchill set down his thoughts on the subject. He believed that the German forces in Northern France and the Low Countries should be kept tied down by fear of an invasion, and that Anglo-US forces should invade Italy and, even better, southern France. Turkey should be persuaded to enter the war so that physical link-up with the Russians could be achieved through the Balkans. On **12 November** Roosevelt sent Churchill a telegram that proposed much the same. It was now up to their respective staffs to work out the details.

In late November, in view of the continuing Russian successes, Churchill began to press for a firm commitment to mounting 'Round Up', the cross-Channel invasion, during the summer months of 1943, and was anxious that the Americans confirm their commitment to 'Bolero', the build-up for it.

26 November 1942 Churchill proposed to Roosevelt a meeting with Stalin in Iceland.
This was in order to agree a joint plan. Roosevelt declined Iceland because of his health and proposed somewhere warmer. Churchill agreed to North Africa in January and sent a telegram to Stalin to this effect.

6 December Stalin replied that he could not leave Moscow for the time being.
This was because of the fighting around Stalingrad. Stalin asked Churchill what the position was regarding the opening of the second front in 1943.

21 December Churchill and Roosevelt agreed that they would meet for further discussions at Casablanca.
By this stage it was clear that all was not going to plan for the Allies in Tunisia. This had to be secured by the end of January if 'Round Up' was to be feasible for 1943. Furthermore, the British Chiefs of Staff favoured a continuation of the Mediterranean strategy rather than 'Round Up'.

13 January 1943 Churchill arrived by air at Casablanca.
He was joined on the following day by President Roosevelt. They had code-names for the conference of 'Air Commodore Frankland' and 'Admiral Q' respectively. They were accompanied by their military staffs.

24 January End of the Casablanca Conference.
A number of very important decisions had been reached. First and foremost, it was agreed that

THE GLOBAL WAR: Winter 1942/3

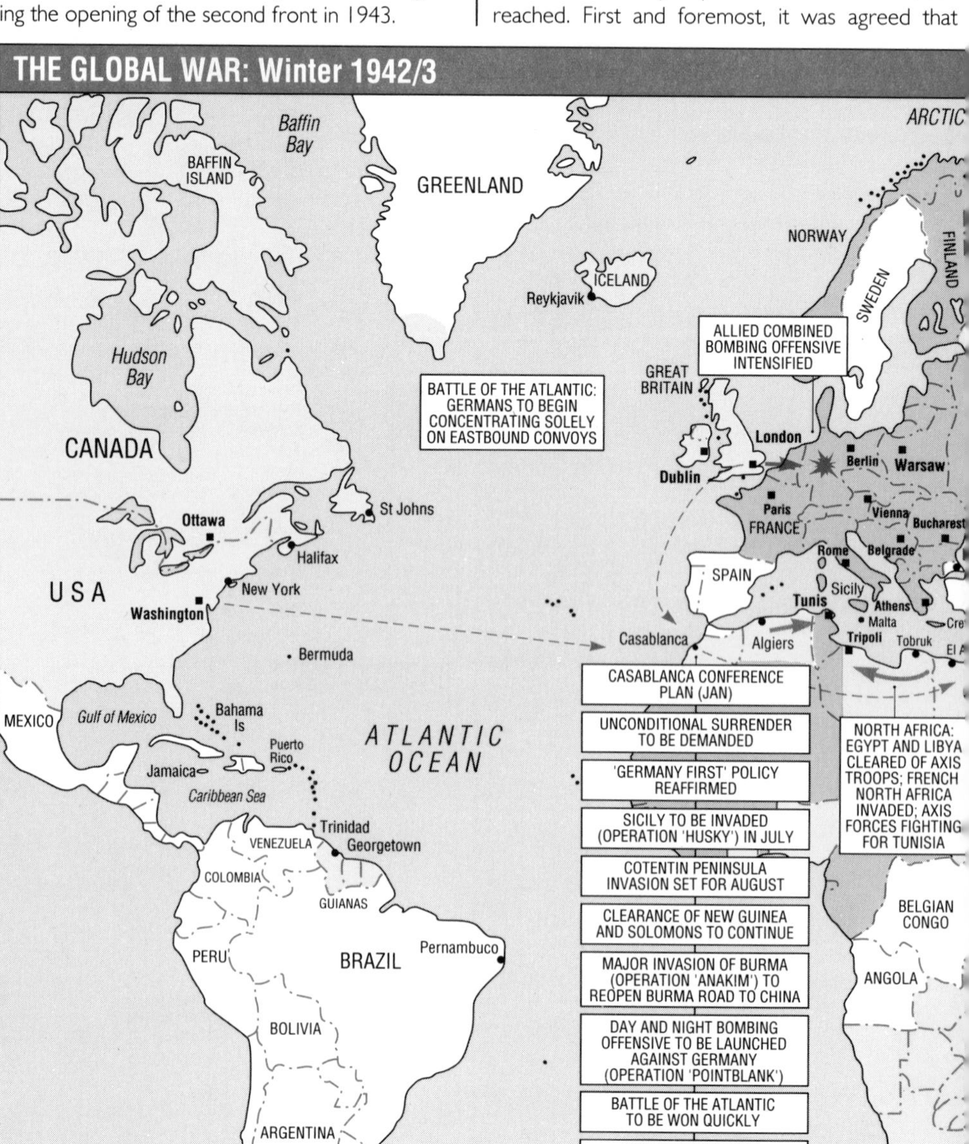

the war would not be won until the 'unconditional surrender' of Germany, Italy and Japan had been obtained. The object of this was 'the destruction of a philosophy ... based on the conquest and subjugation of other peoples'. The policy of 'Germany First' was reaffirmed, and Britain pledged that she would continue the war against Japan after the war ended in Europe.

In terms of major operations to be mounted in 1943, it was agreed that Sicily would be invaded in July 1943 under the code-name 'Husky'. 'Bolero' would continue, with the objective of having 384,000 US troops in Britain by 1 August and 938,000 by the end of the year. A major cross-Channel raid was to be mounted with the object of causing German losses in men and aircraft, and planning was to proceed for an operation set for 1 August to seize the Cotentin Peninsula in France.

In the Far East the clearance of New Guinea and the Solomons was to continue. Operation 'Anakim', a full-blown invasion of Burma designed to re-open the Burma Road with China, was to be mounted using US landing craft.

A combined bomber offensive against Germany, code-named 'Pointblank', was to be mounted with the USAAF bombing by day and RAF Bomber Command by night. The object would be to disrupt German war industry and lower morale as a necessary preparation for a cross-Channel landing. It was essential too that the Battle of the Atlantic be won quickly since otherwise it would impede 'Bolero'. Finally, the convoys to Russia would continue, except during 'Husky' because of the shipping demands, but would be stopped if losses once again grew too great.

25 January Churchill and Roosevelt sent a telegram to Stalin on the results of Casablanca.
They stressed their twin aims of diverting significant German forces from the Eastern Front and keeping Russia well supplied with *matériel*, and made particular mention of 'Pointblank'. That day Roosevelt left for home, while Churchill flew that evening to Cairo. It was his intention to visit Turkey to persuade her to enter the war.

30–31 January Churchill visited Turkey.
He offered the Turks arms and equipment, which they accepted, and gave an outline of the Allied plans in 1943. The Turks, however, while polite and welcoming, were not prepared to come into the war as yet and expressed their distrust of the Soviet Union.

Churchill, after calling in at Cyprus, Cairo, and the British Eighth Army at Tripoli, flew on to Algiers. As a result of discussions here it was agreed that, in order to placate de Gaulle, the powers that had been invested in Giraud as military and civilian commander in French North Africa should be transferred to a French War Committee and Economic High Command, which would be made up of equal numbers of supporters of de Gaulle and Giraud.

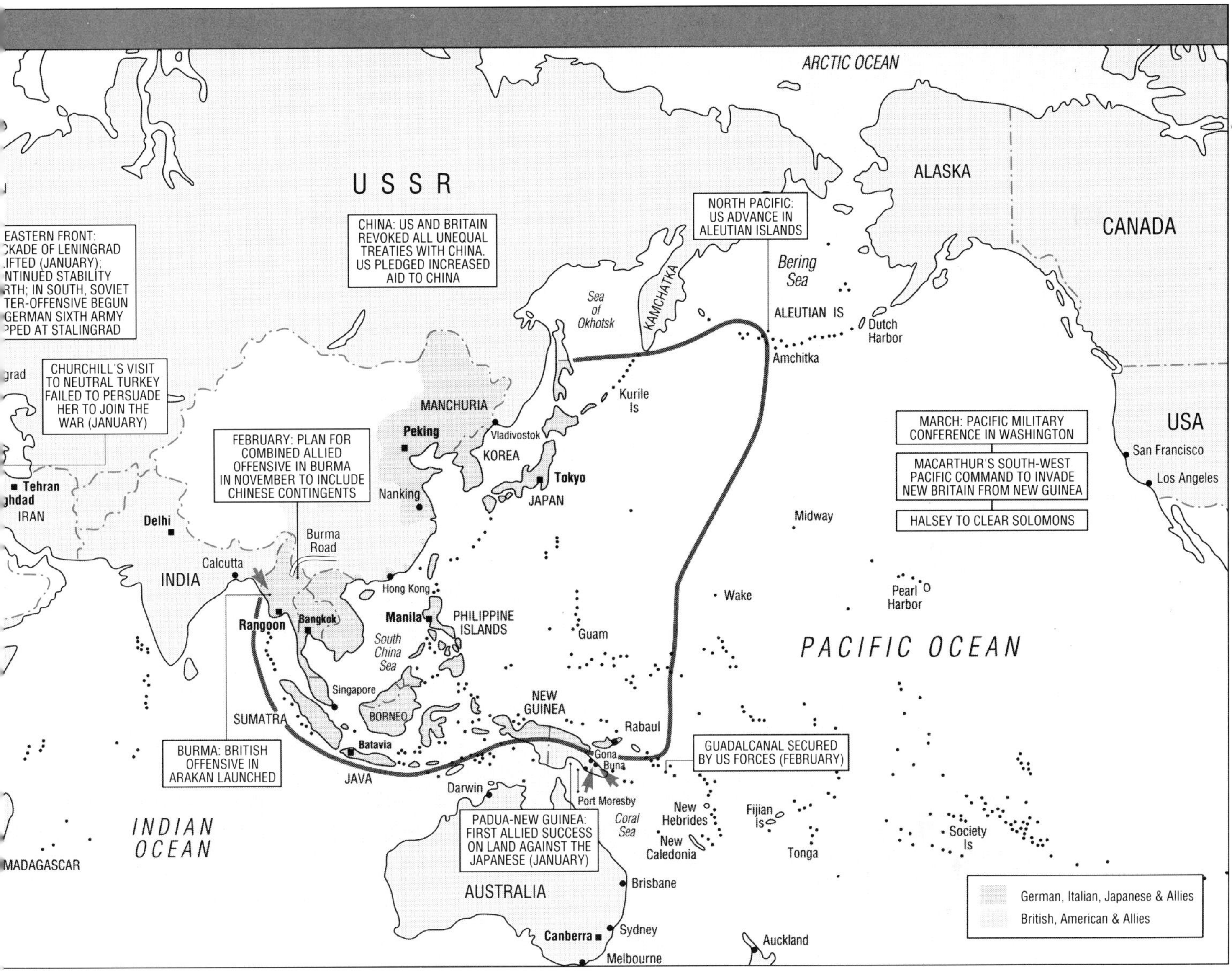

ARCTIC OCEAN
USSR
ALASKA
CANADA
USA
EASTERN FRONT: ...KADE OF LENINGRAD ...IFTED (JANUARY); ...NTINUED STABILITY ...RTH; IN SOUTH, SOVIET ...TER-OFFENSIVE BEGUN ...GERMAN SIXTH ARMY ...PED AT STALINGRAD
CHINA: US AND BRITAIN REVOKED ALL UNEQUAL TREATIES WITH CHINA. US PLEDGED INCREASED AID TO CHINA
NORTH PACIFIC: US ADVANCE IN ALEUTIAN ISLANDS
CHURCHILL'S VISIT TO NEUTRAL TURKEY FAILED TO PERSUADE HER TO JOIN THE WAR (JANUARY)
FEBRUARY: PLAN FOR COMBINED ALLIED OFFENSIVE IN BURMA IN NOVEMBER TO INCLUDE CHINESE CONTINGENTS
MARCH: PACIFIC MILITARY CONFERENCE IN WASHINGTON
MACARTHUR'S SOUTH-WEST PACIFIC COMMAND TO INVADE NEW BRITAIN FROM NEW GUINEA
HALSEY TO CLEAR SOLOMONS
BURMA: BRITISH OFFENSIVE IN ARAKAN LAUNCHED
GUADALCANAL SECURED BY US FORCES (FEBRUARY)
PADUA-NEW GUINEA: FIRST ALLIED SUCCESS ON LAND AGAINST THE JAPANESE (JANUARY)
Bering Sea
Sea of Okhotsk
KAMCHATKA
ALEUTIAN IS
Dutch Harbor
Amchitka
Kurile Is
MANCHURIA
Peking
Vladivostok
KOREA
Tokyo
JAPAN
Nanking
Tehran
IRAN
Delhi
INDIA
Calcutta
Burma Road
Hong Kong
Manila
PHILIPPINE ISLANDS
Rangoon
Bangkok
South China Sea
Guam
Wake
Midway
Pearl Harbor
San Francisco
Los Angeles
PACIFIC OCEAN
Singapore
BORNEO
SUMATRA
NEW GUINEA
Rabaul
Batavia
JAVA
Gona
Buna
Darwin
Port Moresby
Coral Sea
New Hebrides
New Caledonia
Fijian Is
Tonga
Society Is
INDIAN OCEAN
MADAGASCAR
AUSTRALIA
Brisbane
Sydney
Canberra
Melbourne
Auckland
German, Italian, Japanese & Allies
British, American & Allies

The End at Stalingrad

The final destruction of the German pocket at Stalingrad was to involve seven armies commanded by Rokossovsky's Don Front. Three of these were transferred from Yeremenko's Stalingrad Front, which on **1 January 1943** was renamed the South Front. This was to continue the attacks against von Manstein.

30 December 1942 Stavka directive that the attack at Stalingrad was to take place on 6 January.
On 3 January, because of delays in deploying troops and moving up supplies, Rokossovsky and the Stavka representative with the Don and Voronezh Fronts, Nikolai Voronov, asked for a postponement. Stalin grudgingly allowed them four days.

8 January 1943 Rokossovsky offered Paulus surrender terms, which were rejected.

10 January Soviet offensive opened.
This was aimed at rolling up the pocket from west to east. Sixty-Fifth Army advanced five miles on the first day, despite determined German counter-attacks, but in the north and south progress was slower.

12 January The western nose of the pocket overrun.
It cost the Don Front 26,000 casualties and half its force of 257 tanks. German casualties were also high.

13 January Karpovka airfield captured.
This was the most westerly of the seven airfields in the pocket.

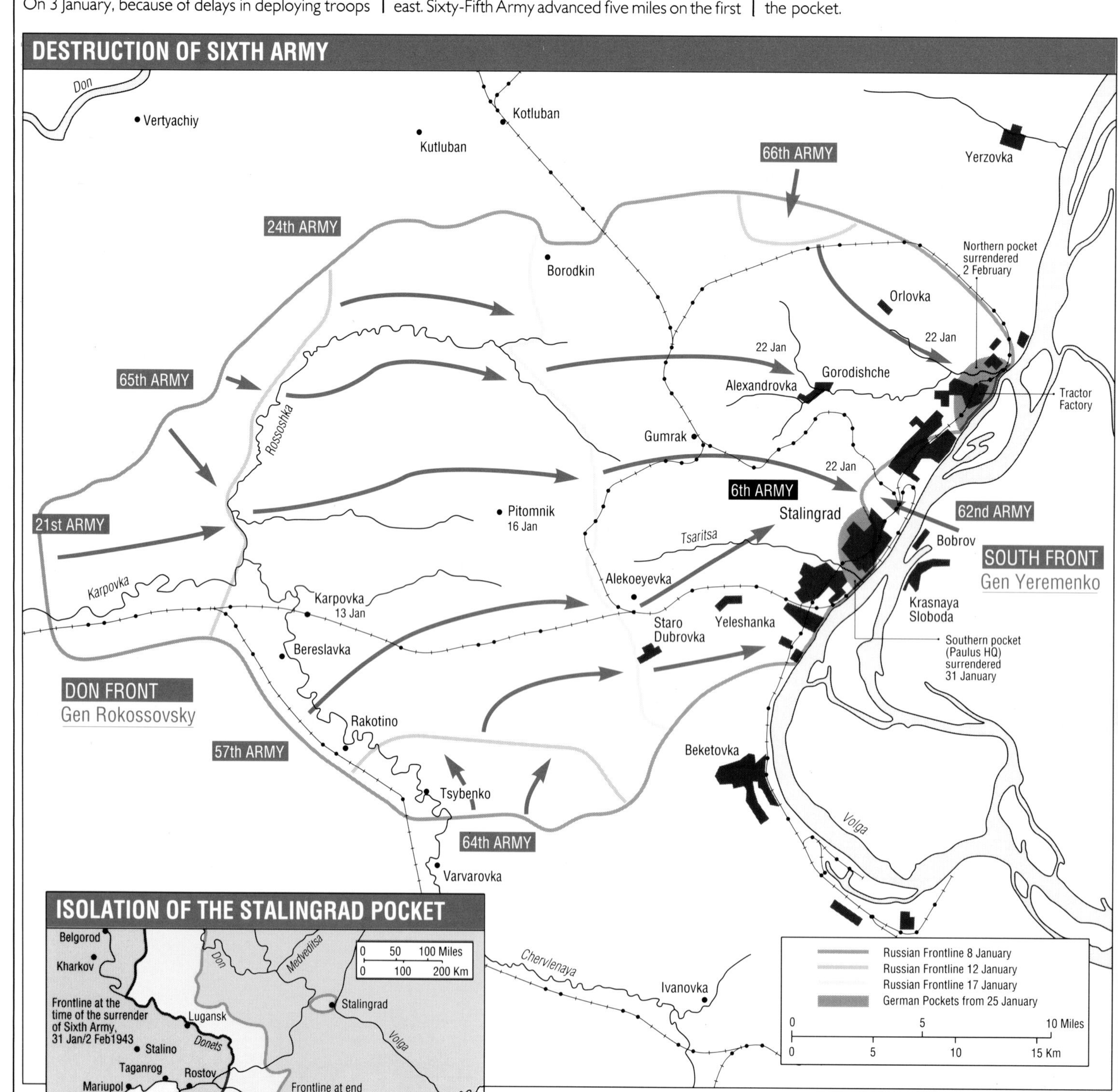

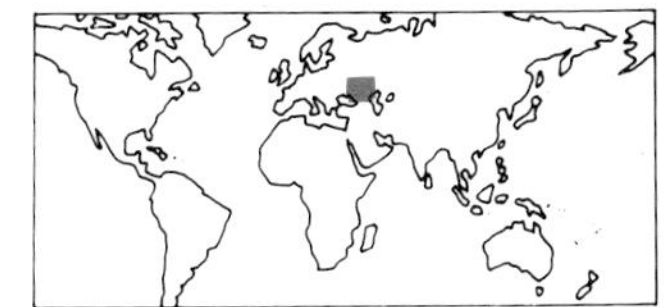

14 January Hitler ordered Field Marshal Erhard Milch to take over the air resupply of the Stalingrad pocket.
Because of the increasing distance to Stalingrad on account of the continuing Soviet attacks against von Manstein and losses in aircraft, the daily supply of the pocket had dropped to 40 tons. Milch was Secretary of State for Air and Goering's deputy, with a high reputation as an organizer. He joined von Manstein at his HQ at Taganrog two days later.

16 January Pitomnik airfield overrun.
This was the only airfield with a night flying capability. A day later only Gumrak was still in German hands. From now on, air supply had to rely increasingly on parachuted containers because of the problems of landing at Gumrak. Milch did, however, manage to increase the tonnage supplied to 60 per day. One additional airstrip was hastily constructed.

17 January Rokossovsky wanted a pause of 2–3 days in the attacks.
This was so that he could regroup. The attacks continued, however. By this stage conditions within the pocket were becoming increasingly grave. Food was desperately short. This and the extreme cold inflicted the defenders with ever greater lethargy. It was now hardly possible to evacuate the wounded, and many of them died. None the less there were still enough officers and men who were determined to fight on.

22 January The final phase of the assault on the German pocket began.
Paulus sent a signal to Hitler emphasizing his desperate shortage of food and ammunition and hinting at surrender, but Hitler refused to countenance this.

The airfield at Gumrak fell and forward elements of the Soviet Twenty-First Army made contact with Chuikov's Sixty-Second Army, which had been tying down German forces in Stalingrad itself. The Sixth Army was now split into two small pockets in the north and south of the city.

23 January The last German aircraft flew out of the pocket.
It was an He 111 and carried nineteen wounded and seven bags of mail. From now on, all supplies had to be air-dropped.

24 January Hitler forbade any break-out, even by small groups of men.
In the southern pocket, Paulus moved his HQ into the basement of the Univermag department store. Such was the shortage of food that Paulus laid down that no food should be given to the wounded and sick, of whom there were now some 30,000.

Night of 29/30 January Milch succeeded in flying-in 124 aircraft to drop supplies into the pocket.
This constituted the highest number of sorties flown for some time, but was too late to affect the inevitable course of events.

30 January Special radio broadcast by Goering on the anniversary of Hitler's accession to power.
'A thousand years hence Germans will speak of this battle with reverence and awe.' Paulus signalled Hitler: 'The swastika flag is still flying above Stalingrad. May our battle be an example to the present and coming generations, that they must never capitulate even in a hopeless situation, for them Germany will emerge victorious.'

Hitler now decided to promote Paulus to Field Marshal in the hope that he would commit suicide rather than surrender. A number of other officers in the pocket were also promoted.

31 January Paulus surrendered.
This happened at 1945 hours local time and after the Univermag building had been surrounded. It was Vassili Chuikov's Sixty-Second Army which had the honour of accepting his surrender. The northern pocket continued to fight on.

2 February The northern pocket surrendered.
This had been reduced to a small area around the Tractor Works and was subjected to a final massive bombardment with a density of guns of no less than 300 per kilometre. The battle for Stalingrad was now over.

3 February Hitler announced the fall of Stalingrad to the German people.
He declared four days of mourning, with the closure of all places of entertainment.

The Germans lost 110,000 killed during the battle and a further 91,000 were made prisoner. No details of the total Soviet casualties are available, but they were high. Of the Germans captured at Stalingrad, some were put to work rebuilding the city, while the others were marched east and ended up in camps from the Arctic Circle down to the borders with Afghanistan. Many died as a result of a typhus epidemic in spring 1943 and others of exhaustion and lack of food. Eventually only some 5,000 returned to Germany long after the war was over. Some high-ranking prisoners, including Paulus himself, disillusioned by what they viewed as Hitler's betrayal of them, were eventually persuaded by the Russians to make propaganda broadcasts to encourage German troops to surrender.

Stalingrad was undoubtedly a major turning-point, not just on the Eastern Front but of the whole war. It was a dramatic reverse for German arms, but need never have happened if Hitler had been less obstinate. For the German armies on the Eastern Front, however, there was little time to grieve, for they were now having to deal with renewed Soviet offensives in the Caucacus and Ukraine.

GERMAN FORMATION LOSSES AT STALINGRAD

All the formations lost at Stalingrad were reformed during spring 1943 – Hitler had an abhorrence of striking any formation off the Order of Battle. Below is a list of these formations with the theatres in which they subsequently fought after reconstitution.

HQ SIXTH ARMY	Eastern Front
HQ IV Panzer Corps	Eastern Front
HQ VIII Corps	Eastern Front
HQ XIV Panzer Corps	Sicily, Italy
HQ LI Corps	LI Mountain Corps Italy
3 Panzer Grenadier Division	Italy, Western Front
14 Panzer Division	Eastern Front
16 Panzer Division	Italy, Eastern Front
24 Panzer Division	Italy, Eastern Front
29 Panzer Grenadier Division	Sicily, Italy
44 Infantry Division	Italy, Eastern Front
60 Panzer Grenadier Division	Eastern Front
71 Infantry Division	Slovenia, Italy, Eastern Front
76 Infantry Division	Italy, Eastern Front
79 Infantry Division	Eastern Front, but destroyed again in September 1944, reconstituted once more and then to Western Front
94 Infantry Division	Italy
100 Jaeger Division	Albania, Eastern Front
113 Infantry Division	Eastern Front
295 Infantry Division	Norway
297 Infantry Division	Albania, Yugoslavia, Eastern Front
305 Infantry Division	Italy
371 Infantry Division	Italy, Yugoslavia, Eastern Front
376 Infantry Division	Eastern Front
384 Infantry Division	Eastern Front
XIV Panzer Corps	
389 Infantry Division	Eastern Front

Stalin Keeps up the Pressure · P132

Stalin Keeps up the Pressure

The success of the Soviet counter-offensive against von Manstein and the fact that Paulus was now 'in a vice' at Stalingrad from which he could not escape encouraged Stalin to more grandiose plans. His object now was to clear the Caucasus of the Axis presence and expel them from the eastern Ukraine. Furthermore, Stalin wanted to lift the blockade on Leningrad.

In the last part of December 1942 the Stavka had been working hard to draw up plans to achieve these aims in conjunction with the Front commanders involved.

29 December 1942 **Stavka gave orders for the entrapment of Army Group A in the Caucasus.**
The ultimate objective was to be Rostov, and the German escape route to the Crimea was to be severed. This was to be carried out by the Transcaucus Front (otherwise known as the Black Sea Group) and the Stalingrad Front (which became South Front on **1 January 1943**).

3 January 1943 **Army Group A began to withdraw from the Caucasus.**
Hitler's staff wanted to evacuate the Caucasus entirely and take up a position on the Don north of Rostov, but Hitler would only agree to falling back to the Manych Canal and the Kuban, because he wanted a base for further operations towards the Caspian. The withdrawal caught the Trancasucasus Front by surprise, and it was slow to follow up. Yeremenko's South Front now struck north towards Rostov, but was held by Fourth Panzer Army.

12 January **Operation 'Iskra', the breaking of the Leningrad blockade, launched.**
This was carried out by the Leningrad and Volkhov Fronts. On the 18th they linked up, creating a corridor, and cleared the Germans from the southern shore of Lake Ladoga. This meant that Leningrad was no longer cut off from the rest of the country. On **6 February** the Russians succeeded in opening a railway line between Schlusselburg and Polyany, and this considerably augmented the tenuous supply line across the frozen Lake Ladoga.

13 January **The Voronezh Front attacked across the Don.**
It was supported by the Bryansk Front to its north and the South-West Front to its south. The initial targets were the Second Hungarian Army and the Eighth Italian Army.

18 January **The Hungarians and Italians were encircled.**
Although many escaped in the heavy snowstorms, 80,000 prisoners were captured when the pockets were reduced on the 27th. This created a 200-mile gap along Army Group B's front and it also left Second German Army on its northern flank dangerously exposed.

24 January **Bryansk and Voronezh Fronts moved to encircle Second German Army.**
The Germans had already begun to evacuate Voronezh, which was recaptured by the Russians on the 25th.

27 January **Hitler allowed Army Group Don to withdraw behind the lower Don.**
Von Manstein was to be joined by part of Army Group A, while the remainder, some 350,000 men, withdrew to the Taman bridgehead. Von Manstein himself wanted to pull back behind the River Mius, but Hitler vetoed this.

30 January **Bryansk and Voronezh Fronts closed on Kastornoe.**
Two of the three corps of German Second Army were now encircled, and Army Group B had virtually ceased to exist as a fighting force.

2 February **Rodion Malinovsky took over command of the South Front from Yeremenko.**
The next major Soviet objectives were Rostov, Kiev and Kursk.

4 February **Soviet amphibious landing near Novorossisk on the Black Sea.**
The plan was to cut off the German Seventeenth Army's withdrawal from the Taman bridgehead. Although the Soviets established a small beachhead, it was contained; fighting here would continue for the next seven months.

6 February **Hitler agreed to further withdrawals.**
Von Manstein and von Kluge were summoned to Hitler's HQ at Rastenburg, East Prussia, the *Wolfschanze* ('Wolf's Lair'). He agreed that von Manstein could withdraw to the Mius and that von Kluge's Army Group Centre could give up the very vulnerable Rzhev salient. Von Weichs's Army Group B was removed from the order of battle and his remaining troops shared between von Kluge and von Manstein.

8 February **Kursk regained by the Russians.**

14 February **Russians reoccupied Rostov.**
Voroshilovgrad also fell, and the South-West Front continued to thrust towards Stalino.

15 February **The Russians launched an attack to eradicate the Demyansk Salient north of Smolensk.**
Two days later the twelve German divisions in the salient began to withdraw and succeeded in extricating themselves without too severe losses. They also denied the Russians their objective of getting in behind the German Eighteenth Army and thus lifting the siege of Leningrad.

16 February **The Germans evacuated Kharkov.**
Next day Hitler, determined to dismiss von Manstein, arrived at Army Group South HQ at Zaporozhe. Von Manstein, his line now shortened and with more troops available, advocated a counter-offensive, to which Hitler eventually agreed. By now the leading Soviet forces had outrun their supplies and even most of their air support, so the time was ripe for such a venture. Von Manstein had already begun to concentrate First and Fourth Panzer Armies for his counter-stroke.

20 February **The Russians re-took Pavlograd and Krasnograd.**
Vatutin's South-West Front had now carved out a large salient pointing south-west towards Dnepropetrovsk on the Dnieper.

20 February **Von Manstein launched his counter-stroke.**
This caught the Russians, who were convinced that the Germans were no longer capable of such an operation, by surprise. The SS Panzer Corps struck Vatutin's right flank south of Krasnograd, while in the south XL Panzer Corps attacked northwards against Popov's mobile group of three tank corps, which at the time was down to 25 tanks. Fourth Panzer Army also struck north to link up with the SS Panzer Corps. Vatutin refused to believe that this was anything other than an attempt to cover the German withdrawal, and continued his attacks westwards. That night General Filipp Golikov, commanding the Voronezh Front, decided on his own initiative to halt the drive to the Dneiper and turn south against the SS Panzer Corps. Within 48 hours he was bloodily repulsed.

25 February **Vatutin finally realized the seriousness of the situation.**
He ordered his now almost-encircled Sixth Army to go over to the defensive and made a desperate plea to the Stavka for reinforcements.

28 February **XL Panzer Corps reached the Donets west of Izyum.**
At the same time Vatutin's right flank was being driven back to the northern Donets.

3 March **Vatutin was now back on the northern Donets.**

4 March **Von Manstein launched the second phase of his counter-stroke.**
Re-concentrating his Panzer forces south-west of Kharkov, he punched through the Voronezh Front and by the 12th had reached Kharkov.

15 March **The SS Panzer Corps recaptured Kharkov.**
This was after bitter street fighting.

18 March **The Germans recaptured Belgorod.**
This now put both the Voronezh and Central Fronts

P130 · The End at Stalingrad

n danger of being cut off. The Voronezh Front now lso fell back to the Donets. Golikov was replaced y Vatutin.

The third phase of von Manstein's plan was to educe the huge Soviet salient based on Kursk nd held by the Central and Voronezh Fronts. The oming of the spring thaw prevented this from being put into effect. Nevertheless, his counter-stroke had done much to restore the German position. As for the Russians, their offensives had demonstrated a dangerous over-confidence and lack of appreciation of German resilience.

There was now a pause in the fighting on the Eastern Front, but the attention of both sides remained firmly fixed on the Kursk salient.

MANSTEIN'S COUNTER-ATTACK

THE RUSSIAN 1943 WINTER OFFENSIVE

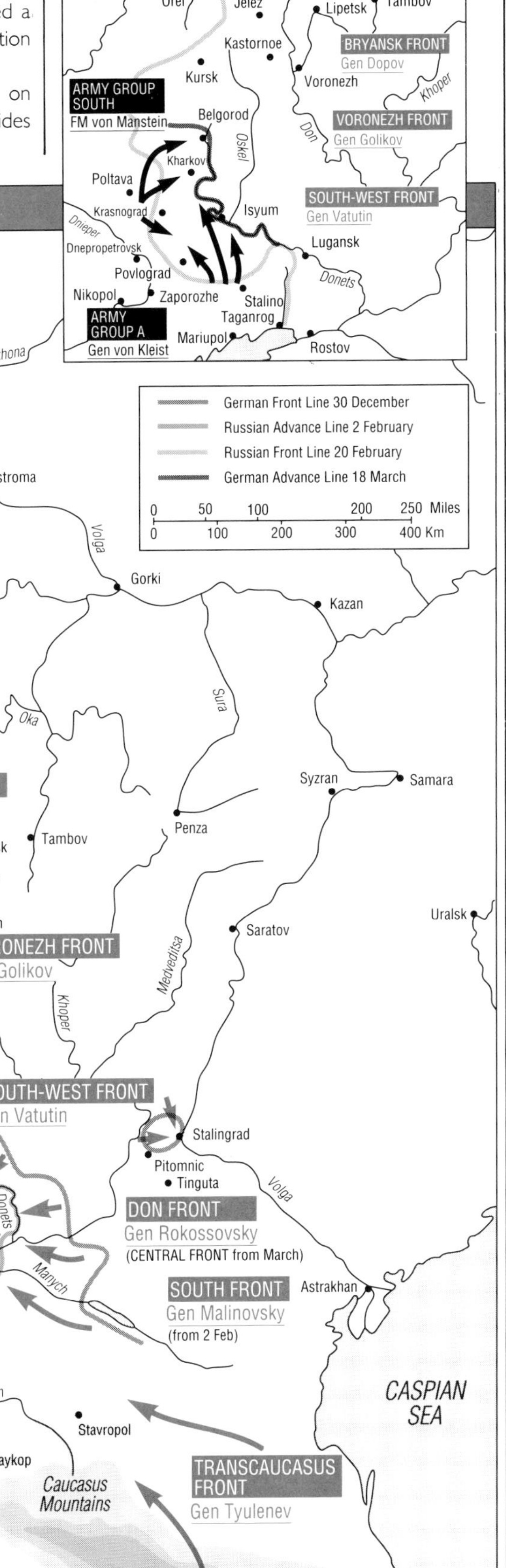

Tunisia

At the beginning of 1943 there was a seeming stalemate in Tunisia. Both sides were desperately striving to reinforce their strength, especially since the front, which ran from the Mediterranean coast down through the Eastern Dorsale to just west of Fondouk, was some 150 miles long and could only be thinly held.

On the Allied side, Eisenhower remained in overall command, but he was too involved with political problems to exercise more than very general control of operations. This devolved on Anderson's First British Army, which now consisted of three nationalities: V British Corps in the north, XIX French Corps in the centre and II US Corps in the south. The Axis forces were now under command of Juergen von Arnim's Fifth Panzer Army, but this would shortly be joined by Rommel's Panzerarmee Afrika, which was withdrawing through Tripolitania pursued by the British Eighth Army. Von Arnim, who now had 100,000 mostly good-quality German troops, was determined to retain the initiative and to disrupt the Allied build-up as much as possible.

3 January 1943 **The French were driven from the Fondouk Pass.**
The French commander-in-chief, Alphonse Juin, retaliated by wresting the Kairouan and Karachoum Passes from the Italians.

18 January **Von Arnim launched Operation 'Eilbote I'.**
This was aimed at regaining the Kairouan and Karachoum Passes from the French and securing the high ground south-west of Pont du Fahs. This was successful, although an attack on Bou Arada, on the Anglo-French corps boundary, was repulsed. The Axis, however, now held all the passes in the Eastern Dorsal and were thus better able to guard the approaches to Bizerte and Tunis.

Eisenhower's plan had been for a US thrust against Sfax (Operation 'Satin'), but von Arnim's attack forced its cancellation.

23 January **Axis command reorganization.**
General Vittorio Ambrosio was appointed Commando Supremo, with Fifth Panzer Army and Rommel's Panzerarmee Afrika, now renamed First Italian Army and firm in the Mareth Line, under him. It was planned that Rommel would return to Europe and command be given to General Giovanni Messe, but this did not happen for some weeks.

24 January **Successful raid by US 1st Armored Division on Sened Station.**
This lay on the Gafsa-Maknassy road.

26 January **Eisenhower issued fresh instructions to Anderson.**
He was to re-establish himself on the line Fondouk – Karachoum Gap – Robaa – Bou Arada and seize the passes on the eastern side of the Eastern Dorsal.

30 January **Axis attack on the French at Faid.**
Despite a US counter-attack, the French were driven out. US attempts to raid Maknassy on **1** and **3 February** were also rebuffed.

In the meantime there had been argument in the Axis camp as to what to do next. Rommel wanted to launch a decisive thrust through Tebessa and into the rear of First Army, while von Arnim, conscious of a declining supply position, wished to restrict himself to spoiling attacks. Kesselring allowed each to conduct his own attack – von Arnim against the French and Americans at Sidi Bou Zid ('Spring Wind'), and Rommel against Gafsa ('Morning Wind').

7 February **With Tripoli port now opened, Montgomery began to advance into Tunisia.**
Heavy rain slowed down the advance.

14 February **Von Arnim launched his attack on Sidi Bou Zid.**
Using a double envelopment, he quickly seized it, cutting off the US forces in the area.

15 February **Rommel seized Gafsa.**
He now advanced to Feriana, while von Arnim made for Sbeitla. Montgomery's forces arrived at Medenine, where they halted facing the formidable Mareth Line.

17 February **Rommel seized Feriana.**
Rommel now made for the Kasserine Pass. The US forces were now in considerable disarray.

18 February **Von Arnim captured Sbeitla.**
He had also sent a force north-east to Fondouk, which Anderson had evacuated.

19 February **General Sir Harold Alexander took command of the newly created 18th Army Group.**
This was to co-ordinate the activities of First and Eighth Armies. He ordered Anderson to hold all the exits from the mountains into western Tunisia.

19 February **Rommel seized the Kasserine Pass.**
This was only after two days' heavy fighting. In the meantime British reinforcements had arrived on the Thala–Kasserine road, and everywhere the Allied defence was becoming more cohesive.

20 February **Rommel rebuffed at Sbiba.**
He now thrust towards Thala, but was rebuffed from here on the 22nd. Rommel now realized that he had 'shot his bolt', and was authorized by Ambrosio to withdraw in order to turn and deal with the Eighth Army.

23 February **Rommel appointed CinC, Army Group Afrika.**
Rommel now intended to attack Montgomery at Medenine (Operation 'Capri'), while von Arnim distracted Allied attention with a series of attacks in northern Tunisia (Operation 'Ox Head').

24 February **The Allies retook Sbiba.**
Next day they recovered the Kasserine Pass, Sbeitla and Sidi Bou Zid.

26 February **'Ox Head' launched.**
It consisted of a number of attacks by armoured battle groups from the coast down to Bou Arada. Some gains were made, notably the capture of Sidi Nisr and the coastal drive towards Sedjenane which eventually fell on **19 March**, but no Axis breakthrough was achieved.

6 March **Battle of Medenine.**
Through Ultra, Montgomery had been warned of Rommel's intention to attack him, and had plenty of time to prepare a reception. Rommel's armour was repulsed. Patton replaced Fredendall as commander of II US Corps.

9 March **Rommel left North Africa.**
He was given sick leave and would not return. Von Arnim took his place, and Gustav von Vaerst was appointed to command Fifth Panzer Army.

17 March **Patton captured Gafsa.**
This was the beginning of a thrust from Tebessa to the Eastern Dorsal to secure Montgomery's left flank as he launched himself at the Mareth Line. This, after the disaster at Kasserine, did much to restore US morale both in Tunisia and at home.

20 March **Montgomery began his attack on the Mareth Line.**
His first attempt, to breach it frontally, failed, so he sent the New Zealand Corps on a long outflanking move through the Tebaga Gap.

Night of 26/27 March **New Zealand Corps broke through the Tebaga Gap.**
The Axis forces evacuated the Mareth Line and withdrew north to the next defensive line at Wadi Akarit, to which Montgomery closed up on **30 March.**

31 March **End of Patton's thrust to the Eastern Dorsal.**
He secured the pass at Maknassy, but was halted just short of Fondouk and Faid.

6 April **Montgomery broke through at Wadi Akarit.**
He failed, however, to prevent Messe's forces withdrawing to the next defensive line at Enfidaville.

7 April **British IX Corps attacked the Fondouk Pass.**

P122 · The Dash to Tunis

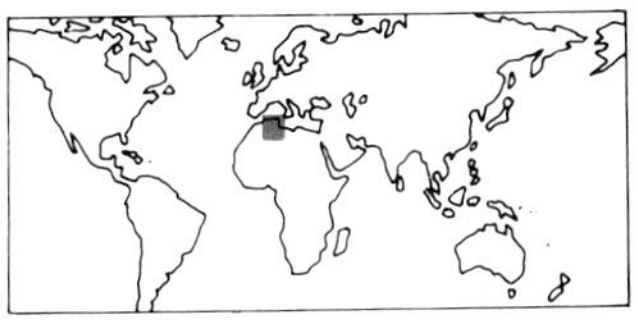

his was secured next day, and on the 10th the dvance continued to Kairouan.

9–21 April **Montgomery failed to dislodge the irst Italian Army from Enfidaville.**
t the same time von Arnim launched a spoiling ttack against First Army between Medjez and Goubellat, which was repulsed with heavy losses. lexander now decided to shift the main axis of ttack to First Army.

22 April **Attacks launched all along the First Army front.**
By now the Axis forces were being steadily strangled. Air and sea operations had virtually cut their supply lines across the Mediterranean. Nevertheless, their resistance was tenacious.

6 May **The final Allied offensive opened.**
In the meantime Montgomery had transferred some of his formations to Alexander.

7 May **Bizerte and Tunis fell.**

On 11 May Axis resistance in the Cape Bon peninsula ceased. Victory had been won at a cost of some 75,000 Allied casualties; the Axis had suffered some 300,000, including 240,000 prisoners – a disaster comparable to Stalingrad. Alexander now signalled Churchill: 'We are masters of the North African shore.' The Allies could now plan for their return to Europe.

THE AXIS OFFENSIVE

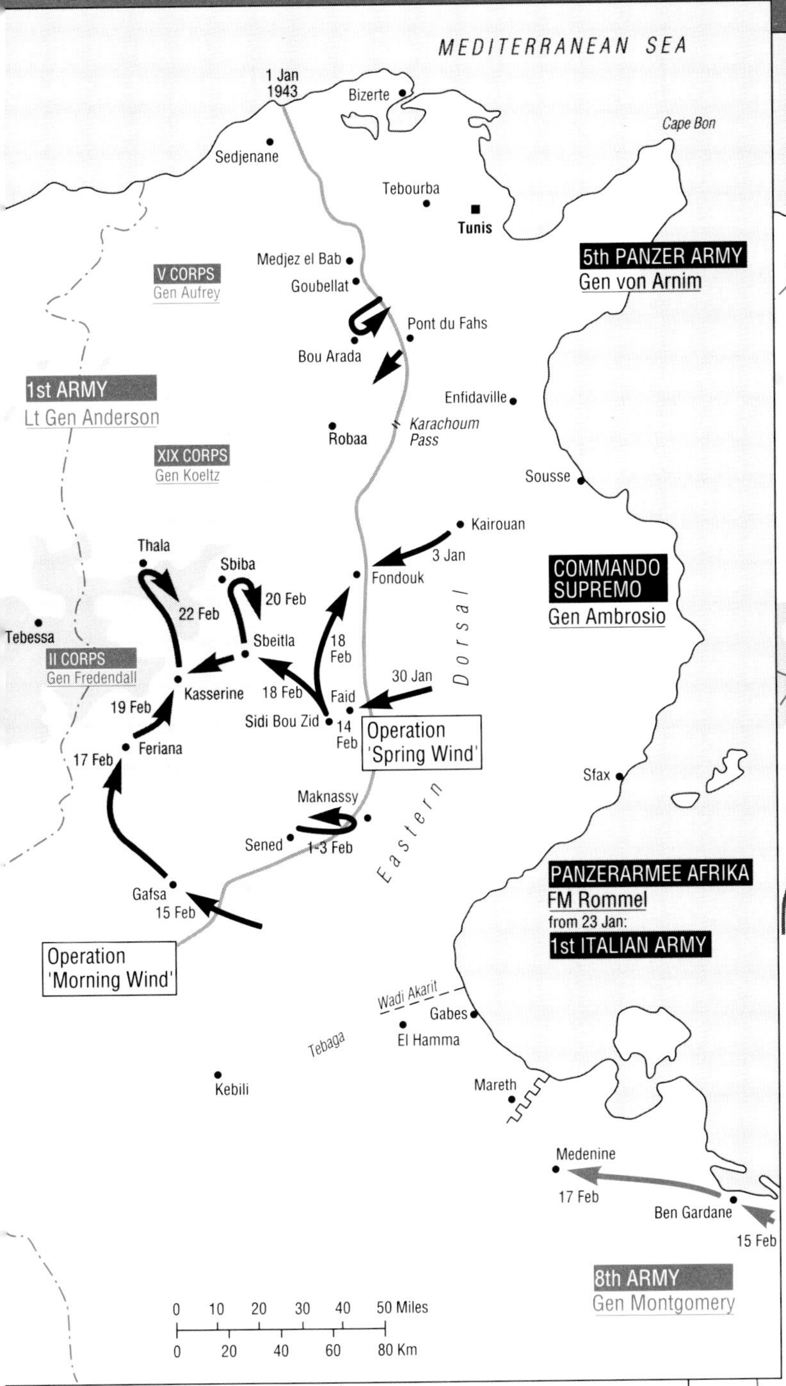

THE ALLIED OFFENSIVES

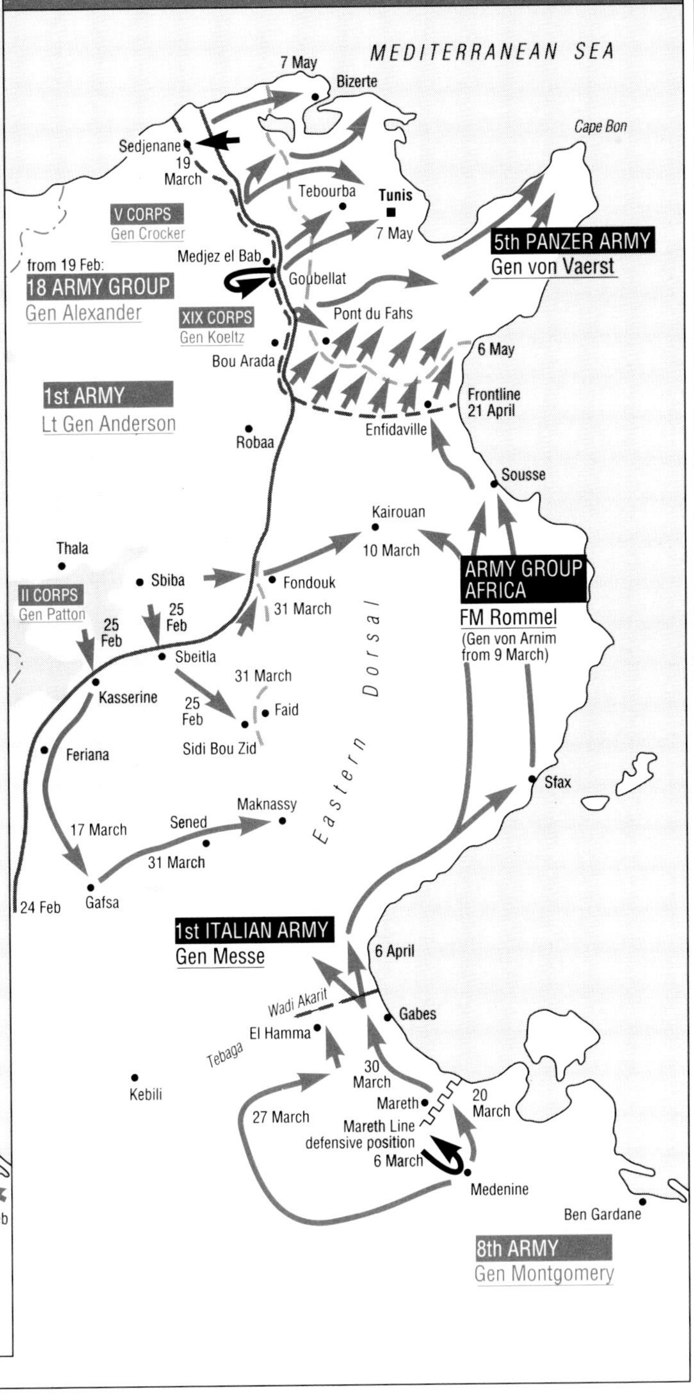

Sicily · P148

Atlantic Victory

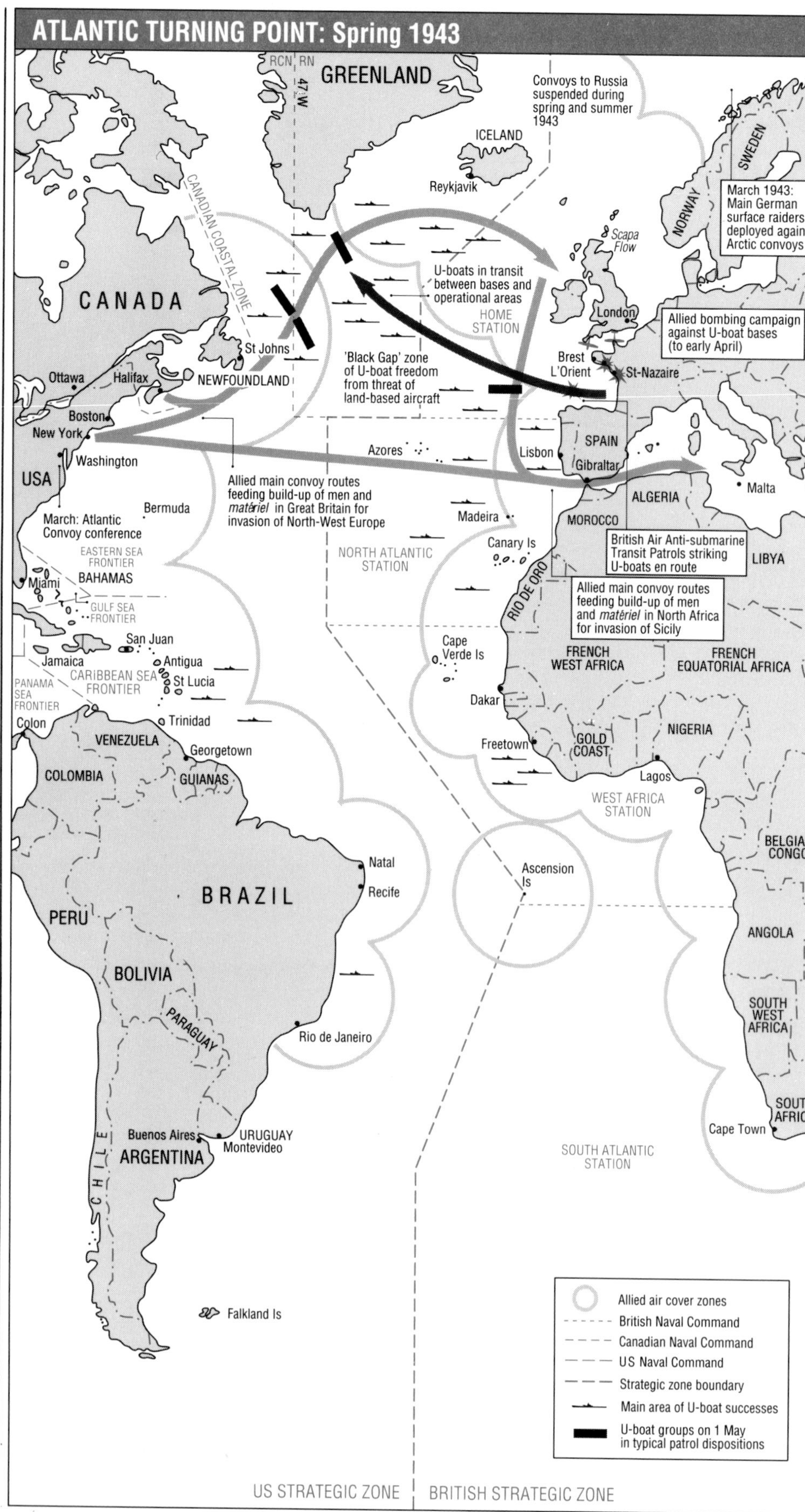

One of the priorities established at the Casablanca Conference was the need to master the U-boat threat in the Atlantic. If this were not radically reduced, and quickly, 'Bolero' and hence 'Round Up' would be in jeopardy. One immediate decision made was that RAF Bomber Command and the USAAF in Britain should attack the U-boat bases on the French Atlantic coast. In January 1943, however, bad weather and the ability to read the U-boat cipher 'Triton' kept losses in the Atlantic down to just over 200,000 tons, less than any month during 1942.

30 January 1943 **Doenitz succeeded Raeder as CinC, German Navy.**
Nevertheless, he did not surrender direct operational control of the U-boats. At the same time there was a radical change in U-boat tactics. Until then they had concentrated equally on westbound and eastbound convoys, using information from radio intercepts to deduce convoy courses. Through U-boat situation-report intercepts transmitted by the Admiralty to the convoys, the Germans were aware that the Allies had an accurate picture of U-boat tactics, but Doenitz refused to accept that this might be because of an ability to read 'Triton'; instead he thought that airborne radar was the culprit. He now laid down that effort should be concentrated on the full eastbound rather than the comparatively empty westbound convoys. U-boat wolf-packs in the north-western Atlantic would be deployed to cover all possible routes, while those in the east would sweep westwards to catch the eastbound convoys that had either previously been attacked by the groups off Newfoundland or had evaded them. Eastbound convoys would only be attacked where there was firm intelligence, or as targets of opportunity.

February **Allied shipping losses rose to almost 315,000 tons.**
The Admiralty's monthly Anti-Submarine Report for January had noted: 'A bolder and more ruthless strategy is now characteristic of the enemy. The tempo is quickening, and the critical phase of the U-boat war in the Atlantic cannot long be postponed.'

1 March **Atlantic Convoy Conference opened in Washington, DC.**
Here it was agreed that the Royal Navy and Royal Canadian Navy would share responsibility for the North Atlantic, the dividing line being 47°W. The US Navy would stop escorting North Atlantic convoys, and take over the escort of tankers to and from the Dutch West Indies instead. They would, however, provide a support group built round the escort carrier *Bogue*, which would operate under British control in the North Atlantic. This would mean that the escort of any threatened convoy could be reinforced. There would also be a radical increase

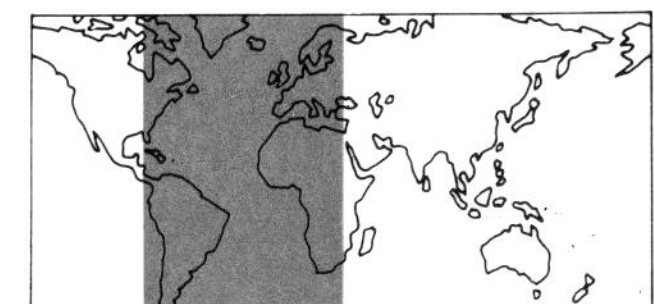

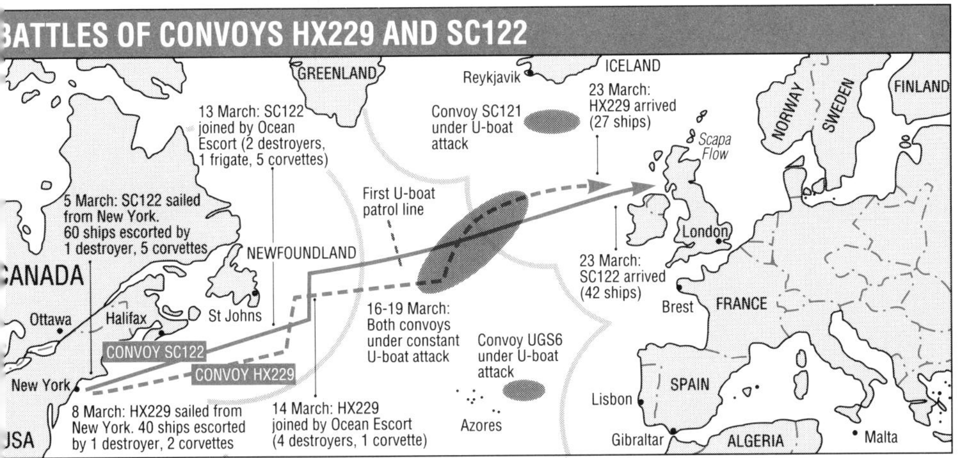

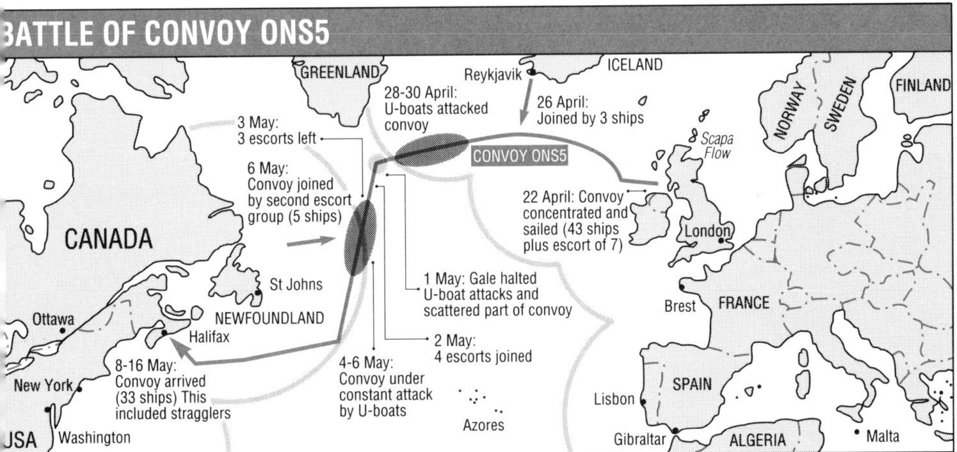

the number of long-range aircraft based on Newfoundland.

March **British Chiefs of Staff viewed the situation in the Atlantic with gloom.**
In a report they concluded that every convoy should be regarded as threatened, and that it was no longer possible to evade the wolf-packs. The convoys would have to fight their way through them. Their gloom was compounded by the fact that Bletchley Park had been unable to decipher 'Triton' since **8 March** because another rotor had been added to the U-boat M4 Enigma machines. Luckily the problem was shortlived, and by the end of the month Bletchley Park was once more able to decipher U-boat traffic.

During the last ten days of February, 28 Allied ships had been sunk in the Atlantic; in the first ten days of March, 41.

5–19 March **The battles of Convoys HX229 and SC122.**
These marked a climax in the Battle of the Atlantic. No less than 37 U-boats in three groups harried the 98 merchant ships of these two eastbound convoys. They sank 21 ships and lost only one U-boat.

This shattering reverse caused the British First Lord of the Admiralty (naval minister) to observe on 22 March that 'there is insufficient shipping to allow us to develop the offensives against the enemy which have been decided on. Every ship sunk makes the situation worse.' No less than 540,000 tons of shipping were lost in the Atlantic during March.

Drastic measures would need to be implemented. There was even serious consideration given to abandoning the convoy system. It was decided to cancel the next two Russian convoys (in fact no more would sail until November 1943), which made 27 additional escort vessels and an escort carrier available and resulted in five further support groups being formed. Furthermore, the escorts now adopted a more aggressive posture, something that Admiral Max Horton, a First World War submarine ace, now CinC Western Approaches and largely responsible for the day-to-day running of operations in the North Atlantic from the British side, had been advocating for the past few months.

During the last few days of March, the spring gales arrived, and this helped to reduce the carnage. Doenitz remained determined, though, to build on his March successes as soon as the weather had abated, and deployed more and more U-Boats to the North Atlantic.

21 April **Improving weather led to increased U-boat activity in the North Atlantic.**

29 April to 1 May **Further gales hindered both convoys and U-boats.**

4 May **Eastbound Convoy ONS5 threatened by 40 U-boats.**
During the next 36 hours twelve ships of this convoy were sunk. Two U-boats had been sunk, one to a Canadian Catalina and another to one of ONS5's escorts.

6 May **ONS5 now reinforced by an escort group.**
During the night, numerous attacks were made on the harrying U-boats, and four were sunk by the escorts. There were no losses to the convoy.

This decisive and remarkable reversal of fortune was to be reinforced by the experiences of the next few North Atlantic convoys. Westbound HX237 sank three U-boats for the loss of three merchantmen stragglers; SC129 sank two for the loss of two; ONS7 one for one; SC130 four for none. In all, during the first three weeks of May, 31 U-boats were sunk.

24 May **Doenitz withdrew his U-boats from the North Atlantic.**
His losses of the past few weeks had come 'as a hard and unexpected blow'. He redeployed his boats to south-west of the Azores. A week later he explained his decision to Hitler, calling for more air support and a higher rate of U-boat construction.

In all, 41 U-boats were sunk during May in return for the sinking of 300,000 tons of Allied shipping, of which 250,000 tons was in the Atlantic.

June **Merchant ship sinkings in the Atlantic fell to 30,000 tons.**
This reflected the U-boat withdrawal from the North Atlantic. That month the number of operational U-boats was 218, compared with 239 in May – the high point of the war. From now until the final defeat of Germany, the monthly total would fall steadily.

May 1943 marked the decisive turning-point in the Battle of the Atlantic. From now on, as operational U-boat strength declined, so the rate of Allied merchant ship new construction against losses increased. There were a number of reasons for this victory: improved and more aggressive escort tactics, more escorts available, increased air coverage (the 'Black Gap' was finally closed in May), more effective U-boat detection devices and anti-submarine weapon systems, increased security of merchant ships' ciphers, which made them more difficult to read, and the continuing ability to read 'Triton'.

Doenitz's decision to withdraw from the North Atlantic was only temporary, however, and the U-boats would soon return with improved weapons. But never again would the threat loom as large as it had in the early spring of 1943.

Securing the Arctic Convoy Route · P186

The Mounting of 'Pointblank'

During the second half of 1942 the strength of RAF Bomber Command and the US Eighth Army Air Force in Britain had been gradually growing. The deployment of US bombers to Britain had been slower than expected because of the need to provide protection to US transatlantic convoys, especially those involved in 'Torch'. The main target had been the U-boat bases.

The Casablanca Conference called for the mounting of a joint bombing offensive against Germany and was specific on target priorities. In descending order, these were to be: U-boat construction yards; aircraft industry; transportation; oil plants and war industry in general. The bombers might also be called upon to attack other targets, notably U-boat bases and the city of Berlin.

27 January 1943 **First USAAF raid against a target in Germany.**
The original target was a submarine plant at Vegesack on the River Weser, but cloud forced a diversion to Wilhelmshaven. One B-24 was lost.

Night of 30/31 January **First operational use by RAF Bomber Command of the navigation device H2S.**
Originally known as 'Home Sweet Home', this was a downward-looking radar the echoes of which were reproduced as an image on a cathode-ray tube. The operation was against Hamburg, and H2S was used by aircraft of the Pathfinder Force, which had been formed by Donald Bennett on **11 August 1942**, to mark targets.

4 February **AOCinC, RAF Bomber Command, Arthur Harris, received a new bombing directive.**
This reflected the agreement reached at Casablanca. General Ira Eaker, commanding the US Eighth Army Air Force, did not consider that he had sufficient bombers to implement 'Pointblank' immediately, and in any event his aircraft were still only nibbling at the fringes of Germany.

23 February **Bombing priority switched to U-boat bases once more.**
This was because of the rapidly increasing losses in the Atlantic. Harris was not happy over this because it meant diverting effort from the bombing of Germany. In many ways he was right, since the heavily reinforced concrete U-boat pens proved impervious to bombing.

Night of 5/6 March **Opening of the Battle of the Ruhr.**
This was to be the first of Harris's three major bombing offensives of 1943. The first attack was against Essen and was mounted by 442 bombers, of which fourteen failed to return. Attacks on U-boat bases continued, however, as did those on other targets in Germany.

6 April **RAF attacks on U-boat bases removed from priority list.**
It was finally accepted that too much effort was being diverted from the main offensive against Germany. Harassing attacks would continue, both by the British and the Americans.

12 April **Unveiling of the Eaker Plan.**
Eaker believed that his daylight attacks were more accurate than those by the British at night. He considered that it was better to cause heavy damage to a few key German war industries than some damage against industry in general. He therefore took the six categories listed in the Casablanca directive and identified 76 specific targets on which he proposed to concentrate. He accepted that Harris's area bombing by night did have value, but it should be against cities connected with his targets. Before he could begin his offensive, he calculated that he would need at least 800 bombers in Britain. This total he hoped to achieve by 1 July.

Night of 16/17 May **RAF raid on the Ruhr Dams.**
It was believed that if the Mohne, Sorpe and Eder Dams could be destroyed, German industry would be deprived of a vital energy source. Under the code-name 'Chastise', nineteen Lancasters of 617 Squadron led by Wing Commander Guy Gibson attacked the dams at low level with a special bouncing bomb known as 'Upkeep'. Eight bombers were lost, but the Mohne and Eder dams were breached and the Sorpe dam was damaged. Some 1,300 people were drowned in the resultant flooding. Gibson was awarded the VC, and 34 other aircrew were decorated. Although the raid did not have the hoped-for effect on German industry, it did provide a significant boost to RAF Bomber Command morale.

21 May **Eaker Plan officially accepted.**
This was during the 'Trident' Conference in Washington, DC. The policy of 'round the clock' bombing was reaffirmed, but stress was laid on the enemy fighter threat, and the USAAF was to make German fighter factories its main target during 1943.

Night of 23/24 May **826 bombers attacked Duesseldorf.**
This was the largest RAF Bomber Command raid since the 1,000-bomber raids of the previous summer. There had been six major raids against the Ruhr in April and seven more were launched in May.

10 June **Combined Chiefs of Staff issued a formal 'Pointblank' directive to Eaker and Harris.**
This confirmed that Eaker was to concentrate on the six Casablanca industries and German fighters; Harris would embark on 'the general disorganization of German industry'.

13 June **26 out of 60 B-17 bombers lost on a rai against Kiel.**
This highlighted the problem of attacking targets ou of fighter escort range by day. Priority was given t extending the range of the P-47 Thunderbolt by th addition of belly fuel tanks, but the vulnerability of U bombers on deep penetration raids into German would not be overcome for another year, until th advent of the P-51B Mustang.

22 June **First USAAF raid on the Ruhr.**
This was on a synthetic rubber plant at Huls an was highly successful. Not for six months did th plant resume full production.

Night of 9/10 July **End of the Battle of th Ruhr.**
This was marked by a raid on Gelsenkirchen b 422 RAF bombers. During the final phase of th battle, which had begun on the night of **11/1 June**, 310 aircraft out of 6,037 sorties flown faile

WAR IN THE AIR: January to Augus

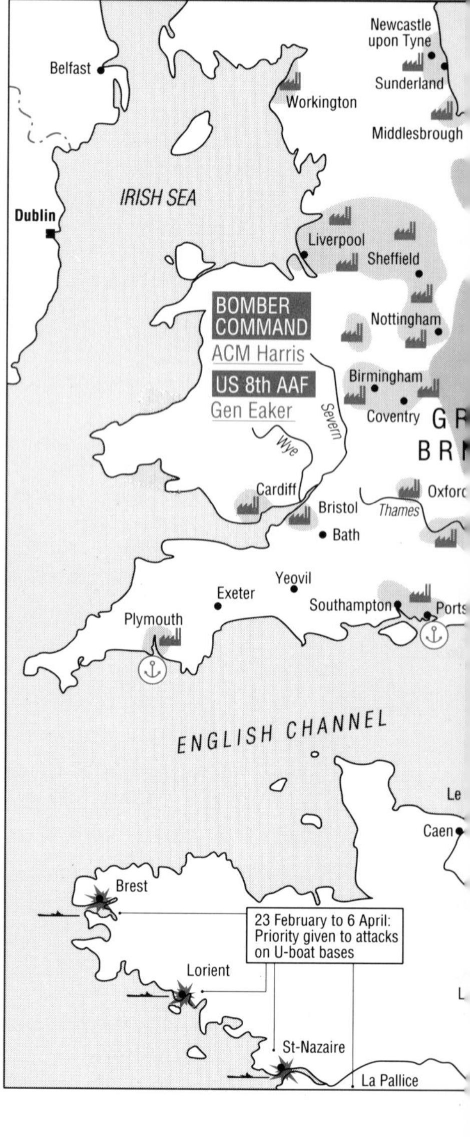

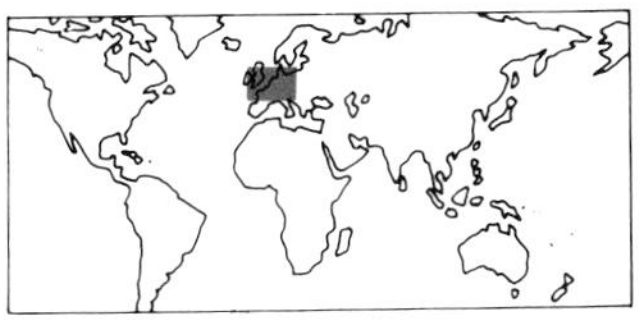

› return. This reflected the growing effectiveness ·f the German night-fighter force.

4 July to 3 August The Battle of Hamburg.
he second of Harris's offensives, code-named Gomorrah', was designed to destroy Hamburg. AF Bomber Command put up 3,015 sorties over our nights, losing 87 aircraft, while the Eighth US rmy Air Force made two daylight raids with 281 ircraft, 21 of which failed to return. Hamburg itself vas devastated, and some 40,000 of its inhabitants vere killed, largely because of the firestorm that vas created. Hitler's Minister for Armaments, Albert peer, warned him that if the Allies attacked other ities in this way, it would bring about a 'rapid end › the war'.

A new device, 'Window', strips of aluminium ropped from the bombers to confuse the German adar, was used for the first time. It totally confused ne German defences, although they recovered very uickly from it.

1 August USAAF attack on the Ploesti oilfields in Roumania.
This was carried out by the Ninth Army Air Force based in North Africa. Although 40 per cent of the refining capacity was destroyed, 54 out of 163 B-24s taking part were shot down. This stopped them from mounting follow-up raids and enabled the industry to recover.

17 August Disastrous Eighth USAAF attack on the industrial areas of Schweinfurt and Regensburg.
This was the first deep-penetration operation mounted from Britain, Schweinfurt being the centre of German ball-bearing manufacture and Regensburg of Me 109s. The operations were mounted in the belief that the German fighter threat had been sufficiently suppressed. As it was, no less than 60 out of 376 bombers were shot down. US confidence in daylight bombing was badly dented by this and the Ploesti raid.

Night of 17/18 August RAF Bomber Command attack on V-weapon experimental base at Peenemuende.
Firm intelligence that the Germans were working on a free-flight rocket was obtained at the end of 1942. In April 1943 a special team had been set up by the British War Cabinet to deal with the matter, and the decision was made to destroy Peenemuende, which was situated on the Baltic Coast, from the air. 596 bombers took off and caused significant, but not decisive, damage, delaying the entry into production of the V-weapons by some months. A total of 38 aircraft failed to return.

Although a 'one off' operation Peenemuende was another fillip to RAF morale, but Schweinfurt–Regensburg had given the Americans pause for thought. Nevertheless, in terms of a *combined* bomber offensive 'Pointblank' had hardly got under way. The crescendo of bombing would mount as 1943 drew on.

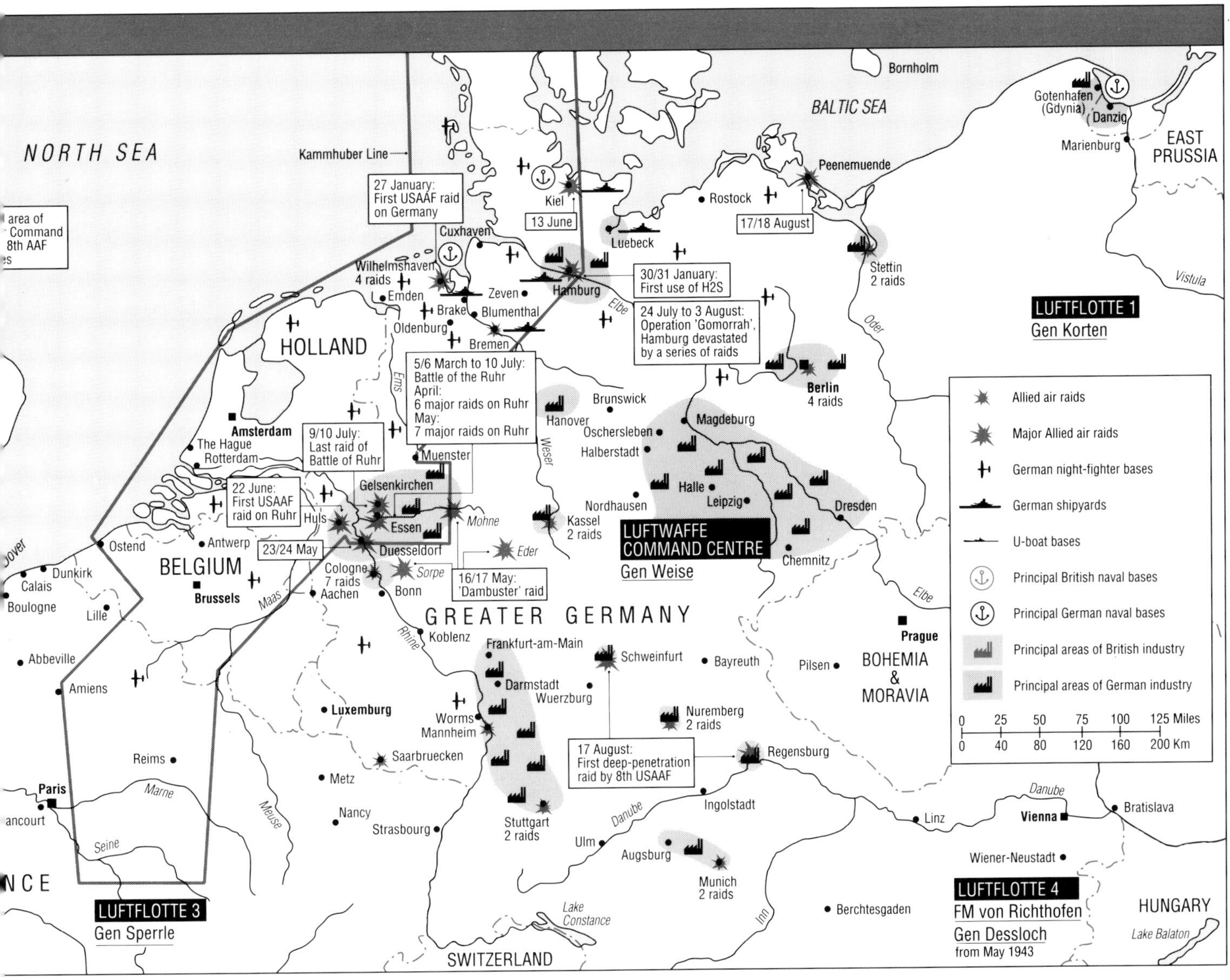
NORTH SEA
BALTIC SEA
Bornholm
Kammhuber Line
27 January: First USAAF raid on Germany
13 June
17/18 August
30/31 January: First use of H2S
24 July to 3 August: Operation 'Gomorrah', Hamburg devastated by a series of raids
5/6 March to 10 July: Battle of the Ruhr April: 6 major raids on Ruhr May: 7 major raids on Ruhr
9/10 July: Last raid of Battle of Ruhr
22 June: First USAAF raid on Ruhr
23/24 May
16/17 May: 'Dambuster' raid
17 August: First deep-penetration raid by 8th USAAF
area of Command 8th AAF
Gotenhafen (Gdynia)
Danzig
Marienburg
EAST PRUSSIA
Peenemuende
Rostock
Kiel
Luebeck
Stettin 2 raids
Cuxhaven
Wilhelmshaven 4 raids
Emden
Zeven
Hamburg
Brake
Blumenthal
Oldenburg
Bremen
HOLLAND
Amsterdam
The Hague
Rotterdam
Muenster
Gelsenkirchen
Huls
Essen
Mohne
Duesseldorf
Eder
Sorpe
Cologne 7 raids
Aachen
Bonn
Antwerp
Ostend
Dunkirk
Calais
Boulogne
Lille
BELGIUM
Brussels
Maas
Ems
Weser
Elbe
Oder
Vistula
Rhine
Hanover
Brunswick
Magdeburg
Oschersleben
Halberstadt
Halle
Leipzig
Nordhausen
Kassel 2 raids
Dresden
Chemnitz
Berlin 4 raids
LUFTFLOTTE 1
Gen Korten
LUFTWAFFE COMMAND CENTRE
Gen Weise
GREATER GERMANY
Koblenz
Frankfurt-am-Main
Schweinfurt
Bayreuth
Pilsen
Prague
BOHEMIA & MORAVIA
Darmstadt
Wuerzburg
Worms
Mannheim
Nuremberg 2 raids
Regensburg
Saarbruecken
Luxemburg
Metz
Nancy
Strasbourg
Stuttgart 2 raids
Ingolstadt
Danube
Ulm
Augsburg
Munich 2 raids
Linz
Vienna
Bratislava
Wiener-Neustadt
Berchtesgaden
Inn
Lake Constance
SWITZERLAND
HUNGARY
Lake Balaton
LUFTFLOTTE 4
FM von Richthofen
Gen Dessloch from May 1943
Abbeville
Amiens
Reims
Paris
Marne
Seine
Meuse
LUFTFLOTTE 3
Gen Sperrle
Allied air raids
Major Allied air raids
German night-fighter bases
German shipyards
U-boat bases
Principal British naval bases
Principal German naval bases
Principal areas of British industry
Principal areas of German industry
0 25 50 75 100 125 Miles
0 40 80 120 160 200 Km

Burma – First Steps Back

As early as **April 1942**, while the Japanese were driving all before them in Burma, the British CinC in India, Wavell, had begun planning to take the country back from them. There was, however, little that could be done immediately. The formations that had fought in Burma needed time to recover their strength, and the other forces available in India were made up largely of raw recruits. Furthermore, the Indian Congress Party, encouraged by the recent disasters suffered by the British, chose this time to mount its 'Quit India' campaign of civil disobedience, and this tied up many troops on internal security duties. Nevertheless, planning continued. Wavell decided that an attack down the Arakan to Akyab offered the best prospects, especially since this would also secure the Bay of Bengal. Furthermore, in June, Churchill had demanded that Akyab be secured as a preliminary to the ambitious 'Anakim' plan for amphibious landings to recapture Rangoon and Moulmein.

Given the ease with which they had driven the British and their allies out of Burma, the Japanese began to consider an invasion of India, something that had not been part of their original plan. On **22 July 1942** Imperial GHQ in Tokyo ordered the study of Operation '21', a three-pronged thrust into India, from the extreme north of Burma, through Imphal, the capital of the Indian state of Manipur and along the coast of the Bay of Bengal to seize Chittagong.

One of the advantages of Operation '21' was that it would cut what was now the main means of supplying Chiang Kai-shek with Lend-Lease *matériel* – the air route from Burma to China over what was called 'the Hump', the pilots' name for the Himalayas. This route could only deliver a very small amount of supplies, mainly owing to the lack of aircraft, and the Chinese began to agitate for the Burma Road to be reopened once more, using a new route from Ledo in Assam. To carry this out Chinese troops would be used under Stilwell. Some, who had arrived in India after the evacuation of Burma, had begun to train at Ramgarh, north-west of Calcutta, under Stilwell's direction, and further troops began to be flown in from China for this purpose in October.

17 September 1942 Wavell ordered General Noel Irwin's Eastern Army to carry out the Arakan offensive.
The plan was for two brigades to carry out an amphibious assault on Akyab while 14th Indian Division created a diversion by advancing into Arakan. Lack of landing craft, caused mainly by requirements for 'Torch' and the Pacific, forced a postponement of the amphibious operation. In the meantime 14th Division carried out patrolling activity into the Arakan, while Irwin viewed it as essential to improve his supply line forward and begin to build an all-weather road to Cox's Bazaar.

25 October The Japanese ceased preparations for Operation '21'.
The Japanese divisional commanders considered the plan too ambitious, bearing in mind the terrain over which they would have to operate, especially in northern Burma.

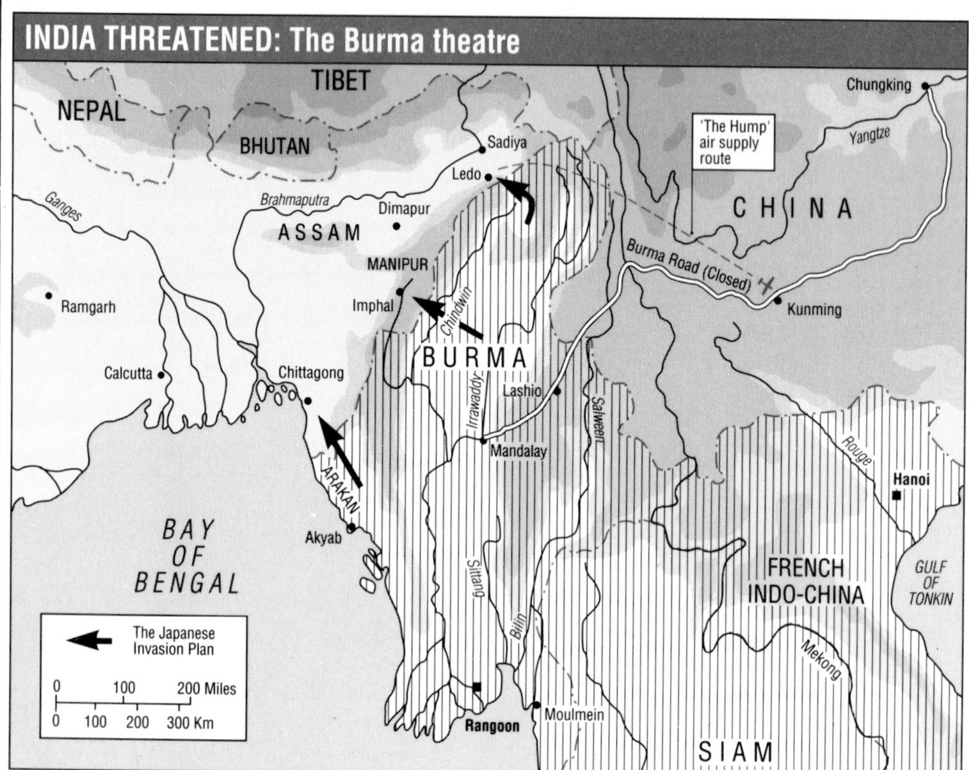

19 November Wavell issued revised instr[u]tions to Irwin.
Irwin was now to use 14th Division to advan[ce] down the Mayu Peninsula, then cross from Fo[ul] Point to Akyab. The Japanese had just two b[at]talions to defend the Mayu Peninsula. Heavy ra[in] now delayed completion of the road to Co[x's] Bazaar and caused repeated postponements to t[he] start of the offensive.

17 December 14th Division began to advance

22 December The Japanese withdrew from t[he] Buthidaung–Maungdaw Line.
They had established and fortified it since [2?] October. It was occupied by 14th Division ne[xt] day. The British then probed down to Foul Poi[nt]. Simultaneously another brigade had been advanci[ng] down the east bank of the River Mayu.

28 December The advance on the east bank [of] the River Mayu reached Rathedaung.
It was held by the Japanese, who immediate[ly] repulsed two attempts to take it.

4 January 1943 The Japanese redeployed on t[he] River Mayu.
They occupied Donbaik and reinforced Akyab.

7 January The British attacked Donbaik.
Four attacks were put in during the next fou[r] days, and all failed. The Japanese had constructe[d] bunkers, which proved impervious to artillery an[d] mortar fire. It was the first time that the British ha[d] met this form of defence.

9–10 January Further attempts to captur[e] Rathedaung failed.
A stalemate now existed, and there was a paus[e] while tanks were brought up to deal with th[e] bunkers.

1–3 February Further attacks on Donbaik an[d] Rathedaung supported by tanks failed.
The Japanese defenders were determined to han[g] on, in the knowledge that their 55th Division woul[d] not arrive until the end of the month.

7 March Japanese 55th Division began to attac[k] the brigade facing Rathedaung.
The Japanese also threatened its communication[s] back into India and forced it to withdraw.

18 March Further British attack on Donbai[k] failed.

24 March The Japanese crossed the River Mayu.
This forced the British on the Mayu Peninsula t[o] withdraw. By this time their morale was very low.

3 April British brigade cut off at Indin.

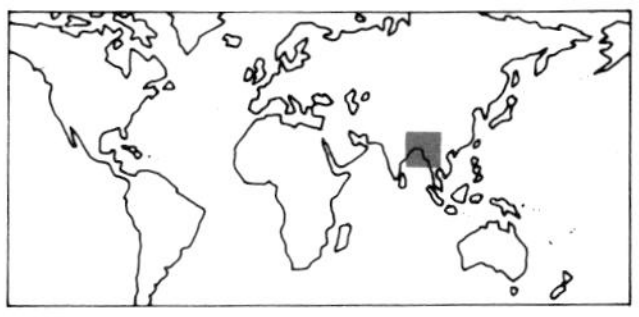

ARAKAN: The Allied advance

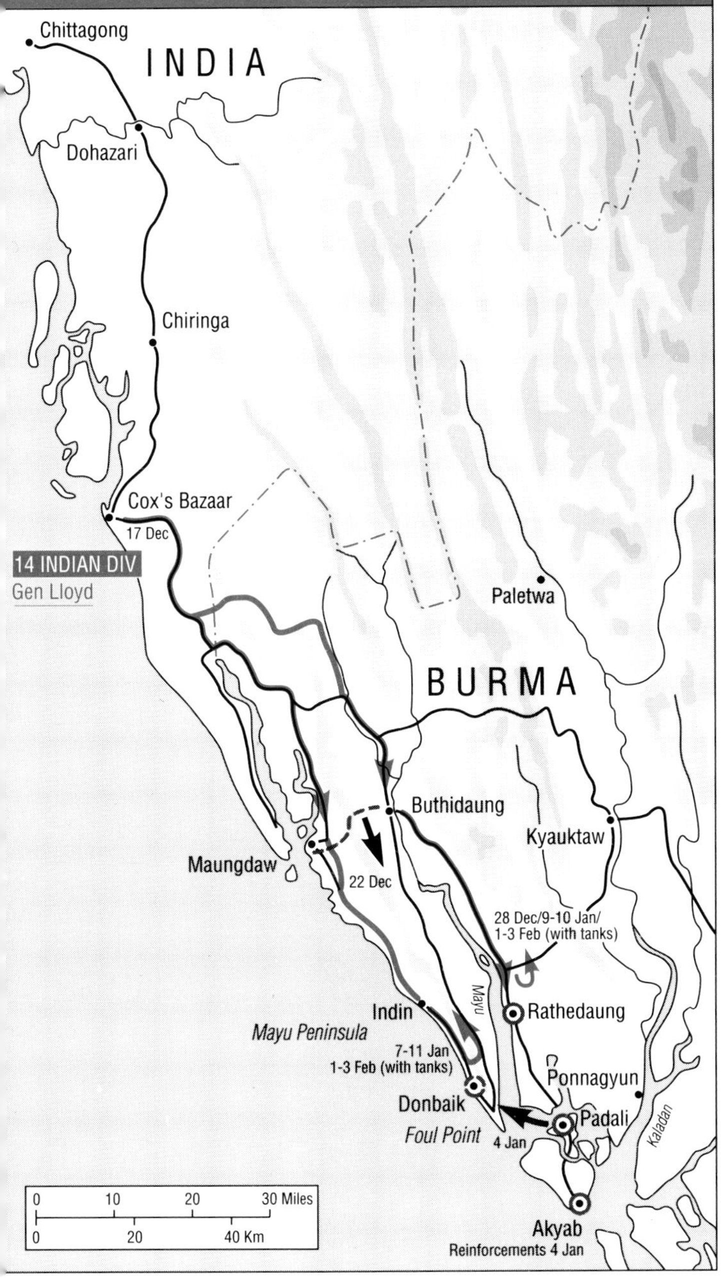

ARAKAN: The Japanese counter-attack

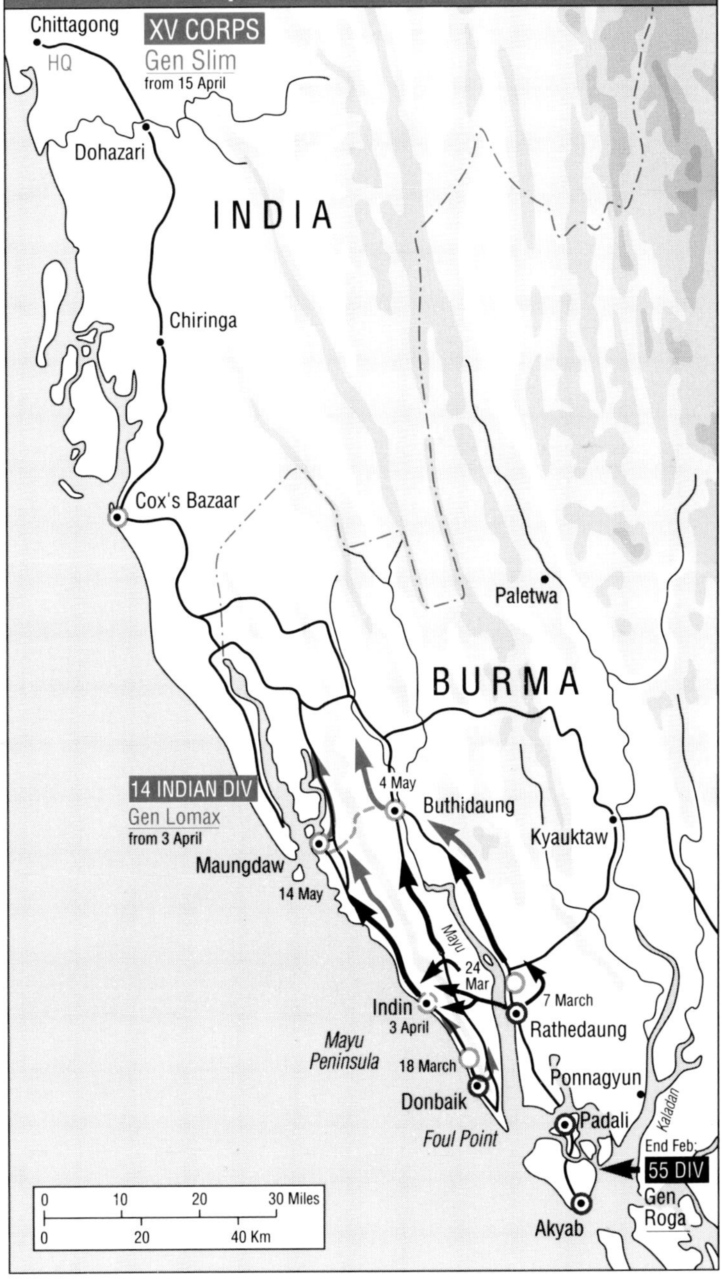

ts HQ was overrun and the commander and staff captured.

15 April General Bill Slim assumed command of all troops in the Arakan.

He attempted to trap the advancing Japanese, but by now his troops were too exhausted and riddled with malaria to be able to put this concept into action.

4 May The Japanese cut the Buthidaung–Maungdaw road.

Slim had set up a defensive 'box' here in order to tempt the Japanese on to it so that they could be destroyed, but the box could not hold. Orders were therefore given to abandon Buthidaung, but to hold on to Maungdaw. The RAF had been harassing the Japanese advance, but not enough to halt it.

14 May The Japanese captured Maungdaw.

After the Japanese had overrun the remainder of the Buthiadaung–Maungdaw Line it was impracticable for Slim to hold on to Maungdaw itself; he evacuated it, withdrawing to positions further north just before the monsoon broke.

The campaign in the Arakan had cost the British some 5,000 casualties, excluding sickness, as opposed to 1,775 Japanese. By the end of it, the British were virtually back on their start-line. It had been a dispiriting experience and had merely served to reinforce the belief that the Japanese soldier was superior in jungle fighting. It cost Irwin his command, although the blame rested more with Wavell for allowing it to proceed with such limited assets, and even more with Churchill for his grandiose belief that the Indian Army would be strong enough so soon after the disasters of early 1942 to begin the reconquest of Burma.

Yet the picture was not totally black. For a start, 14th Indian Division had gained valuable experience, which they could now pass on to others. Secondly, another British foray into Burma was taking place farther north, and this appeared to be achieving some significant successes.

The First Chindit Expedition · P142

The First Chindit Expedition

On **6 February 1942** Wavell, in his capacity as CinC South-West Pacific Command, had signalled the War Office in London requesting the services of a certain Major Orde Wingate, Royal Artillery. He wanted him to co-ordinate the efforts of the Chinese Fifth and Sixth Armies, who were then moving into Burma. Wavell had remembered Wingate from the time when he had commanded the 'Gideon Force of Patriots' in Abyssinia in 1941.

Wingate arrived in Burma at the end of the month, but by then events had moved on, and instead of co-ordinating Chinese operations he was placed in charge of a number of Special Service Detachments. These had been training in Burma for service with Mission 204, which was designed to provide British support and advice for Chiang Kai-shek. This included organizing guerrilla operations, which was the role of the Special Service Detachments. Wingate named his new command the Burma Army Long Range Penetration Group, but in the continuing Japanese onrush it had little opportunity to achieve anything.

Nevertheless, Wingate was convinced that the jungle was an ideal medium for the concept of long-range penetration behind the Japanese lines, and he persuaded Wavell to allow him to raise a force to train in this. Accordingly, Wingate formed 77 Indian Infantry Brigade. This consisted of a British infantry battalion, a Gurkha battalion and remnants of the Special Service Detachments. It was organized into eight columns, each of some 400 men. They used mule transport and air resupply. Wingate dubbed his men 'Chindits', having misheard a Burmese officer utter the word *Chinthe* (Burmese for 'lion'). In July 1942 Wingate took his brigade into the jungles of the Central Provinces of India for an extended period of intensive training, the emphasis being on living in the jungle.

Wavell had originally thought that the Chindits could be used as part of Stilwell's plan to build another Burma Road, but when it became clear that it would be many months before this could be put into effect he turned to the Arakan. Wingate could create a diversion for the amphibious operation against Akyab. But the cancellation of this again left the Chindits without a role.

By now it was the beginning of February1943, and Wingate, fearful that his concept might become stillborn, persuaded Wavell to allow him to put his ideas into practice independently of any other operations. Thus Operation 'Longcloth' was born. The justification would be to remove a possible threat to Fort Herz, the last British outpost in northern Burma. The Chindits would cut the Mandalay–Myitkyina railway, harass the Japanese south-west of Mandalay and, if possible, cut the Mandalay–Lashio railway.

Night of 13/14 February 1943 **The Chindits crossed the Chindwin unopposed.**
They were split into two groups: one column would deceive the Japanese as to Wingate's plan while the remainder cut the railway.

18 February **First brush with the Japanese.**
This involved the southern or diversionary group near Mainyaung and forced them into making a detour, which cost them time.

1 March **Main body reached Pinbon area.**
From here columns were sent forward to cut the Mandalay–Myitkyina railway.

ACROSS THE IRRAWADDY

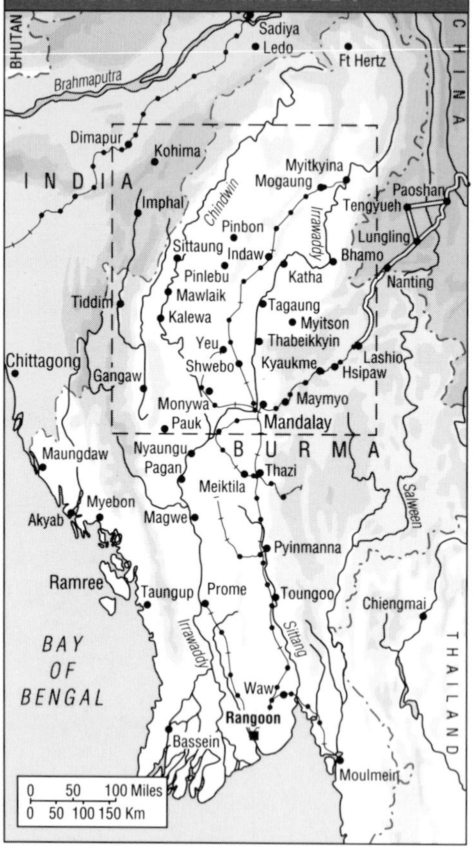

3 March **Southern group reached the Mandalay–Myitkyina railway near Kyaiktin and cut it.**
One of its two columns clashed with the Japanese and was dispersed.

4 March **One main-body column scattered by the Japanese in an action near Pinbon.**
The column commander ordered his men to make their way back to the Chindwin. By now the Japanese were well aware of the Chindit presence and began to deploy troops to hunt them down.

6 March **The main body demolished three railway bridges in the Bongyaung area.**

9 March **Wingate arrived at Tawshaw.**
This was fifteen miles west of Bongyaung. He planned to concentrate his force in the mountains north of Wuntho, but now heard that the southern group was on the other side of the Irrawaddy which would make this impracticable. He therefore decided to cross the Irrawaddy himself. This meant that once he came to withdraw he would have two rather than one major river to cross.

19 March **Wingate crossed the Irrawaddy.**
Two main-column bodies had already done so a week before. He now ordered the destruction of the Gokteik Gorge viaduct, which carried the Mandalay–Lashio road and was the ultimate objective that Wavell had laid down. This task was given to the two columns that had crossed the Irrawaddy the week before, Nos. 3 and 5. These were now near Myitson, and they reported that the area was alive with Japanese. Wingate therefore ordered No. 5 Column to act as his advance guard, leaving the Gokteik viaduct to No. 3, whose commander, Major Mike Calvert, knew it well from the previous spring.

Wingate himself was now in a triangle bounded by the Rivers Irrawaddy and Schweli. There were several roads here, and the jungle was sparse, hot and arid; hardly suitable for Chindit operations, especially with the Japanese noose closing all the time.

24 March **Wingate ordered to withdraw to India.**
This came from General Geoffrey Scoones, commanding IV Corps, which was responsible for northern Burma. Wingate had realized that he had to get away from the triangle he was in, and had intended to move into the Kachin hills and operate towards Lashio and Bhamo. Scoones had warned him that this would stretch air resupply to the limit and had proposed an attack on Schwebo. Wingate now learnt that the Japanese were seizing all boats on the Irrawaddy; hence withdrawal was now the only option.

27 March **The withdrawal began.**
No. 3 Column abandoned the Gokteik viaduct operation. But by now the Japanese had interposed troops on Wingate's withdrawal routes.

28 March **The main body attempted to cross the Irrawaddy at Inywa.**
Wingate believed that the Japanese would not guard this crossing since it was where he had originally crossed the river. As the first column, having collected some boats, began to cross, it met withering fire from the far bank. Wingate therefore decided to break his force up into small bodies.

14–29 April **Wingate and most of his surviving Chindits crossed the Chindwin.**
There had been several brushes with the Japanese on the way out of Burma.

Of the 3,000 Chindits who had originally set out on 'Longcloth', 2,182 got back to India, but the physical condition of some 600 of these was such that they could never again be employed in active soldiering. They had succeeded in putting the Mandalay–Myitkyina railway out of action for four weeks, had inflicted a number of casualties on the Japanese and had gained some useful topographical intelligence. Yet the Japanese grip on Burma was as strong as ever.

There was, however, a greater but less tangible achievement. The Chindits had demonstrated that the ordinary soldier, given the right type of training, could master his Japanese counterpart in jungle warfare. Taken against the depressing backcloth of the Arakan campaign, this was a timely message and did much to boost the morale of the Anglo-Indian forces.

OPERATION 'LONGCLOTH': February-April 1943

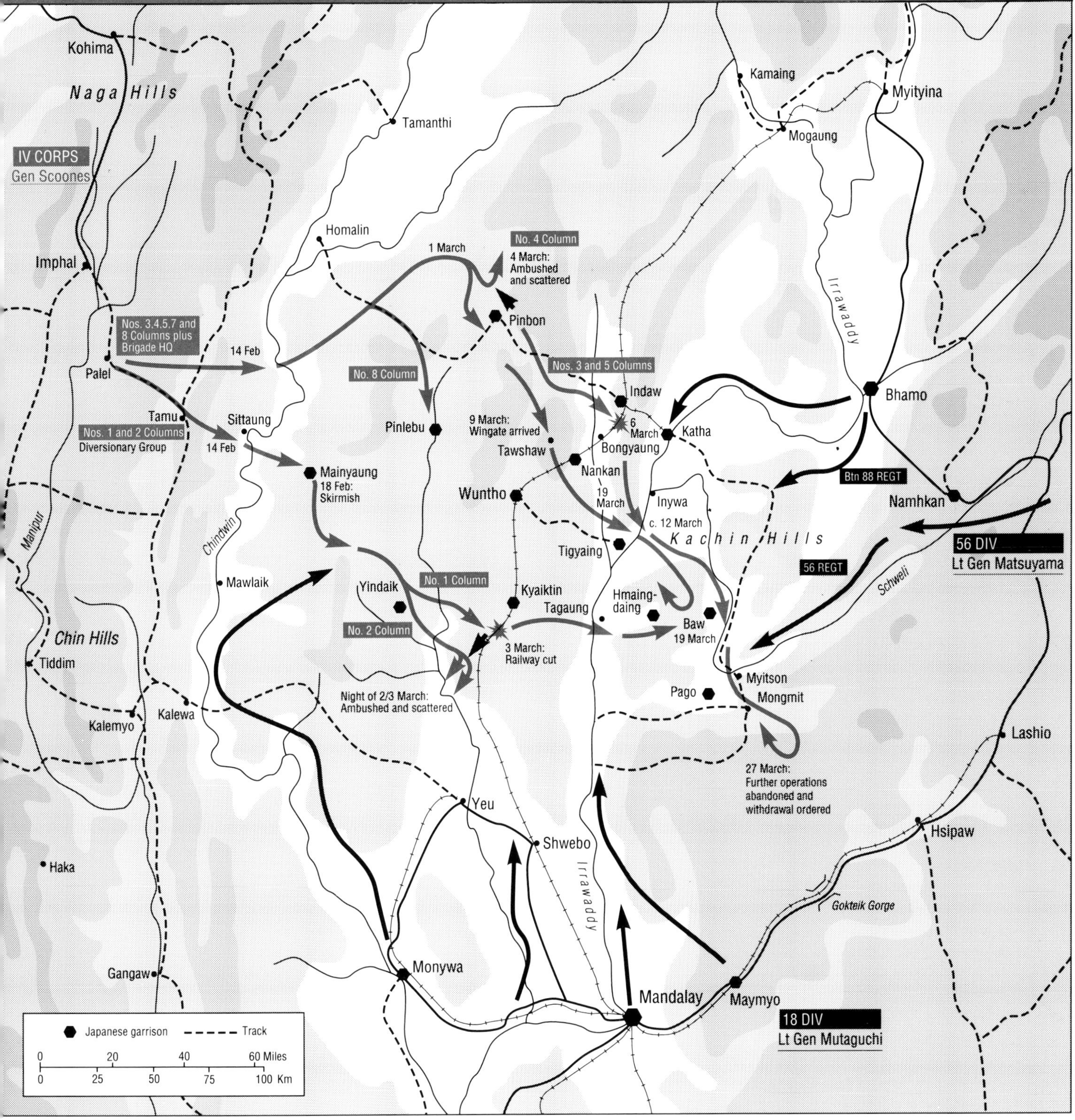

The Aleutians and New Georgia

The Allied successes on Papua–New Guinea and Guadalcanal had shown that the Japanese tide of fortune was now on the ebb. It was recognized, though, that there would be much fighting to be done before Japan was finally brought to her knees. It was also clear that the Pacific must be the decisive theatre, since the supply problems of supporting major offensives in China were too great, and there was little likelihood of a major thrust into Burma for some time to come.

There was, however, a growing debate over Pacific strategy. MacArthur argued strongly for an approach from the South Pacific through New Guinea to the Philippines. This would deny Japan the raw materials on which she was so dependent. The US naval chiefs, on the other hand, favoured the Central Pacific, where they could use their growing aircraft carrier fleet to better effect than in the narrow seas of the south-west. In the meantime, US attention turned to the Aleutians, which had in part been under Japanese occupation since June 1942.

12 January 1943 US forces occupied Amchitka in the Aleutians.

There were no Japanese on this island. The Americans constructed a fighter airfield here. They had earlier, at the end of August 1942, landed on Adak.

18 February US Navy task force bombarded Attu in the Aleutians.

21 February US forces occupied Banika and Pavuvu in the Russell Islands.

These had already been evacuated by the Japanese. The Russells were to be turned into a sea and air

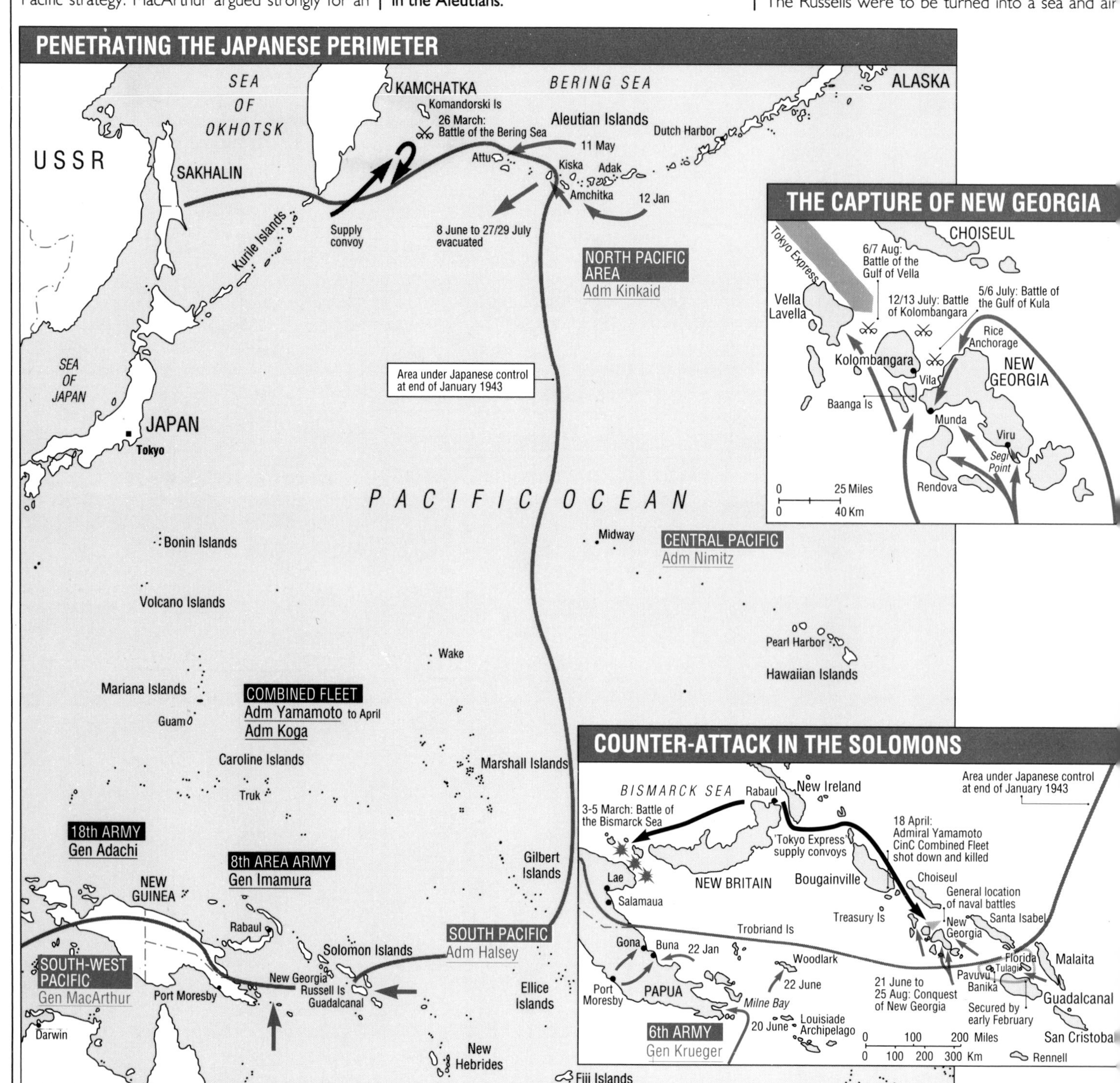

base in order to support operations designed to capture Rabaul, New Britain, the most important Japanese base in the south-west Pacific.

3–5 March Battle of the Bismarck Sea.
US aircraft and light naval craft intercepted a convoy bound for Lae and Salamaua in New Guinea. Four out of eight destroyers and all eight transports were sunk, denying New Guinea vital reinforcements and supplies. From now on the Japanese were forced to rely on resupply by submarine for these two garrisons.

6 March US naval task force bombarded Vila and Munda in the Solomons.
They also sank two Japanese destroyers. Aircraft also began a series of attacks on Munda.

12–15 March Pacific Military Conference held in Washington, DC.
MacArthur submitted his plan for the capture of Rabaul. It called for a co-ordinated effort between his South-West Pacific Command and Halsey's South Pacific Command. MacArthur would invade New Britain from bases in New Guinea, and Halsey would clear the Solomons. The US Navy was doubtful whether there was sufficient shipping to support both.

26 March Battle of the Bering Sea.
The US Navy had been blockading the Japanese-held Aleutians. A squadron of two cruisers and four destroyers was patrolling south of the Soviet Komandorski Islands and intercepted a Japanese task force of one heavy and two light cruisers and eight destroyers escorting Aleutians-bound supply ships. In the subsequent action the cruiser *Salt Lake City* and the Japanese heavy cruiser *Nachi* were badly damaged, and the Japanese had to turn for home. From now on the Japanese were forced to use submarines to resupply their garrisons in the Aleutian Islands.

28 March The US Chiefs of Staff agreed to MacArthur's plan for seizing Rabaul.
They placed Halsey under his command for the operations. Meanwhile the American and Australian forces were continuing their efforts to reduce the Japanese strongholds of Lae and Salamaua.

31 March Nimitz issued orders for the recapture of Attu (Aleutians).
Admiral Kinkaid of Santa Cruz fame was given overall command, and the US 7th Infantry Division was allotted to him.

7 April Heavy Japanese air attacks against US bases in the Solomons.
Yamamoto realized that Rabaul was under threat and decided to forestall the Americans by attacking their operational bases in the south-west Pacific.

18 April Death of Yamamoto.
He was shot down over Bougainville while on a tour of inspection. 'Magic' was responsible for the successful intercept of his aircraft. His death was a grievous blow to the Japanese. He was succeeded as CinC Combined Fleet by Mineichi Koga.

11 May US forces landed on Attu.
Mist and mud hindered initial progress.

30 May Attu finally secured.
The weather and Japanese resistance had cost the Americans heavy casualties. This left just the Japanese garrison on Kiska to be dealt with.

3 June Halsey issued instructions for landings on New Georgia in the Solomons.
The troops taking part would be 43rd US Infantry Division and two Marine Raider battalions. The Japanese were continuing their air attacks on Allied bases, but they were losing many aircraft in the process.

8 June The Japanese began to evacuate Kiska Island.

20 June HQ US Sixth Army (General Walter Krueger) set up at Milne Bay, New Guinea.
This would control the land operations in the South-West Pacific.

21 June Operations against New Georgia began.
US Marines landed unopposed at Segi Point on the southern tip of the island.

22 June US troops occupied Woodlark in the Trobriand Islands.
This lay some 200 miles east of New Guinea.

30 June US landings on Rendova Island off New Georgia.
Further landings also took place in the Trobriand Islands, and the construction of airfields was begun.

1 July Viru on the south-west coast of New Georgia secured.

3 July Beachhead established near Munda, New Georgia.

4 July Further landings at Rice Anchorage on the northern coast of New Georgia.
The centre of Japanese resistance, at Munda, began to show itself.

Night of 5/6 July US warships intercepted the 'Tokyo Express' in the Gulf of Kula.
It had been landing reinforcements on the island of Kolombangara, just north of New Georgia. One US cruiser and a destroyer, and two Japanese destroyers were sunk.

6 July US aircraft began a series of attacks on Bougainville.
Meanwhile, Japanese resistance on New Georgia was stiffening.

Night of 12/13 July Battle of Kolombangara.
This was a further clash with the 'Tokyo Express' bringing in reinforcements to Kolombangara. One US destroyer was sunk and three cruisers and two more destroyers damaged, while the Japanese lost the cruiser *Jintsu*. On New Georgia little progress was being made, and the US forces were experiencing resupply problems.

Night of 17/18 July Japanese counter-attacks on New Georgia.
Some penetrations of US positions were made.

Night of 27/28 July The last Japanese left Kiska in the Aleutians.
The Americans were unaware of this and continued preparations for their landings, which had already included prolonged air and naval bombardments of the island.

5 August The Americans finally secured Munda airfield on New Georgia.
The fight for it had been long and bitter. The Japanese had by now concentrated their resistance on Kolombangara.

Night of 6/7 August Battle of the Gulf of Vella.
This was another interception of the 'Tokyo Express' landing troops on Kolombangara; for almost the first time the US Navy came off best, sinking three destroyers at no loss to itself.

13 August Munda airfield, New Georgia now fully operational once more.

15 August US and Canadian troops landed on Kiska.
The landing force consisted of more than 34,000 men, but the Japanese had long left the island. On this same day Americans landed on Vella Lavella in the Solomons; Japanese resistance was slight.

16 August US landings on Baanga Island.
Japanese guns here had been shelling Munda.

25 August New Georgia finally cleared of Japanese.

By now the Japanese had decided to concentrate their efforts on Bougainville and to evacuate the islands to the south. Allied progress in New Guinea continued to be slow, and Salamaua and Lae still remained in Japanese hands. These had to be captured if MacArthur was to enter New Britain from the west.

Pacific Drives · P160

Kursk

The Germans had recovered remarkably well from their reverses on the Eastern Front at the beginning of 1943, and only the spring thaw had prevented them regaining further recently lost territory. Nevertheless, the growing Soviet strength and increasing threat from the Western Allies made it inevitable that the Germans would have to adopt a more defensive posture in the east. There were two schools of thought as to how this should be done.

Those generals not directly involved with the fighting in the east wanted the forces there to withdraw and regroup out of direct contact with the Russians. At the same time, troops should be transferred to strengthen the defences in the west. Hitler, however, believed that the best form of defence would be a limited offensive before the British and Americans attacked in the west. This would restrict the growth in Soviet military strength and hence degrade offensive capability; but, more important, if it were successful it would restore the morale of both the German people and their allies.

The original idea was for a double-envelopment of the Soviet forces east of Kharkov, but this quickly gave way to the larger and more tempting Kursk salient. General Walther Model's Ninth German Army would attack southwards from the Orel area while Hermann Hoth's Fourth Panzer Army and Group Kempf attacked from the south. The intention had been to mount the operation, which was code-named 'Citadel', in mid-April, but there were deployment delays.

The Russians, too, were well aware of the singular position of the Kursk salient. On the one hand it was very vulnerable to attack; on the other hand it could be an ideal launching pad for further attacks. They knew, both from the Swiss-based 'Lucy' Ring and intelligence officers whom they had infiltrated through the German lines, what the Germans were planning, and were tempted to launch a pre-emptive attack.

12 April 1943 **Stalin decided to remain on the defensive in the Kursk Salient.**

Three concentric rings of field defences were got under way, and armour was to be concentrated behind them as a counter-stroke force. The main strategic aim was, first, to repulse the German attack at Kursk, then to liberate the eastern Ukraine and eastern Belorussia and destroy the German Army Group Centre.

13 April **Berlin Radio announced the discovery of a mass grave at Katyn near Smolensk.**

It contained the bodies of some 4,500 Polish officers. The Germans laid the blame on the Russians, who immediately accused the Germans. The British Government, fearful of upsetting its ally, sided with the Russian version. This, however, upset the Polish government-in-exile, who supported the German invitation for an International Red Cross investigation at the scene of the crime and asked the Russians for details of the Polish officers who had been in their hands. To this no reply was ever received. The International Red Cross asked for Russian representation at the investigation. The Russian answer was to break off relations with the London Poles and to form their own puppet Polish government in Moscow. In the meantime the Germans arranged for medical experts from eastern Europe to carry out autopsies on the victims, and these supported the German claim.

Although the Russians have not as yet wholly admitted it, even today, it seems clear that they were the culprits and had carried out the murders in spring 1940 as part of their efforts to ensure that an independent Poland would never be allowed again.

19 April **The Warsaw Jews rose against the Germans.**

Hunger and increasing persecution in the Warsaw Ghetto brought this about as an act of desperation. They fought with determination, but their organized resistance ended on **16 May**. By then the Warsaw Ghetto had been razed and some 56,000 Jews had either been killed or sent to extermination camps. No support was given by the London Poles until after the uprising had been crushed because they did not wish to commit their 'Home Army' in Warsaw prematurely.

4 May **Hitler postponed 'Citadel' still further.**

He had now decided that he wanted to deploy as many of his new heavy tanks, the Panzerkampfwagen V (Panther), VI (Tiger) and Ferdinand tank destroyer, as possible. This was against the advice of most of his senior commanders, who were aware of the growing Soviet defences and did not want further delays.

4 July **Opening of the Battle of Kursk.**

The German forces consisted of some 900,000 men and 2,500 tanks and assault guns. The Russians had three fronts involved: Central (Rokossovsky) and Voronezh (Vatutin) in the salient, and the Steppe Front (Ivan Konev) in reserve – in all, some 1,300,000 men and 3,000 tanks.

The Germans launched a massive air and artillery bombardment in mid-afternoon. That night engineers began to clear lanes through the Soviet minefields.

5 July **Model and Hoth attacked at dawn.**

The tanks led the attack. In the north, Model penetrated up to six miles on a 20-mile front and had breached the first Russian defence line. Hoth, in the south, drove back the Sixth Guards Army. That night there was heavy rain, which caused much mud.

6 July **The German attacks continued.**

Hoth had now created three penetrations, but none deeper than seven miles. Against ever-stiffening resistance Model's attacks slowed and then came to a standstill.

9–12 July **Hoth continued to push slowly forwards.**

12 July **Massive Soviet counter-attack against Hoth.**

This was carried out by Fifth and Sixth Guards Tank Armies from the Steppe Front, who fell on the German armour in the area of Prokhorovka, north of Belgorod. Some 1,300 tanks and assault guns were engaged in what was the largest tank battle of the war. The fighting continued for the next few days, bringing Fourth Panzer Army to a halt.

On the same day, the West and Bryansk Fronts launched an attack in the Orel area to the rear of Model's army.

13 July **Hitler called off 'Citadel'.**

Not because of lack of progress, but because the Allied landings in Sicily on **10 July** necessitated his sending reinforcements to the west.

15 July **Central Front began to attack northwards against Model.**

Next day, Model and Hoth began to withdraw, and Vatutin's Voronezh Front also went over to the attack.

17 July **South-West Front began to attack towards Kharkov.**

26 July **The Germans began to withdraw from Orel.**

5 August **Belgorod and Orel liberated.**

In the north the Germans were falling back to the hastily prepared Hagen Line, which ran just east of Bryansk.

11–17 August **German counter-attacks against the Voronezh Front south of Bogodukhov.**

This temporarily removed the threat to the German forces south of Kharkov and forced the Russians on to the defensive in this area.

13 August **The Russians reached the outskirts of Kharkov.**

The Germans were eventually forced to withdraw from here to avoid being encircled, and the city was liberated on **23 August**.

'Citadel' was Hitler's last attempt at a major offensive on the Eastern Front. From now on, his armies would be on the defensive. The Kursk salient was no more, and the Soviets were determined to capitalize quickly on the success of their counter-blows.

P132 · Stalin Keeps up the Pressure

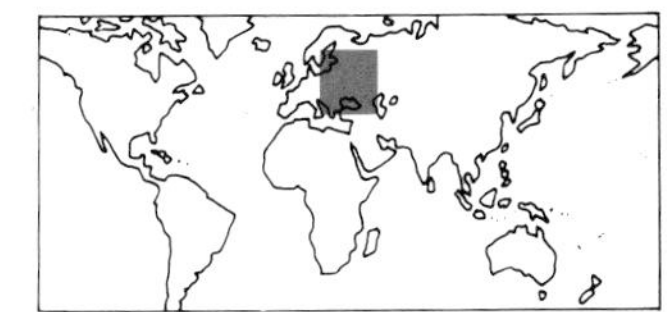

OPERATION 'CITADEL'

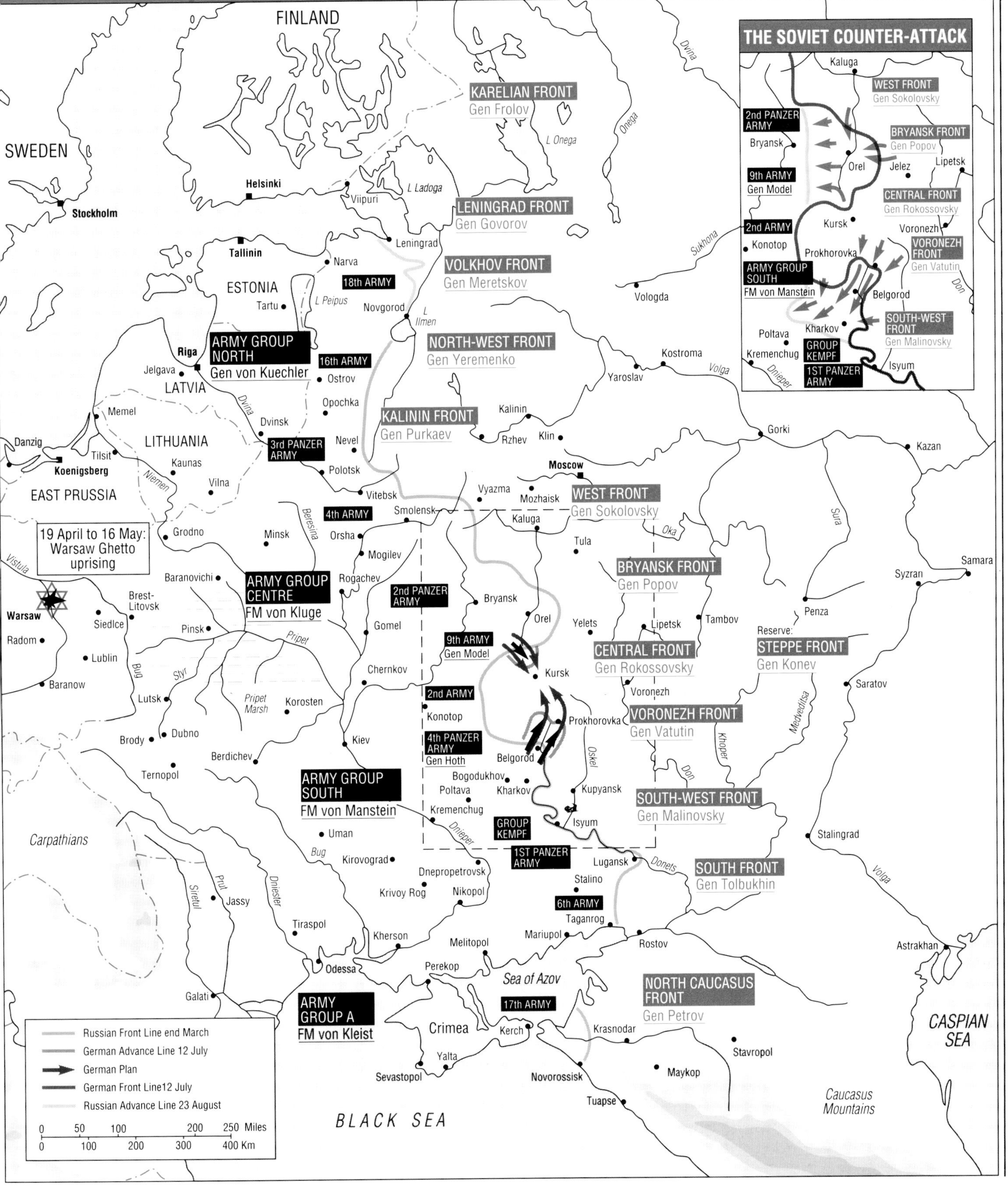

FINLAND
SWEDEN
Stockholm
Helsinki
Viipuri
L Ladoga
L Onega
Dvina
Onega
KARELIAN FRONT
Gen Frolov
LENINGRAD FRONT
Gen Govorov
Leningrad
Tallinin
Narva
ESTONIA
Tartu
L Peipus
18th ARMY
Novgorod
L Ilmen
VOLKHOV FRONT
Gen Meretskov
Sukhona
Vologda
NORTH-WEST FRONT
Gen Yeremenko
Kostroma
Yaroslav
Volga
Riga
ARMY GROUP NORTH
Gen von Kuechler
16th ARMY
Ostrov
Jelgava
LATVIA
Opochka
Dvina
Dvinsk
Memel
LITHUANIA
Danzig
Tilsit
Koenigsberg
3rd PANZER ARMY
Nevel
KALININ FRONT
Gen Purkaev
Kalinin
Rzhev
Klin
Gorki
Kazan
Moscow
Kaunas
Niemen
Vilna
Polotsk
Vitebsk
EAST PRUSSIA
Vyazma
Mozhaisk
WEST FRONT
Gen Sokolovsky
Smolensk
Kaluga
Oka
4th ARMY
Beresina
19 April to 16 May: Warsaw Ghetto uprising
Grodno
Minsk
Orsha
Tula
Mogilev
Vistula
BRYANSK FRONT
Gen Popov
Samara
Syzran
Baranovichi
ARMY GROUP CENTRE
FM von Kluge
Rogachev
2nd PANZER ARMY
Bryansk
Orel
Sura
Brest-Litovsk
Warsaw
Siedlce
Pinsk
Gomel
Yelets
Lipetsk
Tambov
Penza
Radom
Pripet
9th ARMY
Gen Model
Reserve:
STEPPE FRONT
Gen Konev
Lublin
Bug
Styr
CENTRAL FRONT
Gen Rokossovsky
Kursk
Chernkov
Saratov
Baranow
Voronezh
Lutsk
Pripet Marsh
Korosten
2nd ARMY
Konotop
Prokhorovka
VORONEZH FRONT
Gen Vatutin
Medveditsa
Dubno
Brody
Kiev
4th PANZER ARMY
Gen Hoth
Oskel
Khoper
Belgorod
Berdichev
Ternopol
ARMY GROUP SOUTH
FM von Manstein
Bogodukhov
Poltava
Kharkov
Kupyansk
Don
SOUTH-WEST FRONT
Gen Malinovsky
Kremenchug
Isyum
Carpathians
Uman
GROUP KEMPF
Dnieper
Stalingrad
Bug
Kirovograd
1ST PANZER ARMY
Lugansk
Donets
SOUTH FRONT
Gen Tolbukhin
Volga
Dnepropetrovsk
Stalino
Siretul
Prut
Dniester
Jassy
Krivoy Rog
Nikopol
6th ARMY
Taganrog
Tiraspol
Kherson
Melitopol
Mariupol
Rostov
Astrakhan
Odessa
Perekop
Sea of Azov
NORTH CAUCASUS FRONT
Gen Petrov
Galati
ARMY GROUP A
FM von Kleist
17th ARMY
Crimea
Kerch
Krasnodar
Stavropol
CASPIAN SEA
Yalta
Sevastopol
Novorossisk
Maykop
Tuapse
Caucasus Mountains
BLACK SEA

THE SOVIET COUNTER-ATTACK

Kaluga
WEST FRONT
Gen Sokolovsky
2nd PANZER ARMY
Bryansk
BRYANSK FRONT
Gen Popov
Orel
Jelez
Lipetsk
9th ARMY
Gen Model
CENTRAL FRONT
Gen Rokossovsky
2nd ARMY
Kursk
Voronezh
Konotop
Prokhorovka
VORONEZH FRONT
Gen Vatutin
ARMY GROUP SOUTH
FM von Manstein
Belgorod
Don
Kharkov
SOUTH-WEST FRONT
Gen Malinovsky
Poltava
GROUP KEMPF
Kremenchug
Dnieper
1ST PANZER ARMY
Isyum

Russian Front Line end March
German Advance Line 12 July
German Plan
German Front Line12 July
Russian Advance Line 23 August

0 50 100 200 250 Miles
0 100 200 300 400 Km

The Russian Autumn Offensive · P154

Sicily

The invasion of Sicily (Operation 'Husky') had been agreed by the Allies at Casablanca as the next step after the clearance of North Africa. Detailed planning for it had begun in March 1943, long before the campaign in Tunisia had come to an end. A major limiting factor was that the landing craft for it would not arrive until May, and hence it would not be possible to mount 'Husky' before July. From the start it was accepted that it must be a joint Anglo-US effort, and selected to undertake it were the newly created US Seventh Army under Patton and Montgomery's British Eighth Army. While Eisenhower, as Supreme Allied Commander, exerted overall control, the operations themselves would be directed by Alexander's 15th (formerly 18th) Army Group.

The original plan called for three landings: in the south-east, south-west and north-west near Palermo. Montgomery objected strongly to this, as he considered it over-ambitious and based on the dangerous assumption that the island would be weakly held. Eventually, it was agreed that the two armies would land side by side on the south-east and south coasts.

9 May 1943 Deception plan 'Mincemeat' put into effect.
The body of a British officer was washed ashore on the Spanish coast. On it were plans indicating that the Allies intended to invade Sardinia and make a feint on Sicily. Hitler now ordered priority in the Mediterranean to be given to Sardinia and northern Italy.

11 June British troops landed on the island of Pantelleria.
This lay between Tunisia and Sicily and had been subjected to a massive air bombardment since **8 May**. The garrison of 11,000 Italian troops laid down its arms without firing a shot.

That night there was an intensive air and sea bombardment of the island of Lampedusa, to the south-east, which surrendered unconditionally next day. This gave the Allies airfields from which to support the initial stages of 'Husky'.

10 July The Allies landed in Sicily.
The island was held by General Alfredo Guzzoni's Italian Sixth Army with two crack German divisions under command, in all some 230,000 men. Guzzoni's plan was to allow low-grade coastal divisions to take the initial shock of the landings while the remainder of his troops, including the Germans, were held back for a counter-attack role.

The Allied landings were preceded during the night by US and British airborne landings. Unfortunately the paratroops were badly scattered. Never-

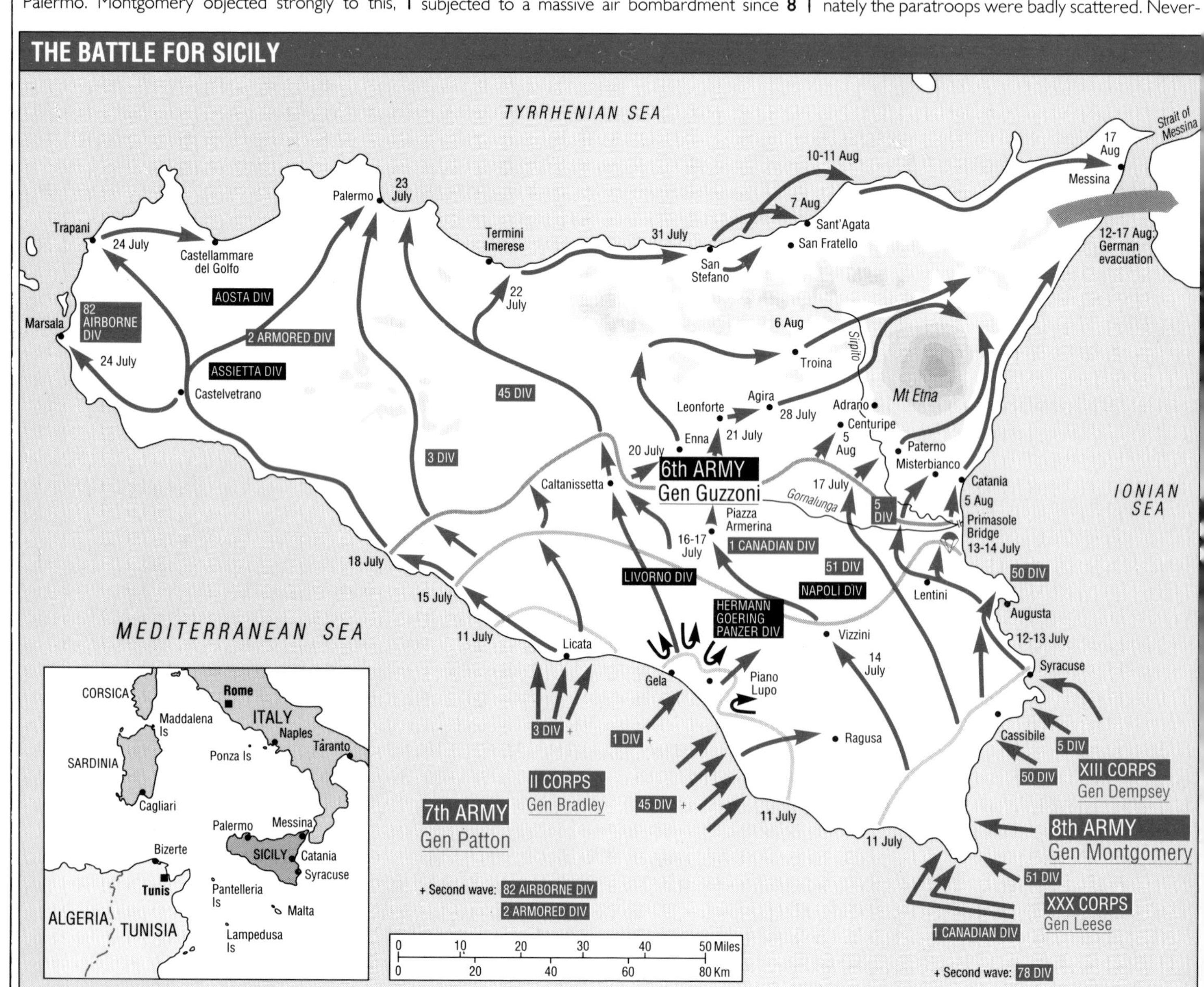

theless the amphibious landings went well, catching the Italians by surprise, and beachheads were quickly established. Later that day the US 1st and 45th Infantry Divisions successfully withstood Axis counter-attacks in the Gela and Piano Lupo areas.

Once ashore, with the beachheads established, the idea was for Montgomery to drive up the east coast and seize Messina, thus cutting off the Axis troops from the Italian mainland, while Patton guarded his landward left flank.

12 July Having repulsed further counter-attacks in the Gela area, Patton began to advance inland.
Montgomery, meanwhile, having captured Syracuse on the 10th, was approaching Augusta on the coast. He had also directed XXX Corps to advance to the communications centre of Enna, in the centre of the island.

Night of 13/14 July British combined airborne/commando operation to seize the Primasole bridge.
This carried the coastal road over the Rivers Sirpito and Gornalunga south of Catania. The German 1st Parachute Division was deployed in the area and recaptured the bridge.

16 July Patton began to drive to Palermo.
That night the Germans were forced to withdraw from the Primasole bridge after British troops had got across the rivers further upstream. German resistance south of Catania was still strong, however.

19 July Hitler and Mussolini met at Filtre, northern Italy.
Hitler tried to restore Mussolini's flagging morale.

The Allies meanwhile bombed Rome. In Sicily, Montgomery was trying to hook inland around the German positions south of Catania. In the west, Patton's advance was increasing in momentum, the main weight of Axis resistance now being in the east.

20 July US II Corps occupied Enna.

23 July US troops entered Palermo.
Next day they occupied the ports of Trapani and Marsala, and Patton now began to turn east towards Messina, determined to arrive there before Montgomery.

25 July Mussolini arrested by the Fascist Grand Council.
This reflected a growing loss of confidence in him brought about by the worsening Italian military situation. King Victor Emmanuel now asked Marshal Pietro Badoglio to form a new government. Two days later Mussolini was taken to the island of Ponza. Hitler, fearful that Italy would now make a separate peace with the Allies, ordered German divisions to be sent to northern Italy, and plans were made for the rescue of Mussolini and his restoration to power.

BUILD-UP OF GERMAN FORCES IN ITALY, August 1943

NORTHERN ITALY

ARMY GROUP B Field Marshal Erwin Rommel

HQ I SS Panzer Corps	from Germany
HQ II SS Panzer Corps	from Eastern Front
1 SS Panzer Grenadier Division	from Eastern Front
24 Panzer Division	from France
65 Infantry Division	from Netherlands
HQ LI Mountain Corps	from South Germany
44 Infantry Division	from Austria
71 Infantry Division	from Slovenia
HQ LXXXVII Corps	from France
76 Infantry Division	from France
94 Infantry Division	from France
305 Infantry Division	from France

SOUTHERN ITALY

COMMANDER-IN-CHIEF SOUTH Field Marshal Albert Kesselring

All formations, apart from those that had fought in Sicily, were in place prior to August, having deployed to Italy earlier in the summer.

Tenth Army Gen von Vietinghoff

XIV Panzer Corps	
16 Panzer Division	
Hermann Goering Para Panzer Division	
XXVI Corps	
1 Para Division	from Sicily
26 Panzer Division	
29 Panzer Grenadier Division	from Sicily
XI Flak Corps	
2 Para Division	
3 Panzer Grenadier Divison	
90 Panzer Grenadier Division	Sardinia
SS Reichsfuehrer Brigade	Corsica

28 July The Canadians captured Agira.

31 July The US 45th Division captured San Stefano on the north coast.
Next day US forces were held up in front of Troina, west of Mount Etna.

3 August The Axis forces began to cross the Strait of Messina to Italy.
The Italians went first, leaving the Germans to form the rearguard. Centuripe fell to the British.

5 August Catania finally fell to the British.

6 August The Americans finally captured Troina.
Progress along the northern coast road was slow, largely owing to mines and demolitions.

7 August US amphibious landing near Sant'Agata on the north coast.
They had been held up at San Fratello.

8 August Mussolini imprisoned on Maddalena Island, north-east of Sardinia.

10 August Second US amphibious hook on the north coast.

12 August The Germans began to evacuate Sicily.

14 August The Italian Government declared Rome an open city.
This was as a result of a second Allied air raid on the 13th, designed to encourage the Italians to sue for peace. They were taking their first tentative steps, directed by the Chief of the General Staff, General Ambrosio, and had sent General Guiseppe Castellano to Madrid to meet the British ambassador there. The Germans meanwhile were very suspicious, and a conference had been convened between Rommel and the Italian Army Chief of Staff, General Roatta.

17 August The Americans entered Messina.
But all the Axis troops had managed to escape.

25 August After talks in Lisbon, General Castellano was told that the Allies would accept only unconditional surrender.
The Allies were represented by Eisenhower's Chief of Staff, Bedell Smith, and Chief of Intelligence Kenneth Strong.

Thus ended the Sicilian campaign, which had proved to be much harder and longer than originally expected by the Allies. Italy was now wavering, and it seemed that just one more push would knock her out of the war. Orders for her invasion had already been given out.

The Italian Landings · P152

8 EUROPE RE-ENTERED, August 1943 to January 1944

29 APRIL 1943 TO 23 AUGUST 1943

Conference Summer

During the summer of 1943 the Allies held no less than three major conferences. While the Casablanca Conference of January 1943 had resolved the immediate priorities so far as the Americans and British were concerned with regard to the defeat of Italy and Germany, much remained to be agreed on both 'Round Up' (the cross-Channel invasion of the Continent of Europe) and global strategy as a whole.

29 April 1943 Churchill proposed to Roosevelt that another Allied conference be held in Washington, DC.
Churchill's main concern was that the Americans might place greater priority on the Pacific at the expense of Europe, especially since he accepted that, as a result of the abortive Arakan campaign and the shortage of shipping, 'Anakim' (the amphibious assault on Burma) was no longer possible in 1943. This was immediately agreed by the Americans, and on **5 May** Churchill set sail in the liner *Queen Mary* (accompanied by 5,000 German POWs) for the USA. He arrived on **11 May.**

12–25 May Anglo-US 'Trident' Conference in Washington, DC.
The main decisions reached were:
a. 'Round Up' was not possible in 1943, but would be mounted by 1 May 1944.
b. 'Pointblank' (the combined bombing offensive) was confirmed as a very necessary preliminary to 'Round Up'.
c. The invasion of Sicily ('Husky') was to be exploited in such a way as to knock Italy out of the war and tie down the maximum number of German divisions. The Americans believed that this could be best achieved by invading Sardinia, while the British wanted to invade Italy itself. This was left unresolved.
d. Agreement jointly to develop the atomic bomb under the cover name of 'Tube Alloys'.

Burma was left unresolved. The Americans wanted more effort to support Chiang Kai-shek, especially by using the 'Anakim' forces to open up the Burma Road once more; but the British, advised by Wavell, considered that the cost, especially in terms of malarial casualties, would be too great.

19 May Churchill addressed US Congress.
'By singleness of purpose, by steadfastness of conduct, by tenacity and endurance such as we have so far displayed – by these, and only by these, can we discharge our duty to the future of the world and to the destiny of man.'

26 May Churchill left Washington for Algiers via Newfoundland and Gibraltar.
He wanted personally to dissuade Eisenhower from the Sardinia option. He managed to get Roosevelt's agreement for Marshall, who had originally supported 'Husky', to come to North Africa as well.

29 May to 3 June Algiers Conference.
Eisenhower indicated that he would be prepared to invade Italy after Sicily, and it was agreed to leave the decision in his hands.

De Gaulle and Giraud also agreed to set up a joint Committee for National Liberation of France. A 'Trident' decision that the USAAF in North Africa should attack the Ploesti oil wells in Roumania ('Soapsuds') was also confirmed.

11 June Stalin expressed his displeasure to Churchill and Roosevelt over the postponement of 'Round Up'.

4 July General Sikorski, leader of the Free Poles, was killed in an air crash off Gibraltar.
Claims that this was the work of Stalin or Churchill have never been substantiated.

16 July Churchill proposed another Allied conference.
The success of 'Husky' convinced him that Italy must be invaded quickly and Rome captured. He was, however, still fearful that the Americans would lose interest in the Mediterranean in favour of the Pacific. At the time, Eisenhower favoured a landing in the 'toe' of Italy. Churchill was also keen to clear Greece and the Balkans of the Axis presence.

4 August Meeting of the Pacific War Council in London.
This had met intermittently since its first meeting on **10 February 1942.** Present were Dutch and Chinese representatives, and Churchill assured them that it was the British intention to reopen the Burma Road; but he warned that it would take a long time.

5 August Churchill left Britain on board *Queen Mary* bound for Halifax, Canada.

13–23 August The Quebec Conference ('Quadrant').
The first five days were occupied with discussions among the Combined Chiefs of Staff, and not until the 19th did Churchill and Roosevelt join in. The major decisions reached were:

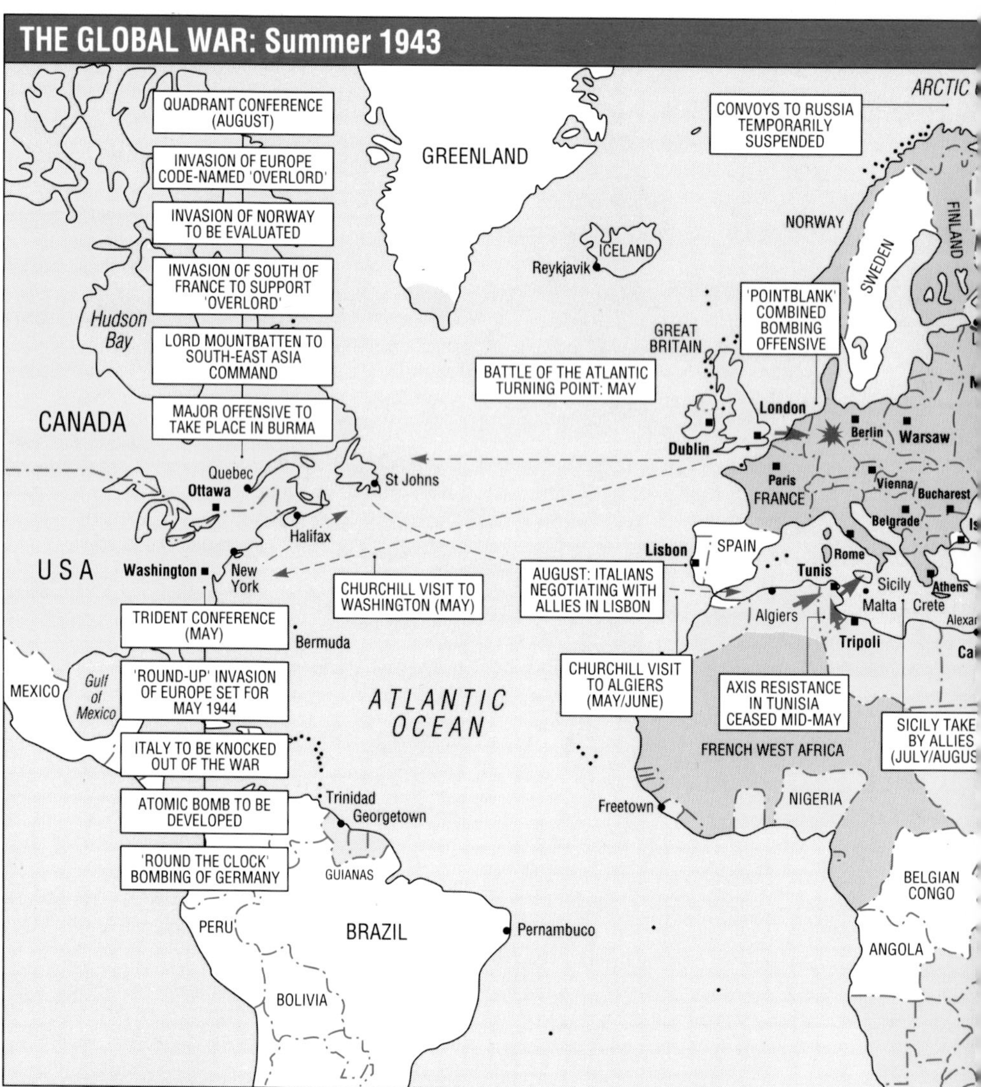

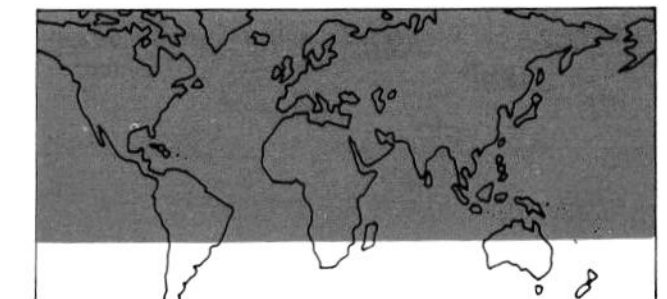

a. The 'Trident' decision to mount the cross-Channel invasion, now code-named 'Overlord', in May 1944 was reaffirmed, and, at the suggestion of the Americans, General George C. Marshall was appointed to command it.

b. The invasion of Norway ('Jupiter') was to be considered as an alternative should it prove impossible to mount 'Overlord'. A major operation against Norway had long been one of Churchill's pet projects.

c. While 'Overlord' retained top priority, 'unremitting pressure' would be maintained on the German forces in northern Italy, and this was to be regarded as contributing to the success of 'Overlord'.

d. A study would be carried out on a landing in southern France ('Anvil') as a means of assisting 'Overlord'.

e. A new Allied command was to be set up, South-East Asia Command (SEAC), to control operations in Burma and elsewhere in SE Asia. Appointed as supreme commander was the youthful Admiral Lord Louis Mountbatten, who was at the time the British Director of Combined Operations.

f. Preparations would continue for a major campaign in northern Burma and for an amphibious operation elsewhere within SEAC. Churchill also agreed that Wingate, who attended part of 'Quadrant', should launch another, but larger long-range penetration operation in Burma with his Chindits.

g. Formal recognition was given to de Gaulle's and Giraud's Committee for National Liberation of France.

In the midst of 'Quadrant', on **22 August**, Stalin sent a telegram to Churchill and Roosevelt complaining that they were making agreements while he was just a 'passive observer'. He particularly resented the negotiations being conducted by the British and Americans with Marshal Badoglio's government in Italy about the possibility of an armistice, even though they had kept him informed of progress. Stalin demanded the setting up of a 'political commission' to consider the case of states wishing to leave the Axis side and proposed Sicily as its base. It was believed that both Finland and Hungary wanted to leave the war. Churchill and Roosevelt agreed that the Russians should be represented in any armistice negotiations in western Europe and that a tripartite conference should be held.

The British also approved the US plans in the Pacific. Because of the shortage of amphibious shipping and the strength of the garrison, it had now been decided to neutralize and bypass Rabaul rather than capture it. A new drive was to be instituted in the Central Pacific, with the first objective being the Gilbert Islands. MacArthur, in the meantime, would continue operations in the Bismarck Archipelago and advance along the New Guinea coast to the Vogelkorp Peninsula.

'Quadrant' had not only confirmed the decisions made at 'Trident' but had also done much to reduce Anglo-US friction over the Mediterranean debate, although US doubts as to British willingness to subordinate everything to 'Overlord' remained. In the meantime, Eisenhower had been preparing for the invasion of the Italian mainland, and the Italian armistice negotiations had reached a critical stage.

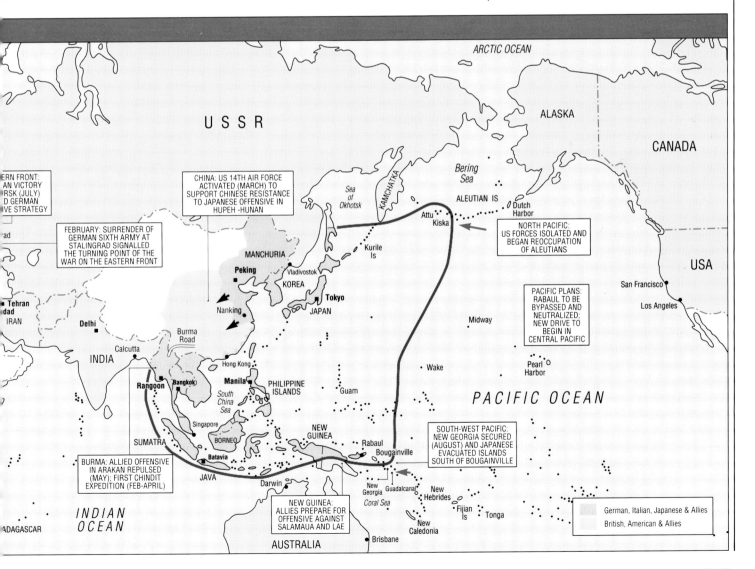

The Italian Landings

The planning for the invasion of Italy was beset by a number of problems. For a start, there was the question of where to land. Churchill had been agitating for entering Italy as far north as possible, ideally close to Rome or, failing that, Naples. Eisenhower had considered these alternatives, but had been advised by his air and naval staffs that they were operationally risky because they would stretch naval and air support to the limit. He therefore selected the Gulf of Salerno as being the northernmost point from which Sicily-based fighter support could be guaranteed. At the same time it was also tempting to chose the shortest sea route from Sicily and land in the extreme south. A landing here had little risk, but strategically would make little impact on the Axis forces. This, however, was what Montgomery advocated, proposing a landing across the Strait of Messina and another landing on the west coast of the toe of Italy in the Gulf of Gioia.

Eisenhower therefore decided that two landings would be made – at Salerno ('Avalanche') and across the Strait of Messina ('Baytown'). Overall command would remain with Alexander's Fifteenth Army Group; Montgomery's British Eighth Army would take on 'Baytown', and to carry out 'Avalanche' a new army was created, the US Fifth. The reason for this was that Patton was out of favour, having slapped a shell-shocked soldier during the Sicilian campaign, while Omar Bradley, another contender, was already earmarked for an army command in 'Overlord'. Eisenhower therefore selected General Mark Clark to command the US Fifth Army, and his command would be made up of a mixture of US and British divisions. Mark Clark was to mount Operation 'Avalanche' from North Africa.

Much depended on the outcome of the Italian armistice negotiations and what the German reaction to this would be. The meetings in Lisbon between Badoglio's envoy and Bedell Smith and Clark, representing the Allies, had ended on **20 August 1943**, and General Castellano had returned to Rome bearing the Allied demand for unconditional surrender and a ten-day ultimatum to accept this.

The Germans were well aware of the Italian efforts to arrange an armistice, and also knew that Italy would be the next Allied target. Immediately on the overthrow of Mussolini on **25 July** they had rushed troops into northern Italy under Rommel's supervision. Rommel himself believed that it would be better to construct a redoubt in northern Italy to keep the Allies at bay; Kesselring, who was still CinC South, believed that it would be possible to fight a slow, delaying campaign up the length of Italy. Hitler agreed to both. Consequently, by the end of August, Kesselring had the newly formed Tenth Army (General Heinrich von Vietinghoff) of ten divisions in southern Italy, while Rommel retained a further eight in the north.

31 August 1943 The Allies summoned Badoglio's envoy, General Castellano, to Sicily.
The Allied ultimatum had expired and the Italian Government had not yet reached a decision. Field Marshal Keitel, Hitler's Chief of Staff, issued orders for the disarming of the Italian forces should an armistice be agreed.

1 September The Italian Government signified acceptance of the armistice to the Allies.
Castellano would go to Sicily to sign it. Meanwhile Allied air bombardment of the Italian coast in preparation for the invasion began.

3 September 'Baytown' mounted and the armistice signed.
Eisenhower's plan was to use this as a feint in order to draw the German forces away from Salerno. As it happened, the German forces in Calabria had withdrawn inland two days before, leaving a network of demolition behind them. Consequently the British XIII Corps landing encountered the minimum of resistance.

Castellano signed the armistice on behalf of the Italians and Bedell Smith for the Allies in Eisenhower's presence at Cassibile, near Syracuse, Sicily. The armistice would come into effect on **8 September**, the day the Salerno landings were due to take place. Until then the armistice would remain a secret so as not to alert the Germans.

Eisenhower now removed the US 82nd Airborne Division from Mark Clark's command for an airborne drop on Rome in order to encourage the Italian Army to rise against the Germans ('Giant II'). Two liaison officers were parachuted into Rome to inform Badoglio of Eisenhower's intention. However, Badoglio was horrified, and the operation was cancelled. Instead, Montgomery was given the task

THE ALLIED RETURN TO MAINLAND EUROPE

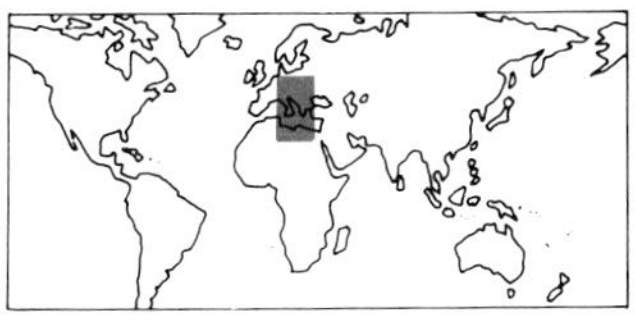

of mounting an operation on Taranto ('Slapstick') in order to secure the Italian Fleet.

5 September The 'Avalanche' force set sail from North Africa.

Montgomery's forces were making slow progress through Calabria because of the German demolitions.

8 September Eisenhower broadcast the Italian surrender from Radio Algiers.

This was a grave mistake, since the Salerno landing force was still at sea; it merely alerted the Germans, who, with the code phrase 'bring in the harvest', proceeded to disarm the Italian forces. Only one general resisted, and he was promptly shot by the Germans. They did not immediately tackle the Italian Navy.

9 September The Salerno landings.

Kesselring had already deduced that the landing would take place at Salerno. The Allied troops, two US and two British divisions, together with Commandos and Rangers, had expected an easy landing, but were instead greeted by Luftwaffe attacks on the ships and fire from elements of 16th Panzer Division. Nevertheless, a beachhead was established.

A subsidiary British landing at Taranto ('Slapstick') was also speedily mounted on the same day in order to ensure that the Italian warships here did not fall into German hands. No resistance was met and the Italian naval squadron set sail for Malta, as did those at Genoa and La Spezia. The Genoa and La Spezia squadrons were subjected to Luftwaffe air attack in the afternoon, and the flagship, the battleship *Roma* was sunk by rocket bombs. Next day the Italian Fleet formally surrendered to the Allies at Malta. The Italian royal family and most of the government went to Pescara and then to Brindisi. The Germans took direct control of Croatia, Greece and the Yugoslav coast, which had been under Italian control.

Iran now declared war on Germany – a symbolic gesture.

THE ALLIED CONQUEST OF SOUTHERN ITALY

10 September German troops occupied Rome.

Von Vietinghoff began to concentrate the Tenth Army at Salerno.

10 September The British began to land in the Dodecanese Islands.

Churchill believed that by taking advantage of the Italian armistice and occupying these islands he could threaten the German position in the Balkans and finally persuade Turkey to enter the war. While the British were foiled on the main island of Rhodes because the Italian governor eventually decided to surrender to the Germans, special forces units successfully occupied the islands of Castelorizzo, Cos, Leros and Simi. Because of US insistence that Italy was the main priority, little more than a brigade could be spared to garrison the islands and air and naval support were also limited. This force was in place by the end of September.

11 September The Germans evacuated Sardinia.

They moved their garrison to Corsica, where the Italian troops occupying the island were disarmed.

12 September The Germans rescued Mussolini.

From the moment of Mussolini's arrest, Hitler had been determined to liberate him. His plan was to set up a new Fascist government in northern Italy. Mussolini had been transferred to Gran Sasso in the Abruzzi mountains and was rescued in a daring glider *coup de main* operation. A day later he was reunited with his wife and Hitler in Bavaria, and on **25 September** he declared a new Italian Socialist Republic in northern Italy. It was, however, never to be more than a puppet government.

14 September Fierce German counter-attack on the Salerno beachhead.

It struck the centre of the Allied line and at one point threatened to drive the Allies back into the sea. After two days, however, largely thanks to air and naval bombardment support, the attack was beaten back.

16 September US Fifth and British Eighth Armies linked up.

This was near Vallo di Lucania. Kesselring now ordered his troops to begin slowly withdrawing northwards.

Thus the Allies had achieved a major aim in knocking Italy out of the war, and their forces were secure on the Italian mainland. It was now a question of what success they could gain against Kesselring's troops.

Objective Rome · P162

The Russian Autumn Offensive

The recapture of Kharkov on **23 August 1943** was by no means the end of the Russian counter-offensive triggered by the German failure at Kursk. Rather it marked the first stage of a rolling offensive that would not end until the Soviet flag was hoisted above the Reichstag in Berlin nearly two years later.

Stalin was determined not to allow the German armies time to recover and stabilize the situation, and planned to drive quickly for the Dnieper, thus recovering the Donbas and eastern Ukraine. In the process he intended to destroy Army Group South. To this end he had assembled no less than 2.5 million men organized into five fronts: Central, Voronezh, Steppe, South-West and South. His orders had been given out on **12 August.** Once the Voronezh Front had completed the destruction of the German forces in the Kharkov area it was, in concert with the Steppe Front, to advance to the Dnieper and secure bridgeheads across it. Rokossovsky's Central Front would attack west and then south-west towards Kiev and the upper Dnieper. The South and South-West Fronts would meanwhile secure the lower Dnieper. Another operation was to be launched by the North Caucasus Front against the German Seventeenth Army, which was still clinging on to the Taman Peninsula.

While priority was given to operations in the south, Stalin had also instituted a subsidiary offensive against Army Group Centre designed both to destabilize and to prevent von Kluge releasing reinforcements to von Manstein in the south. Since

THROUGH THE EAST WALL

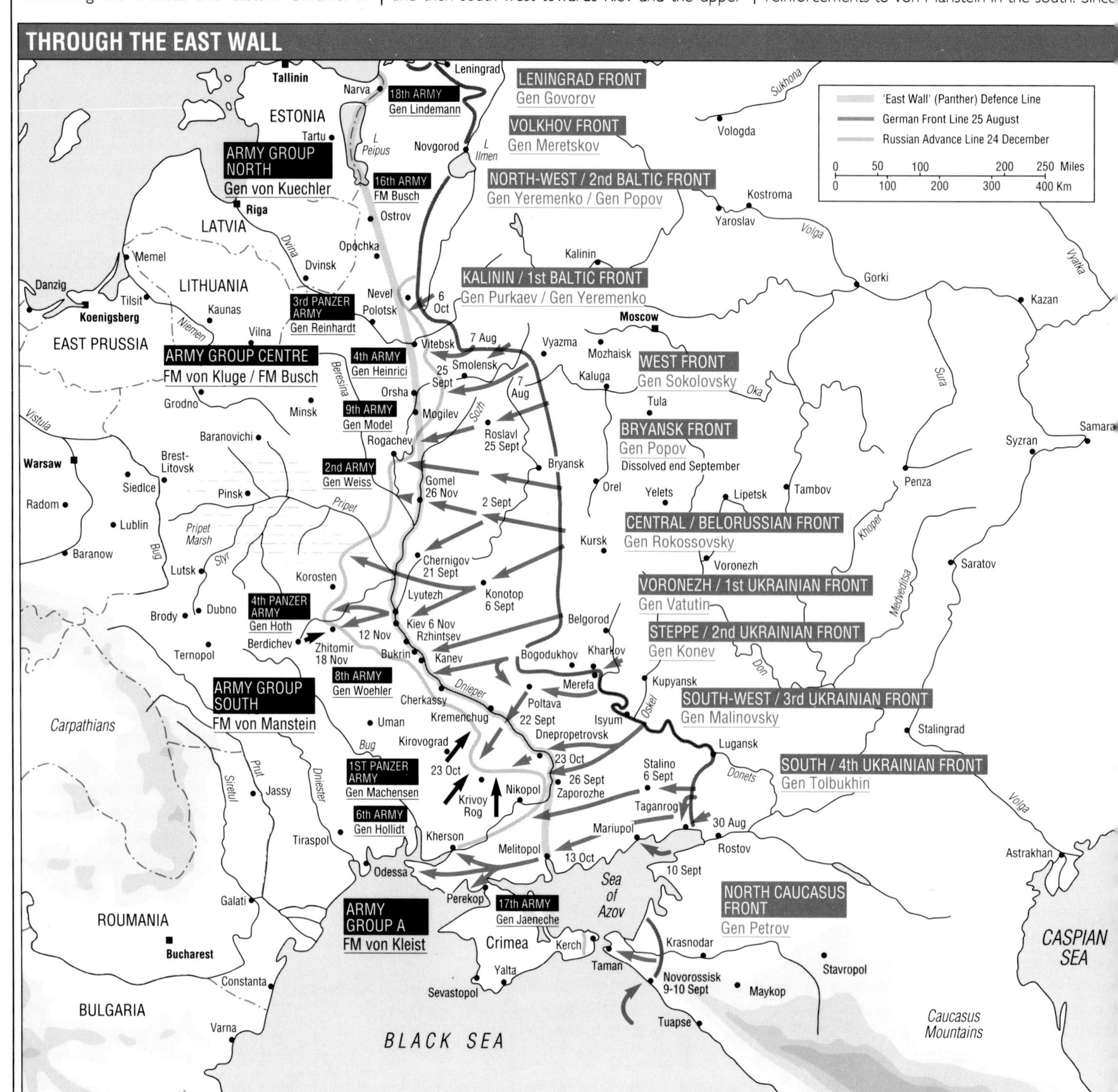

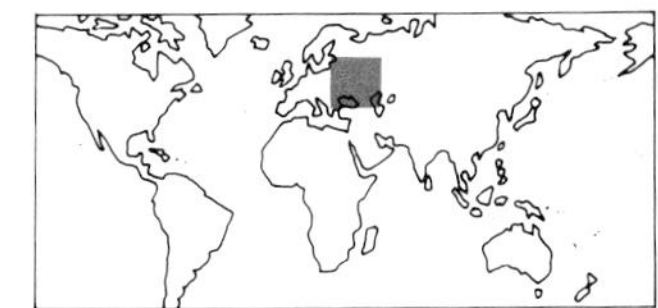

ne line here had been largely static for some time, ne Germans had erected extensive defences and ne first task was to break into these, which the alinin, West and Bryansk Fronts began to do on **7 ugust**.

For all these offensives Stalin was relying on artisans to disrupt the German lines of communi-ation.

Although on **12 August** Hitler had ordered the reparation of a new defensive line, the East Wall, om the Narva through Lake Peipus and Belorussia nd then down the River Sozh to Gomel and the Dnieper to just north of Zaporozhe and then to Melitopol on the Sea of Azov, he would not ountenance any withdrawal to it.

6 August 1943 Central Front began to attack he southern flank of Army Group Centre.
arther south the Soviet attacks in the Donets area ontinued.

7 August Hitler visited HQ, Army Group South.
Von Manstein told him that he could either speedily einforce Army Group South or agree a withdrawal o behind the Dneiper. Preoccupied with the Allied hreat in the Mediterranean, Hitler did not reach decision. Matters for von Manstein were made even worse two days later when von Kluge flew to Hitler's HQ at Rastenburg and dissuaded him from ransferring troops from Army Group Centre to von Manstein.

0 August Tolbukhin's South Front liberated Taganrog.
t had previously been encircled. The South Front uccess created a grave threat to von Manstein nd made the position of the German Seventeenth Army in the Taman Peninsula still more critical.

2 September The Central Front reached the Bryansk–Konotop railway.
This marked the virtual completion of the break-in operation, which had been fiercely resisted by the Germans.

4 September Merefa, south of Kharkov, cap-tured.
This marked a significant weakening of German esistance in the Ukraine. Two days later the impor-tant railway junction of Konotop was captured. Stalino also fell to the Russians.

8 September Hitler had a further meeeting with von Manstein.
Von Kleist, commanding Army Group A and res-ponsible for the Taman Peninsula and Crimea, was also present. Von Manstein pleaded to be allowed to fall back to the lower Dnieper, but Hitler was still not prepared voluntarily to surrender the Donets Basin. He had, however, on the 4th agreed that von Kleist could evacuate the Taman Peninsula.

Night of 9/10 September The Transcaucasus Front attacked the Taman Peninsula.
This began with a combined amphibious/land assault on the port of Novorossisk, which fell on the 16th and accelerated the German Seventeenth Army's withdrawal.

10 September Mariupol on the Sea of Azov captured by amphibious assault.

14 September The Central and Voronezh Fronts began their drive on Kiev.
By now von Manstein was falling back towards the Dnieper, destroying as much industrial plant as possible as he did so.

16 September The Germans evacuated Bryansk.

21 September The Central Front liberated Chernigov.
This brought Rokossovsky's troops up to the Dnieper.

22 September Vatutin's Voronezh Front seized crossings over the Dnieper.
This was in the area Rzhintsev–Kanev. On the 26th, Malinovsky's South-West Front seized further crossings south of Dnepropetrovsk. (On **9 September** the Stavka had issued an order, prompted by Stalin, stating that those who forced crossings over the Dnieper would be awarded the Hero of the Soviet Union, the highest Russian decoration.)

By the end of September, von Manstein was behind the East Wall; but because of casualties and poor siting of the defences he was very stretched to hold it.

25 September Smolensk and Roslavl liberated.
After this the Bryansk Front was dissolved, part of its forces being transferred to the Central Front and the remainder forming the new Baltic Front under Popov.

6 October New Soviet offensive launched to open up the way to the Baltic states.
This was mounted by Yeremenko's Kalinin Front and Popov's new Baltic Front. It was designed to envelop Vitebsk and force a wedge between Army Groups North and Centre.

9 October The last elements of the German Seventeenth Army crossed the Kerch Straits into the Crimea.

13 October The Soviets reached Melitopol on the Sea of Azov.
There was ten days' fierce fighting before the town was finally liberated.

16–19 October Vatutin bloodily repulsed in attempts to enlarge the Bukrin bridgehead on the Dnieper.

16 October Malinovosky and Konev launched an attack on the Dnieper bend.
Their aim was to trap the German First Panzer Army and the reformed Sixth Army.

20 October Soviet fronts retitled.
The Voronezh, Steppe, South-West and South Fronts became respectively the 1st, 2nd, 3rd and 4th Ukrainian Fronts. The Central Front was renamed the Belorussian Front. The Kalinin and Baltic Fronts became the 1st and 2nd Baltic Fronts.

23 October Malinovsky's 3rd Ukrainian Front captured Dnepropetrovsk.
At the same time XL Panzer Corps counter-attacked Konev's 2nd Ukrainain Front twenty miles in to the Krivoy Rog area and forced it to withdraw to the River Ingulets.

27 October Von Kluge relinquished command of Army Group Centre.
He was invalided as a result of a motor accident, but had become increasingly disillusioned over the predicament of the German armies in Russia. He was replaced by Field Marshal Ernst Busch.

3 November Major Soviet attack launched out of the Lyutezh bridgehead over the Dnieper.
This was planned after the failure at Bukrin and proved to be more successful.

6 November Kiev liberated.

12 November Zhitomir liberated.
This quickly enabled the Belorussian and 1st Ukrainian Fronts to create a bridgehead some 100 miles deep and 150 miles wide over the Dnieper, and destroyed the concept of the East Wall.

18 November The Germans retook Zhitomir.
This was as a result of a counter-attack launched by XLVIII Panzer Corps against the Kiev bridgehead. Further gains were made, but on **26 November** the rains came and the German thrust quickly ground to a halt.

26 November The Belorussian Front liberated Gomel.

24 December Popov cut the railway running westwards out of Vitebsk.
The Germans, however, still held Vitebsk.

The Soviet offensives of autumn 1943 had involved the whole of the Eastern Front apart from the far north. Although significant successes had resulted and much territory had been liberated, the German armies were still intact.

The Relief of Leningrad · P164

10 OCTOBER 1942 TO 6 OCTOBER 1943

Stilwell and China

The USA in particular had long recognized the vital role China had to play in the war against Japan. In **July 1942**, Washington had created the China-Burma-India (CBI) Command under General Joseph Stilwell, who had been Chiang Kai-shek's chief of staff since March. The US CBI Command was to provide logistic support to China and to control all US combat forces committed in direct or indirect support of the Chinese. At the same time the 'Flying Tigers', Colonel Claire Chennault's band of US 'mercenary' pilots, were incorporated into the Command as the China Air Task Force, an element of the newly created Tenth Air Force.

Stilwell's prime concern was to create a modern Chinese army that could effectively take on the Japanese. This placed Chiang Kai-shek in a difficult position. He was very reliant on the support of the warlords, who held many of the commands in the Nationalist Army, and they feared that the reforms proposed by Stilwell would rob them of their traditional power. Chiang Kai-shek had, however, agreed that the two Chinese divisions that had accompanied Stilwell out of Burma and into Assam in the spring of 1942 could be retained by him in India.

Stilwell now struck another problem. The British were unhappy about Chinese troops being in India because of suspected Chinese sympathy with the independence movement in India and fears about Chinese designs on Burma. Only after General Marshall had persuaded the British Chiefs of Staff did the British in India drop their objection, and on **26 August** the Chinese Army in India (CAI) training centre at Ramgarh was opened. Stilwell persuaded Chiang Kai-shek to arrange for troops to be flown from China in sufficient numbers to create three divisions plus supporting troops.

Stilwell had originally hoped that Chiang Kai-shek might agree to an offensive from Yunnan into north-east Burma in the spring of 1943, but the Chinese leader had other ideas. He was influenced by Chennault into believing that air power alone could defeat the Japanese in China. At the end of June, however, US aircraft promised to the Tenth Air Force were diverted to the Middle East because of the grave situation confronting the British there. This angered Chiang Kai-shek and reinforced his view that China was the 'poor relation' among the Allies. He accordingly tabled the so-called Three Demands to the Allies – three US divisions to be

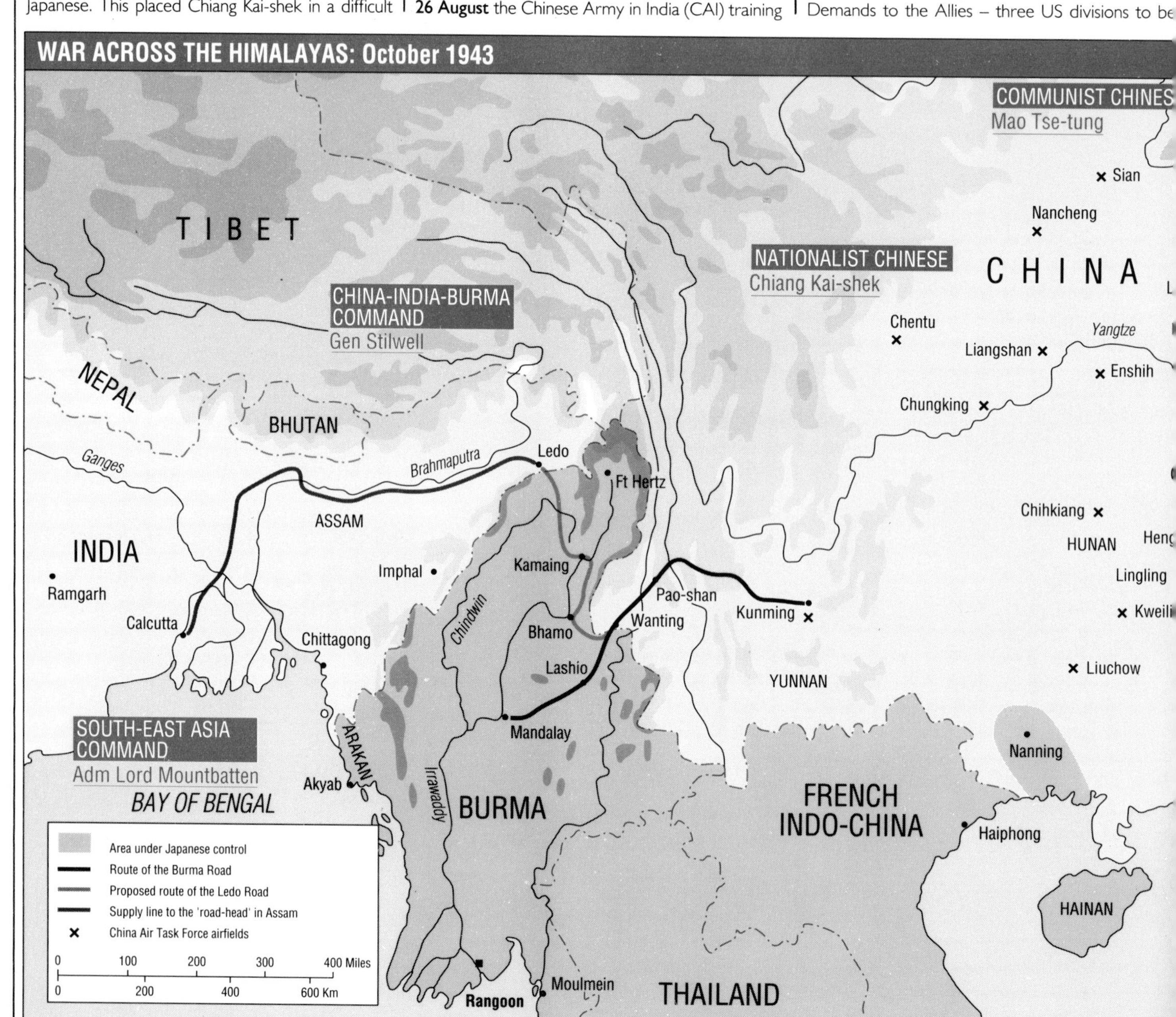

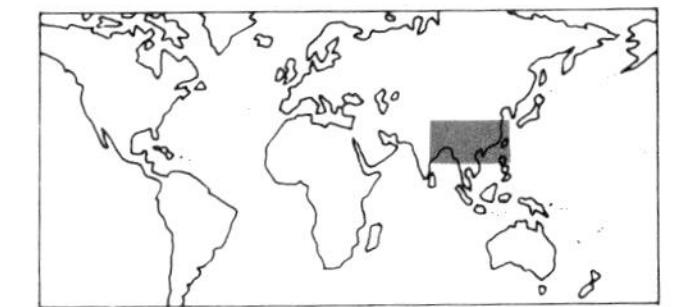

sent to India at the end of September 1942 in order to reopen land communications with China from India; 500 combat aircraft to operate in China from August 1942; and 5,000 tons of Lend-Lease supplies to be delivered monthly from August.

At the time it was impossible for the Allies to meet these demands and, despite Chiang Kai-shek's threat of closing down China as an Allied theatre of operations, they played for time. Stilwell himself, although he disagreed with Chennault's 'victory through air power' doctrine, was disappointed that Washington gave him a vague promise of just one US regiment instead of the three divisions demanded by the Chinese leader.

10 October 1942 Roosevelt declared that all unequal treaties with China would be repealed.

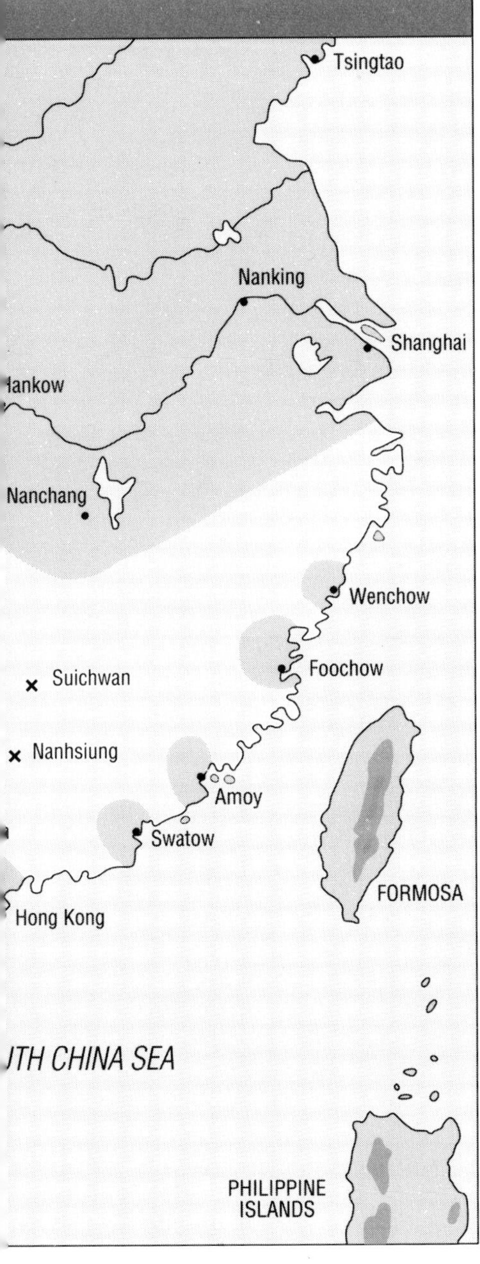

This included a surrender of all concessions gained during the past century. Roosevelt persuaded Britain to do the same, and treaties to this effect were signed on **11 January 1943.** This was to mollify Chiang Kai-shek over the Three Demands. At the same time Roosevelt undertook to provide 100 transport aircraft to deliver the 5,000 tons per month from the beginning of 1943, and 265 combat aircraft. He remained firm on not offering US divisions. As a result Chiang Kai-shek agreed to take part in an offensive into Burma and undertook to provide 15–20 divisions if British and US naval presence was sufficient to establish sea and air superiority in the Bay of Bengal and mount the amphibious operation against Rangoon.

28 December Chiang Kai-shek informed Roosevelt that the Allies had not achieved the required dominance of the Bay of Bengal.
Roosevelt asked him to wait until he had discussed this with Churchill at Casablanca. In the meantime, Stilwell, who had several US engineers rather than combat troops, began to build the Ledo Road, which was designed to run from Assam through north-east Burma to China. By this time the British had launched the Arakan offensive.

8 January 1943 Chiang Kai-shek confirmed that he would not take part in a Burma offensive.
This led General Marshall and Admiral King to argue strongly for 'Anakim' at Casablanca. They saw China as potentially a better way of defeating the Japanese than the long and expensive 'island hopping' campaigns in the Pacific: 'Anakim' should be mounted in November 1943. The British, however, with their offensive in the Arakan grinding to a halt, remained highly sceptical. Nevertheless, after a high-level Anglo-US military mission had visited China, agreement was reached in Calcutta on **9 February** that a combined offensive would be launched in Burma in November 1943. This did not please Chennault, who remained convinced that air power was the key to victory in China and Chiang Kai-shek supported him.

28 February The Ledo Road reached the Burma frontier.
This was 43 miles from Ledo; but now conditions conspired against the road builders and only another four miles had been completed by the time the rains arrived in May.

8 March The Japanese launched an offensive up the River Yangtze in China.
This was one of their periodic 'rice offensives' designed to seize food stocks, and the target was the Hupeh–Hunan 'rice-bowl'. Fearful that Chungking was the ultimate objective, the Chinese, against Stilwell's advice, diverted part of Y Force in Yunnan which was earmarked for the autumn offensive against Burma.

11 March US 14th Air Force activated in China.
This was created, on Roosevelt's orders, from Chennault's China Air Task Force, and Chennault was given command. Chiang Kai-shek now demanded that this mount an offensive against the Japanese drive up the Yangtze. Roosevelt, fearful of a Chinese collapse, agreed.

12–25 May Allied 'Trident' Conference in Washington.
The Allies agreed to shelve 'Anakim' in favour of increased air support for China.

Stilwell remained determined to develop Chinese land operations in Burma and eventually on **12 July** obtained Chiang Kai-shek's agreement to this in writing. He was still frustrated though by the diversion of Y Force. It was, however, agreed that a 3,000-man US combat force, code-named 'Galahad', should be sent to Stilwell for long-range penetration operations in conjunction with Wingate's Chindits.

6 September Stilwell proposed to Chiang Kai-shek that he lift the blockade on Mao Tse-tung's Communists.
The civil war between the Nationalists and the Communists had begun in 1927 and resulted in the latter withdrawing during 1934–5 to the remote north-west province of Yunnan – the so-called 'Long March'. In 1937, in the face of the Japanese invasion of China, Mao Tse-tung and Chiang Kai-shek had agreed to shelve their differences and form the United Front against the common foe. Mutual suspicion remained, however, and after the Japanese-Soviet pact of April 1941, Chiang Kai-shek viewed the Communists once more as his enemy and sent troops to contain them in Yunnan. It was Stilwell's polictical adviser, John P. Davies, who persuaded him that a mission should be sent, but Chiang Kai-shek would not countenance it. This marked the beginning of a growing rift between Stilwell and Chiang Kai-shek, although the latter assured Stilwell that he would not use force against the Communists.

6 October Mountbatten arrived in Delhi to assume command of SEAC.
Stilwell was to be his deputy and met him on arrival. The two got on well, and nine days later Mountbatten flew to Chungking and met Chiang Kai-shek. By so doing he was able to smother a campaign for Stilwell's removal.

Mountbatten's early visit to Chungking did much to boost Chiang Kai-shek's self-importance and improve his relationship with the Allies. During the next month it seemed to him that he had finally achieved his ambition of being raised to the same international level as Churchill, Stalin and Roosevelt and that the 'Big Three' powers had now become the 'Big Four'.

Japanese Offensive in Burma · P174

'Sextant' and 'Eureka'

During October 1943 serious differences among the Allies began to re-emerge. On the one hand Stalin was expressing his dissatisfaction over progress in Italy and was clamouring for the Arctic convoys to be resumed. On the other, Churchill began to have increasing doubts about 'Overlord', to carry out which troops would have to be sent home from Italy which presented the danger of the Germans counter-attacking the weakened Allied forces and then throwing the 'Overlord' landings into the sea – defeat in detail. Stalin, however, would brook no change of plan with regard to 'Overlord' and expressed concern that German troops in northern Italy were now being sent to reinforce the eastern Front.

Likewise, the Americans were suspicious of British intentions towards the Balkans, especially since the landings in the Dodecanese, and there was also the problem of how to gird Chiang Kai-shek into positive military action against the Japanese.

9 September 1943 Stalin proposed that the Big Three meet at Tehran in Iran.
He also suggested a foreign ministers' meeting in Moscow. Roosevelt and Churchill agreed to this.

19 October Third London Protocol signed.
By this the USA extended aid to the USSR until 30 June 1944 and would provide 2.7 million tons through Soviet Pacific ports and 2.4 million tons through Persia.

31 October Foreign Ministers' Conference in Moscow ended.
The Western Allies reassured the Russians about 'Overlord' and the resumption of the Arctic convoys. More significant was the fact that China was allowed to join the Big Three in a reaffirmation of the principle of Unconditional Surrender. Stalin initially resisted this, both because he did not consider China as being in the same league as the other Allies and for fear of antagonizing the Japanese too much. He recognized, however, Roosevelt's determination to increase Chiang Kai-shek's status.

In the meantime, Churchill had been pressing for three meetings to resolve outstanding conflicts of strategy. He wanted senior US, British and Soviet military staffs to meet in Cairo, where he and Roosevelt would do the same. Finally there would be a meeting of the three Allied leaders in Tehran. These were agreed to except the sending of a Soviet military delegation to Cairo.

12 November Churchill left Britain for the Mediterranean in the battlecruiser *Renown*.
While at sea he learnt of German landings on Leros in the Dodecanese. The British garrison, with no external support available, was overwhelmed and within a week all British resistance in the Dodecanesee ceased. This came as a heavy blow to Churchill's ambitions in the Balkans. He was forced to put into Malta for two days because of illness.

13 November The Allies recognized Italy as a co-belligerent.
This meant that Italy had now formally changed sides and that her armed forces were available to the Allies. This only referred, of course, to that part of Italy which had been secured by the Allies, but partisan groups began to organize in the German-occupied north.

21 November Churchill arrived in Egypt.
He was joined by Chiang Kai-shek and Roosevelt, who arrived by air on the 22nd.

23–26 November The Cairo Conference ('Sextant').
The two main subjects discussed were Burma and Europe. Mountbatten explained his plans for the dry season 1943–4 in Burma. These included a further attack in the Arakan, Chinese attacks in northern Burma and further Chindit operations. He also wanted to mount an amphibious operation to recapture the Andaman Islands ('Buccaneer'). The Chinese, however, refused to co-operate unless there was a major amphibious operation in the Bay of Bengal.

With regard to Europe it was agreed that a more positive approach should be taken concerning Italy and the Balkans. This meant attacking rather than holding in Italy and giving material support to the partisan movements in the Balkans. It was accepted though that this might mean postponing 'Overlord' until mid-July 1944.

No firm decisions were made, however, at 'Sextant'. Indeed this was not possible until Churchill and Roosevelt had had their first joint face-to-face meeting with Stalin. 'Sextant' would be resumed after this had taken place.

28 November to 1 December The Tehran Conference ('Eureka').
From the start it was clear that Stalin would accept no delay to the mounting of 'Overlord' and was unimpressed by any operation which would not directly support it. Thus he was in favour of the proposed landing in the South of France, but not

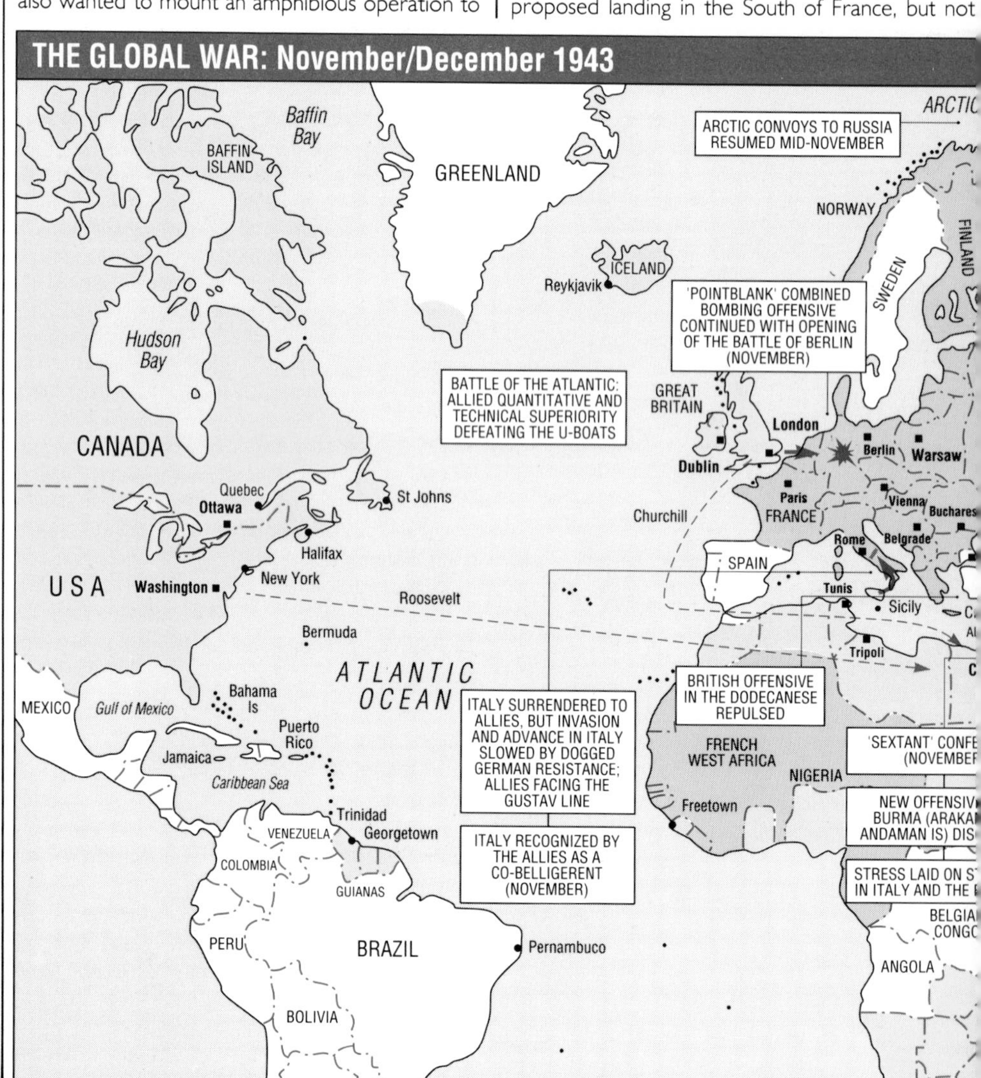

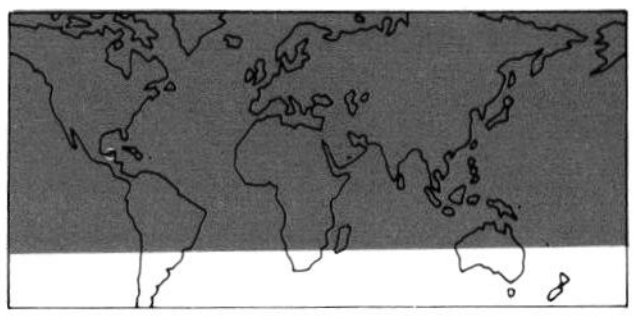

mpressed by the Anglo-US intention of capturing Rome by January 1944, or another proposal of anding on the Italian Adriatic coast. He was also ukewarm over ideas to support the partisans in the Balkans.

The Western Allies therefore agreed that 'Overord' would take place in May 1944 and that the South of France landings would also take place. n return, Stalin would mount an offensive on the eastern Front in May 1944 to prevent the Germans rom switching troops to the west. The partisans in Yugoslavia would be given the maximum possible *matériel* support as well as being helped by Commando operations. It was also agreed that it was most desirable that Turkey should join the Allied side.

There was some discussion as to the future of Poland and the shape of post-war Germany. There was tentative agreement that Poland's boundaries with the Soviet Union and Germany be shifted westwards and that Germany be partitioned by some means.

Perhaps most important of all as far as the Western Allies were concerned was that Stalin undertook to join in the fight against Japan as soon as Germany had been defeated.

On the surface 'Eureka' appeared to have been a great success; certainly Churchill and Roosevelt thought so. But, apart from some very generalized polite comment, no real attempt had been made to address the problem of how the Western democracies and the rigid dictatorship of Stalinist Russia might get along with one another without friction in the post-war world.

4–7 December Anglo-US talks with Turkish Prime Minister Ismet Inonu.

Both Churchill and Roosevelt did their best to persuade Inonu to join the war. The farthest he would go was possibly to allow British aircraft to operate from Turkish bases. Otherwise Turkey, still very ill equipped, continued to fear a German attack if she were to declare war.

4–6 December 'Sextant' reconvened.

The implications of 'Eureka' were considered. It was confirmed that priority would be given to 'Overlord' and the South of France landings ('Anvil'). Because of this the British wanted to suspend 'Buccaneer' because of the perennial problem of shortage of landing craft. The Americans regretted this because of their pledges to Chiang Kai-shek, but were forced to agree to a postponement until after the 1944 monsoon season. It was agreed that a successful wooing of Turkey provided the best way of influencing events in the Balkans. In the meantime every effort would be made to increase landing craft manufacture and the highest priority was to be given to the prosecution of the Combined Bomber Offensive against Germany.

Finally, Roosevelt announced that Eisenhower rather than Marshall, should command 'Overlord'. Marshall, who was very disappointed at the news, had proved too indispensable to his President. Roosevelt left for home on the 7th, but Churchill stayed a few days longer in Cairo, mainly to discuss assistance to the partisans of the German-occupied countries of the Balkans.

Thus agreement among the Big Three over how the war should be prosecuted until mid-1944 had been reached.

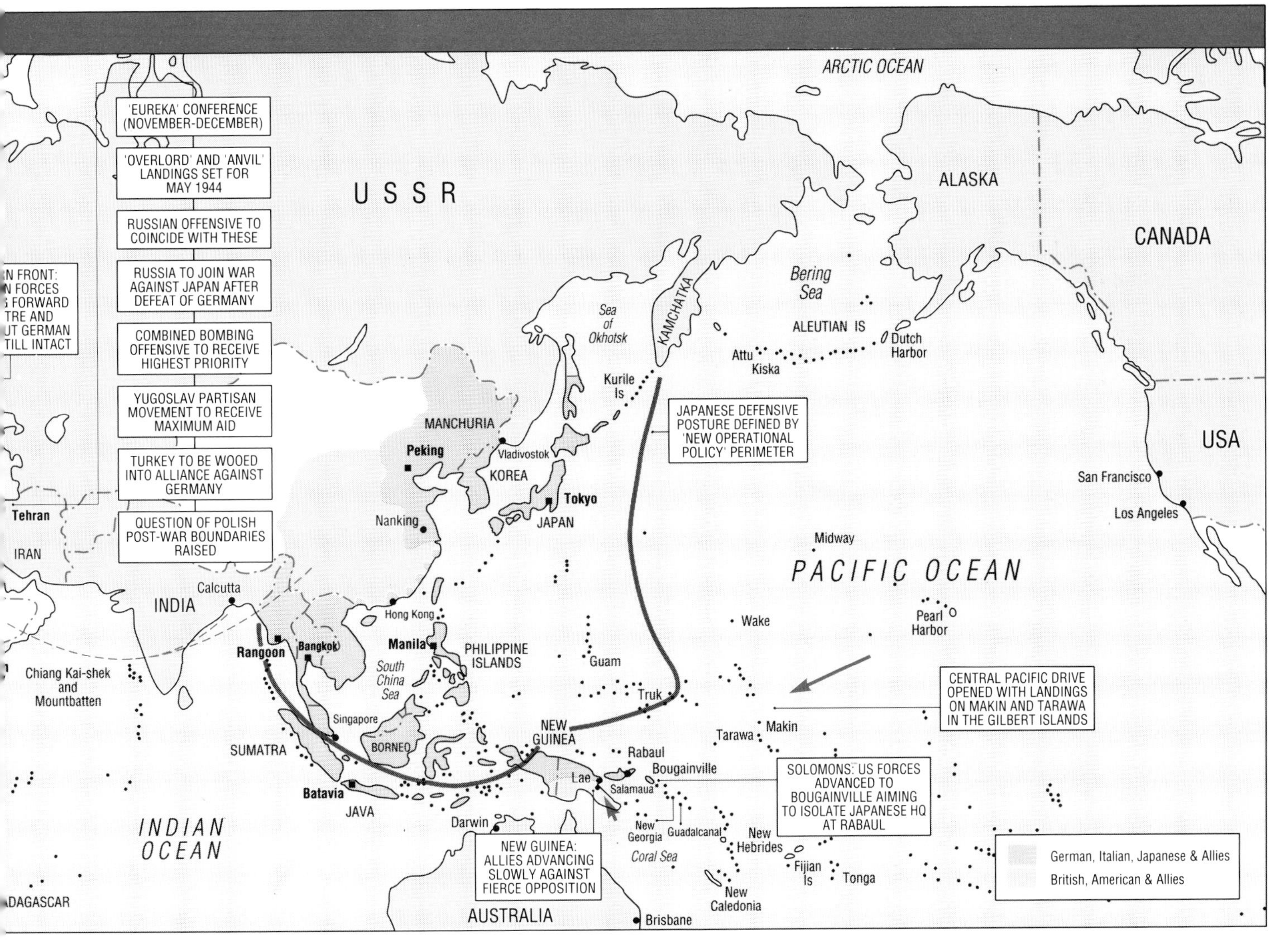
ARCTIC OCEAN
'EUREKA' CONFERENCE (NOVEMBER-DECEMBER)
'OVERLORD' AND 'ANVIL' LANDINGS SET FOR MAY 1944
RUSSIAN OFFENSIVE TO COINCIDE WITH THESE
RUSSIA TO JOIN WAR AGAINST JAPAN AFTER DEFEAT OF GERMANY
COMBINED BOMBING OFFENSIVE TO RECEIVE HIGHEST PRIORITY
YUGOSLAV PARTISAN MOVEMENT TO RECEIVE MAXIMUM AID
TURKEY TO BE WOOED INTO ALLIANCE AGAINST GERMANY
QUESTION OF POLISH POST-WAR BOUNDARIES RAISED
USSR
ALASKA
CANADA
USA
Bering Sea
Sea of Okhotsk
KAMCHATKA
ALEUTIAN IS
Attu
Kiska
Dutch Harbor
Kurile Is
JAPANESE DEFENSIVE POSTURE DEFINED BY 'NEW OPERATIONAL POLICY' PERIMETER
MANCHURIA
Peking
Vladivostok
KOREA
Tokyo
JAPAN
Nanking
Tehran
IRAN
INDIA
Calcutta
Hong Kong
Rangoon
Bangkok
Manila
PHILIPPINE ISLANDS
South China Sea
Guam
Truk
Chiang Kai-shek and Mountbatten
Singapore
BORNEO
NEW GUINEA
SUMATRA
Batavia
JAVA
Rabaul
Bougainville
Lae
Salamaua
New Georgia
Guadalcanal
Coral Sea
Darwin
NEW GUINEA: ALLIES ADVANCING SLOWLY AGAINST FIERCE OPPOSITION
AUSTRALIA
Brisbane
New Caledonia
New Hebrides
Fijian Is
Tonga
INDIAN OCEAN
DAGASCAR
San Francisco
Los Angeles
Midway
PACIFIC OCEAN
Wake
Pearl Harbor
CENTRAL PACIFIC DRIVE OPENED WITH LANDINGS ON MAKIN AND TARAWA IN THE GILBERT ISLANDS
Tarawa
Makin
SOLOMONS: US FORCES ADVANCED TO BOUGAINVILLE AIMING TO ISOLATE JAPANESE HQ AT RABAUL
German, Italian, Japanese & Allies
British, American & Allies

4 SEPTEMBER 1943 TO 23 FEBRUARY 1944

Pacific Drives

As far as the Pacific theatre was concerned, the most significant decision taken at 'Quadrant' was to bypass and neutralize Rabaul rather than attempt a direct attack on it. In wider terms US Pacific strategy now envisaged three separate drives. MacArthur's South-West Pacific Area was to continue its clearance of the New Guinea coast supported by Halsey's South Pacific Area which would overrun the Bismarck Archipelago. In this way Rabaul would become totally isolated and could be reduced by air power. These two drives would then combine for an assault of the Philippines. Nimitz's Central Pacific Area was to begin a series of island hopping operations westwards culminating as well in landings on the Philippines. After this the plan was to establish air bases in southern China from which Japan could be dominated and her supply lines strangled – another reason why the USA was determined to keep Chiang Kai-shek placated.

In terms of immediate objectives, Salamaua and Lae in New Guinea were MacArthur's; Halsey was about to tackle Bougainville and Nimitz was preparing to assault the Gilbert Islands.

By September 1943, in view of the Allied successes, the Japanese had been forced to rethink their strategy. Everywhere in the Pacific they were stretched too thin and this was not helped by Japan's struggling war industry. Contraction of her perimeter seemed the only answer and their 'New Operational Policy' defined the minimum area that must be held as Burma – Malaya – western New Guinea – Carolines – Marianas – Kuriles. All territory outside this area was to be used to buy time for defensive preparations to make the minimum area impregnable. At the same time aircraft and ship production would be stepped up with a view to challenging US naval power once more.

4 September 1943 **Australian and US troops made amphibious landings east of Lae.**
Next day the US 503rd Parachute Regiment made the first operational drop in the Pacific on Nadzab airfield north-west of Lae. This was quickly opened up and elements of the 7th Australian Division were flown in by air. Attacks from the land on Salamaua, which had been launched in August to draw Japanese attention away from the Lae landings, were resumed.

11 September **The Japanese evacuated Salamaua.**
They likewise withdrew northwards from Lae on the 15th

22 September **Australians landed near Finschhafen, New Guinea.**
Japanese resistance here was fierce.

28 September to 2 October **The Japanese evacuated their garrison on Kolombangara, Solomons.**
The Americans had landed on Vella Lavella to its west and opened an airfield here thus making Kolombangara highly vulnerable.

2 October **Finschhafen finally fell to the Australians.**
The next major Allied objective on New Guinea was the port of Madang. Two thrusts towards it were launched, one along the coast from Finschhafen and the other inland from Lae. The nature of the terrain and Japanese resistance meant that progress was slow.

5–6 October **US Naval task force bombarded Wake Island.**
Nimitz issued orders for the start of the Central Pacific drive. Admiral Raymond A. Spruance was to direct the Gilberts landings and simultaneously neutralize the Marshalls and Nauru.

6 October **Battle of Vella Lavella.**
US destroyers intercepted the Tokyo Express evacuating men from the island. The Japanese lost one destroyer, but succeeded in evacuating 600 men, while the Americans lost one destroyer and had a further two damaged.

27 October **Beginning of the Bougainville operations.**
8th New Zealand Brigade landed on the Treasury Islands (Operation 'Goodtime'). Stirling was undefended, but there was resistance on Mono. That night the US 2nd Marine Parachute Battalion landed on Choiseul ('Blissful'). This was a feint designed to distract the Japanese from the main landings on Bougainville. The Marines were withdrawn on **3rd November.**

1 November **Landings on Bougainville ('Cherry Blossom').**
These were carried out by General Alexander Vandergrift's US I Marine Corps (3rd Marine, 37th Infantry Divisions) and were made in the Cape Torokina area. The island was held by General Hyakutake's Seventeenth Army of 33,000 men, the bulk of whom were concentrated in the south. Consequently the landings initially met only light resistance.

Night of 1/2 November **Battle of Empress Augusta Bay, Bougainville.**
Sentaro Omori's Japanese Eighth Fleet (two heavy and two light cruisers, eleven destroyers, five transports) had sailed from Rabaul to harass the US landings. In the resultant night action Omori lost a light cruiser and a destroyer, while the Americans had two cruisers and two destroyers damaged. They shot down a number of Japanese aircraft.

5 November **Halsey launched a carrier aircraft strike against a newly arrived Japanese naval task force at Rabaul.**
Halsey had deployed the carriers *Saratoga* and *Princeton* to New Britain for this. Their aircraft badly damaged seven cruisers and two destroyers and the Japanese task force withdrew to Truk thereby removing a threat to the US lodgement on Bougainville. Rabaul itself was now coming under increasing air attack.

7 November **Japanese counter-attacked the US beachead on Bougainville.**
The Tokyo Express had landed troops to the north. This marked the beginning of a period of intense fighting on the island.

10 November **The main Gilberts invasion ('Galvanic') force sailed from Pearl Harbor.**
This was followed on the 13th by the southern force from the New Hebrides. The Gilberts were also subjected to air attack from the 13th.

20 November **'Galvanic' launched.**
Tarawa and Makin had been heavily fortified by the Japanese, and the US Marines suffered heavy casualties during the landing on the former. Progress was better on Makin.

23 November **Makin and Tarawa finally secured.**
The Japanese, with no hope of rescue, fought to the last. Casualties were 218 US and 555 Japanese on Makin and 3,500 and 5,000 on Tarawa.

Night of 24/25 November **Battle of Cape St. George, New Ireland.**
Five Allied destroyers intercepted five Japanese *en route* with reinforcements for Buka Island. Three Japanese destroyers were sunk at no loss to the Allies. This was the last such naval clash in the Solomons.

26 November **Unopposed US landing on Abemama Atoll in the Gilberts.**

4 December **US carrier aircraft attacks on Kwajalein and Wotje in the Marshalls.**
In the process the carrier *Lexington* was damaged by a Japanese aircraft-launched torpedo. The assault on the Marshalls was planned for January 1944.

9 December **US airfield opened on Bougainville.**
Progress in expanding the beachhead remained slow in the face of fierce Japanese resistance.

15 December **Preliminary US landing on New Britain.**
This was a diversionary landing by the 112th Cavalry Regiment on the Arawe Peninsula on the south coast. The main landing was to be made in the west at Cape Gloucester.

26 December **US 1st Marine Division landed on Cape Gloucester, New Britain.**

P144 · The Aleutians and New Georgia

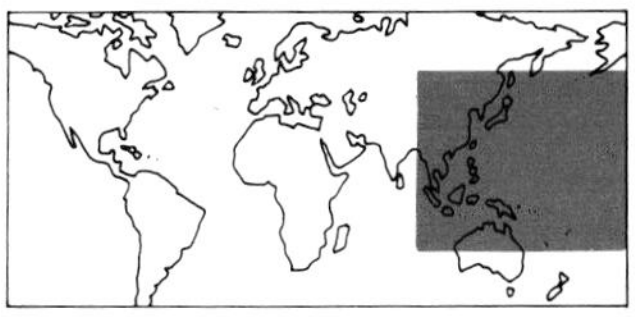
Dutch Harbor

THE BEGINNING OF THE CENTRAL PACIFIC DRIVE

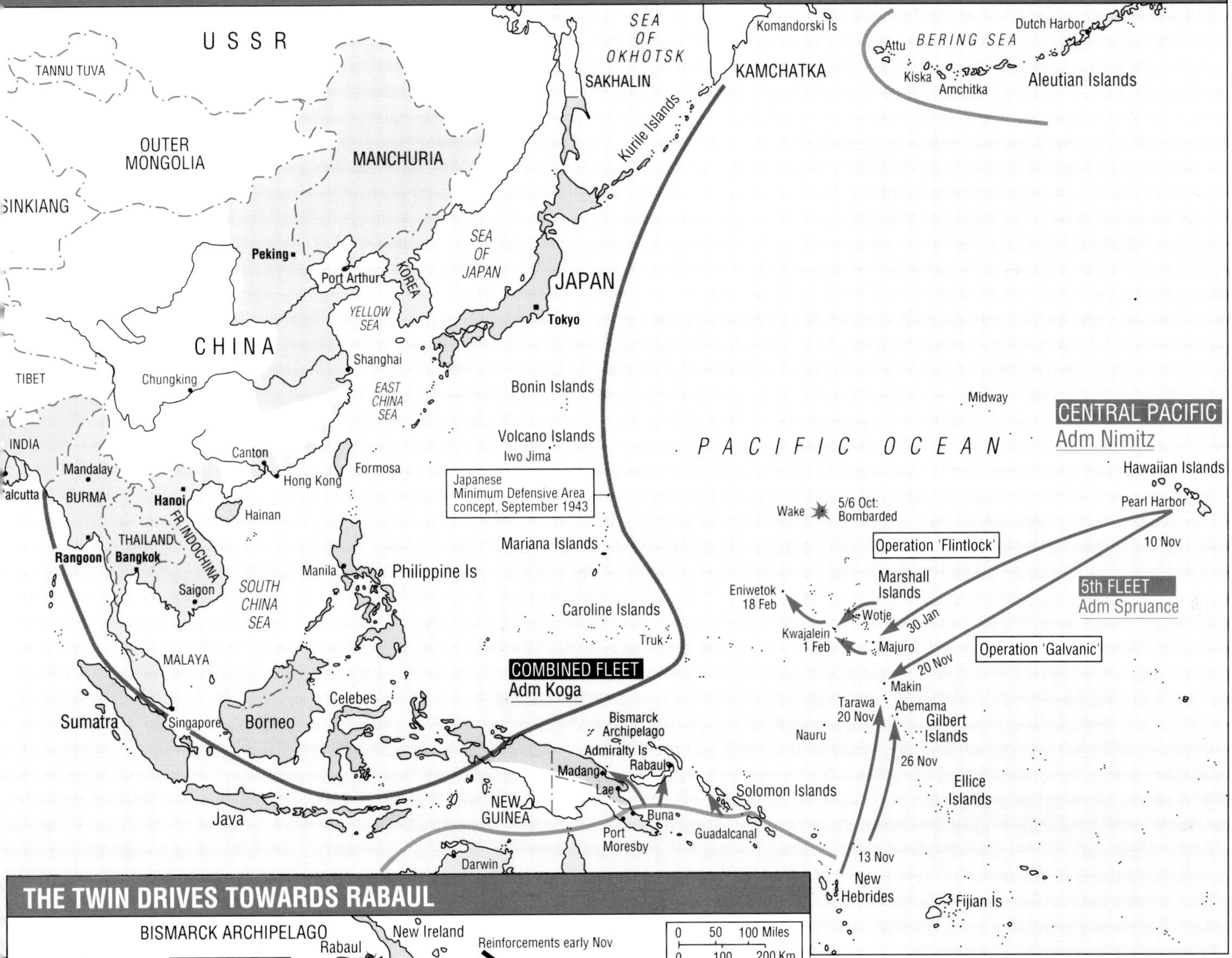
USSR
TANNU TUVA
OUTER MONGOLIA
SINKIANG
MANCHURIA
SEA OF OKHOTSK
SAKHALIN
Komandorski Is
KAMCHATKA
Kurile Islands
Attu
BERING SEA
Dutch Harbor
Kiska
Amchitka
Aleutian Islands
Peking
Port Arthur
KOREA
SEA OF JAPAN
JAPAN
Tokyo
YELLOW SEA
CHINA
Shanghai
TIBET
Chungking
EAST CHINA SEA
Bonin Islands
Midway
CENTRAL PACIFIC
Adm Nimitz
INDIA
Volcano Islands
Iwo Jima
PACIFIC OCEAN
Canton
Mandalay
Hong Kong
Formosa
Hawaiian Islands
Calcutta
BURMA
Hanoi
Japanese Minimum Defensive Area concept, September 1943
Pearl Harbor
Hainan
FR INDOCHINA
Wake
5/6 Oct: Bombarded
THAILAND
Rangoon
Bangkok
Mariana Islands
Operation 'Flintlock'
10 Nov
Manila
Philippine Is
Marshall Islands
Saigon
SOUTH CHINA SEA
Eniwetok
18 Feb
5th FLEET
Adm Spruance
Caroline Islands
Wotje
30 Jan
Truk
Kwajalein
1 Feb
Majuro
Operation 'Galvanic'
MALAYA
COMBINED FLEET
Adm Koga
20 Nov
Makin
Celebes
Tarawa
20 Nov
Abemama
Sumatra
Singapore
Borneo
Bismarck Archipelago
Nauru
Gilbert Islands
Admiralty Is
Rabaul
26 Nov
Madang
Lae
Ellice Islands
Solomon Islands
Java
NEW GUINEA
Buna
Port Moresby
Guadalcanal
Darwin
13 Nov
New Hebrides
Fijian Is

THE TWIN DRIVES TOWARDS RABAUL

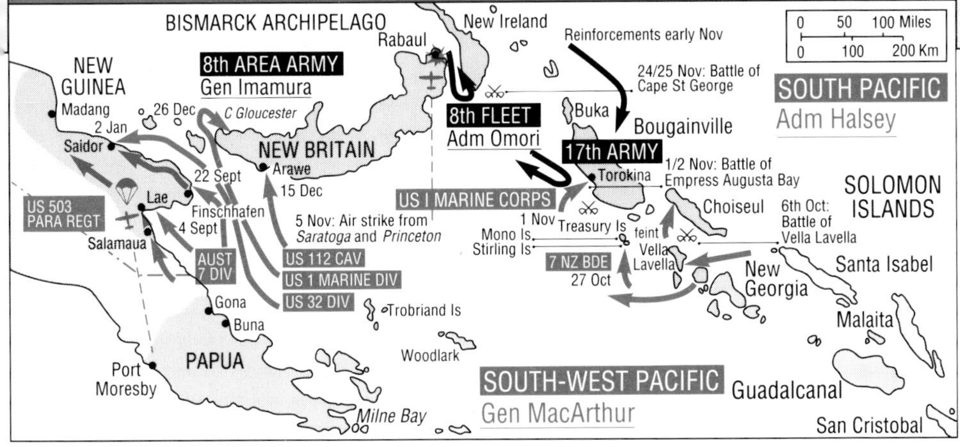
BISMARCK ARCHIPELAGO
Rabaul
New Ireland
Reinforcements early Nov
0 50 100 Miles
0 100 200 Km
NEW GUINEA
8th AREA ARMY
Gen Imamura
Madang
26 Dec
C Gloucester
24/25 Nov: Battle of Cape St George
2 Jan
8th FLEET
Adm Omori
Buka
SOUTH PACIFIC
Adm Halsey
Saidor
NEW BRITAIN
Bougainville
Arawe
17th ARMY
22 Sept
15 Dec
Torokina
1/2 Nov: Battle of Empress Augusta Bay
SOLOMON ISLANDS
US 503 PARA REGT
Lae
US I MARINE CORPS
Finschhafen
4 Sept
5 Nov: Air strike from Saratoga and Princeton
1 Nov
Treasury Is
Choiseul
6th Oct: Battle of Vella Lavella
Salamaua
AUST 7 DIV
Mono Is
Stirling Is
feint
US 112 CAV
7 NZ BDE
27 Oct
Vella Lavella
Santa Isabel
US 1 MARINE DIV
New Georgia
US 32 DIV
Gona
Trobriand Is
Malaita
Buna
Port Moresby
PAPUA
Woodlark
SOUTH-WEST PACIFIC
Gen MacArthur
Guadalcanal
Milne Bay
San Cristobal

This was after an extensive air bombardment of Japanese bases on the island. the Japanese had some 10,000 defenders, some of whom had been counter-attacking the Arawe beachhead. Although the Americans quickly seized the airfield on Cape Gloucester progress was thereafter slow against mounting Japanese resistance.

2 January 1944 US 32nd Division landed at Saidor, New Guinea.

This was designed to accelerate the advance on Madang.

30 January Opening of the assault on the Marshalls ('Flintlock').

US troops landed on the unoccupied eastern atoll of Majuro. This was to be the forward logistics base for the attacks on the Kwajalein and Eniwetok atolls.

1 February US landings on the Kwajalein Atoll.

4th Marine Division landed in the extreme north and 7th Infantry Division in the extreme south. The atoll was secured by the end of 4 February. Casualties were more than 8,000 Japanese and 1,800 US. This speedy success meant that the attack on Eniwetok ('Catchpole') could be advanced.

18–23 February Battle of Eniwetok Atoll.

Once again the Japanese fought to the last and lost 3,500 men. US casualties were 1,200.

The pace in the Pacific was now beginning to quicken. Truk in the Carolines and the Marianas were now the next major objectives, as well as the final isolation of Rabaul.

On Towards the Philippines · P176

1 OCTOBER 1943 TO 24 JANUARY 1944

Objective Rome

By the end of September 1943 both the Allies and the Germans in Italy could feel reasonably pleased with themselves. The Allies had got ashore, cleared the southern half of the country as far north as the line Naples – Foggia, and brought Italy, apart from Mussolini's puppet government in the north, over to the Allied side. The Germans, on the other hand, had not suffered severe losses and the withdrawal to the winter line in the mountains south of Rome was proceeding according to plan.

Yet both sides were now locked in debate as to the shape of their overall strategies in Italy for the future. On the German side the argument between Rommel, who still had his Army Group B in northern Italy, and Kesselring continued. Rommel maintained that it was not possible to hold the Allies south of the Pisa – Rimimi line, while Kesselring argued that his current delaying actions were proving successful, pointing to the nature of the Italian terrain, which favoured the defence.

The Allies, too, were in a quandary. As we have seen, once the landings had taken place there was a change of view on Italy. Rather than merely being seen as a means of tying down German

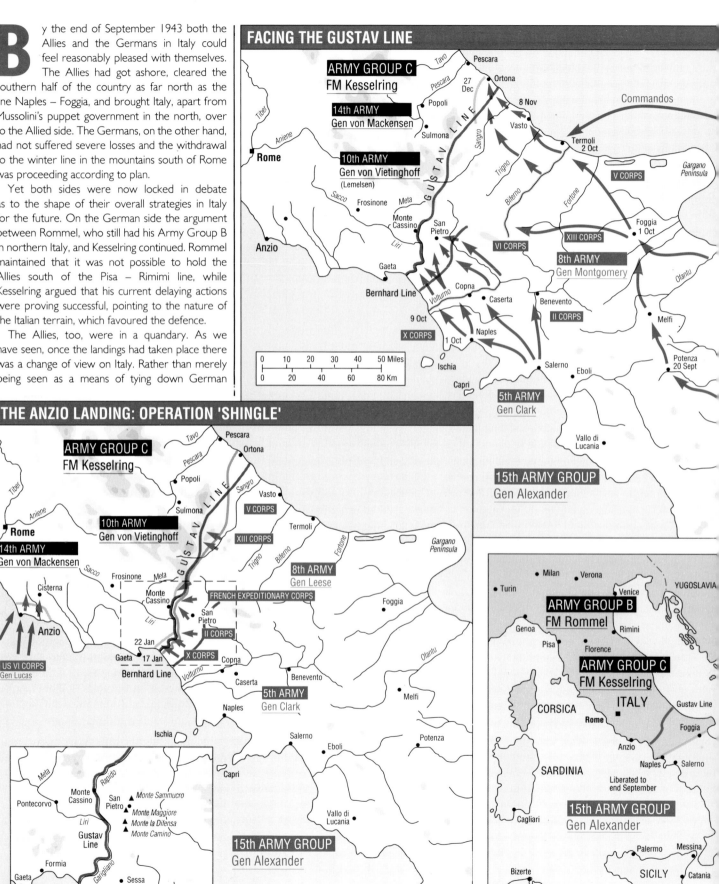

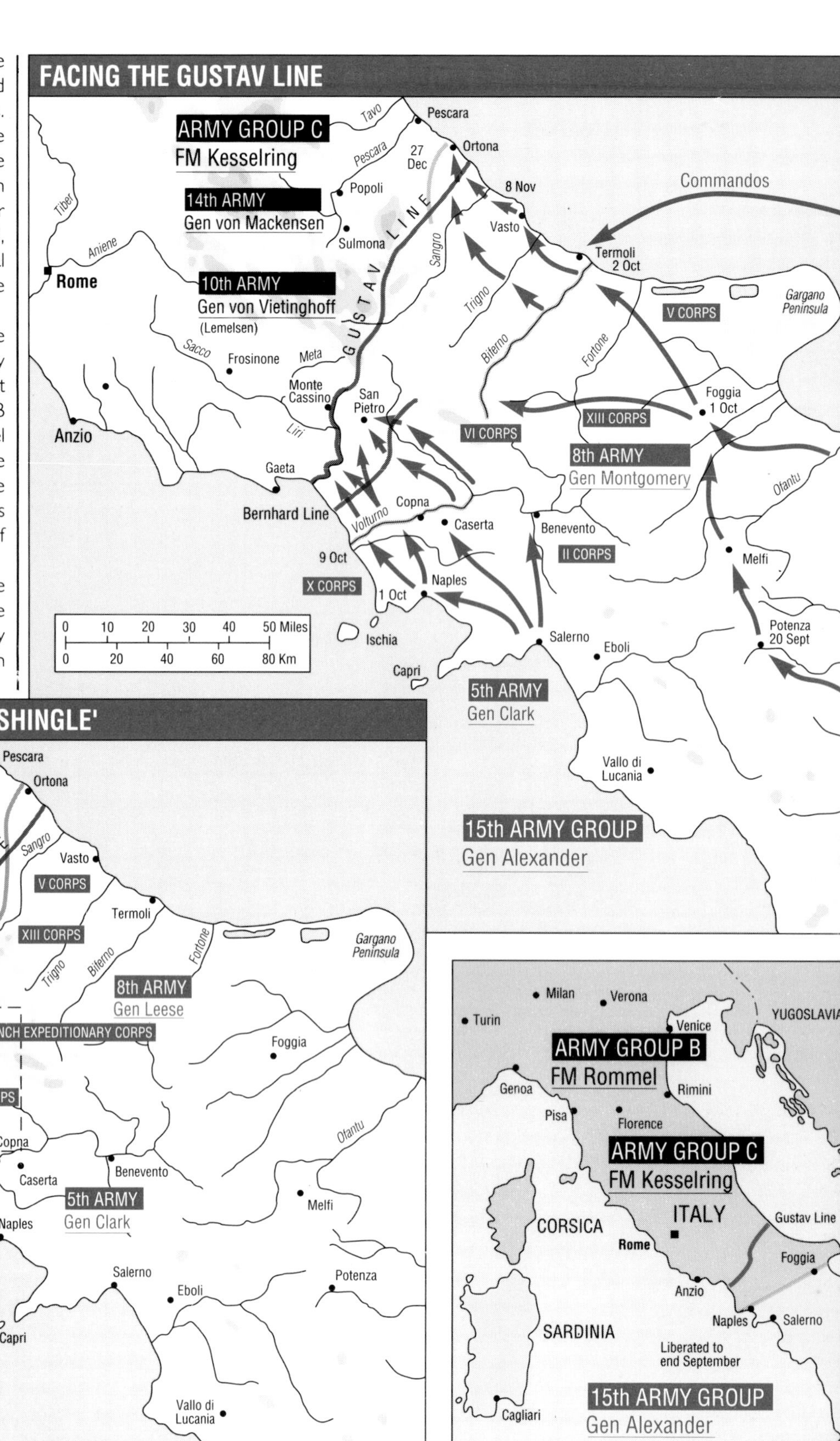

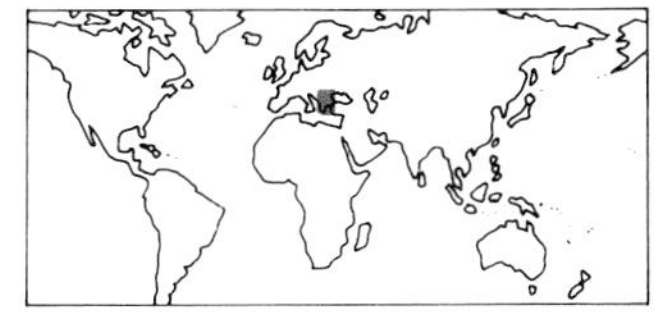

troops, there was a temptation to believe that something decisive could be developed. To do this, however, would mean retaining troops and landing craft required for 'Overlord', thus forcing a postponement of it.

1 October 1943 **US Fifth Army entered Naples and the British Eighth Army entered Foggia.**
It had been agreed that the Fifth Army would advance up the west side of the Appenines and the Eighth Army on the east side. German demolitions continued to impose a severe brake on the rate of advance.

2 October **British Commandos landed at and seized Termoli.**
This was in order to turn the German defences on the River Biferno. Heavy rain swelled the river and turned the area into a sea of mud. This delayed the link-up of the British 78th Division with the Commandos.

4 October **Hitler ordered Rommel to reinforce Kesselring with two divisions.**
This was as a result of a conference on Italy held on **30 September**. Kesselring was now to hold the Bernhard Line between Gaeta and Ortona for as long as possible. This indicated that Hitler was beginning to come down in favour of the Kesselring concept.

'Ultra' detected the move of these reinforcements on the 7th and this, together with the autumn rains, severely dented the optimistic Allied forecast of reaching Rome within a month.

9 October **US Fifth Army closed on the River Volturno.**
Although crossings of it were achieved on the 13th, the rain, skilful German rearguard actions and demolitions meant that the advance could not be resumed until **24 October**.

5–14 November **The battle for Monte Camino.**
This feature dominated the River Garigliano from the south, but efforts by the British 56th Division to take it failed. To the immediate north the US 3rd Infantry Division had an equally tough time, but the Bernhard Line had now been penetrated.

6 November **Hitler appointed Kesselring to the supreme command in Italy.**
This meant that Kesselring's concept of defending south of Rome had been approved. Rommel's HQ, Army Group B was moved to France. Army Group C would be responsible for the defence of Italy and a new German army, the Fourteenth under General Eberhard von Mackensen, was formed. This was deployed in depth behind the Tenth Army, which was now temporarily commanded by General Joachim Lemelsen since von Vietinghoff was on sick leave.

8 November **Montgomery began to close on the River Sangro.**
On the same day Eisenhower gave Alexander orders to maintain pressure on the Germans and capture Rome. He had in the meantime obtained permission from the Combined Chiefs of Staff to retain the landing craft earmarked for 'Overlord' and envisaged another amphibious landing in order to break the growing deadlock and reach Rome. The landing itself would be carried out by the Fifth Army at Anzio under the code-name of 'Shingle'.

15 November **Alexander ordered Mark Clark to halt his attacks south of the River Garigliano.**
His troops were exhausted and badly needed a breathing-space. Alexander now wanted Montgomery to cross the Sangro, advance to Pescara and then threaten Rome from the east. Mark Clark, in the meantime, was to drive up the river valleys of the Liri and Sacco. Once he reached Frosinone, 50 miles south of Rome, he was to launch 'Shingle'.

20 November **Eighth Army crossed the River Sangro.**
A spell of better weather significantly helped Montgomery's progress.

28 November **Montgomery began his assault on the Gustav Line.**
He succeeded in overrunning it at its eastern end but thereafter his casualties began to mount and his rate of advance slowed.

1 December **Inter-Allied agreement at Tehran to give 'Overlord' and 'Anvil' priority over Italy.**
The troops to mount 'Anvil', the southern France landings, would have to come from Italy, but there was Anglo-US agreement that the Anzio landing should precede 'Overlord' and that the Pisa – Rimimi line should be reached before 'Anvil' was mounted.

2 December **Mark Clark resumed his attacks.**
After four day's heavy fighting the British 56th Division secured Monte Camino, while two days later the US II Corps had seized Monte la Difensa and Monte Maggiore. The German Tenth Army finally began to withdraw to the Gustav Line.

7–17 December **Battle for San Pietro.**
A total of 1,500 casualties were suffered in the taking of this village on the slopes of Monte Sammucro. This highlighted the difficulties of maintaining momentum.

18 December **Mark Clark recommended the cancellation of 'Shingle'.**
He concluded that, because of his slow progress, two divisions would be needed, rather than the one originally envisaged, so that the Tenth Army would be panicked into evacuating the Gustav Line. Churchill, who had never liked 'Anvil', since it would weaken the Allied capability to force a decision in Italy, objected. Roosevelt agreed that 'Shingle' should go ahead provided that it did not prejudice 'Overlord' and 'Anvil'. This meant that the landing craft to support it had to be surrendered by **6 February** 'Shingle' was to take place on **22 January**.

27 December **1st Canadian Division captured Ortona.**
This marked the end of Montgomery's offensive. His troops were exhausted and had suffered increasing casualties. The onset of winter did not help.

8 January 1944 **Field Marshal Maitland Wilson succeeded Eisenhower as Supreme Allied Commander, Mediterranean.**
Eisenhower moved back to Britain to take charge of 'Overlord'. At the same time Montgomery, who had been given operational charge of 'Overlord', also returned home, being replaced in command of the Eighth Army by General Sir Oliver Leese. He took with him three of his crack divisions. These were replaced by Wladislaw Anders' II Polish Corps and by Alphonse Juin's French Expeditionary Force. The latter relieved General John P. Lucas's VI US Corps, which was to carry out 'Shingle'.

17 January **Fifth Army attacked across the Garigliano.**
X British Corps (General Richard McCreery) established bridgeheads across the lower Garigliano.

20 January **US II Corps joined the attack.**
In the north the US 34th Infantry Division succeeded in getting across the River Rapido, but was halted below Monte Cassino. The 36th Division was bloodily repulsed in its attempts to cross the river.

22 January **The landings at Anzio.**
The landings by the British 1st and US 3rd Divisions took the Germans by surprise – they had only two battalions in the area – and the beachhead was quickly established. However, because of lack of clarity in his orders, Lucas did not exploit his early success, while Kesselring ordered the Fourteenth Army to the area. During the next few days Lucas was content to build up and strengthen his bridgehead.

24 January **The French Expeditionary Force attacked across the Rapido north of Monte Cassino.**
Initially the French were very successful, but German counter-attacks stopped them just short of Monte Cassino.

A period of intense frustration was now about to be experienced by the Allies. The failure to exploit the success at Anzio would result in near disaster, while Mark Clark would continue to hit his head in vain against the Gustav Line, especially at Monte Cassino.

Cassino and Rome · P170

30 DECEMBER 1943 TO 22 FEBRUARY 1944

The Relief of Leningrad

By the end of 1943 the Germans had been driven back on the Eastern Front from the Black Sea to north of Smolensk. The Russian strategy had been to launch attacks one after another all along the front. As one began to lose momentum so another was launched. This was especially so in the Ukraine where the southern Russian fronts continued to attack in turn. In this way the German armies were given little time to pause for breath.

Ever since the beginning of 1943, when the Russians had succeeded in opening a narrow corridor to beleaguered Leningrad, von Kuechler's Army Group North had had a relatively quiet time compared with the German army groups to the south. The penalty was that von Kuechler had had to send a number of divisions to help out von Manstein in the south, but still had 500 miles of heavily wooded and marshy front to hold. To do this he was left with 40 infantry, one panzer grenadier and two mountain divisions. His main problem was lack of armour.

Von Kuechler was certain that the Russians would launch a major attack before long – indeed, they had begun planning not just the relief of Leningrad, but a drive to the Baltic states since the beginning of November 1943. He had therefore prepared a defensive line, the Panther Line, which happened to lie along the pre-war boundary of the Baltic states with the USSR.

Apart from a natural desire to bring the long siege of Leningrad to an end, it was also Stalin's intention to continue his series of offensives through the winter. Once again its purpose was to allow the Germans no rest. His immediate target was the annihilation of the German Eighteenth Army which was positioned between Leningrad and Lake Ilmen. Govorov's Leningrad Front would strike its northern flank and Meretskov's Volkhov Front hit its southern, both destroying it by double envelopment. To the south Popov's 2nd Baltic Front would engage the German Sixteenth Army. The offensive was planned to take place in mid-January.

30 December 1943 von Kuechler asked Hitler's permission to withdraw to the Panther Line prior to the Russian attack.
Hitler refused this because General Georg Lindemann, commanding the Eighteenth Army, was confident of being able to hold in his present positions. Also this would leave Finland isolated and precipitate her withdrawal from the war.

5 January 1944 Konev's 2nd Ukrainian Front launched an attack designed to trap the German Eighth Army on the Dnieper.
Although Stalin's eyes were fixed primarily on the north, he was nevertheless still determined to drive the Germans from the Ukraine as fast as possible and the pressure on von Manstein had never eased. To Konev's north, Vatutin had, on **24 December**, launched fierce attacks from the Kiev salient which opened up a 40-mile gap between First and Fourth Panzer Armies. Von Manstein had repeatedly asked Hitler for permission to withdraw from the Dnieper bend, but this was not given.

8 January Konev liberated Kirovograd.

10 January Malinovsky's 3rd Ukrainian Front attacked the German Sixth Army.
It made little progress and was called off after five days.

14 January The Russian Leningrad offensive opened.
It began with the Second Shock Army attacking out of the Oranienbaum bridgehead, which the Russians had clung on to ever since the German drive to Leningrad in 1941. The Germans holding the perimeter began to give ground.

15 January The Soviet Forty-Second Army struck from south of Leningrad.
By the 19th it had linked up with Second Shock Army. Simultaneously, the Volkhov Front began to press the Eighteenth Army from the front and get round its southern flank. The frozen Lake Ilmen was crossed during a snowstorm, and Novgorod was quickly brought under attack.

22 January Von Kuechler asked Hitler for permission to withdraw the Eighteenth Army.
It was now in danger of being encircled. Hitler refused, saying that he would reinforce von Kuechler with a Panzer division from Army Group Centre. Von Kuechler's situation was not helped by some 35,000 partisans operating on his lines of communication. On the same day the Stavka ordered the capture of Luga by 30 January.

25 January 1st and 2nd Ukrainian Fronts attacked the vulnerable German salient west of Cherkassy.
This threatened First Panzer and Eighth Armies. On the 28th the Russians created a pocket trapping two German corps. Hitler ordered them to stand fast and von Manstein desperately gathered relief forces together.

26 January The clearing of the Leningrad – Moscow railway signified the end of the Leningrad blockade.
The siege had lasted 900 days and had been endured by the inhabitants with great fortitude. The event was marked next day with 24 salvoes being fired by 324 guns, and firework displays. A year later the Presidium of the Supreme Soviet awarded Leningrad the Order of Lenin.

27 January Vatutin's right flank armies attacked towards the River Styr.
They reached the river in two days and were now across the pre-war Polish border.

28 January On his own initiative von Kuechler ordered the Eighteenth Army to withdraw to the River Luga.
It cost him his command and next day he was replaced by Walther Model.

29 January Stalin reiterated the vital importance of capturing Luga.
The marshy terrain and the fact that the northern Soviet fronts had experienced static warfare for so long slowed the momentum of the attacks enabling the Germans to withdraw without too many becoming entrapped.

30 January 3rd and 4th Ukrainian Fronts launched a fresh attack on the German Sixth Army.
The left bank of the Dnieper was quickly cleared and the German formations in the Dnieper bend were forced to make a hurried withdrawal.

12 February Luga finally fell.
The Germans withdrew along the railway to Pskov. Next day Stalin dissolved the Volkhov Front, splitting its divisions between the Leningrad and 2nd Baltic Fronts. The latter had been making slow progress against the German Sixteenth Army.

15 February Hitler finally agreed Army Group North's withdrawal to the Panther Line.
By 1 March the Soviets had reached the Estonian border and faced the Panther Line. It was the end of the offensive in the north.

15 February Hitler finally agreed to the breakout of the two corps encircled west of Cherkassy.
Attempts to relieve them had failed. Two days later some 30,000 men managed to get back to German lines having left their badly wounded and heavy equipment in the pocket.

22 February 3rd Ukrainain Front captured Krivoy Rog.

Army Group North's withdrawal to the Panther Line had left the Finns exposed and in neutral Stockholm they now began to put out peace feelers to the Soviet Union. Relations between the Germans and the Finns had gradually cooled since the heady days of summer 1941. It had slowly become clear to the Germans that the Finns were only interested in restoring their pre-1940 border with the USSR and had refused to advance one step beyond it. In the Ukraine there was now a short pause while the Soviet fronts regrouped in order to complete its liberation.

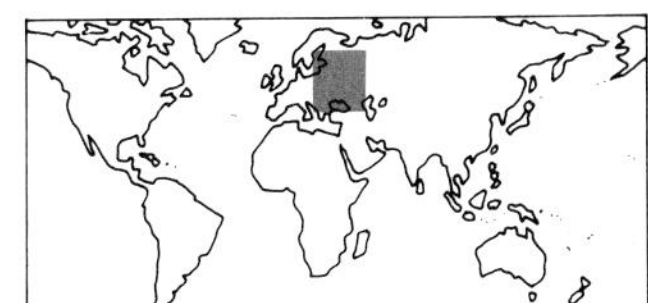

THE SOVIET 1944 WINTER OFFENSIVE

THE DRIVE FROM LENINGRAD

German Front Line end December 1943

0 10 20 Miles
0 20 40 Km

FINNISH SOUTH-EAST ARMY
Karelian Isthmus
Lake Ladoga
Gulf of Finland
2nd SHOCK ARMY
Kronstadt
Oranienbaum
Leningrad
42nd ARMY
67th ARMY
8th ARMY
54th ARMY
18th ARMY
LENINGRAD FRONT
Gen Govorov
14 Jan
15 Jan
Ladoga
Volkov
to Moscow

Panther Defence Line
German Front Line end December 1943
Russian Advance Line end February 1944

0 50 100 200 250 Miles
0 100 200 300 400 Km

FINLAND
SWEDEN
Stockholm
Helsinki
FINNISH SOUTH-EAST ARMY
Viipuri
L Ladoga
L Onega
Onega
KARELIAN FRONT
Gen Frolov
Oranienbaum
Leningrad
15 Jan
14 Jan
LENINGRAD FRONT
Gen Govorov
Tallinin
Narva
ESTONIA
Luga
L Peipus
Tartu
Luga
12 Feb
Novgorod
L Ilmen
VOLKHOV FRONT
Gen Meretskov
(disbanded Feb)
18th ARMY
Gen Lindemann
Riga
Pskov
LATVIA
Ostrov
Opochka
ARMY GROUP NORTH
Gen von Kuechler/
Gen Model
Memel
Dvina
Dvinsk
2nd BALTIC FRONT
Gen Popov
Rzhev
Kalinin
Nevel
1st BALTIC FRONT
Gen Bagramyan
Danzig
Tilsit
Koenigsberg
LITHUANIA
16th ARMY
Gen Hansen
Kaunas
Niemen
Vilna
Polotsk
EAST PRUSSIA
3rd PANZER ARMY
Gen Reinhardt
Vitebsk
Smolensk
Vyazma
Mozhaisk
Moscow
Klin
ARMY GROUP CENTRE
FM Busch
Grodno
Minsk
Orsha
4th ARMY
Gen Heinrici
Mogilev
WEST FRONT
Gen Sokolovsky
Kaluga
Tula
Vistula
Baranovichi
9th ARMY
Gen Model
Warsaw
Brest-Litovsk
Siedlce
Pinsk
Pripet
2nd ARMY
Gen Weiss
Rogachev
Gomel
Bryansk
Orel
Yelets
Radom
Lublin
Bug
Baranow
Styr
Lutsk
29 Jan
27 Jan
Korosten
Chernkov
1st UKRAINIAN FRONT
Gen Vatutin
Kursk
Brody
Dubno
Berdichev
Kiev
2nd UKRAINIAN FRONT
Gen Konev
Belgorod
Oskel
Ternopol
4th PANZER ARMY
Gen Rans
24 Dec
Cherkassy
Poltava
Kharkov
Kupyansk
ARMY GROUP SOUTH
FM von Manstein
1st PANZER ARMY
Gen Hube
28 Jan
Uman
Kremenchug
Dnieper
3rd UKRAINIAN FRONT
Gen Malinovsky
Carpathians
Bug
8 Jan
Kirovograd
Dnepropetrovsk
Prut
Siretul
Dniester
Jassy
8th ARMY
Gen Woehler
Krivoy Rog
22 Feb
6th ARMY
Gen Hollidt
Nikopol
4th UKRAINIAN FRONT
Gen Tolbukhin
Tiraspol
Kherson
Melitopol
Mariupol
Taganrog
Rostov
Odessa
Perekop
Sea of Azov
NORTH CAUCASUS FRONT
Gen Petrov
Galati
ROUMANIA
Bucharest
ARMY GROUP A
FM von Kleist
17th ARMY
Crimea
Kerch
Yalta
Sevastopol
Krasnodar
Novorossisk
Maykop
Stavropol
Tuapse
BLACK SEA
Caucasus Mountains
CASPIAN SEA
Vologda
Kirov
Kostroma
Yaroslav
Volga
Vyatka
Gorki
Kazan
Oka
Sura
Samara
Syzran
Penza
Tambov
Lipetsk
Voronezh
Saratov
Medveditsa
Khoper
Don
Stalino
Lugansk
Donets
Stalingrad
Volga
Astrakhan

Crescendo of Bombing

The Combined Bombing Offensive against Germany had been reaffirmed at the Quebec Conference as an essential pre-requisite to the success of 'Overlord'. It was to continue to enjoy the 'highest strategic priority'.

The Eighth USAAF was, however, suffering from a crisis of confidence after the disastrous Schweinfurt–Regensburg raid of **17 August 1943** and once more withdrew its operations to the fringes of Occupied Europe. Indeed, so grave was the situation that serious consideration was given to switching to night operations.

In contrast, Sir Arthur Harris was in buoyant mood after his successful attacks on Hamburg and the V-weapon experimental base at Peenemuende. He was now turning to the third of his major offensives of 1943. This time the target was to be Berlin. Yet, as August 1943 wore on it became increasing noticeable that the German air defences had recovered from the shock they had received from the introduction of 'Window' over Hamburg.

Night 23/24 August 1943 57 out of 719 RAF bombers failed to return from an attack on Berlin.
This trend of an increased casualty rate was confirmed during the next few nights when in four raids 127 bombers failed to return from 2,262 sorties. Aircrew morale began to slip and it became clear to Harris that he could not afford to mount a prolonged offensive on the German capital with a loss rate as high as this. Consequently he called his bombers off Berlin and concentrated on other targets while he pondered ways in which bomber casualties could be reduced.

6 September First USAAF raid on Germany since Schweinfurt–Regensburg.
The target was Stuttgart and 45 bombers were lost. However, the modified P–38 escort fighter with its range increased to 450 miles and the B-17G with its nose turret to combat head-on fighter attacks were beginning to arrive in the Eighth Army Air Force and US confidence began to increase once more.

Night of 22/23 September RAF Bomber Command introduced a new 'spoof target' tactic.
The object was to keep the German night fighters dispersed. In this case Hanover was the main target and Oldenburg the spoof. Twenty-six aircraft out of 711 failed to return, a noticeable decrease in the loss rate. Five US B-17s also took part in this raid, the first time the Americans had attacked by night, an indication of how seriously the Eighth Army Air Force was considering switching to night bombing.

9 October US Eighth Army Air Force attacked the Focke-Wulf plants at Anklam amd Marienburg.
Both were extensively damaged and the cost was just twenty bombers. Portal, the British Chief of the Air Staff, called the Marienburg raid 'the best high-altitude bombing we have seen in this war'.

9 October General Hap Arnold proposed to the US Joint Chiefs of Staff a reorganization of the USAAF in Europe.
He argued that Italy should be used as a base for 'Pointblank' so that targets out of range of Britain-based bombers could be reached. Twelfth US Army Air Force should be split into two – one element to be dedicated to support of the ground forces and the other to strategic bombing. This was agreed and the Fifteenth Air Force was formed under Doolittle for the latter purpose and Spaatz was given overall command in the Mediterranean. This decision did not please Eaker and the British since they saw it as stunting the growth in strength of the Eighth Air Force. The decision was, however, confirmed at 'Sextant'.

14 October Second US raid on Schweinfurt; sixty bombers lost out of 291.
This was another bloody reverse and again the USAAF withdrew to the fringes, concentrating mainly on French airfields.

2 November First Fifteenth Air Force contribution to 'Pointblank'.
The target was the Me 109 plant at Wiener-Neustadt. Much damage was done, but eleven out of 110 bombers failed to return.

8 November Harris formed No 100 (Special Duties) Group.
RAF Bomber Command now had an increasing range of technical aids, especially to confuse the German radars, and No 100 Group would co-ordinate them. It would, however, be some time before it was operational.

In the meantime Harris had hoped that he could mount his attack on Berlin in conjunction with the US Eighth Army Air Force, but the diversion of aircraft to the Fifteenth Air Force and recent reverses meant that Eaker was not ready for this and Harris decided that he could not wait.

Night of 18/19 November Opening of the Battle of Berlin.
444 aircraft set out to bomb the city, while a further 395 attacked Mannheim and Ludwigshafen. Most of the night fighters were diverted here and 23 bombers were lost compared with only nine of the Berlin force. Because of cloud over Berlin the bombing was 'blind' and bombs fell in most parts of the city. Four nights later 764 aircraft flew to Berlin again and two more attacks were made on it before the month was out. Some 4,500 Berliners lost their lives in these four raids and there was extensive damage to buildings, many people being made homeless. In all 80 bombers were lost from 2,040 sorties.

Night of 16/17 December First RAF Bomber Command attack on V-weapons sites in France.
A number had been identified during November and because they were difficult to hit 617 (Dambuster) Squadron was given the task, being equipped with a new 12,000lb bomb, the 'Tallboy'. This first 'Crossbow' attack, as these operations were called, was not a success and neither was the second mounted two weeks later.

During December a further four RAF Bomber Command attacks were made on Berlin in steadily worsening weather. 130 bombers were lost from 2,037 sorties. Frankfurt-am-Main and Leipzig also suffered heavy attack.

1 January 1944 Spaatz appointed to command the US strategic air forces in Europe.
Eaker took over the Allied Air Forces in the Mediterranean and Doolittle was appointed to command the US Eighth Army Air Force.

11 January US Eighth Army Air Force attacked

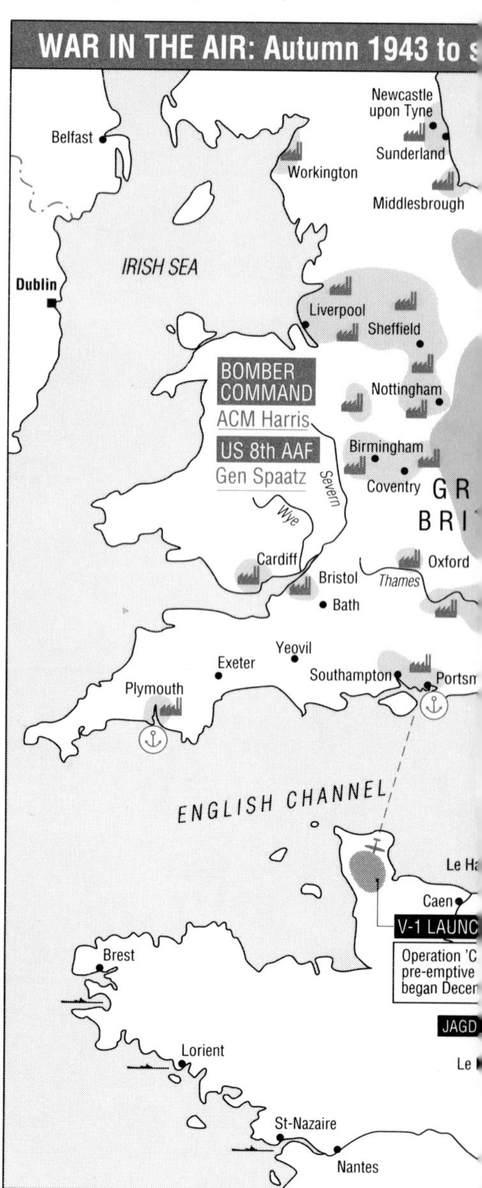

P138 · The Mounting of 'Pointblank'

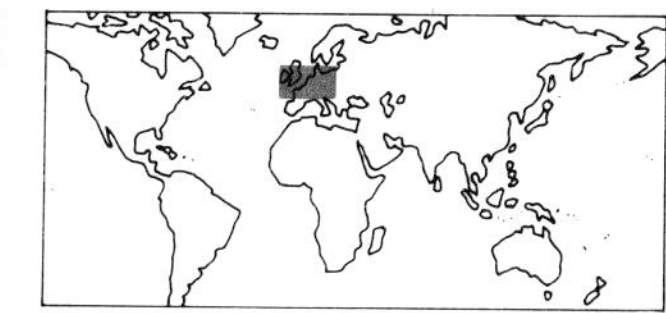

fighter production plants at Halberstadt, Oscherleben and Brunswick.
34 bombers out of 633 were lost, but extensive damage was caused. Also, P-51Bs were now available, although in sufficient numbers only to support one of the attacks. Nevertheless, they shot down 60 German fighters at no cost to themselves. Bad weather during the month severely restricted US bombing.

14 January **Harris was ordered to give priority to German fighter production and ball-bearings.**
This did not stop him from mounting five further raids on Berlin during the month, 202 aircraft being lost from 3,314 sorties.

Night of 15/16 February Further RAF attack on Berlin.
Bad weather during the first part of February had prevented any major attacks. 42 out of 891 aircraft were posted as missing. Harris now began to realize that the German air defences around Berlin and on the approaches to it had grown so strong that he was forced to switch to targets in the south of Germany.

21 February The beginning of 'Big Week'.
In six days RAF Bomber Command and the Eighth and Fifteenth Air Forces dropped 15,200 tons of bombs on fighter and ball-bearing production plants. The brainchild of Spaatz, this radically reduced the Luftwaffe's fighter force, a blow from which it never really recovered.

4 March **First USAAF daylight raid on Berlin.**
80 out of 600 bombers were lost.

Night of 24/25 March Last major RAF raid on Berlin.
The bomber stream became scattered by unpredicted strong winds and 72 out of 811 aircraft were lost.

Night of 30/31 March RAF Bomber Command **suffered its worst raid loss of the war against Nuremberg.**
Bad weather and effective night fighter tactics brought about the loss of 96 out of 795 aircraft.

Nuremberg marked the end of 'Pointblank'. Harris had failed to do to Berlin what he had done to Hamburg. The range and the weather had conspired against him and the target was too large and the German night defences too effective. He had also failed to bring Germany to its knees as he had believed he could. The USAAF had, thanks to the P-51B, largely recovered from the batterings it had suffered during the autumn of 1943. Now the Allied strategic air forces were to take on another task, direct support for 'Overlord'.

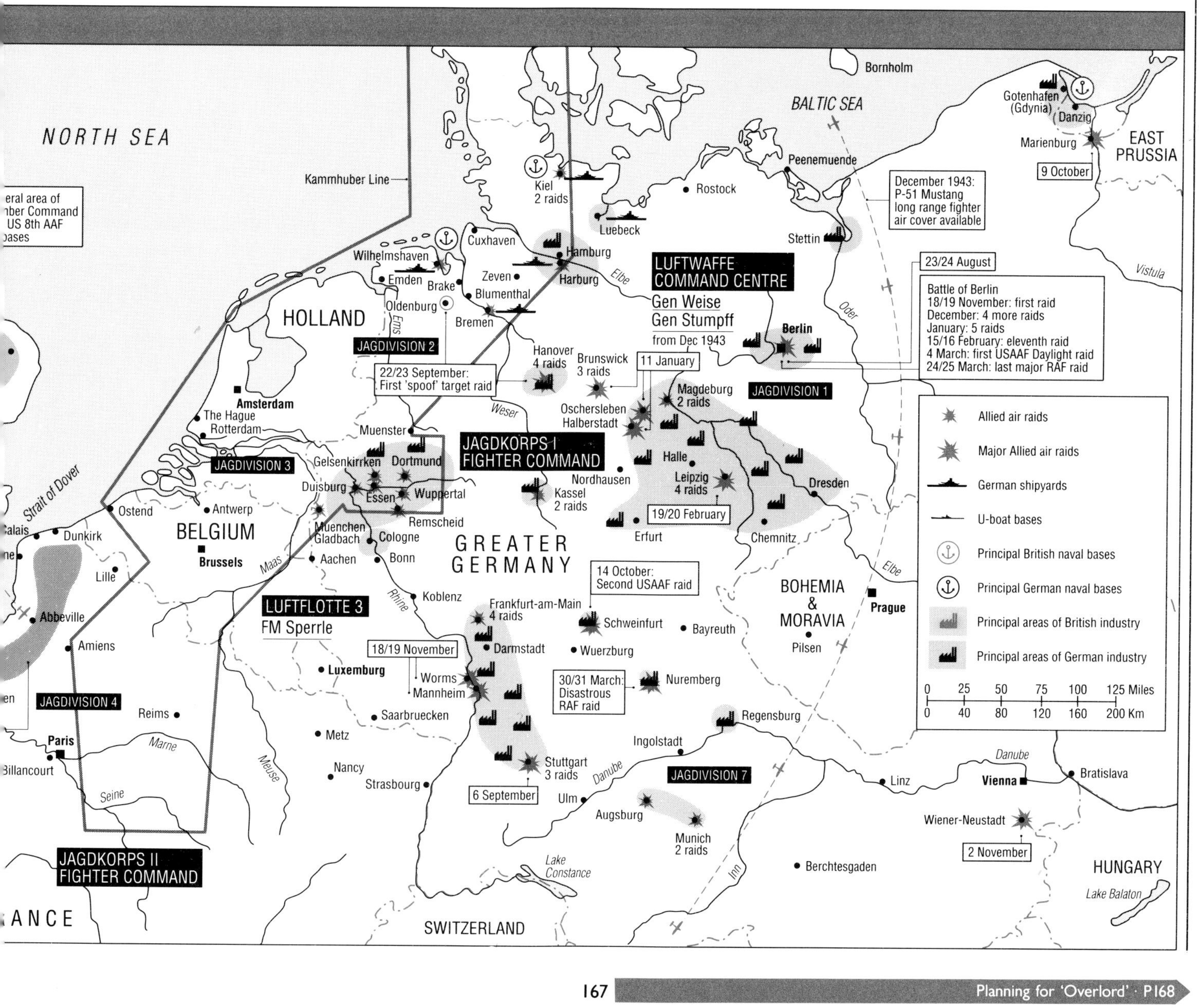

NORTH SEA
BALTIC SEA
Kammhuber Line
General area of Bomber Command and US 8th AAF bases
LUFTWAFFE COMMAND CENTRE
Gen Weise
Gen Stumpff
from Dec 1943
JAGDKORPS I FIGHTER COMMAND
JAGDKORPS II FIGHTER COMMAND
LUFTFLOTTE 3
FM Sperrle
JAGDIVISION 1
JAGDIVISION 2
JAGDIVISION 3
JAGDIVISION 4
JAGDIVISION 7
December 1943: P-51 Mustang long range fighter air cover available
23/24 August
Battle of Berlin
18/19 November: first raid
December: 4 more raids
January: 5 raids
15/16 February: eleventh raid
4 March: first USAAF Daylight raid
24/25 March: last major RAF raid
22/23 September: First 'spoof' target raid
11 January
9 October
19/20 February
14 October: Second USAAF raid
18/19 November
30/31 March: Disastrous RAF raid
6 September
2 November
Kiel 2 raids
Hanover 4 raids
Brunswick 3 raids
Magdeburg 2 raids
Leipzig 4 raids
Kassel 2 raids
Frankfurt-am-Main 4 raids
Stuttgart 3 raids
Munich 2 raids
HOLLAND
BELGIUM
GREATER GERMANY
BOHEMIA & MORAVIA
EAST PRUSSIA
HUNGARY
SWITZERLAND
FRANCE

Allied air raids
Major Allied air raids
German shipyards
U-boat bases
Principal British naval bases
Principal German naval bases
Principal areas of British industry
Principal areas of German industry
0 25 50 75 100 125 Miles
0 40 80 120 160 200 Km

Planning for 'Overlord' · P168

9 LIBERATION, February to September 1944

13 APRIL 1943 TO 17 MAY 1944

Planning for Overlord

On 13 April 1943 a Briton, General Frederick Morgan, was confirmed in his appointment as Chief of Staff to the Supreme Allied Commander (designate) (COSSAC). He was to head a joint Anglo-US tri-service staff based in London and was tasked with drawing up the detailed plans for the Allied invasion of north-west Europe.

26 April 1943 Combined Chiefs of Staff issued COSSAC's formal directive.
The main object of the invasion was 'to defeat the German fighting forces in north-west Europe'. COSSAC was to gather the strongest possible forces in Britain and hold them in readiness for invasion in 1943 should there be a significant weakening of German resistance and was to draw up a plan to this effect. He was also to plan for an amphibious operation in 1943 designed to draw the Luftwaffe into battle with the Allied air forces in Britain and, of course, for a full-scale landing on the Continent of Europe as early as possible in 1944.

These plans were given code-names as follows: 'Starkey' represented the operation designed to bring the German Air Force into battle. 'Rankin' was the plan for quickly following up any weakening of German resistance. It was sub-divided into three: Case A (The Germans thinned out their defences on the North Sea, Channel and Atlantic coasts, but did not evacuate any territory); Case B (The German defence line was maintained, but portions of it were evacuated); and Case C (a sudden German collapse resulting in wholesale evacuations in the west). 'Overlord' was the main invasion of the Continent of Europe in 1944.

3 July Beginning of the British Commando 'Forfar' cross-Channel raids.
These operations were designed to test the French Channel coast defences and last for two months. Other intelligence was gained through SOE and the British Secret Intelligence Service (SIS) and even

PREPARATIONS FOR THE INVASION OF NORTH-WEST EUROPE

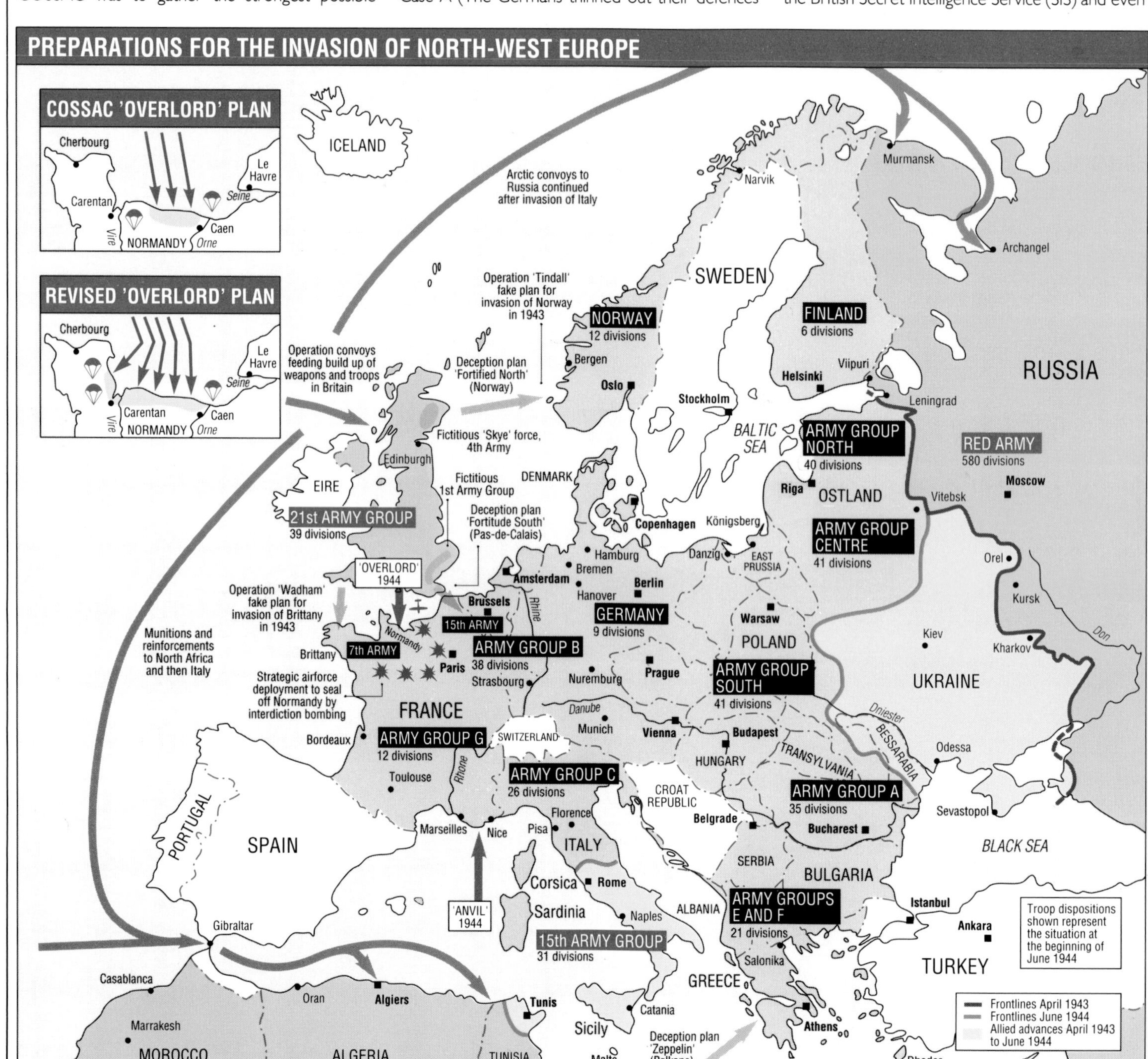

P158 · 'Sextant' and 'Eureka'

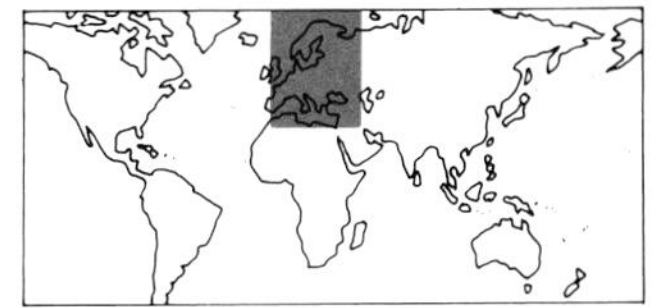

from people's pre-war holiday picture postcards and photographs.

15 July COSSAC presented his plan for 'Overlord' to the British Chiefs of Staff.
He saw the essential requirements as the need for the landing area to be well within range of England-based fighters and to have beaches extensive enough to support an initial landing by three divisions and the subsequent build-up of forces. There were only two areas that fitted these – the Pas-de-Calais and Normandy. The former had the advantage of being closer to Britain, but was much more heavily defended and hence the planners opted for Normandy. The initial assault force was limited to three divisions because of the lack of landing craft. They would land north of Caen, consolidate the beachhead and move north-west to secure Cherbourg as a port and then south and east into Brittany and across the Seine. Small forces were earmarked for 'Rankin' A and B, and in the case of 'Rankin' C proposals put forward for the occupation of Berlin by a tri-national force and the division of the country into zones of occupation.

This plan was approved in outline at the Quebec Conference in August, although Churchill warned that the landings could only take place if the Germans had no more than twelve mobile divisions in France at the time, and if their build-up of reinforcements could not reach more than fifteen divisions in two months. He also urged that the strength of the initial assault be increased by 25 per cent.

At the same time, a number of major deception plans were being developed to draw German attention away from Normandy and to dissuade them from strengthening their forces in France. Under the overall cover name of 'Bodyguard', the main elements of these were:
'Fortitude North' – to keep German forces tied down and, if possible, reinforced in Scandinavia. This included the creation of a fictitous Allied invasion force in Scotland ('Skye').
'Fortitude South' – to make the Germans believe that the landings would be made on the northern French or Belgian coasts. Most effort was put into the Pas-de-Calais option ('Quicksilver').
'Zeppelin' – to deceive the Germans into believing that an invasion of the Balkans was imminent.
'Cockade' – to induce the Germans to draw off forces from the Eastern and Italian fronts in 1943 in the belief that the Allies would invade Europe then. It included possible invasions of Norway ('Tindall') and Brittany ('Wadham').

8 September Operation 'Starkey' put into action.
British forces carried out an embarkation exercise on the Kent coast under the code-name 'Harlequin' in order to make the Germans believe that invasion was about to take place. They failed to react and the Luftwaffe was not tempted into battle.

11 September All cross-Channel Special Forces operations were now to be co-ordinated by COSSAC.
No such operations were mounted until the end of December. These also involved detailed beach reconnaissance by the Combined Operations Pilotage Parties (COPPs) who swam ashore from midget submarines.

11 October The name 'Mulberry' adopted as a code-name for the artificial harbours to be used in 'Overlord'.
The use of these was crucial to the build-up of the beachhead until the port of Cherbourg could be opened. Another important technical innovation was Pipeline Under The Ocean ('Pluto'), which was to be the main means of supplying the invasion forces with fuel.

6 December Roosevelt appointed Eisenhower as Supreme Allied Commander for 'Overlord'.
He had up until then favoured Marshall for the appointment, against the advice of Churchill, his political advisers and even Stalin. His decision was transmitted in a message to Stalin as the Second Cairo Conference broke up.

Other important appointments were the British airman Sir Arthur Tedder to be Deputy Supreme Commander; Bedell Smith Chief of Staff; Admiral Sir Bertram Ramsay to be the naval CinC; and Air Chief Marshal Sir Trafford Leigh-Mallory, the air CinC.

12 December Rommel appointed CinC, Army Group B.
He was tasked, under the CinC West, von Rundstedt, with the defence of the coasts running from Holland to the Bay of Biscay. Under his command were Hans von Salmuth's Fifteenth Army (Ostend – Le Havre) and Friedrich Dollmann's Seventh Army (Le Havre – River Loire). Rommel, who had carried out a comprehensive inspection of the Atlantic Wall in December, immediately organized a radical strengthening of the coastal defences.

24 December Montgomery appointed to command 21st Army Group.
This was the formation responsible for carrying out the actual invasion of Normandy and would be made up of the First US Army (Bradley) and Second British Army (General Miles Dempsey). Montgomery was not appointed land CinC since Eisenhower intended to control operations on the Continent himself.

31 December Montgomery was shown the 'Overlord' plan by Churchill at Marrakesh.
He criticized it on the grounds that the initial assault forces and the landing area were too small and would enable the Germans easily to contain the beachhead and create congestion on the beaches during the subsequent Allied build-up. Eisenhower, who had had his first sight of the plan in October, agreed.

3 January 1944 Montgomery held his first 'Overlord' conference in London.
This was at the newly set up HQ 21st Army Group at St Paul's School, Kensington. After three days of discussions Montgomery produced a new plan. Five divisions would now land on a 50-mile front from the River Orne to the east side of the Cherbourg Peninsula. Airborne divisions would be used to cover the flanks. Second British Army would keep the Germans tied down in the Caen area while the Americans cleared the Cherbourg and Brittany peninsulas. Only then would the main break-out take place. This was approved by Eisenhower, but Montgomery's efforts to have the landings in the South of France ('Anvil') cancelled were in vain.

The increase in the size of the initial landings meant that more shipping was required. Since this could not be organized by 1 May, the agreed date for the completion of all preparations, it was decided to postpone 'Overlord' by one month to early June.

27 January An embargo was placed on Cross-Channel raiding apart from COPP operations.
The fear was that these would merely encourage the Germans to strengthen their defences.

20 March Hitler declared that he did not believe that the Allies had decided on where to land.
This was in a speech to his CinCs. Rommel agitated for the armoured reserves in the West to be placed under his command so that he could immediately counter-attack the initial landings. Hitler, however, retained them under his own control.

25 March Eisenhower decided on how the strategic air forces could best support 'Overlord'.
There had been a fierce debate during the past few months as to how they should be used. Harris argued that RAF Bomber Command should continue to concentrate on morale targets in Germany, while Spaatz believed that a continuous campaign against oil would reap the best results. The D-Day planners, however, wished to concentrate on transportation targets with the aim of sealing off Normandy. Eisenhower chose the last-named as a priority to be shared with the continued campaign to weaken German air strength. On **14 April** control of the strategic air forces was formally passed to Eisenhower and their role confirmed in a directive issued three days later.

15 May Final presentation of plans for 'Overlord' at St Paul's School, London.

17 May Eisenhower selected 5 June as D-Day, dependent on the weather.
All was now set for the greatest amphibious operation ever launched.

Cassino and Rome

By the end of January 1944, although the Allies had failed in their first attempt at seizing Monte Cassino, the beachhead at Anzio seemed secure and the prospects for capturing Rome looked good.

Also in Alexander's mind was the need to ensure that as many German divisions as possible were kept tied down in Italy during the mounting of 'Overlord'. He therefore began to plan an offensive,'Diadem', which would achieve this aim.

29 January 1944 US VI Corps began to attack out of the Anzio beachhead.
3rd US Division advanced towards Cisterna and 1st British Division towards Albano in the Alban Hills. Both attacks were held by the German Fourteenth Army which had been increasing in strength opposite Anzio during the past week.

30 January The US 34th Division renewed the attack on Cassino.
After heavy fighting in which the Americans managed to capture Hill 593 which overlooked Monte Cassino, the Germans counter-attacked on **9 February** and drove them off it.

3 February First German counter-attack at Anzio launched.
This struck the exposed British 1st Division and slowly drove it back towards the sea.

By the 12th the British were back on virtually their last defences before the sea. The Germans, however, had also suffered heavy casualties and there was now a pause before they attacked again.

15 February The Allies bombed Monte Cassino Monastery as a preliminary to a fresh attack.
In the meantime Alexander had switched 2nd New Zealand and 78th British Divisions across from the Eighth Army and formed them and 4th Indian Division into the New Zealand Corps under Freyberg. Elements of 4th Indian Division attacked Monte Cassino on the 16th and 17th, but failed, after German counter-attacks, to make any progress and Alexander called the attacks off.

16 February Von Mackensen began a major counter-attack against the Anzio beachhead.
He had managed to assemble ten divisions for this compared to the five which the Allies now had in the beachhead. It was once again the British sector that suffered and such was the initial German success that there was a very real danger that the beachhead would be split in two. Only a massive air and artillery effort during the 18th and 19th prevented this from happening.

22 February General Lucas was replaced by Lucian Truscott as the commander at Anzio.
Lucas's failure to capitalize on his initial success in landing meant that his replacement was inevitable.

22 February Alexander submitted his proposed 'Diadem' plan to the Supreme Allied Commander Mediterranean, Maitland Wilson.
He concluded that the best chance of the plan working was for the line to remain where it was without Kesselring being forced into making a premature withdrawal. The bulk of the British Eighth Army would be switched across the Apennines and strike with 12 divisions at Cassino, break through the Gustav Line here, and then advance up the Liri Valley towards Rome.

The US Fifth Army would make a subsidiary attack in the west while Truscott broke out of the Anzio bridgehead in order to cut the German communications running north to Rome. The Allied air forces would embark on a massive interdiction campaign ('Strangle') designed to throttle the Axis north-south supply routes. 'Diadem' would be launched in late April or early May, but required a postponement of 'Anvil' since the troops required for this would otherwise leave the Allies too weak to attack with any confidence of success. This marked a major change in Allied strategy and could only be agreed at the highest level.

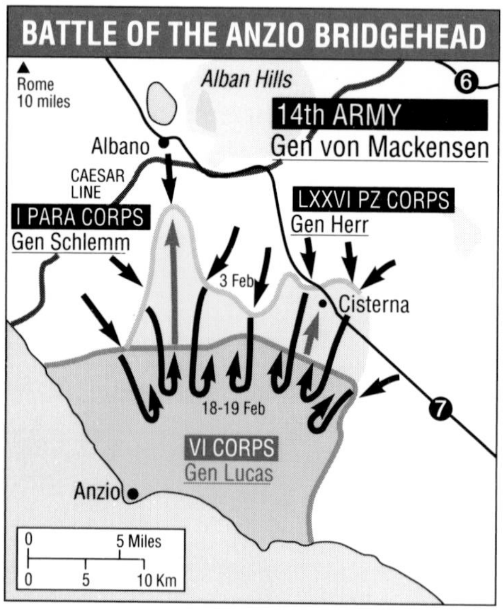

29 February The Germans renewed their attacks at Anzio.
This time they fell on the US 3rd Division and once again Allied air power was used to halt them. On **3 March** the Germans called off their attacks on Anzio for good.

15 March Opening of the third assault on Monte Cassino.
Preceded by a massive air and artillery bombardment, 4th Indian Division and the New Zealanders attacked once more. Again they were frustrated by the determined resistance of the German 1st Parachute Division, and on the 21st Alexander called off the attack.

24 March The Allies finally agreed to postpone 'Anvil'.
It would now take place on **10 July** and the way was clear for 'Diadem' to proceed. The air 'Strangle' campaign had already begun while on the ground the Allied forces redeployed, rested and refurbished.

Night of 11/12 May 'Diadem' launched.
Although the Germans were expecting a major Allied attack, the opening of the offensive caught them by surprise. Nevertheless, II Polish Corps failed in its attack on Monte Cassino and although XIII British Corps secured bridgeheads across the Rapido it was unable to exploit its success. On the Fifth Army front, however, there was success thanks to Alphonse Juin's French Expeditionary Corps. Breaking through the Aurunci Mountains, which the Germans thought were impassable, they had by the evening of the 14th established themselves overlooking the Liri Valley.

15 May Kesselring ordered a general withdrawal to the Adolf Hitler Line, which was now renamed the Dora Line.
By this time the German 71st and 94th Divisions, facing Fifth Army, were in tatters.

17 May The Poles attacked Monte Cassino once more.
Again they were repulsed, but by next morning the defenders had withdrawn northwards and at 1030 hours the Polish flag was hoisted above the ruins of the monastery.

19 May US II Corps took Gaeta and Itri.
By now the right flank of the German Tenth Army was in disorder and this increased as the Fifth Army advance gained in momentum with the Americans reaching Terracina and the French Pico on the 22nd.

Night of 22/23 May The Eighth Army attacked in the Liri Valley.
The Canadians penetrated the defences of the Dora Line and on the 23rd a follow-up attack punched through it despite fierce German counter-attacks and heavy casualties on both sides.

23 May US VI Corps broke out of the Anzio beachhead.
German resistance around Cisterna was fierce, but next day the Allies cut Highway 7, creating a wedge between Tenth and Fourteenth Armies.

24 May Hitler gave permission for Kesselring to withdraw to the Caesar Line.

25 May US II and VI Corps linked up on Highway 7.
This marked the end of VI Corps' four months' isolation in the Anzio beachhead. On the same day the Eighth Army crossed the River Melfa at the head of the Liri Valley.

The original plan had been for the US VI Corps to drive east to Valmontone in order to cut off the withdrawal of the Tenth Army, but Mark Clark succumbed to the temptation to drive direct to Rome up Highway 7. This, however, meant traversing the Alban Hills, where the Caesar Line was at its strongest, and Truscott's attack on Albano on the 26th made no impression.

This enabled the Germans to dig in around Valmontone and to hold off the US II Corps attack on it for long enough for Tenth Army to withdraw intact.

Night of 30/31 May US VI Corps finally forced the defences in the Alban Hills.

Pressure on Valmontone was increasing and the German Tenth Army along Highway 6 was being increasingly harried by I Canadian Corps, which reached Frosinone on the 31st.

2 June Kesselring requested Hitler's permission to give up Rome.

This was granted next day and by the end of the 4th the last German troops had evacuated the capital.

5 June US Fifth Army entered Rome.

This was the end of 'Diadem', which had achieved its object, at a cost of 40,000 Allied and 25,000 German casualties, in keeping Kesselring's forces fully occupied while 'Overlord' was mounted. There now followed a dramatic advance north of Rome to the River Arno. But such was the skill with which Kesselring conducted his withdrawal that at no time were the Allies able to outflank him. With the capture of Livorno on **19 July** the Allied advance came to an end, especially since the troops earmarked for 'Anvil' now had to be made ready, thus radically reducing Alexander's offensive power.

PURSUIT: To the Gothic Line

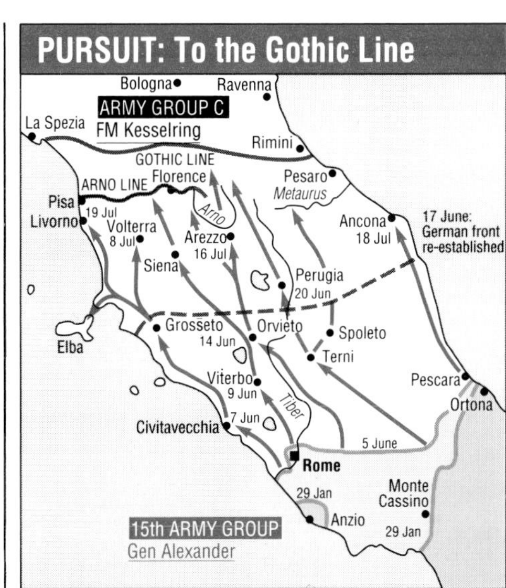

OPERATION 'DIADEM': The drive to Rome

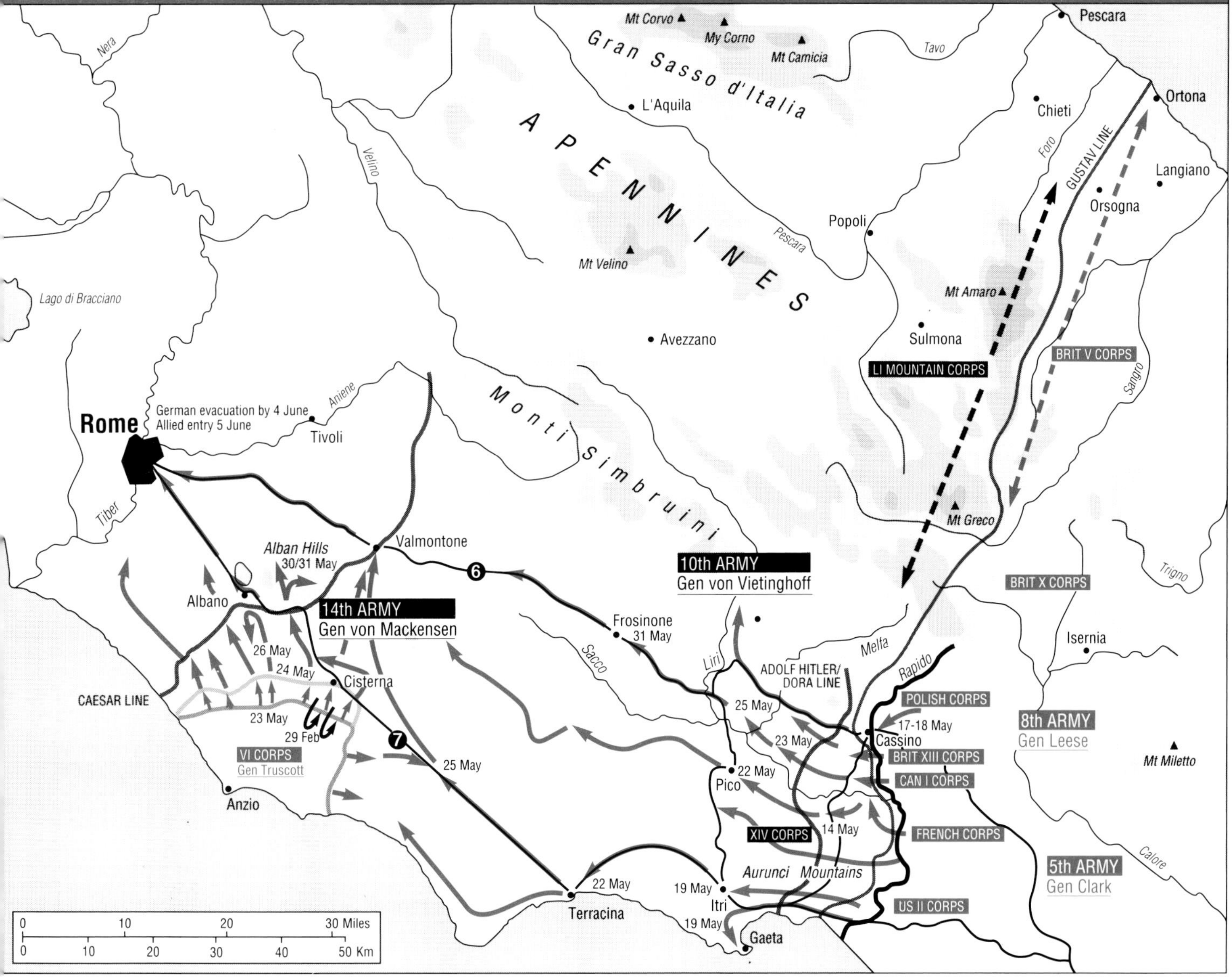

Storming the Gothic Line · P206

Tito and Yugoslavia

Of growing significance to Allied fortunes in the Mediterranean theatre was the situation in Yugoslavia. As has been described on page 98, from the outset of the German occupation, resistance in Yugoslavia had been polarized into two distinct groups – Mihailovic's Cetniks and Tito's Communists. The Western Allies initially backed the former, but it was Tito who increasingly made the running.

4 July 1941 **Tito issued a national call to arms.**
This had been prompted by the German invasion of Russia. The partisans enjoyed some early successes, especially in Montenegro where some 4,000 Italian troops were captured, and Serbia, two-thirds of which were under partisan control by September. It was at this stage that Tito and Mihailovic first met, but the political gulf between the two was apparent from the start.

20 September 1941 **A British officer was put ashore on the Yugoslav coast to establish contact with Mihailovic.**
He arranged for arms supplies to be dropped to Mihailovic, but soon realized that these were being used against Tito and hence arranged for them to be stopped.

September to December 1941 **First German drive against Tito's partisans.**
They were driven from Serbia into Bosnia. Nevertheless, Tito's forces continued to grow and by the end of 1941 had reached some 80,000 men and women.

January to March 1942 **Second German anti-partisan offensive.**
Determined resistance, especially in the Kozara mountains area of western Bosnia, resulted in little success for the Axis forces, even though they had now been openly joined by the Cetniks.

April to June **Third Axis offensive.**
Tito's forces were driven into western Bosnia.

26 November **Tito convened the Anti-Fascist Council for the National Liberation of Yugoslavia.**
This was both to gain the wholesale support of the civilian population and to demonstrate to the Allies that Tito's partisans were a force to be reckoned with. While the Western Allies were still loathe to withdraw their support from Mihailovic, especially since he had been made a minister in the Yugoslav government-in-exile, the Russians, too, in spite of promises, had failed to give Tito any material support. Yet, by the end of 1942 his partisan strength had grown to 150,000. Unlike other partisan forces, Tito's followers were noted for their strict military discipline. This and Tito's personal charisma would help them survive the hardships that lay ahead.

January–March 1943 **Fourth German offensive against the partisans.**
This drove Tito's forces out of Bosnia and into Montenegro. In the process Tito destroyed a force of 12,000 Montenegrin Cetniks; and never again would Mihailovic be able to field significant forces.

May–June **Fifth Axis offensive.**
This time 150,000 Axis troops trapped 20,000 partisans in the Montenegrin mountains. They broke out into north-east Bosnia, but lost 8,000 in the process.

28 July **Churchill decided to send Fitzroy Maclean to liaise with Tito.**
Mihailovic's continued collaboration with the Axis powers and his policy of doing nothing until the Allies invaded Yugoslavia contrasted badly with Tito's herculean efforts and his success in keeping so many Axis troops tied down in Yugoslavia. Churchill's decision had been made on the strength of a report by his former research assistant, Captain William Deakin, who had been sent to Tito's HQ in May.

Nevertheless, the British maintained their liaison with Mihailovic until May 1944, and while this was in being Tito remained suspicious of their intentions.

8 September **With the Italian surrender, Tito disarmed their troops in Yugoslavia.**
Before the Germans could react he succeeded in disarming ten divisions, thus radically increasing his combat strength. He was also able to liberate large areas of Dalmatia, Croatia and Slovenia.

October 1943–January 1944 **Sixth German offensive against Tito.**
This involved simultaneous campaigns in many parts of Yugoslavia, especially in Macedonia, Slovenia, Croatia and Bosnia. Although the partisans were kept on the move the Germans achieved no significant successes, apart from clearing the partisans from the Dalmatian coast.

In the meantime the British had set up Force 133, based in Cairo, to co-ordinate support for the partisans in the Balkans.

January 1944 **The partisans agreed to a British force being sent to the island of Vis in the Adriatic.**
By this stage it looked as though the Germans were about to occupy all the islands in the Adriatic, which would cut the Allied sea communications with Tito. A Commando force, including a US OSS and British naval elements, was sent here, and at the same time the Germans did overrun the other islands. A combined HQ was set up and a series of raids mounted on neighbouring islands.

April–June **Seventh German anti-partisan offensive.**
Fighting took place in Istria, Slovenia, Macedonia and Serbia.

25 May **German airborne *coup de main* against Tito's HQ at Drvar.**
This operation, 'Knight's Move', was carried out by the 500th SS Parachute Battalion. The partisans were taken totally by surprise. Tito himself managed to escape to a partisan-held airfield some twelve miles away and was flown to Bari, the advance HQ of Force 133. In the mountains the German paratroops were surrounded and suffered heavy casualties before being finally relieved next day.

31 May–2 June **Joint British-partisan operation against the island of Brac.**
This was mounted at Tito's request in order to draw pressure off his partisans on the mainland. Although it failed in its object of destroying the German garrison, it did force the Germans to redeploy troops to the Dalmatian coast.

13 June **Tito set up his HQ on Vis.**
Joint commando-partisan raids on neighbouring islands continued.

12 August **Churchill met Tito at Naples.**
Churchill wanted to ensure that all Yugoslavs, whatever their political persuasion, combined against the Germans, and he expressed his displeasure that British-supplied arms were being used by Tito to fight fellow Yugoslavs. Tito asserted that this was his wish also and assured Churchill that it was not his intention to impose a Communist regime after the liberation of his country. At the same time he tried, without success, to establish what the British policy was for areas in Austria and northern Italy which were claimed by Yugoslavia. The meeting was generally cordial but had no conclusive results.

21 September **Tito flew to Russia to see Stalin.**
He did this without telling the British, but with Soviet forces now approaching the Yugoslav border it was vital that he arrange clear co-ordination with them.

Tito had succeeded in keeping no less than fifteen German and eight Bulgarian and Croatian divisions tied down in Yugoslavia. This had been of much assistance both to the Western Allies and Russia. By autumn 1944, however, he was being forced to walk a political tightrope. On one hand the impending Russian liberation of Yugoslavia threatened the independence that he had struggled for so long to preserve for his country. On the other there was Anglo-US determination that Yugoslavia should not join the Communist camp after the war. It was therefore a question of placating both sides and looking to rebuilding the country after the ravages of the Axis occupation. In November 1944 Tito was to agree that King Peter II could return to Yugoslavia after the war; but this bargain was never kept.

P98 · Resistance in Occupied Europe

OCCUPIED YUGOSLAVIA: 1941 to 1944

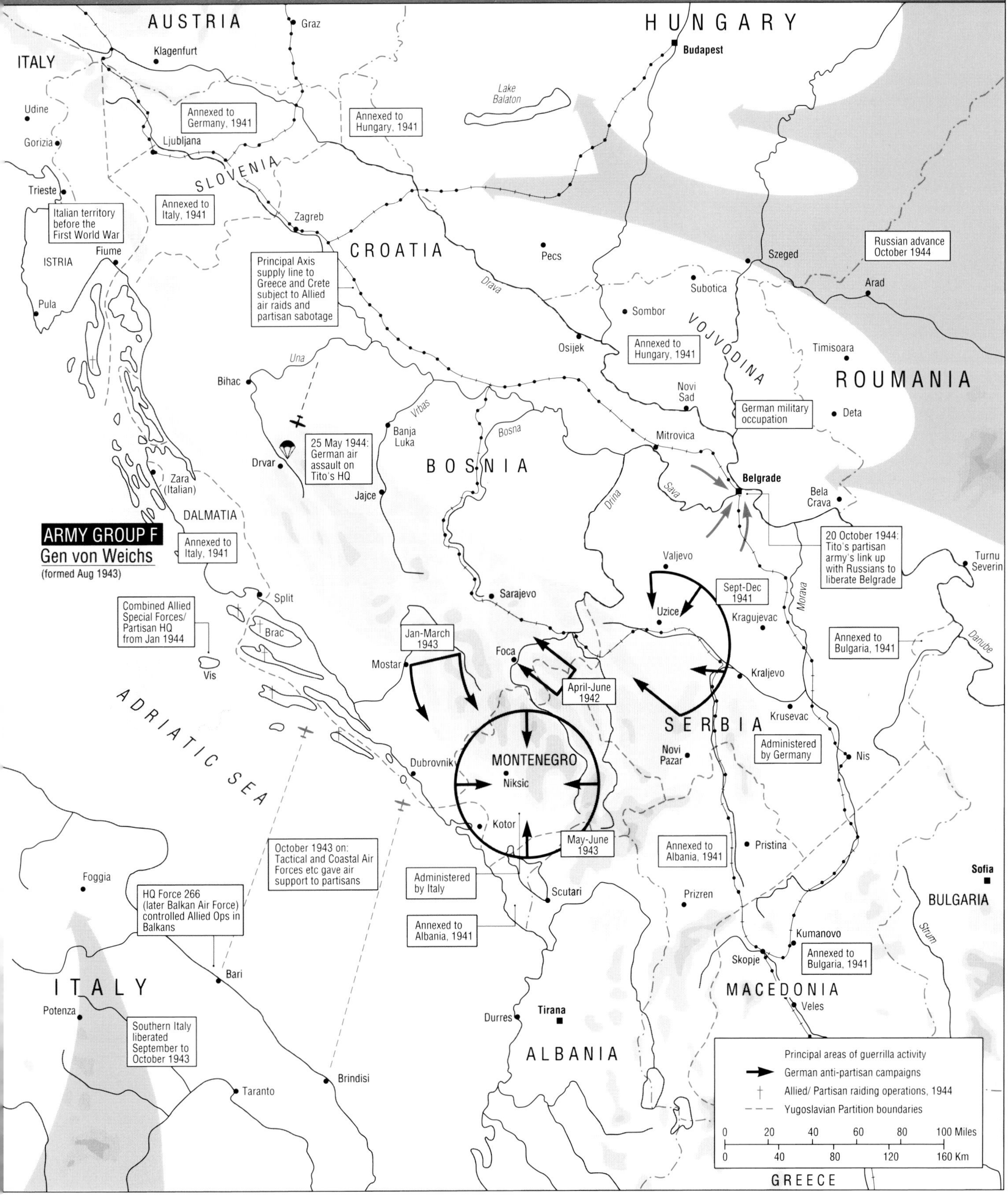

AUSTRIA
Graz
HUNGARY
Budapest
ITALY
Klagenfurt
Udine
Gorizia
Annexed to Germany, 1941
Annexed to Hungary, 1941
Lake Balaton
Ljubljana
SLOVENIA
Trieste
Italian territory before the First World War
Annexed to Italy, 1941
Zagreb
CROATIA
Pecs
Szeged
Russian advance October 1944
Arad
ISTRIA
Fiume
Pula
Principal Axis supply line to Greece and Crete subject to Allied air raids and partisan sabotage
Drava
Subotica
Sombor
VOJVODINA
Osijek
Annexed to Hungary, 1941
Timisoara
ROUMANIA
Una
Bihac
Vrbas
Banja Luka
Bosna
Novi Sad
German military occupation
Deta
Drvar
25 May 1944: German air assault on Tito's HQ
BOSNIA
Mitrovica
Zara (Italian)
Jajce
Drina
Sava
Belgrade
Bela Crava
DALMATIA
ARMY GROUP F
Gen von Weichs
(formed Aug 1943)
Annexed to Italy, 1941
20 October 1944: Tito's partisan army's link up with Russians to liberate Belgrade
Valjevo
Turnu Severin
Split
Sarajevo
Sept-Dec 1941
Combined Allied Special Forces/ Partisan HQ from Jan 1944
Brac
Vis
Uzice
Kragujevac
Morava
Jan-March 1943
Foca
Annexed to Bulgaria, 1941
Danube
Mostar
Kraljevo
April-June 1942
ADRIATIC SEA
SERBIA
Krusevac
Administered by Germany
Novi Pazar
Nis
Dubrovnik
MONTENEGRO
Niksic
Kotor
May-June 1943
Annexed to Albania, 1941
Pristina
October 1943 on: Tactical and Coastal Air Forces etc gave air support to partisans
Administered by Italy
Sofia
BULGARIA
Foggia
HQ Force 266 (later Balkan Air Force) controlled Allied Ops in Balkans
Scutari
Prizren
Annexed to Albania, 1941
Strum
Kumanovo
Skopje
Annexed to Bulgaria, 1941
Bari
ITALY
MACEDONIA
Veles
Potenza
Southern Italy liberated September to October 1943
Tirana
Durres
ALBANIA
Brindisi
Taranto
GREECE

Principal areas of guerrilla activity
German anti-partisan campaigns
Allied/ Partisan raiding operations, 1944
Yugoslavian Partition boundaries

0 20 40 60 80 100 Miles
0 40 80 120 160 Km

Japanese Offensive in Burma

Mountbatten's arrival in India in October 1943 as the newly appointed Supreme Allied Commander South East Asia Command (SEAC) had quickly generated a new sense of purpose in the theatre. Yet he soon found himself frustrated. His desire to launch an amphibious operation, which he made plain at the Cairo Conference the following month, came to nothing because of the landing craft requirement for 'Overlord' and 'Anvil'. Yet Chiang Kai-shek was insistent on such an operation in the Bay of Bengal in order to open up a port to speed up the supply of *matériel* to China; without such an operation the chances of getting the Chinese actively to co-operate in a major offensive in Burma seemed slight.

Mountbatten's one hope lay in an operation that had been planned in conjunction with Stilwell. Operation 'Thursday' was to be mounted by Wingate's Chindits, now grown to the equivalent of two divisions, and Stilwell's Chinese. It was designed to cut off the Japanese 18th Division in north Burma and 56th Division in Yunnan and make northern Burma safe for the completion of the Ledo – Kunming road.

The Japanese had recognized for some time that the Allies would in time mount a major offensive in Burma, and throughout much of 1943 there had been a debate as to how this should be countered. The two most likely areas were in the north, in co-operation with the Chinese, and on the coast. The Japanese considered that they could repulse the latter without much trouble, but increasingly believed that they could pre-empt an attack in the north by striking at the key communications base in Assam, Imphal. They also evolved a plan for a subsidiary offensive in Arakan, designed to deflect British attention from the north. In Arakan, beginning on **1 November 1943**, the British had been inching forward in preparation for the amphibious operation, which in fact never took place.

7 January 1944 **Tokyo gave authorization for the Imphal attack.**
It would be carried out by General Renya Mutaguchi's Fifteenth Army at the beginning of March under the code-name of 'U-Go'(Operation 'C'). Mutaguchi himself had long held more grandiose views and was bent on nothing less than the invasion of India itself. In this he was encouraged by Subhas Chandra Bose, leader of the Free India movement, who had formed a force, the Indian National Army, from Indian POWs of the Japanese. He believed that once the Japanese entered India the Indian people would rise in revolt against the British.

9 January **XV Indian Corps occupied Maungdaw.**
It was General Philip Christison's ultimate aim to recapture Akyab so that its airfields could be used in support of operations against Rangoon. By the end of January Christison had established a line Maungdaw–Buthidaung.

14 January **Mountbatten approved the final plan for 'Thursday'.**
Stilwell was to advance from Ledo to Shaduzup and then into the Mogaung-Myitkyina area from where he would swing north into China, building the road as he went. Indeed, he had already resumed his advance in October 1943 and was now in the Hukawng Valley. Wingate would cut the communications of the Japanese facing Stilwell, while it was hoped that the Chinese would move into Burma from Yunnan, driving 56th Division before them.

5 February **The first Chindit brigade (16th) set off by foot from Ledo.**
It was to operate in the Pinbon-Pinlebu area. Two other brigades would be flown in later to operate in the Indaw area.

6 February **Japanese launched their counter-offensive ('Ha-Go' – Operation 'Z') in the Arakan.**
The Japanese managed to slip through 7th Indian Division in the east of the British line and north to Taung Bazaar. They then turned south, planning to catch XV Corps in the rear. Most of the subsequent fighting centred on the village of Sinzweya, the Corps forward administrative area, which became known as the 'Admin Box'.

26 February **The Japanese called off their attacks in the Arakan.**
For the first time the British and Indian troops had successfully withheld a major Japanese offensive. They had done so, especially in the Admin Box, by staying put and fighting, relying on air resupply.

5–6 March **Stilwell's troops won a victory over the Japanese 18th Division at Maingkwan and Walawbaum.**
Fighting with the Chinese was the only US ground combat unit in the theatre, 5307 Composite Unit (Provisional), code-named 'Galahad' but better known as Merrill's Marauders after their commander.

5–12 March **77 and 111 Chindit Brigades flew in by DC-3 Dakota and glider.**
They made successful landings at two landing grounds – 'Broadway' and 'Chowringhee' – in the Kaukkwe Valley. A third, 'Piccadilly', could not be used because it was discovered to be covered in tree trunks. They immediately set up 'strongholds' at these and 'Aberdeen' and 'White City'. Elements of the Japanese 18th Division attacked these, but were easily beaten off. The Chindits also cut the Mandalay – Myitkynia railway in several places.

Night of 7/8 March **The Japanese 'U-Go' offensive began.**
The first phase was an advance by the 33rd Division from Fort White against 17th Indian Division in the Tiddim area. Slim, commanding the Fourteenth Army, knew that the Japanese were preparing to attack, but expected it to begin a week later. 17th Division began to withdraw northwards towards Imphal, warding off attacks on its left flank.

11 March **The British recaptured Buthidaung in the Arakan.**
Next day the fortress of Razibil, which the Japanese had held throughout, also fell. The British were now able to switch two divisions north to the Imphal-Kohima front.

14 March **A force from Japanese 33rd Division advanced north against 20th Indian Division in the Tamu area.**
20th Indian Division was ordered to withdraw and hold the hills astride the Tamu – Imphal road. This they successfully did for the next three months despite much bitter fighting.

19 March **Elements of Japanese 31st Division attacked Sangshak, north-east of Imphal.**
This area was held by 50th Indian Parachute Brigade, which went into a 'box'. This held out for a week before being overrun, but bought precious time for the British, who were able to reinforce the main 31st Division objective, Kohima, which covered the important railhead of Dimapur with its large stocks of supplies. The Japanese 15th Division now cut the road between Imphal and Kohima.

24 March **Wingate killed in an air crash near Bishenpur.**
This was while returning from visiting his brigades in the Indaw area. His place was taken by Major-General W. D. A. Lentaigne. In the meantime a fourth Chindit brigade (14th) had been flown in. 16th Brigade now tried to capture Indaw without success, while the Japanese launched heavy attacks on White City.

3 April **Japanese 31st Division closed on Kohima.**
It was held by little more than one British infantry battalion, which did not arrive there until the 5th, the day the siege began.

9 April **Mountbatten and Slim decided to pass the Chindits over to Stilwell's command.**
16th Brigade was to be evacuated by air while the remainder moved north. In the meantime White City came under heavy attack once more, while Stilwell continued to drive 18th Division back.

18 April **The Kohima garrison relieved.**
There had been a desperate battle here during the past two weeks, but during this time General Montague Stopford, commanding XXXIII Corps, had pushed two brigades up from Dimapur and cleared the route to Kohima.

In the meantime the Japanese 15th Division turned south down the road from Kohima to attack

P156 · Stilwell and China

THE TURNING POINT IN BURMA

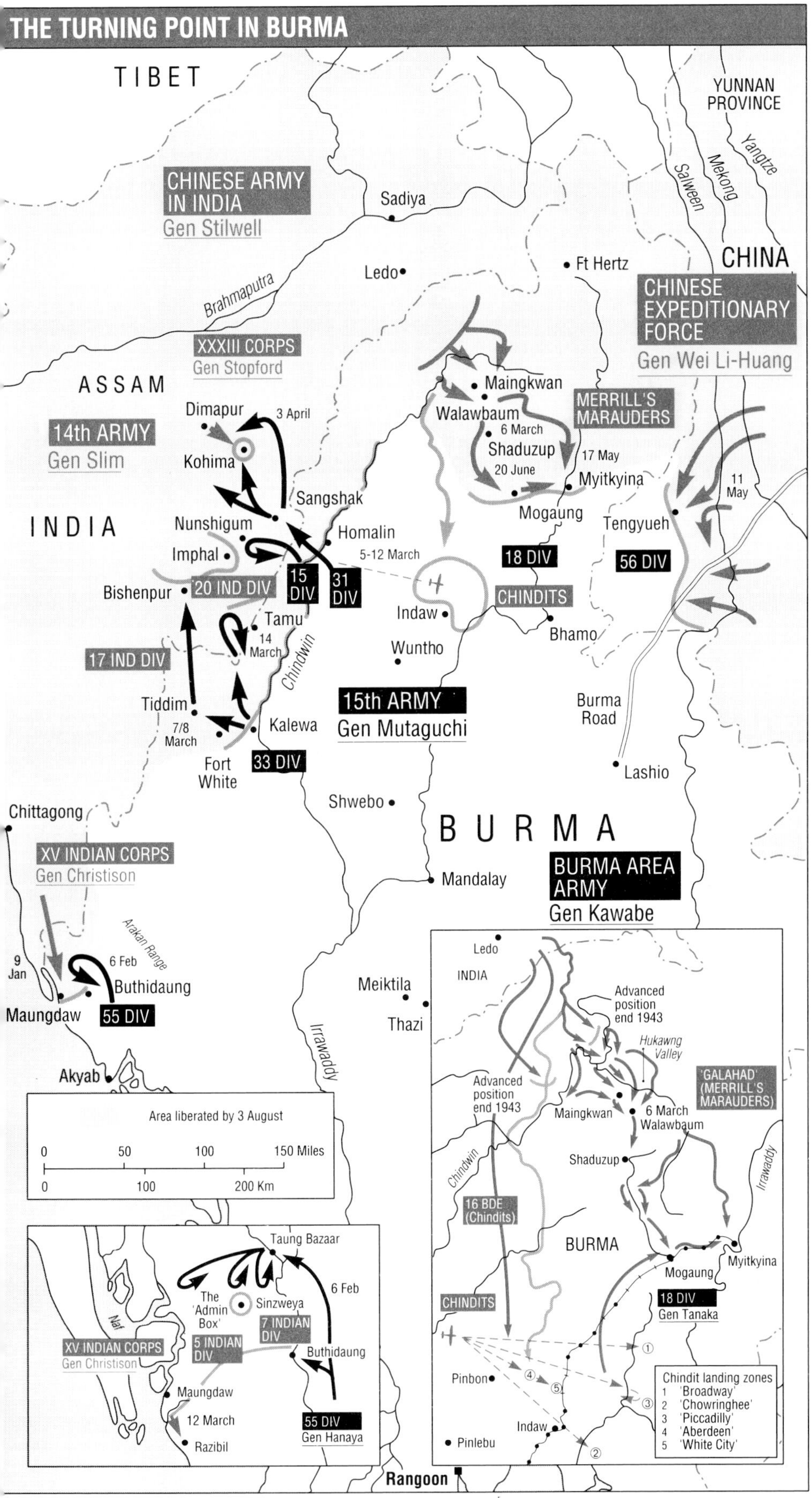

Imphal from the north and north-east. They were driven off the prominent feature of Nunshigum and halted at Sengmai. On **19 April**, short of supplies and much weakened in strength, they went on to the defensive. Likewise the 33rd Division drive up from the south to Imphal had lost its impetus and been halted south of Bishenpur. Worse, Mutaguchi had planned only on a three-week campaign and his army was now very short of supplies.

22 April Stopford began to clear the Japanese from around Kohima.
Resistance was fierce and progress slow. Fighting was to continue in this area for the next two months.

11 May The Chinese began their offensive on the Salween front.

13 May Fighting was renewed to the south of Imphal.
This became very much of a 'dogfight' between 17th Indian Division and 33rd Division. While the former made attempts to cut the Japanese lines of communication on the Tiddim road, the latter tried, without success, to seize Bishenpur.

17 May Merrill's Marauders seized the airfield at Myitkyina.
Efforts to take the town failed and the Japanese quickly reinforced their garrison there.

22 June The British finally reopened the Kohima – Imphal road.

26 June Mogaung fell to the Chindits.
This was after five days' heavy fighting. By now they had been wasted by battle casualties and sickness and were hardly viable as a fighting force.

11 July General Masakazu Kawabe commanding Burma Area Army finally gave orders to call off the Japanese offensive.
The position of Fifteenth Army had become increasingly parlous and its divisions now withdrew, followed by Slim, across the Chindwin. At the end of July came the monsoon, which brought a halt to operations.

3 August Stilwell finally captured Myitkyina.
The Ledo Road could now be extended this far. Both the Chindits and Merrill's Marauders were now flown back to India.

The repulse of the Japanese at Imphal-Kohima and the capture of Myitkyina marked the turning point of the war in Burma. From now on the Japanese would be on the defensive, and the Allied liberation of the country could begin in earnest.

On Towards the Philippines

By the end of February 1944 the Allies in the Pacific were poised to isolate entirely the main Japanese base of Rabaul in the South-West Pacific. With the Marshalls and Gilberts now secured, they were looking also towards the strategically placed Mariana Islands.

29 February 1944 Elements of US 1st Cavalry Division landed on Los Negros in the Admiralty Islands.

They quickly seized the airfield at Momote, but had to repulse a number of Japanese counter-attacks.

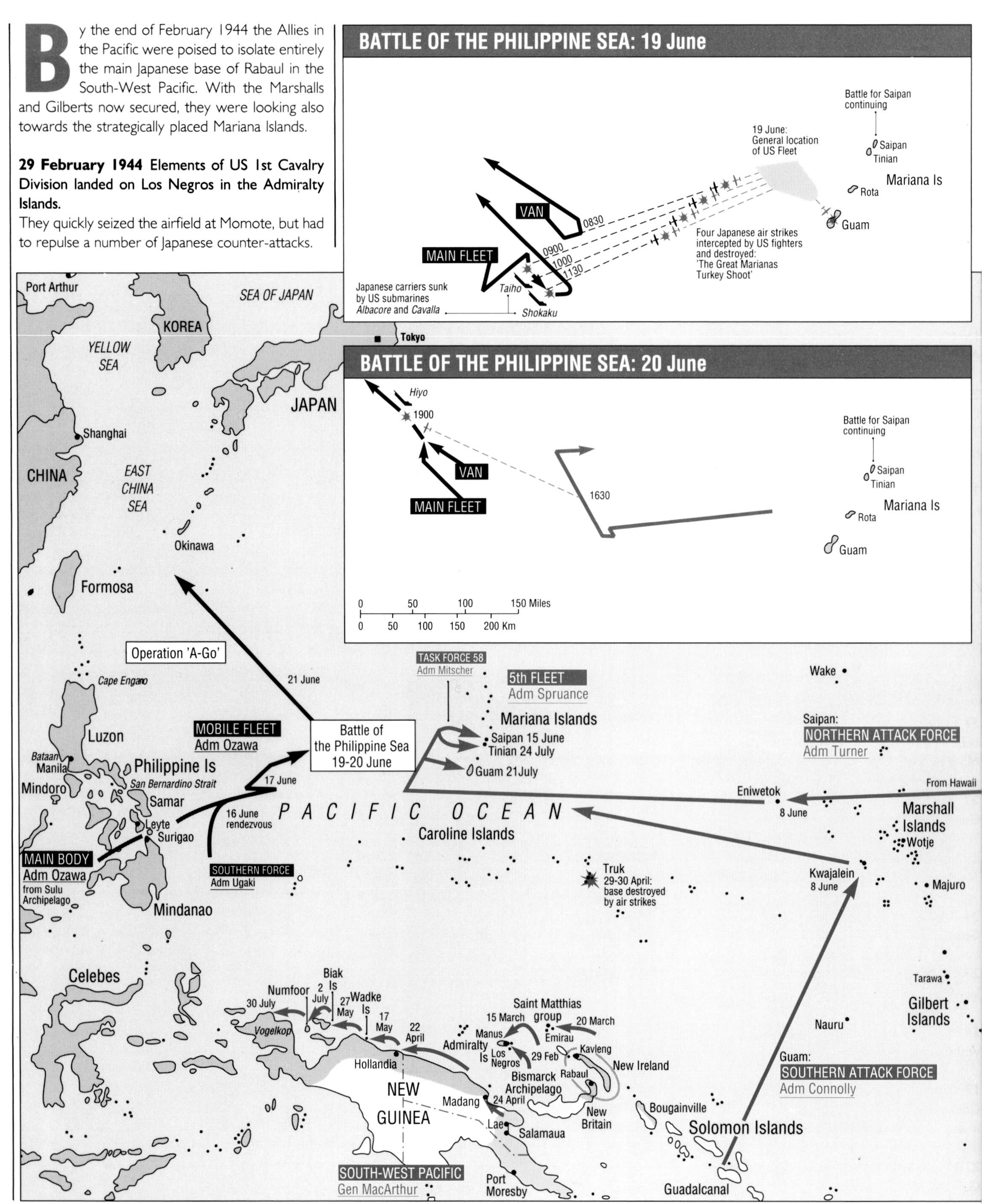

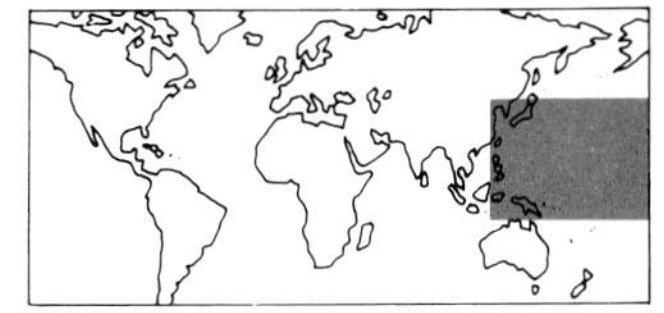

7 March Momote airfield on Los Negros became operational.

Further reinforcements were landed and operations set in train to clear the Admiralties.

8 March The Japanese began to attack the US beachhead on Bougainville.

12 March MacArthur and Nimitz received a new directive from the Combined Chiefs of Staff.

Their next major objectives were to be Luzon and Formosa, with a target date of February 1945. More immediately, Emirau Island in the Saint Matthias group was to be seized and a landing made at Hollandia in New Guinea.

15 March US troops landed on Manus in the Admiralties.

20 March US Marines landed unopposed on Emirau Island in the Saint Matthias group.

The ring around Rabaul and the subsidiary base of Kavieng on New Ireland was now sealed.

24 March Japanese counter-attack on the beachhead at Bougainville foiled.

This was the last such attempt to destroy the US beachhead, although skirmishing continued until May, and the Japanese began to withdraw their forces inland from Empress Augusta Bay. Little attempt was made to pursue them, since MacArthur did not consider that they now posed any significant threat.

By now, apart from some mopping-up, the US forces had secured the Admiralties.

31 March Admiral Mineichi Koga, who had succeeded Yamamoto, killed in an air crash on Mindanao.

22 April US forces landed at Hollandia, New Guinea.

The Japanese base had been subjected to air attack for some weeks and latterly naval bombardment. The Japanese forces withdrew inland.

24 April The Australians occupied Madang, New Guinea.

29–30 April Carrier-borne aircraft destroyed the Japanese base at Truk in the Carolines.

14 May Japanese forces on New Britain began to withdraw to Rabaul.

17 May US landing on Wadke Island off New Guinea.

It was secured after two days.

27 May US forces landed on Biak Island off New Guinea.

The Japanese garrison (11,000 men) was considerably larger than expected, and the island was well fortified. This was a disappointment to MacArthur, who had hoped to secure it quickly and use it as an air base for operations against the Philippines.

11 June US carrier-borne aircraft began to soften up Saipan in the Marianas prior to its invasion.

It had been decided to attack this island first since it was the northernmost of the group and would cut off forces on the other islands from Japan.

The Japanese had recognized for some time that the Marianas would be invaded and had devised a plan, 'A-Go', for the destruction of the US carrier force. The idea was to destroy it with aircraft based in the Marianas, combined with those of the Japanese fleet. Accordingly, at the same time as the US preliminary bombardment of Saipan began, Admiral Toyoda ordered his fleet to deploy. It consisted of three groups: the main battle fleet (Kurita) built round four battleships and three light carriers; the main carrier force (Ozawa) with three carriers; and a reserve carrier force (Joshima) with two carriers and a battleship.

The Americans, however, had gathered together the largest naval force yet seen in the Pacific. The invasion fleet, which carried three Marine and one Army divisions, alone had twelve escort carriers, five battleships and eleven cruisers. The main carrier force under Admiral Marc Mitscher, which was now carrying out the Saipan bombardment, had no less than fifteen carriers, while in support was Spruance's Fifth Fleet with seven battleships and 21 cruisers.

15 June 2nd and 4th US Marine Divisions landed on Saipan.

Although they suffered casualties on the beaches, beachheads were secured and 20,000 men had been landed by the end of the day. The Japanese garrison numbered 32,000 men. Admiral Toyoda gave out final orders for the destruction of Mitscher's carrier task force.

17 June US 27th Division began to land on Saipan.

Progress in advancing inland was slow in the face of fierce Japanese resistance. This was not helped by the fact that air support had been substantially reduced since Mitscher's aircraft were 'softening up' Guam and preparing to meet the Japanese fleet, whose approach had been spotted by US submarines.

19–20 June Battle of the Philippine Sea.

The Japanese began by launching four aircraft strikes at the US carriers. These were detected by radar and intercepted. The result was that 219 Japanese aircraft were shot down for the loss of 29 American. Two Japanese carriers were sunk by US submarines. Ozawa believed that most of his aircraft had landed on Guam and waited overnight to recover them. Next day Mitscher's aircraft located the Japanese carrier force and attacked it. One carrier was sunk and several other warships damaged, as well as a further 65 Japanese aircraft shot down. Ozawa now withdrew towards Okinawa. Such had been his losses in aircrews that the back of the Japanese naval air power was broken and would never recover. The Americans dubbed the action 'The Great Marianas Turkey Shoot'. On Saipan the US forces were beginning to make some progress in clearing the island.

25 June Mount Tapotchau, the dominant height on Saipan, captured.

30 June Biak Island off New Guinea finally secured, apart from mopping-up.

2 July US and Australian forces landed on Numfoor Island, New Guinea.

6 July Admiral Nagumo and General Saito committed suicide on Saipan.

Before they died these two top commanders ordered a final suicide attack. This took place next day and marked the end of Japanese resistance. They had lost more than 26,000 men, while the Americans had suffered 16,500 dead, wounded and sick.

18 July General Tojo resigned as Japanese Prime Minister.

His conduct of the war had come under increasing attack and his resignation was forced upon him. General Kuniaki Koiso replaced him.

21 July 1st US Marine Division landed on Guam.

The island was garrisoned by 18,000 Japanese. US 77th Infantry Division also began to land.

24 July 2nd and 4th US Marine Divisions landed on Tinian, which was held by 9,000 Japanese.

A Japanese counter-attack that night failed.

Night of 25/26 July Fierce Japanese counter-attacks on Guam.

All were held.

30 July US landings on the Vogelkop Peninsula at the north-west corner of New Guinea.

1 August Effective resistance ended on Tinian.

10 August Effective resistance ended on Guam.

With the capture of the Marianas and the Philippine Sea victory, defeat now began to stare the Japanese in the face. Yet in the American camp there was now a fierce debate as to what should be tackled next. This hinged on whether or not to bypass the Philippines.

Leyte Gulf · P196

The Russian Spring Offensive

The Germans hoped that with the arrival of the spring thaw they would be given a respite from the Russian attacks that had continued throughout the winter. They were, however, to be disappointed. Stalin was now determined on nothing less than the destruction of Army Groups South and A and the liberation of the remainder of western Ukraine. The offensive in the Ukraine would reopen on **4 March**.

29 February 1944 General Nikolai Vatutin ambushed by Ukrainian partisans.
The partisans were fighting for an independent Ukraine. Originally supported by the Germans against the Russian Communists, the partisans were by now fighting them as well since they had failed to set up an independent Ukrainian state. Vatutin himself, who was commanding 1st Ukrainian Front and playing a leading role in the Russian offensives in the south, was grievously wounded and died on **15 April**. His place was taken by Zhukov.

4 March 1st Ukrainian Front reopened the offensive in the Ukraine.
Konev's 2nd Ukrainian Front joined in on **5 March** and Malinovsky's 3rd Ukrainian Front on **6 March**. The main aim was to divorce Army Group South from Army Group A and then destroy them in detail. In spite of the mud the offensive initially made good progress and Zhukov alone advanced 25 miles on a 100-mile front during the first two days.

10 March Uman fell to Konev.
He had in the past few days captured 200 abandoned tanks, 600 guns and 12,000 trucks.

13 March Malinovsky liberated Kherson.

17 March Konev reached the River Dniester.
Zhukov, having swung south in order to entrap First Panzer Army, reached it a week later. On the same day Kurochkin's 2nd Belorussian Front began to attack in order to prevent the German Army Group Centre from threatening Zhukov's right flank.

19 March German troops marched into Hungary.
This was to ensure Hungary's continued allegiance and to secure her oilfields.

22 March Roumanian dictator Antonescu flew to Berlin.
The Russians were already making overtures to Roumania over signing a peace, and Antonescu wanted all Roumanian troops under German command to be used in the defence of his country. Hitler agreed that the defence of Roumania would be a priority.

25 March Konev reached the Russian-Roumanian border along the River Prut.
Stalin wanted Konev and Malinovsky to entrap the German Sixth and Eighth and Roumanian Third Armies.

28 March First Panzer Army entrapped by Zhukov and Konev.

30 March Hitler sacked von Manstein (Army Group South) and von Kleist (Army Group A).
He accused their forces of running away without fighting, but the truth was that they had been entirely surprised by the speed of the Russian advance. Both men were of proven ability, but neither was employed again. Their places were taken by Walther Model and Ferdinand Schoerner, both committed Nazis, and their commands renamed Army Groups North and South Ukraine.

30 March First Panzer Army began to break out to the west.
Aided by an attack by two SS divisions in the Podgaitsy area, Hans-Valentin Hube's men reached safety on **7 April**.

1 April Finnish delegation returned from a visit to Moscow to explore terms for an armistice.
The Russians demanded a return to the 1940 frontiers, the internment or expulsion of all German troops in the country and a $600 million war indemnity payable over five years. On **17 April** the Finnish parliament rejected these terms as unacceptable. The Finns therefore were committed to continue the fight on the German side, but they realized that their prospects for the future were nothing but grim.

2 April Konev's forces crossed the River Prut and entered Roumania.

5 April 2nd Belorussian Front disbanded.
Its offensive had advanced as far as Kovel, but here fierce German resistance prevented it from any further movement forward.

8 April Fyodor Tolbukhin's 4th Ukrainian Front began to attack into the Crimea.
Erwin Jaenicke's Seventeenth Army had been left increasingly on a limb to hold the Crimea. Next day Yeremenko's Independent Coastal Army also struck out from the Kerch bridgehead. Jaenicke was quickly forced out of his defence lines and withdrew towards Sevastopol.

10 April Malinovsky liberated Odessa.
This further isolated the German Seventeenth Army in the Crimea.

17 April Ternopol finally fell to Zhukov.
Hitler had declared this a *Fuehrer Festung*, to be defended to the last, which its garrison did. The Russian offensive in the Ukraine had now closed up to the Carpathians and was halted.

1 May Stalin announced his aims for operations during summer 1944.
These were to clear the remainder of Russian territory of Germans and liberate Poland, Czechoslovakia and the 'fraternal' Slav nations. He had undertaken to launch a major offensive to coincide with 'Overlord' and had been informed of the latter's postponement by one month at the beginning of April. His operational plan was kept very secret and during its creation only five senior officers of the Stavka were privy to it.

In essence it called for feints in the north and south and a decisive blow in the centre. The northern feint was designed to knock Finland out of the war and prevent Army Group North going to the help of Army Group Centre. The main thrust would be in Belorussia, with a subsidiary operation directed on Lvov and thence westwards to prevent the Germans moving up reserves from the south. An elaborate deception plan was evolved in order to make the Germans believe that they would be attacked again in the south and, within the framework of 'Bodyguard', that a joint Allied attack on Norway was in the offing.

5 May The Russians began their attack on Sevastopol.
By the evening of the 9th Sevastopol was in their hands and the remnant of the German Seventeenth Army had been driven back to Cape Khersonessky. Here, on **12 May**, 25,000 surrendered. The Crimea had been cleared.

22–23 May Conference to confirm the details of the Russian summer offensive (Operation 'Bagration').
This was attended by the commanders or their representatives of the fronts with the leading roles. The attack in the north would begin on **9 June** and the main attack in the centre on **22 June**, the third anniversary of 'Barbarossa'.

In the meantime there had been a reorganization of fronts. The Volkhov front had been disbanded and Meretskov now commanded the Karelian Front facing the Finns. A new 3rd Baltic Front had been formed under Maslenikov and the West Front became the 3rd Belorussian Front under Chernyakhovsky. The 2nd Belorussian was also resurrected.

As May wore on into June the commander of the German Army Group Centre, Field Marshal Ernst Busch, became convinced that the Russians were planning a major offensive against him. Hitler, while recognizing that an offensive to coincide with 'Overlord' was likely, believed that the prime Russian objective would be the seizure of the Roumanian oilfields and the overrunning of the Balkans. He therefore refused to allow Busch to shorten his front by withdrawing to the more defendable line of the River Beresina. Army Group Centre was thus left holding a vast and vulnerable salient.

P164 · The Relief of Leningrad

1939 | 1940 | 1941 | 1942 | 1943 | 1944 | 1945

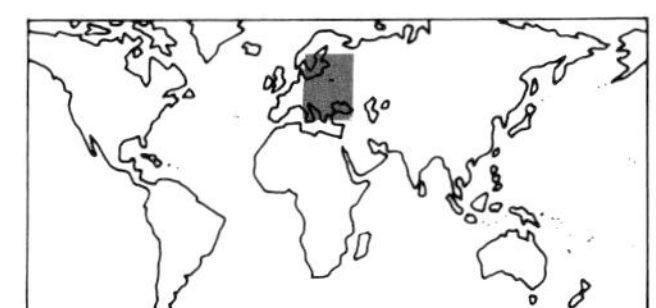

LIBERATION OF THE WESTERN UKRAINE

FINLAND
SWEDEN
Stockholm
Helsinki
Viipuri
L Ladoga
L Onega
Onega
Leningrad
KARELIAN FRONT
Gen Meretskov
LENINGRAD FRONT
Gen Govorov
Suthona
Vologda
Tallinin
Narva
ESTONIA
L Peipus
Tartu
3RD BALTIC FRONT
Gen Maslenikov
Novgorod
L Ilmen
Volga
Kostroma
Yaroslav
18th ARMY
Pskov
Ostrov
2nd BALTIC FRONT
Gen Popov
LATVIA
Riga
16th ARMY
Opochka
Kiln
BALTIC SEA
ARMY GROUP NORTH
Gen Lindemann
Dvina
Dvinsk
Nevel
1st BALTIC FRONT
Gen Yeremenko
Moscow
Copenhagen
Memel
Polotsk
Vitebsk
Oka
LITHUANIA
Kaunas
Tilsit
Niemen
3rd PANZER ARMY
Smolensk
Tula
Danzig
Koenigsberg
EAST PRUSSIA
Vilna
4th ARMY
Orsha
WEST FRONT
Gen Sokolovsky
Beresina
Minsk
Mogilev
Rastenburg
Grodno
9th ARMY
Rogachev
Bialystok
ARMY GROUP CENTRE
FM Busch
Bobruisk
Berlin
Bydgoszcz
Vistula
Jelez
Poznan
2nd ARMY
Gomel
Kursk
GREATER GERMANY
Warsaw
Siedlce
Bug
Brest-Litovsk
Pinsk
Pripet
2nd BELORUSSIAN FRONT
Gen Kurochkin
Lodz
Magnuszew
Pripet Marsh
Radom
Maidenek
Kovel
1st UKRAINIAN FRONT
Gen Zhukov
Belgorod
Breslau
Lublin
Chelm
Styr
Korosten
POLAND
Lutsk
Kiev
Kharkov
Baranow
4th PANZER ARMY
2nd UKRAINIAN FRONT
Gen Konev
Prague
17 April
Brody
Berdichev
Poltava
Cracow
San
Lvov
Dnieper
Ternopol
4 March
Cherkassy
Kremenchug
Donets
Brno
ARMY GROUP SOUTH
FM von Manstein
Podgaitsy
Bug
17 March
5 March
3rd UKRAINIAN FRONT
Gen Malinovsky
Kirovograd
Uman
10 March
Krivoy Rog
Stalino
Linz
Vienna
Bratislava
Dniester
19 March: German Troops entered Hungary
1st PANZER ARMY
(28 March)
2 April
Prut
6 March
4th UKRAINIAN FRONT
Gen Tolbukhin
Danube
Budapest
25 March
Taganrog
Melitopol
HUNGARY
4th ROUMANIAN ARMY
Jassy
Tiraspol
8th ARMY
Kherson
13 March
Odessa
10 April
INDEPENDENT COASTAL ARMY
Gen Yeremenko
Sava
Zagreb
Siretul
6th ARMY
8 April
Kerch
9 April
ARMY GROUP A
FM von Kleist
Galati
17th ARMY
Ploesti (Oil)
Sevastopol
9 May
Yalta
3rd ROUMANIAN ARMY
Bucharest
Cape Khersonessky
12 May: Germans surrender
Constanta
Danube
ROUMANIA
BLACK SEA

German front line 2 March
Russian front line 22 June

0 | 50 | 100 | 150 | 200 | 250 Miles
0 | 100 | 200 | 300 | 400 Km

The Russian Summer 1944 Offensive · P190

The Normandy Landings

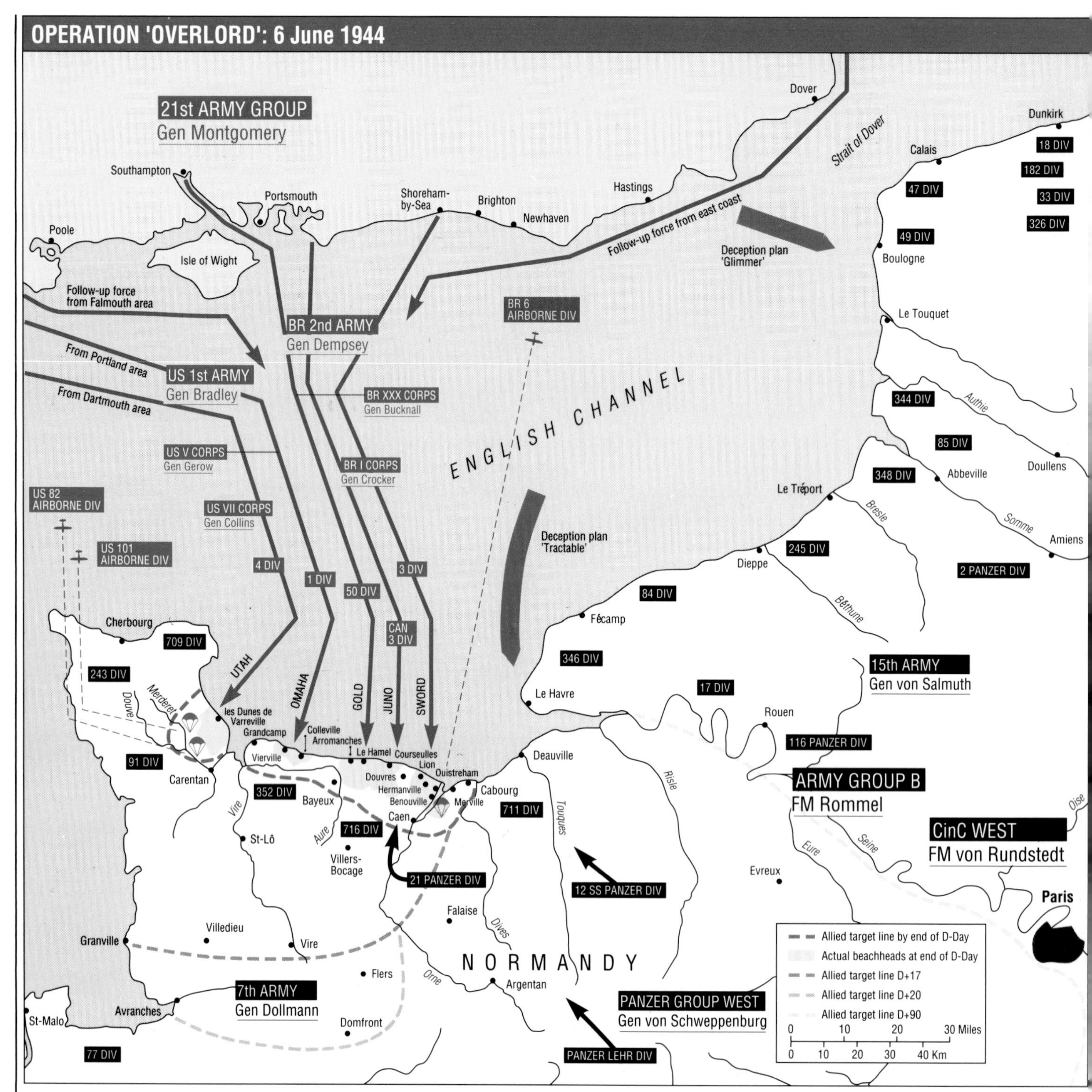

D uring the last part of May 1944 the roads of southern England were thronged with vehicles as the invasion forces moved to their final assembly areas close to the south coast. The Channel ports were filled with shipping. It was impossible to hide these preparations from the Germans and hence the deception operation, 'Fortitude', assumed an even greater importance in the overall scheme.

Thus the mythical British Fourth Army in Scotland continued to create in German eyes a threat to Norway. Likewise 'Quicksilver', the Pas-de-Calais deception, was intensified. German agents who had been 'turned' by the British transmitted mythical information on preparations in south-east England, supported by the phantom 1st Army Group, which had a real commander, George Patton, and was located, complete with dummy camps and equipment, in this area. The object was now to make the Germans believe that the Normandy landings were a feint and merely an overture to the main landings in the Pas-de-Calais.

In the skies above, the strategic and tactical air forces continued their attacks against transportation targets and were helped in this by the French Resistance. One noticeable trend, however, was a dramatic increase in the Luftwaffe's night-fighter strength, and RAF Bomber Command losses rose sharply during May. As for the German air capability by day, concentrated attacks were made on Luft-

P168 · Planning for 'Overlord'

affe airfields in northern France. Selected coastal tteries – not just in Normandy – were also peatedly attacked. Crucial, too, was the need to eep the U-boats and German surface craft at bay, d intensive air patrols were carried out.

The selection of D-Day itself was based on the eed for the invasion fleet to cross the Channel in arkness and for the troops to go ashore at low de as soon as possible after dawn. A full moon was equired for the airborne operations. There were vo periods in June that fitted these conditions, ne at the beginning of the month and one in the iddle. On **17 May** Eisenhower made his decision: -Day would be 4 June. Later this was amended 5 June.

9 May 1944 The weather forecast for the first eek in June was optimistic.
senhower received regular reports from his chief eteorologist, Group Captain J. M. Stagg, RAF.

June Eisenhower moved to his invasion HQ at ortsmouth.
y now the invasion craft were beginning to be aded with troops and their equipment.

June Weather forecast for D-Day was bad.
tagg warned Eisenhower that a depression was bout to set in and that the forecast for the 5th as overcast and stormy with a maximum cloud ase of 500 feet.

June Eisenhower postponed the invasion by 24 ours.
t 0430 hours he met Stagg and his senior com- nanders. Stagg stated that the sea conditions would e slightly better than first thought, but the 5th vould still be very overcast. Although Montgomery vanted the invasion to go ahead on the 5th, Tedder nd Leigh-Mallory argued for a postponement and isenhower endorsed this.

At 2130 hours Stagg produced another forecast. He stated that the rain would stop at about midnight nd that there would be an improvement during he next 36 hours. Eisenhower therefore confirmed)-Day as 6 June. Orders were immediately given or the invasion fleet to set sail.

June That evening the invasion fleet set off cross the Channel.
Because of the weather the Germans did not elieve that the invasion would take place. Most of the senior officers of Seventh Army were taking part in war games, and Rommel left his HQ that day for Germany in order to plead with Hitler for more troops to be sent to Normandy. Before the main landings took place there were a number of preliminary but important operations, which took place during the night of **5/6 June**.

First, RAF Bomber Command carried out two deception schemes to make the Germans believe that two other invasion fleets were sailing towards the French coast, one towards Boulogne and the other towards Le Havre. Code-named 'Glimmer' and 'Tractable' respectively, the bombers dropped 'Window' in such a way as to appear on the German radars as fleets at sea. Below them 35 vessels assisted in the deception.

At 2100 hours the BBC transmitted a coded message to the French Resistance confirming that the invasion was being mounted. It was the second half of the first verse of Paul Verlaine's poem *Chanson d'Automne*, the first half having been transmitted on the 1st. This made the Germans suspicious, but only the Fifteenth Army was put on alert.

Also, three airborne divisions began to take off to carry out their task of securing the flanks of the landings:

British 6th Airborne Division was to secure the left flank west of the River Dives, destroy bridges in the river valley, which the Germans had flooded, secure bridges over the Orne and the Caen-Ouistreham Canal and knock out the coastal battery at Merville. First to land was a glider-borne infantry company, which successfully seized the canal bridge at Benouville – thereafter and to this day it is called Pegasus Bridge. High winds scattered the parachute drop, with a number of men drowning in the Dives, but the five key bridges over the river were destroyed and the Merville battery put out of action.

US 82nd and 101st Airborne Divisions were to land north of Carentan at the base of the Cotentin Peninsula. They, too, experienced problems of high winds and were very scattered on landing. 82nd Division landed in the midst of the German 91st Division and was not able to destroy the bridges over the River Douve. Nevertheless, it was able to keep 91st Division tied down and prevented it from attacking the forces landing on *Utah* beach. 101st Division successfully seized crossings over the River Merderet, but was also unable to destroy crossings over the Douve.

Finally the Allied Air Forces dropped 1,760 tons of bombs on the beach defences.

6 June The Allies landed in Normandy.
The airborne landings, combined with 'Tractable' and 'Glimmer', threw von Rundstedt's HQ outside Paris into confusion. That a landing was about to take place in Normandy seemed very clear, but was it merely a feint? Von Rundstedt requested Hitler's permission to deploy two Panzer divisions (12th SS and Panzer Lehr) to the beaches, but was told to wait until daylight when the situation would become clearer.

In the meantime the Allied armada of 700 warships and 2,700 support ships, with 2,500 landing craft, closed on the beaches.

Utah Beach Troops of the US 4th Infantry Division were the first Allied troops to land, at 0630 hours. The current had fortuitously swept the landing craft 2,000 yards south of where they should have landed, but hit a weak point in the German defences and the troops got ashore with comparative ease. Indeed, of the 23,000 men who landed that day only 197 became casualties.

Omaha was dominated by cliffs, and the US 1st and later 29th Divisions experienced a very different action. For much of the day they were pinned down on the beaches and it was only thanks to the initiative shown by various individuals that they did manage to advance off them. A total of 55,000 men had landed by the end of the day, but there were 4,649 casualties.

Gold was the responsibility of the British 50th Division supported by 8th Armoured Brigade. They managed to get off the beaches without too much difficulty but had a stiff fight for the village of Le Hamel. Much of the success of the day was attributable to the specialized armour of 79th Armoured Division.

Juno was the beach for the 3rd Canadian Division. Here choppy water and underwater obstacles created problems in landing, but the infantry got ashore successfully and by nightfall had linked up with the British 50th Division.

Sword was the responsibility of the British 3rd Division, whose leading waves landed at 0730 hours. They managed to get off the beaches without too much difficulty and had captured Hermanville by mid-morning. Growing congestion on the beaches, a problem from which the Canadians also suffered, meant that the depth brigade was delayed in coming forward, which gave the Germans valuable time. The Commandos of 1 Special Service Brigade landed in the Ouistreham area and moved to join 6th Airborne Division.

On the German side the landings had created surprise, and defence on the beaches was not as stiff as it might have been. Total Allied air superiority and the massive naval bombardment compounded their difficulties. The immediate mobile reserve, 21st Panzer Division, had originally been sent to counter the paratroops in the Orne area, but was then switched to cover Caen. It was now that the congestion on *Juno* and *Sword* helped in giving 21st Panzer valuable time in which to redeploy, and by mid-afternoon it was in a position to deny the Allies the early capture of Caen, a D-Day objective, and prevent the Canadian and 3rd Division beachheads from linking up.

Permission to deploy 12th SS Panzer and the Panzer Lehr Divisions was not given by Hitler's HQ until mid-afternoon, but by then it was too late to bring them into action that day. Even so, Hitler remained convinced that Normandy was not the main landing.

Thus, by the end of the day, although they had not captured all the objectives laid down for D-Day, the Allies had achieved their main aim. A total of 155,000 men had been landed and the Germans would be hard pressed to drive them back into the sea.

The Fighting in Normandy · P182

The Fighting in Normandy

THE BUILD-UP: 7-30 June

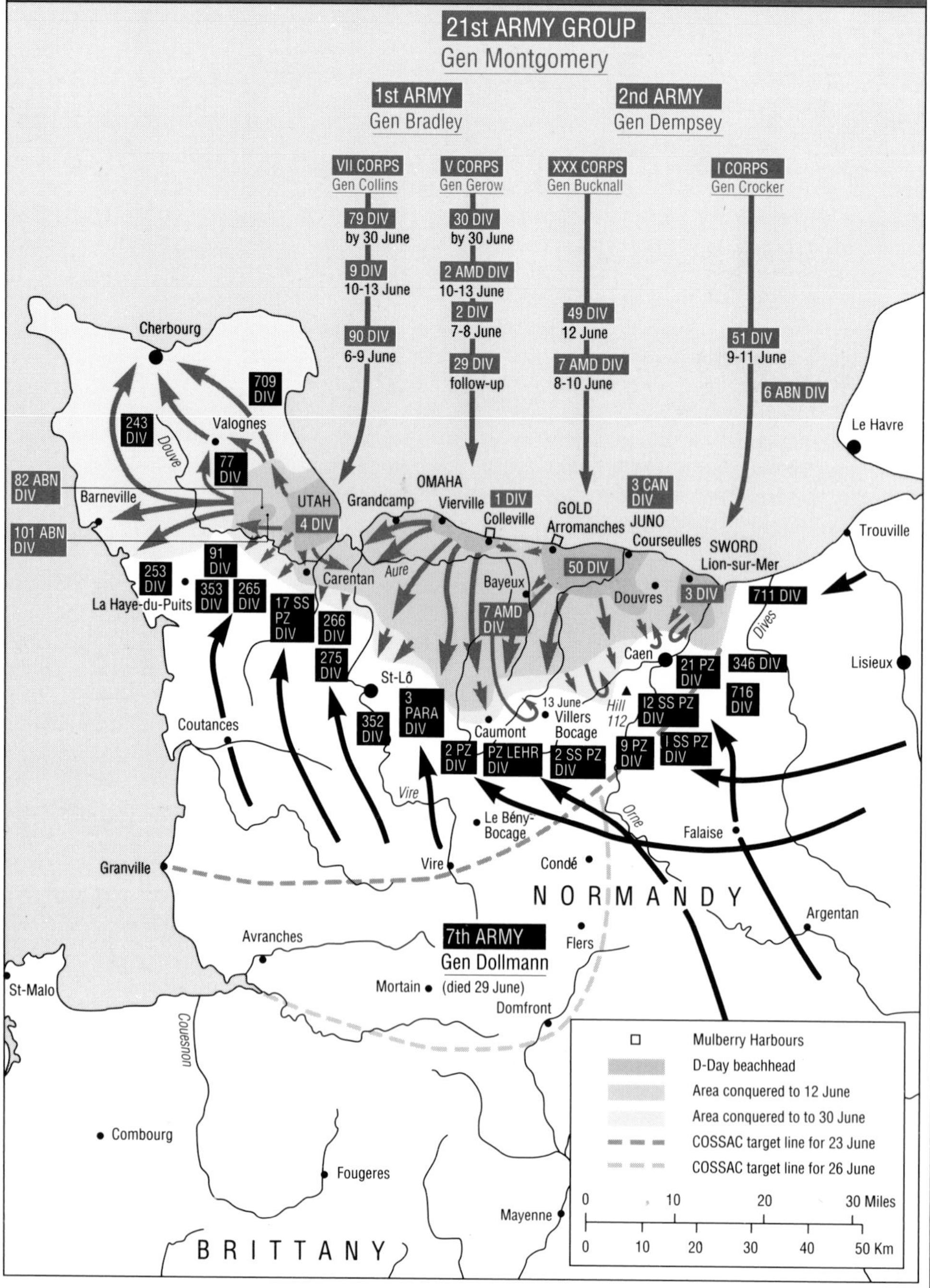

The days following 6 June in Normandy became a battle between the Allies to consolidate their beachhead and the Germans to prevent them from doing so. The latter, however, laboured under severe disadvantages. Apart from the total Allied air dominance of the beachhead and the massive weight of naval gunfire that the Allies could bring to bear, the success of the transportation bombing campaign meant that reserves could seldom be moved other than by very circuitous routes to the battlefield. Consequently the German armour especially could only be committed piecemeal. This situation was not helped by the fact that Hitler remained convinced that another blow would come east of the Seine and refused to allow any formations to be transferred from Fifteenth Army.

7–8 June 1944 **Renewed attempts by 3rd Canadian Division to capture Caen.**
These were foiled by the newly arrived 12th SS Panzer Division (Hitler Youth) which launched some fierce counter-attacks, displaying a fanaticism that was to be their hallmark in Normandy. Bayeux was occupied by the British 50th Division on the 7th and a link up made with the *Omaha* beachhead.

11–14 June **British attempt to take Caen fro[m] the west failed.**
7th Armoured Division thrust south of Bayeux an[d] then turned east but was foiled by a Tiger tan[k] company of 12th SS Division at Villers-Bocage an[d] by the arrival of 2nd Panzer Division, which fille[d] the one remaining gap in the German defences.

12 June **Carentan captured and *Omaha* and *Uta[h]* linked up.**
The Americans now turned west and north to clea[r] the Cotentin Peninsula.

17 June **Conference between von Rundstedt, Rommel and Hitler at Soissons.**
Rommel demanded the evacuation of the Cotenti[n] Peninsula, but Hitler refused this.

18 June **US VII Corps reached the west coast o[f] the Cotentin Peninsula at Barneville.**

19–22 June **Violent storm in the Channel.**
This badly damaged both 'Mulberry' harbours an[d] put a serious brake on the build-up of supplies i[n] the beachhead. By this stage the Allied strength i[n] Normandy had grown to twenty divisions as agains[t] sixteen German.

22–27 June **The battle for Cherbourg.**
The German commander had been ordered t[o] defend the port to the last and when it was finall[y] captured the dock installations had been destroye[d] and would take some weeks to be made operationa[l] once more.

26–30 June **Operation 'Epsom' – an attempt b[y] the British VIII Corps to break through the Germa[n] lines west of Caen.**
An advance of six miles was made and the dominan[t] Hill 112 captured, but counter-attacks from the wes[t] by the newly arrived II SS Panzer Corps persuade[d] Dempsey to withdraw to the west bank of th[e] Odon.

29 June **Second Hitler, von Rundstedt, Romme[l] conference.**
This was held at Berchtesgaden, Hitler's retreat i[n] the Alps. Hitler demanded the containment of th[e] beachhead and its liquidation, but von Rundsted[t] lacked the infantry to be able to withdraw an[d] concentrate his Panzer divisions for a major attack. Von Rundstedt and Rommel therefore proposed a[n] evacuation of Normandy which Hitler turned down. As a result, on **2 July** von Rundstedt resigned an[d] his place was taken by von Kluge.

3 July **First US Army began to attack south towards St-Lô.**
The US troops found it slow going given the close nature of the *bocage* countryside and stiff Germa[n] resistance.

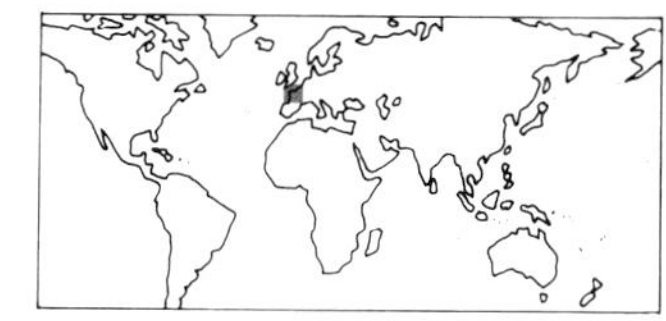

OPERATIONS 'COBRA' AND 'GOODWOOD': 1-31 July

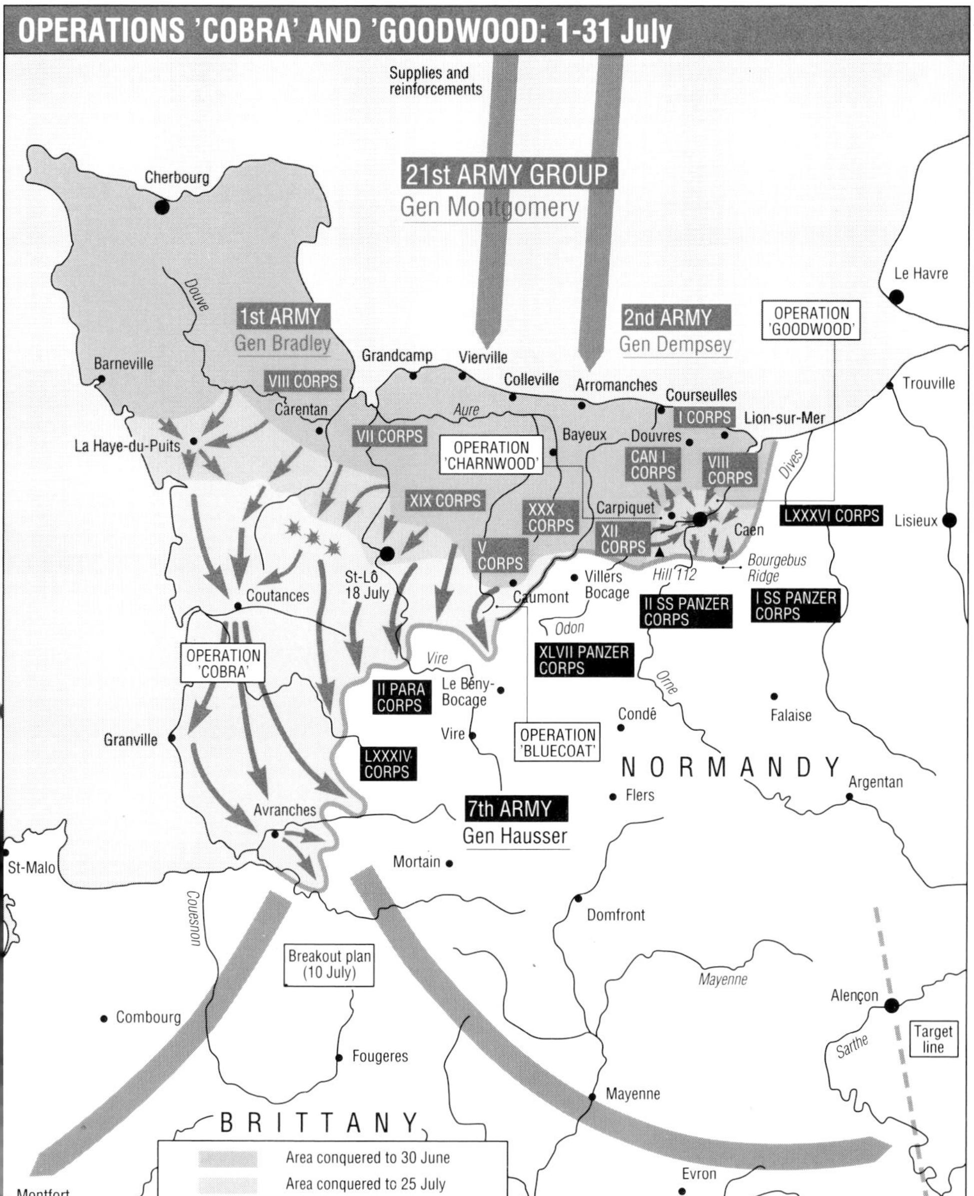

4 July The Canadians attacked Carpiquet west of Caen.
They met bitter resistance from 12th SS Panzer Division and failed to secure the airfield.

8–11 July Operation 'Charnwood', another British attempt to capture Caen.
Preceded by an RAF Bomber Command attack on the city on the night of 7th/8th elements of I British and I Canadian Corps recaptured Hill 112 and broke into Caen. A fanatical defence by 12th SS Panzer Division prevented them from clearing the southern part of the city.

10 July Montgomery issued a directive for the future conduct of operations in Normandy.
In order to relieve pressure on Bradley and draw the German weight back to the east, Dempsey was to launch a massed armour attack east of Caen (Operation 'Goodwood'). Once Bradley had secured St-Lô he was to swing east towards the line Alençon – Le Mans and west to clear Brittany.

17 July Rommel was gravely wounded.
He was returning to his HQ from a visit to Sepp Dietrich's I SS Corps when his car was shot up by RAF fighters. Von Kluge took over Army Group B.

18 July Operation 'Goodwood' opened.
No less than 6,800 tons of bombs were dropped by British and US bombers on the German defences at dawn. Immediately after this 7th, 11th and Guards Armoured Divisions began to roll forward and initially were very successful. The Germans now began to recover, harrying them from the east flank and bringing up tanks from I SS Panzer Corps on to the dominating Bourgebus Ridge. At the same time the Canadians managed to liberate the remainder of Caen. By the end of the day the British armour had been halted at the foot of the ridge. For the next two days the British struggled, with little success, to gain the ridge. In all they lost 400 tanks. The Americans believed that Montgomery had tried to break out on his own and had failed. In truth, though, 'Goodwood' did achieve the aim of bringing the German strength back to the east, thus facilitating 'Cobra', Bradley's break-out.

18 July St-Lô finally fell to the Americans.

20 July Failed attempt against Hitler's life.
This was the famous 'Bomb Plot' executed at Hitler's HQ, the Wolf's Lair at Rastenburg, East Prussia. High ranking officers in Berlin tried to take over the capital, but were foiled by a quick-thinking Goebbels. In Paris the Military Governor of occupied France, General Karl von Stuelpnagel, arrested SS, Gestapo and Nazi officials in the capital, but was forced to release them when he failed to get hoped for support from von Kluge. The conspirators were all arrested and either shot on the spot or subjected to show trials a few months later and hanged, apart from a lucky few. Rommel, who was implicated, was forced to take his own life on **14 October**. The overall result of the plot was to make Hitler distrust his generals even more.

25 July Operation 'Cobra' launched.
It began with the dropping of 4,000 tons of bombs on the German defences. Some fell short, causing 600 US casualties, including General Lesley McNair who had overall responsibility for the training of the US Army and had come to watch the start of the offensive. The main attack was carried out by Lawton Collins' VII Corps and after 36 hours' of fighting the German defences had been broken. By the 31st, Avranches had been captured and the Americans were poised to exploit their success west into Brittany and east towards Le Mans.

30 July British Second Army launched Operation 'Bluecoat'.
This was a thrust south from Caumont towards Vire and was designed to continue to keep as much German attention as possible away from the Americans. By this stage the German forces in Normandy were on the edge of a total collapse. Indeed, there seemed every prospect that they would be totally annihilated.

Normandy Break-Out

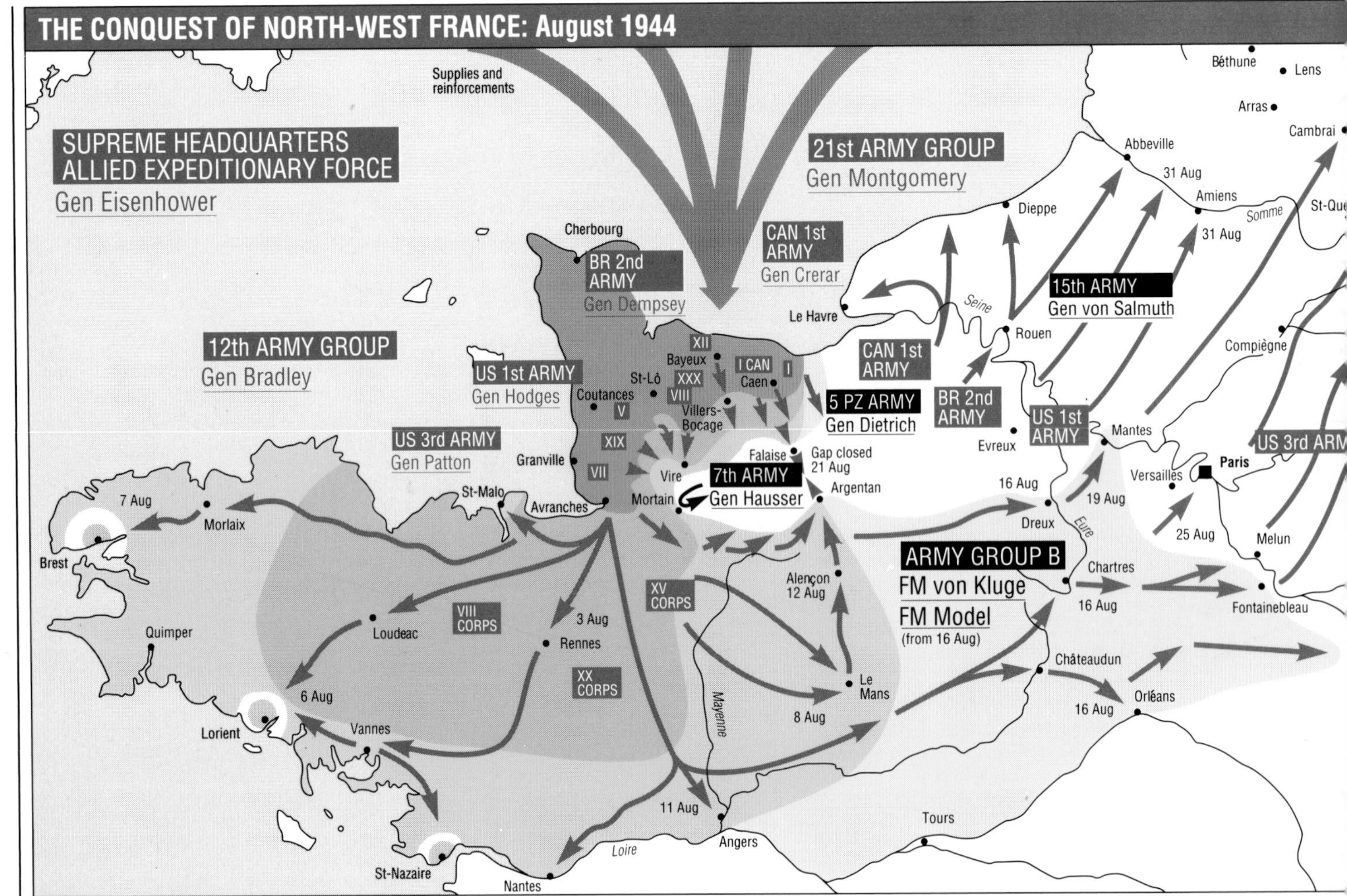

On 1 August 1944 there was a re-organization of the Allied ground forces in Normandy. Third US Army, which had been arriving under great secrecy during the past month, was formally activated. Now that there were two US armies in the theatre, 12th Army Group was created to command them and Omar Bradley was placed in charge. This put him on the same level as Montgomery, but Eisenhower laid down that the latter would continue to exercise operational control over the Allied ground forces until the Supreme Headquarters Allied Expeditionary Force (SHAEF) could establish itself on the Continent. Appointed in Bradley's place to command First US Army was Courtney Hodges.

On this same day Patton's Third Army was unleashed into Brittany and south towards the River Loire and then east. In the meantime two US corps from First Army were advancing towards Vire and British Second Army towards Villers-Bocage.

Hitler was still determined that there should be no withdrawal from Normandy and at the same time had sent General Walter Warlimont of his Operations Staff to Normandy to ensure that von Kluge kept the Allies contained and wore them down with spoiling attacks.

3 August 1944 Third US Army began to attack Rennes.

The Germans withdrew from it that night. On the same day Mortain was captured.

6 August Patton's troops reached Lorient.

As with the other ports in north-west France this had been declared a fortress by Hitler. It was to hold out until the end of the war in Europe.

Night of 6/7 August German counter-attack at Mortain opened (Operation 'Luttich').

Carried out by three weak Panzer divisions and parts of two other divisions, this struck US First Army's VII Corps north and south of Mortain. 'Ultra', however, had forewarned the Allies and although there was some fierce fighting the Germans were contained, with significant assistance from Allied tactical air power, and forced back. By the 15th it was all over and US VII Corps had recovered Mortain.

Also on the 7th, US VIII Corps (Third Army) reached Brest, whose garrison of 36,000 refused to surrender and another siege began. By this time, too, Patton's break-out to the east had crossed the River Mayenne.

7 August Eisenhower set up an advanced command post in Normandy.

This was near Granville, but since he was still commuting back and forth across the Channel Montgomery continued to retain operational control.

Night of 7/8 August Canadian First Army mounted Operation 'Totalize'.

This was a thrust south of Caen with the objective of Falaise. The aim was to cut off the withdrawal routes of the German forces facing British Second Army. In spite of massive bombing attacks from the air the Canadians' old adversaries, 12th SS Panzer Division, put up a dogged resistance and not until the 16th did Falaise finally fall.

8 August Patton liberated Le Mans.

By this time his forces were rapidly gaining momentum.

12 August Haislip's US XV Corps reached Alençon.

Patton now directed it north to Argentan. His object was to close the gap with the Canadians at Falaise and hence trap the remnants of the German Fifth

P182 · The Fighting in Normandy

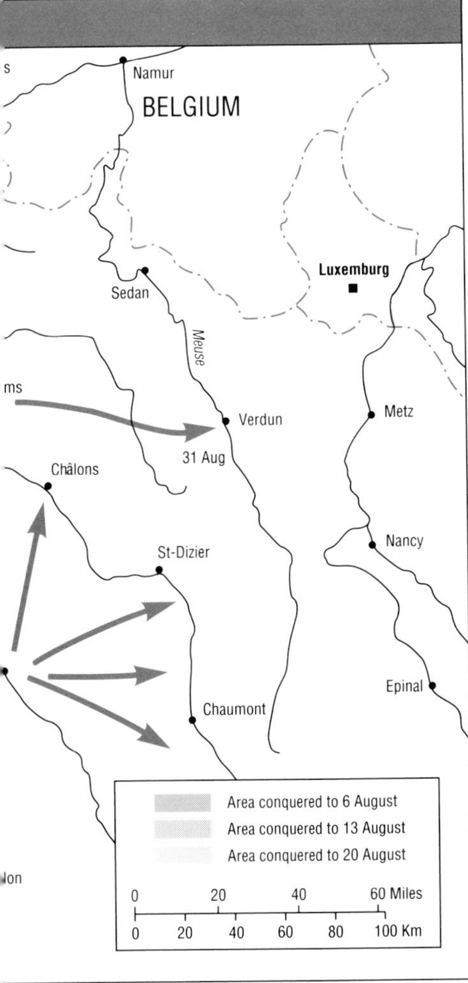

OPERATION 'DRAGOON'

Panzer and Seventh Armies. Meanwhile, his other two corps in the break-out to the east were driving north-east towards Paris.

13 August Bradley ordered Patton to halt his XV Corps south of Argentan.
He had now crossed the boundary between 12th and 21st Army Groups and there was a danger of friendly forces firing on one another. On this same day, von Kluge, realizing the trap that was being created, began to withdraw his troops from the Falaise pocket.

15 August The Allies landed in the South Of France (Operation 'Dragoon' – formerly 'Anvil').
Throughout the summer Churchill had continued to argue without success for its cancellation in order to enable the offensive in Italy to continue. At the beginning of August he then proposed that it should be mounted against Brest in order to hasten the opening of it as an Allied port. Eisenhower, however, supported by Roosevelt and the Combined Chiefs of Staff, was insistent on the early capture of Marseilles so that additional Allied forces could be quickly brought into the NW Europe theatre.

The initial landings were carried out by the three divisions of Lucian Truscott's US VI Corps, supported by French Commandos and a paratroop landing by 1st Airborne Task Force north-west of Fréjus, between Cannes and Hyères. German resistance was weak. Blaskowitz's Army Group G had lost much of First Army, which had been redeployed north, and the remainder were tied up in combating the French Maquis. This left Friedrich Wiese's Nineteenth Army with just seven divisions to cover the whole of the southern French coast.

Within three days the French Army B (Jean de Lattre de Tassigny) and US Seventh Army (Alexander Patch) were ashore, with the former advancing on Marseilles and Toulon and the latter Cannes and Nice.

16 August Hitler sacked von Kluge.
He had been under suspicion for complicity in the July Bomb Plot, but his order to withdraw from the Falaise pocket and the fact that he had spent the 15th out of contact with his HQ, having been pinned down by Allied air attacks, made Hitler believe that he was trying to make a separate peace with the Allies. Walter Model was sent to replace him. Von Kluge himself was summoned back to Berlin to explain himself, but committed suicide on the 19th while flying between Paris and Metz.

With the Canadian capture of Falaise that evening the neck of the pocket from which the Germans were trying to escape became even narrower. Throughout this time the Allied air forces were remorselessly bombarding the troops within the pocket.

To the south Patton's men captured Châteaudun, Dreux, Chartres and Orléans.

19 August Uprising by the French in Paris.
This was initiated by General Marie-Pierre Koenig's French Forces of the Interior (FFI), an amalgam of all the Resistance groups. The US 79th Division secured a crossing across the River Seine at Mantes.

21 August The Falaise pocket finally closed.
This came about as a result of the US First Army, which had relieved XV Corps in the area, taking Argentan, and the Canadians and Poles driving down from Falaise. The Allies captured 50,000 prisoners and the Germans left 10,000 dead and enormous quantities of *matériel* in the pocket. Some 30,000 had succeeded in escaping across the Seine. Hitler had finally given Model permission to do this on the previous day. The Allied armies now wheeled east and began to cross the Seine in line.

23 August Hitler ordered the governor of Paris, General Dietrich von Choltitz, to raze Paris.
By this time von Choltitz had signed a temporary truce with the FFI, largely thanks to the intermediary efforts of Raoul Nordling, the Swedish consul-general in the capital. On the same day Philippe Leclerc's 2nd French Armoured Division and Raymond Barton's 4th US Infantry Division were sent to liberate Paris.

25 August French and US troops entered Paris.
The German garrison put up some resistance, but in the afternoon von Choltitz, who had been playing for time over Hitler's order of the 23rd, surrendered. That evening de Gaulle arrived in the capital, making a triumphant formal entry on foot next day. There was some danger that the Communists might try and seize control, but during the next few days de Gaulle foiled this and retained power for himself.

28 August Toulon and Marseilles liberated.
By now US Seventh Army was advancing up the east bank of the Rhône and the French began to move up the west bank. In the north the Allies were crossing the Seine on a broad front.

29 August Patton's troops entered Reims.

31 August The British captured Amiens and crossed the River Somme. On the same day the Americans established a bridgehead across the Meuse near Verdun. It seemed as though the German armies in the west had been totally routed and that the Allies would be entering Germany within weeks. As the Allied drive increased in momentum, however, a growing problem developed. Still heavily reliant on the Mulberry harbours, since Cherbourg was not fully functioning and no other major port in the north had yet been secured, ever-stretching supply lines began to lead to increasing fuel shortages. This problem was to trigger a major strategy debate among the Allies.

Montgomery's Gamble · P200

Securing the Arctic Convoy Route

At Casablanca in **January 1943** it had been agreed that the convoys to Russia would be maintained during the summer of 1943 except during the period of the Sicily landings. Three factors combined to reverse this decision. The crisis of March 1943 in the Battle of the Atlantic renewed the need for as many escorts as possible to be deployed with the Atlantic convoys. The German naval CinC, Karl Doenitz, had managed to persuade Hitler to revoke his decision to scrap his surface fleet. Consequently, also in March 1943, *Tirpitz*, accompanied by *Scharnhorst* and *Luetzow*, returned to the area of the North Cape, from where she could pose a grave threat to the Arctic convoys. Thirdly, the Russians, despite their demands for the convoys to be maintained, began to make difficulties at Murmansk, ordering two British radio stations there to close.

Throughout the summer of 1943, therefore, there were no convoys to the northern Russian ports, and the German capital ships lay at anchor in Altenfiord. In the meantime, the U-boat threat in the Atlantic had been brought under control. As the summer wore on the Admiralty drew up a plan for destroying *Tirpitz* and her consorts, using midget submarines known as X-Craft.

8 September 1943 ***Tirpitz*** **and** ***Scharnhorst*** **bombarded the Norwegian weather station on Spitzbergen.**
This was the first time that either ship had been to sea for some time and *Scharnhorst*'s captain considered that his crew needed more gunnery training and put to sea almost immediately on return to Altenfiord.

22 September British X-Craft entered Altenfiord.
Six midget submarines were involved, but two of these broke their tow while on passage to Altenfiord and were lost. A third developed a number of defects while in the fiord. With *Scharnhorst* at sea and *Luetzow* having just moved to a new and as yet undetected anchorage, *Tirpitz* was the only target left. Two of the X-craft managed to fix charges to her hull and were then forced to surface and surrender. Their charges successfully detonated, wrecking *Tirpitz*'s engines, buckling a rudder and putting two turrets out of action. The other X-craft arrived after the explosives had detonated and was sunk by gunfire.

Next day *Luetzow* set sail for Germany and a refit, leaving only *Scharnhorst* and five destroyers to threaten the northern convoy route.

1 October Churchill telegraphed Stalin that the Arctic convoys would be resumed in mid-November.
He stressed that there was 'no contract or bargain' involved and warned of the difficulties involved,

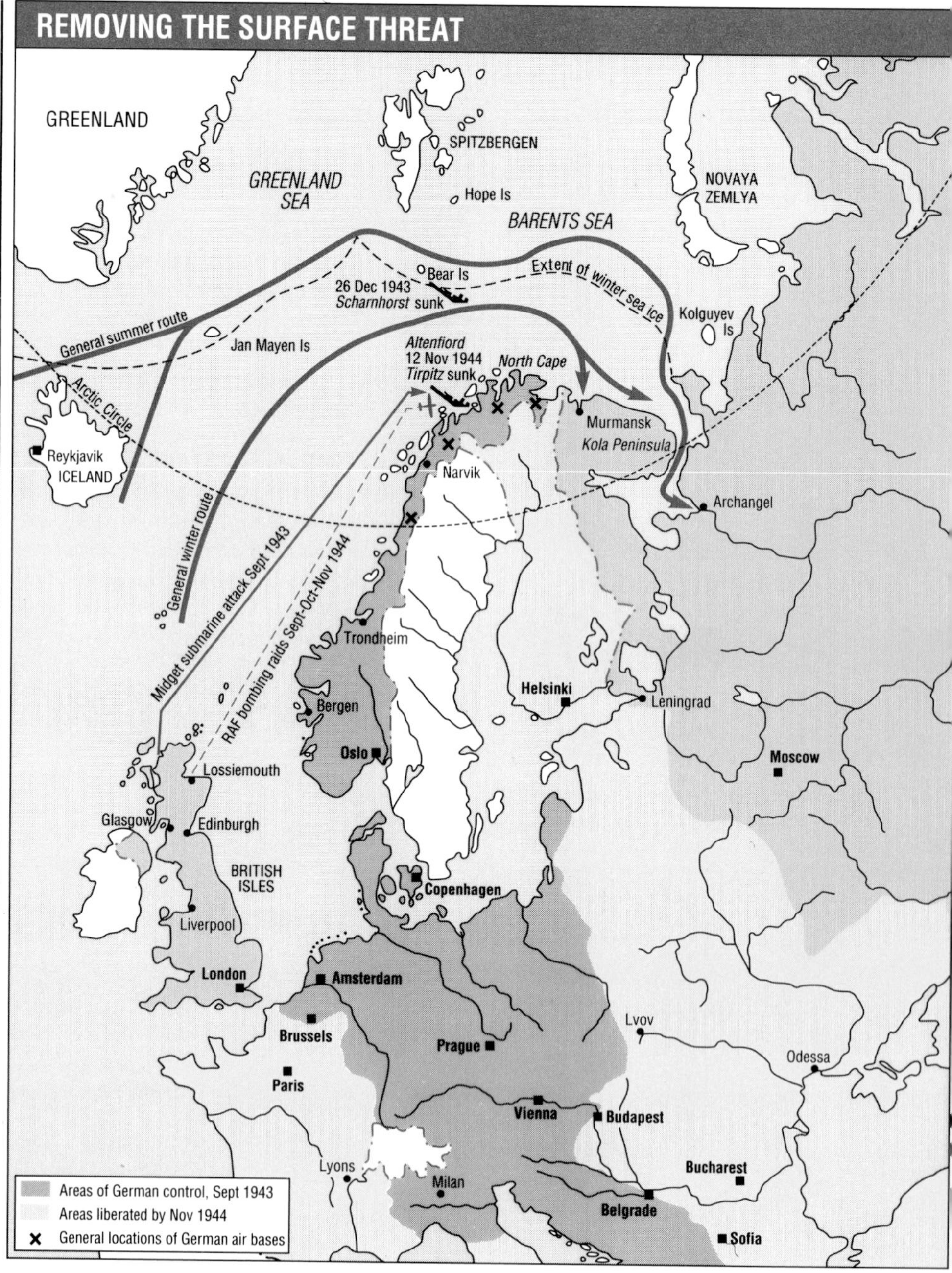

pointing to the Germans' new acoustic torpedo, which threatened escorts in the Atlantic, and the demands on shipping in the Mediterranean. He also requested better treatment for British personnel based at the northern ports. Two weeks later Stalin replied, stating that Britain was obliged to send the convoys. He displayed little sympathy for the plight of the British personnel in north Russia. The telegram was returned to the Russian Ambassador to London 'unread'; nevertheless it was decided to send one convoy to Russia every four weeks.

15 November Convoy JW54A sailed for Russia.
This was just after a convoy of thirteen empty merchant vessels, which had spent the summer in north Russia, had returned to Britain without German interference. Admiral Sir Bruce Fraser, CinC, British Home Fleet, hoped to be able to tempt *Scharnhorst* into battle, and when convoy JW55A sailed from Scotland on **12 December** he took the battleship *Duke of York* to the Barents Sea. There was no German reaction to this convoy.

Doenitz's policy had been to wait until he could deploy his new Type XXI U-boats, with their schnorkel apparatus, which enabled them to stay underwater for long periods, and higher sub-surface speeds, before launching another major offensive on Allied shipping. To do nothing, however, would reduce the standing of the *Kriegsmarine* in Hitler's eyes; hence with the resumption of the Arctic convoys he decided to use the battlecruiser *Scharnhorst* against them.

P108 · Allied Aid to Russia

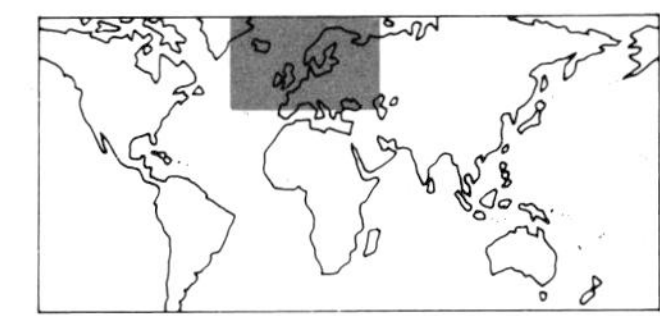

BATTLE OF THE NORTH CAPE

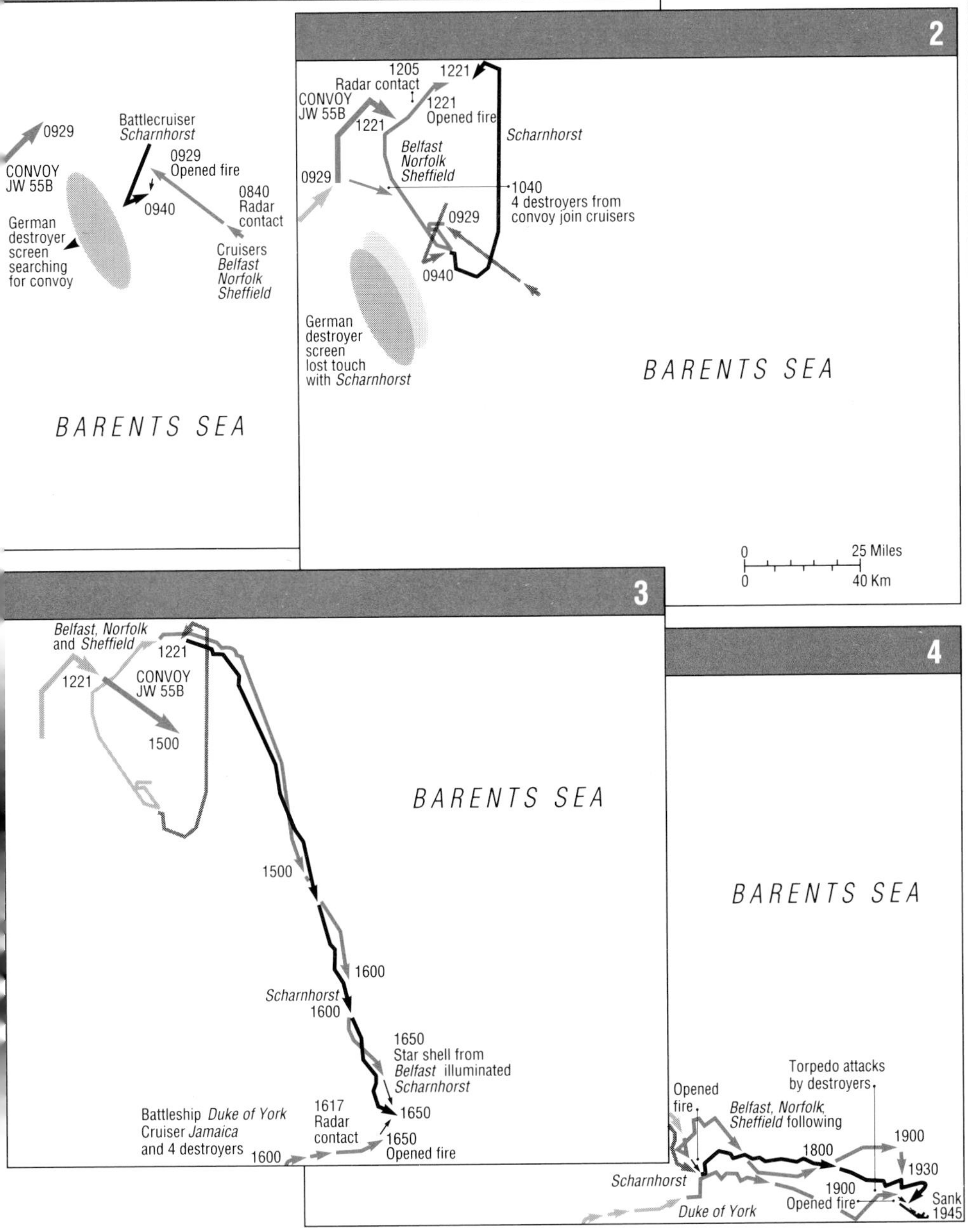

1

0929
Battlecruiser *Scharnhorst*
0929 Opened fire
CONVOY JW 55B
0940
0840 Radar contact
German destroyer screen searching for convoy
Cruisers *Belfast* *Norfolk* *Sheffield*
BARENTS SEA

2

1205
1221
Radar contact
CONVOY JW 55B
1221
1221 Opened fire
Scharnhorst
Belfast *Norfolk* *Sheffield*
0929
1040 4 destroyers from convoy join cruisers
0929
0940
German destroyer screen lost touch with *Scharnhorst*
BARENTS SEA
0 25 Miles
0 40 Km

3

Belfast, Norfolk and *Sheffield*
1221
1221
CONVOY JW 55B
1500
BARENTS SEA
1500
1600
Scharnhorst 1600
1650 Star shell from *Belfast* illuminated *Scharnhorst*
Battleship *Duke of York* Cruiser *Jamaica* and 4 destroyers 1600
1617 Radar contact
1650
1650 Opened fire

4

BARENTS SEA
Opened fire
Torpedo attacks by destroyers
Belfast, Norfolk, Sheffield following
1900
1800
1930
Scharnhorst
1900 Opened fire
Sank 1945
Duke of York

20 December Convoy JW55B left Loch Ewe, Scotland for Russia.
Two days later it was spotted by aircraft and *Scharnhorst* prepared to put to sea. Also on the 20th RA55A left Kola for Britain and passed Bear Island undetected.

Night of 25/26 December *Scharnhorst* and her destroyers set sail to intercept JW55B.
On Fraser's orders, the convoy escort had been reinforced by four destroyers from RA55A. In support of the convoy and west of it were *Duke of York*, a cruiser and four destroyers. To its east was a squadron of three cruisers. These two forces remained undetected by German aircraft, which had continued to track the convoy.

26 December The Battle of North Cape.
At 0700 hours the German Rear-Admiral, Bey, ordered his destroyers to fan out ahead to locate the convoy. Two hours later the British cruiser squadron, having detected *Scharnhorst* on radar, closed and opened fire, scoring two hits before the German ship veered away. The cruisers then moved to form a protective screen for the convoy. Spotting *Scharnhorst* again at 1205 hours, they once more opened fire and again she shied away. In the meantime Fraser had been steaming east to cut off *Scharnhorst* from Altenfiord. At 1617 hours he first detected *Scharnhorst* and opened fire half an hour later. At 1945 hours *Scharnhorst* sank. There were only 36 survivors. Next day JW55B reached Murmansk. Thus the main threat to the Arctic convoys was removed, but the British were still concerned that *Tirpitz* might be refurbished and determined to sink her.

3 April 1944 British carrier-borne aircraft attacked *Tirpitz* in Altenfiord.
Altenfiord was out of range of UK-based bombers and it had taken time to assemble the necessary carriers. Two waves of Barracuda dive-bombers, escorted by fighters, struck the ship shortly after dawn. She was, having been recently repaired, about to undergo deep-water trials, but although repeatedly hit by bombs, did not suffer as much damage as expected and was out of commission for only three months. During the next four months the Royal Navy made six further attempts against *Tirpitz*, but these were foiled either by bad weather or by the ship's defences.

15 September 9 and 617 Squadrons RAF attacked *Tirpitz* with 12,000lb bombs.
They had flown to the Russian air base of Yagodnik. One bomb hit and caused severe damage. *Tirpitz* was now, with a speed of 8 knots, hardly seaworthy and Doenitz decided that she could best be used as a gun platform to help ward off an Allied invasion of Norway. He therefore ordered her to proceed to Haakoy Island near Tromso. This put her within range of UK-based bombers.

29 October 9 and 617 Squadrons struck again.
They were foiled by poor visibility and no hits were recorded. The Germans now deployed fighters to a nearby airfield in order to protect *Tirpitz*.

12 November Third attack on *Tirpitz* by 9 and 617 Squadrons.
They took off from Lossiemouth in north-east Scotland, and at least two of their bombs struck the target. There was an internal explosion and *Tirpitz* turned turtle. Some 1,000 of her crew perished. The German fighters failed to scramble in time and only one of the 29 Lancasters taking part was damaged, but made a successful forced landing in neutral Sweden.

Thus the German surface threat from Norway, which had so influenced Allied maritime strategy, had been removed. This did not mean, however, that the Arctic convoys would now get through without casualties; the air and sub-surface threats remained. Nevertheless, from August 1944 until April 1945 more than 250 Allied merchant ships would successfully make the passage, carrying in excess of one million tons of *matériel* for the Russian war machine.

In the Atlantic the new superior U-boats continued to sink both merchant ships and escorts. But they were never the threat that they had once been and Germany's growing shortage of oil put an increasing brake on their activities.

The End in Europe · P226

German Miracle Weapons

As early as **8 November 1942** Hitler had made public mention of new secret weapons that would strike the Allies 'dumb'. Although he did not specify what they were he was referring to the V-1 flying bomb and V-2 rocket, then under development at the experimental base of Peenemuende on the Baltic coast, jet fighter aircraft and a new breed of U-boat. More and more, as German fortunes waned and disaster began to loom, did he believe that these could change the course of the war. Many Germans, believing that Unconditional Surrender offered them less than nothing, began to pin their hopes on them. It was, however, the V-weapons that were to cause the Western Allies, especially the British, the greatest concern.

The fact that the Allies were aware of the V-weapon development as early as the end of 1942, and the successful attack on Peenemuende by RAF Bomber Command on the night of **17/18 August 1943** have already been mentioned (see page 139). The result of the raid was to make the Germans move the manufacture of them to the Harz Mountains and for experimental flights to be made over Poland. Hitler remained convinced that V-weapons could change Germany's fortunes.

In September 1943 it became clear to the British that the Germans were developing not just a rocket, but a pilotless aircraft as well, what later became known as the 'flying bomb'. Indeed the Germans had begun work on this, as an offshoot of their work on jet engines, in 1939.

28 October 1943 An RAF reconnaissance pilot successfully obtained a photograph of a V-1 launch ramp near Abbeville.

Six in the area had been reported by a French agent and the other five were also identified. By the end of November 72 launch sites had been identified and all appeared to point at London.

21 December Allied air forces began to bomb the V-1 launch sites under the code-name 'Crossbow'.

During the period leading up to D-Day RAF Bomber Command and the US Eighth and Ninth Army Air Forces attacked and destroyed all 96 sites that had been constructed.

27 April 1944 Photographic interpretation revealed that the Germans were installing a new type of V-1 launch site.

This was prefabricated and hence comparatively mobile. The sites were positioned close to French

WAR IN THE AIR: Summer 1944 to spring 1945

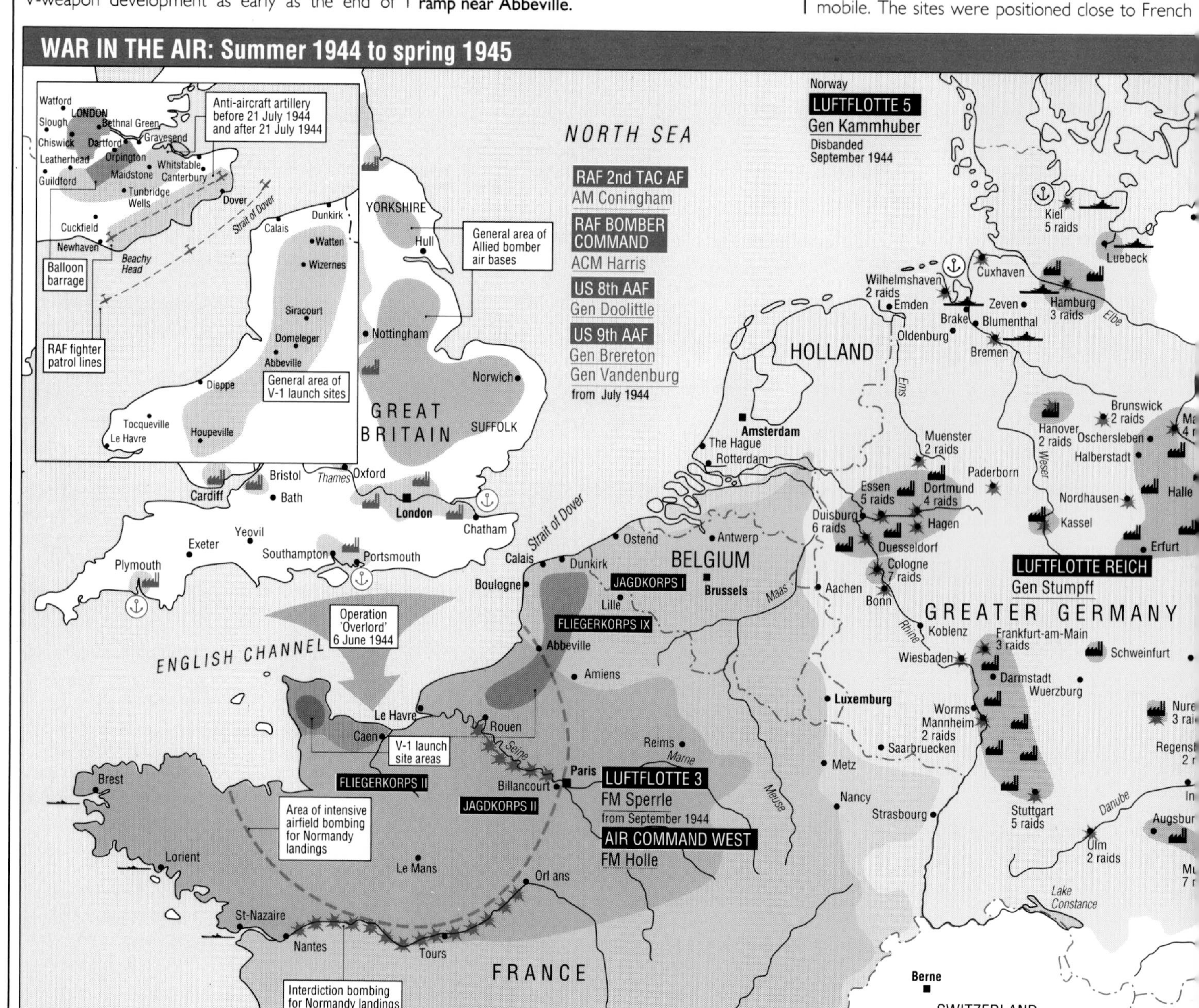

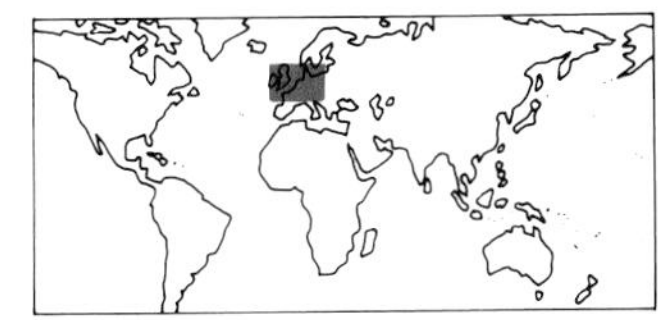

villages, which made them difficult to attack. The bombing effort was therefore concentrated on V-1 missile supply sites.

13 June **First V-1s fired against England.**
Although the Germans had by now constructed more than 70 launch sites in north-east France, only 55 were fitted with launch rails. Many of these lacked necessary safety equipment and 155th Flak Regiment, which operated them, was still short of training. Consequently only ten missiles were fired, of which four exploded on the launch pad and two crashed into the sea. The first V-1 to land in England did so at the village of Swanscombe between Dartford and Gravesend on the Thames Estuary. The others fell on Cuckfield, Sussex, Sevenoaks, Kent and Bethnal Green in east London. The only fatal casualties were six killed at Bethnal Green.

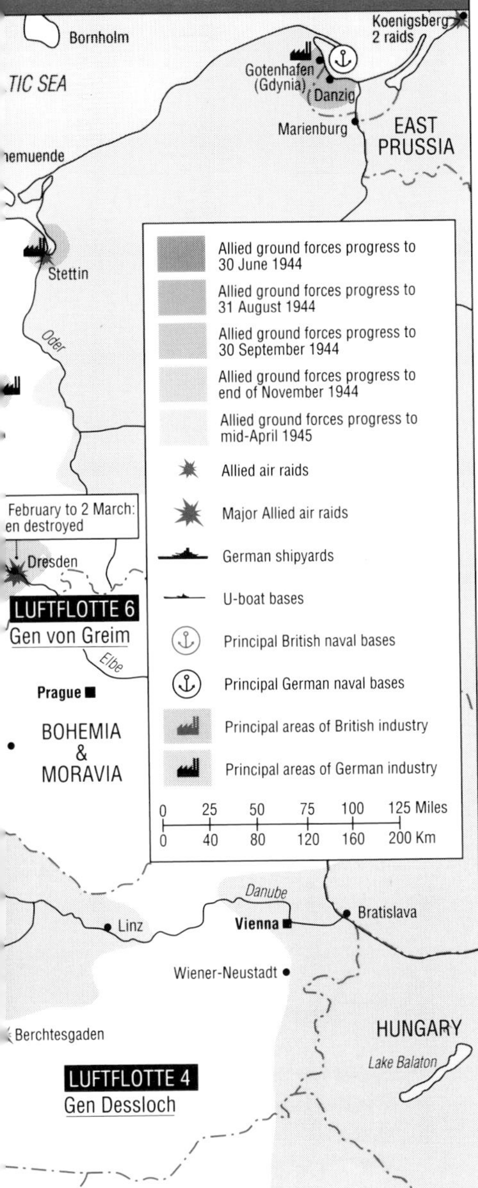

There was now a short pause while the Germans improved the sites.

15 June **V-1 offensive resumed.**
244 missiles were launched from 55 sites in 24 hours. 144 reached the English coast and 73 fell on Greater London. During the next few weeks England was hit by an average of 100 per day. Most fell in the London area and there were heavy casualties. Some one and a half million people evacuated London. The air defences were thrown into a dilemma since it was recognized that to shoot the V-1s down over built-up areas would cause just as much damage.

21 July **London's anti-aircraft guns were moved to the south coast.**
From then on matters improved. The guns were able to shoot down the V-1s over the sea, while in front and behind them fighters also joined in. It was now that the RAF's first operational jet fighter, the Gloster Meteor, which entered service on **12 July** with 616 Squadron (twelve days after the first German operational jet, the Me 262, did), was first blooded in combat. On **4 August** a Meteor, its guns jammed, succeeded in tipping over a V-1, marking the first successful jet versus jet action. On the same day another Meteor shot down a V-1.

28 August **Only four out of 94 V-1s successfully launched got through to London.**
65 were destroyed by anti-aircraft guns, 23 by fighters and four by the last defence line in front of London, barrage balloons. In the meantime the Allied forces had been attacking launch and supply sites wherever they could find them.

7 September **The British Government announced that 'except possibly for a few last shots, the Battle of London is over . . .'**
By now the Pas-de-Calais, where most of the V-1 launch sites were, had been overrun. 6,725 V-1s had reached the south coast of England and more than half had been destroyed by the air defences. 2,340 had reached the London area, killing 5,475 people and severely injuring a further 16,000. This, however, was not the end of the story. The Germans began to release them from piloted aircraft and during the next seven months more than 750 were launched in this way. Only one-tenth hit the London area, the remainder striking as far north as Yorkshire and as far west as Shropshire. The last V-1, a modified, longer-range version fired from northern Holland, did not appear over Britain until **29 March 1945** and was shot down by anti-aircraft guns over Suffolk.

8 September **The first V-2 rocket struck England.**
The V-1 offensive had diverted attention away from the V-2; nevertheless during the past nine months Allied intelligence had been working hard to gain technical details of it. On **20 May 1944** a V-2 had fallen into the River Bug 80 miles north-west of Warsaw and had been successfully secured by the Polish Underground. On **13 June** another rocket exploded over Sweden and British intelligence officers were allowed to inspect the wreckage in return for giving the Swedes some mobile radars. On **18 July** the US Eighth Army Air Force successfully bombed the experimental stations at Peenemuende and Blizna (Poland). A week later, in the face of the Soviet advance, the Germans abandoned the latter. What had become clear to Allied intelligence was that although the V-2 had the same range as the V-1 (185 miles) it could not be brought down once launched. Also, the evidence showed that the Germans had begun wholesale production of them. On **4 August** the Allied air forces began to attack suspected V-2 storage sites in France, but with the waning of the V-1 threat priority on this was lowered.

The rocket that landed in Chiswick, west London on the 8th was launched from the outskirts of The Hague in the Netherlands and was the second to be fired that day. The first had landed on the outskirts of Paris.

18 September **The German V-2 rocket batteries were withdrawn eastwards.**
This was as a result of the Allied airborne operation 'Market Garden' (see pages 200–1). Up until then 35 rockets had been launched at England. The majority of launch sites remained in Holland.

3 October **V-2 bombardment of London resumed.**
During the pause 44 rockets had been fired at East Anglia from Friesland, Denmark, but only one caused casualties, landing outside Norwich. The air attacks on the V-2 supply depots were now resumed. The V-2 attacks from the Netherlands continued until **27 March 1945** when one landed on a block of flats in Stepney, east London, killing 134 people and another near Orpington in Kent. By then the German transportation system was in ruins and it proved impossible to maintain the supply of rockets.

In all, 10,500 V-1s and 1,115 V-2s were fired at England and those that got through caused in excess of 33,000 civilian casualties and much damage to property. During the same period the liberated part of Belgium also suffered, notably Antwerp and Brussels. If Hitler had launched his 'revenge' weapons (the V designation stood for *Vergeltungswaffen* – revenge weapon) offensive some months earlier it might well have been to the detriment of 'Overlord'. As it was, once the Western Allies were safely ashore in Normandy victory was in sight and the V-weapons had appeared too late to deflect the Allies from their purpose. It was much the same story with the advanced U-boats and the Luftwaffe's jet aircraft.

The Rhine Crossings · P216

The Russian Summer 1944 Offensive

The long awaited Russian offensive on the Eastern Front was to prove more devastating than anything Germany and her allies had so far experienced.

10 June 1944 Russia attacked the Finns.
Preceded by heavy bombing and a massive artillery bombardment the Russian Twenty-First Army, attacking on the west side of Lake Ladoga, penetrated ten miles on the first day. The initial main Russian objective was Viipuri.

20 June Viipuri fell.
Reinforced with German *matériel* and an infantry division the Finns managed to hold the Russians north of the town. In return for German assistance Finnish President Ryti was forced to sign a pact stating that he would not make a separate peace with the Soviet Union.

21 June Meretskov's Karelian Front attacked the Finns between Lake Ladoga and Lake Onega.
The Finns defended desperately, but were steadily forced back.

22 June The main Russian offensive ('Bagration') opened.
In the north 1st Baltic Front quickly enveloped Vitebsk and by the 27th it had fallen, with a complete German corps (from Third Panzer Army) being lost.

23 June Chernyakhovsky's 3rd Belorussian Front attacked down the Minsk highway.
Next day Rokossovsky's 1st Belorussian Front joined in.

28 June Russian troops crossed the Beresina.
By now Third Panzer Army had been shattered, most of Ninth Army had been encircled near Bobruisk and Fourth Army, withdrawing on Minsk, was also in danger of being cut off. In short, Army Group Centre had been torn open, but Busch found it difficult to make Hitler appreciate the seriousness of the situation. On that same day, 28th, Hitler replaced Busch by Model, who was still expected to continue commanding Army Group North Ukraine as well.

3 July Hitler sacked Georg Lindemann, CinC, Army Group North.
Lindemann had wanted to withdraw his southern wing in view of the pressure from 1st Baltic Front. Hitler forbade this and ordered him to attack south-east in order to help Army Group Centre. Lindemann protested and was replaced by Johannes Friessner.

4 July Minsk liberated.
The Russians had created a large pocket to the east of the city. This was reduced on the 11th and 57,000 men surrendered. Army Group Centre had now lost the equivalent of 28 divisions and only its wings remained intact. The way to Poland and Lithuania now lay open for the Red Army.

10 July Hitler moved to his HQ at Rastenburg, East Prussia.
This was in spite of the situation in the west and signified his concern at what was happening on the Eastern Front. On the same day Yeremenko's 2nd Baltic Front struck at Hansen's Sixteenth German Army.

13 July Konev's 1st Ukrainian Front and the left wing of 1st Belorussian Front began to attack Army Group North Ukraine.
Progress was initially slow, but a pocket was created in the Brody area. Some elements managed to break out and escape, but when it was finally reduced on the 22nd some 25,000 Germans had been killed in it and another 17,000 were captured.

20 July 1st Belorussian Front reached the River Bug, the 1939 Polish border, west of Kovel. This was the day on which there was the bomb attempt against Hitler's life.

22 July Moscow Radio announced the establishment of the Polish Committee for National Liberation in Chelm, eastern Poland.
For some time the Russians had been setting up a Polish Communist infrastructure and this committee became known as the 'Lublin Committee' and its followers the 'Lublin Poles'. Five days later the Committee met Stalin, Molotov and Zhukov and signed an agreement whereby the Polish Army fighting with the Russians would be strictly subordinated to them. Stalin explained to the British that the reason for setting up the Committee was to enable Poland, once liberated, to govern itself. The Polish government-in-exile was aghast and on the 26th sent a deputation to Moscow, on Churchill's advice.

In the meantime, with the Russians now closing on the Vistula, General Tadeusz Bor-Komorowski, commander of the Polish Home Army in Warsaw, had sent out a warning to his men to prepare for an uprising against the Germans. On the 25th the London Poles passed the decision to the Poles in Warsaw as to when and if to rise.

23 July 1st Belorussian Front entered Lublin.
At the same time the first of the extermination camps in the east, Maidenek, 1.5 miles west of Lublin, was liberated.

24 July Hitler ordered Army Groups North and Centre to hold where they were.
He also arranged for Friessner to change places with the ardent National Socialist, Ferdinand Schoerner, who was commanding Army Group South Ukraine.

26 July Elements of 1st Belorussian Front reached the Vistula east of Radom.
The Leningrad Front captured Narva in Estonia.

27 July Lvov liberated by 1st Ukrainian Front.
2nd Baltic Front also captured Dvinsk in southern Latvia. Next day Brest-Litovsk fell and 1st Ukrainian Front reached the River San.

31 July 3rd Belorussian Front entered Kaunas, capital of Lithuania.
It was secured on the following day. In the meantime 1st Baltic Front was closing on the Gulf of Riga and threatening to cut off Army Group North. Only a counter-stroke by six Panzer divisions in mid-August reopened land communications with Riga, but then only temporarily.

1 August The Poles in Warsaw rose against the Germans.
The Polish CinC in Britain, General Kazimierz Sosnkowski, had advised against an uprising since British direct support in the form of the Polish Parachute Brigade and Polish aircraft with the RAF, which the Home Army had demanded, could not be made available. Since he was in Italy at the time, his advice only reached London after the uprising had begun. Furthermore the Germans had begun to move strong armoured reinforcements to the city. On the other hand, the Russian sponsored Radio Koscuiszko had broadcast a call to arms to the people of Warsaw on **29 July** and they could hear the sounds of battle on the eastern outskirts of the city as the 1st Belorussian Front faced fierce counter-attacks from three Panzer divisions from Second and Fourth Armies. But, on the night of **31 July/1 August** the Russian forces on the eastern outskirts of the capital had, in view of the growing German resistance, been ordered on to the defensive.

4 August Stalin met the London Polish delegation to Moscow.
He had kept them waiting for some days. There was debate over the boundaries of a post-war Poland and Stalin emphasized that there could not be two groups of Poles – Lublin and London. The Russians had also made plain their annoyance at not having had prior warning of the Warsaw uprising. On the same day the British Government requested permission to drop supplies over Warsaw. Stalin replied that he did not believe that the Home Army stood any chance of success. Throughout the remainder of the month the Russians remained on the defensive in front of Warsaw, although to the south a bridgehead across the Vistula was established by 1st Ukrainian Front in the Magnuszew area. Repeated requests by the Western Allies to drop supplies to the Warsaw Poles were rejected by the Russians. In the meantime, the Polish Home Army were fighting desperately within the city.

P178 · The Soviet Spring Offensive

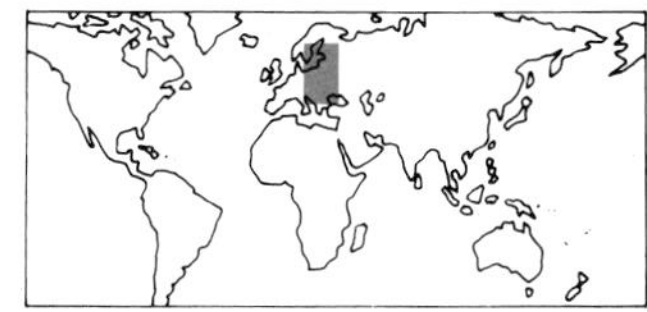

OPERATION 'BAGRATION': The drive to the Vistula

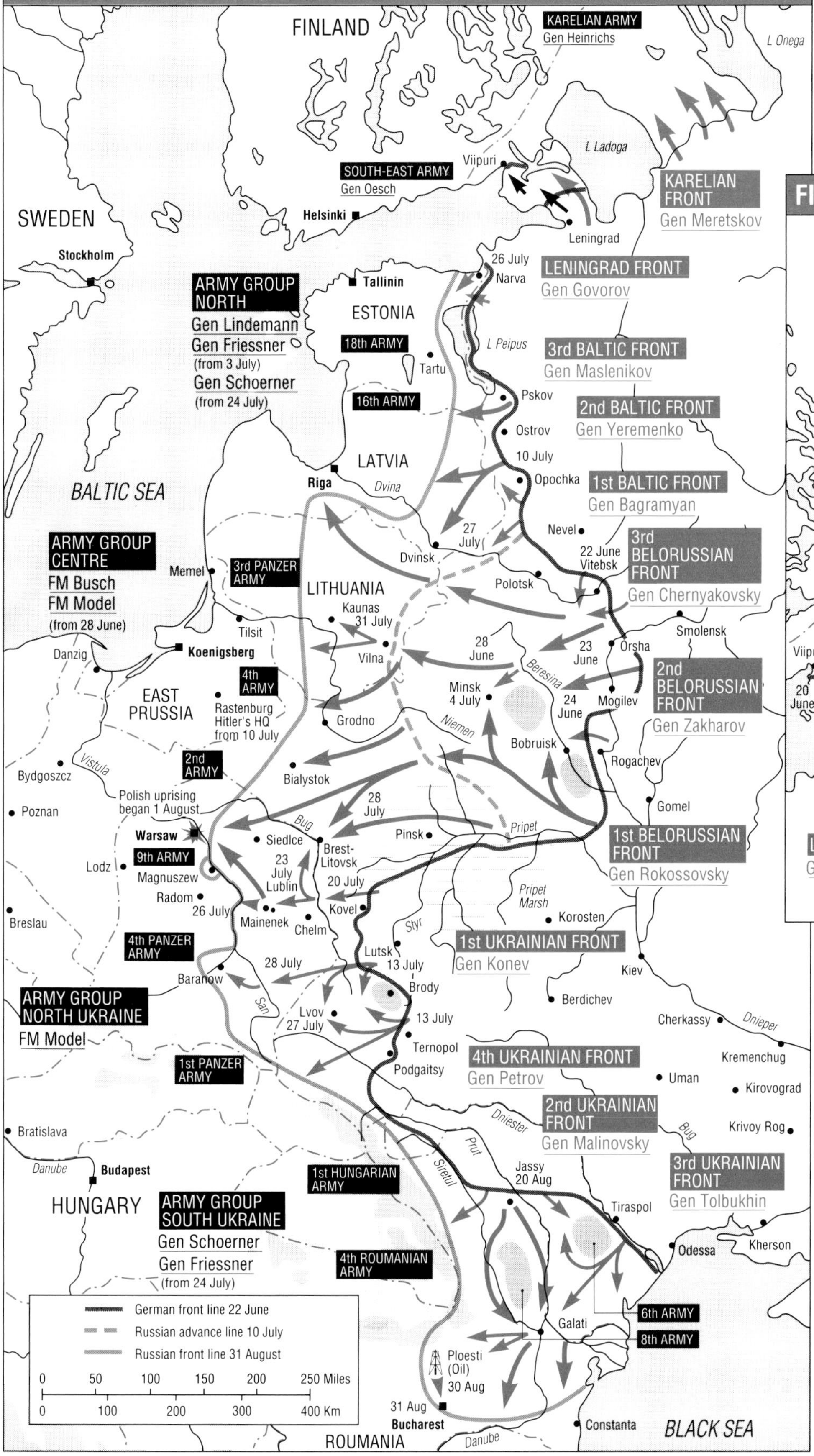

German front line 22 June
Russian advance line 10 July
Russian front line 31 August

0 50 100 150 200 250 Miles
0 100 200 300 400 Km

4 August President Ryti of Finland resigned.
He was succeeded by Mannerheim who considered that the pact Ryti had signed with the Germans no longer applied. On **25 August** Finland asked the USSR for peace terms. The Russians agreed to receive a Finnish deputation provided that the Finns broke off diplomatic relations with Germany and expelled all German troops from their country.

FINLAND INVADED

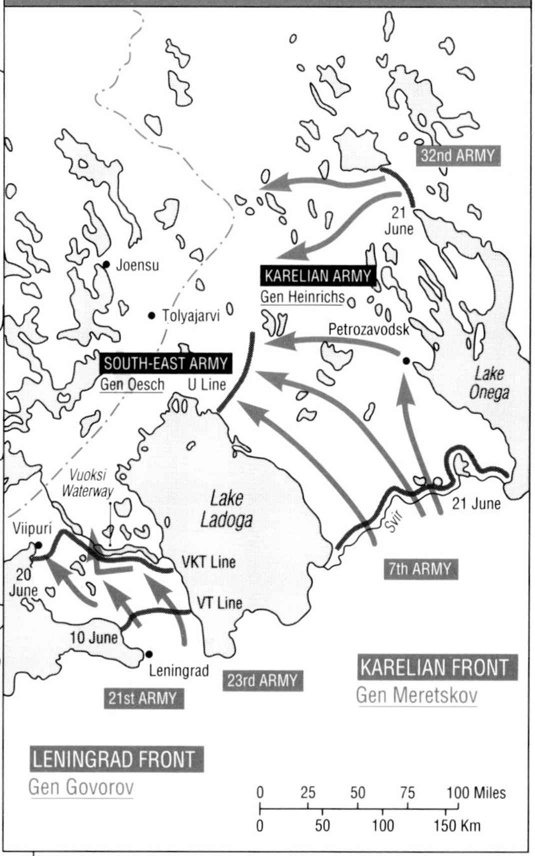

0 25 50 75 100 Miles
0 50 100 150 Km

20 August 2nd and 3rd Ukrainian Fronts attacked into Roumania.
Many Roumanian formations quickly surrendered and some 20 German divisions found themselves trapped between the Dniester and the Prut.

23 August King Carol of Roumania declared that hostilities were at an end.
Antonescu was arrested on the same day and the German troops were given two days to leave the country. Hitler ordered Friessner, CinC Army Group South Ukraine, to arrest the King, but it was too late. All Friessner could do was to try and extricate his forces and withdraw into Hungary, Bulgaria and to the Yugoslav border. In the process he lost his Sixth Army and part of the Eighth in the pocket east of the Prut.

31 August Russian forces entered Bucharest.
They had occupied the Ploesti oilfields on the previous day.

Finland and the Balkans · P194

10 CLOSING IN, September 1944 to February 1945

10 AUGUST 1944 TO 7 NOVEMBER 1944

The Second Quebec Conference

At the beginning of September 1944 it seemed to the Allies that they were driving all before them on all fronts and that there were good prospects of the war in Europe being brought to an end before 1944 was out.

The Western Allies had liberated most of France and had entered Belgium and it seemed that the shattered German forces could do little to prevent them closing quickly to the German border. Indeed, elements of the US First Army reached and crossed the border west of Aachen as early as **12 September**. In Italy they were fighting their way through the Gothic Line, but in Greece, where the German evacuation was expected to begin at any time, a dangerous schism was developing between the Communist and non-Communist resistance movements.

On the Eastern Front Hitler's allies were beginning to desert him. Roumania had already dropped out of the war and signed a formal armistice with the Allies in Moscow on **12 September**. Roumania now joined the Allies. Bulgaria, too, fell by the wayside. Although an ally of Germany, she had never declared war on the USSR, but had been under increasing pressure from the Soviets to sever her links with Germany. The speedy collapse of Roumania threw the Bulgarian Government into a panic. On **27 August** Bulgaria assured the Soviet Union of its complete neutrality, but this was not enough. On **5 September** the USSR made a formal declaration of war on her and three days later Soviet troops entered Bulgaria. There was no resistance and next day 'hostilities' came to an end with the largely Communist Fatherland Front being installed as the government. This left Soviet forces poised to tackle Yugoslavia and Hungary.

Finland broke off diplomatic relations with Germany on **2 September** and, bending to Soviet terms for an armistice, demanded the withdrawal of all German troops. Some areas were evacuated, although not without the odd clash with Finnish forces, but the Germans were unwilling to release their hold on northern Finland. On **19 September** an armistice between Finland and the USSR was signed.

Further south the former Baltic republics had been largely cleared of German forces, although Army Group North still clung to Riga, much of Estonia, and the Courland Peninsula. The offensive here was to be resumed on **14 September**. The main summer 1944 Soviet offensive had, however, come to rest on the Vistula and still no external help was forthcoming for the beleaguered Polish Home Army, which was now being gradually eradicated in Warsaw. On **10 September** the Soviets did accede to an Anglo-US request to use their airfields for supply drops on Warsaw and began to drop supplies themselves on the 14th. On **18 September** 110 bombers from the US Eighth Army Air Force flew from Britain, dropped supplies to the Home Army and landed on Soviet airfields. It was, however, too late and on **2 October** Bor-Komrowski was forced to surrender to the Germans.

In Burma the Japanese had 'shot their bolt' and the Allied forces were now awaiting the end of the monsoon before beginning the liberation of Burma. In China, on the other hand, the Japanese were on the offensive in the Hunan, Kwangtung and Kwangsi provinces, primarily to overrun US air bases from which a strategic bombing offensive on Japan itself was being mounted.

Finally, in the Pacific the Americans were preparing for their return to the Philippines, although what the next objective should be was still the subject of much debate.

As early as **16 July** Churchill had proposed to Roosevelt, who agreed, that another meeting of the Big Three should take place. They agreed to meet at Invergordon, Scotland and an invitation was sent to Stalin. He, however, declined on the grounds that he could not leave Russia while military developments on the Eastern Front were so rapid.

10 August 1944 Churchill proposed a meeting at Quebec to Roosevelt.

Roosevelt had stated that he did not now wish to come to Scotland since Stalin would not be there and also because of the Presidential election due to take place in November. Churchill wanted to discuss the British Empire's role in the defeat of Japan after that of Germany, the situation in Burma and that in Italy. Two days later Churchill accepted Roosevelt's formal invitation for a meeting in Quebec.

12–16 September Second Quebec Conference ('Octagon').

The main points of discussion were:

a. *Italy* It was agreed that there should be no weakening of Allied forces there until the Germans had been decisively defeated. Thereafter the main objective would be Vienna. The amphibious shipping supporting 'Dragoon' would be retained for one month, pending a decision, for possible operations in the north Adriatic.

b. *Balkans* The British would send forces to Greece to fill the vacuum left by the retreating Germans. An operational plan, 'Manna', had already been drawn up for this. Otherwise no Anglo-US forces would be deployed in the Balkans.

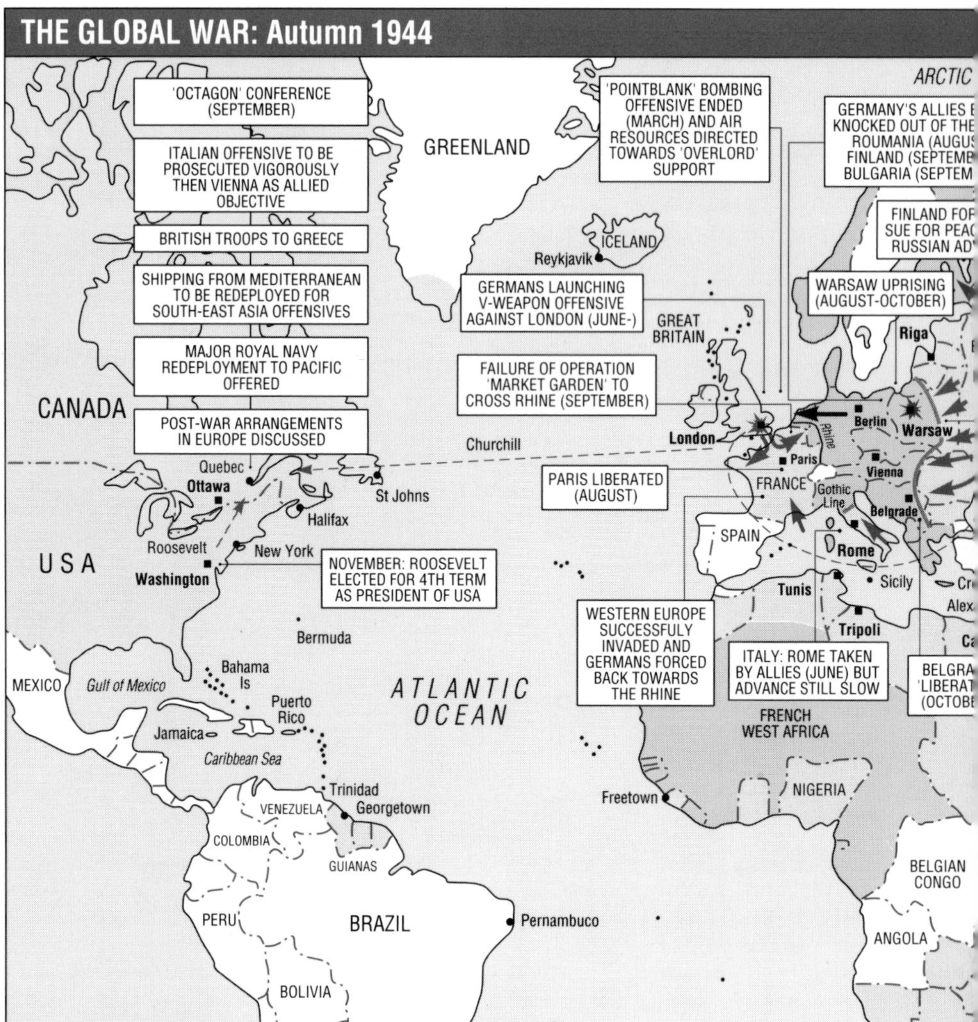

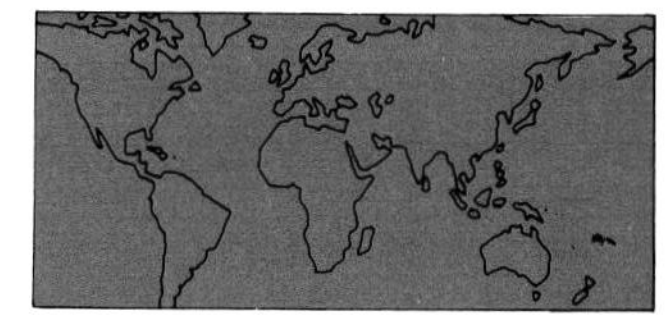

c. *Burma* Rather than rely on what was likely to be a long-drawn-out jungle campaign, the British wished to mount an amphibious operation against Rangoon ('Dracula') in the spring of 1945. The shipping for this would be that being used for 'Dragoon', hence the need for an early decision on the Adriatic amphibious operations. The ultimate objective was the liberation of Singapore.

d. *Pacific* The British made their 'main fleet' immediately available and this was accepted. Air and ground contributions would be forthcoming after Germany had been defeated.

e. *Post-war Germany* In terms of occupation zones, the original plan was for the British to be in the south, the Americans in the north and the Russians in the east. The British proposed swapping their zone with the Americans so that they could control the Baltic ports and this was agreed. The British proposal that the French should be allowed a zone of occupation was, however, resisted by the Americans.

US Secretary of the Treasury Henry Morgenthau unveiled his plan for ensuring that Germany never again would have the industrial base from which to rearm. The steel industries in the Ruhr and Saar would be eliminated and the ultimate aim would be to convert the country to one 'primarily agricultural and pastoral in its character'. The Western Allies would have to supply Germany with essential steel goods. This plan was given approval by Roosevelt and Churchill, although many of their advisers were against it. In the event, because of the effect this would have on the European economy as a whole it was later dropped.

f. *Lend-Lease* The USA agreed to continue to supply Britain until the end of the war with Japan, and no conditions would be attached that would jeopardize the recovery of Britain's export trade.

Churchill now wanted to meet Stalin as soon as possible in order to confirm his entry into the war against Japan, resolve the Poland question and discuss the Balkans. Stalin agreed that he should come to Moscow.

9–19 October Stalin-Churchill talks ('Tolstoy') in Moscow.

Churchill obtained confirmation from Stalin that he would declare war on Japan after the defeat of Germany. With regard to the Balkans, Roumania and Bulgaria were recognized as being totally within the Soviet sphere of influence, Hungary would be under equal Soviet and Western influence, and Greece would be in the British sphere.

Stalin and Churchill agreed to work towards a government of national unity in Poland, which would be made up of both the London and Lublin Poles. It was accepted, however, that little could be done until agreement had been reached on the post-war Polish-Soviet border. Stalin had for long been insistent that this should be the October 1939 Line, commonly known as the Curzon Line, but that Lvov should be on the Soviet side. Since many Poles lived to the east of this line the London Poles had objected. Churchill, however, agreed to persuade the London Poles to accept the line. The Poles on the wrong side would be moved to those parts of eastern Germany that would be ceded to Poland. The London Poles, however, continued to find this unacceptable.

7 November Roosevelt won a fourth term in office in the US Presidential Election.

He was, however, by now becoming a very sick man, although this was concealed from the world at large.

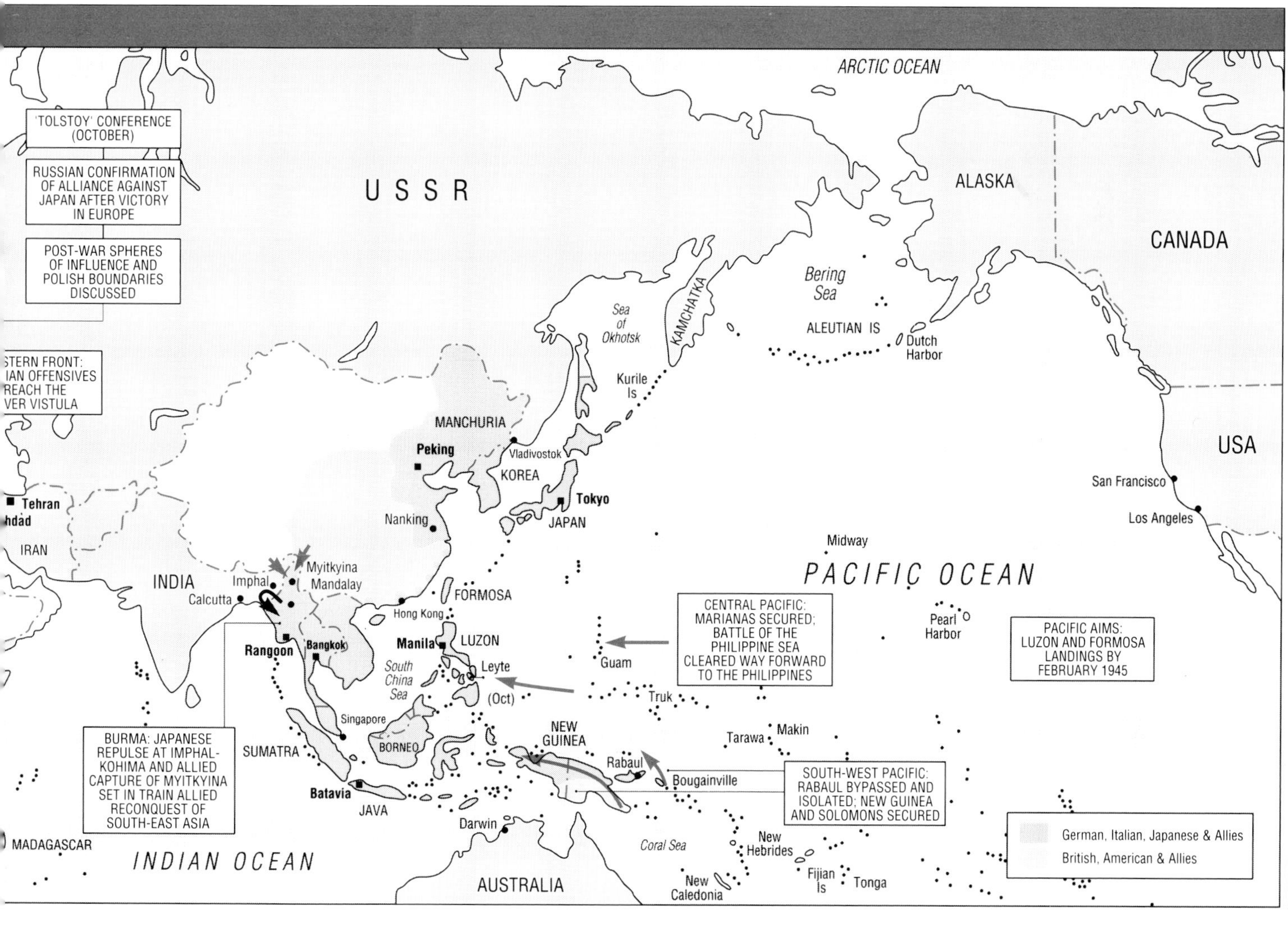

'TOLSTOY' CONFERENCE (OCTOBER)

RUSSIAN CONFIRMATION OF ALLIANCE AGAINST JAPAN AFTER VICTORY IN EUROPE

POST-WAR SPHERES OF INFLUENCE AND POLISH BOUNDARIES DISCUSSED

...STERN FRONT: ...IAN OFFENSIVES REACH THE ...VER VISTULA

BURMA: JAPANESE REPULSE AT IMPHAL-KOHIMA AND ALLIED CAPTURE OF MYITKYINA SET IN TRAIN ALLIED RECONQUEST OF SOUTH-EAST ASIA

CENTRAL PACIFIC: MARIANAS SECURED; BATTLE OF THE PHILIPPINE SEA CLEARED WAY FORWARD TO THE PHILIPPINES

PACIFIC AIMS: LUZON AND FORMOSA LANDINGS BY FEBRUARY 1945

SOUTH-WEST PACIFIC: RABAUL BYPASSED AND ISOLATED; NEW GUINEA AND SOLOMONS SECURED

German, Italian, Japanese & Allies

British, American & Allies

ARCTIC OCEAN
USSR
ALASKA
CANADA
USA
PACIFIC OCEAN
INDIAN OCEAN
AUSTRALIA

1 SEPTEMBER 1944 TO 26 DECEMBER 1944

Finland and the Balkans

While the main summer 1944 Soviet offensive had run out of momentum on the Vistula in August, events on the flanks had moved quickly. Under the terms of the armistice signed with Finland on **19 September 1944**, Finland was permitted to retain her independence within her 1940 frontiers, except for Viipuri and the Petsamo areas. The USSR also took control, but not sovereignty, over the Porkkala Peninsula south of Helsinki and Finland had to pay her war reparations. The immediate Soviet concern was now to clear the remaining German troops from Soviet territory adjoining northern Finland and open up a threat to the Germans in Norway. Further to the south, the offensive to clear Army Group North from the Baltic republics was renewed in mid-September.

On the southern flank the sudden collapse of Roumania and Bulgaria's hurried departure from the Axis camp opened up dramatic possibilities for liberating the Balkans and Hungary. Indeed, as early as **29 August** the Stavka had issued orders to Malinovsky (2nd Ukrainian Front) and Tolbukhin (3rd Ukrainian Front), directing the former on to Bucharest and then to swing north-west through the Transylvanian Alps and on to the plains of Hungary. Tolbukhin was to advance south into Bulgaria and then turn west along the line of the Danube and enter Yugoslavia. During August, too, Admiral Horthy, the dictator of Hungary, had begun to make overtures to the

P190 · The Russian Summer 1944 Offensive

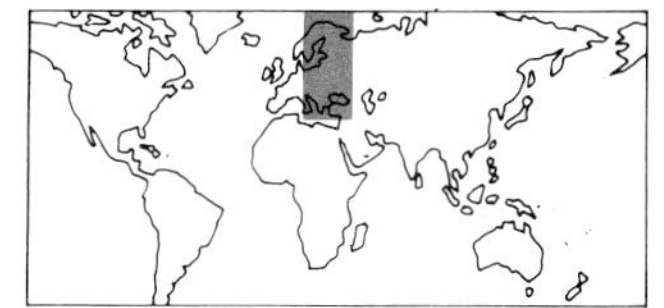

Western Allies, but it had been made clear to him that he must deal with Moscow and not them.

1 September 1944 **The Western Allies' Balkan Air Force launched Operation 'Rat Week'.**
This was designed to block the routes north from southern Yugoslavia and northern Greece in order to prevent the Germans deploying reinforcements to interfere with Tito's plans for his partisans to drive towards Belgrade and link up with the Russians.

5 September **Strong German-Hungarian counter-attack in the southern Carpathians.**
This fell on the Fourth Roumanian Army, now fighting on the Russian side, and threw it into confusion. On the 11th Malinovsky launched a tank army into the attack and this drove the Axis troops from the southern Carpathians to Targu Mures.

8 September **Loehr's German Army Group E began to evacuate the Greek islands.**
It was Bulgaria's declaration of war on Germany and the approach of Tolbukhin's 3rd Ukrainian Front to the Yugoslav border which precipitated this, together with 'Rat Week', which the Germans believed was designed to prevent the withdrawal of Army Group E. By the end of the month the evacuation of the Greek mainland was also underway with Army Group E moving north into Yugoslavia to combine with Army Group F.

9 September **Bulgaria's change of sides vastly increased the area of responsibility of von Weichs' Army Group F.**

14 September **The Soviet offensive against Army Group North reopened.**
In the south the 1st Baltic Front caught the German Sixteenth Army by surprise and penetrated several miles on the opening day, but on the 16th was brought to a halt in front of Riga. North of the River Dvina 2nd and 3rd Baltic Fronts made slower progress against stiff resistance.

17 September **Leningrad Front attacked in Estonia from the Lake Peipus area.**
On the 22nd it captured Tallinn, capital of Estonia. In the meantime Hitler had agreed that the Narva Group, defending Estonia, could be withdrawn.

17 September **The Bulgarian Army was formally placed under Soviet command.**

24 September **The Stavka issued a new directive for dealing with Army Group North.**
Instead of trying to reduce Riga the main axis was now to be directed on the Baltic near Memel with a view to cutting off the remainder of Army Group North in the Courland Peninsula. There was therefore now a pause while troops were switched to the left flank.

24 September **Malinovsky, having broken into the Transylvanian Alps, closed to the Hungarian border.**
It had been a tough struggle to force the passes. In the meantime Petrov's 4th Ukrainian Front had been trying to break through the Carpathians from Poland and into Hungary and Slovakia, where there had been since **29 August** a growing uprising designed to facilitate the entry of the Red Army by keeping German troops tied down. There was now a brief pause for breath.

Also on this day German Army Groups North and South Ukraine were redesignated Army Groups A and South. Army Group North Ukraine had been commanded by Harpe since the beginning of the month.

28 September **Tolbukhin began his drive on Belgrade.**
The offensive needed careful co-ordination with Tito and the Bulgarian Army, now operating with Tolbukhin.

1 October **Hungarian armistice delegation arrived in Moscow.**
By this time Malinovsky had resumed his offensive and was driving towards the River Tsiza, as was Petrov's 4th Ukrainian Front. With no prospect of physical contact with the Western Allies Horthy had no option if he was to minimize his people's suffering. On 4 October, now aware of what was happening, German troops occupied key points in Hungary.

5 October **1st Baltic Front began to attack once more.**
On the 10th the Russians reached the Baltic at Palanga and Memel, but the latter proved too strongly held to take immediately and was put under siege. Army Group North was now trapped in the Courland Peninsula, where it would remain until the end of the war. The Germans quickly rushed up reinforcements to the Niemen in order to prevent the Russians penetrating into East Prussia.

7 October **Meretskov's Karelian Front launched an attack aimed at Petsamo in northern Finland.**
The German Twentieth Mountain Army (Rendulic) was quickly forced into a precipitate retreat and Petsamo was secured on the 15th. Part withdrew across the border into Norway and was pursued as far as Kirkenes, where the Soviets halted and dug in for the winter. The remainder were pushed south-west to Nautsi on the Finnish border and left to the Finns to deal with.

11 October **The Hungarian delegation signed an armistice in Moscow.**
All Hungarian troops were to be evacuated from neighbouring states and Hungary would declare war on Germany. Horthy, however, had not made any preparations for the armistice and the Germans were able to kidnap him on the 15th and bundle him off to a concentration camp. In his place a puppet government was installed. Some Hungarian formations deserted to the Russians, but others continued to fight on the German side, especially after the Germans made it plain that they were determined to hold Hungary.

12 October **Tolbukhin's forces crossed the River Morava south of Belgrade.**
His plan was to destroy the Germans falling back on the city to its south.

14–20 October **The battle for Belgrade.**
The Germans defended desperately, but were eventually overwhelmed by the combined forces of Tolbukhin and Tito. Only by clinging on to Kraljevo were the Germans able to prevent the Russians from cutting Army Group E and F's one remaining withdrawal route, the road running north from Skopje and then west from Kraljevo to Sarajevo. Having captured Belgrade the Russian forces halted, thus enabling Army Groups E and F to continue their withdrawal and link up with Friessner in Hungary.

15 October **2nd and 3rd Baltic Fronts captured Riga.**

20 October **Debrecen, third largest city in Hungary, fell to Malinovsky.**
Nyiregyhaza fell two days later, thus cutting the lines of communication of Woehler's Eighth Army which was withdrawing in front of Petrov. Friessner immediately organized a counter-attack which retook Nyiregyhaza. This enabled Woehler to withdraw intact across the upper Tisza.

29 October **Malinovsky began to attack across the Tisza towards Budapest.**
The Germans had reinforced, however, and Malinovsky advanced on too narrow a front. Although his troops reached the southern and eastern outskirts of the city on **4 November** they could not break through. Malinovsky now tried to outflank from the north, but this attempt, with attacks from the south and east, also failed by the end of November.

5 December **Malinovsky's third attempt to take Budapest began.**
Hitler had ordered Budapest to be defended to the last and on the 26th the city was encircled, with one Hungarian and four German divisions trapped inside it. In the meantime, on the 21st, Friessner had been replaced by Woehler as CinC, Army Group South.

By now the Stavka was finalizing its plans for another major offensive, this time across the Vistula and on towards Berlin.

From the Vistula to the Oder · P210

15 SEPTEMBER 1944 TO 25 DECEMBER 1944

Leyte Gulf

Throughout 1944 the US planners had been locked in debate over future strategy in the Pacific. In essence, in order to prepare the way for invasion of Japan itself, which might well be necessary to secure final victory, control of the South China Sea was needed. In particular it was the triangle bounded by the South China coast, Luzon and Formosa which attracted the planners' attention. Apart from the ability to secure airfields in southern China from which Japan could be bombarded, this step would also sever Japanese communications with South East Asia and the Dutch East Indies. Furthermore, a port on the South China coast could be used to channel Lend-Lease to Chiang Kai-shek more efficiently than by the air and overland routes from India and Burma.

In March 1944 the US Joint Chiefs of Staff had directed MacArthur to be prepared to invade the Philippines by the end of 1944 and Luzon itself in February 1945. They had also ordered Nimitz to plan to land on Formosa, also in February 1945. They did not, however, lay down priorities between Formosa and Luzon.

During the summer of 1944 it became clear that the Japanese were reinforcing in the western Pacific, especially Formosa. At the same time Chiang Kai-shek was coming under increasing pressure from the Japanese in southern China. It thus became clear to the Joint Chiefs of Staff that the Pacific programme would have to be accelerated, even to the extent of bypassing the Philippines and Formosa in favour of a direct assault on Japan. Both Nimitz and MacArthur argued that this was impossible without seizing at least the southern and central Philippines, and the Joint Chiefs of Staff were forced to agree with them. Where they differed was that MacArthur believed that if Luzon were seized, a landing on Formosa would be unnecessary, while Nimitz thought the opposite.

15 September 1944 MacArthur amended his plan for invading the Philippines.

Up until now he had planned to make his initial landing in the south-west of Mindanao on **15 November**, followed by the main thrust on Leyte on **20 December**. He now proposed, with Joint Chiefs of Staff approval, to bypass Mindanao and land on Leyte on **20 October**. He believed that he could then make a landing on Luzon on **20 December**, followed, if necessary, by Formosa on or about **20 February**. Even if Luzon were bypassed it would not be possible to bring the landing on Formosa forward for logistical reasons.

Nimitz's plan called for simultaneous assaults on Formosa and the Amoy area of China, with priority going to the latter. It soon became clear, though, that sufficient aircraft were unavailable to suppress the Japanese airfields within range of both objectives. Furthermore the Japanese had now overrun the US Fourteenth Air Force bases in southern China. In addition, the necessary manpower could only be achieved by withdrawing troops from Europe, which was unacceptable unless Germany could be defeated before the end of 1944.

On the same day MacArthur's forces landed unopposed on Morotai in the Moluccas, but 1st US Marine Division met stiff opposition landing on Peleliu in the Palau Islands. Indeed, 30,000 Japanese troops under General Sadao Inoue were on the islands and, although Peleliu itself was secured on **27 November**, Japanese resistance on some of the other islands continued until the end of the war.

3 October New Joint Chiefs of Staff directive to MacArthur and Nimitz.

MacArthur was to invade Luzon on or about **20 December**, while Nimitz, having given naval support to the operation, was to assault Iwo Jima in late January, followed by Okinawa. The Formosa option, although never formally cancelled, was left in abeyance.

12–16 October Halsey's Third US Fleet carried out heavy air attacks on Formosa and Luzon in preparation for the Leyte landings.

The Japanese plan, 'Sho' (Victory), for the defence of the inner ring running from the Kuriles to the Philippines called for immediate sea and air attacks as US landings were getting under way. Admiral Soemu Toyoda, CinC Combined Fleet, and responsible for carrying out 'Sho', believed that these air attacks presaged imminent landings on Formosa and Luzon and committed his air power. The result was that he lost some 500 aircraft, as against 89 US, and his only successes were the damaging of a number of US ships.

14 October The US Leyte invasion force sailed from Manus Island and Hollandia.

It was to be carried out by General Walter Krueger's US Sixth Army supported by Admiral Thomas Kinkaid's US Seventh and Bull Halsey's Third Fleets. Overall responsibility for the defence of the Philippines rested with the Southern Area Army, commanded by Field Marshal Hisaichi Terauchi. Under him were Sosaku Suzuki's Thirty-Fifth Army, responsible for Mindanao and the Visayans and Fourteenth Area Army, commanded by Tomoyuki Yamashita, conqueror of Malaya and Singapore, and covering Luzon and Leyte. Leyte itself was defended by Shiro Makino's 16th Division, consisting largely of unblooded conscripts.

17 October US Rangers landed on Suluan Island at the mouth of Leyte Gulf.

They quickly overwhelmed the minute Japanese garrison, but not before it had sent out a radio warning. This alerted Admiral Toyoda of the imminence of a landing on Leyte and he immediately began to concentrate his naval power for an attack on the US fleet in the Leyte area. Next day the Rangers landed on Homonhon and Dinagat, thus securing the entrance to Leyte Gulf.

20 October US landings on Leyte.

They took place on a 16-mile front. Japanese resistance was variable. MacArthur himself waded ashore, a symbolic gesture to signify the fulfilment of his vow, made on **11 March 1942**, that he would return. Next day the Americans entered Tacloban, capital of Leyte, but thereafter progress slowed in the face of frequent Japanese counter-attacks.

23–26 October Battle of Leyte Gulf.

Toyoda's plan for destroying the US Third and Seventh Fleets was to lure them away from Leyte and trap them between two powerful battleship groups. The bait was his four surviving carriers. The two battleship groups were to be made up from Admiral Takeo Kurita's First Striking Force, which had steamed from its base in the Dutch East Indies (close to its oil lifeblood), while Admiral Jisaburo Ozawa's Mobile Fleet with one heavy, three light and two converted battleship carriers provided the bait.

On the 23rd US submarines intercepted Kurita's force, sank two cruisers and crippled a third. Halsey now became attracted by Kurita rather than the carrier bait. Beating off attacks from aircraft based on Luzon, which sank the carrier *Princeton*, he turned south and engaged Kurita, sinking the battleship *Musashi* and crippling a heavy cruiser. Kurita now withdrew west, but then turned north again under cover of darkness. He had split his force in two, making for the San Bernardino Strait himself while the other half passed south of Leyte. Kinkaid went for the latter, destroying it, including two battleships, but this left the amphibious shipping, including six escort carriers, supporting the Leyte landings at the mercy of Kurita. This began to try to extricate itself but quickly lost one escort carrier and three destroyers. In the meantime Halsey had finally turned north to engage the Japanese carriers, but hearing of the plight of the amphibious shipping, left his own carriers to deal with them, which they did, sinking all, and turned south once more. Kurita, however, believed that Halsey was about to cut off his retreat and withdrew back through the San Bernardino Strait.

The main result of Leyte Gulf was that it totally crippled the Japanese Fleet in that it now had no carriers. For the Allies, one disturbing aspect of the battle, however, was the appearance of a new weapon, the *Kamikaze* (Divine Wind) suicide aircraft which, packed with explosives, was designed to destroy enemy ships by diving on to the decks.

Not until **25 December** was Leyte finally cleared of Japanese and then only after another landing had been made in the Ormoc area on **7 December**. Even so, mopping up of isolated Japanese pockets on Leyte would continue to occupy MacArthur's troops for some time to come.

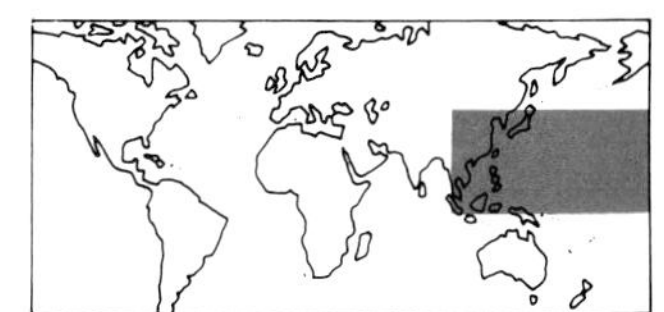

THE NAVAL CAMPAIGN FOR THE PHILIPPINES

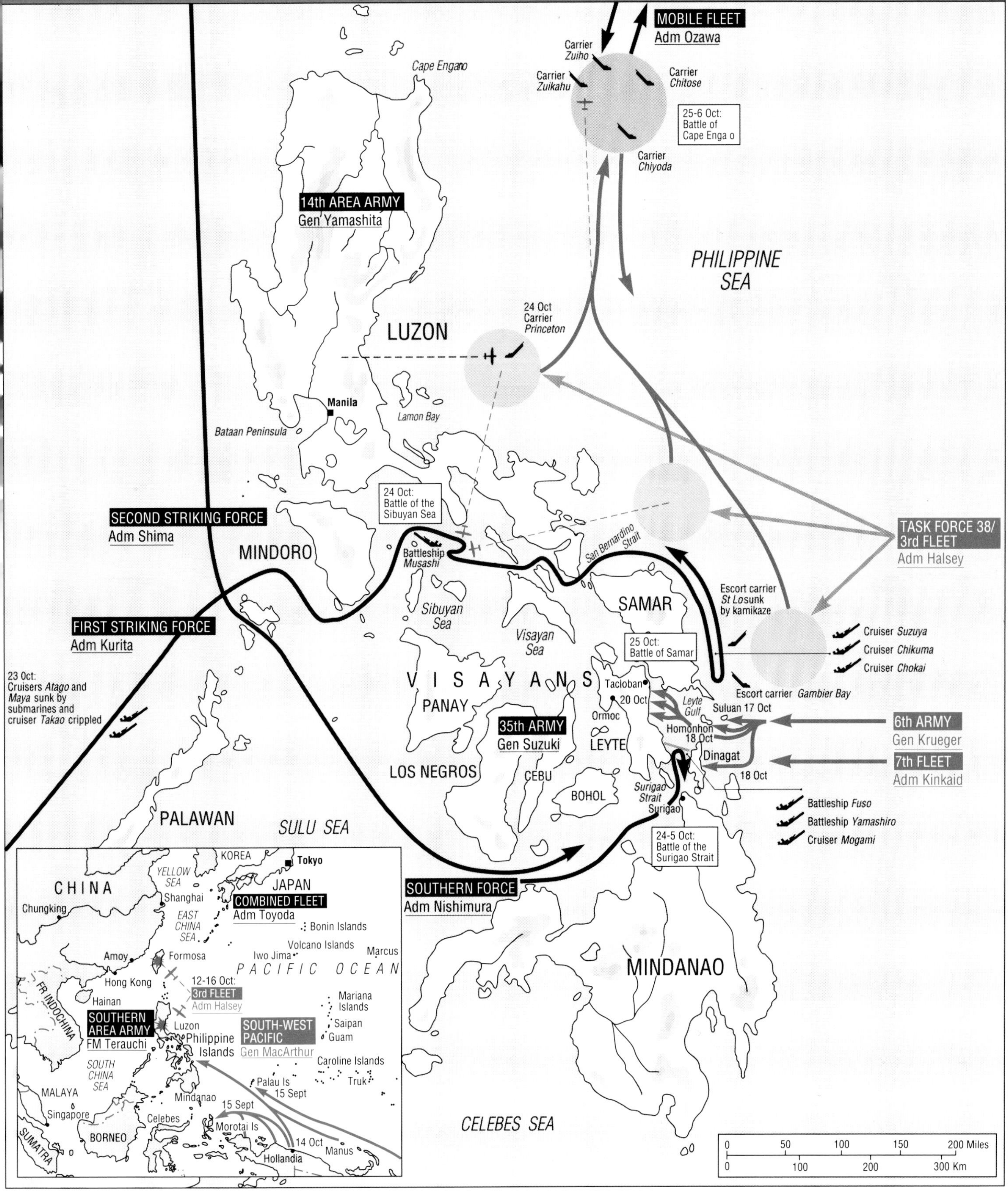

MOBILE FLEET
Adm Ozawa

Carrier *Zuiho*
Carrier *Zuikahu*
Carrier *Chitose*
Carrier *Chiyoda*

25-6 Oct:
Battle of
Cape Enga o

Cape Engaño

14th AREA ARMY
Gen Yamashita

PHILIPPINE SEA

24 Oct
Carrier
Princeton

LUZON

Manila

Lamon Bay

Bataan Peninsula

24 Oct:
Battle of the
Sibuyan Sea

SECOND STRIKING FORCE
Adm Shima

MINDORO

Battleship
Musashi

San Bernardino Strait

TASK FORCE 38/
3rd FLEET
Adm Halsey

Escort carrier
St Losunk
by kamikaze

SAMAR

Sibuyan Sea

Visayan Sea

FIRST STRIKING FORCE
Adm Kurita

25 Oct:
Battle of Samar

Cruiser *Suzuya*
Cruiser *Chikuma*
Cruiser *Chokai*

23 Oct:
Cruisers *Atago* and
Maya sunk by
submarines and
cruiser *Takao* crippled

V I S A Y A N S

Tacloban

Escort carrier *Gambier Bay*

20 Oct

Leyte Gulf

Suluan 17 Oct

PANAY

35th ARMY
Gen Suzuki

Ormoc

Homonhon
18 Oct

6th ARMY
Gen Krueger

LEYTE

Dinagat

7th FLEET
Adm Kinkaid

LOS NEGROS

CEBU

18 Oct

BOHOL

Surigao Strait

Surigao

Battleship *Fuso*
Battleship *Yamashiro*
Cruiser *Mogami*

PALAWAN

SULU SEA

24-5 Oct:
Battle of the
Surigao Strait

SOUTHERN FORCE
Adm Nishimura

KOREA
Tokyo
YELLOW SEA
CHINA
JAPAN
Shanghai
COMBINED FLEET
Adm Toyoda
Chungking
EAST CHINA SEA
Bonin Islands
Volcano Islands
Amoy
Formosa
Iwo Jima
Marcus
PACIFIC OCEAN
Hong Kong
12-16 Oct:
3rd FLEET
Adm Halsey
FR INDOCHINA
Hainan
Mariana Islands
SOUTHERN AREA ARMY
FM Terauchi
Luzon
SOUTH-WEST PACIFIC
Gen MacArthur
Saipan
Philippine Islands
Guam
SOUTH CHINA SEA
Caroline Islands
Palau Is
15 Sept
Truk
MALAYA
Mindanao
15 Sept
Singapore
Celebes
Morotai Is
BORNEO
14 Oct
Manus
SUMATRA
Hollandia

MINDANAO

CELEBES SEA

0 50 100 150 200 Miles
0 100 200 300 Km

Luzon · P198

15 DECEMBER 1944 TO SPRING 1945

Luzon

The stiff resistance that MacArthur encountered on Leyte forced him, at the end of November 1944, to put back the date for the landings on Luzon from **20 December** to **9 January 1945**. Once again the landings would be carried out by the US Sixth Army, supported by the Third and Seventh Fleets and General George Kenney's Far East Air Forces. The initial landings would take place in the Lingayen Gulf, where the Japanese had landed in December 1941.

By this time Terauchi and his Southern Army HQ had left the Philippines for Indo-China, leaving Yamashita in charge. His Fourteenth Area Army had more than 250,000 men, but they were short of fuel, ammunition, vehicles and food. With the recent losses, he had only some 150 combat aircraft on Luzon and therefore had to accept that the Americans would enjoy air supremacy from the outset. He expected the Americans to land in Lingayen Gulf, but did not believe that he had the strength to be able successfully to defeat them in the open country running south to Manila. Instead he decided to pin his defence on three mountain strongholds: northern Luzon, which would be his final bastion, the hills east of Manila, from where the capital's water supplies were obtained, and the high ground running south into the Bataan Peninsula. In this way he hoped to be able to keep MacArthur's troops tied down for as long as possible and thus delay the Allied invasion of Japan.

15 December 1944 US 24th Division landed on Mindoro.
The landing took place on the south-west coast of this island which lies just to the south of Luzon. The landing was unopposed and the troops advanced inland eight miles, set up a defensive perimeter and began to construct an airfield. An escort carrier and two destroyers were damaged in *Kamikaze* air attacks.

2 January 1945 US Seventh Fleet began its passage to Lingayen Bay.
Its initial role was to soften up the defences in the Bay. In the meantime the Third Fleet was attacking airfields on Formosa and Luzon. From the 4th onwards the Seventh Fleet was subjected to constant *Kamikaze* attacks and a number of ships became casualties, including one escort carrier sunk and the battleships *New Mexico* and *California* badly damaged. Nevertheless, this did not prevent the bombardment of the shore positions. Also by the 7th the Japanese combat aircraft strength on Luzon was down to 35 and they were flown off. The *Kamikaze* threat continued for a further week, however.

9 January The US landings in Lingayen Gulf, Luzon.
No opposition was met on the beaches, but *Kamikaze* aircraft were out in force, damaging the battleship *Mississippi* and a light cruiser among other ships. The axis of advance was directed on Manila. Further ships were damaged during the next few days.

16 January US I Corps met fierce opposition as it tried to take Rosario.
To its south XIV Corps was meeting little opposition and was now crossing the River Agno.

21 January XIV Corps reached San Miguel.
I Corps continued to make slow progress in the face of strong resistance.

26 January XIV Corps reached Clark Field.

ALLIED ORDER OF BATTLE IN THE PACIFIC, January 1945

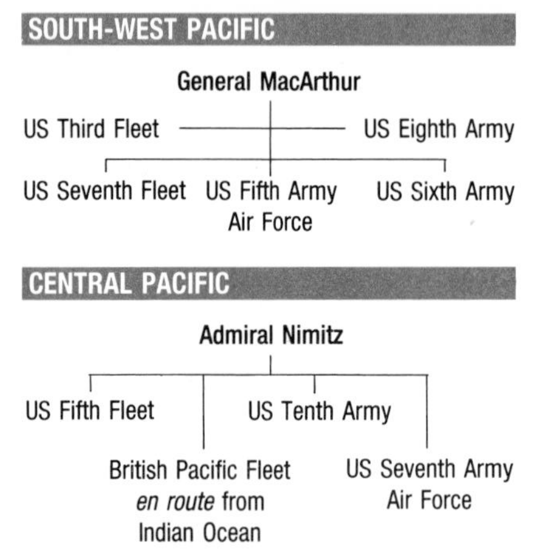

29 January US XI Corps landed at San Antonio, north of the Bataan Peninsula.
Krueger's plan was for XI Corps to join XIV Corps in the advance on Manila, while I Corps was aiming for San José.

31 January US 11th Airborne Division landed at Nasugbu at the entrance of Manila Bay.
Its orders were to advance north to Manila.

3 February US XIV Corps reached the outskirts of Manila.

4 February San José fell to I Corps.

10 February MacArthur defined the areas of responsibility for US Sixth and Eighth Armies.
Sixth Army was to devote itself to Luzon while Eichelberger's Eighth Army was to clear all the islands to its south.

Krueger's forces had been involved in fierce fighting in Manila for some days, but US I Corps reached the east coast of Luzon beyond San José. Yamashita's forces were now split into two.

15 February Part of US 38th Division was landed at Mariveles on the southern tip of the Bataan Peninsula.
The Peninsula was totally secured on the 21st. The Japanese in the hilly terrain north of Bataan, one of Yamashita's strongholds, had been bypassed.

16 February US airborne landing on Corregidor.
This was combined with a battalion-sized amphibious landing. Initially surprised, the Japanese fought back fiercely during the next few days.

19 February X Corps (Eighth Army) landed on the north coast of Samar in the San Bernardino Strait.

28 February Landing by part of 41st Division at Puerto Princesa on Palawan.
Resistance was minimal and the island was quickly cleared.

2 March Corregidor now totally secured.

3 March Manila finally cleared of all Japanese resistance.
During the fighting Manila itself had been virtually convert to ruins. It had cost the Americans 6,500 casualties, but about 100,000 Filipinos had died, many of them victims of frenzied atrocities by the Japanese, crimes for which Yamashita would eventually stand trial as a war criminal.

Krueger's next tasks were to clear the Japanese from Manila Bay and to tackle the stronghold in the hills above Manila. Both these tasks took some weeks. This then left the forces north of Bataan and in northern Luzon. These would serve to tie down more than four US divisions and numerous Filipino guerrilla bands until the end of the war. This was especially so in the fastnesses in the north of the island, but also in Yamashita's other two strongholds, north of Bataan and east and south-east of Manila.

Eichelberger had an equally lengthy task in clearing the other Philippine islands, especially on Mindanao, where elements of Suzuki's Thirty-Fifth Army also held out until the end of the war. In June 1945 Eighth Army also took over responsibility for Luzon so as to release Krueger's Sixth Army to prepare for the invasion of Kyushu, the southernmost of the main Japanese islands. Indeed, the Philippines became like New Guinea, where MacArthur's amphibious outflanking moves in the summer of 1944 along the north coast of Dutch New Guinea had left a sizeable Japanese force, albeit starved of supplies, in north-east New Guinea, which 6th Australian Division spent 1945 in eliminating. By the spring of 1945 the Philippines and New Guinea were very much side-shows. The main offensive had been taken over by Nimitz who had stormed the last two island bastions guarding the way to Japan itself.

SECURING THE PHILIPPINES

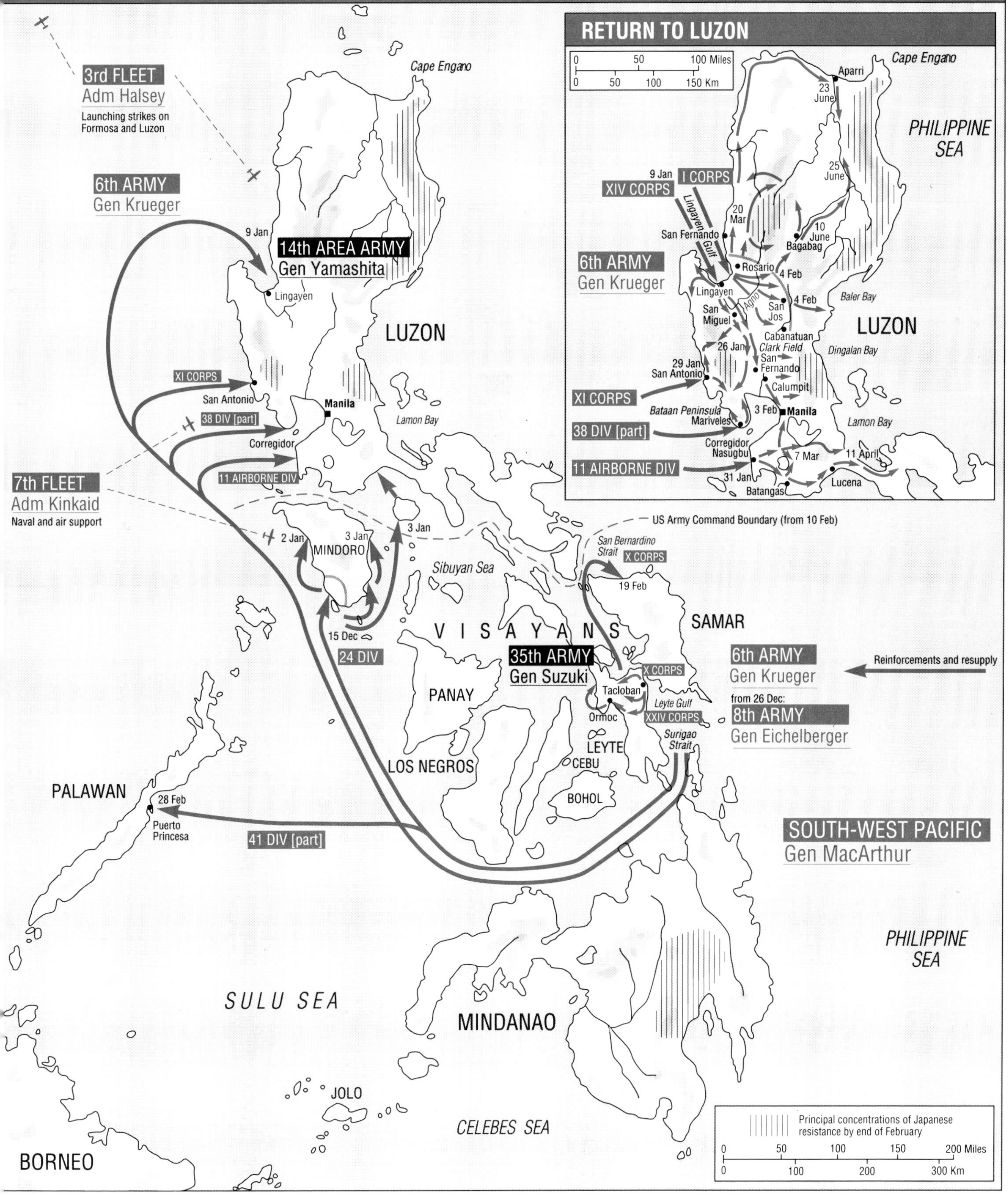

3rd FLEET
Adm Halsey
Launching strikes on Formosa and Luzon

6th ARMY
Gen Krueger

9 Jan

14th AREA ARMY
Gen Yamashita

Cape Engano

Lingayen

LUZON

XI CORPS

San Antonio

38 DIV [part]

Manila

Corregidor

Lamon Bay

7th FLEET
Adm Kinkaid
Naval and air support

11 AIRBORNE DIV

2 Jan

3 Jan

MINDORO

3 Jan

US Army Command Boundary (from 10 Feb)

San Bernardino Strait

X CORPS

Sibuyan Sea

19 Feb

15 Dec

24 DIV

V I S A Y A N S

SAMAR

35th ARMY
Gen Suzuki

X CORPS

6th ARMY
Gen Krueger

Reinforcements and resupply

PANAY

Tacloban

Leyte Gulf

from 26 Dec:

8th ARMY
Gen Eichelberger

Ormoc

XXIV CORPS

Surigao Strait

LEYTE

LOS NEGROS

CEBU

PALAWAN

28 Feb

BOHOL

Puerto Princesa

41 DIV [part]

SOUTH-WEST PACIFIC
Gen MacArthur

PHILIPPINE SEA

SULU SEA

MINDANAO

JOLO

CELEBES SEA

BORNEO

Principal concentrations of Japanese resistance by end of February

0 50 100 150 200 Miles
0 100 200 300 Km

RETURN TO LUZON

0 50 100 Miles
0 50 100 150 Km

Cape Engano

Aparri

23 June

PHILIPPINE SEA

25 June

9 Jan

I CORPS

XIV CORPS

Lingayen Gulf

20 Mar

10 June

Bagabag

San Fernando

6th ARMY
Gen Krueger

Rosario

4 Feb

Lingayen

Agno

4 Feb

Baler Bay

San Miguel

San Jos

LUZON

Cabanatuan

26 Jan

Clark Field

Dingalan Bay

29 Jan

San Fernando

San Antonio

Calumpit

XI CORPS

Bataan Peninsula

3 Feb

Manila

Mariveles

38 DIV [part]

Lamon Bay

Corregidor

Nasugbu

7 Mar

11 April

11 AIRBORNE DIV

31 Jan

Lucena

Batangas

Montgomery's Gamble

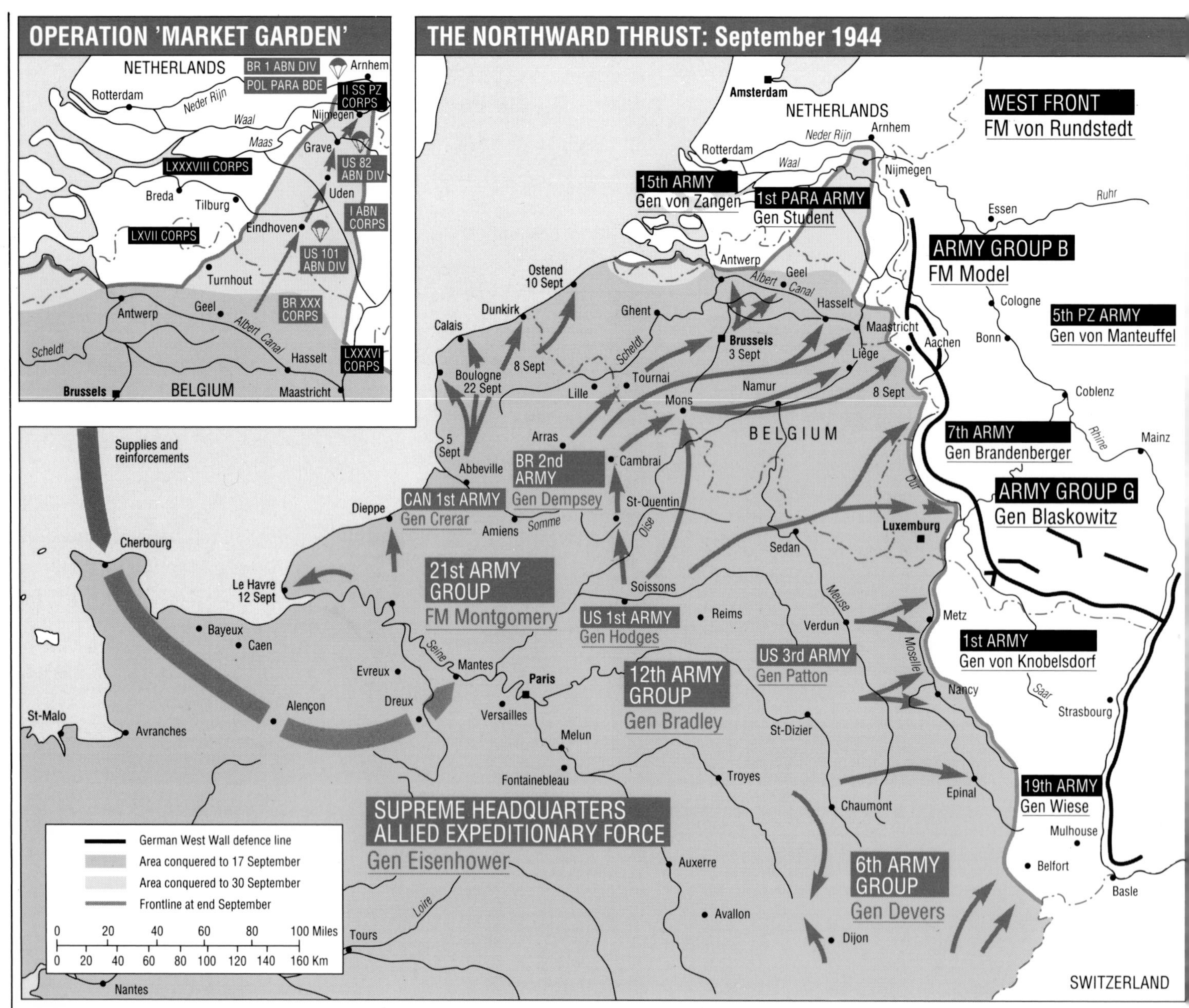

On **1 September 1944** Eisenhower formally assumed control of Allied ground operations in north-west Europe. Montgomery, from whom he took over the reins, was promoted Field Marshal on the same day. The situation on that day continued to give rise to great optimism in the Allied camp. Patton's Third US Army had liberated Verdun and was now advancing towards another historic French fortress town, Metz. Hodges's US First Army was advancing towards St-Quentin and Cambrai and Dempsey's British Second Army entered Arras. On the Channel coast Crerar's Canadian First Army was approaching Le Havre and Dieppe, while in southern France Patch's US Seventh Army and de Lattre de Tassigny's French Army B were closing on Lyons. Everywhere the German armies appeared broken and confused.

3 September 1944 The British Guards Armoured Division liberated Brussels.
On the same day de Lattre de Tassigny's troops entered Lyons.

4 September Eisenhower issued a directive concerning future operations.
In essence, while Montgomery followed up the broken German armies to the Ruhr Bradley was to drive for the Saar. This was the beginning of a long and often acrimonious debate between Eisenhower and Montgomery otherwise known as the 'Broad versus Narrow Front' controversy.

Even though the British 11th Armoured Division captured the port of Antwerp on this day there was a growing supply crisis. As the Allied armies dashed across France they remained reliant on supplies coming in through Cherbourg, which by the beginning of September was almost fully operational. Brest and Lorient were still under siege, as were the Channel ports, and while the port of Antwerp was virtually undamaged it could not be used because the Germans still occupied both banks of the Scheldt. Because of the damage done to the French railway system by the Allied bombing almost total reliance was on trucks to bring up supplies. Consequently, from **25 August** a conveyor-belt system known as the 'Red Ball Express' was set up to keep the armies supplied. There were, however, insufficient trucks and drivers to be able to deliver sufficient fuel and vehicle spares to maintain the rapidly increasing rate of advance. Consequently both Montgomery and Bradley were forced to halt some formations to keep the others moving.

It was in this context that Montgomery argued that the rate of supply was not sufficient to support

P184 · Normandy Break-Out

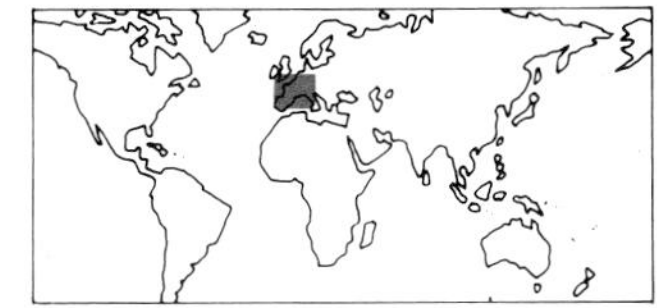

vo major thrusts on the Ruhr and the Saar. Instead iere should be just one thrust directed on the Ruhr nd mounted quickly before the Germans had time ɔ rebuild their strength in the west. Eisenhower ɔntinued to insist that the advance to the Rhine iould be on a broad front, but did agree that 1ontgomery could have the one available theatre eserve. This was the First Allied Airborne Army ɔmmanded by the US airman, General Lewis rereton, and consisting of two US airborne and two ritish airborne divisions and the Polish Parachute rigade. Since D-Day it had been alerted for a umber of possible operations in support of the round forces but all of them had been cancelled.

September **Hitler recalled von Rundstedt to e CinC West.**
1odel had been both CinC West and CinC Army iroup B throughout this time and running two HQs ad proved an almost impossible task. He therefore everted to being just CinC Army Group B.

September **The Canadians began to attack oulogne.**
was eventually surrendered on the 22nd, but the ort facilities had been badly damaged, as would be ie case with the other Channel ports.

September **British Second and US First Armies losed to the Albert Canal.**
lthough the Americans made a crossing near Iasselt it was noticeable that the German resistance vas beginning to stiffen.

Because of the overstretched supply lines Mont- omery would not be able to assemble sufficient ridging to cross the numerous Dutch rivers on is route to the Ruhr before mid-September. He ierefore decided to use First Allied Airborne Army ɔ capture bridges intact. This was the genesis of)peration 'Market-Garden'.

September **The Canadians began to attack)unkirk and the Americans launched their final ssault on Brest.**
)unkirk would resist all efforts to liberate it and vould not surrender until the end of the war against iermany. The US First Army entered Liège and ırther crossings were made over the Albert Canal t Geel and Maastricht.

0 September **Eisenhower approved the plan ɔr 'Market-Garden'.**
'hree airborne divisions would be used, US 82nd nd 101st and British 1st, together with the Polish 'arachute Brigade. The US 101st would seize the ridges over the Wilhelmina and Willemsvaart Canals at Eindhoven; the 82nd the bridges over he Maas at Grave and the Waal at Nijmegen; and he British 1st Airborne the bridge over the Rhine t Arnhem. General Frederick 'Boy' Browning's I Airborne Corps HQ would command the airborne

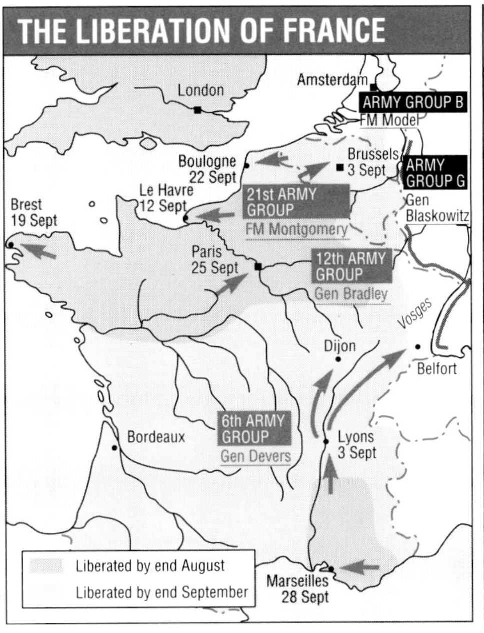

side while General Brian Horrocks's British XXX Corps advanced northwards to link up with the airborne forces. If successful the operation would turn the German flank on the Rhine. The Canadians occupied Ostend.

11 September **First Allied troops crossed the German border.**
This was a patrol from 2nd Platoon, Troop 'B', 85th Cavalry Reconnaissance Squadron of the US 5th Armored Division which waded across the River Our near the Luxemburg border and into Germany near the village of Stalzemberg. Lack of fuel prevented this from being exploited, although other patrols also entered Germany in the same area on this day.

12–15 September **Hodges's US First Army attempted to break through the West Wall south of Aachen.**
Although some penetration was made, lack of ammunition and German reinforcements hampered progress. Further south Patton's Third Army, despite grave fuel shortages, closed up to the Moselle between Metz and Epinal, crossing it opposite Nancy. The German defences, under von Rundstedt's guidance, were beginning to recover.

12 September **Le Havre finally surrendered to the Canadians.**

15 September **US 6th Army Group became operational.**
Commanded by General Jacob Devers, this now took control of the US Seventh Army and French Army A, which had been under command of 7th Army and now became First French Army. By this stage the Americans and French had driven the remnants of Army Group G back into Germany and were now facing them in the Vosges Mountains and the Belfort Gap.

17 September **Operation 'Market-Garden' launched.**
101st Airborne Division quickly secured its objectives. 82nd Airborne Division captured its Meuse bridge, but was foiled on that over the Waal by a German counter-attack. 1st Airborne Division fought its way into Arnhem and seized the bridge over the Rhine there. XXX Corps, with XII and VIII Corps covering its flanks, entered Eindhoven, but from here on the advance would be restricted to a single road with low-lying wet country on each side.

18 September **XXX Corps linked up with 101st Airborne Division.**

19 September **XXX Corps linked up with 82nd Airborne Division.**
Next day the two combined to take the Nijmegen bridge over the Waal. German resistance was increasing, however. In Arnhem the British still held the bridge, but German pressure was mounting, mainly from 9th and 10th SS Panzer Divisions, which had been refitting in the area after the fighting in Normandy. Brest finally fell to US VIII Corps.

21 September **The Germans recaptured the bridge at Arnhem.**
The Polish Parachute Brigade reinforced 1st Airborne Division, landing south of the Rhine, but German counter-attacks prevented it from moving into Arnhem.

22 September **The Germans cut XXX Corps' route south of Uden.**
This slowed down the advance. The same happened on the 24th. Meanwhile the Allied airborne troops in Arnhem had been forced into an ever-contracting defensive perimeter. Boulogne fell to the Canadians.

26 September **The end of 'Market-Garden'.**
Although XXX Corps did succeed in reaching the south bank of the Lower Rhine and linking up with the Polish paratroops, it was too late to save 1st Airborne Division in Arnhem. Only just over 2,000 out of 10,000 escaped back across the Rhine.

'Market-Garden' represented the one prospect of finishing the war in Europe in 1944. It failed for a variety of reasons, but, given the Allies' supply situation and the German powers of recovery, it is questionable whether the thrust into Germany could have been maintained had it been successful. Still reliant on Cherbourg as the main supply port, the Allies were now faced with a frustrating autumn. What they did now finally recognize was the importance of clearing the Scheldt and opening up the port of Antwerp.

Closing up to the German Border · P202

Closing up to the German Border

The overstretched Allied supply lines and the failure at Arnhem meant that the opportunity for the Allies to defeat Germany before the end of 1944 had gone. Pressed by Admiral Sir Bertram Ramsay, the Allied naval CinC, Eisenhower had decided on **22 September 1944** that priority must be given to the opening up of the Scheldt so that the port of Antwerp could be brought into operation. This task he passed to Montgomery's 21st Army Group, leaving Bradley's 12th Army Group to try and fight its way through the West Wall and Devers' 6th Army Group to close up to the Rhine in the southernmost part of the front down to the Swiss border. In the meantime, on **14 September** the Allied strategic air forces had reverted to operations under ccontrol of the Combined Chiefs of Staff, with priorities of oil, transportation, tank and mechanical transport production and depots, and ordnance depots, as well as direct support for land and naval forces.

27 September 1944 Montgomery ordered Canadian First Army to clear the Scheldt estuary.
On the same day Patton began to attack Metz.

30 September Calais liberated by the Canadian 3rd Division.

1 October Canadian 2nd Division began to advance towards Beveland.
The object was to secure the north bank of the Scheldt. In the meantime the Canadian First Army was also about to begin to reduce the Breskens pocket on the south side of the mouth of the Scheldt estuary. This contained the experienced German 64th Division.

2 October US First Army began to attack the West Wall between Aachen and Geilenkirchen.

6 October Opening of the Battle of Huertgen Forest.
This wooded area lay just south-east of the point where the German, Dutch and Belgian borders met. The West Wall passed through it. It was to be a grim and bloody battle for Hodges' US First Army.

12 October British Second Army began to advance south-east from Overloon, which was captured that day.
Montgomery wanted to clear the Peel marshes, but the strength of the German defences caused him to abandon this on the 17th, after the capture of Venraij, and devote his attention to the Scheldt. Patton called off his frontal attack on Metz, which had made little progress, and began to plan an envelopment of the city.

16 October Canadian 2nd Division captured Woensdrecht, thus sealing the German Fifteenth Army in the Beveland peninsula.
On the same day, after a period of bitter fighting, the Americans succeeded in surrounding Aachen and the French First Army began to attack in the Vosges.

18 October Eisenhower gave orders for the next phase of operations.
While Montgomery was to continue with the clearance of the Scheldt, Bradley was to advance to the Rhine and secure a bridgehead over it at Cologne (Operation 'Queen'). The main thrust would be made by Hodges' First Army, with General William Simpson's Ninth Army on his left and Patton's Third Army on the right. Patton would only move forward once his supply situation permitted since he enjoyed the lowest supply priority within the Army Group. Devers was to continue to push towards the Belfort Gap and Montgomery, once the port of Antwerp had been opened, was to clear the area between the Rhine and the Maas.

21 October Aachen finally fell to the Americans.
The German garrison had offered fierce resistance and the two US divisions involved, 1st and 30th Infantry, were exhausted by the end of the month. Breskens fell to the Canadians.

22 October British XII Corps began to attack east of the Maas.
The initial objectives were Tilburg and s'Hertogenbosch.

29 October Canadian 2nd Division captured Goes on South Beveland.

1 November Amphibious assault on Walcheren (Operation 'Infatuate').
The coastal defences had been attacked repeatedly by RAF Bomber Command during the previous few weeks. There were landings by Commandos at Westkapelle and by Commandos and a British infantry brigade at Flushing (now Vlissingen). The Canadians crossed from South Beveland on the 3rd, having, on the 2nd, ended German resistance in the Breskens pocket. Walcheren was secured on **8 November**, but the clearing of mines from the estuary had already begun on the 4th.

8 November Patton began an offensive in the Saar.
Very heavy rain had postponed the start of 'Queen', First Army's thrust to Cologne, but Patton decided to press on. Next day his troops crossed the Moselle at Malling and Uckange, and the Seille south of Metz.

14 November French First Army began an attack to seize the Belfort Gap (Operation 'Independence').
British XII Corps began to reduce the German bridgehead over the Maas between Venlo and Roermond.

16 November US First and Ninth Armies launched Operation 'Queen'.

18 November British XXX Corps began an operation to capture the Geilenkirchen salient ('Clipper').
The fighting in the Huertgen Forest was renewed. Patton's troops entered Metz and the French First Army was well into the Belfort Gap.

22 November French First Army entered Mulhouse.

23 November Elements of US Seventh Army entered Strasbourg.

26 November US Third Army began to penetrate the Maginot Line.

26 November The first merchant vessels entered the port of Antwerp.
By 1 December 10,000 tons of supplies were being unloaded per day and this increased to 19,000 tons within two weeks.

29 November US First Army had just about cleared the Huertgen Forest and was overlooking the Roer valley.
The process had reduced two more divisions, 4th and 8th, to tatters. Simpson's Ninth Army had also been slowly advancing north of Aachen towards the Roer.

4 December Patton began to break through the West Wall in the Saar.
It happened that the defences here were especially strong and progress was slow, but bridgeheads were established over the River Saar.

7 December The Maastricht Conference.
This was attended by Eisenhower, Tedder, Montgomery and Bradley. Montgomery still argued for a single thrust to the Ruhr, but Eisenhower dismissed this, although he did give the US Ninth Army to 21st Army Group for its advance to the Ruhr, while continuing to insist that the advance to the Rhine be on a broad front.

9 December US Ninth Army completed the clearance of the west bank of the Roer from Brachelen to Altdorf.
The main concern now was that the Germans would open the Roer dams and flood the countryside. General Leonard Gerow's US V Corps began to advance through the Monschau corridor in order to seize the dams from the north, but by the end of **15 December** this had ground to a halt in the face of stiff German resistance. In the extreme south 6th Army Group was beginning to reduce the Colmar pocket which was held by the German Nineteenth Army.

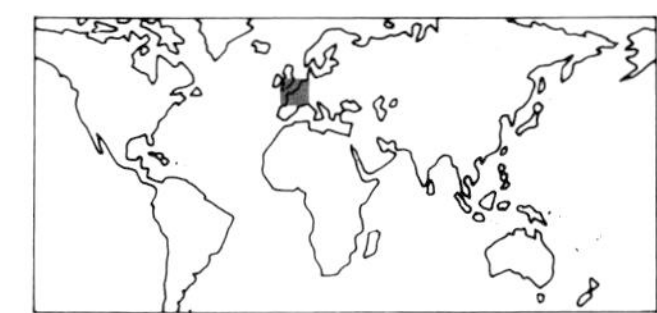

TO THE WEST WALL

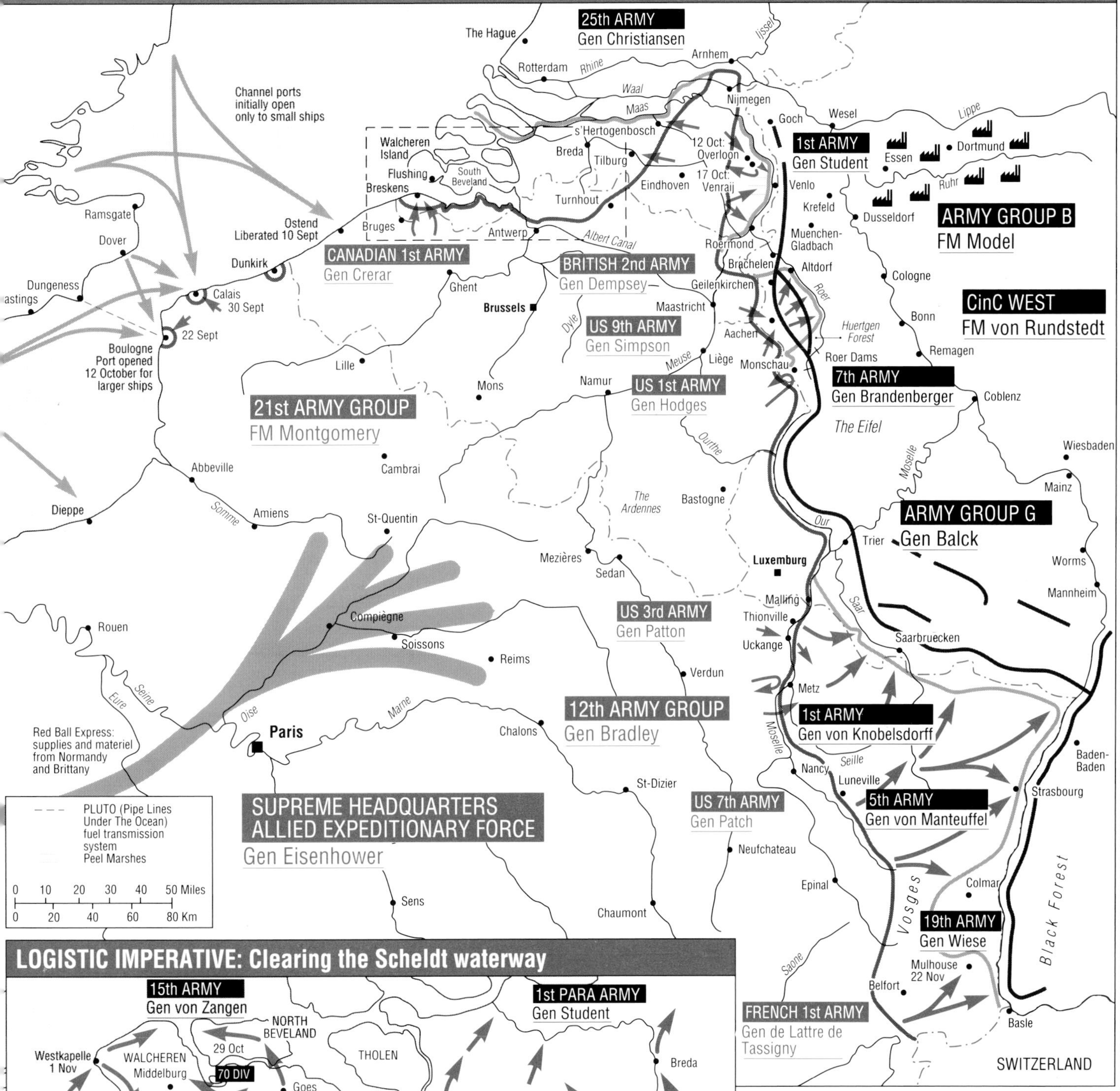

25th ARMY
Gen Christiansen

1st ARMY
Gen Student

ARMY GROUP B
FM Model

CinC WEST
FM von Rundstedt

7th ARMY
Gen Brandenberger

ARMY GROUP G
Gen Balck

1st ARMY
Gen von Knobelsdorff

5th ARMY
Gen von Manteuffel

19th ARMY
Gen Wiese

CANADIAN 1st ARMY
Gen Crerar

BRITISH 2nd ARMY
Gen Dempsey

US 9th ARMY
Gen Simpson

US 1st ARMY
Gen Hodges

21st ARMY GROUP
FM Montgomery

US 3rd ARMY
Gen Patton

12th ARMY GROUP
Gen Bradley

US 7th ARMY
Gen Patch

FRENCH 1st ARMY
Gen de Lattre de Tassigny

SUPREME HEADQUARTERS ALLIED EXPEDITIONARY FORCE
Gen Eisenhower

Channel ports initially open only to small ships

Ostend Liberated 10 Sept

Calais 30 Sept

22 Sept

Boulogne Port opened 12 October for larger ships

Red Ball Express: supplies and materiel from Normandy and Brittany

12 Oct: Overloon

17 Oct: Venraij

The Hague, Rotterdam, Rhine, Waal, Maas, Arnhem, Nijmegen, Ijssel, Goch, Wesel, Lippe, Essen, Dortmund, Ruhr, Venlo, Krefeld, Dusseldorf, Muenchen-Gladbach, Altdorf, Cologne, Bonn, Remagen, Coblenz, Wiesbaden, Mainz, Worms, Mannheim, Walcheren Island, Flushing, South Beveland, Breskens, Bruges, Antwerp, Albert Canal, s'Hertogenbosch, Breda, Tilburg, Eindhoven, Turnhout, Roermond, Brachelen, Geilenkirchen, Roer, Maastricht, Aachen, Huertgen Forest, Roer Dams, Monschau, Liège, Meuse, Dyle, Namur, Brussels, Ghent, Mons, Lille, Ramsgate, Dover, Dungeness, Hastings, Dunkirk, Abbeville, Somme, Amiens, Cambrai, Dieppe, St-Quentin, Ourthe, The Ardennes, Bastogne, The Eifel, Moselle, Our, Trier, Luxemburg, Mezières, Sedan, Malling, Thionville, Uckange, Saar, Saarbruecken, Metz, Verdun, Rouen, Compiègne, Soissons, Reims, Seine, Eure, Oise, Marne, Paris, Chalons, St-Dizier, Nancy, Seille, Luneville, Strasbourg, Baden-Baden, Neufchateau, Epinal, Vosges, Colmar, Black Forest, Chaumont, Sens, Saone, Belfort, Mulhouse 22 Nov, Basle, SWITZERLAND

PLUTO (Pipe Lines Under The Ocean) fuel transmission system
Peel Marshes

0 10 20 30 40 50 Miles
0 20 40 60 80 Km

LOGISTIC IMPERATIVE: Clearing the Scheldt waterway

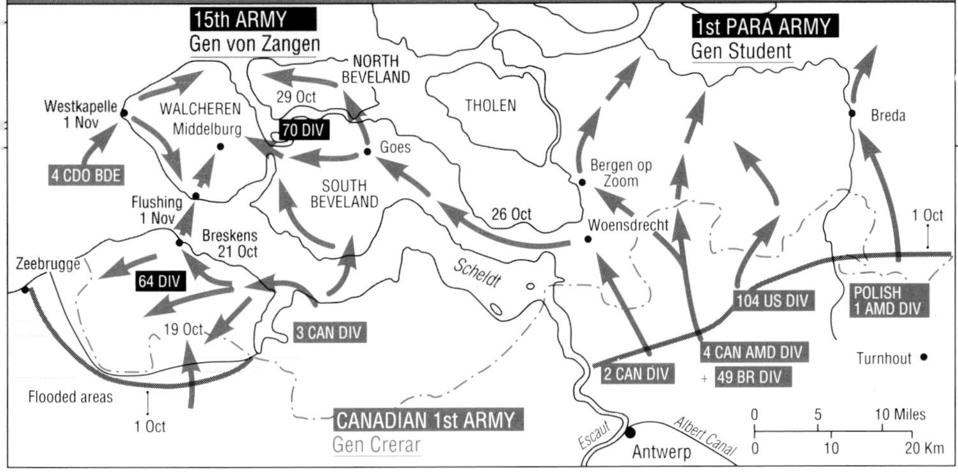

15th ARMY
Gen von Zangen

1st PARA ARMY
Gen Student

CANADIAN 1st ARMY
Gen Crerar

4 CDO BDE, 70 DIV, 64 DIV, 3 CAN DIV, 2 CAN DIV, 4 CAN AMD DIV + 49 BR DIV, 104 US DIV, POLISH 1 AMD DIV

Westkapelle 1 Nov, WALCHEREN, Middelburg, NORTH BEVELAND, 29 Oct, THOLEN, Goes, SOUTH BEVELAND, Flushing 1 Nov, Breskens 21 Oct, Zeebrugge, 19 Oct, 1 Oct, Flooded areas, 26 Oct, Scheldt, Bergen op Zoom, Woensdrecht, Breda, 1 Oct, Turnhout, Escaut, Albert Canal, Antwerp

0 5 10 Miles
0 10 20 Km

Although some substantial gains had been made during the past three months, German resistance had been stiff and the autumn rains and snow had not helped. It had been a frustrating period for the Western Allies and they were still some way from the Rhine apart from in the extreme south. Nevertheless, Belgium, southern Holland and France, apart from a few border areas, were now liberated. The Allies were, however, about to receive a rude shock.

The Ardennes Counter-Offensive · P204

16 SEPTEMBER 1944 TO 1 JANUARY 1945

The Ardennes Counter-Offensive

As early as **16 September 1944** Hitler announced at one of his conferences his intention to make a counter-attack out of the Ardennes with Antwerp the objective. It was designed to cut 21st Army Group off from 12th Army Group. It is probable, however, that the idea had been brewing in his mind for some weeks, certainly since the Russian offensive had come to a halt on the Vistula. The destruction of 20–30 enemy divisions would have much more impact on the Western Allies than on the Russians and could swing the balance of fortune very much in Germany's direction.

On **25 September** Hitler gave his detailed reasoning and ordered General Alfred Jodl, head of his operations section, to draw up an outline plan. Surprise was paramount and, because of the Allies' overwhelming air supremacy, maximum advantage would have to be taken of the winter fogs.

In the meantime, desperate efforts were being made to make good the losses suffered during the past year. On **25 July** Hitler had issued a directive for 'total war', demanding one million recruits for the Wehrmacht. A new type of division, Volksgrenadier, was formed, slimmer than the normal division and with priority on defence. These were made up of men combed out from industry and remnants of formations that had already been destroyed. In October 1944 an additional organization, the Volksturm, was also formed. This was raised on a district basis and drew in all males aged 16–60 to provide a last line of defence for the Third Reich. German war production, largely thanks to the efforts of the Minister, Albert Speer, had peaked during 1944, despite the Allied bombing. The Russian halt on the Vistula and the successful slowing down of the Allied advance in the west enabled *matériel* to be stockpiled for the German counter-offensive.

9 October 1944 Jodl presented his draft plan for Operation 'Wacht am Rhein'.

Some 31 divisions could be made available and Jodl put forward five possible courses of action. They represented limited double envelopments in five areas along the front, from Duesseldorf in the north to the Belfort Gap in the south. None was ambitious enough for Hitler and he told Jodl to think again. Two days later Jodl produced a revised plan. The operation would be carried out by three armies under the command of Model's Army Group B. Von Rundstedt, as CinC, West, would exercise overall supervision. The attack would hit the Americans in the Ardennes and western edge of the Eifel, seize crossings over the Meuse and then drive on to Antwerp. The main weight of the attack would be in the north and would comprise Sepp Dietrich's newly formed Sixth Panzer Army (four SS Panzer divisions, five infantry divisions). To his south would be Hasso von Manteuffel's Fifth Panzer Army (three Panzer and four infantry divisions) and finally, to hold the southern shoulder, would be Erich Brandenberger's Seventh Army (four infantry divisions). In theatre reserve were three infantry and the equivalent of one Panzer division, while Model had one infantry division, and call could be made on Gustav-Adolph von Zangen's Fifteenth Army, which was Dietrich's northern neighbour.

22 October Hitler briefed von Rundstedt's and Model's chiefs of staff.

This was the first time that anyone outside Hitler's HQ heard of the operation. Hitler ordered that the operation begin on 25 November. Von Rundstedt and Model were appalled, viewing the plan as much too ambitious and instead proposed a double envelopment of the US forces around Aachen. This became known as the 'Small Solution', but found no favour with Hitler, although he did agree to the attack being postponed to **10 December** in order to allow more time for preparation.

Five days later the army commanders were briefed, but such was the need for secrecy that the corps commanders were not informed until mid-November and the divisional commanders not until early December.

8 December The attacking forces began to deploy.

All movement took place at night. By this time Hitler had agreed to a further postponement of the launch date to 15 December.

12-13 December Hitler held a final conference.

This took place at one of his western command posts, the 'Eagle's Nest' in the Taunus hills north of Frankfurt am Main. He conceded a further 24 hours' postponement. While the Allies were receiving a number of intelligence indicators that the Germans were preparing something, they remained convinced that, in view of the continuous pressure on them since June, the German armies were incapable of mounting a major offensive. As it was, VIII US Corps, which would bear the brunt of the initial onslaught, consisted of two divisions (4th and 28th) that were recovering from the Huertgen Forest fighting, a weak armoured division (9th) and one unblooded division (106th), which had just arrived from the USA. Indeed, the Ardennes - Eifel sector was considered a quiet one.

16 December The opening of 'Wacht am Rhein'.

After a short, sharp pre-dawn bombardment the attack began in heavy fog, which grounded Allied air power. In the Monschau area in the extreme north progress was slow, but one battle group, under Joachim Peiper, of I SS Panzer Corps, managed by the end of the day to penetrate deep into the US lines and was racing for the Meuse bridges. The German Fifth Army, however, broke through 106th Division, but had a harder task against the experienced 28th Division. Confusion was sown in Allied lines by the infiltration of groups of men dressed in US uniforms from Otto Skorzeny's 150 Panzer Brigade (Operation 'Greif').

Not until the afternoon did the Allied high command realize that the attack was more than a feint and began to organize reinforcements. Eisenhower himself, because of the scare produced by Skorzeny's men, became a virtual prisoner in his HQ at Versailles.

18 December Sixth Panzer Army crossed the River Ambleve, while Fifth Panzer Army approached Bastogne.

Only Peiper's battle group had continued to make significant progress on Dietrich's front, but skilful blowing of bridges and the wintry conditions were making it increasingly difficult for it to get quickly to the Meuse.

Eisenhower met Bradley, Devers and Patton at Verdun. Eisenhower laid down that the advance to the Rhine was to be halted until the German offensive had been stopped. Patton was to counter-attack from the south and, indeed, had already begun to make preparations to switch his army through 90 degrees.

19 December Von Manteuffel failed to rush Bastogne.

It was reinforced this day by 101st US Airborne Division. Peiper was being increasingly frustrated in his drive to the Meuse and all attacking formations were beginning to suffer from shortage of fuel.

Eisenhower agreed that Montgomery should take control of the northern part of the salient, taking US First and Ninth Armies under command. Montgomery immediately began to deploy elements of British XXX Corps to guard the Meuse bridges.

22 December Sixth Panzer Army's offensive had ground to a halt.

Peiper's battle group had failed to make further progress and was now cut off. Dietrich was now ordered to begin to transfer formations to von Manteuffel and within a few days would be entirely on the defensive. Von Manteuffel, in the meantime, had surrounded Bastogne, which refused to surrender, and his armoured spearheads pushed as far west as just short of Dinant on the Meuse by the end of the 24th. This, however, was the high water mark of the German offensive. Patton was beginning to attack from the south and the weather had now cleared sufficiently for the Allies to be able to use their air power.

26 December Bastogne relieved.

It was achieved by the US 4th Armored Division. While von Manteuffel tried during the next few days to drive the Americans back and secure Bastogne, Patton's increasing pressure proved too much.

1939	1940	1941	1942	1943	1944	1945

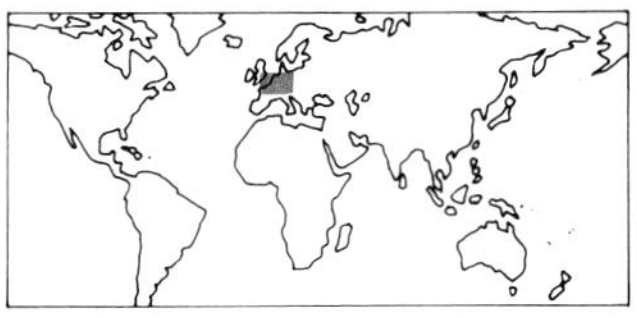

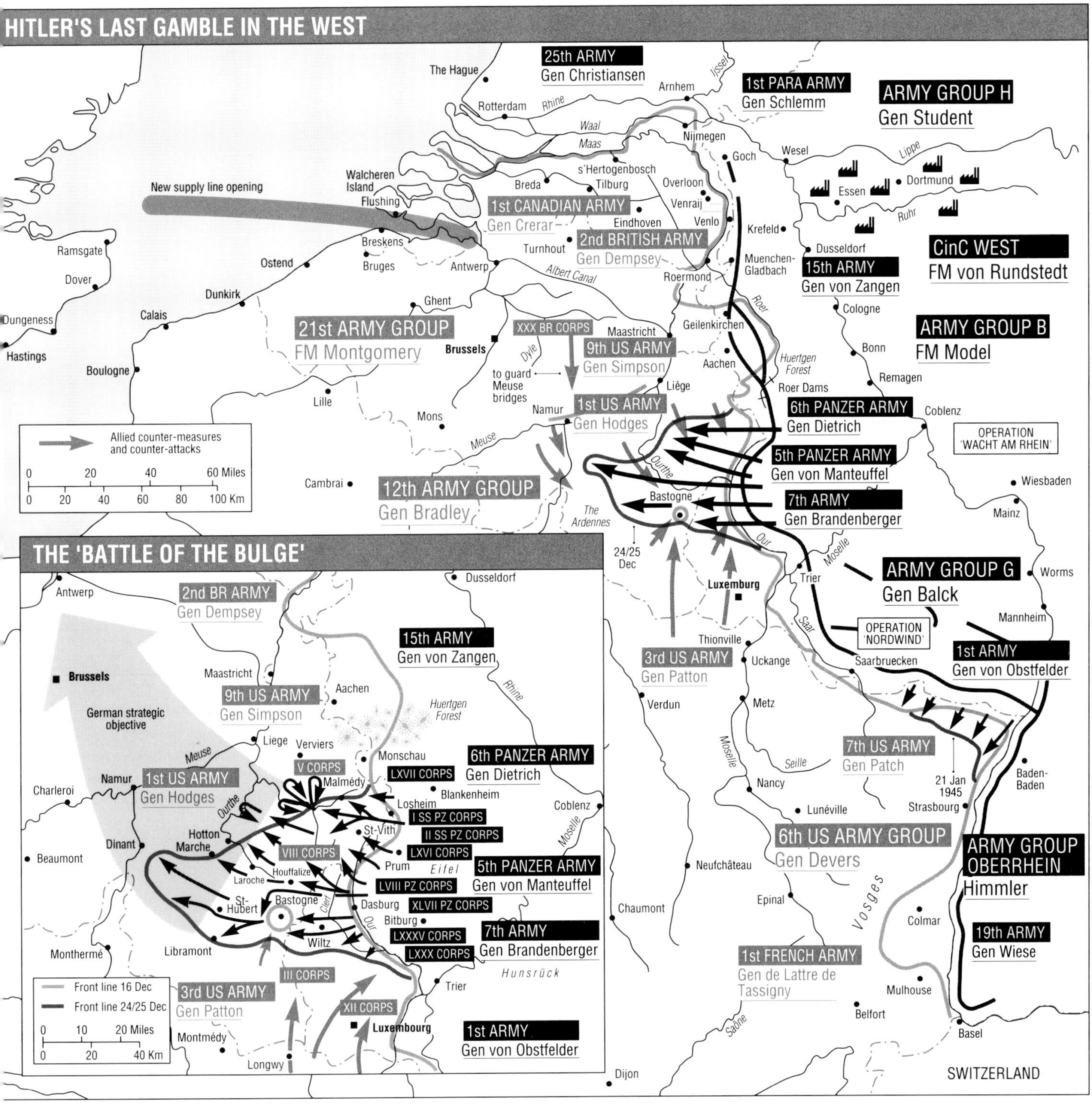

HITLER'S LAST GAMBLE IN THE WEST
25th ARMY
Gen Christiansen
1st PARA ARMY
Gen Schlemm
ARMY GROUP H
Gen Student
1st CANADIAN ARMY
Gen Crerar
2nd BRITISH ARMY
Gen Dempsey
15th ARMY
Gen von Zangen
CinC WEST
FM von Rundstedt
21st ARMY GROUP
FM Montgomery
XXX BR CORPS
9th US ARMY
Gen Simpson
ARMY GROUP B
FM Model
to guard Meuse bridges
1st US ARMY
Gen Hodges
6th PANZER ARMY
Gen Dietrich
OPERATION 'WACHT AM RHEIN'
5th PANZER ARMY
Gen von Manteuffel
12th ARMY GROUP
Gen Bradley
7th ARMY
Gen Brandenberger
24/25 Dec
ARMY GROUP G
Gen Balck
OPERATION 'NORDWIND'
3rd US ARMY
Gen Patton
1st ARMY
Gen von Obstfelder
7th US ARMY
Gen Patch
21 Jan 1945
6th US ARMY GROUP
Gen Devers
ARMY GROUP OBERRHEIN
Himmler
19th ARMY
Gen Wiese
1st FRENCH ARMY
Gen de Lattre de Tassigny
New supply line opening
Allied counter-measures and counter-attacks
0 20 40 60 Miles
0 20 40 60 80 100 Km
The Hague
Rotterdam
Arnhem
Nijmegen
Goch
Wesel
Walcheren Island
Flushing
Breda
s'Hertogenbosch
Tilburg
Overloon
Venraij
Eindhoven
Venlo
Essen
Dortmund
Krefeld
Dusseldorf
Ramsgate
Dover
Breskens
Bruges
Ostend
Antwerp
Turnhout
Roermond
Muenchen-Gladbach
Cologne
Dunkirk
Calais
Dungeness
Hastings
Boulogne
Ghent
Brussels
Maastricht
Geilenkirchen
Aachen
Bonn
Huertgen Forest
Remagen
Liège
Roer Dams
Lille
Mons
Namur
Coblenz
Cambrai
Bastogne
The Ardennes
Wiesbaden
Mainz
Luxemburg
Trier
Worms
Mannheim
Thionville
Uckange
Saarbruecken
Verdun
Metz
Nancy
Lunéville
Strasbourg
Baden-Baden
Neufchâteau
Epinal
Colmar
Chaumont
Mulhouse
Belfort
Basel
Dijon
SWITZERLAND
Rhine
Waal
Maas
Albert Canal
Meuse
Roer
Ourthe
Our
Moselle
Saar
Seille
Vosges
Saône
Lippe
Ruhr
Dyle
Issel
THE 'BATTLE OF THE BULGE'
2nd BR ARMY
Gen Dempsey
15th ARMY
Gen von Zangen
9th US ARMY
Gen Simpson
German strategic objective
1st US ARMY
Gen Hodges
V CORPS
LXVII CORPS
6th PANZER ARMY
Gen Dietrich
I SS PZ CORPS
II SS PZ CORPS
VIII CORPS
LXVI CORPS
5th PANZER ARMY
LVIII PZ CORPS
Gen von Manteuffel
XLVII PZ CORPS
LXXXV CORPS
7th ARMY
LXXX CORPS
Gen Brandenberger
III CORPS
3rd US ARMY
Gen Patton
XII CORPS
1st ARMY
Gen von Obstfelder
Front line 16 Dec
Front line 24/25 Dec
0 10 20 Miles
0 20 40 Km
Antwerp
Dusseldorf
Brussels
Maastricht
Aachen
Huertgen Forest
Liege
Verviers
Monschau
Malmédy
Blankenheim
Losheim
St-Vith
Charleroi
Namur
Coblenz
Beaumont
Dinant
Hotton
Marche
Houffalize
Prum
Eifel
Laroche
St-Hubert
Bastogne
Dasburg
Bitburg
Montherme
Libramont
Wiltz
Trier
Hunsrück
Luxembourg
Montmédy
Longwy
Meuse
Ourthe
Clerf
Our
Moselle
Rhine

Night of 31 December/1 January General Hermann Balck's Army Group G launched Operation 'Nordwind'.

This had been prepared for some days and was designed to destroy the Allied forces in Alsace. It was mounted by Hans von Obstfelder's First Army. 6th Army Group were ready for it and the Germans enjoyed only very limited success. Eisenhower ordered US Seventh Army to withdraw in order to shorten its line, but de Gaulle objected to giving up Strasbourg and Eisenhower was, for political reasons, forced to modify his order.

1 January 1945 The Luftwaffe mounted Operation 'Bodenplatte' against Allied airfields. 900 aircraft took part and succeeded in destroying some 300 Allied aircraft, mainly on the ground, for the loss of about the same number. This was the last German offensive in the Ardennes.

By now the Allies were beginning to push the Germans back and before the end of the month had regained all the ground they had lost. Both sides suffered some 80,000 casualties, but the Allies were in a much better position to make good theirs. Hitler's last gamble in the west delayed the Allied advance to the Rhine by some six weeks, but this was not enough to affect the ultimate course of the war, especially since the long-awaited Russian offensive in the east had now opened.

The Rhine Crossings · P216

Storming the Gothic Line

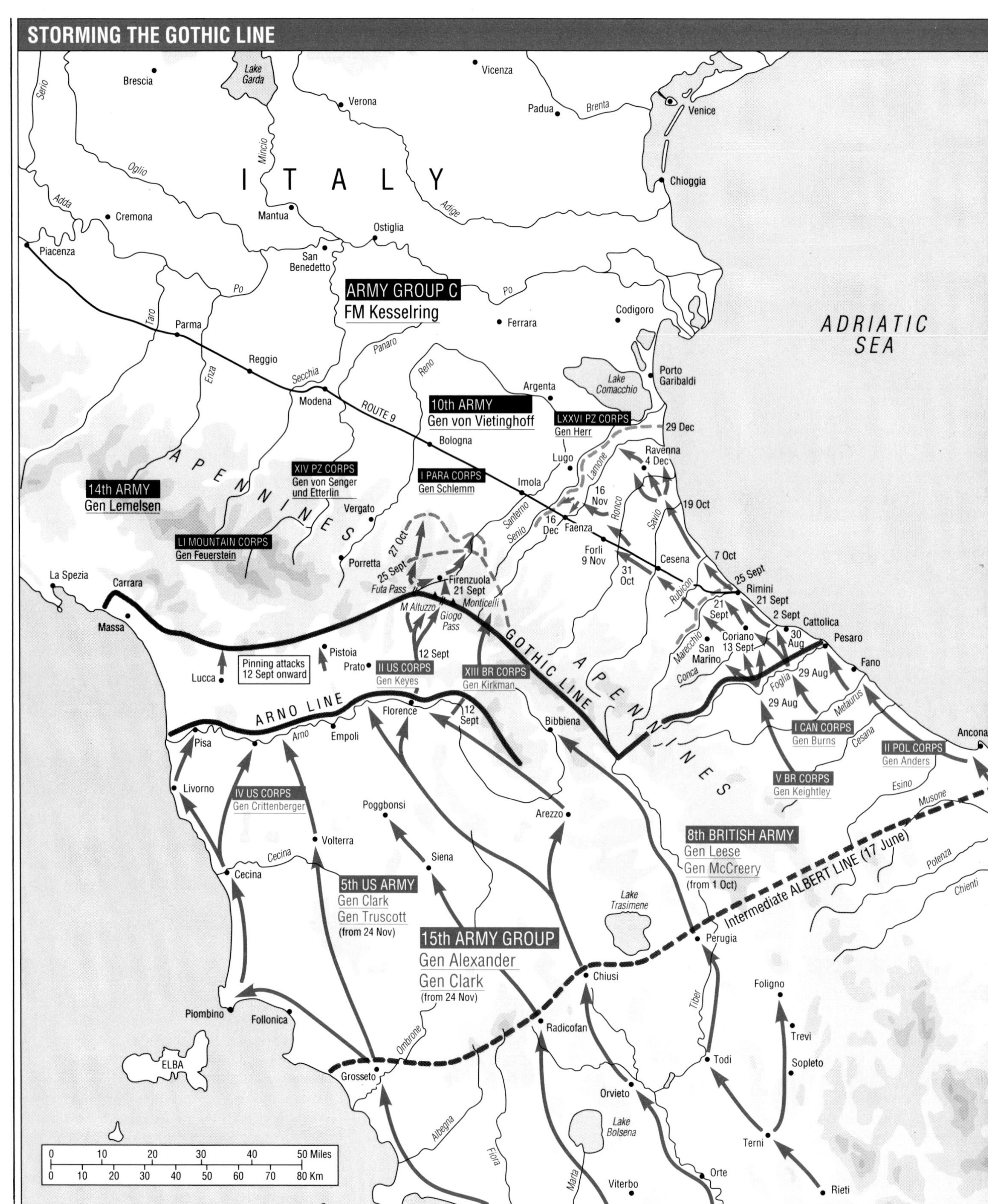
STORMING THE GOTHIC LINE
ITALY
ADRIATIC SEA
ARMY GROUP C
FM Kesselring
10th ARMY
Gen von Vietinghoff
14th ARMY
Gen Lemelsen
LXXVI PZ CORPS
Gen Herr
XIV PZ CORPS
Gen von Senger und Etterlin
I PARA CORPS
Gen Schlemm
LI MOUNTAIN CORPS
Gen Feuerstein
II US CORPS
Gen Keyes
XIII BR CORPS
Gen Kirkman
IV US CORPS
Gen Crittenberger
5th US ARMY
Gen Clark
Gen Truscott
(from 24 Nov)
15th ARMY GROUP
Gen Alexander
Gen Clark
(from 24 Nov)
8th BRITISH ARMY
Gen Leese
Gen McCreery
(from 1 Oct)
I CAN CORPS
Gen Burns
II POL CORPS
Gen Anders
V BR CORPS
Gen Keightley
GOTHIC LINE
ARNO LINE
Intermediate ALBERT LINE (17 June)
ROUTE 9
APENNINES
Pinning attacks 12 Sept onward
Futa Pass
M Altuzzo
Giogo Pass
Monticelli
25 Sept
27 Oct
21 Sept
12 Sept
16 Dec
16 Nov
4 Dec
19 Oct
29 Dec
31 Oct
9 Nov
7 Oct
2 Sept
30 Aug
29 Aug
13 Sept
Brescia
Vicenza
Lake Garda
Verona
Padua
Venice
Chioggia
Cremona
Mantua
Ostiglia
Piacenza
San Benedetto
Parma
Reggio
Modena
Ferrara
Codigoro
Lake Comacchio
Porto Garibaldi
Argenta
Bologna
Lugo
Ravenna
Imola
Faenza
Forli
Cesena
Rimini
Cattolica
Pesaro
Fano
Ancona
San Marino
Coriano
Vergato
Porretta
Firenzuola
La Spezia
Carrara
Massa
Pistoia
Prato
Lucca
Pisa
Florence
Empoli
Bibbiena
Livorno
Poggbonsi
Arezzo
Volterra
Siena
Cecina
Lake Trasimene
Perugia
Chiusi
Piombino
Follonica
Radicofan
Foligno
Trevi
Sopleto
Todi
ELBA
Grosseto
Orvieto
Lake Bolsena
Terni
Orte
Viterbo
Rieti
Serio
Oglio
Adda
Mincio
Adige
Brenta
Po
Taro
Enza
Secchia
Panaro
Reno
Santerno
Senio
Lamone
Ronco
Savio
Rubicon
Marecchio
Conca
Foglia
Metaurus
Cesana
Esino
Musone
Potenza
Chienti
Arno
Cecina
Ombrone
Albegna
Fiora
Marta
Tiber
0 10 20 30 40 50 Miles
0 10 20 30 40 50 60 70 80 Km

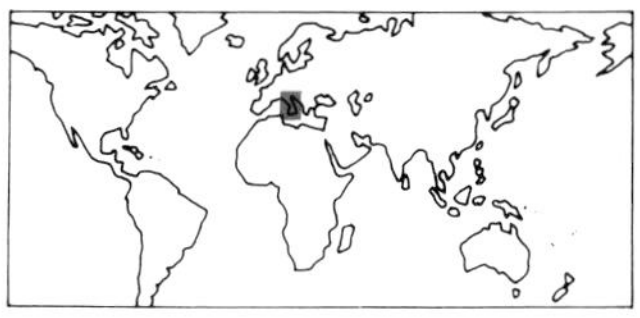

In Italy, Kesselring had decided as early as **1 June 1944**, just before the Allies captured Rome, to withdraw his forces to the Gothic Line in the northern Apennines. Its defences would not, however, be completed until the autumn and hence he needed to buy time during his withdrawal.

Alexander's plan was to continue to concentrate on the west and to thrust for Florence, penetrate the Gothic Line to its north and drive on to Bologna. For a time the German Fourteenth Army was in grave danger of being cut off and isolated, but an intermediate defence line, the Albert Line, 80 miles north of Rome, enabled the Germans to stabilize their position before continuing the withdrawal. Eventually, by **15 July**, the Allies had reached the River Arno and here they were forced to a halt.

The main reason for this was the requirement to remove the French Expeditionary Corps and US VI Corps, who were both earmarked for the landings in the South of France. In their place, in early August, arrived the Brazilian Corps of 25,000 men under General Joao Mascarenhas de Moraes (Brazil had declared war on the Axis powers on 22 August 1942) and the US 92nd Division, which was composed of black soldiers. Neither of these formations had been in combat, but, worse, Fifth Army had had to give more than one-third of its artillery to 'Anvil'.

In spite of this, Alexander was convinced that the Gothic Line could be quickly forced and had produced a plan which called for a surprise attack through the Apennines, which represented the centre of the German line.

4 August 1944 Leese, commanding the British Eighth Army, proposed a new plan.
The loss of the French mountain warfare expertise had put Alexander's plan in jeopardy. Leese now suggested that his army be secretly switched back east of the Apennines. It would then attack towards Rimini. With Kesselring's attention now drawn towards the Adriatic, the US Fifth Army would then attack towards Bologna. Finally, the Eighth Army would strike again, into the plains of Lombardy. Alexander agreed to this, and it was adopted under the code-name 'Olive'.

25 August Operation 'Olive' opened.
Leese attacked with three corps abreast – left V British, centre I Canadian, right II Polish. By the 29th all had reached the River Foglia and faced the Gothic Line itself.

30 August V British and I Canadian Corps crossed the Foglia and began to attack the Gothic Line.
By **2 September** the Canadians had managed to break through the Gothic Line and next day had established a bridgehead over the River Conca. The British on their left, however, had been held up in front of Clemente. By now Kesselring, initially caught by surprise, had begun to react and rushed reinforcements across from the west. This and torrential rain, beginning on the evening of the 4th, brought about a temporary halt.

In the meantime, on Mark Clark's Fifth Army front the Germans had withdrawn from the Arno and into the Gothic Line.

12 September US Fifth Army began its offensive.
Ultra had identified the boundary between the German Tenth and Fourteenth Armies as lying just east of the Il Giorgo Pass. Mark Clark had therefore decided to concentrate on this, with II US Corps attacking in the west and XIII British Corps in the east. US IV Corps on the coast would tie down German IV Corps opposite it. XIII Corps quickly broke through the Gothic Line in its sector, but the Americans became involved in a desperate tussle for the two peaks which guarded Il Giorgo Pass, Montecelli and Monte Altuzzo, and these were not secured until the 17th.

Night of 12/13 September Eighth Army resumed its attacks.
The Canadians captured Cariano and looked poised to complete a major breakthrough. The tanks, however, had great difficulty in crossing the swollen streams and the advance was not resumed until the 14th, giving the Germans time to recover. There now followed a week's hard fighting as the Germans were driven back towards the Rimini Line.

21 September Mark Clark's troops captured Fiorenzuola.
This presented Kesselring with another major threat in that the Americans were now poised to thrust north to Bologna and cut the vital Route 9.

On the same day Rimini fell to the Greek Brigade and the Canadians crossed the River Marecchia. Eighth Army was now faced by the River Po, the next major obstacle, which lay 50 miles to the north. In between were no less than nine other rivers.

24 September Mark Clark began to advance on Bologna.
Once again rain intervened and allowed Kesselring to reorganize his defences.

1 October General Sir Richard McCreery succeeded Leese in command of Eighth Army.
Leese was posted to Burma. On the same day Clark renewed his efforts to reach Bologna. He was now just nine miles from his objective, but still had two miles of mountainous country to fight through.

7 October Eighth Army began to attack towards the River Rubicon.
Within four days the river was reached.

12 October Eighth Army was now advancing north of the Rubicon.
Fifth Army, meanwhile, continued to struggle in the mountains with little tangible success.

19 October Eighth Army crossed the River Savio.
Next day the River Cesano was crossed.

27 October Fifth Army forced to close down its offensive.
It was not yet out of the mountains south of Bologna, and from 20 September to 26 October had suffered 15,700 casualties. This rate was more than the replacement system could keep up with and Mark Clark had no option but to halt. It was now left to the equally tired Eighth Army to maintain the pressure.

31 October Eighth Army crossed the River Ronco.

1 November Eighth Army crossed the River Rabbi.

9 November British 4th Division captured Forli.

16 November Eighth Army crossed the Lamone.

20 November Castiglione fell to the Eighth Army.

24 November Alexander became Supreme Allied Commander in the Mediterranean.
Maitland Wilson moved to Washington as the British representative to the Combined Chiefs of Staff, succeeding Field Marshal Sir John Dill who had died. Mark Clark was appointed to command 15th Army Group in Alexander's place and Lucian Truscott came from France to take over Fifth Army.

4 December Ravenna fell to the Canadians.

16 December Faenza captured by British V Corps.
The New Zealanders reached the Senio.

26 December The Germans launched a surprise counter-attack against the US 92nd Division in the Serchio valley.
This caused a gap in US IV Corps' lines, which was plugged by 8th Indian Division, which had been lent to Fifth Army by Eighth Army. The line was restored on the 28th.

29 December Eighth Army's offensive finally closed down.
It still rested on the south bank of the Senio and several river lines still lay between it and Bologna, let alone the Po. With the Italian winter now having taken a firm grip, Alexander decided to close down offensive operations until the spring. Despite the frustrations they had suffered, the Allies could take satisfaction in that they had kept the German armies in Italy tied down throughout 1944.

The End in Italy · P224

29 SEPTEMBER 1943 TO 14 FEBRUARY 1945

The Greek Civil War

Of increasing concern to the British since the summer of 1943 had been the situation in Greece. As has been explained on page 98, resistance in Greece was made up of three factions: those who supported the monarchy: the republicans; and the Communists. Increasingly, as the tide turned in favour of the Allies and the prospects of liberation grew brighter, the squabbles among the resistance groups increased.

In **March 1943** a group of Greek politicians had signed a manifesto in Athens declaring that King George should not return to his country without a plebiscite having first been held. The king, who was with his government-in-exile in Cairo, offered instead a general election immediately after liberation. This, however, was not enough for either the republicans or the Communists. Neither trusted the king, especially for his appointment of General Metaxas as right-wing virtual dictator. The British, as was their policy with the other occupied countries, supported the government-in-exile and became especially concerned when, after the Italian surrender in **September 1943**, ELAS, the Communist military wing, managed to seize the bulk of the weapons belonging to the Italian troops in Greece.

29 September 1943 Churchill ordered preparations to be made for a British force to be sent to Greece in the event of a German evacuation.
It was to be just a token force and would go to Athens only.

26 March 1944 ELAS set up a Committee of Liberation.
The previous month the British military mission in Greece had established an uneasy truce between ELAS and EDES, the leading republican grouping. This new declaration, in northern Greece, made it clear that the Communists were bent on seizing power once the Germans had left.

31 March Greek officers in Cairo demanded the resignation of the prime minister of the government-in-exile.
They were Communist supporters. Prime Minister Emmanuel Tsouderos, who had been appointed by the king after his predecessor had committed suicide in April 1941, proposed that King George appoint the popular Archbishop Damaskinos as Regent, but the king rejected this. The result was a mutiny by Greek military and naval forces in Egypt, which had to be put down by the British, but without casualties.

12 April King George announced that a new government would be formed representing all views.
The majority of members would be those who had been in Greece throughout the occupation. Tsouderos resigned and the son of General Venizelos, the First World War statesman, was appointed. He, too, quickly proved unacceptable and was replaced on **26 April** by George Papandreou, leader of the Social Democratic Party, who was brought out of Greece.

14–17 May Lebanon Conference.
Papandreou managed to obtain agreement for an all-party government to be set up. ELAS agreed to fight the Germans in Greece until they left.

6 August Churchill re-emphasized the need to be prepared to send a British force to Greece.
He had heard that the Greek Communists were only prepared to remain in the government provided that Papandreou resigned. Ultra had also given warning that the Germans were beginning to withdraw. The aim of the force would be to install a Greek government, accept the German surrender and prepare the way for the introduction of relief aid. Plans were drawn up by Maitland Wilson, Supreme Allied Commander Mediterranean, under the code-name 'Manna'.

21 August Churchill met Papandreou in Rome.
Papandreou asked for British support in uniting Greek resistance against the Germans and pointed out that the Communists had all the arms. He was also worried about Bulgarian troops, who were now across the border in northern Greece. Churchill replied that he could not pledge the sending of British troops to Greece and the possibility must be kept secret. He advised Papandreou to move his Cabinet to Italy as quickly as possible and stressed that it was for the Greek people as a whole to decide whether they wanted a monarchy or a republic. Churchill had, however, made up his mind by now that a force would have to be sent to Greece.

26 September The Caserta Agreement.
Wilson, in an effort to repair the breach between ELAS and EDES before 'Manna' was mounted, called the leaders of the two, Stephanos Saraphis and Napoleon Zervas, and Papandreou together and got them to agree to place their forces under Papandreou's government, which in turn would take orders from General Ronald Scobie, who would command the British force.

In the meantime the Germans had been displaying

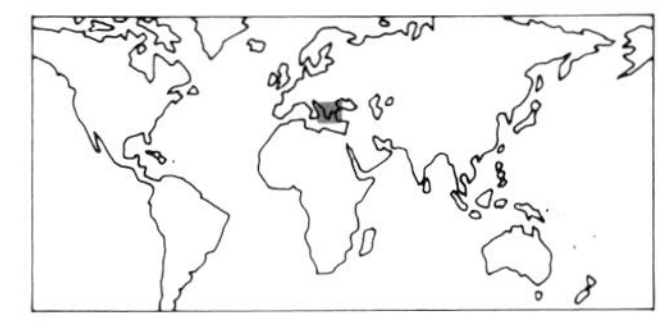

a reluctance to evacuate Athens, which had been the signal for 'Manna' to be mounted.

4 October 'Manna' launched.
British troops were landed at Patras on the north coast of the Peloponnese. This was a town with generally royalist sympathies. It had been established previously by a British force of Commandos, Special Boat Service and Long Range Desert Group, known as Foxforce, which had landed on Cerigo (Kithera) on **17 September**, that the Peloponnese, apart from Corinth, was clear of German troops.

8 October The Germans evacuated Corinth.

9–18 October Churchill obtained confirmation from Stalin in Moscow that Greece was a British problem.
Churchill's greatest fear was that the Russians would give active support to the Greek Communists. In exchange Churchill had to agree to give Stalin virtually a free hand in the remainder of the Balkans. Roosevelt had grudgingly agreed to this course of action, although US suspicions of British imperialist designs on Greece remained strong.

12 October The Germans evacuated Athens.
Next day a British airborne brigade landed and seized Magara airfield, Athens was entered and the Royal Navy occupied Piraeus on the 14th.

16 October Papandreou's government arrived in Athens.
Harold Macmillan, the British minister to Supreme Allied HQ Mediterranean, impressed on Papandreou that he must move quickly to reform the currency, disarm the guerrilla forces, reconstitute a Greek National Army and organize facilities for the reception of relief aid which was being provided by the United Nations Relief and Rehabilitation Agency (UNRRA) for the starving population. If he did not his government would be unable to establish itself. Papandreou did his best, introducing a new currency on **9 November** and plans for the Army on **28 November**. This was to be an amalgam of Greek units that had been serving with the British Army and those that had been part of the various resistance forces. The Communists, however, objected to some of the other elements being incorporated into the Army and refused to surrender their arms. Their six representatives in the government resigned and they called a general strike. In the meantime the Germans had continued their withdrawal and by mid-November were virtually clear of the northern frontier. The Bulgarian forces had also withdrawn.

3 December Civil war broke out in Athens.
Communist demonstrators clashed with police and there were twelve fatalities. ELAS units began to march on Athens and Churchill ordered Scobie to use force to put down ELAS. British reinforcements were organized to be sent to Greece. There was, however, disquiet among left-wing elements in Britain. Fighting quickly spread to Piraeus and Salonica. Stalin, however, had kept his word. There was no Russian involvement or even criticism of British actions in the Russian Press.

25 December Churchill arrived in Greece.
The fighting had continued in spite of British efforts to bring about a cease-fire. Next day a conference (which ELAS delegates attended) was organized, presided over by Archbishop Damaskinos, who had expressed his disgust to Macmillan over atrocities committed by ELAS. Churchill assured the conference of Britain's continued respect for Greek independence and stated that the Greeks must resolve their differences, especially since the priority lay in defeating Germany.

29 December Churchill, on return to England, persuaded King George to agree to Archbishop Damaskinos becoming Regent of Greece.
This was something for which the British had been striving during the past few weeks.

4 January 1945 New Greek Government formed under General Nikolaos Plastiras.
By this stage Scobie's forces had regained complete control of Athens and Piraeus.

12 January Truce signed in Greece.

12 February The Peace of Varkiza.
A major sticking-point had been the refusal of ELAS to release civilian hostages they had taken. They now agreed to do this, to disband their forces and co-operate in the formation of a National Army. Churchill arrived in Athens, on his way back from Yalta, on the 14th and was accorded a warm welcome.

The problems of Greece had been only temporarily solved, however. The question of the monarchy was left unresolved and the Communists withdrew to the mountains in the north, determined on another bid for power once the war was over. In the meantime two divisions' worth of British troops were tied down in Greece as an insurance against further trouble.

GREEK RESISTANCE AND LIBERATION

 Post-war Problems · P246

From the Vistula to the Oder

In November 1944 the Stavka drew up a general plan of campaign for 1945. They recommended that pressure be continued against Hungary and East Prussia in order to force the Germans to weaken their centre. Then Zhukov's 1st Belorussian and Konev's 1st Ukrainian Fronts would be unleashed on a drive from the Vistula to Berlin, with the aim of advancing some 430 miles in 45 days. Stalin approved this in principle and laid down that the main offensive from the Vistula should begin on about **20 January 1945**.

In the meantime the Russians continued their efforts to take Budapest and their leading propagandist, Ilya Ehrenburg, began a campaign to prepare the Red Army for its entry into the Third Reich. It was based on revenge for the sufferings that the Germans had inflicted on the Soviet Union. A wave of darkness was about to descend on the German people living in the east

Hitler's intelligence chief on the Eastern Front, General Reinhardt Gehlen, had, by December 1944, realized what was brewing. Heinz Guderian, who had been acting Army Chief of Staff since July 1944, visited Hitler at the Eagle's Nest on Christmas Eve to warn him of what was about to happen. Still wrapped up in the Ardennes counter-offensive, Hitler dismissed Gehlen's reports as rubbish and refused Guderian's plea that Army Group North be evacuated from the Courland Peninsula or that the German forces in Norway be reduced so that the defences on the Vistula could be strengthened. In the east, only Budapest held his attention in the east and he demanded that a counter-stroke be mounted to relieve the Hungarian capital. He ordered Guderian to switch Herbert Gille's IV SS Panzer Corps from Army Group Centre and for it to carry out this operation.

1 January 1945 Gille mounted his counter-thrust towards Budapest.

This caught the Russians by surprise and Gille managed to get to within fifteen miles of Budapest. Malinovsky now engineered a counter-move designed to envelop Gille's rear.

6 January Churchill asked Stalin when he intended to attack across the Vistula.

The Western Allies wanted the offensive to begin as soon as possible in order to reduce the pressure on them. Stalin assured him that it would take place not later than the second half of the month. The winter had arrived late that year and Stalin's original intention had been to wait until the ground had hardened and the autumn fogs had evaporated. He now gave orders that Konev was to attack on the 12th and Zhukov on the 14th.

7 January Breith's III Panzer Corps attacked towards Budapest.

This was in an effort to link up with and reinforce Gille's thrust. After five days' furious fighting it was

P194 · Finland and the Balkans

halted and both Breith and Gille fell back to their start-lines.

9 January Guderian pleaded with Hitler again for the Vistula defences to be strengthened.
Again Hitler showed little interest.

12 January Konev attacked under a massive artillery bombardment.
By the end of the day he had penetrated up to twelve miles on a 25-mile front, tearing Fourth Panzer Army apart.

13 January Chernyakhovsky's 3rd Belorussian Front attacked westwards into East Prussia.
Third Panzer Army initially resisted bitterly, but was gradually forced back, leaving Fourth Army to its south in danger of being trapped in front of the Masurian Lakes.

14 January Zhukov attacked.
His initial thrust was from the south of Warsaw, but next day he launched an attack to its north aiming at a double envelopment of the city.

On this same day Rokossovsky's 2nd Belorussian Front broke out of its bridgehead on the River Narew and attacked Georg-Hans Reinhardt's Army Group Centre. Initially progress was slow, but after Hitler had ordered Reinhardt to transfer a Panzer corps to Army Group A the Russian offensive gathered momentum. On the 19th Rokossovsky's troops crossed the 1938 border near Neidenburg.

Night of 16/17 January The German garrison of Warsaw, threatened with encirclement, began to withdraw.
It did so amid an orgy of looting and destruction. Next day the First Polish Army finally liberated it. Hitler, furious that Warsaw had been given up so easily, sacked Harpe and replaced him in command of Army Group A by Schoerner. Lothar Rendulic was given Army Group North in Schoerner's place.

17 January Gille launched another attack towards Budapest.
His corps had been brought round in great secrecy to the Lake Balaton area. Tolbukhin's 3rd Ukrainian Front was taken by surprise and on the 19th Gille reached the Danube at Dunapentele, cutting off much of 3rd Ukrainian Front. Gille then moved up the west bank of the Danube and by the 27th was only twelve miles from Budapest.

19 January Konev captured Cracow and Zhukov took Lodz.
The Germans tried desperately to hold the Russian onrush on the Bzura and Rawka river lines, but with no success.

20 January Konev's troops crossed the German frontier with Poland at Namslau.
These were elements of the Fifty-Second and Third Guards Tank Armies, which now turned south towards Katowice. To their north Fourth Tank and Fifth Guards Armies dashed for the Oder, reaching it on the 22nd.

26 January Hitler sacked Reinhardt.
While he had agreed that Memel should be evacuated on the 22nd (Bagramyan's 1st Baltic Front occupied it on the 28th), he insisted that the Loetzen Line, which ran through the Masurian Lakes, should be held. Reinhardt, however, was preparing to order a withdrawal in order to save Fourth Army.

Hitler also reorganized his army groups. Army Group North became Army Group Courland with Heinrich von Vietinghoff, transferred from Italy, being given command; Army Group Centre became Army Group North and Rendulic replaced Reinhardt; Army Group A became Army Group Centre with Schoerner remaining in command. A new army group, Army Group Vistula, was also formed, taking under command Second and Ninth Armies. Command of this was given to none other than Heinrich Himmler, a stark indication of how little Hitler now trusted his generals, especially since it was Army Group Vistula which now had to bar the way to Berlin.

By now the Russians had cut off 26 divisions in Courland and a further 27 in East Prussia. Hitler ordered the towns and cities of these areas to be turned into fortresses, most notable of which was Koenigsberg.

Germany was now facing a flood of refugees from the east, many bearing tales of Russian atrocities. There is no doubt that the Soviet troops responded readily to Ehrenburg's 'eye for an eye' propaganda. Some of those trying to flee by sea from the ports in Pomerania and East Prussia perished in the waters of the Baltic, victims of the Baltic Red Fleet. The worst of these incidents, and, indeed the greatest maritime disaster in history, had occurred on **30 January** when the liner *Wilhelm Gustloff*, which had just left Danzig, was sunk by a Russian submarine with the loss of 8,000 lives.

29 January Zhukov was now across the German frontier in force.
Two days later his armies had reached the Oder and established bridgeheads south of Kuestrin and in the Kienitz area.

By now Konev had cleared the Silesian industrial region and both he and Zhukov were bent in driving on to Berlin. Both had exceeded the Stavka's planned rate of advance and were now running desperately short of supplies. They were therefore forced to halt on the Oder, especially since German resistance had begun to stiffen, and they had been forced to divert formations to deal with a number of German-held fortresses, notably Posen, which they had left in their wake. Furthermore there was increasing concern over the threat that Army Group Vistula presented to Zhukov's right flank from Pomerania.

6 February The Stavka gave orders for the reduction of East Prussia and Pomerania.
1st Baltic and 3rd Belorussian Fronts were tasked with the former and 2nd Belorussian the latter.

10 February Chernyakhovsky, Rokossovsky and Bagramyan began their attacks.
They made little progress. On the 19th Chernyakhovsky, the youngest front commander, died of wounds and was replaced by Vasilievsky, who was Deputy Defence Commissar.

13 February Budapest finally fell.
Gille's relief operation had ground to a halt by the end of January and he was forced once again to withdraw. The German garrison of Budapest resisted building by building and then attempted to break out to the north-west. It was destroyed.

Hitler's attention, however, was still focused on Hungary, especially the oilfields in the Lake Balaton area. He had already earmarked Dietrich's Sixth Panzer Army for Hungary, even though both Guderian and Dietrich believed it more important to send it to the Oder, and it now began to move there from the west.

Night of 13/14 February RAF Bomber Command attack on Dresden.
The Western Allies believed that the only positive way in which they could help the Russian offensive was by bombing the German cities of the east. They hoped that this would convince the Germans that the Allies were acting as one. At the Yalta Conference Stalin confirmed that he would like this to take place. The Americans began this programme, code-named 'Thunderclap', by bombing Berlin and Magdeburg. Dresden, a historic city of little military significance, except that it was packed with refugees, was the next victim. 800 bombers attacked and much of the city was destroyed, with some 50,000 people being killed. The Americans followed up next day and again on **2 March**. This raised disquiet in some Western Allied circles over the morality of 'city busting', and Dresden remains the most controversial raid of the war. Chemnitz was also attacked twice during the next two weeks.

15 February Counter-attack against Zhukov's right flank from Pomerania.
This was mounted by Walther Wenck's Third Panzer Army and made good progress until he himself was injured in a car crash on the 17th. It was, however, sufficient to make Zhukov realize that he must deal with Pomerania before advancing on Berlin.

Pomerania and Vienna · P218

26 SEPTEMBER 1944 TO 14 FEBRUARY 1945

On the Road to Mandalay

On **16 September 1944** the Combined Chiefs of Staff issued a directive to Mountbatten for the clearance of the Japanese from Burma. Earlier, in July, Mountbatten had submitted two plans, 'Capital' and 'Dracula'. 'Capital' was an advance by Slim's Fourteenth Army to the line Mandalay – Pakokku with subsequent exploitation to Rangoon, while 'Dracula' was an amphibious and airborne assault directly on Rangoon and scheduled for January 1945.

The directive was the result of consideration of these plans at the Second Quebec Conference ('Octagon'). It laid down Mountbatten's mission as 'to recapture Burma at the earliest date'. 'Capital' was approved to the extent that it would secure air and overland communications with China. 'Dracula', if it could be carried out before the 1945 monsoon, was also sanctioned. Should this not prove possible, however, 'Capital' was to be continued as long as it did not jeopardize the mounting of 'Dracula' in November 1945, after the monsoon.

The Japanese, too, had been planning. They had also suffered a severe command shake-up. General Hyotaro Kimura took over Burma Area Army and Shihachi Katamura took command of Fifteenth Army.

26 September 1944 Terauchi issued orders for Burma Area Army.
Kimura was to maintain the security of southern Burma, which would provide the northern flank of the South-East Asia 'defence zone'. He was also to try and cut the links between China and India. Terauchi warned him that, although he was receiving some reinforcements, his men would have to be self-sufficient since they could not expect supplies from Japan.

Kimura tasked his armies as follows:
Thirty-Third Army (two divisions) to hold the line Lashio – Monglong mountains, north-east of Mandalay and cut the India–China land link (Operation 'Dan').
Fifteenth Army (three divisions) to halt the Allies on the Irrawaddy ('Ban').
Twenty-Eighth Army (two divisions, one independent brigade) to contact the Allied advance and hold it, as well as defend the area Yenangyaung – Bassein – Rangoon ('Kan').

2 October Churchill declared that it would not be possible to mount 'Dracula' before the 1945 monsoon.
'Dracula' had been very dependent on the war in Europe being ended before the end of 1944. The failure at Arnhem meant that there was no prospect of this. Mountbatten continued to fight for it, however.

19 October Roosevelt recalled Stilwell from China.
The rift between Chiang Kai-shek and Stilwell had continued to grow during 1944, much of the cause being Chiang's relationship with Mao Tse-tung's Communists. Stilwell remained convinced that Chiang was putting considerable effort into containing them instead of concentrating on clearing the Japanese out of China. Matters were aggravated by Roosevelt's sending Vice President Henry Wallace to Chungking in June to persuade Chiang to co-operate with the Communists, and the subsequent sending of a US military mission, code-named 'Dixie', to Mao in July. Journalists also visited him and sent back glowing reports.

Stilwell became even more frustrated by Chiang's lack of drive in facing up to the Japanese thrust to eradicate the US air bases in China, demanding that Chiang put him in charge of all the Chinese armies. Chiang threatened to withdraw his divisions in Burma back behind the River Salween, which would undo all the good work done during the past few months. Roosevelt supported Stilwell and sent Chiang a stiff rebuke, but the Generalissimo was undeterred. He was quite happy to accept another American as commander of his armies, but not Stilwell. Consequently, in order to ensure that China continued to play an active part in the war, Roosevelt had to sacrifice Stilwell.

As far as SEAC was concerned this did enable the complication of Stilwell's 'three hats' to be resolved. Indeed, he was replaced by three Americans. General Albert Wedermeyer became Chiang's adviser, General Daniel Sultan took over Northern Combat Area Command (NCAC) and General Raymond Wheeler became Deputy Supreme Allied Commander. At the same time Mountbatten created a new overall command, Allied Land Forces South East Asia (ALFSEA) which was given to General Sir Oliver Leese, who arrived from Italy.

After the capture of Myitkyina Stilwell had planned as a first priority to use NCAC and Y Force to reopen the Burma Road and link it with the Ledo Road. He also intended to trap the Japanese Thirty-Third Army and destroy it. Sultan and Wedermeyer stuck to this plan.

Slim continued to plan for 'Capital'. The main role in the first phase would be taken by General Geoffrey Scoones' IV Corps, and in early October this began to concentrate in the Kohima area. It was to advance via Pinlebu to the Schwebo area and link up with the British 36th Division, which was part of NCAC and would be advancing south. XXXIII Corps (Montagu Stopford) would cross the Chindwin further south in the Kalewa area and meet IV Corps in the Schwebo Plain. They would then all wheel south to trap the Japanese forces in the heart of the Irrawaddy loop.

In the Arakan, too, plans were being made for offensive operations. These would be carried out by Philip Christison's XV Corps and his primary objectives were set as the islands of Akyab and Ramree, the capture of which would extend air cover to Rangoon and the Thai border.

1 November Y Force retook Lungling.
The Chinese had been pushed back to the Salween in late August, but Stilwell's advance from Myitkyina had forced the Japanese to withdraw.

7 November Chinese Sixth Army (NCAC) entered Schwebo.

3 December The opening of 'Capital'.
11th East African and 20th Indian Divisions crossed the Chindwin at Kalewa and Mawlaik and 19th Indian Division (IV Corps) at Sittaung. Japanese resistance was slight since Kimura, given his parlous supply situation, was not prepared to risk confrontation at this early stage.

8 December General Frank Messervy took command of IV Corps.

15 December Chinese First Army (NCAC) entered Bhamo.

16 December 19th Indian Division linked up with 36th Division at Rail Indaw.

18 December Slim changed his plan.
In view of the lack of Japanese resistance he now planned to use XXXIII Corps to deceive the Japanese into thinking that Mandalay was his main objective while IV Corps drove to the key communications centre of Meiktila. Once the upper Irrawaddy had been secured Fourteenth Army would race south in order to seize a port, Rangoon or Moulmein, before the monsoon broke in May. Slim termed this plan 'Extended Capital' and the first priority was secretly to redeploy IV Corps south down the line of the River Manipur until it was opposite Meiktila.

2 January 1945 2nd British Division (XXXIII Corps) reached Yeu.

4 January XV Corps landed unopposed on Akyab.
The Japanese defences in the Arakan were being stripped to reinforce Mandalay. In the meantime 81st and 82nd West African Divisions were advancing towards Myebon.

7 January XXXIII Corps entered Schwegu.
The town was not completely cleared until the 10th, the same day that Katamura ordered his men to withdraw behind the Irrawaddy.

14 to 16 January 19th Indian Division established bridgeheads across the Irrawaddy.
These were at Kyaukmyaung and Thabeikkyin. Throughout the rest of the month the Japanese

212

OPERATIONS 'CAPITAL' AND 'EXTENDED CAPITAL': Phase One

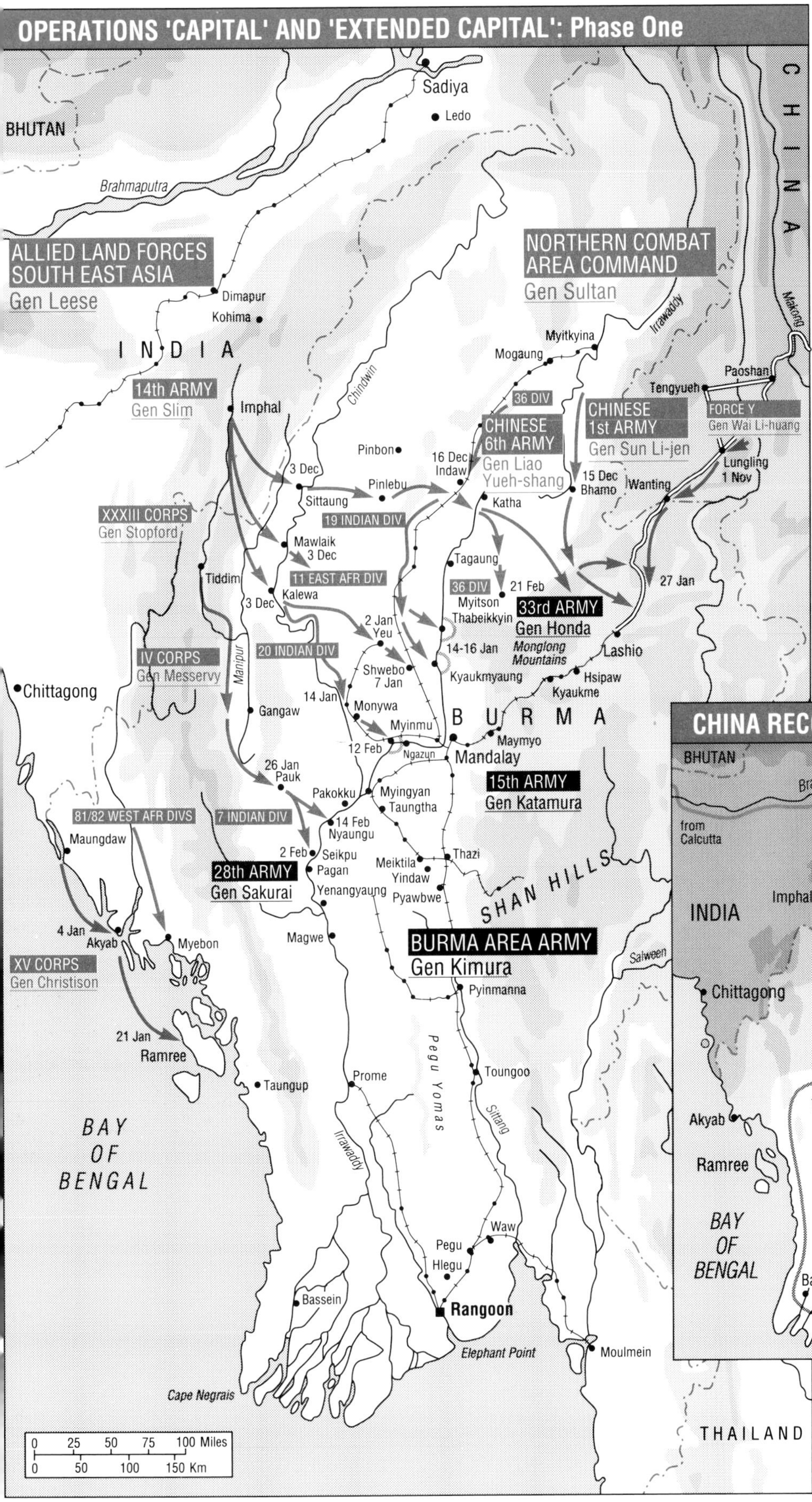

ALLIED LAND FORCES SOUTH EAST ASIA
Gen Leese

NORTHERN COMBAT AREA COMMAND
Gen Sultan

14th ARMY
Gen Slim

XXXIII CORPS
Gen Stopford

IV CORPS
Gen Messervy

XV CORPS
Gen Christison

CHINESE 6th ARMY
Gen Liao Yueh-shang

CHINESE 1st ARMY
Gen Sun Li-jen

FORCE Y
Gen Wai Li-huang

33rd ARMY
Gen Honda

15th ARMY
Gen Katamura

28th ARMY
Gen Sakurai

BURMA AREA ARMY
Gen Kimura

36 DIV · 19 INDIAN DIV · 11 EAST AFR DIV · 20 INDIAN DIV · 7 INDIAN DIV · 81/82 WEST AFR DIVS

BHUTAN · INDIA · CHINA · BURMA · THAILAND · BAY OF BENGAL · SHAN HILLS · Pegu Yomas · Monglong Mountains

0 25 50 75 100 Miles
0 50 100 150 Km

attacked repeatedly in an effort to eradicate them. At the same time 20th Indian Division reached Monywa.

21 January XV Corps landed on Ramree Island. It was secured on **9 February.**

26 January 7th Indian Division (IV Corps) captured Pauk.
Messervy could now begin his thrust to Meiktila.

27 January Burma and Ledo Roads joined at Mongyu.
This was as a result of Chinese First Army and Y Force linking. They now continued to advance down the Burma Road. In the meantime Chinese Sixth Army was striking south-east from Bhamo.

12 February 20th Indian Division crossed the Irrawaddy at Myinmu.
With Mandalay now threatened from the north and west the Japanese began to launch furious counter-attacks against this bridgehead as well.

14 February 7th Indian Division crossed the Irrawaddy at Nyaungu.
In order to deceive the Japanese a feint crossing had been made at Seikpu on the 2nd.

CHINA RECONNECTED

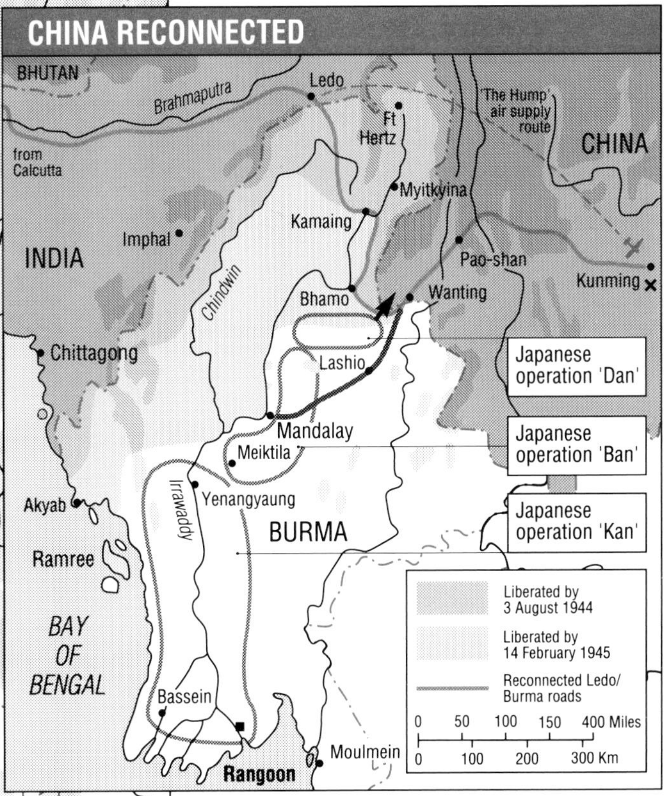

Japanese operation 'Dan'
Japanese operation 'Ban'
Japanese operation 'Kan'

Liberated by 3 August 1944
Liberated by 14 February 1945
Reconnected Ledo/Burma roads

0 50 100 150 400 Miles
0 100 200 300 Km

The Allied armies in Burma were now driving back the Japanese on a broad front. The prospect of reaching Rangoon before the monsoon broke now depended on how long it would take to capture Mandalay and more especially Meiktila.

The End in Burma · P232

11 VICTORY IN EUROPE, February to May 1945

30 JANUARY 1945 TO 11 FEBRUARY 1945

The Yalta Conference

At the end of December 1944, on Churchill's return from Athens and his attempt to resolve the Greek Civil War, he immediately set about trying to engineer another meeting of the Big Three. Uppermost in his mind was the question of Poland, especially since he was aware that the Polish troops fighting with the Western Allies were becoming very concerned over the future of their country. Further, Stalin had sent him a telegram on **27 December** which spoke of the Polish government-in-exile as a 'few emigrants' and implied that he would only recognize the Lublin Government.

Churchill immediately proposed to Roosevelt that they meet Stalin at Yalta on the Black Sea. Roosevelt and Stalin agreed and the conference, code-named 'Argonaut', was fixed for early February. De Gaulle also wanted to attend, but while it had been agreed that France should have a zone of occupation in post-war Germany, neither Churchill nor Roosevelt would agree to this since they suspected that he would merely play one off against the other for his own ends.

At the beginning of February the Allies were closing in on all fronts. On the Eastern Front the Soviets had overrun the Baltic republics and most of East Prussia. They had closed up to the River Oder, while in the south Budapest was about to fall and on **20 January** the provisional Hungarian Government signed an armistice with the Allies. The Western Allies had recovered from the shock of the Ardennes counter-offensive, driven the Germans back to their start-line and were once more closing up to the Rhine. In Italy they had paused for breath, waiting for the spring and the final push that would drive the Germans into the Alps. The situation in Greece had been stabilized. Germany, now ringed on all sides, was enduring a crescendo of bombing as she prepared to face the final onslaught.

In Burma the Allies were pressing the Japanese hard and were involved in a race against time to reach Rangoon before the monsoon broke. In China the Japanese continued their rice offensives. The Australians persevered with the clearance of New Guinea and the Americans with that of the Philippines. At the same time they were poised to land on Iwo Jima. Japan herself was now being subjected to the might of US strategic air power and was also being slowly throttled by attacks on her maritime lines of communication.

30 January to 1 February 1945 The US and British chiefs of staff met in Malta.
This was a preliminary to 'Argonaut' and was aimed at agreeing the next steps in north-west Europe, Italy and south-east Asia. Eisenhower's plan to continue the advance to the Rhine on a broad front was approved, although somewhat grudgingly on the British part since they continued to sympathize with Montgomery's single-thrust argument. Alexander was to continue to maintain pressure on the Germans in Italy, but was to surrender three Canadian and two British divisions to Eisenhower. As for south-east Asia, while the Americans recognized the growing success of the offensive in Burma, they reminded the British that the US and Chinese ground and US air elements under Mountbatten's command were there primarily to support China. It was agreed that should they be needed in China the matter would be first considered by the Combined Chiefs of Staff before any decision was made.

Simultaneously, British Foreign Secretary Anthony Eden and US Secretary of State Edward Stettinius reviewed sixteen foreign policy topics which were likely to give rise to differences with the Russians.

2 February Roosevelt arrived at Malta aboard the US cruiser *Quincy*.
Churchill had flown there on 29 January, but had been ill during the past two days. Churchill hoped to agree a common approach to Stalin with Roosevelt, but did not get the opportunity.

3 February Roosevelt and Churchill flew separately to Yalta.

4–11 February The Yalta Conference.
The results of the conference were set forth in a statement prepared by the three leaders. They declared:
1. Germany was about to be hit by 'new and powerful blows' and further resistance by her people would merely make the cost of defeat 'heavier'.
2. The occupation and control of post-war Germany by the three powers was agreed. It was not their purpose to 'destroy' Germany, but there could not be a 'decent' life for the German people until Nazism and militarism had been eradicated.
3. Germany should make 'just' reparations for the damage she had caused.

THE GLOBAL WAR: February 1945

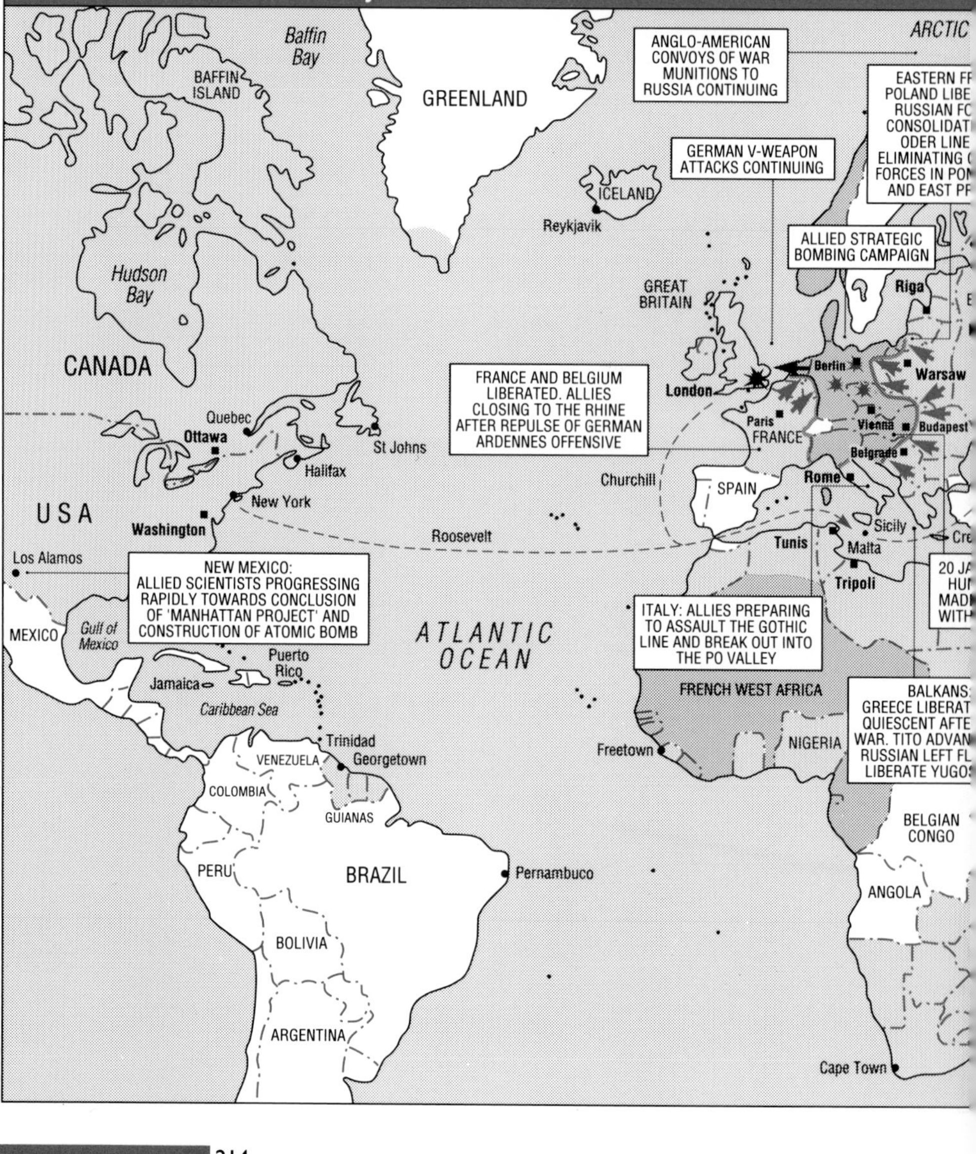

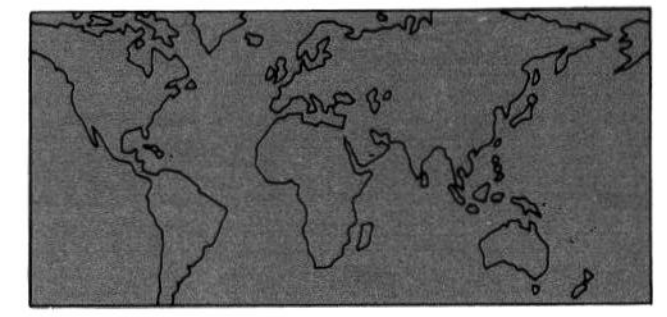

4. The Big Three, together with France and China, would sponsor the United Nations Conference, which was to convene in San Francisco on **25 April** in order to draw up a charter for the United Nations Organization.
5. The Declaration on Liberated Europe. This stated that the Big Three would honour the principles of the 1941 Atlantic Charter and that they pledged to help the liberated peoples of Europe 'to solve by democratic means their pressing political and economic problems'. They would help any European country to form interim governments representative of all democratic opinion and dedicated to holding free elections as soon as possible so that the people could vote for a government of their choice.
6. This dealt specifically with Poland. The Lublin Government was to be reorganized on a democratic basis to include other Polish representatives both in Poland and abroad. This Polish Provisional Government of National Unity would be formed after consultations with the Big Three, who would be represented by Molotov and the British and US Ambassadors to Moscow. The eastern border of Poland would roughly follow the Curzon Line, but she would be given significant additional territory in the north and west and the extent of this would be arranged in consultation with the Polish Government of National Unity.
7. Tito's anti-Fascist Assembly of Liberation Government would be extended to include members of the 1941 Yugoslav parliament who had not collaborated with the Axis powers.
8. The foreign secretaries of the three powers would consult with one another at regular intervals.
9. Only with 'continuing and growing co-operation and understanding among our three countries and among all the peace-loving nations can the highest aspiration of humanity be reached – a secure and lasting peace which will, in the words of the Atlantic Charter, "afford assurance that all the men in all the lands may live out their lives in freedom from fear and want".'

On the surface it seemed that much had been achieved, but underneath there were currents of discontent, especially from the British point of view. Roosevelt, by now very ill, went to Yalta determined to ensure that the Soviet Union entered the war against Japan as soon as possible after the defeat of Germany and was prepared to make concessions to achieve this. One of these was that the Soviet Union would be allowed three seats at the United Nations, representing the USSR, Ukraine and Belorussia. But underlying 'Argonaut' from the British point of view was the realization that Roosevelt and Stalin appeared at times to combine against Churchill, especially over their refusal to tie down the future of post-war Europe in detail. Russia's entry into the Far East also threatened Britain's influence and standing there. The truth was that the USA and USSR were now super-powers, but Britain, drained by five and a half years of war, was not.

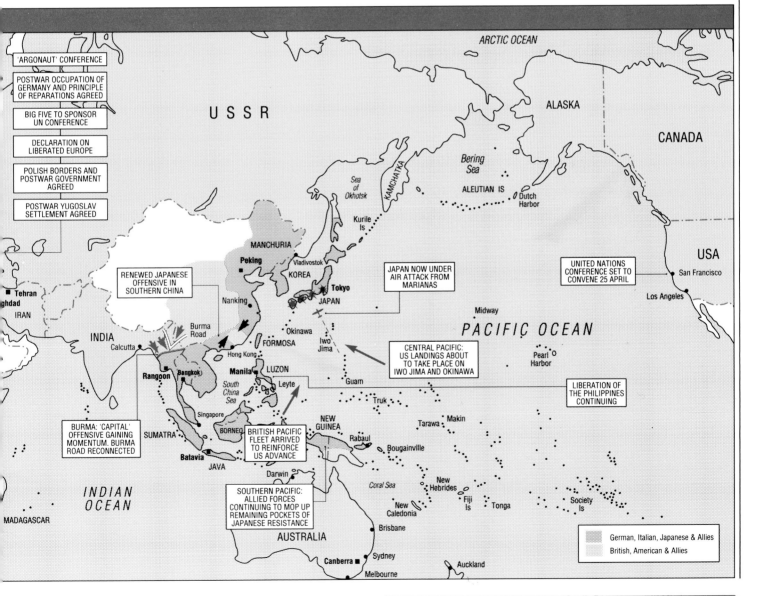

The Potsdam Conference · P234

The Rhine Crossings

The Ardennes counter-offensive in the end proved little more than a temporary setback for the Western Allies. By mid-**January 1945** they had turned their attention once more to the Rhine, the last major natural barrier barring the way into the heart of Germany.

Eisenhower confirmed once more that the main target was the Ruhr, but he was also concerned to maintain his Broad Front strategy, and this was approved by the Combined Chiefs of Staff at Malta at the end of January. The Ruhr would therefore be overcome by double envelopment. Montgomery's 21st Army Group, with Simpson's Ninth US Army still under command, was to cross the Rhine north of the Ruhr while Bradley's 12th Army Group crossed between Cologne and Duesseldorf. Another reason for two crossings was that if one failed he would still have a 'string to his bow'.

There remained much to do, however, because Hitler was determined to hold west of the Rhine for as long as possible because of its value as a supply route. This meant not just clinging on to the West Wall, but the Rivers Roer and Maas as well.

Montgomery tasked Crerar's First Canadian Army, with XXX British Corps under command, to clear the area south-east of Nijmegen up to the lower Rhine (Operation 'Veritable'). Simpson would then advance towards Duesseldorf ('Grenade') and join hands with the Canadians. As a preliminary Dempsey's Second British Army was to clear an awkward salient known as the Roermond Triangle ('Blackcock'). Bradley's armies would continue to recapture the ground lost during the Ardennes counter-offensive, get through the West Wall, clear the Eifel and close to the Rhine, while Devers' 6th Army Group was to complete the reduction of the Colmar pocket and the overrunning of Saarland.

16 January 1945 **Dempsey launched 'Blackcock'.**
Until now the weather had been very cold and the ground was frozen hard, but just before 'Blackcock' opened there was a sudden thaw, accompanied by thick fog. This and strong German resistance made progress slow and it took ten days to secure the Roermond triangle.

20 January **French First Army began the reduction of the Colmar pocket.**
Inside this was Friedrich Wiese's German Nineteenth Army of eight divisions.

28 January **German salient in the Ardennes finally eliminated.**
First and Third US Armies now began to attack the West Wall, with Hodges' first object as capturing the Roer dams intact.

31 January **The advance to the Roer dams began.**
Terrain difficulties and German resistance meant that it was not until **9 February** that they were all captured. By then it was too late. The Germans had opened the valves and destroyed the machinery that controlled them. The result was that the surrounding countryside was flooded and this forced Simpson to postpone 'Grenade', which had been scheduled to begin on **8 February**, until the water had subsided sufficiently.

5 February **US Seventh and French First Armies linked up to seal the Colmar pocket.**
By this time von Rundstedt had finally obtained Hitler's permission to withdraw Nineteenth Army over the Rhine. Four days later 6th Army Group had closed up to the Rhine south of Strasbourg.

8 February **The opening of 'Veritable'.**
This was preceded by the largest artillery bombardment yet seen in the west and the German defenders, many of whom were from units made up of medically downgraded men, were numbed by it. The attack therefore initially went well, but then the Canadians began to come up against the hardened paratroops of General Eugen Meindl's First Parachute Army. The Canadians soon became embroiled in the densely wooded area of the Reichswald, the scene of much bitter fighting.

21 February **51st Highland Division captured Goch.**
To XXX British Corps' south the battle for the Reichswald continued. Patton's US Third Army had begun to clear the triangle formed by the confluence of the Rivers Moselle and Saar and Patch's US Seventh Army was attacking north into the Saarland.

23 February **Simpson launched 'Grenade'.**
The waters in the Roer valley had by now sufficiently subsided and there was the added advantage that 'Veritable' had drawn a number of German divisions north. Consequently Simpson made comparatively good progress. Simultaneously Hodges' US First Army began to attack across the Roer in the Dueren area.

26 February **II Canadian Corps attacked east of Nijmegen ('Blockbuster').**
Its objectives were the towns of Calcar, Udem and Xanten and to close up to the Rhine north of Wesel.

27 February **US Ninth Army crossed the Roer and US First Army reached the Erft.**

2 March **Ninth US Army reached the Rhine opposite Duesseldorf.**
The Germans, however, had blown the bridges here.

3 March **First Canadian and US Ninth Armies linked up at Walbeck, south-west of Geldern.**

4 March **The Reichswald finally cleared.**
US First Army reached the outskirts of Cologne.

6 March **'Grenade' completed.**
US Ninth Army had now closed up to the Rhine.

7 March **US First Army seized an intact bridge over the Rhine at Remagen.**
This was between Bonn and Koblenz and it was captured by elements of 9th Armored Division. By evening a bridgehead had been consolidated. This caused Eisenhower to place more emphasis on the drive in the south. On the German side, Hitler was furious. Next day he sacked von Rundstedt as CinC West and replaced him by Kesselring. During the next few days the Germans made repeated efforts to destroy the bridge, using air attacks, V-2 rockets launched from Holland and even frogmen, besides numerous counter-attacks by the German Seventh Army.

9 March **First Parachute Army abandoned the Wesel pocket and withdrew across the Rhine.**

10 March **Operations 'Veritable' and 'Blockbuster' completed.**
21st Army Group was now on the west bank of the Rhine and Montgomery began to prepare for a crossing at Wesel.

15 March **US Seventh Army launched Operation 'Undertone'.**
This was designed to clear the Saar-Palatinate triangle in conjunction with US Third Army, which had already closed to the Rhine north of Koblenz.

In the meantime US First Army had begun to attack south-east from the Remagen bridgehead and cut the Cologne – Frankfurt autobahn on the 16th.

17 March **Remagen bridge finally collapsed.**
It had been weakened by attempted demolition on the day of its capture. By this time First Army had constructed two other bridges upstream.

19 March **Hitler issued a 'scorched earth' order.**
Hitler was determined that if Germany were defeated nothing of value would be left for the victors. Despite a protest by Speer the previous day in which he argued that the leadership was duty bound to maintain 'even if only in the most primitive manner, a basis of existence for the nation to the last' Hitler refused to listen. Everything – military installations, communications, transportation, industry, food supplies – was to be destroyed. He justified it by saying that 'if the war is lost, the nation will also perish'. Four days later, Hitler's private secretary, Martin Bormann decreed that the whole German population, including foreign workers, was to be moved to the centre of the country. Neither of these orders were put

P204 · The Ardennes Counter-Offensive

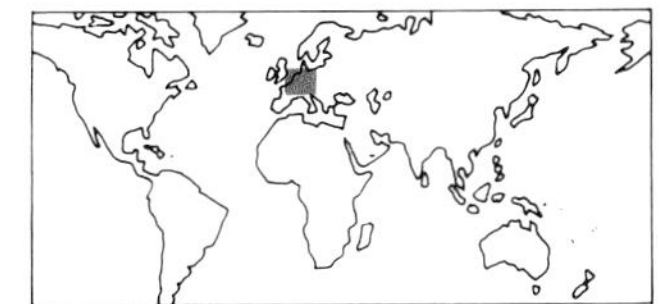

into effect, partly because they were impossible to carry out but also because Speer managed to persuade Model and the industrialists not to try to implement them.

Night of 22/23 March Patton achieved a 'bounce' crossing of the Rhine at Oppenheim.
He caught most of the German defenders asleep.

Night of 23/24 March Montgomery crossed the Rhine (Operation 'Plunder').
The crossings were made by 3rd Canadian Division at Emmerich, 51st Highland Division at Rees and 9th US Division near Rheinberg. On the 24th British

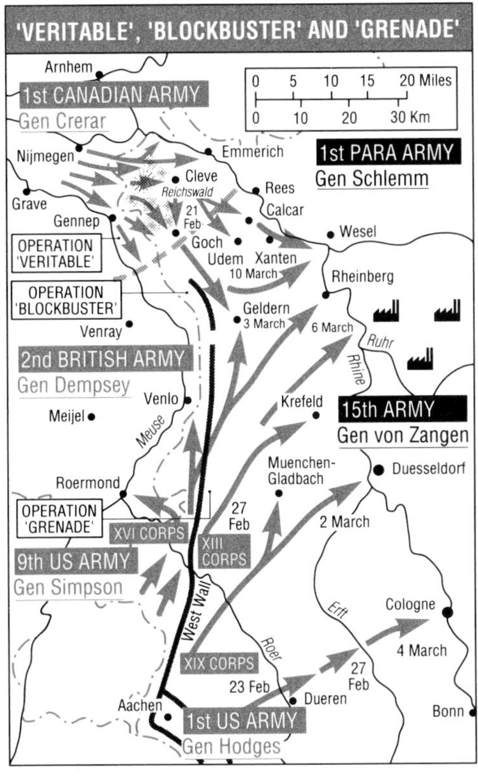

6th and US 17th Airborne Divisions dropped near Wesel in order to widen the bridgehead.

Night of 24/25 March US Third Army made further crossings at Boppard and near St Goar.

26 March US Seventh Army crossed near Worms.
Patch made another crossing near Mainz the following day.

31 March French First Army crossed near Germersheim.
The Allies had now crossed the Rhine in several places, achieving what Eisenhower had described in January as a 'tactical and engineering operation of the greatest magnitude'. The curtain was now ready to be raised on the last act, but this would not happen without a further major strategical disagreement among the Western Allies.

THE RHINELAND CAMPAIGN

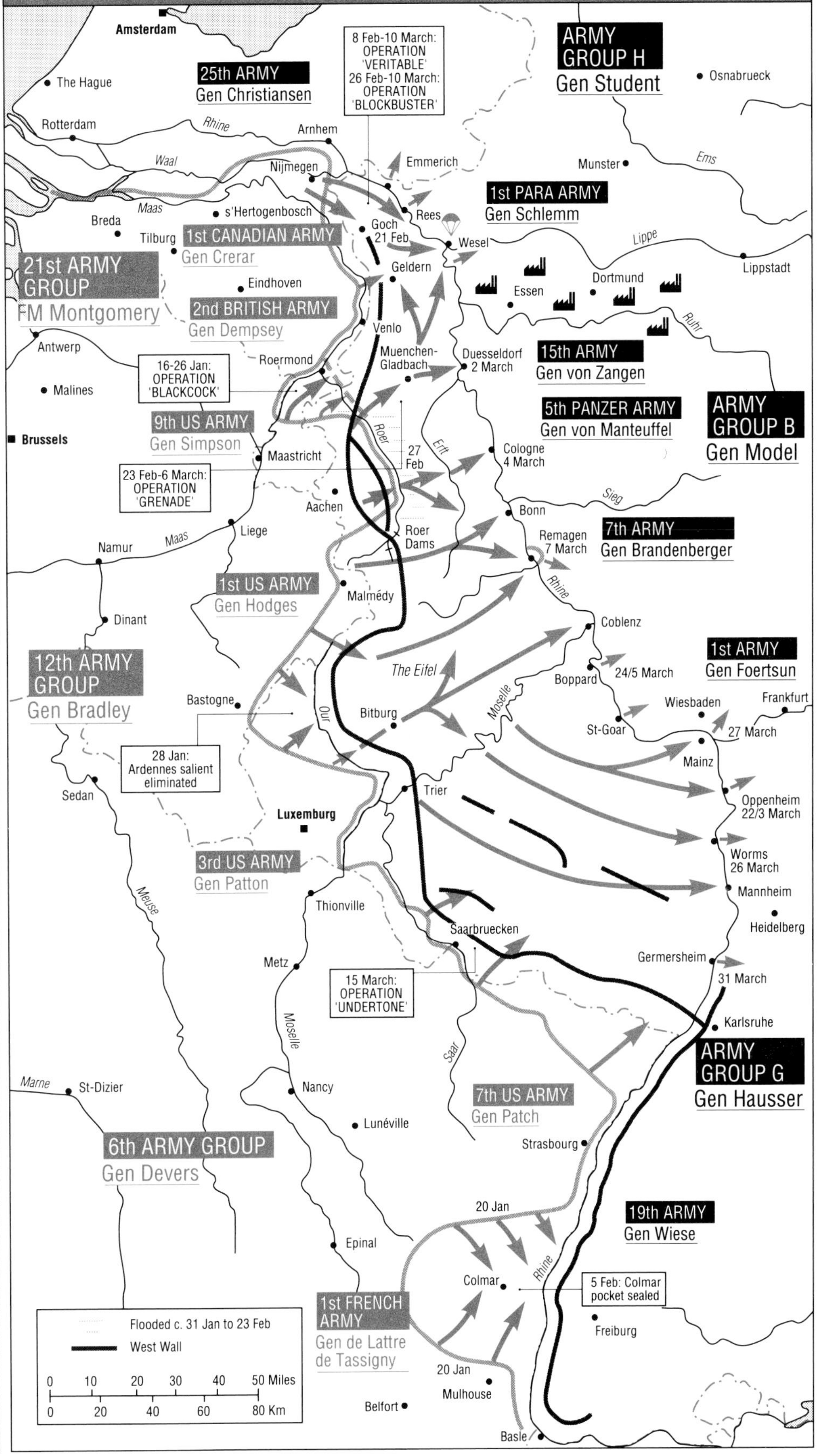

Amsterdam
The Hague
Rotterdam
25th ARMY
Gen Christiansen
8 Feb-10 March: OPERATION 'VERITABLE'
26 Feb-10 March: OPERATION 'BLOCKBUSTER'
ARMY GROUP H
Gen Student
Osnabrueck
Rhine
Arnhem
Waal
Nijmegen
Emmerich
Munster
Ems
Maas
s'Hertogenbosch
Breda
Tilburg
1st CANADIAN ARMY
Gen Crerar
Goch
21 Feb
Rees
1st PARA ARMY
Gen Schlemm
Wesel
Lippe
21st ARMY GROUP
FM Montgomery
Eindhoven
Geldern
Essen
Dortmund
Lippstadt
2nd BRITISH ARMY
Gen Dempsey
Venlo
Ruhr
Antwerp
16-26 Jan: OPERATION 'BLACKCOCK'
Roermond
Muenchen-Gladbach
Duesseldorf
2 March
15th ARMY
Gen von Zangen
Malines
9th US ARMY
Gen Simpson
5th PANZER ARMY
Gen von Manteuffel
ARMY GROUP B
Gen Model
Brussels
Roer
Erft
Maastricht
27 Feb
Cologne
4 March
23 Feb-6 March: OPERATION 'GRENADE'
Aachen
Sieg
Bonn
Liege
Namur
Maas
Roer Dams
Remagen
7 March
7th ARMY
Gen Brandenberger
1st US ARMY
Gen Hodges
Malmédy
Dinant
Rhine
Coblenz
12th ARMY GROUP
Gen Bradley
The Eifel
Boppard
24/5 March
1st ARMY
Gen Foertsun
Bastogne
Our
Bitburg
Moselle
Wiesbaden
Frankfurt
St-Goar
27 March
28 Jan: Ardennes salient eliminated
Mainz
Sedan
Trier
Oppenheim
22/3 March
Luxemburg
3rd US ARMY
Gen Patton
Worms
26 March
Meuse
Mannheim
Thionville
Heidelberg
Saarbruecken
Metz
Germersheim
15 March: OPERATION 'UNDERTONE'
31 March
Karlsruhe
Moselle
Saar
ARMY GROUP G
Gen Hausser
Marne
St-Dizier
Nancy
7th US ARMY
Gen Patch
Lunéville
Strasbourg
6th ARMY GROUP
Gen Devers
20 Jan
19th ARMY
Gen Wiese
Epinal
Rhine
Colmar
5 Feb: Colmar pocket sealed
1st FRENCH ARMY
Gen de Lattre de Tassigny
Freiburg
Flooded c. 31 Jan to 23 Feb
West Wall
0 10 20 30 40 50 Miles
0 20 40 60 80 Km
20 Jan
Mulhouse
Belfort
Basle

Final Offensive from the West · P220

8 FEBRUARY 1945 TO 26 APRIL 1945

Pomerania and Vienna

In mid-February 1945 the Russians were concerned to remove any potential threat from the flanks before they started the final drive to Berlin. Stalin knew that the Western Allies still had much to do before reaching the Rhine let alone Berlin, and there was therefore no particular urgency to send his armies forward to the German capital before they had built up their supplies once more after their rapid dash from the Vistula to the Oder.

Hitler, on the other hand, remained mesmerized by Hungary, despite the fact that Budapest had now finally fallen. He had conceived a new offensive, 'Spring Awakening', designed to destroy Tolbukhin's 3rd Ukrainian Front and establish a barrier east of the Lake Balaton oilfields. It was to be carried out by Sepp Dietrich's Sixth Panzer Army, now being transferred from the Western Front, and Hermann Balck's Sixth Army.

8 February 1945 **Konev's 1st Ukrainian Front renewed its offensive.**
The aim was to close to the River Neisse so as to bring his front in line with that of Zhukov. The initial attacks encircled Breslau and Glogau. There was an immediate massive flight of refugees westwards.

17 February **The Stavka gave fresh orders to Malinovsky (2nd Ukrainian) and Tolbukhin.**
They were to prepare and carry out an offensive designed to destroy Army Group South, clear the rest of Hungary and then capture Brno, Vienna and Graz, thus cutting off Army Group E, which had now absorbed Army Group F, in Yugoslavia and hasten the surrender of the German armies in northern Italy.

That same day I SS Panzer Corps, which was part of Sixth Panzer Army and had just arrived in Hungary, attacked the Russian bridgehead over the Hron north-west of Budapest. It was eradicated by the 24th.

By the end of the month the Russians had a very clear idea of 'Spring Awakening'. They knew that the main thrust, by Balck and Dietrich, would be made between Lakes Valencei and Balaton, with subsidiary attacks by Second Panzer Army towards Kaposvar and by Army Group E north-east towards Mohacs on the Danube. Yet the Stavka insisted that Tolbukhin continue preparations for his offensive, while also preparing to face the German attacks.

23 February **Posen finally fell to the Russians.**

24 February **Rokossovsky mounted a fresh offensive into Pomerania.**
An initial penetration of thirty miles was made, but thereafter lack of reserves on marshy ground slowed the rate of advance.

1 March **Zhukov joined in the Pomerania offensive.**
This took the Germans, who had been expecting him to thrust towards Berlin, by surprise. Zhukov and Rokossovsky now dashed to the Baltic coast. Kolberg fell to Zhukov on the 16th and Rokossovsky reached the Gulf of Danzig on the 25th.

3 March **German counter-attack to relieve Glogau and reopen the Berlin–Silesia railway link.**
This was mounted by Fritz-Hubert Graeser's Fourth Panzer Army, which was made up of a hastily flung together hotch-potch of units. It was quickly halted and did little to slow Konev's advance to the Neisse.

Night of 5/6 March **Opening of 'Spring Awakening'.**
Alexander Loehr's Army Group E attacked over the River Drava while Maximilian de Angelis's Second Panzer Army launched its attack south of Lake Balaton. Next day came the main attack by Balck and Dietrich. The terrain was very wet and progress was slow, with a penetration of just sixteen miles being made in the first four days. The subsidiary thrusts fared even worse and were quickly brought to a halt.

11 March **Hitler re-appointed Rendulic as CinC, Army Group Courland.**
This was still holding out in Koenigsberg and the Samland peninsula. Hubert Weiss took over Army Group North. Stalin's dissatisfaction with progress in clearing this area resulted in Bagramyan's command losing its Front status and being placed under command of 3rd Belorussian Front as the Samland Group.

13 March **Vasilievsky launched a new attack to capture Koenigsberg.**
By the end of the month Samland had been cleared, with the remnant of German Fourth Army withdrawing across the Frisches Haff to the Frischau Nehrung and Pillau.

15 March **'Spring Awakening' halted.**
By now the Stavka had issued fresh orders. Tolbukhin was to destroy Sixth Panzer Army and Sixth Army north of Lake Balaton and then, in conjunction with Malinovsky, attack north-west rather than west as laid down in the 17 February order. The attack was to begin no later than 16 March. Consequently that day Tolbukin began to counter-attack and threatened to cut off Balck and Dietrich, forcing them to withdraw – without Hitler's permission. So angry was he that he ordered Dietrich's Waffen-SS troops to remove their prized divisional cuff bands.

On this same day Konev launched another attack, this time in southern Silesia, quickly encircling Oppeln and reaching Neustadt.

20 March **General Siegfried Heinrici succeeded Himmler as CinC, Army Group Vistula.**

25 March **Woehler replaced by Rendulic as CinC, Army Group South.**
By this time Tolbukhin was approaching the Austrian border and Malinovsky was nearing Bratislava. Those Hungarian troops still fighting on the German side now began to surrender in large numbers.

28 March **Guderian replaced by General Hans Krebs as German Army Chief of Staff.**
This was a culmination of increasing disagreements between Hitler and Guderian.

29 March **Vasili Chuikov's Eighth Guards Army eradicated the German bridgehead over the Oder at Kuestrin.**

30 March **Rokossovsky captured Danzig (now Gdansk).**
Gdynia had fallen two days before. The German remnant withdrew to the mouth of the Vistula. Pomerania was now overrun and the civilian population was subjected to many atrocities.

31 March **Konev captured Ratibor, Upper Silesia.**
By now he was on the east bank of the Neisse and had overrun almost all Silesia, although the Germans still held Breslau, Glogau and a pocket west of Oppeln.

1 April **The Stavka ordered 2nd and 3rd Ukrainian Fronts to make the capture of Vienna a top priority.**
Dietrich had been given orders to defend the Austrian capital with the remnant of his army, now retitled Sixth SS Panzer Army. Hitler briefed Rendulic on the 6th and stressed the importance of holding on to Vienna.

6 April **The Russians were on the outskirts of Vienna.**
Malinovsky and Tolbukhin were carrying out a combined encircling operation.

On the same day the final assault on Koenigsberg began. It fell on the 10th.

13 April **The Russians secured Vienna.**
Malinovsky and Tolbukhin now turned their main attention once more to the north-west and Czechoslavakia, their initial objective being Brno. Rendulic withdrew his forces further into Austria under lessening Russian pressure.

The final Russian assault in East Prussia, against Pillau, began. Pillau fell on the 26th, but unlike at Koenigsberg, there was a mass evacuation by sea of German troops and civilians.

By early April all was now ready for the final assault on the capital of the Third Reich. The Western Allies, too, were now advancing with increasing rapidity. Germany was being squeezed in a vice.

The Battle of Berlin · P222

Final Offensive from the West

On **28 March 1945** Eisenhower, on his own initiative, sent a message to Stalin. He stated that after the reduction of the Ruhr the main weight of the Anglo-US advance would be directed on the line Erfurt–Leipzig–Dresden. He had no intention of making Berlin an objective. This pleased Stalin greatly: he replied that Berlin had lost its 'former strategic importance' and that he would also concentrate on the Erfurt–Leipzig–Dresden area in order to link up with the Western Allies and split the German defence in two. Stalin planned to launch his offensive in the second half of May, once the ground had dried out.

If Stalin was pleased with Eisenhower's plan, the British were not. Churchill bombarded Eisenhower with a series of signals stressing the need to meet the Russians as far east as possible and that Berlin was still the 'most decisive point in Germany'.

At the lower level, Montgomery was even more aggrieved. Relations between him and Eisenhower had worsened from December 1944, when Montgomery had given the impression that he had bailed the Americans out in the Ardennes. Nevertheless, he had continued to be led to believe that 21st Army Group would make the main thrust into Germany and assumed that Berlin would be its ultimate objective. Now Eisenhower told him that once the Ruhr had been encircled he was to pass Simpson's US Ninth Army back to Bradley. The latter would then reduce the Ruhr and make the main drive towards Dresden while Montgomery protected his northern flank.

Apart from ensuring that there was no clash with the Russians, especially over Berlin, Eisenhower was influenced by another factor in his decision to concentrate on the south of Germany. This was his belief that Hitler was planning a last-ditch stand in the Alps, in the so-called National Redoubt. This emanated from SHAEF intelligence, which had been alerting him to this possibility since mid-February. In fact, there was no such German intention.

It was amid this atmosphere of rancour that the Western Allies broke out of their bridgeheads on the Rhine.

28 March 1945 British Second Army attacked out of its bridgehead at Wesel.

28 March US First and Third Armies met in the Giessen area.
This trapped the German LXXXIX Corps and created a hole in the defence line of German Army Groups B and G.

1 April US Ninth and First Armies met at Lippstadt.
The Ruhr was now encircled, and trapped inside was Model's Army Group B, leaving a 200-mile gap in the German defences. While they began their break-in operation, Simpson and Hodges were quick to take advantage of this gap, sending some of their divisions racing eastwards. Hodges reached Paderborn that same day.

2 April Canadian First Army broke out of the Nijmegen bridgehead.
Crerar's task was to liberate northern Holland.

4 April The British entered Osnabrueck.
Next day they reached the Weser.

4 April Patton captured Kassel.
This was after two days' fighting.

5 April US Seventh Army crossed the River Main at Wuerzburg.
Two days later Patch entered Neustadt. To his south, de Lattre de Tassigny was clearing the Black Forest down to the Swiss border.

10 April Simpson's troops entered Hanover.
They were the 84th Infantry Division.

11 April US 2nd Armored Division reached the Elbe at Magdeburg.
A bridge across the river was blown in their faces, but late in the evening of the next day they succeeded in crossing. They were now faced by fierce counter-attacks, but 83rd Infantry Division managed to make another crossing upstream at Barby.

Simpson now pleaded to be allowed to drive on to Berlin, but Eisenhower was adamant, even though the Russian thrust to Berlin had not yet started; Simpson was not to advance any farther eastwards.

11 April Patch captured Schweinfurt.
This was not before the USAAF had delivered one final attack on this town, which had given them so much trouble in 1943.

12 April President Roosevelt died at Warm Springs, Georgia.
He was automatically succeeded by Vice President Harry S. Truman. In Berlin, Hitler celebrated Roosevelt's death as an omen that his fortunes were about to change for the better.

13 April US Third Army reached the River Mulde and established beachheads across it.

15 April Eisenhower issued fresh orders.
Bridgeheads established over the Elbe were to be consolidated, but further offensive operations beyond were not to be undertaken. Bradley was now to switch his attention south to the Danube valley and link up with the Russians there in order to isolate the National Redoubt. Montgomery was to secure Hamburg and Kiel, cut off Schleswig-Holstein and be prepared to advance into Denmark, as well as secure German North Sea naval bases.

15 April The British 11th Armoured Division liberated the concentration camp at Bergen-Belsen.
The Americans liberated Buchenwald on the same day. These were not, however, the first camps liberated by the Western Allies. Patton's troops had entered that at Ohrdruf on **4 April**. In every case, the liberators were totally unprepared for the conditions they met.

15 April Arnhem was liberated by the Canadians.
This was after three days' fierce fighting. Next day they reached Groningen. They now turned north-east, in accordance with Eisenhower's directive of that day, to clear Germany's North Sea coast. But they made slow progress because of the numerous river lines in their path. This bypassed the German Twenty-Fifth Army, which was left virtually intact in western Holland.

17 April Second British Army reached Bremen.
It would take nine days' fighting to secure the port.

17 April Patton began to wheel south-east.

18 April The Ruhr pocket was finally reduced.
No less than 325,000 German troops were made prisoner. Model, conscious that he had let Hitler down, committed suicide rather than surrender.

19 April British VIII Corps reached the Elbe near Lauenburg.

19 April Leipzig fell to Hodges.

20 April Patch captured Nuremberg.
This was after a fanatical defence of this symbol of National Socialism by 17th SS Panzer Grenadier Division. Nuremberg was to be the pivot for the switch of direction by US Third and Seventh Armies.

Two days later US 12th Armored Division crossed the Danube at Dillingen.

23 April Eisenhower informed the Russians that he would meet them on the Elbe and Mulde.
He offered to advance further east to Dresden, but this was declined.

25 April First physical contact made between the Russians and the Western Allies.
This took place at Torgau on the Elbe, north-east of Leipzig. The units involved were elements of the US 273rd Infantry Regiment from US First Army and the Russian 175th Rifle Regiment from the 1st Ukrainian Front.

Germany was now split by the Allies. In the meantime the Battle for Berlin was reaching its final stages and the end of the war in Europe was in sight.

P216 · The Rhine Crossings

FROM THE RHINE TO THE ELBE

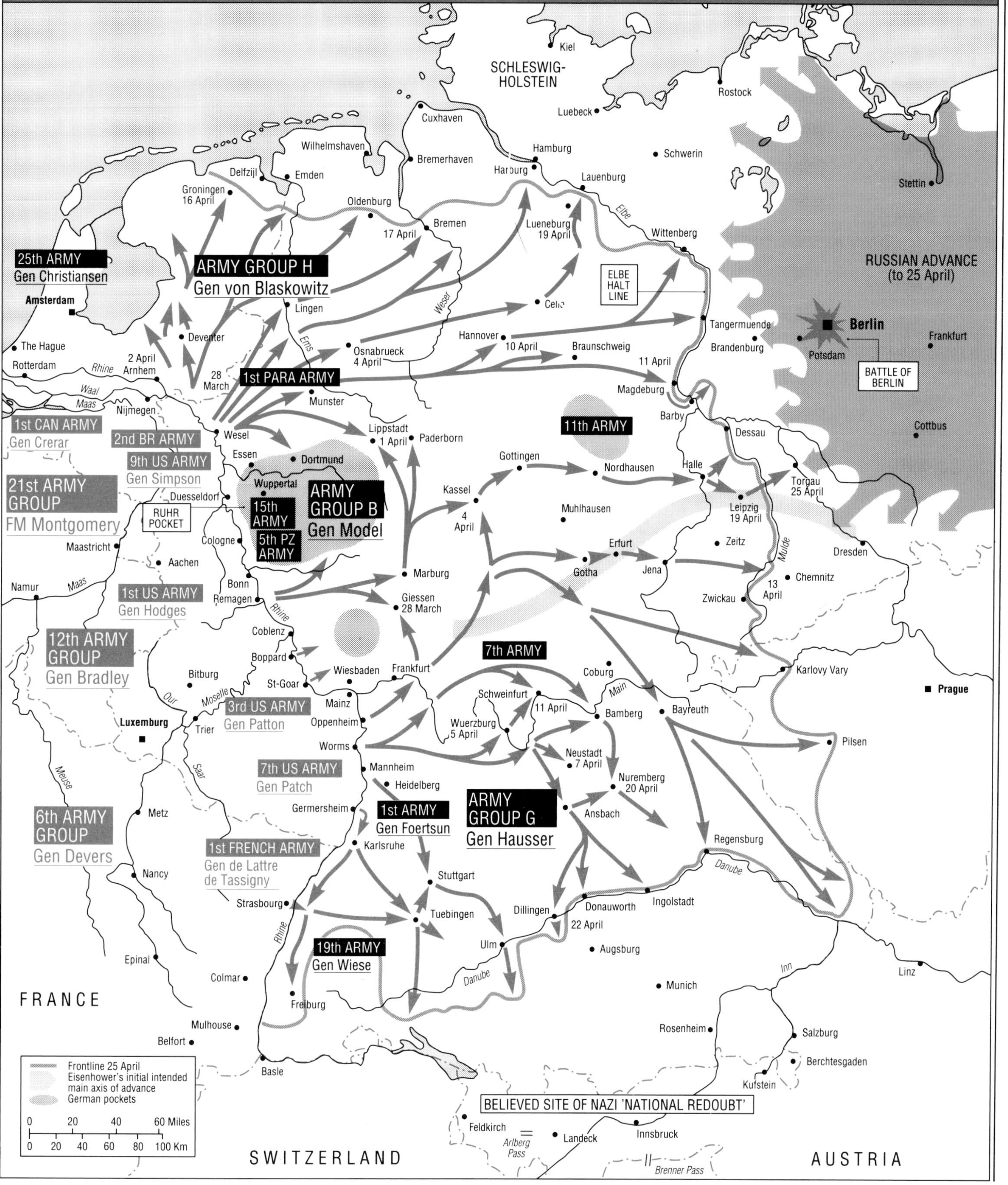

Kiel
SCHLESWIG-HOLSTEIN
Rostock
Luebeck
Cuxhaven
Wilhelmshaven
Hamburg
Schwerin
Bremerhaven
Harburg
Delfzijl
Emden
Lauenburg
Stettin
Groningen 16 April
Oldenburg
Bremen
17 April
Lueneburg 19 April
Elbe
Wittenberg
25th ARMY
Gen Christiansen
ARMY GROUP H
Gen von Blaskowitz
RUSSIAN ADVANCE (to 25 April)
Amsterdam
Lingen
Wesel
ELBE HALT LINE
Celle
Tangermuende
Berlin
Frankfurt
The Hague
Deventer
Ems
Hannover
Osnabrueck 4 April
10 April
Braunschweig
Brandenburg
Potsdam
Rotterdam
Rhine
2 April
Arnhem
11 April
BATTLE OF BERLIN
Waal
Maas
28 March
1st PARA ARMY
Magdeburg
Nijmegen
Munster
Barby
1st CAN ARMY
Gen Crerar
2nd BR ARMY
Wesel
Lippstadt 1 April
Paderborn
11th ARMY
Dessau
Cottbus
9th US ARMY
Gen Simpson
Essen
Dortmund
Gottingen
Nordhausen
Halle
Torgau 25 April
21st ARMY GROUP
FM Montgomery
Wuppertal
Duesseldorf
15th ARMY
ARMY GROUP B
Gen Model
Kassel
4 April
RUHR POCKET
Muhlhausen
Leipzig 19 April
Maastricht
Cologne
5th PZ ARMY
Erfurt
Zeitz
Dresden
Aachen
Gotha
Jena
Mulde
Namur
Maas
1st US ARMY
Gen Hodges
Bonn
Remagen
Marburg
Chemnitz
13 April
Zwickau
Giessen 28 March
Rhine
Coblenz
12th ARMY GROUP
Gen Bradley
Boppard
7th ARMY
Karlovy Vary
Bitburg
St-Goar
Wiesbaden
Frankfurt
Coburg
Prague
Our
Moselle
3rd US ARMY
Gen Patton
Mainz
Schweinfurt
Main
Luxemburg
Trier
Oppenheim
11 April
Bamberg
Bayreuth
Wuerzburg 5 April
Worms
Pilsen
Meuse
Saar
7th US ARMY
Gen Patch
Mannheim
Neustadt 7 April
Heidelberg
Nuremberg 20 April
6th ARMY GROUP
Gen Devers
Metz
Germersheim
1st ARMY
Gen Foertsun
ARMY GROUP G
Gen Hausser
Ansbach
1st FRENCH ARMY
Gen de Lattre de Tassigny
Karlsruhe
Regensburg
Nancy
Stuttgart
Danube
Strasbourg
Dillingen
Donauworth
Ingolstadt
Tuebingen
22 April
Rhine
19th ARMY
Gen Wiese
Ulm
Augsburg
Epinal
Colmar
Danube
Inn
Linz
FRANCE
Freiburg
Munich
Mulhouse
Rosenheim
Salzburg
Belfort
Berchtesgaden
Basle
Kufstein
BELIEVED SITE OF NAZI 'NATIONAL REDOUBT'
Feldkirch
Arlberg Pass
Landeck
Innsbruck
Brenner Pass
SWITZERLAND
AUSTRIA

Frontline 25 April
Eisenhower's initial intended main axis of advance
German pockets

0 20 40 60 Miles
0 20 40 60 80 100 Km

The Battle of Berlin

It was not until **29 March 1945** that the plan for the seizure of Berlin began to be finalized. On that day Konev and Zhukov returned to Moscow and went through details with the Stavka. Then, on **1 April**, they had an audience with Stalin in order to have their plans approved by him. In essence Zhukov was to have the main role, being responsible for capturing Berlin and then pushing on to the Elbe. Konev was to destroy the German forces south of the city and then seize Leipzig and Dresden. These attacks were to take place on **16 April** and the operations were to be completed not later than **1 May**, May Day. In addition, Rokossovsky was to attack north of Berlin on **20 April** and the other fronts were ordered to maintain pressure on the Germans so as to prevent them transferring reserves from elsewhere to Berlin.

There was only one significant change made. The original plan included a boundary between Konev and Zhukov that ran from Guben on the Neisse to the Elbe. Significantly, this was now stopped at Luebben, well to the south-east of the capital, and implied that if Konev could get to Berlin first he would not be halted. There now followed two weeks of hectic preparation.

At the beginning of February, Hitler had declared Berlin a fortress, and considerable defensive preparations had been carried out, especially between the city and the Oder. He himself, since his return to Berlin from the west on **16 January**, had increasingly occupied his command post beneath the Reich Chancellery, the Fuehrerbunker.

By mid-April, Hitler was forced to look in two directions: to the Elbe and to the Oder. To cover the former was Wenck's Twelfth Army, consisting of some twelve divisions, almost all recently formed from a mixture of veterans and newly trained conscripts, and a miscellany of additional units. Army Group Vistula, commanded by Heinrici, had Hasso von Manteuffel's Third Panzer Army of nine divisions (none of them in fact Panzer) and Theodor Busse's Ninth Army (11 infantry division, one Panzer division), and four SS Panzergrenadier divisions as army group reserve.

South of Berlin the left wing of Ferdinand Schoerner's Army Group Centre consisted of Fritz-Hubert Graeser's Fourth Panzer Army with one Panzer and four infantry divisions. In total this amounted to some fifty weak divisions, which were faced by nearly 200 Russian divisions.

12 April 1945 Zhukov began to probe out of the Kuestrin bridgehead.
There were casualties on both sides. On the 15th, Heinrici obtained Hitler's permission to withdraw his troops back to the main defensive position so that he would not suffer too many casualties during the preliminary Russian bombardment.

15 April **Hitler issued a special Order of the Day.**
He warned his troops that the 'Jewish Bolsheviks' were bent on 'extermination' of the German people. Anyone who did not do his duty was to be shot, but if everyone did their duty 'Berlin stays German, Vienna will be German again and Europe will never be Russian'. He ended with a reference to the death of Roosevelt, whom he termed 'the greatest war criminal of all time'.

16 April The Russians began their final drive to Berlin.
Zhukov attacked from the Kuestrin bridgehead after a short, sharp, but massive artillery and air bombardment. The German withdrawal of the previous day meant that much of this fell on empty positions and when the Russians attacked they could make little impression, especially around the Seelow Heights.

In contrast, Konev, attacking on an 18-mile front across the Neisse between Forst and Muskau, was by the end of the day poised to break through Fourth Panzer Army's defences.

17 April Zhukov finally gained the Seelow Heights.
Konev had now broken through Fourth Panzer Army, and Stalin agreed that he could drive to Berlin, although he did not tell Zhukov this.

18 April Rokossovsky launched his attack north of Berlin.
This was two days earlier than scheduled and was mounted between Schwedt and Stettin. It took him two days to get through the marshy ground between the eastern and western branches of the Oder, but thereafter he was able to keep Third Panzer Army tied down so that it could not be deployed to Berlin.

Zhukov continued to make slow progress through the network of German defences. The German Ninth Army on the Oder was becoming increasingly exposed, but Hitler would not countenance a withdrawal. Konev had now reached and crossed the River Spree.

20 April Hitler's 56th Birthday.
Hitler finally gave responsibility for the defence of Berlin to Army Group Vistula. He also agreed that a number of government departments could leave Berlin for southern Germany and Schleswig-Holstein. Doenitz was given command of the German forces in the north and set up an HQ at Ploen, while Kesselring was made responsible for the south. It was also Hitler's last appearance outside the Fuehrerbunker, when he decorated members of the Hitler Youth for bravery.

By now Rokossovsky had got across the western branch of the Oder and Konev was pushing on north and south of Spremberg, but was also having to deal with desperate counter-attacks by Ninth Army around Frankfurt-on-Oder. Konev was advancing north-west to Berlin and had taken Calau.

In Czechoslovakia, Petrov's 4th and Malinovsky's 2nd Ukrainian Fronts were sweeping through Slovakia and were approaching the River Morava, while Tolbukhin's 3rd Ukrainian Front was preparing to enter Czechoslovakia from Vienna.

21 April 2nd Guards Tank Army crossed the autobahn ring on the north-east side of Berlin.
Russian heavy artillery began to shell the centre of Berlin. Konev continued to make good progress against the weaker defences south of the city.

The last air attacks on Berlin by the Western Allies were made by the RAF on the night of 20th/21st and by the USAAF on the 21st.

23 April Hitler declared that he would remain in Berlin until the end.
He announced his intention of committing suicide rather than fall into Russian hands. It was now clear that the Americans were not intending to cross the Elbe. Hitler therefore ordered Wenck to turn east and link up with Busse's Ninth Army. The two would then drive north to the capital. Hitler also announced that he was taking personal command of the defence of the capital.

25 April Berlin encircled.
Zhukov and Konev's troops made contact with one another just east of Ketzin. By this time they had also trapped Ninth Army and part of Fourth Panzer Army and were fighting in the eastern, north-eastern and south-eastern suburbs of Berlin.

Goering, who had flown to southern Germany, proposed to Hitler that, as Deputy Fuehrer, he take over the leadership of the Third Reich since Hitler could not exercise control from Berlin. Hitler, on the 24th, stripped him of all his offices and ordered the SS to place him under house arrest.

26 April Wenck's Twelfth Army launched its relief attack.
Aiming for Potsdam, Wenck succeeded in advancing to within fifteen miles of Berlin on the first day. But by the end of the day Konev and Zhukov were approaching the centre of the city.

In Czechoslovakia, 2nd Ukrainian Front captured Brno, while, north of Berlin, Rokossovsky captured Stettin.

28 April Hitler discredited Himmler.
This was a consequence of his discovery that Himmler had opened armistice negotiations with the Allies. On the same day Hitler sacked Heinrici and replaced him by Kurt Student as CinC, Army Group Vistula, since Heinrici had announced his intention of continuing to withdraw.

By now the Russians were closing in on the Reichstag and Chancellery. Wenck's relief attack had been forced to a halt, but that night Busse began to break out to the west in order to meet him.

P218 · Pomerania and Vienna

ARMAGEDDON AT BERLIN

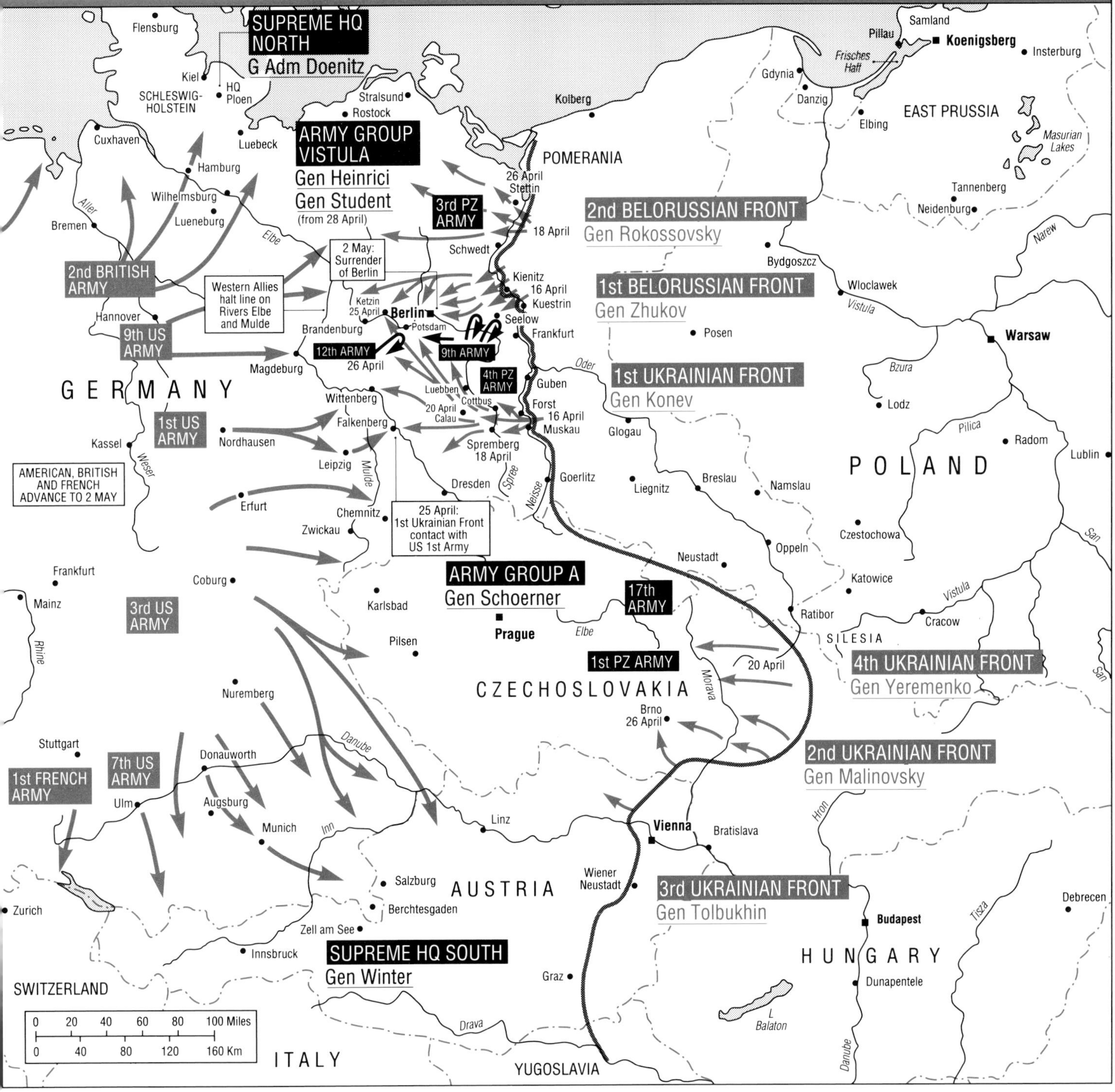

SUPREME HQ NORTH
G Adm Doenitz
ARMY GROUP VISTULA
Gen Heinrici
Gen Student
(from 28 April)
3rd PZ ARMY
2nd BELORUSSIAN FRONT
Gen Rokossovsky
1st BELORUSSIAN FRONT
Gen Zhukov
1st UKRAINIAN FRONT
Gen Konev
2 May: Surrender of Berlin
Western Allies halt line on Rivers Elbe and Mulde
2nd BRITISH ARMY
9th US ARMY
12th ARMY
26 April
9th ARMY
4th PZ ARMY
1st US ARMY
AMERICAN, BRITISH AND FRENCH ADVANCE TO 2 MAY
25 April: 1st Ukrainian Front contact with US 1st Army
ARMY GROUP A
Gen Schoerner
17th ARMY
1st PZ ARMY
3rd US ARMY
4th UKRAINIAN FRONT
Gen Yeremenko
2nd UKRAINIAN FRONT
Gen Malinovsky
7th US ARMY
1st FRENCH ARMY
3rd UKRAINIAN FRONT
Gen Tolbukhin
SUPREME HQ SOUTH
Gen Winter
Flensburg
Kiel
HQ Ploen
SCHLESWIG-HOLSTEIN
Stralsund
Rostock
Luebeck
Cuxhaven
Hamburg
Wilhelmsburg
Lueneburg
Bremen
Aller
Elbe
Kolberg
POMERANIA
26 April
Stettin
18 April
Schwedt
Kienitz
16 April
Kuestrin
Seelow
Frankfurt
Ketzin
25 April
Berlin
Potsdam
Brandenburg
Hannover
Magdeburg
GERMANY
Wittenberg
Luebben
20 April
Calau
Cottbus
Guben
Forst
16 April
Muskau
Falkenberg
Spremberg
18 April
Nordhausen
Kassel
Weser
Leipzig
Mulde
Dresden
Spree
Neisse
Goerlitz
Erfurt
Chemnitz
Zwickau
Samland
Pillau
Koenigsberg
Insterburg
Frisches Haff
Gdynia
Danzig
Elbing
EAST PRUSSIA
Masurian Lakes
Tannenberg
Neidenburg
Narew
Bydgoszcz
Wloclawek
Vistula
Posen
Warsaw
Oder
Bzura
Lodz
Glogau
Pilica
Radom
Lublin
POLAND
Liegnitz
Breslau
Namslau
Oppeln
Czestochowa
Neustadt
Katowice
Ratibor
Cracow
SILESIA
San
Frankfurt
Mainz
Rhine
Coburg
Karlsbad
Prague
Pilsen
Elbe
20 April
Morava
CZECHOSLOVAKIA
Brno
26 April
Nuremberg
Stuttgart
Donauworth
Danube
Ulm
Augsburg
Munich
Inn
Linz
Vienna
Bratislava
Hron
Salzburg
AUSTRIA
Wiener Neustadt
Berchtesgaden
Zell am See
Zurich
Innsbruck
Budapest
Debrecen
Tisza
HUNGARY
Dunapentele
Graz
SWITZERLAND
L Balaton
Drava
Danube
ITALY
YUGOSLAVIA
0 20 40 60 80 100 Miles
0 40 80 120 160 Km

29 April The final battle for the Reichstag and Chancellery began.
Hitler married his mistress Eva Braun and in his Last Will and Political Testament appointed Grand Admiral Karl Doenitz as his successor. Meanwhile the remnant of the German Ninth Army battled westwards to link up with Wenck.

30 April Hitler committed suicide.
He did so with Eva Braun. Before he died Hitler authorized the remaining troops in Berlin to break out. The Reichstag fell, after bitter fighting, at 2250 hours.

1 May Goebbels committed suicide.
This was after an attempt to negotiate with the Russians. His wife and six children perished with him. Others of Hitler's inner circle, including Krebs, also opted for suicide. Some attempted to escape but were captured or, like Martin Bormann, killed.

2 May Berlin surrendered.
The formal surrender was carried out by General Helmuth Weidling, the Berlin military commander.

The Battle of Berlin had been a bloody and costly business. The Russians suffered more than 300,000 casualties. It is impossible to establish what the German casualties, military and civilian, were. Suffice to say that the Russians took 480,000 prisoners during the two weeks' fighting.

The End in Europe · P226

The End in Italy

The onset of 1945 brought a lull in the fighting in northern Italy. The pressure that they had exerted on the Germans throughout 1944 had left the Allies exhausted, and Alexander had decided not to resume his offensive until the spring. The fact that the Combined Chiefs of Staff had directed, as a result of their pre-Yalta meeting in Malta at the end of January, that the pressure on the Germans in Italy must be maintained confirmed in Alexander's eyes the requirement for another offensive. There was also the fear that unless the Germans were kept under pressure they could withdraw at leisure to the Alps, from where it would be very difficult to dislodge them.

Indeed, it had been Kesselring's intention to do just this, using the Rivers Po and Adige as intermediate defence lines; but this was refused by Hitler, who insisted that Army Group C must stand and fight where it was. When, in early March 1945, Kesselring was appointed CinC, West, Italy still remained under his overall control, with von Vietinghoff, who had been succeeded in command of the now isolated Army Group Courland by Rendulic, being promoted to command Army Group C in his place.

Kesselring immediately transferred four divisions to the west, leaving the Tenth and Fourteenth

VICTORY IN ITALY

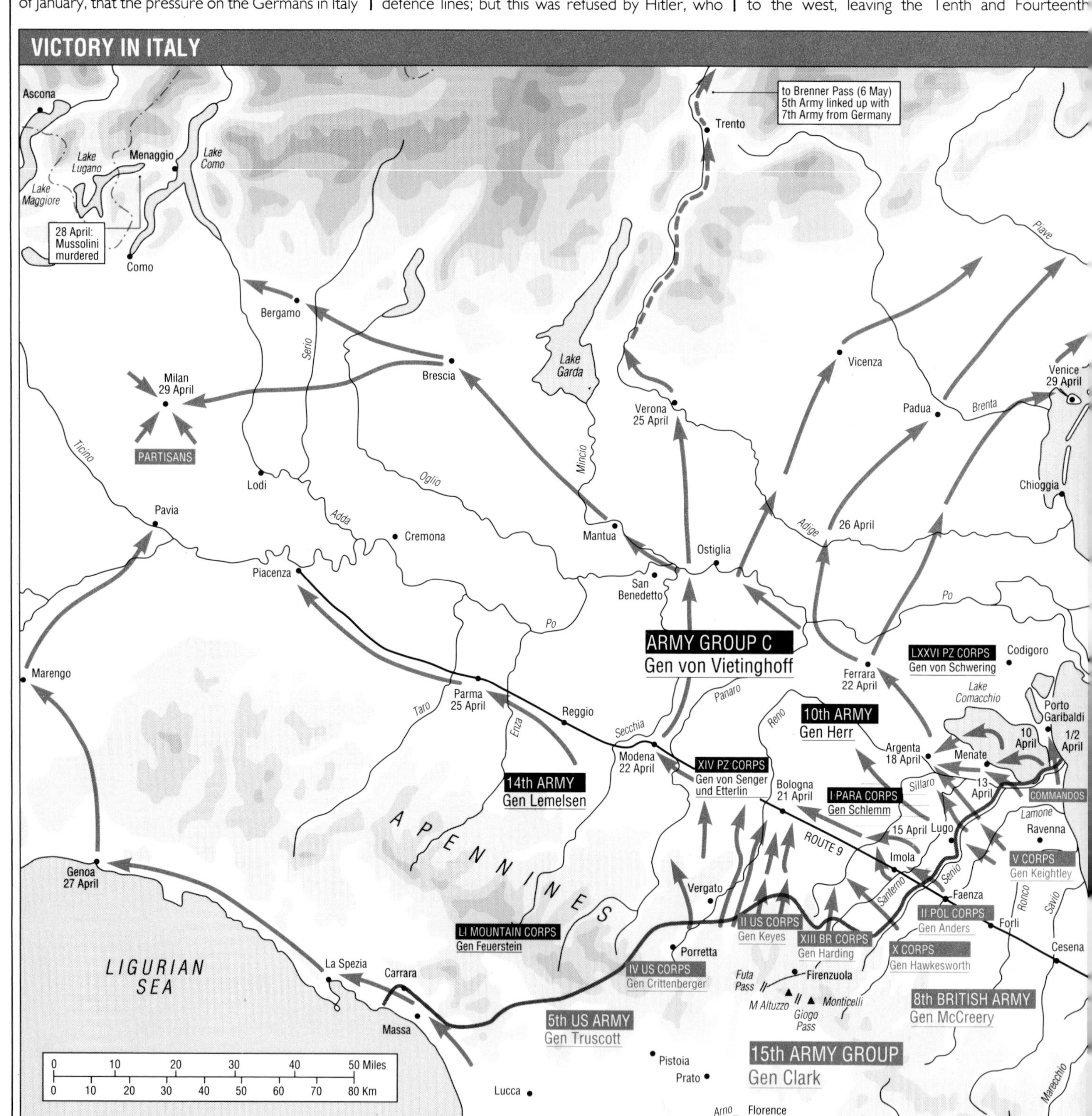

Armies with just eight divisions each. In addition, Army Group C had two veteran Panzergrenadier divisions as a mobile reserve, two further divisions to combat partisan activity in the rear areas and five unreliable Italian divisions of Mussolini's Army of Liguria. A crucial disadvantage under which the Germans laboured was that a prolonged Allied air offensive had virtually destroyed the communications system in northern Italy, making the rapid redeployment of troops virtually impossible.

The Allied plan that Mark Clark, now commanding 15th Army Group, evolved over the winter months of 1944/5 was simply to destroy Army Group C by trapping it between the Fifth and Eighth Armies. The former would thrust north to the west of Bologna, while the British seized the Argenta Gap lying between the River Reno and Lake Comacchio. The Allies in this theatre, too, had had to surrender troops to North West Europe in the shape of Canadian I Corps, although the threat that three British divisions would have to be handed over as well did not materialize. In the Canadians' place a number of Italian partisan brigades were deployed.

Towards the end of February, however, there were some dramatic, but highly secret developments indicating that the Germans in Italy might be prepared to make a unilateral armistice.

There had, during the last months of 1944, been a number of overtures made to the Western Allies by none other than Heinrich Himmler. He realized that Germany faced defeat and proposed that the Western Allies join Germany in an attack on the USSR in order to prevent Soviet Communism from encroaching in Western Europe. Not surprisingly, these proposals had been ignored. But now there came a 'feeler' from northern Italy which had possibilities.

3 March 1945 An OSS agent met SS General Eugen Dollmann at Lugano, Switzerland.
Dollmann was the adjutant to SS General Karl Wolff, the German military governor of northern Italy. Contact had first been made through Swiss intelligence and a prominent Milan industrialist. As an indication of goodwill, Dollmann was told to arrange for the release of two Italian partisan leaders. This was done, and Allen Dulles, the OSS head in Switzerland, received permission from the Supreme Allied HQ Mediterranean to proceed further with negotiations.

8 March Dulles met Wolff in Zurich, Switzerland.
Dulles reiterated that any surrender in Italy must be unconditional and to all three of the major Allied powers. Wolff agreed to enlist the support of Kesselring and the German Ambassador in Italy. Kesselring now left Italy, and so Wolff had to approach his successor. Two senior officers from Alexander's HQ, the American General Lyman Lemnitzer and the British General Terence Airey, were now sent to Switzerland to take part in the 'Sunrise' negotiations with Wolff.

In the meantime US Ambassador to Moscow Averell Harriman informed the Russians of what was afoot. They demanded representation at the talks, but this was denied.

19 March Dulles, Lemnitzer and Airey met Wolff at Ascona on Lake Maggiore, Italy.
The generals were in disguise. Wolff was not certain as to where von Vietinghoff stood and proposed that he visit Kesselring on the Western Front.

1 April Himmler ordered Wolff not to set foot out of Italy.
He had sensed what Wolff was up to and did not want to be upstaged by him. This prevented the 'Sunrise' talks from going any further, and Airey and Lemnitzer returned to Caserta.

By now Mark Clark's final offensive in Italy was about to open; indeed, the preliminaries were already under way.

Night of 1/2 April British Commandos attacked the spit running between Lake Comacchio and the Adriatic.
This was designed to tie down the German flank, as was a similar operation launched on the night of 4th/5th to seize islands on the Lake from which raiding operations could be mounted.

9 April Opening of the Allied offensive.
British Eighth Army attacked first. In the centre of McCreery's front, Indians and New Zealanders of Charles Keightley's V Corps attacked across the Senio towards Lugo. By the 11th a bridgehead had been established over the Santerno. On the 10th there was an amphibious operation with a landing at Menate on the west shore of Lake Comacchio and designed to turn the German flank in front of the Argenta Gap.

13 April McCreery crossed the Reno.

14 April Truscott's Fifth Army launched its attack.
This had been delayed two days by bad weather.

15 April Polish II Corps began to cross the River Sillaro.
It was thrusting north-west to Bologna astride Route 9. Truscott continued to fight his way through the mountains down on to the Lombardy plain.

18 April McCreery captured Argenta.
This had been helped by another outflanking operation across Lake Comacchio.

21 April Bologna fell.
First to enter the city were the Poles coming along Route 9. A few hours later Geoffrey Keyes' US II Corps entered along Route 65 from the south.

By now von Vietinghoff's defences were broken and he had given orders to withdraw to the Po. It was now that the Allied air offensive on communications began to bite.

22 April The Americans reached Modena and the British Ferrara.

23 April Wolff made another approach to the Allies.
It was clear now that Army Group C was on the verge of collapse and von Vietinghoff agreed that an armistice should be signed without reference to Berlin. It was not, however, until the 27th that Dulles was given authority from Alexander's HQ to resume negotiations. By now the Allied advance was accelerating.

25 April The Americans took Parma and Verona.

26 April The Allies crossed the Adige.

27 April The Americans reached Genoa.

28 April Mussolini murdered.
He had left his villa on Lake Garda for Milan on the 18th, planning to join his German allies in a last-ditch stand in the Alps. Having failed to rally his followers, he departed for Lake Como on the 25th, intending to meet 3,000 loyal Blackshirts. Next morning, six miles north of Menaggio, his convoy was ambushed by partisans. They allowed his German escort to pass, but arrested him and his mistress Clara Petacci. They were held in a farmhouse while instructions from the Committee of National Liberation were awaited. On the morning of the 28th a Communist partisan leader, Walter Audisio, arrived, bundled them into a car and then, after a short drive, dragged them out and shot them. Their bodies were then taken to Milan, where, by now mutilated, they were strung up in one of the main squares.

29 April The Germans signed an unconditional surrender at Caserta.
The German signatories were representatives of von Vietinghoff, and a Russian officer was also present. The surrender was to come into effect at 1300 hours GMT on 2 May.

US Fifth Army reached Milan, already liberated by partisans, and British Eighth Army Venice.

2 May British troops met Tito's partisans in Trieste.
There were fears that Tito would snatch this vital port and indeed it was to become an immediate post-war problem.

The war in Italy was now at an end, although the Fifth Army continued to advance north through the Alps to Austria, reaching the Brenner Pass on 6 May.

The End in Europe · P226

The End in Europe

By the beginning of May 1945, with the death of Hitler, the fall of Berlin and the surrender in Italy, it was clear that the war in Europe could not last many more days. Indeed, Doenitz, the new Fuehrer, had in a radio broadcast on 1 May told the German people that the only reason for continuing to fight was to 'save Germany from destruction by the advancing Bolshevik enemy'.

2 May 1945 21st Army Group secured the base of the Schleswig-Holstein peninsula.
Montgomery's armies were now racing to beat Rokossovsky's 2nd Belorussian Front to the port of Luebeck. Meanwhile, 12th and 6th Army Groups had now entered Austria and were also closing to the Czech border.

3 May A German delegation arrived at Montgomery's HQ on Lueneberg Heath.
It was led by the just-appointed CinC of the German Navy, Admiral Hans Georg von Friedeburg. The Germans offered the surrender of their forces withdrawing in the face of Rokossovsky. Montgomery stated that these must surrender to the Russians and instead demanded the unconditional surrender of all German forces in north-west Germany, Holland and Denmark. Von Friedeburg agreed to take this demand back to Doenitz.

Montgomery's forces took the surrender of Hamburg, reached Luebeck and met Rokossovsky's forces on the line Wismar–Wittenberg. US Ninth Army also met the Russians south-east of Wittenberg. US Third Army was across the River Inn and approaching Linz while Seventh Army on its right was negotiating the surrender of Salzburg.

4 May Montgomery accepted the surrender of the German forces in north-west Germany, Holland and Denmark.
Hostilities were to cease at 0800 hours on the following day. This included the German Twenty-Fifth Army in Holland, where, during the period **29 April to 7 May,** RAF Bomber Command and the USAAF dropped foodstuffs to the beleaguered and starving Dutch population (Operation 'Manna'). Doenitz now gave orders for his U-boats still at sea to return to port and surrender. He realized that the surrender signed on Lueneberg Heath applied to only one front, but also believed that every day the war was prolonged more troops could be saved from Russian clutches. He had, none the less, to open negotiations with the Americans and therefore sent von Friedeburg direct to Eisenhower's HQ at Reims in the hope that he could negotiate a separate surrender with the Western Allies.

Salzburg surrendered to US Seventh Army, which also seized Hitler's mountain retreat at Berchtesgaden.

5 May Eisenhower turned down the German proposal for a separate surrender to the Western Allies.
In the meantime a number of unofficial surrenders were beginning to take place, notably in the south, where SS General Paul Hausser's Army Group G began to surrender in large numbers to 6th Army Group.

There was an uprising in Prague following a number of spontaneous uprisings against the Germans in other parts of the country. By the end of the day large parts of the city were in the hands of the insurgents, and they had captured the radio station. The umbrella Czech National Council broadcast appeals to resistance fighters in other parts of the country to come to Prague and also to General Andrei Vlasov's Russia Liberation Army, which had been created by the Germans from Russian POWs, and was stationed in Prague.

US Third Army had crossed into Czechoslovakia the previous day and Patton wanted to drive straight to Prague. Eisenhower had, however, on **30 April** agreed a stop-line Pilsen–Karlsbad with the Russians, and they would not agree to Patton's moving east of this.

General Richard Dewing, Head of the SHAEF Mission to Denmark, and a British airborne unit flew into Copenhagen. British troops crossed the German border into Jutland and next day more troops were flown into Copenhagen. The German surrenders here went smoothly, apart from on the island of Bornholm, which was garrisoned by 20,000 German troops. The commander wanted to surrender to the British, but it had been agreed that this area was a Russian responsibility.

6 May Jodl arrived at Reims to continue surrender negotiations.
He proposed a two-stage surrender with German forces being allowed liberty of movement during the first phase in order to avoid capture by the Russians. Eisenhower rejected this, but said that he would keep his lines open for a further 48 hours to German troops withdrawing from the east. Jodl passed this back to Doenitz, who authorized him to sign an unconditional surrender.

The Germans moved Waffen-SS troops into Prague, but they were engaged by Vlasov's men, who hoped that Patton would relieve them, declaring that they were fighting both German Nazism and Russian Bolshevism. Patton had reached Pilsen where he halted.

7 May At Reims the Germans signed an unconditional total surrender to the Allies.
The surrender document was signed at 0240 hours in the War Room of SHAEF HQ, with Jodl signing on behalf of the Germans, Bedell Smith for Eisenhower, General Ivan Suslaparov for the USSR and the French General François Sevez as witness. All hostilities were to end at 2301 hours Central European Time **8 May**; as from then all German forces were to remain in place.

Churchill and Truman had decided to declare the next day Victory in Europe (VE) Day and intended to broadcast this to their respective peoples on the 7th. The Russians, however, now insisted on having another surrender ceremony in Berlin, and so the broadcasts had to be cancelled. The news, however, had already leaked out so that they were forced to go ahead with the VE Day celebrations on the 8th.

Troops of the 1st Belorussian Front reached the Elbe around Magdeburg, and 1st Ukrainian Front finally took the surrender of the fortress of Breslau. In Prague Vlasov's troops, disowned on Russian prompting by the Czech National Front and realizing that Patton was not coming to their aid, evacuated the city and withdrew west.

Efforts to contact the German commander in Norway, General Franz Boehme, by radio during the 6th and 7th had failed. This concerned the Allies, who feared that he and his 280,000 men might decide to fight on. On the evening of the 7th, however, he acknowledged the surrender in a broadcast on Radio Oslo and ordered a cease-fire.

8 May Surrender ceremony in Berlin.
Keitel, Hans-Juergen Stumpff (representing the Luftwaffe) and von Friedeburg signed for the Germans, and Zhukov, Tedder, Spaatz and de Lattre de Tassigny for the Allies.

The remnant of Army Group Courland surrendered to the Leningrad Front, while Dresden and Goerlitz surrendered to the 1st Ukrainian Front. In Czechoslovakia, Konev, who had now redeployed his armies south to the Czech border, gave details of the German surrender to Army Group Centre that evening, ordering it to comply by midnight. The deadline passed without response, and Konev unleashed a drive on Prague, which he reached in the early hours of the following morning.

The SHAEF Mission to Norway flew to Norway and made Boehme sign a surrender document. Meanwhile, two Royal Navy destroyers kept a rendezvous with a representative of the German garrison of the Channel Islands. He was not empowered to agree to any surrender terms and the German commander stated that he would not surrender without orders from Germany.

9 May Hostilities were now officially at an end, but fighting continued in Czechoslovakia, Austria and Croatia.
Prague was liberated when the troops of 1st and 2nd Ukrainian Fronts met in the city. The remnant of Army Group Centre were now surrounded. 2nd Ukrainian Front was also still pursuing Woehler's Army Group Austria (formerly Army Group South), whose Waffen-SS elements were trying to surrender to the Americans. Most managed to do

UNCONDITIONAL SURRENDER: May 1945

GERMAN FORCES NORWAY
Gen Boehme
NORWAY
Oslo
7 MAY: GERMAN COMMANDER ANNOUNCES SURRENDER
SWEDEN
Stockholm
FINLAND: MADE PEACE SEPT 1944
Helsinki
ESTONIA
LATVIA
Riga
ARMY GROUP COURLAND
Surrendered 8 May
LENINGRAD FRONT
LITHUANIA
Edinburgh
GREAT BRITAIN
NORTH SEA
Liverpool
London
Southampton
GERMAN FORCES
DENMARK
Copenhagen
5 MAY: BRITISH TROOPS FLOWN IN TO TAKE SURRENDER OF GERMAN FORCES
BALTIC SEA
Bornholm
Koenigsberg
EAST PRUSSIA
Danzig
BELGIUM: LIBERATED DECEMBER 1944
HOLLAND
25th ARMY
Amsterdam
1st CAN ARMY
2nd BR ARMY
9th US ARMY
5 May
Flensberg
2 May
Kiel
3 May
Wismar
Luebeck
3 May
Hamburg
Lueneburg
Wittenberg
Hannover
3 May
Magdeburg
Berlin
2nd BELORUSSIAN FRONT
1st BELORUSSIAN FRONT
8 MAY: REPEAT SURRENDER CEREMONY
Vistula
Warsaw
POLAND
Lublin
Channel Islands
Cherbourg
Surrendered 9 May
Dieppe
Brussels
BELGIUM
Cologne
Rhine
Seine
Reims
Paris
Meuse
7 MAY: GERMANS SIGNED UNCONDITIONAL SURRENDER
Luxemburg
GERMANY
Frankfurt
1st US ARMY
Leipzig
Elbe
Chemnitz
Dresden
Goerlitz
Oder
Breslau
Surrendered 8 May
Surrendered 7 May
1st UKRAINIAN FRONT
Karlsbad
Prague
ARMY GROUP CENTRE
Surrendered 11 May
Cracow
Nuremberg
Pilsen
6 May
Stuttgart
Strasbourg
Loire
3rd US ARMY
1st FR ARMY
7th US ARMY
4th UKRAINIAN FRONT
2nd UKRAINIAN FRONT
3rd UKRAINIAN FRONT
Inn
4 May
Salzburg
Linz
Vienna
Danube
Berchtesgaden
Berne
Innsbruck
FRANCE
SWITZERLAND
AUSTRIA
Brenner Pass
Graz
14 May
Klagenfurt
Budapest
HUNGARY: CHANGED SIDES OCTOBER 1944
HUNGARY
ROUMANIA: CHANGED SIDES AUGUST 1944
6 MAY: LINK UP BETWEEN 7th ARMY FROM GERMANY AND 5th ARMY FROM ITALY
Lyons
ARMY GROUP E
Surrendered 14 May
2 May
Milan
Po
Venice
2 May
Trieste
Zagreb
ROUMANIA
Turin
Rhne
Toulouse
2 May
5th US ARMY
8th BR ARMY
YUGOSLAV ARMY OF NATIONAL LIBERATION
AEGEAN: GERMAN GARRISONS SURRENDERED BY 11 MAY
CRETE: GERMAN GARRISON SURRENDERED 12 MAY
Belgrade
Nice
Marseilles
ITALY
YUGOSLAVIA
SPAIN

so, but one division, the SS Totenkopf, which had a notorious reputation for war crimes on the Eastern Front, was immediately handed over to the Russians. In Croatia, Tito's forces liberated Zagreb and continued to hound the remains of Army Group E.

The remaining German forces in East Prussia surrendered to 2nd and 3rd Belorussian Fronts. Having been forced to bomb it from the air, Russian troops landed on the Danish island of Bornholm and took the surrender of the German garrison. The German garrison in the Channel Islands also signed a surrender aboard the destroyer HMS *Bulldog*.

11 May **Army Group Centre surrendered to the Russians in Czechoslovakia.**

14 May **Final surrenders by Army Group E in Yugoslavia to Tito's forces.**

23 May **British troops arrested Doenitz and his government at Flensburg.**

It had only been allowed to operate this long in order to assist in the surrender of the German forces, especially the U-boats.

The fighting in Europe was now at an end, and the Allies could turn to the defeat of Japan. But peace was to bring a fresh series of problems.

The Potsdam Conference · P234

Attacking Japan's Achilles' Heel

CLOSING IN ON JAPAN
Novosibirsk
USSR
Irkutsk
Lake Baikal
Chita
Kyakhta
SEA OF OKHOTSK
Nikolayevsk
KAMCHATKA
SAKHALIN
Poronaysk
Kurile Islands
Amur
Blagoveshchensk
4th ARMY
Khabarovsk
Sovetskaya Gavan
Lake Hulun
Kerulen
Yalu
Isitsihar
MONGOLIA
1st AREA ARMY
KWANTUNG ARMY
Gen Yamada
Harbin
Mutankiang
Ussuri
3rd AREA ARMY
Changchun
Kirin
Gobi Desert
Vladivostok
3rd AREA ARMY
HOKKAIDO
MANCHUKUO
Najin
SINKIANG
COMMUNIST CHINESE
Mao Tse-tung
Kiuchuan
Shenyang
Antung
34th ARMY
Peking
Tientsin
Port Arthur
Pyongyang
Dairen
Wonsan
SEA OF JAPAN
1st GENERAL ARMY
JAPAN
Yellow River
Yenan
CHINA EXPEDITIONARY FORCE
Seoul
KOREA
HONSHU
17th AREA ARMY
YELLOW SEA
Pusan
Kaifeng
Chengchow
17 April 1944
Siking
Nagoya
Tokyo
Yokohama
Kyoto
Hiroshima
Kobe
Osaka
NATIONALIST CHINESE
Chiang Kai-shek
CHINA
18 Dec 1944: Incendiary raid
Wuhan
Nagasaki
Shikoku
Kyushu
June 1944
TIBET
Lhasa
Bramaputra
Ichang
Nanking
Shanghai
Yangtze
Fuel supplies
Chungking
Hankow
18 June 1944
Hangchow
24 Nov 1944: Musashino raid, first B-29 attack from Marianas
Bhutan
Ledo
NORTHERN COMBAT AREA COMMAND
Gen Sultan
14th US AIR FORCE
Gen Chennault
Nanchang
Changsha
26 June/8 Aug
Ryukyu Archipelago
Lingling
Hengyang
9-10 March 1945: Beginning of incendiary raids
Bonin Is
20th US BOMBER COMMAND
Myitkyina
Bhamo
Kumming
21st US BOMBER COMMAND
to Oct 1944
Kweilin
4 Sept
10 Nov 1944
Foochow
Okinawa
32nd AREA ARMY
Gen Kuribayashi
Volcano Is
Japanese forward air defence base
Iwo Jima
14th ARMY
Gen Slim
Dacca
Lashio
Liuchow
Amoy
Formosa
Liberated by end March 1945
Mandalay
Salween
Nunning
Canton
Macau
Hong Kong
10th AREA ARMY
Hanoi
Haiphong
BURMA
BURMA AREA ARMY
Gen Kimura
Hainan
PACIFIC OCEAN
Mariana Islands
Rangoon
Mekong
SOUTH CHINA SEA
THAILAND
Moulmein
Luzon
5 June 1944
Bangkok
General area under Allied control by end March 1945
B-29s operating from here by mid-October 1944
Saipan
Manila
SOUTH-EAST ASIA COMMAND
Adm Lord Mountbatten
FRENCH INDO-CHINA
PHILIPPINES
Tinian
Guam
Phnom Penh
Saigon
Cam-Ranh Bay
Kra Isthmus
Samar
SOUTHERN ARMY
Gen Terauchi
Leyte
8th Army (Gen Eichelberger) clearing Philippines during first half of 1945
Palawan
Phuket Is
Caroline Islands
Mindanao
Kota Bharu
Palau Is
Georgetown
Brunei
NORTH BORNEO
Kuala Lumpur
MALAYA
SOUTH-WEST PACIFIC AREA
Gen MacArthur
PACIFIC OCEAN AREA
Adm Nimitz
SARAWAK
INDIAN OCEAN
Singapore
SUMATRA
BORNEO
CELEBES
Balikpapan
Airfield
US submarine blockade of Japanese sea communication lines
0 100 200 300 400 500 Miles
0 200 400 600 800 Km
Palembang
MOLUCCAS
Hollandia
NETHERLANDS NEW GUINEA
NEW GUINEA
Batavia

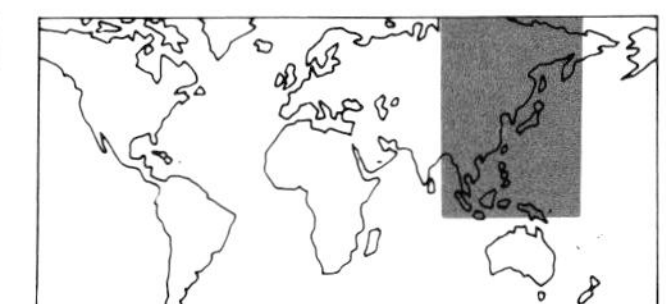

The USA had always been aware of Japan's one major weakness – an almost complete lack of domestic raw materials. Indeed, this had been one of the main driving forces behind Japan's decision to go to war with the Western democracies. She was thus highly dependent on her merchant fleet, one of the largest in the world, for the acquisition of vital raw materials.

In December 1941 the US and Japanese Navies possessed small and roughly equal submarine fleets. The Americans had 55 boats and the Japanese 64. Both navies believed in the same doctrine, namely that the prime role of the submarine was to sink enemy capital ships. During the course of the war the Japanese remained wedded to this doctrine, but the Americans showed more flexibility.

There were several reasons for this. First, like Germany, the US Navy quickly adopted a policy of unrestricted submarine warfare. Second, given the experience in the Atlantic, attacks on merchant shipping were seen to have great strategic potential; on a more practical level, they were easier targets than warships. Finally, three of the leading American Admirals, King, Nimitz and Hart, were themselves former submariners.

Consequently, from the end of 1942, increasing emphasis was placed on attacks against Japanese merchant shipping. During 1944 the sinkings reached an average of fifty per month but thereafter fell away, simply because of lack of targets. By the beginning of 1945 the sea lines of communication between Japan and what remained of her newly acquired empire had been virtually throttled. Indeed, by the end of the war the US submarine fleet, which had grown to a total of just over 150 boats, had sunk 1,153 Japanese merchant ships totalling 4,889,000 tons. In contrast the Japanese submarine fleet, which had contracted to less than 60 boats by war's end, sank a mere 184 Allied merchant vessels.

The other weapon in the American armoury for destroying Japan's means for waging war was the strategic bomber. This could attack the factories that turned the raw materials into weapons. James Doolittle had mounted his carrier-launched bomber raid against Japan in June 1942, but this was a unique operation. Indeed, it was two years before the Japanese mainland suffered the effects of Allied bombing again. The reason for this was range, both in terms of bases close enough and aircraft capable of reaching Japan with a full bomb-load.

In terms of aircraft the solution lay in the Boeing B-29 Superfortress. Work on it had begun in 1938, and it made its first flight on **21 September 1942.** With a range of 3,250 miles (5,230km) carrying a full bomb-load it was more than capable of reaching Japan from southern China. The next requirement therefore was to establish bases here.

Four airfields were built in southern China and a further five in India during early 1944. By this time there were two B-29 groups formed in the USA, 20th Bomber Command, which flew to India, and 21st Bomber Command, which would use the Chinese airfields. These were placed under the command of General 'Hap' Arnold.

Before they could become operational, however, the Japanese launched an offensive in southern China, 'Ichi-Go', on **17 April** 1944, which was designed first to clear Chinese resistance between the Yellow river and the Yangtze and then sweep into Hunan and Kwangsi provinces and overrun Fourteenth Air Force's bases in the latter.

5 June 1944 First B-29 operation.
This was mounted by 20th Bomber Command against targets in the Bangkok area of Siam (Thailand). Because of their capacity, the B-29s in India were largely used to deliver fuel to support 21st Bomber Command operations against Japan.

15 June 21st Bomber Group mounted its first attack on Japan.
This was against an iron and steel works at Yawata in the north of Kyushu Island. Little damage was caused. Subsequent attacks on Kyushu targets – Sasebo, Nagasaki and Yawata again – also produced disappointing results, and on the second trip to Yawata 18 out of 70 bombers were lost.

18 June The Japanese captured Changsha.
They then continued south to Hengyang, capturing an airfield there on the 26th, but the Chinese here, supported by Chennault's Fourteenth Air Force, held them and they withdrew after two weeks' fighting. This temporarily removed the threat to the US air bases.

8 August The Japanese captured Hengyang.
The Japanese had returned again, and the Chinese commander, as a result of a feud, was denied supplies by Chiang Kai-shek. The next objective was Kweilin, but Chennault's attacks on Japanese supply lines forced them to postpone their attack and they did not resume their advance until **29 August.**

4 September The Japanese captured the air base at Lingling.
By this stage, with the Marianas now secured, US engineers were working feverishly to construct airfields on Guam, Saipan and Tinian from which B-29s could operate.

12 October First B-29 landed in the Marianas.
Piloted by Brigadier General Heywood Hansell, commanding 21st Bomber Command, it touched down on Isley Field, Saipan. Within a few days a complete bombardment wing had arrived and some preparatory operations were carried out against Truk and Iwo Jima. All the B-29s were now removed from China to the Marianas, and they were followed later by the India-based aircraft.

10 November The Japanese captured Kweilin.
By the end of the month they had succeeded in overrunning airfields at Liuchow and Nanning as well.

24 November First B-29 raid on Japan from the Marianas.
The target was the Nakajima aircraft engine factory at Musashino in the suburbs of Tokyo. 111 bombers took part, but the target was obscured by haze and few bombs hit. One B-29 was shot down by fighters. Another attempt three days later was foiled by cloud. Nevertheless, the Japanese realized the threat that the B-29s posed. Even so, the results of the high-altitude precision bombing remained disappointing, and bomber casualty rates increased until by February 1945 they were running at 5.7 per cent. Not until Iwo Jima was secured was it possible to provide fighter escorts in the shape of P-51 Mustangs.

Night of 9/10 March 1945 First major US incendiary attack on Japan.
This was the brainchild of General Curtis LeMay, who had taken over what had now become the Twentieth Air Force, the B-29s in the Marianas, in January. On **18 December 1944** his 20th Bomber Command had taken part in a raid on Hankow in China with Fourteenth Air Force. Some of the B-29s had dropped incendiaries at low level and the attack was considered very successful.

LeMay now decided to use a similar tactic on Japan's cities, mounting his attacks by night to reduce aircraft casualties. In this way he hoped to be able to destroy the 'cottage industry' to which much of Japan's war production had now been reduced. 333 B-29s took off from the Marianas, their target Tokyo. The results were devastating: more than sixteen square miles of the city, made up largely of wooden houses, were burnt out. Other incendiary raids were made against Nagoya (night of 11th/12th), Osaka (13th/14th), Kobe and Nagoya again (18th/19th). LeMay then ran out of incendiaries, but after a short pause the offensive was resumed with both incendiary and high-explosive bombs, and mounted in intensity.

In spring 1945 Prime Minister Admiral Kantaro Suzuki commissioned Cabinet secretary Hisatsune Sakomizu to prepare a report on Japan's resources in order to establish whether it was possible for the war to continue. It made grim reading for the Japanese – steel production was two-thirds of the official estimate, aircraft production down to a third of its quota because of aluminium and bauxite shortages, munitions production as a whole down by 50 per cent because of coal shortages. The transportation system was crippled through lack of oil. Worse, the smallest harvest since 1905 had resulted in drastic food shortages. The situation could only get worse.

Iwo Jima and Okinawa · P230

Iwo Jima and Okinawa

The US Joint Chiefs of Staff directive of **3 October 1944** had ordered MacArthur to invade Luzon in the Philippines in December 1944, while Nimitz attacked Iwo Jima in late January 1945 and then moved on to Okinawa in the Ryukyu Archipelago, the last stepping-stones leading to Japan itself.

There were several reasons for seizing Iwo Jimo rather than bypassing it in favour of a direct assault on Okinawa. For a start, US Twentieth Air Force was suffering losses in its offensive against Japan and needed fighter escorts. The Marianas were beyond the range of these, while Iwo Jima, which had two airstrips, was only 660 nautical miles from Tokyo. Since it was traditionally part of Japan, its capture would severely dent Japanese morale. It also gave the Japanese the ability to launch air strikes on the Marianas.

By mid-1944 the Japanese had rightly guessed that Iwo Jima would be an American target and began to reinforce their garrison there. By mid-November it had grown to 21,000 men under the command of General Tadamichi Kuribayashi. He worked hard to convert the island to a fortress of pillboxes, caves and underground tunnels.

8 October 1944 **Nimitz earmarked General Holland 'Howling Mad' Smith to control the Iwo Jima operation.**
General Harry Schmidt's V Amphibious Corps (3rd, 4th, 5th Marine Divisions) would carry out the landings.

11–12 November **First US naval bombardment of Iwo Jima.**

8 December **The US Twentieth Air Force began to 'soften up' Iwo Jima.**
Carried out mainly by B-24 Liberators and B-25 Mitchells, with occasional assistance from the B-29 fleet, this preparatory air bombardment was to last 72 days. Slow progress in the Philippines, however, forced a postponement from late January to first 3 February and then 19 February. This was because some of the naval assets deployed in the Philippines were needed for Iwo Jima.

20 January 1945 **Japanese Imperial HQ issued a directive for the defence of Japan ('Sho-Go').**
While the final decisive battle would be fought on the Japanese mainland, the main defensive battle would take place in the Ryukyus. The main object would be to destroy the Allied fleet once landings had taken place.

General Mitsuru Ushijima's Thirty-Second Army on Okinawa had been gradually reinforced during the past six months and now had a strength of 80,000 men.

17 February **US frogmen suffered heavy casualties during a beach reconnaissance of Iwo Jima.**

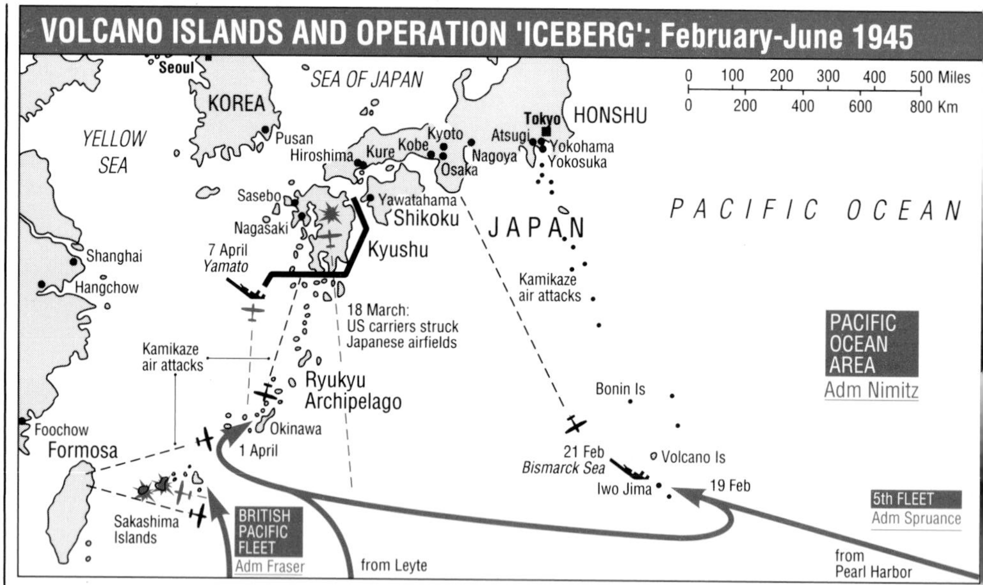

The Japanese thought that the invasion had begun and opened fire with heavy artillery causing 170 casualties. There now began a concentrated naval bombardment of the island.

19 February **The landings on Iwo Jima.**
4th and 5th Marine Divisions carried out the initial landings. In the first few minutes Japanese resistance was light, but then the Marines were subjected to concentrated fire. In spite of this the Marines managed to establish their beachhead and, although casualties were high, 30,000 men had been landed by the end of the day.

21 February **Japanese *Kamikaze* attacks on the US Fifth Fleet supporting the landings.**
The escort carrier *Bismarck Sea* was sunk and the fleet carrier *Saratoga* badly damaged. Admiral Raymond Spruance now commanded the Fifth Fleet, having taken over from Halsey in January.

23 February **Mount Suribachi captured.**
It was the capture of this, the highest point on Iwo Jima that brought about one of the most famous photographs of the war, 'Raising Old Glory on Iwo Jima' by Joe Rosenthal. The Marines now turned north, but their progress was slow and bloody.

4 March **First B-29 landed on Iwo Jima.**

14 March **Iwo Jima declared secure.**
Even so, there were still a number of Japanese pockets of resistance.

24 March **Capture of the Kerama Islands marked the beginning of the Okinawa operations ('Iceberg').**
These lay south-west of Okinawa and were to be used as a fleet anchorage. On the same day the naval bombardment of Okinawa began. Six days earlier Spruance's carriers had attacked airfields on Kyushu to neutralize them, but the carriers *Franklin* and *Wasp* were badly damaged in *Kamikaze* attacks.

Nimitz had originally intended that 'Iceberg' be mounted on 1 March, but progress in the Philippines and on Iwo Jima forced a postponement by one month. The landings would be carried out by General Simon Buckner's newly formed US Tenth Army of seven divisions. Once again the Fifth Fleet would provide the naval support. This had now been joined by the British Pacific Fleet under Admiral Sir Bruce Fraser, who had sunk *Scharnhorst*. In all, 1457 ships would take part in 'Iceberg', which British observers described as 'the most audacious and complex enterprise yet undertaken by the American amphibious forces'.

27 March **General Kuribayashi, Japanese commander on Iwo Jima, committed suicide.**
The day before, some 300 Japanese had launched a suicidal *Banzai* attack. In what was the most costly US battle of the war the Americans suffered 25,000 casualties, including almost 7,000 dead. Only 1,083 members of the Japanese garrison survived and many of these were not captured for some time. Indeed, the last two did not surrender until 1951.

1 April **The landings on Okinawa.**
Ushijima had decided not to defend the beaches, preferring to concentrate the bulk of his forces in the southernmost part of the island. Consequently the Americans were able to land 50,000 men on the first day.

6–7 April **Massive *Kamikaze* attacks on the invasion fleet.**
28 ships were hit and three sank. Further attacks followed during the next few weeks.

7 April **The battleship *Yamato* sunk by US aircraft.**

P198 · Luzon

IWO JIMA: February to March 1945

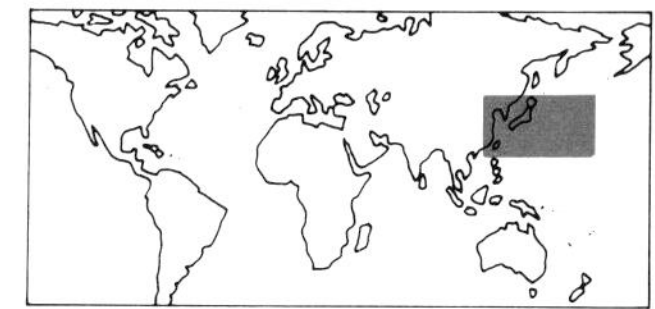

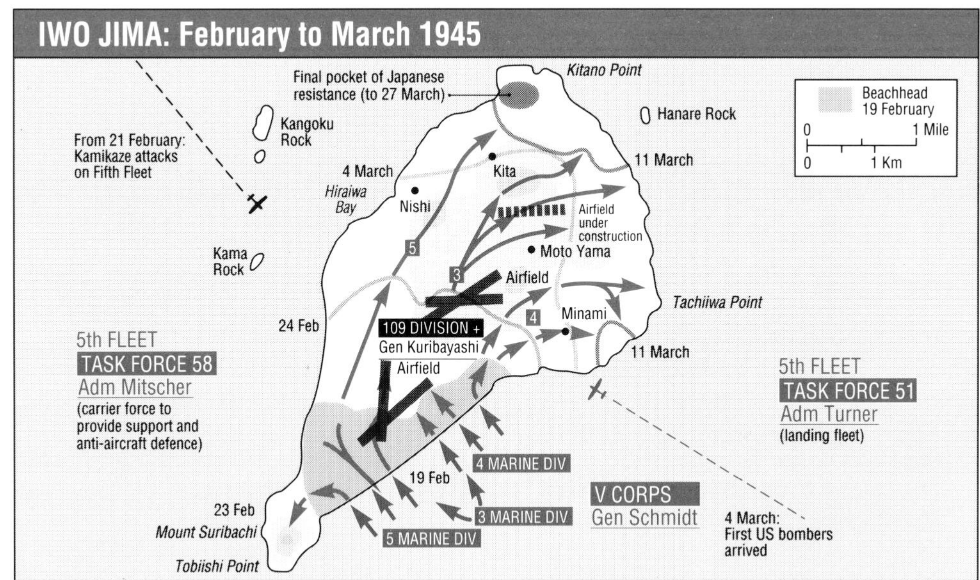

The pride of the Japanese Navy had left the Inland Sea on the previous day, accompanied by a light cruiser and eight destroyers. Her mission was to attack the invasion fleet, but she had only sufficient fuel for a one-way passage and it was planned to run her aground and use her as a gun platform. She was attacked by carrier-based aircraft just south-west of Kyushu and sunk, together with the cruiser and three destroyers. This marked the death knell of the Japanese Navy.

7 April The first P-51 escort operation from Iwo Jima for B-29s attacking Japan.

9 April Three US divisions began to attack the Shuri Defence Line in the south of Okinawa.
This marked the beginning of a long and costly period of fighting for Tenth Army with little progress to show for it in the face of strong fortifications and continuous Japanese counter-attacks.

10 April US troops landed on Tsugen Island to the east of Okinawa.
It was quickly cleared.

16 April US 77th Division landed on Ie Shima, west of Okinawa.
It was secured on the 21st after bitter fighting.

20 April US 6th Marine Division completed the clearance of the Motobu Peninsula.
The north of Okinawa was now secured.

27 May Naha, capital of Okinawa, captured.

29 May Shuri Castle, key to the Shuri Line, finally captured by US 1st Marine Division.
Heavy rain from 22 May hindered operations.

4 June Elements of US 6th Marine Division landed on the north coast of the Oroku peninsula.

18 June General Buckner killed.
He was the highest ranking American to be killed in the war; his heart had been pierced by a shell splinter.

19 June Japanese troops began to surrender voluntarily.
It was the first incidence of this and a sign that Japanese morale was ebbing.

22 June General Ushijima committed suicide.
This marked the end of the battle for Okinawa. Tenth Army had suffered almost 40,000 battle casualties, and *Kamikaze* attacks had cost the US Navy a further 9,700. Japanese casualties, both military and civilian, were some 110,000.

Now, finally, the Allies could attend to the most awesome operation of all – the invasion of Japan itself.

OKINAWA: April to June 1945

Hiroshima and Nagasaki · P238

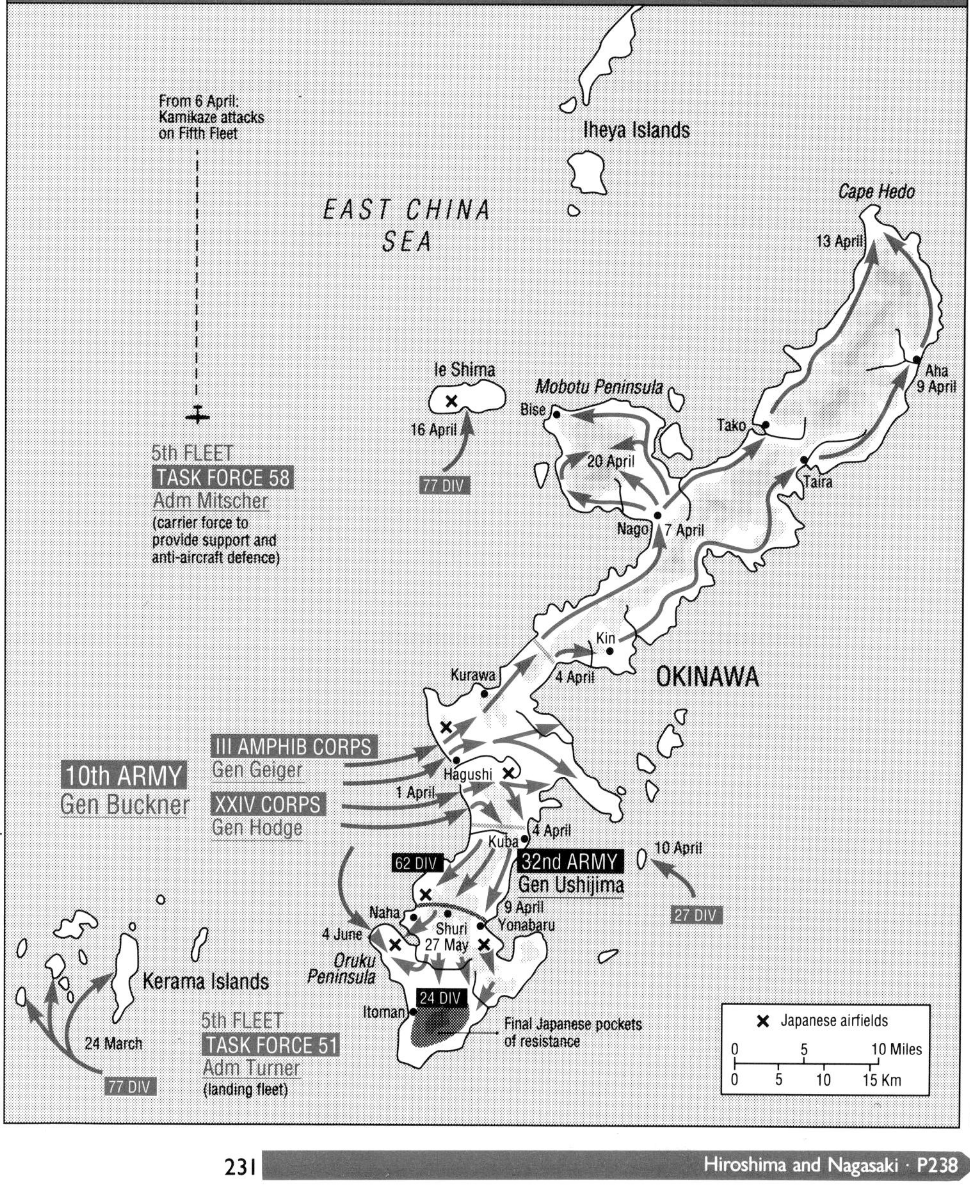

21 FEBRUARY 1945 TO 4 AUGUST 1945

The End in Burma

Mountbatten's directive for the reconquest of South East Asia had tasked him with the liberation of Malaya and Singapore once that of Burma had been completed. This, however, inevitably meant another major amphibious operation and the need for an advanced base to be established. Phuket Island, west of the Kra Isthmus in southern Thailand, was selected, but to secure it in reasonable time would of necessity mean diverting forces earmarked for 'Dracula', Mountbatten's projected amphibious assault on Rangoon. This produced a dilemma in that it was clear that both could not be mounted. However, by mid-February Bill Slim's Fourteenth Army thrust into central Burma, 'Extended Capital', was showing much promise and he believed that he could capture Rangoon himself before the monsoon broke. Consequently, on **23 February 1945** the British Chiefs of Staff finally cancelled 'Dracula'.

In the meantime Slim was closing on Mandalay and Meiktila, the twin keys to central Burma, and the Chinese armies were steadily advancing south in northern Burma.

21 February 1945 **36th British Division (NCAC) captured Myitson.**

22 February **17th Indian Division began to advance towards Meiktila from the Nyaungu bridgehead.**
It seized Taungtha two days later.

24 February **2nd British Division began to cross the Irrawaddy at Ngazun, west of Mandalay.**
Japanese resistance here was strong. 20th Indian Division's bridgehead at Myinmu now linked up with that at Ngazun.

26 February **19th Indian Division began to advance on Mandalay from the north.**

27 February **IV Corps reached the outskirts of Meiktila.**
Next day the attack on Meiktila began.

3 March **Meiktila fell to 17th Indian Division.**
Slim's deception plan to persuade the Japanese that Mandalay was his primary objective was successful and the Japanese had been wrong-footed. They had believed that the thrust to Meiktila was merely a raid. Nevertheless, recovering from their surprise, they now began to organize counter-attacks to retake the town. This would draw in elements of four divisions from the Fifteenth and Thirty-Third Armies.

4 March **Japanese counter-attack recaptured Taungtha.**
This cut 17th Indian Division's only supply route. The airfields at Meiktila were reopened the following day, and the Division was entirely reliant on air resupply for the next three weeks, during which Masaki Honda, commanding Thirty-Third Army, launched a series of counter-attacks on Meiktila, especially the airfields.

7 March **Advancing down the Burma Road, Y Force captured Lashio.**

9 March **19th Indian Division reached the outskirts of Mandalay.**
General Pete Rees, its commander, had detached a brigade to secure his right flank by capturing Maymyo. This fell on the 13th, the Japanese garrison being caught by surprise. Its capture also cut the sources of supply for the Japanese opposing the Chinese to the north.

11 March **Mandalay Hill captured.**
Most of the city apart from Fort Dufferin was quickly cleared of Japanese.

17 March **2nd British Division, advancing on Mandalay from the west, captured Fort Ava.**

20 March **Fort Dufferin finally fell to 19th Indian Division.**

24 March **A division of 6th Chinese Army (NCAC) linked up with Y force on the Burma Road at Hsipaw.**
This effectively marked the end of the Chinese role in Burma, and returned to China.

28 March **Honda ordered the counter-attacks on Meiktila to cease and for his troops to withdraw south.**
He now planned to block the Allied advance south at Pyawbwe.

30 March **The Allied advance south of Meiktila began.**

THE CAPTURE OF MANDALAY AND MEIKTILA

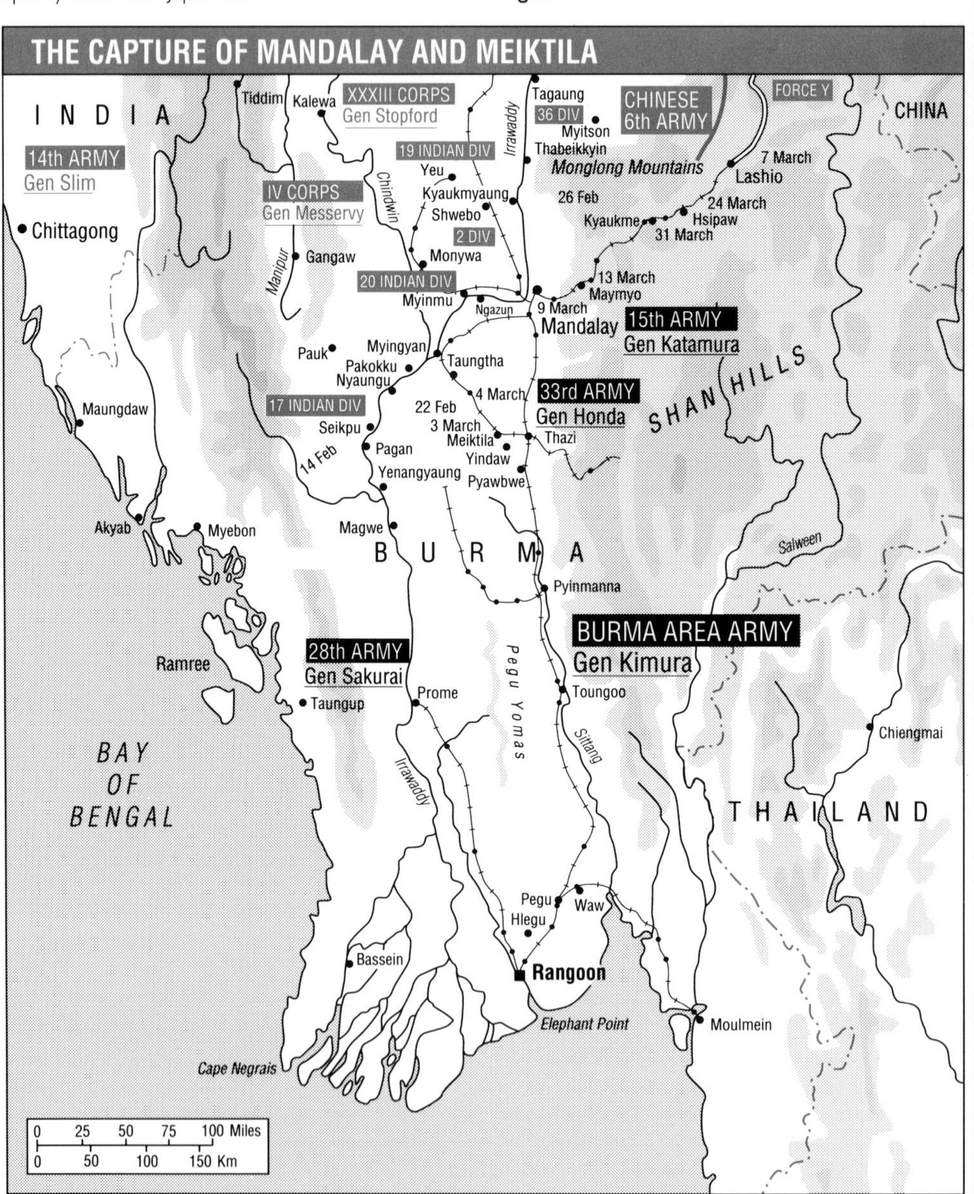

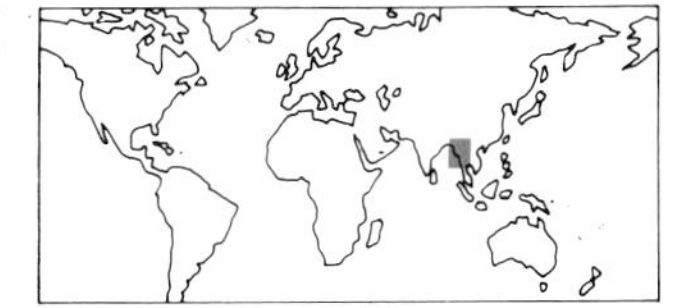

The main thrust down the line of the River Sittang was carried out initially by IV Corps divisions, while XXXIII Corps advanced south-west towards the Irrawaddy in order to cut the Japanese Twenty-Eighth Army's withdrawal routes in the Arakan. Almost immediately IV Corps met stiff resistance from Honda's troops in front of Pyawbwe.

31 March 36th British Division reached the Burma Road at Kyaukme.
It now rejoined Fourteenth Army and was sent to relieve 19th Indian Division in Mandalay.

2 April Mountbatten decided to mount a modified 'Dracula'.
The Japanese resistance around Meiktila had delayed the advance to the south, and both Slim and Leese, the overall land forces commander, were doubtful about Fourteenth Army's ability to reach Rangoon before the monsoon. Accordingly a division from XV Corps in the Arakan would carry out the landing on **2 May**, preceded the day before by an airborne landing on Elephant Point to secure the seaboard approaches to Rangoon.

6 April Yindaw captured.
17th Indian Division now hooked round Pyawbwe to the west, thus blocking Honda's retreat and virtually destroying his army. Meanwhile XXXIII Corps was clearing the Irrawaddy valley south of Myingyan and its banks south of Pakokku.

20 April Honda almost captured by 5th Indian Division in Pyinmana.
That evening the 'Mango Rains' which preceded the monsoon arrived.

23 April 19th Indian Division reached Toungoo.
By this time Honda had lost complete control over the remnant of his army. Katamura's Fifteenth Army was also trying to withdraw from the Shan Hills to Toungoo, but it had been slowed by demolitions set up by the Karen Levies and hence lost the race.

25 April XXXIII Corps captured Yenangyaung and its oilfields.
This was after four days' fierce fighting, at the end of which the Japanese withdrew.

29 April 17th Indian Division reached Pegu.

1 May Parachute drop on Elephant Point.
This was carried out by a Ghurkha parachute battalion.

2 May The 'Dracula' landings.
These were carried out by 26th Indian Division, and Rangoon was entered the following day. The Japanese had, however, withdrawn on the 1st. XXXIII Corps entered Prome, thus sealing off the Japanese Twenty-Eighth Army in the Arakan. Then the monsoon broke, ten days earlier than expected.

6 May 26th Indian Division linked up with 17th Division advancing south from Pegu at Hlegu.

7 May Slim replaced in command of Fourteenth Army by Christison.
This was at the instigation of Leese. Fourteenth Army was now to prepare for the invasion of Malaya ('Zipper') and Leese considered that Christison was more experienced in amphibious operations. Slim was to take command of Twelfth Army, which was formed on **28 May**, and carry out the final clearance of the Japanese from Burma. Slim threatened to resign and the upshot was that Stopford took over Twelfth Army and Dempsey was appointed to Fourteenth Army, with Christison retaining temporary command until Dempsey could arrive from Europe. Slim was given leave in Britain and then appointed CinC, ALFSEA in place of Leese.

The final phase of the campaign was undertaken by Twelfth Army and took place during July. Honda's Thirty-Third Army attempted to assist Sakurai's Twenty-Eighth Army break out from the Pegu Yomas east over the River Sittang. During **3–11 July** Honda attempted to seize Waw, but this was a diversion for the main operation, which was launched against 17th Indian Division on **19 July** south of Toungoo. By **4 August** it was all over. Of 18,000 men who withdrew from the Pegu Yomas, only some 6,000 reached the east bank of the Sittang and they were hardly fit enough to continue the long march to Malaya, their ultimate destination.

The long battle for Burma was finally over, although sizeable elements of the Burma Area Army still remained between the Sittang and the Salween. Mountbatten's attention, however, was now firmly fixed on 'Zipper' and the liberation of Singapore ('Mailfist'), as well as the securing of Phuket ('Roger').

VICTORY IN BURMA: 31 March to 4 August 1945

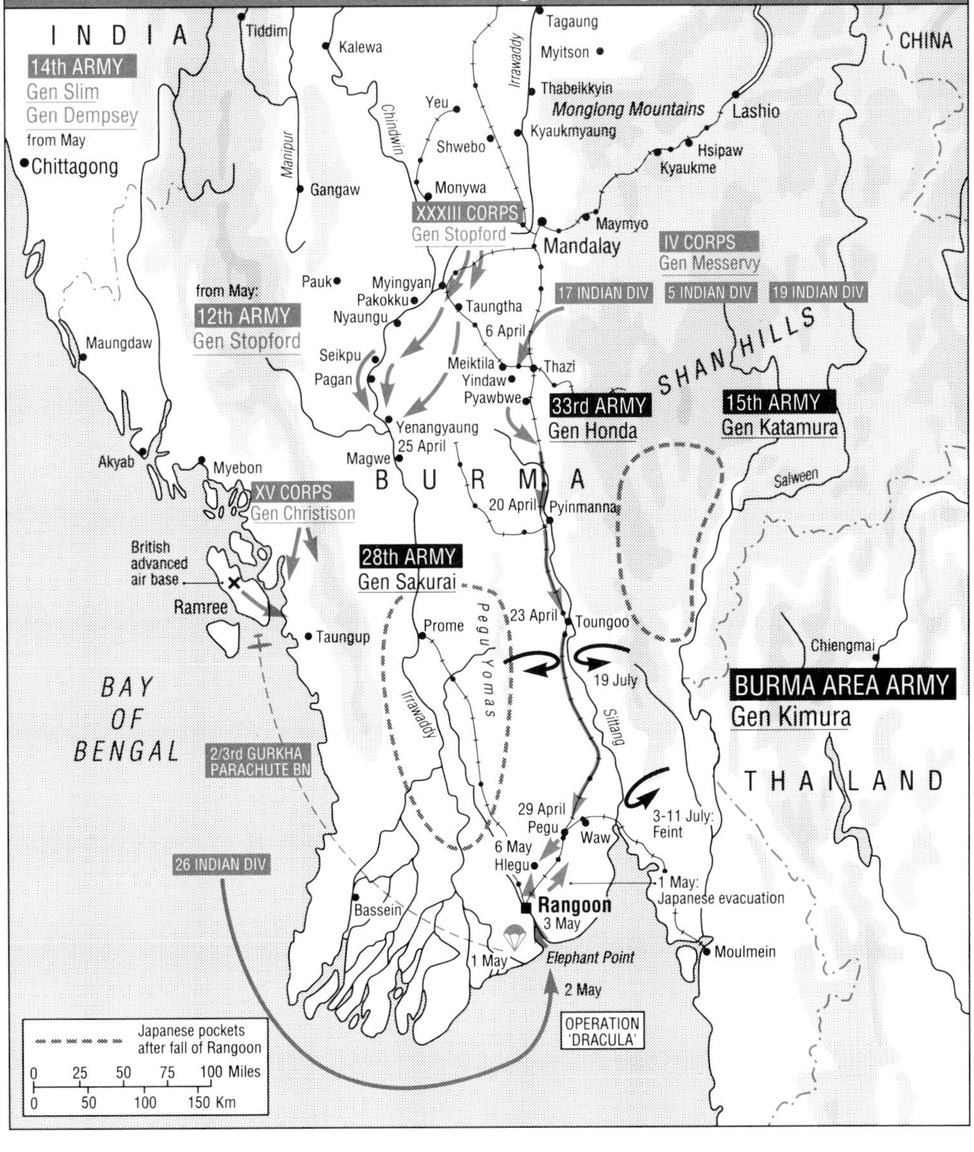

Japan Surrenders · P240

12 THE ULTIMATE WEAPON, June to September 1945

2 MAY 1945 TO 2 AUGUST 1945

The Potsdam Conference

The end of the war in Europe immediately presented the Western Allies at least with a whole series of new problems. For a start, although broad agreement had been reached at Yalta on the occupation of Germany, few specifics had been decided upon. While the four zones of occupation (with that of France being carved out of part of the British and US zones) had been drawn up, the fighting had left the Western Allies well to the east of the boundary with the Russian zone. How were the adjustments to take place? Reparations in kind from Germany had also been agreed, but to what degree should they be enforced, and how should the conquered German people be treated? Austria had not entered the calculations, and the question of how she should be dealt with needed to be decided. Then there was the question of eastern Europe, and especially Poland. The Balkans, too, presented problems. Finally there was the need to ensure that Stalin honoured his commitment to declare war against Japan.

2 May 1945 US representatives on the Allied Control Missions in Bulgaria and Roumania warned Truman of Russian attitudes there.
Local Communists, although in a minority, had taken over the governments, and it seemed that the Russians were determined to bring these former German allies under their complete control.

6 May Churchill urged Truman to convene another meeting of the Big Three.
He followed this up on **12 May** with a warning that an 'iron curtain' might descend across Europe and proposed that the Western Allies should not weaken their forces in Europe until relations with Russia were clearer. Truman believed that this step would merely serve to worsen relations; and in any event sizeable US forces were urgently needed in the Pacific.

8 May President Truman initiated an order to cease Lend-Lease to Britain and the USSR immediately.
He felt obliged to reflect the intention of Congress when the bill had been originally passed. There was, however, an immediate outcry from Britain (since this action cut across the Roosevelt pledge to Churchill at the Second Quebec Conference) and Stalin, who maintained that the full amounts agreed in the Fourth Protocol had not yet been delivered. Truman was therefore forced to modify his order and continue Lend-Lease until Japan had been defeated.

9 May Tito insisted that the Venezia Guilia region of north-east Italy be administered by Yugoslavia.
This, including the ports of Fiume and Trieste, had been given to Italy after the First World War. Anglo-US concern was based on fears for the weak Italian Government, partial isolation of their occupation forces in western Austria and also that Tito might, if no firm stand were taken, try to seize parts of Austria. Indeed, he did appropriate some border areas. The Western Allies reminded him of the Moscow Declaration of **1 November 1943** by which the Allies undertook to restore a free and independent Austria to her pre-1938 borders, and stated that the Venezia Guilia problem would be resolved as part of the peace settlement. As an interim measure, they proposed a compromise of a line dividing the administration between the Allies and Yugoslavia. Tito at first refused to back down, and Churchill was prepared to use force against him. Truman, however, was not so willing at first, but in view of Tito's intransigence did instigate some contingency planning. He also informed Stalin of the situation. By the end of the month there were signs that Tito's attitude was softening.

16 May US Secretary of War Henry Stimson expressed disquiet to Truman over policy towards defeated Germany.
The Allied view at the time was to keep the German people near the hunger margin as a punishment and to follow, at least in part, the Morgenthau Plan for German industry. Stimson warned of the danger of hardship driving the Germans into 'a non-democratic and necessarily predatory habit of life'. The German people could not be supported by

WAR AND PEACE: August 1945

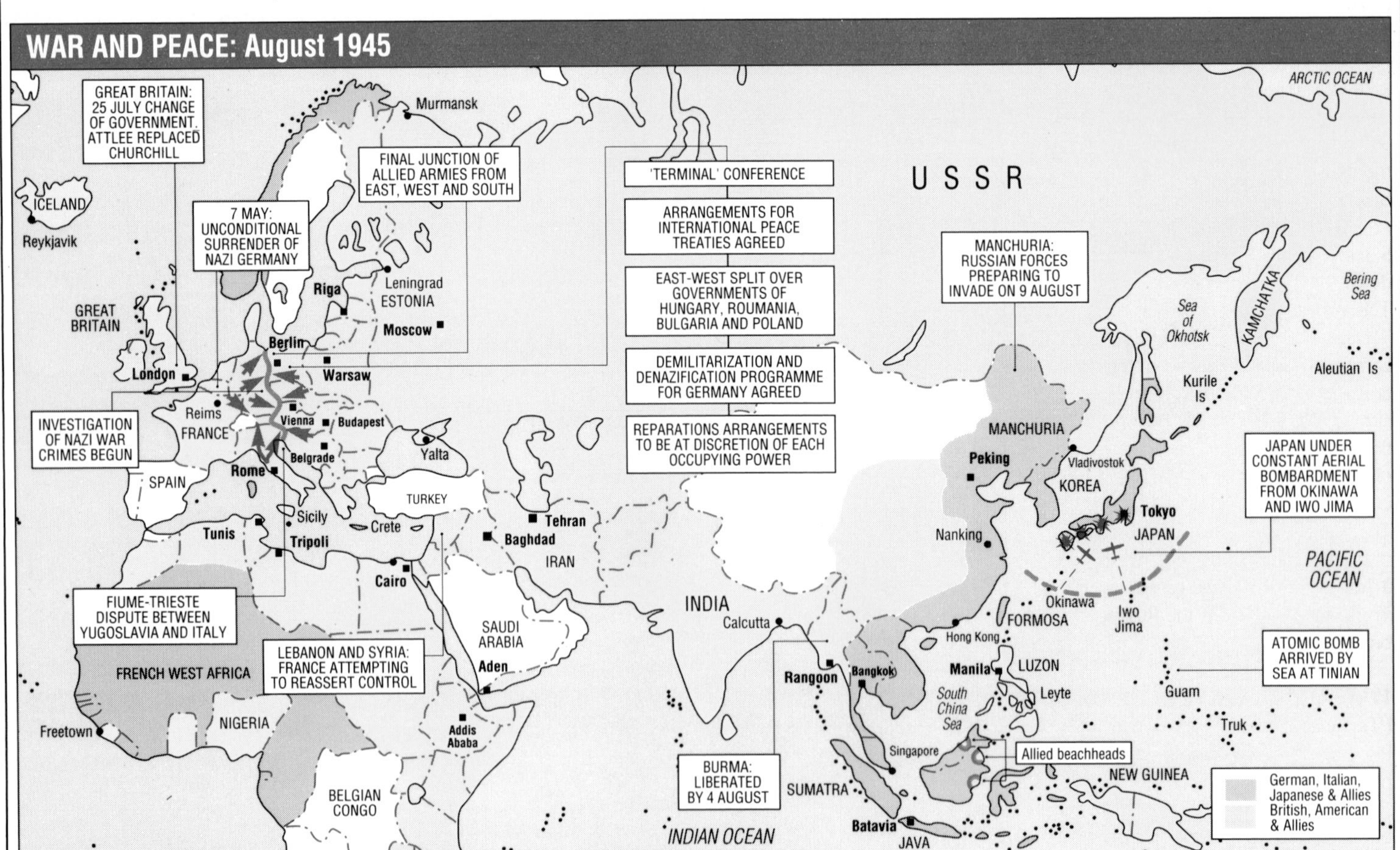

GREAT BRITAIN: 25 JULY CHANGE OF GOVERNMENT. ATTLEE REPLACED CHURCHILL
FINAL JUNCTION OF ALLIED ARMIES FROM EAST, WEST AND SOUTH
7 MAY: UNCONDITIONAL SURRENDER OF NAZI GERMANY
'TERMINAL' CONFERENCE
ARRANGEMENTS FOR INTERNATIONAL PEACE TREATIES AGREED
EAST-WEST SPLIT OVER GOVERNMENTS OF HUNGARY, ROUMANIA, BULGARIA AND POLAND
DEMILITARIZATION AND DENAZIFICATION PROGRAMME FOR GERMANY AGREED
REPARATIONS ARRANGEMENTS TO BE AT DISCRETION OF EACH OCCUPYING POWER
MANCHURIA: RUSSIAN FORCES PREPARING TO INVADE ON 9 AUGUST
INVESTIGATION OF NAZI WAR CRIMES BEGUN
JAPAN UNDER CONSTANT AERIAL BOMBARDMENT FROM OKINAWA AND IWO JIMA
FIUME-TRIESTE DISPUTE BETWEEN YUGOSLAVIA AND ITALY
LEBANON AND SYRIA: FRANCE ATTEMPTING TO REASSERT CONTROL
ATOMIC BOMB ARRIVED BY SEA AT TINIAN
BURMA: LIBERATED BY 4 AUGUST
Allied beachheads
German, Italian, Japanese & Allies
British, American & Allies
ARCTIC OCEAN
USSR
ICELAND
Reykjavik
Murmansk
GREAT BRITAIN
London
Riga
Leningrad
ESTONIA
Moscow
Berlin
Warsaw
Reims
FRANCE
Vienna
Budapest
Belgrade
Yalta
SPAIN
Rome
TURKEY
Sicily
Crete
Tunis
Tripoli
Tehran
Baghdad
IRAN
Cairo
SAUDI ARABIA
Aden
FRENCH WEST AFRICA
Freetown
NIGERIA
Addis Ababa
BELGIAN CONGO
INDIA
Calcutta
Rangoon
Bangkok
SUMATRA
Singapore
Batavia
JAVA
INDIAN OCEAN
MANCHURIA
Peking
Vladivostok
KOREA
Nanking
Tokyo
JAPAN
Okinawa
FORMOSA
Hong Kong
Manila
LUZON
Leyte
South China Sea
Iwo Jima
Guam
Truk
NEW GUINEA
PACIFIC OCEAN
Sea of Okhotsk
KAMCHATKA
Bering Sea
Kurile Is
Aleutian Is

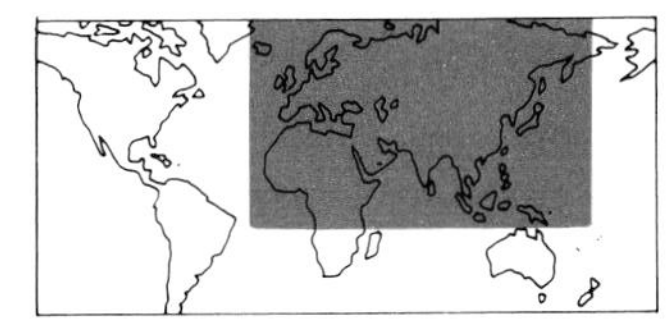

their agriculture alone, and needed some industry. However, 'Russia will occupy most of the good food lands of Central Europe while we have the industrial portions. We must find some way of persuading Russia to play ball'.

16 May Eisenhower began to agitate for the Allied Control Council for Germany to be set up.

18 May De Gaulle requested an invitation to any meeting of the Big Three.

At this time he was causing problems for both Britain and the USA. He was attempting unilaterally to annexe part of north-west Italy, and it was only when Truman threatened to stop supplies to the French Army that de Gaulle climbed down and agreed to withdraw his troops from the disputed area by mid-July. He was also trying to reassert control over Lebanon and Syria, even though the Big Three now recognized them as independent states. This, and the feeling that de Gaulle would merely make the task of reaching agreement with Stalin more difficult, resolved Truman and Churchill to exclude him.

25 May–7 June Truman sent Harry Hopkins on a mission to Moscow.

The objective was to pave the way for another major conference by attempting to come to agreement over issues of potential conflict between the USA and USSR. Churchill was not consulted over this, although he was informed of it beforehand; he was also told of Truman's intention to have a private meeting with Stalin prior to the main conference. Stalin gave his agreement to a Big Six conference at Potsdam in mid-July. In truth, there was strong disapproval in US official circles of Churchill's mistrust of Stalin.

5 June Signing of the Allied declaration on the defeat of Germany in Berlin.

This was signed by the four Allied commanders-in-chief, Eisenhower, Montgomery, Zhukov and de Lattre de Tassigny. Details of the zones of occupation and system for the control of Germany were also issued. This meeting marked the setting up of the Allied Control Council, but Zhukov refused to discuss its installation in Berlin until the British and US forces had withdrawn from the Russian zone. The Western Allies eventually agreed to this.

3 July Western Allied garrisons entered Berlin.

The withdrawals from the Russian zone had begun on the 1st.

17 July–2 August The Potsdam Conference ('Terminal').

Prior to the conference, the British and Americans had drawn up and compared topic lists. These were shown to Stalin, who did not produce one, but did not object to the Western Allies' agendas. The conference got off to an encouraging start. Agreement was quickly reached over the setting up of a Council of Foreign Ministers representing Britain, China, France, Russia and the USA to draw up peace treaties with Italy, Roumania and Bulgaria, Hungary and Finland.

As to the eastern European states themselves, the conference soon found itself in choppy waters. It seemed to the Western Allies, especially Churchill, that Stalin was doing little to honour the Yalta Declaration of Liberated Europe. Churchill demanded that the Russians take clearcut steps to ensure that truly democratic governments were set up, but Stalin reminded him of the agreement they had made in Moscow in October 1944 over spheres of influence in the Balkans. The Russians also accused Britain of suppressing democratic elements in Greece. The Americans did their best to reconcile these differences, but all that could be achieved was some revision in the Allied Control Commission machinery. Stalin remained resolutely opposed to any Western involvement in elections in Hungary, Roumania and Bulgaria.

Poland, however, remained the main stumbling-block. A provisional government had now been set up in Warsaw, the majority of its members being Lublin Poles, and this had been recognized by Britain and the USA on 5 July with the proviso that the pledged free elections be held at an early date. This appeared to be confirmed at Potsdam, but the question of Poland's western border proved more intractable. The Poles, supported by the Russians, demanded that it run along the Oder and western Neisse, but this meant that, not only was Poland effectively becoming another occupying power of Germany, but it denied Germany vital agricultural lands. Eventually the Western Allies were forced to concede a compromise whereby this line was made provisional on the peace settlement.

On **25 July** the conference adjourned while Churchill and Clement Attlee, his former deputy in the wartime government and leader of the British Labour Party (whom Churchill had invited to accompany him), flew back to Britain for the General Election. The results were announced on the 26th and revealed a landslide victory for the Labour Party. Churchill was now out of office; Attlee returned to Potsdam on his own.

So far as Germany was concerned, the programme for the demilitarization and deNazification was agreed, but a common policy over reparations proved impossible to achieve, and it was agreed that each occupying power would deal with this within its own zone at its own discretion. The same was to apply to German assets in Austria. As for Japan, this is covered on page 238. Potsdam was the last meeting of the wartime Allies. At this conference, hopes that East-West co-operation could be nurtured and developed in the post-war world showed ominous signs of being dashed.

THE NEW EUROPE

Post-war Problems · P246

The Development of the Atomic Bomb

The origins of the atomic bomb go back to February 1896 when the Frenchman Henri Bacquerel discovered radioactivity while experimenting with uranium. In 1898 the New Zealander Professor Ernest Rutherford at the University of Montreal, Canada, established that uranium emitted two types of radiation, alpha and beta particles. The culmination of his work came at the University of Manchester, England, in 1919 when he successfully 'split the atom' by bombarding nitrogen with alpha particles. The following year the Danish scientist Niels Bohr completed the theory of the atom by establishing that it was made up of a nucleus of protons and neutrons, around which electrons revolved. In 1930 the German scientists Walther Bothe and Helmuth Becker discovered that when they bombarded beryllium with alpha particles a very penetrating neutral particle was emitted. Finally in 1932 the British physicist James Chadwick established that this neutral particle was a neutron. The basis for producing energy from this process was now available.

In 1934 an *émigré* Hungarian physicist, Leo Szilard, living in London, applied for a patent for the production of energy through a nuclear chain reaction, but it was not until 1938 that his theory was proved correct when two German scientists, Otto Hahn and Fritz Strassmann, bombarded Uranium 238 with neutrons and created energy through nuclear fission.

3 March 1939 Szilard demonstrated that a nuclear bomb was feasible.
Now in the USA, he had heard of Hahn and Strassmann's success, and produced neutrons by bombarding beryllium with alpha particles emitted from radium and then exposed uranium to these. He approached the US Navy, who failed to grasp the significance of his discovery.

In the meantime, in Paris, Frédéric and Irène Joliot achieved similar results, but unlike Szilard, who feared that Nazi Germany would create a nuclear weapon, they published their results, and thus forced him to publish his.

2 August After a meeting with Szilard, Albert Einstein wrote to President Roosevelt.
Szilard was now convinced that a race to build the first nuclear weapon was in progress between Germany and the USA, and that the US Government needed to be alerted. As a result, that autumn Roosevelt set up the Uranium Committee; but it achieved little during the next eighteen months. In Britain, Lord Chatfield, Minister for the Co-ordination of Defence, had in the spring of 1939 tasked the eminent scientist Sir Henry Tizard with investigating using nuclear energy in weapons.

19 March 1940 Tizard received the Fritsch-Peierls memoranda.

Otto Fritsch and Rudolf Peierls were two German émigrés in Britain who had worked on nuclear fission in Berlin. Both believed that a 'super bomb' could be produced through nuclear chain reaction requiring just a few pounds of uranium isotope. This dramatically increased the feasibility of building such a weapon, and Tizard set up the Maud Committee to establish the effort needed to develop and build a nuclear bomb in Britain.

Across the English Channel the French had been concentrating on the peaceful uses of nuclear energy. They realized that a moderator was needed to slow down the neutrons produced by fission for the chain reaction to work. Most suitable for this was heavy water. There was only one source of this, the Norsk Hydro Company in Norway, and the French Government had purchased their entire stock. In mid-April 1940 the French emissary who had arranged this travelled to Britain and reported on recent French progress. He expressed French fears that the Germans were working on a nuclear weapon and proposed that the French and British pool their resources, which was agreed. Shortly afterwards the French brought their heavy water across to Britain. This was virtually under the noses of the Germans, by now overruning Norway. This put the British well ahead of the Americans, as Tizard was to discover when he visited the USA that autumn.

July 1941 The Maud Committee published its findings.
The key sentence read: 'We have now reached the conclusion that it will be possible to make an effective uranium bomb which, containing some 25 pounds of active material, would be equivalent as regards destructive effect to 1,800 tons of TNT and would also release large quantities of radioactive substances, which would make places near to where the bomb exploded dangerous to human life for a long period.' The material for the first bomb would be ready by the end of 1943 and, although it would cost $5 million to construct the isotope-separation plant, given the destructive power of the weapon the project should go ahead. Churchill agreed and the following month authorized the development and production of the bomb under the code-name 'Tube Alloys'.

11 October Roosevelt proposed to Churchill a joint effort to develop the nuclear weapon.
The Americans had received copies of the Maud

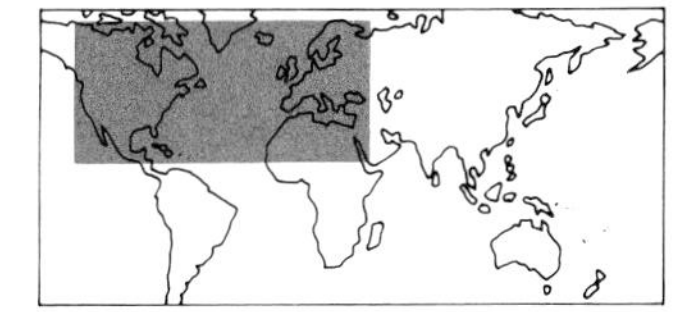

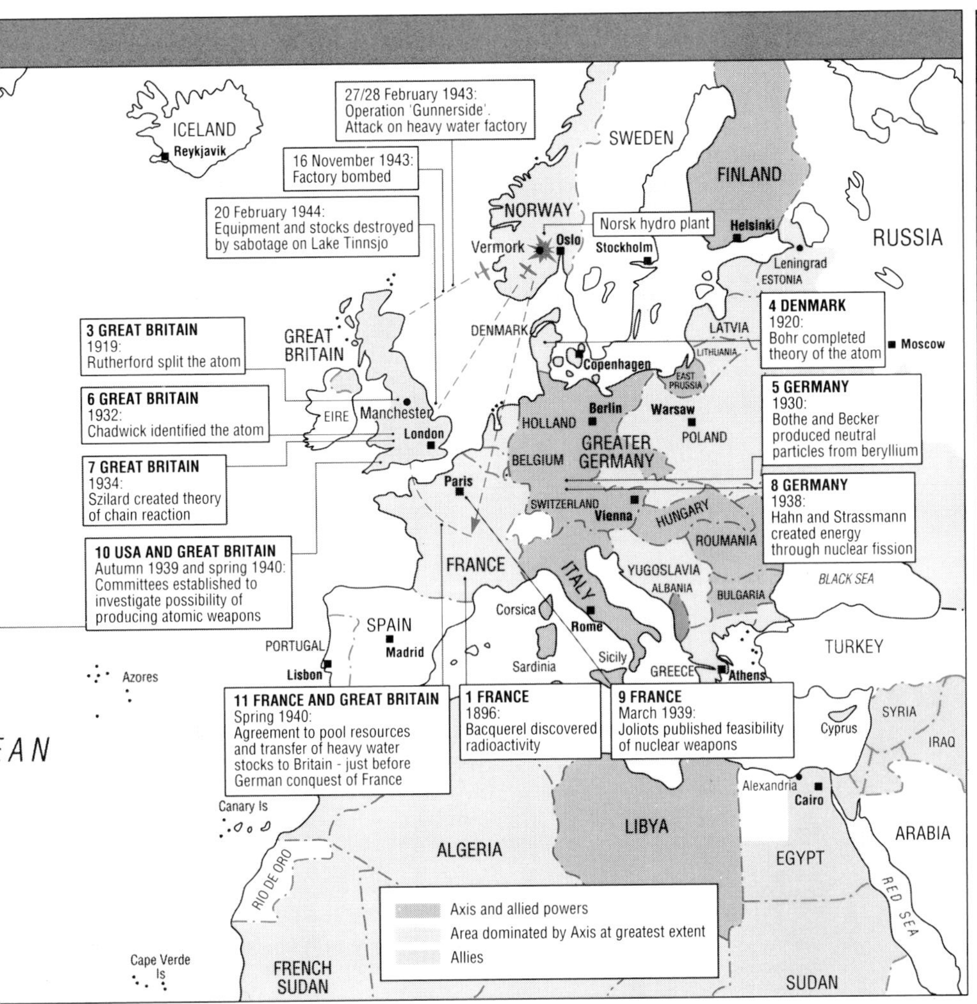
27/28 February 1943: Operation 'Gunnerside'. Attack on heavy water factory
16 November 1943: Factory bombed
20 February 1944: Equipment and stocks destroyed by sabotage on Lake Tinnsjo
3 GREAT BRITAIN 1919: Rutherford split the atom
6 GREAT BRITAIN 1932: Chadwick identified the atom
7 GREAT BRITAIN 1934: Szilard created theory of chain reaction
10 USA AND GREAT BRITAIN Autumn 1939 and spring 1940: Committees established to investigate possibility of producing atomic weapons
11 FRANCE AND GREAT BRITAIN Spring 1940: Agreement to pool resources and transfer of heavy water stocks to Britain - just before German conquest of France
1 FRANCE 1896: Bacquerel discovered radioactivity
9 FRANCE March 1939: Joliots published feasibility of nuclear weapons
4 DENMARK 1920: Bohr completed theory of the atom
5 GERMANY 1930: Bothe and Becker produced neutral particles from beryllium
8 GERMANY 1938: Hahn and Strassmann created energy through nuclear fission
Norsk hydro plant
ICELAND
Reykjavik
NORWAY
Vermork
Oslo
Stockholm
SWEDEN
FINLAND
Helsinki
Leningrad
RUSSIA
ESTONIA
LATVIA
LITHUANIA
EAST PRUSSIA
Moscow
DENMARK
Copenhagen
GREAT BRITAIN
EIRE
Manchester
London
HOLLAND
BELGIUM
Berlin
Warsaw
POLAND
GREATER GERMANY
Paris
SWITZERLAND
Vienna
HUNGARY
ROUMANIA
FRANCE
YUGOSLAVIA
ALBANIA
BULGARIA
BLACK SEA
ITALY
Corsica
Rome
Sardinia
Sicily
GREECE
Athens
TURKEY
SPAIN
Madrid
PORTUGAL
Lisbon
Azores
Cyprus
SYRIA
IRAQ
Canary Is
Alexandria
Cairo
LIBYA
ALGERIA
EGYPT
ARABIA
RIO DE ORO
RED SEA
Cape Verde Is
FRENCH SUDAN
SUDAN
Axis and allied powers
Area dominated by Axis at greatest extent
Allies

Report, and the US National Academy of Sciences Committee (the Uranium Committee reorganized) agreed with its findings. The British view, however – especially since the USA was still not at war – was that while co-operation should be encouraged, the projects to produce a bomb should be independent.

6 December The USA decided to set up its own project for developing a nuclear bomb.

The driving force behind this was Dr Vannevar Bush, Director of the US Office of Scientific Research and Development.

Within a few months US resources, both technical and industrial, had overtaken those of Britain. The Lord President of the Council, Sir John Anderson, who was in overall charge of 'Tube Alloys', concluded that Britain after all lacked the resources to develop and produce a bomb and recommended to Churchill that Britain join the US project.

June 1942 During his visit to the USA, Churchill proposed a pooling of resources to Roosevelt.

He believed that he had gained Roosevelt's agreement to this, but during the next few months events proved otherwise.

25 September The US Army set up the 'Manhattan Project' with General Leslie Groves in charge.

Bush believed that no US civil agency could mobilize the resources necessary to produce the bomb, so he invited the US Army to take over the project. Dr Robert Oppenheimer was appointed scientific director and he gathered a team of scientists, who were to be based at Los Alamos, New Mexico. It was now recommended that the British only receive information on the project in areas where they could make direct use of it. Indeed, information from the USA virtually dried up during the next few months, and although Churchill raised the matter at Casablanca in January 1943 there was no improvement.

7 November–2 December First successful experiment to produce a nuclear self-sustaining chain reaction.

This was conducted by Enrico Fermi at the University of Chicago, in a squash court beneath the football stadium.

In the meantime a plant for producing Uranium 235 had been set up at Oak Ridge, Tennessee. Another plant for producing plutonium was constructed at Hanford, Washington State, because the Americans were now developing two devices, one based on uranium and the other on plutonium, which relied on implosion.

Night of 27/28 February 1943 Successful attack on the Norwegian heavy water plant at Vermork, Rjukan.

From the summer of 1940 the Germans had been urging the Norsk Hydro Company to increase production, and it was decided by the British that to slow down German nuclear weapon development they would have to destroy the plant. An attempt mounted on the night of **19/20 November 1942**, Operation 'Freshman', had ended in disaster with two gliders' worth of troops crashing. This new operation, 'Gunnerside', was controlled by SOE using Norwegian officers and men of Company Linge, a Special Forces unit based in Britain. It was estimated to have set the German nuclear weapon programme back by two years.

26 May Churchill gained Roosevelt's agreement to a joint venture.

This was while he was was in Washington, DC for the 'Trident' Conference. It was clarified during Churchill's next visit to North America in August: development and manufacture would take place in the USA as a joint project, with no secrets on either side.

30 September Neils Bohr escaped from Denmark to Sweden.

From there he was conveyed to Britain and then to the USA, where his advice on theoretical aspects was to prove invaluable.

16 November 155 bombers of US Eighth Army Air Force attacked Vermork.

The Germans had managed to recommence heavy water production, and General Groves had become concerned. The plant itself escaped damage, but the Germans now decided to transport all heavy water equipment to Germany. Norwegian intelligence learnt of this and informed London.

20 February 1944 Norwegian SOE agents sank the heavy water equipment and stocks being transported to Germany.

They sabotaged the ferry carrying it, the *Hydro*, on Lake Tinnsjo. This finally put paid to Germany's chances of producing a nuclear weapon.

16 July 1945 First successful explosion of a nuclear device at Alamogordo, New Mexico.

Under the code-name 'Trinity', a plutonium bomb was detonated.

A second plutonium bomb was already being built, while the one uranium bomb was already being transported across the USA to the Pacific coast, where the USS *Indianapolis* was standing by.

Hiroshima and Nagasaki · P238

Hiroshima and Nagasaki

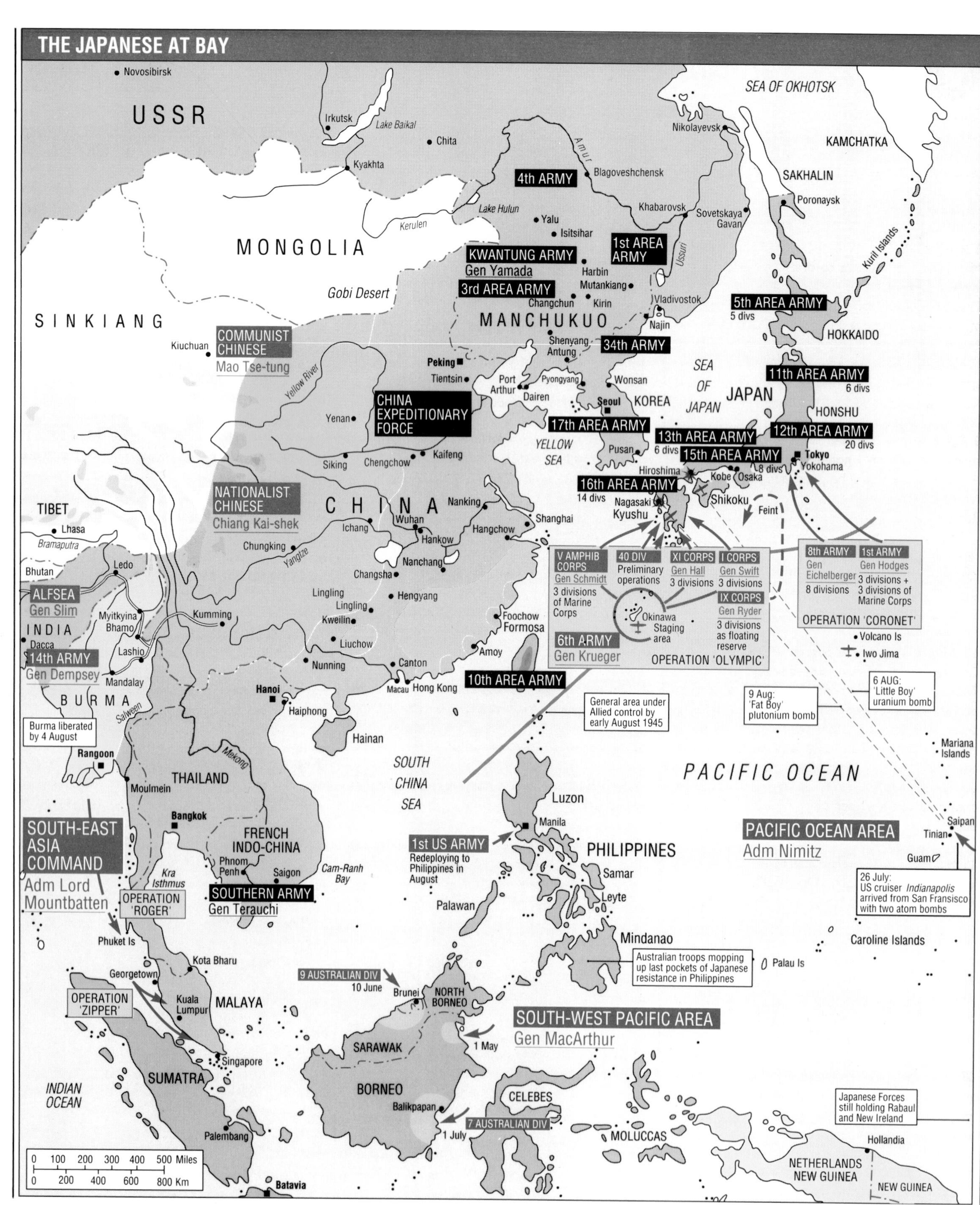
THE JAPANESE AT BAY
USSR
MONGOLIA
SINKIANG
MANCHUKUO
CHINA
KOREA
JAPAN
TIBET
INDIA
BURMA
THAILAND
FRENCH INDO-CHINA
MALAYA
SUMATRA
BORNEO
CELEBES
PHILIPPINES
SEA OF OKHOTSK
SEA OF JAPAN
YELLOW SEA
SOUTH CHINA SEA
PACIFIC OCEAN
INDIAN OCEAN
4th ARMY
1st AREA ARMY
KWANTUNG ARMY
Gen Yamada
3rd AREA ARMY
5th AREA ARMY
5 divs
34th ARMY
11th AREA ARMY
6 divs
12th AREA ARMY
20 divs
13th AREA ARMY
6 divs
15th AREA ARMY
8 divs
16th AREA ARMY
14 divs
17th AREA ARMY
10th AREA ARMY
COMMUNIST CHINESE
Mao Tse-tung
CHINA EXPEDITIONARY FORCE
NATIONALIST CHINESE
Chiang Kai-shek
ALFSEA
Gen Slim
14th ARMY
Gen Dempsey
Burma liberated by 4 August
SOUTH-EAST ASIA COMMAND
Adm Lord Mountbatten
OPERATION 'ROGER'
OPERATION 'ZIPPER'
SOUTHERN ARMY
Gen Terauchi
1st US ARMY
Redeploying to Philippines in August
9 AUSTRALIAN DIV
10 June
7 AUSTRALIAN DIV
1 July
1 May
SOUTH-WEST PACIFIC AREA
Gen MacArthur
PACIFIC OCEAN AREA
Adm Nimitz
V AMPHIB CORPS
Gen Schmidt
3 divisions of Marine Corps
40 DIV
Preliminary operations
XI CORPS
Gen Hall
3 divisions
I CORPS
Gen Swift
3 divisions
IX CORPS
Gen Ryder
3 divisions as floating reserve
Okinawa
Staging area
6th ARMY
Gen Krueger
OPERATION 'OLYMPIC'
8th ARMY
Gen Eichelberger
8 divisions
1st ARMY
Gen Hodges
3 divisions + 3 divisions of Marine Corps
OPERATION 'CORONET'
Feint
General area under Allied control by early August 1945
9 Aug: 'Fat Boy' plutonium bomb
6 AUG: 'Little Boy' uranium bomb
26 July: US cruiser Indianapolis arrived from San Fransisco with two atom bombs
Australian troops mopping up last pockets of Japanese resistance in Philippines
Japanese Forces still holding Rabaul and New Ireland
Novosibirsk
Irkutsk
Lake Baikal
Chita
Kyakhta
Kerulen
Gobi Desert
Amur
Blagoveshchensk
Nikolayevsk
KAMCHATKA
SAKHALIN
Poronaysk
Kuril Islands
Khabarovsk
Sovetskaya Gavan
Lake Hulun
Yalu
Isitsihar
Harbin
Mutankiang
Ussuri
Changchun
Kirin
Vladivostok
Najin
HOKKAIDO
HONSHU
Kiuchuan
Shenyang
Antung
Peking
Tientsin
Port Arthur
Dairen
Pyongyang
Wonsan
Seoul
Pusan
Yellow River
Yenan
Siking
Chengchow
Kaifeng
Tokyo
Yokohama
Hiroshima
Kobe
Osaka
Nagasaki
Kyushu
Shikoku
Nanking
Shanghai
Wuhan
Hankow
Ichang
Chungking
Yangtze
Hangchow
Nanchang
Changsha
Hengyang
Lhasa
Bramaputra
Bhutan
Ledo
Myitkyina
Bhamo
Kumming
Lingling
Kweilin
Liuchow
Foochow
Formosa
Amoy
Volcano Is
Iwo Jima
Dacca
Lashio
Mandalay
Nunning
Canton
Macau
Hong Kong
Salween
Hanoi
Haiphong
Hainan
Rangoon
Mekong
Moulmein
Bangkok
Luzon
Manila
Samar
Leyte
Mindanao
Palawan
Mariana Islands
Saipan
Tinian
Guam
Kra Isthmus
Phnom Penh
Saigon
Cam-Ranh Bay
Caroline Islands
Palau Is
Phuket Is
Kota Bharu
Georgetown
Kuala Lumpur
Brunei
NORTH BORNEO
SARAWAK
Singapore
Balikpapan
MOLUCCAS
Palembang
Batavia
Hollandia
NETHERLANDS NEW GUINEA
NEW GUINEA
0 100 200 300 400 500 Miles
0 200 400 600 800 Km

P230 · Iwo Jima and Okinawa

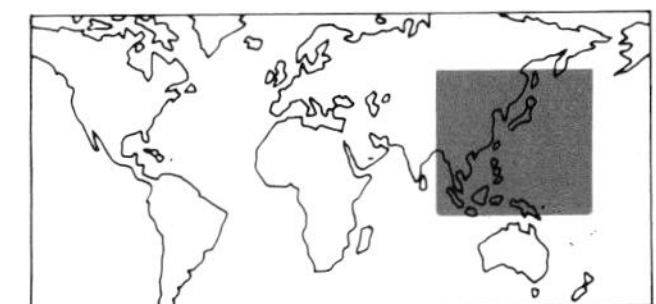

On 19 September 1944, during the second Quebec Conference, Roosevelt and Churchill had initialled a policy statement on the Atomic Bomb. Development would continue to remain highly secret, but 'when a "bomb" is finally available, it might perhaps, after mature consideration, be used against the Japanese, who should be warned that this bombardment will be repeated until they surrender'.

3 April 1945 **The US Joint Chiefs of Staff directed MacArthur and Nimitz to draw up plans for the invasion of Japan.**
They laid down a two-phase operation: the invasion of Kyushu ('Olympic') on about **1 December**, followed by Honshu ('Coronet') on about **1 March 1946**. By this time MacArthur and Nimitz had been appointed overall land and sea commanders, and Kenney air commander, in the Pacific.

5 April **Russia informed Japan of its intention to renounce their 1941 non-aggression pact.**
A year's notice had to be given, and hence the pact would still stand until April 1946. This was the first Russian step towards declaring war on Japan.

The government of General Kuniaki Koiso resigned in protest at being excluded from military decision-making, and the venerable Admiral Kantaro Suzuki became prime minister. He believed that the Emperor wanted the war to end.

12 May **The Japanese Supreme Council for the Conduct of War first discussed peace.**
This was after having considered the grim findings of the Sakomizu Report on Japan's situation. The belief was that the USSR would want to see a strong post-war Japan to act as a buffer between her and the USA and would be prepared to act as a go-between. In return Japan would be prepared to surrender Port Arthur, Dairen, the South Manchurian railways and the northern Kuriles.

25 May **US Joint Chiefs of Staff issued the directive for the invasion of Japan ('Downfall').**
This enshrined MacArthur and Nimitz's plans. 'Olympic' was to be brought forward to **1 November** to take advantage of the better weather and would be carried out by Krueger's Sixth Army (twelve divisions). Two armies, First (Hodges, with six divisions) and Eighth (Eichelberger, with eight divisions) would be used for 'Coronet', which remained scheduled for **1 March 1946**.

28 May **Stalin informed Hopkins that he would go to war with Japan in mid-August.**
He also insisted that the Russians have a share in the occupation of Japan.

1 June **US Interim Committee reported to Truman on the Atomic Bomb.**
This had been set up under the chairmanship of Secretary of War Henry Stimson to consider if and how the bomb should be used. It recommended that it should be used as soon as possible against Japan and against a military target surrounded by other buildings. No prior warning as to its nature should be given. Many of the 'Manhattan' Project scientists, including Oppenheimer, Fermi and Szilard, objected. Rather, a demonstration of the bomb should be given to the United Nations. Only if a subsequent ultimatum was rejected by Japan, and with UN approval, should the USA consider using the bomb. The administration rejected this as impracticable, but only the President could make the final decision.

3 June **First Japanese peace approach to the Russians.**
This was to Yakov Malik, Russian Ambassador to Japan. Throughout June the Japanese continued to press him, but he remained non-committal.

6 June **The Japanese Supreme Council passed a resolution to fight until the end.**
This was as a result of a paper written by the Supreme Command, who argued that the Japanese 'national essence' (*kokutai*) must be upheld. They had a plan for the defence of Japan, 'Ketsu-Go', which called for the defeat of the US landings on the beaches. For this they intended to mass 2.35 million troops, backed up by four million Army and Navy civil employees and a newly raised 28-million-strong civilian militia. This represented the ultimate in total war.

22 June **Emperor Hirohito told the Supreme Council that steps towards peace must be taken.**
This was irrespective of the 6 June decision, which the Emperor had appeared to accept.

4 July **British consent to use the A-bomb against Japan given.**

10 July **First Japanese approach to the Americans.**
This was an unofficial initiative by Japanese employees of the Bank for International Settlements in Basle, Switzerland. They used their director, the Swede Per Jacobsson, as an intermediary to approach Allen Dulles' OSS. Dulles informed Truman, now at Potsdam, of what had transpired, emphasizing that the main Japanese preoccupation appeared to be to safeguard the position of the Emperor.

12 July **The Japanese sought Russian approval for an envoy to visit Moscow.**
This was to be former premier Prince Fumimaro Konoye, who had been personally selected by the Emperor. Ambassador Naotake Sato in Moscow was asked to obtain Russian approval, but he warned that, should the USA and Britain insist on unconditional surrender, Japan would fight on until the end. The Russians, however, refused to give Sato any decision.

26 July **Britain, China and the USA issued a surrender demand to Japan from Potsdam.**
The authority and influence of all those who had led the Japanese on their march of conquest had to be eliminated; Japan itself was to be occupied and was to evacuate all territories outside the mainland islands. Finally it called on the Japanese Government to 'proclaim now the unconditional surrender of all Japanese armed forces, and to provide proper and adequate assurance of their good faith in such action. The alternative for Japan is prompt and utter destruction.' This was issued in the knowledge of the successful Alamogordo Atomic Bomb test. Truman intimated to Stalin that the USA now had an atomic bomb, but did not tell the Japanese.

28 July **Premier Suzuki announced to the Japanese Press that the Potsdam Declaration was to be ignored.**
They did so because it made no reference to the Emperor and they were still awaiting a Russian reply to the proposal on Prince Konoye's visit to Moscow. The Americans, however, took it as outright rejection. Consequently, orders sent to Spaatz, now commanding the US Strategic Air Forces in the Pacific, on **25 July**, to drop 'first special bomb as soon as weather will permit visual bombing on or after about 3 August 1945 on one of the targets: Hiroshima, Kokura, Niigata, and Nagasaki' were confirmed.

6 August **Atomic bomb dropped on Hiroshima.**
Bad weather had delayed the operation. The bomb itself was dropped from the B-29, *Enola Gay*, which had taken off from Tinian, skippered by Colonel Paul Tibbets. It was the uranium bomb, known as 'Little Boy', and detonated 2,000 feet above the city. 42 square miles were flattened, 80,000 people were killed outright, with a further 10,000 missing, and 37,000 seriously injured. Many more suffered from radiation sickness. Truman termed it 'the greatest thing in history'.

9 August **Second atomic bomb dropped, on Nagasaki.**
Still no reply had been forthcoming from Japan and so Truman went ahead with another attack. This time the plutonium bomb was used, nicknamed 'Fat Boy'. The primary target was Kokura Arsenal and City, but the crew of B-29 *Bock's Car*, skippered by Major Charles Sweeney, could not identify the aiming point through the haze and flew on to Nagasaki, the secondary target. Here 35,000 were killed, 5,000 missing and 6,000 severely injured.

The previous day Ambassador Sato had finally managed to see Molotov in Moscow, but it was only to be told that with effect from 9 August Russia would be at war with Japan.

Japan Surrenders · P240

Japan Surrenders

It was not until **9 August** that the Japanese Supreme Council for the Conduct of the War met to consider the situation. The impetus was not so much the dropping of the A-bomb on Hiroshima – for the full enormity of what had happened there had not yet sunk in – but more the Russian declaration of war.

9 August 1945 Russian troops invaded Manchukuo (Manchuria) at dawn.
During the past three months the Russians had been transferring experienced formations from Europe to the Far East until by August they had a 3:2 numerical superiority over the Kwantung Army. In terms of *matériel* this superiority was even more marked – almost 5:1 in guns, 5:1 in tanks and 2:1 in aircraft.

The Red Army in the Far East was organized into three fronts under a Far East Stavka run by Marshal Alexander Vasilievsky. Kiril Meretskov's 1st Far East Front was to attack from the Vladivostok area into Korea and west towards Harbin, and to seize the Japanese-occupied southern part of Sakhalin Island. Maxim Purkayev's 2nd Far East Front would invade northern Manchuria, while Rodion Malinovsky and the Trans-Baikal Front would overrun southern Manchuria from Outer Mongolia. His front, containing the bulk of the armour and the veterans from Europe, attacked first, with the object of cutting off the Kwantung Army.

On the 9th, the Kwantung Army, commanded by General Yawada, was given orders that its main task was to defend Korea, which meant holding the mountainous area north of the border with China, having first tried to defeat the Red Army on the line Mukden (Shenyann) and Changchun. This therefore called for a strategic withdrawal from northern Manchuria.

Throughout this day the Japanese Supreme Council deliberated. The civilian members and the Navy Minister, Admiral Mitsumasa Yonai, argued that they should now accede to the Potsdam Proclamation, but the military members saw no option but to fight to the bitter end. By late evening no decision had been reached and the only answer was to consult the Emperor.

10 August Emperor Hirohito decreed that the Potsdam Proclamation be accepted.
That evening Japanese radio transmitters sent out the acceptance in Morse Code in English. The only proviso was that the terms did not 'comprise any demand which prejudices the prerogatives of His Majesty as sovereign ruler'. The message was picked up in the USA, but Truman waited until the Swiss Embassy in Washington, DC, received the Japanese offer to surrender. Stimson, in the face of opposition, insisted that the Emperor be retained, since only he could ensure that his country ceased fighting. Truman accepted this, and a message was drafted stating that from the moment of surrender the Emperor and his government would be under the authority of the Supreme Allied Commander. It could not be sent, however, without the approval of the USSR, Britain and China.

By now two more atomic bombs had been delivered to Tinian and were scheduled to be used on the 13th and 16th, while conventional naval and air activity against Japan continued.

Britain and China agreed the draft US reply, but the Russians were sceptical about Japanese acceptance of unconditional surrender and Molotov stated that they would fight on in Manchuria. He also demanded that the office of Supreme Commander be shared by a Russian officer and one from the Western Allies. Ambassador Averell Harriman firmly rejected this, and Stalin quickly backtracked. The US reply to Japan could now be sent.

In Manchuria, 2nd Far East Front joined in the Russian offensive, crossing the River Amur. 1st Far East Front was experiencing fanatical Japanese resistance, but Malinovsky's *Blitzkrieg* attack was making rapid progress.

11 August US reply to the Japanese surrender message sent.
It was received in Tokyo at 0100 hours local time on the 12th. A group of hard-line army officers met in Tokyo and decided to mount a *coup* with the aim of rejecting the peace terms. The Allies meanwhile organized OSS and SOE teams to rescue Allied prisoners of war held by the Japanese, and on the Russian front fierce Japanese counter-attacks halted Meretskov before Mutankiang.

12 August The Japanese Government debated the US reply.
Of greatest concern was the demand that the ultimate form of Japanese government should be decided by free elections, since this did not guarantee the position of the Emperor. This widened the gulf between the civilian and military factions. The plotters were trying to enlist the support of senior officers. Truman had ordered a stay on further nuclear attacks.

14 August The Emperor ordered acceptance of the Allied terms.
This dissuaded senior officers from supporting the *coup*, but in order to ensure that the Japanese people acknowledged the surrender, the Emperor agreed to prepare a recording to be broadcast to the nation. He did this late that night. The plotters realized that their only chance of success was to seize the recorded disk before it could be transmitted. They therefore surrounded the Imperial Palace and the radio station, but could not find the disk because it had been hidden. On this the revolt foundered and many of the rebels committed suicide. In the meantime the Japanese had sent formal acceptance of the surrender terms to the USA, Britain, Chin and the USSR.

14 August Sino-Russian Treaty of Friendship and Alliance signed.
One of the stumbling-blocks to Russia's entering the war against Japan had been mistrust of Chiang Kai shek and fear that with US support he would turn on Mao Tse-tung's Communists and defeat them. The terms, which had been agreed when Hopkins visited Moscow at the end of May, recognized Chiang as the established leader of China. In return independence for Outer Mongolia was agreed, as well as the sharing of the Manchurian Railway, the Russian acquisition of Port Arthur and a share of the Dairen port facilities. The Russians would also withdraw their forces from Manchuria at the end of hostilities against Japan.

15 August Emperor Hirohito broadcast the surrender to his people.
This and his utterance at the cabinet meeting on the 10th were unprecedented – deified as the Emperor was, he had never before spoken in public. The broadcast went out at 1115 hours local time. Earlier that morning 176 US aircraft had taken off from the carriers of Halsey's Third Fleet to bomb targets in the Tokyo area, shooting down twelve Japanese fighters. While this raid was in progress, Allied forces in the Pacific received orders to cease offensive operations.

Fighting, however, continued in Manchuria, where General Yamada resolved not to surrender until he had written orders to do so.

17 August New government formed in Japan under Prince Toshihiko Higashikuni.

18 August Yamada sent his chief of staff to Vasilevsky's HQ to negotiate the surrender of the Kwantung Army.
This was after having received a direct written order to do so from the Emperor. The surrender document was signed the following day, with hostilities to end on the 20th. The Russians, however, were determined to seize as much territory as possible before Japan signed the formal surrender, and they continued to advance. They were assisted by Mao Tse-tung's Eighth Route Army, which advanced north to meet the Russians on the Sino-Manchurian border.

19 August US and Japanese delegations met in Manila to arrange the Allied occupation of Japan.

28 August The first US forces arrived in Japan.
They were aircraft technicians and were followed two days later by the 11th Airborne Division, which landed at Atsugi airfield, and US 4th Marine Regiment, which went ashore at the Yokosuka naval base.

P238 · Hiroshima and Nagasaki

1939	1940	1941	1942	1943	1944	1945

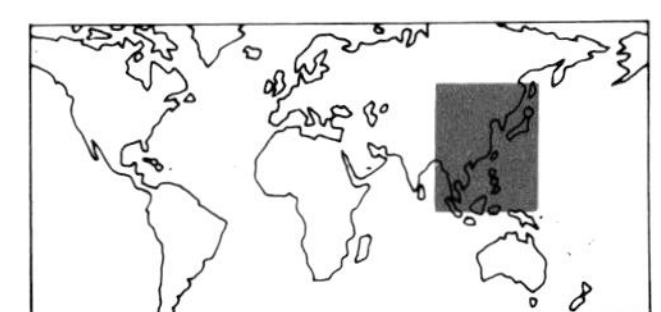

REALPOLITIK IN MANCHURIA

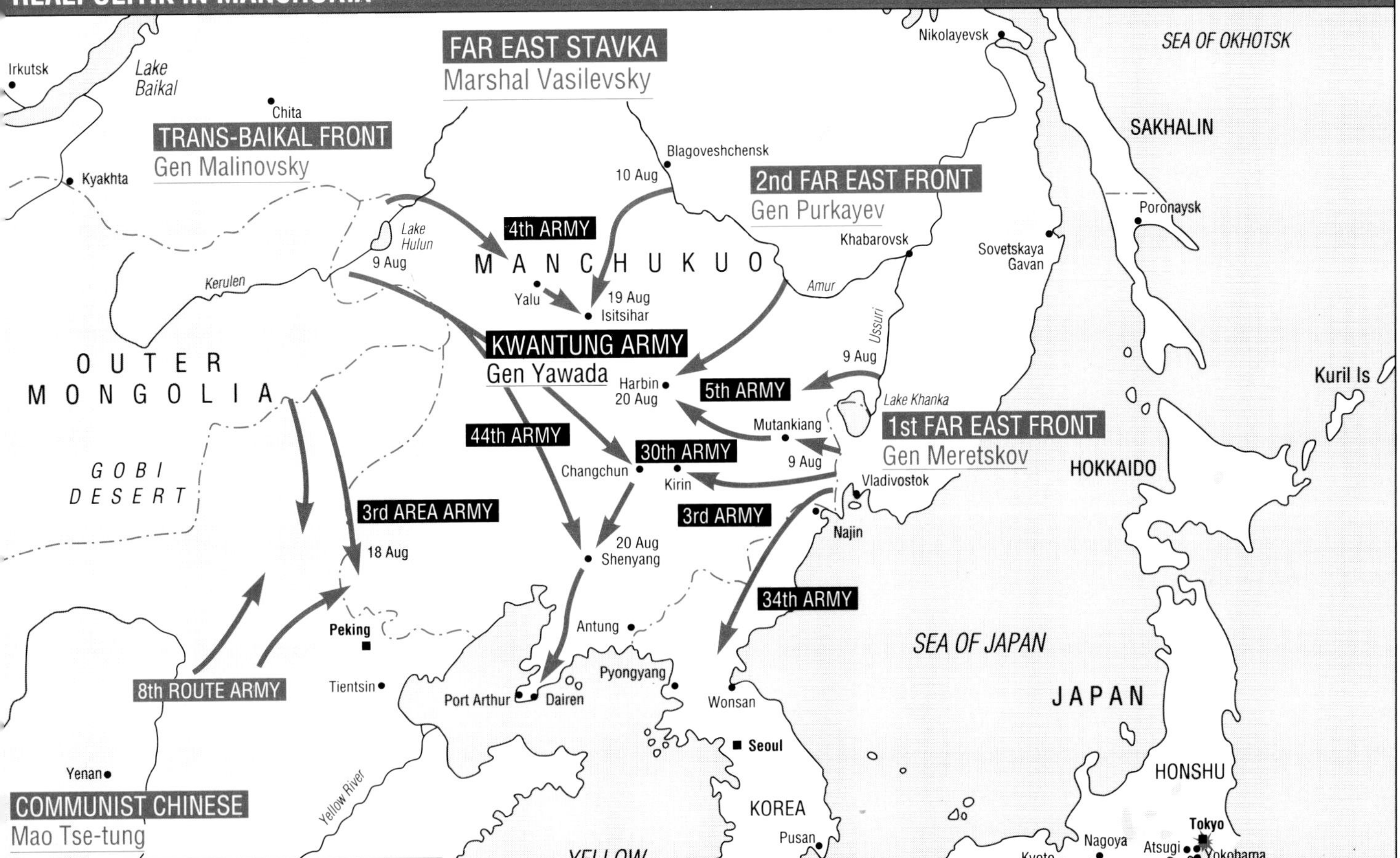

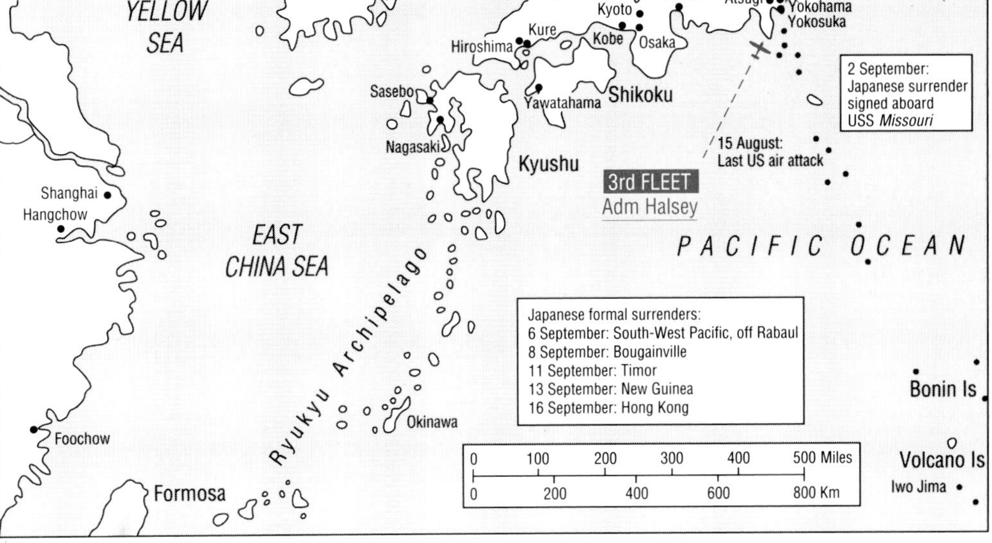

FAR EAST STAVKA
Marshal Vasilevsky

TRANS-BAIKAL FRONT
Gen Malinovsky

2nd FAR EAST FRONT
Gen Purkayev

1st FAR EAST FRONT
Gen Meretskov

KWANTUNG ARMY
Gen Yawada

COMMUNIST CHINESE
Mao Tse-tung

3rd FLEET
Adm Halsey

4th ARMY · 5th ARMY · 44th ARMY · 30th ARMY · 3rd ARMY · 3rd AREA ARMY · 34th ARMY · 8th ROUTE ARMY

2 September:
Japanese surrender
signed aboard
USS *Missouri*

15 August:
Last US air attack

Japanese formal surrenders:
6 September: South-West Pacific, off Rabaul
8 September: Bougainville
11 September: Timor
13 September: New Guinea
16 September: Hong Kong

MALAYA LIBERATED

11 September:
Japanese formal surrender
of Southern Armies

OPERATION 'ROGER'

OPERATION 'ZIPPER'

12 September:
Surrender of
Japanese forces
in South-East Asia

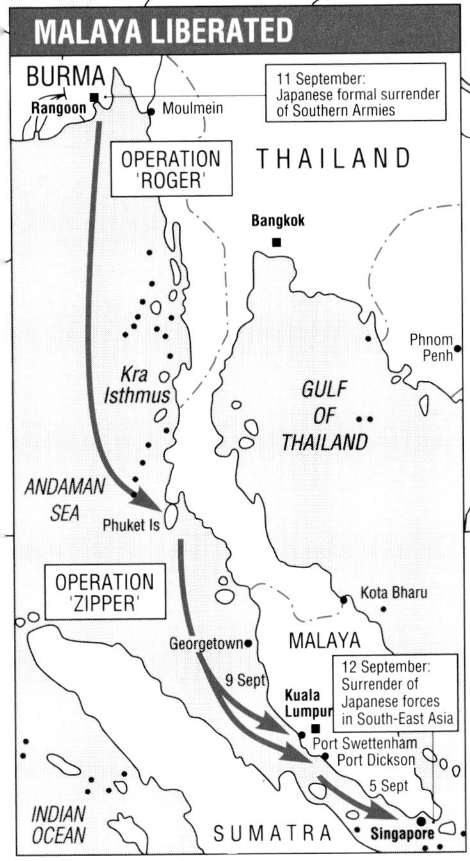

2 September Japan's formal surrender.
This took place on board the US battleship *Missouri* in Tokyo Bay. As Supreme Commander of the Allied Powers, MacArthur presided; other signatories represented USA, Britain, China, Australia, the Netherlands, New Zealand, USSR, France and Canada. The new foreign minister, Mamoru Shigemitsu, signed for Japan.

8 September MacArthur arrived in Tokyo.

9 September Allied landings on the Malayan coast ('Zipper').
It had been postponed for one month because of the decision to send British veterans home from South-East Asia.

12 September Mountbatten took the formal surrender of the Japanese in South-East Asia on Singapore Island.
This was to reinforce the main surrender.

The Cost of the War · P242

SEPTEMBER 1939 TO SEPTEMBER 1945

The Cost of the War

By September 1945 many areas of the world lay devastated. The main theatres of war had left a massive trail of destruction in their wake. Some fifty million people had lost their lives. Many others had lost their homes and in several cases, especially concentration camp survivors, their countries.

It was not just the economies and industrial bases of the vanquished nations that had suffered. Those countries occupied by the Germans and Japanese had seen their economies undermined, and their industries had suffered both from pillaging by their enemies and attacks by the Allies to prevent the Axis powers from utilizing these industries.

But Britain, which apart from the Channel Islands had not been occupied by her enemies, had also suffered economically. The cost of waging six years war in many parts of the world had left he financially broke, and this situation was aggravate by the final ending of Lend-Lease in August 1945 She had also been under persistent air attack fo more than four years and had suffered grea material damage. In spite of this she was sti a major power and was expected to shoulde

GLOBAL DAMAGE

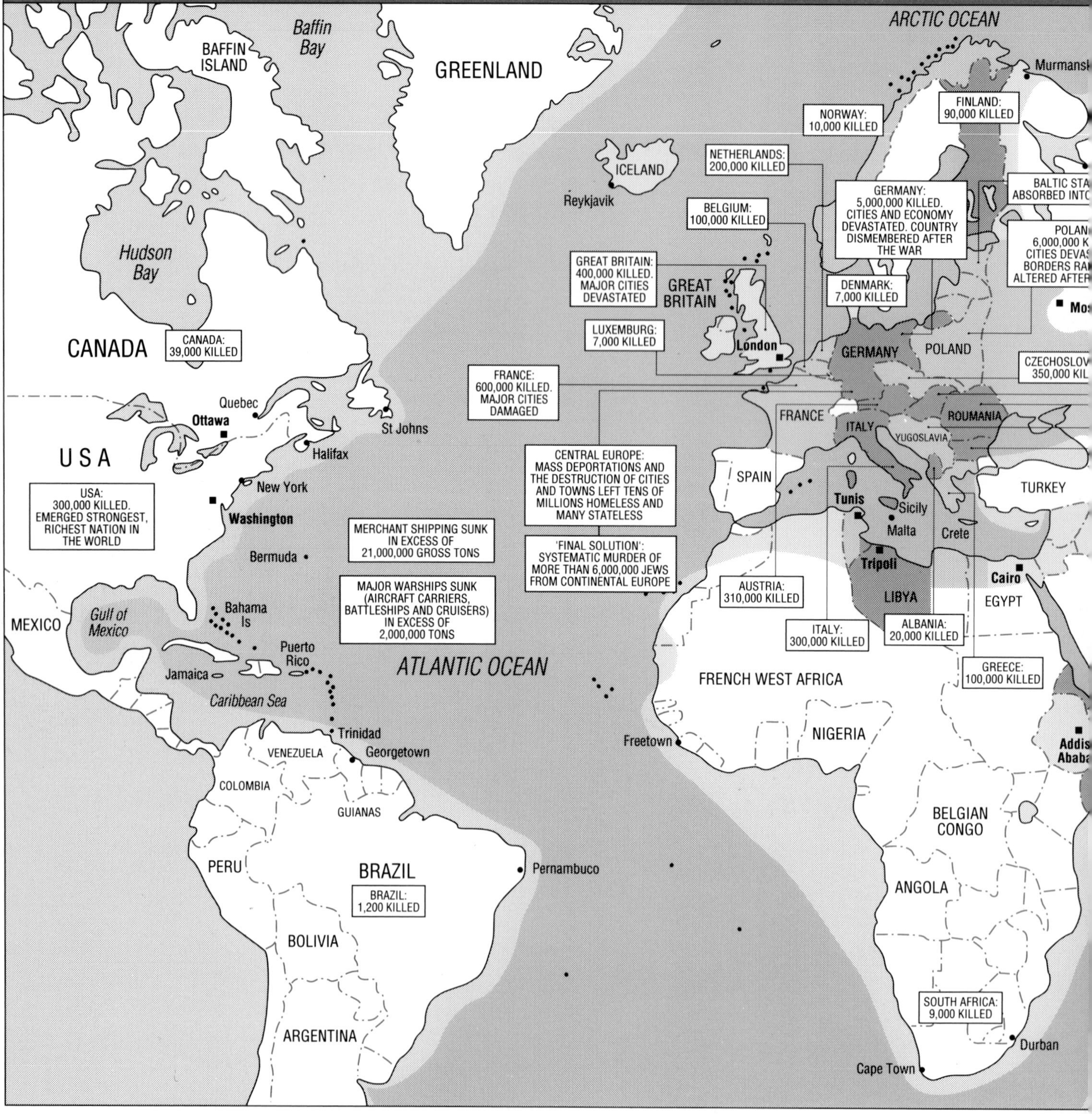

ARCTIC OCEAN
Baffin Bay
BAFFIN ISLAND
GREENLAND
Murmansk
NORWAY: 10,000 KILLED
FINLAND: 90,000 KILLED
NETHERLANDS: 200,000 KILLED
ICELAND
Reykjavik
BELGIUM: 100,000 KILLED
GERMANY: 5,000,000 KILLED. CITIES AND ECONOMY DEVASTATED. COUNTRY DISMEMBERED AFTER THE WAR
BALTIC STA ABSORBED INT
POLAN 6,000,000 K CITIES DEVAS BORDERS RA ALTERED AFTER
Hudson Bay
GREAT BRITAIN: 400,000 KILLED. MAJOR CITIES DEVASTATED
GREAT BRITAIN
DENMARK: 7,000 KILLED
Mos
CANADA
CANADA: 39,000 KILLED
LUXEMBURG: 7,000 KILLED
London
GERMANY
POLAND
CZECHOSLOV 350,000 KIL
FRANCE: 600,000 KILLED. MAJOR CITIES DAMAGED
Quebec
Ottawa
St Johns
FRANCE
ITALY
ROUMANIA
YUGOSLAVIA
USA
Halifax
CENTRAL EUROPE: MASS DEPORTATIONS AND THE DESTRUCTION OF CITIES AND TOWNS LEFT TENS OF MILLIONS HOMELESS AND MANY STATELESS
SPAIN
TURKEY
USA: 300,000 KILLED. EMERGED STRONGEST, RICHEST NATION IN THE WORLD
New York
Washington
MERCHANT SHIPPING SUNK IN EXCESS OF 21,000,000 GROSS TONS
Tunis
Sicily
Malta
Crete
Bermuda
'FINAL SOLUTION': SYSTEMATIC MURDER OF MORE THAN 6,000,000 JEWS FROM CONTINENTAL EUROPE
Tripoli
Cairo
MAJOR WARSHIPS SUNK (AIRCRAFT CARRIERS, BATTLESHIPS AND CRUISERS) IN EXCESS OF 2,000,000 TONS
AUSTRIA: 310,000 KILLED
LIBYA
EGYPT
MEXICO
Gulf of Mexico
Bahama Is
ITALY: 300,000 KILLED
ALBANIA: 20,000 KILLED
Puerto Rico
ATLANTIC OCEAN
GREECE: 100,000 KILLED
Jamaica
FRENCH WEST AFRICA
Caribbean Sea
Trinidad
Freetown
NIGERIA
Addis Ababa
VENEZUELA
Georgetown
COLOMBIA
GUIANAS
BELGIAN CONGO
PERU
BRAZIL
Pernambuco
BRAZIL: 1,200 KILLED
ANGOLA
BOLIVIA
SOUTH AFRICA: 9,000 KILLED
ARGENTINA
Durban
Cape Town

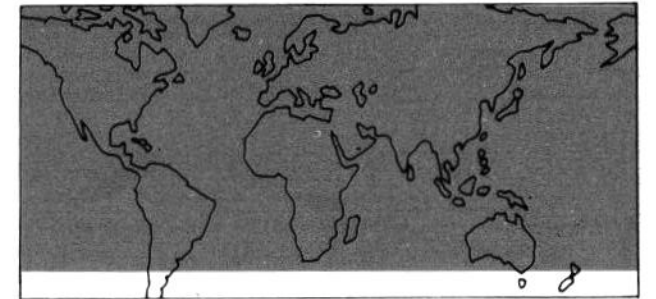

a large burden in ensuring that the peoples of former enemy countries occupied by the Allies did not starve. Furthermore, many parts of her empire, especially in the Far East, had suffered directly from the fighting and enemy occupation and it was up to her to instigate reconstruction programmes.

Perhaps above all, the peoples of those nations directly engaged in the war were exhausted, both mentally and physically. The task of reconstruction was to be a hard one.

There was one exception to this – the United States of America. As the 'arsenal of democracy' she had supplied massive amounts of *matériel* to her allies and they were in her debt. As a result, her industry was flourishing as never before and was now even stronger than before the slump of the 1920s. Furthermore, the USA was also militarily the most powerful nation in the world as sole possessor of the ultimate weapon.

It is thus no small wonder that it was to Washington, DC, that the rest of the world now looked. Unlike the situation in 1918, however, there was little likelihood that the United States would withdraw into isolationism.

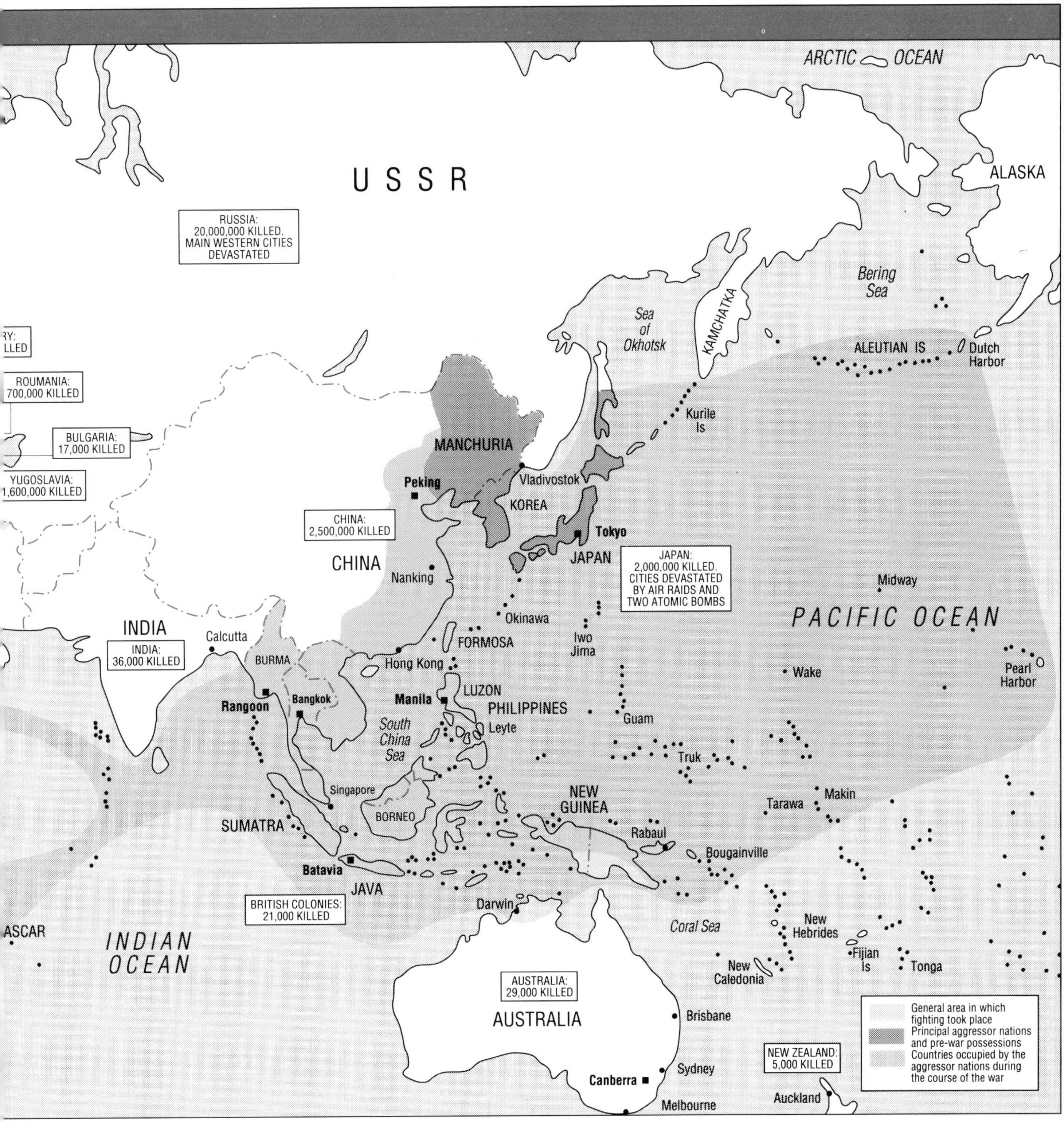

Post-war Problems · P246

13 JANUARY 1942 TO THE PRESENT

War Crimes Trials

The morality of war crimes trials is something that wracks much of the world to this day. Indeed, such trials are still being held, and war criminals tracked down some 45 years or more after the crimes they are accused of committing had taken place. Yet the origins of war crimes trials lay in the foundation of the United Nations.

13 January 1942 The St James's Declaration.
The governments-in-exile of Belgium, Czechoslovakia, France, Greece, Holland, Luxemburg, Norway, Poland and Yugoslavia met in London, called for international solidarity to prevent acts of vengeance by the general public but to mete out 'punishment through the channel of organized justice of those guilty and responsible for these crimes, whether they have ordered them, perpetrated them or in any way participated in them'.

The Chinese observer at this meeting directed a similar warning to Japan.

21 August Roosevelt warned the Axis powers of his awareness of war crimes committed by them.
The perpetrators 'should have this warning that the time will come when they shall have to stand in the courts of law in the very countries which they are now oppressing and answer for their acts'. Churchill identified Britain with this warning the following month.

7 October 1943 The principle of a United Nations Commission to examine war crimes agreed.

October First meeting of the United Nations War Crimes Commission (UNWCC).
Its members were Australia, Belgium, Britain, Canada, China, Czechoslovakia, France, Greece, Holland, India, Luxemburg, New Zealand, Poland, South Africa, USA and Yugoslavia. Stalin declined to join because of the inclusion of the British Dominions.

30 October The Three Power Declaration in Moscow warned Germany of war crimes trials at the end of the war.
This was issued as part of the Anglo-US-USSR foreign ministers' conference and echoed the St James's Declaration.

15–18 December Kharkov War Crimes Trial.
Four German defendants were found guilty by the Russians of war crimes committed in the Kharkov area. In addition, five others, including Sepp Dietrich, then commanding the SS Leibstandarte Division, were found guilty *in absentia*.

16 June 1944 British Foreign Secretary Anthony Eden drew up a list of top German war criminals.
The list contained 33 names, from Hitler down, and was the first firm indication that the Allies intended to call the leadership of the Third Reich fully to account.

15 September Roosevelt and Churchill approved a plan for shooting the Nazi leaders without trial.
This had been drawn up by Viscount Simon, and they agreed to put this to Stalin, together with a list of names. The Russians, however, had been insisting that they be tried first. This was confirmed when Churchill visited Moscow the following month, and he recommended to Roosevelt that the Simon proposal be left to lie until the next meeting of the Big Three.

During this time the Western Allies had already begun to investigate war crimes committed against their own nationals, and these were filed with UNWCC.

17 December The Malmédy Massacre in the Ardennes.
The killing of some 80 newly captured US soldiers by SS troops during the Ardennes counter-offensive galvanized US opinion over war crimes. A theory that the Nazi leadership was guilty of criminal conspiracy over war crimes and waging an 'illegal war' took root. On **22 January 1945** Roosevelt agreed a proposal for an international trial.

9 February 1945 War crimes policy briefly discussed at Yalta.
Stalin was in favour of a trial of major war criminals provided that it was not 'too judicial', while Churchill still appeared to believe in summary execution. No firm agreement was reached, which threw the US Government into some confusion.

3 May Tripartite foreign ministers' meeting at San Francisco.
There had been almost continuous Anglo-US debate since Yalta, and at this meeting, also attended by the USSR, Britain agreed to drop her summary execution stance. A legal working party with British, French, Russian and US representatives was set up.

2 August At Potsdam the Big Three stated their determination to bring the major war criminals quickly to trial.
The definition of major criminals in this context was those whose crimes did not have a 'particular geographical localization'. The remainder were covered by the October 1943 Moscow Declaration.

8 August The London Charter.
This was the charter of the International Military Tribunal that was to try the major war criminals, who would be named by the four major powers. The Tribunal would try them for crimes against peace (waging a war of aggression), war crimes (violations of the laws and customs of war) and crimes against humanity (inhumanity and persecution of civilians). In addition, those who participated in the formulation or execution of a 'Common Plan or Conspiracy' to commit any of these crimes could be tried.

By the end of the month, the list of those to be tried by the International Military Tribunal had been drawn up, and they began to be moved to the court prison at Nuremberg. The list contained 24 names, including Goering, Doenitz, Hess and Speer. Martin Bormann, whose death in Berlin at the end of the war had not yet been established, was tried *in absentia*. Two others never came to court: Hitler's Labour Minister, Robert Ley, who committed suicide, and the industrial magnate, Gustav Krupp von Bohlen und Halbach on the grounds of senility.

In addition, a number of organizations and bodies were indicted – Reichs cabinet, party leaders, SS, SA, Gestapo and the General Staff and Higher Command of the German Armed Forces.

22 September MacArthur issued instructions for setting up an International War Tribunal to try major Japanese war criminals.

GLOBAL GUILT: Atrocities and retrit

18 October The trial Indictment was formally lodged with the Tribunal and a copy given to each defendant.

20 November 1945 to 1 October 1946 The Nuremberg Trials.
Eleven of the defendants were sentenced to death, three were given life sentences, two 20 years, one 15 years, and one 10 years of imprisonment. Three were acquitted. Goering committed suicide, but the remainder were hanged at Nuremberg in the early hours of **16 October**.

In the meantime, individual nations were beginning to hold their own war crimes trials of those accused of committing them against their nationals.

19 January 1946 Far East International War Crimes Tribunal charter established.
It was similar to that in Europe, but it did enable such countries as India and the Philippines, which had not been signatories to the surrender of Japan, to be represented.

26 April Indictments were issued to 28 leading Japanese.
They consisted of 55 counts grouped into three general headings: crimes against peace; murder; and 'other conventional war crimes and crimes against humanity'. The defendants included former premier Hideki Tojo, former war minister General Yoshijiro Umezu and the Emperor's closest adviser, Marquis Koicho Kido. There was much international agitation to indict the Emperor as well, but the US Government believed that this would cause the disintegration of the Japanese nation and force the Allies to maintain a large occupation force for the foreseeable future.

3 June 1946 to 4 November 1948 Tokyo International War Crimes trial.
The trial itself, then the world's longest, ended on 16 April 1948, but judgement was not delivered until almost six months later. By then two defendants had died and one had been found mentally unfit. All of the remaining 25 were found guilty, and seven were sentenced to death, including Tojo. Sixteen others received life sentences and the remainder lesser terms of imprisonment. The seven condemned to death were hanged at Sugamo Prison, Tokyo, on **23 December 1948**.

As in Europe, individual nations carried out their own war crimes trials. Excluding the USSR, seven nations carried out some 2,240 trials, with a total of 5,700 defendants, of whom 4,400 were convicted.

In 1949, with the establishment of the West German state, the Germans took over responsibility for war crimes trials, as did the Japanese in 1952. Nevertheless, some nations, especially Israel, have continued to pursue war criminals and bring them to trial. Other nations, unless it is for crimes committed on their own territory, no longer have the jurisdiction to do this. The debate as to whether war crimes trials, especially those at Nuremberg and Tokyo, were legally and morally justified or merely the victors' way of gaining revenge over the vanquished continues to this day.

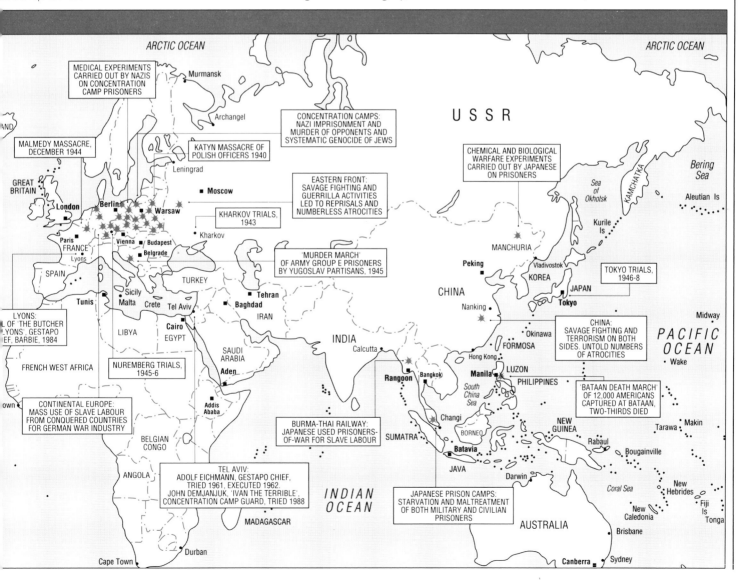

ARCTIC OCEAN
MEDICAL EXPERIMENTS CARRIED OUT BY NAZIS ON CONCENTRATION CAMP PRISONERS
MALMEDY MASSACRE, DECEMBER 1944
KATYN MASSACRE OF POLISH OFFICERS 1940
CONCENTRATION CAMPS: NAZI IMPRISONMENT AND MURDER OF OPPONENTS AND SYSTEMATIC GENOCIDE OF JEWS
USSR
CHEMICAL AND BIOLOGICAL WARFARE EXPERIMENTS CARRIED OUT BY JAPANESE ON PRISONERS
EASTERN FRONT: SAVAGE FIGHTING AND GUERRILLA ACTIVITIES LED TO REPRISALS AND NUMBERLESS ATROCITIES
KHARKOV TRIALS, 1943
'MURDER MARCH' OF ARMY GROUP E PRISONERS BY YUGOSLAV PARTISANS, 1945
TOKYO TRIALS, 1946-8
LYONS: TRIAL OF 'THE BUTCHER OF LYONS', GESTAPO CHIEF, BARBIE, 1984
CHINA: SAVAGE FIGHTING AND TERRORISM ON BOTH SIDES. UNTOLD NUMBERS OF ATROCITIES
PACIFIC OCEAN
NUREMBERG TRIALS, 1945-6
'BATAAN DEATH MARCH' OF 12,000 AMERICANS CAPTURED AT BATAAN, TWO-THIRDS DIED
CONTINENTAL EUROPE: MASS USE OF SLAVE LABOUR FROM CONQUERED COUNTRIES FOR GERMAN WAR INDUSTRY
BURMA-THAI RAILWAY: JAPANESE USED PRISONERS-OF-WAR FOR SLAVE LABOUR
TEL AVIV: ADOLF EICHMANN, GESTAPO CHIEF, TRIED 1961, EXECUTED 1962. JOHN DEMJANJUK, 'IVAN THE TERRIBLE', CONCENTRATION CAMP GUARD, TRIED 1988
INDIAN OCEAN
JAPANESE PRISON CAMPS: STARVATION AND MALTREATMENT OF BOTH MILITARY AND CIVILIAN PRISONERS
AUSTRALIA

Post-War Problems

A peace conference to bring a formal end to the war was convened in Paris on **26 July 1946**, and peace treaties were signed with Italy, Finland, Bulgaria, Hungary and Roumania on **10 February 1947**. No such treaties were signed with Germany and Austria since they no longer existed as states. That with Japan was not signed until the end of the US occupation in 1951; it excluded Russia because of a dispute over the southern Kuriles, which continues to this day.

As at the end of the First World War, in 1945 the world pinned its hopes on an international forum for providing a peaceful resolution of disputes. This time, however, the United States would not opt out. At Tehran on **1 December 1943** Churchill, Roosevelt and Stalin recognized the responsibility resting on the United Nations to 'make peace which will command the goodwill of the overwhelming masses of the peoples in the world and banish the terror and scourge of war for many generations'.

21 August to 7 October 1944 Dumbarton Oaks Conference.
This was held in Washington, DC, its object being to agree the structure of the United Nations (UN). During the first phase up to **28 September** Britain, USSR and the USA were involved; then, since the USSR was not yet at war with Japan, China took her place. The nub of the organization would be the Security Council, and permanent membership of this was given to China, France, Britain, the USA and USSR, with other temporary members.

25 April to 25 June 1945 San Francisco Conference.
Representatives of fifty nations gathered to work out the UN Charter.

24 October The UN Charter came into force.
Fifty-one nations made up the initial membership. The original criterion for joining was that members must have declared war against the Axis powers by **1 March 1945**.

From the outset, the UN was faced with numerous disputes, and matters were not made easier by the beginning of the Cold War.

THE COLD WAR

Hopes that the Russians would honour the various wartime agreements and allow free elections in the countries of eastern Europe were gradually dashed, and one by one they fell under autocratic Communist rule. Likewise, efforts to run occupied Germany as an overall unit foundered. Mutual mistrust between Russia and her former allies rapidly worsened.

5 March 1946 Churchill's famous 'Iron Curtain' speech.
He declared at Westminister College, Fulton, Missouri, that 'an iron curtain has descended across the Continent [of Europe]'.

12 March 1947 Introduction of the Truman Doctrine.
Civil war had broken out once more in Greece. The overstretched British could no longer support her or Turkey against increasing Russian threats, so they asked the USA to take over the task. In a speech requesting funds from Congress to do this, Truman stated: 'It must be the policy of the United States to support free peoples who are resisting attempted subjugation by armed minorities or outside pressures.' This became a cornerstone of US foreign policy.

5 June 1947 The Marshall Plan was born.
It came in a speech by General George Marshall, now US Secretary of State, at Harvard University. Recognizing that Europe was still prostrate and vulnerable to the Communist threat from the USSR, he declared an aid programme to enable the revival of 'a working economy in the world so as to permit the emergence of political and social conditions in which free institutions can exist'. Stalin declined to have anything to do with it and would not allow eastern European nations to do so either, but western Europe grasped it eagerly, and it was to a large measure its saviour. This served to widen the gulf between eastern and western Europe still further. Ultimately, with the formation of the North Atlantic Treaty Organization (NATO) and the Warsaw Pact, as well as the Federal (West) and Democratic (East) Republics of Germany, it was to create two armed camps in Europe.

MIDDLE EAST

Many of the Jews of Europe who survived the Holocaust wanted to turn their backs on Europe and begin a new future in Palestine, their traditional homeland and a British mandate since 1920. The British had allowed immigration prior to 1939, albeit restricted for fear of upsetting the indigenous Arabs, who in 1936 had risen in revolt because of the Jewish influx. Within Palestine itself during the war a movement had grown dedicated to creating an independent Jewish state in Palestine. At the end of the war the British maintained their restricted immigration policy, with illegal immigrants being turned back.

31 October 1945 Jewish attacks on the British in Palestine began.
This caused the British to restrict immigration even more, but the violence increased.

20 April 1946 Anglo-US commission recommended an immediate influx of 100,000 Jews to Palestine.
Britain had turned to the USA for help, but even this step did not reduce the violence.

14 February 1947 Britain handed over responsibility for Palestine to the UN.

29 November The UN recommended the partition of Palestine.
The British mandate would end on 15 May 1948.

15 May 1948 With the ending of the British mandate, the neighbouring Arab states invaded the newly-created Jewish state of Israel.
So began a conflict that continues to the present day.

INDIA

The end of the war brought renewed agitation for independence among Indians. The British Labour Government had come to power in July 1945 determined to grant this at an early date. The main problem was that neither the Muslims nor the Hindus were prepared to allow the other to have ascendancy, and hence partition seemed the only answer. In the event, supervised by Mountbatten, as the last Viceroy, independence became fact on **15 August 1947**. Two states were created, India and Pakistan, but the period immediately before and after independence saw bloodshed on a catastrophic scale among Muslims stranded in India and

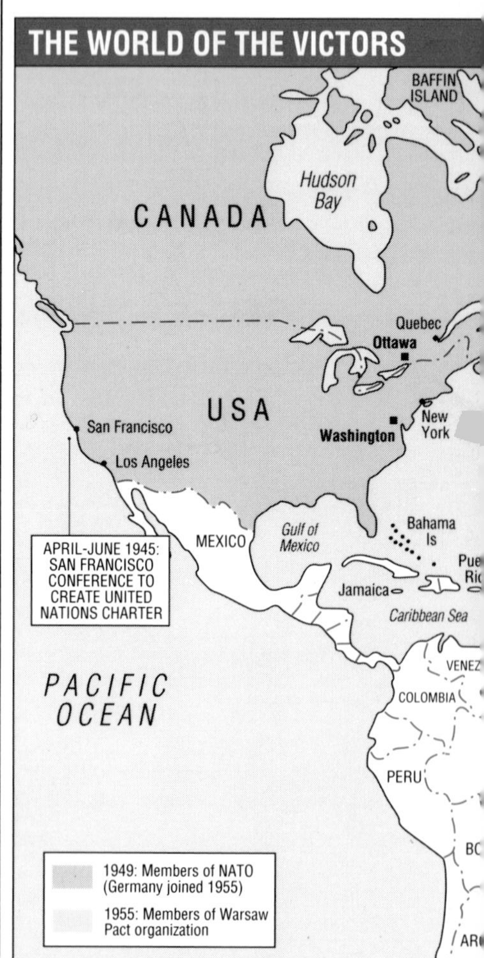

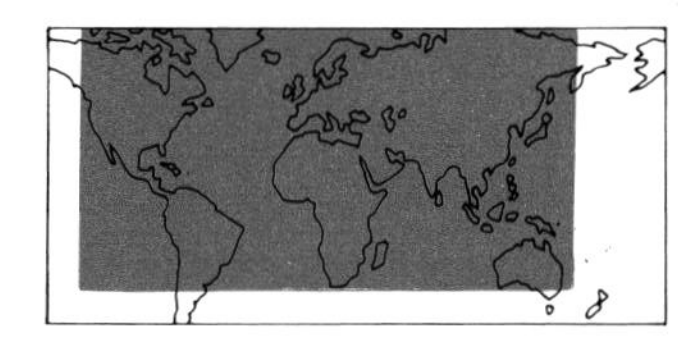

Hindus in Pakistan. Emnity has existed between the two countries ever since.

If India was to be granted independence, Burma, which also had a vociferous independence movement, could not be denied. Burma became independent on **4 January 1948**, but the hill tribes, notably the Karens, refused to co-operate with the central government and still do so.

DUTCH EAST INDIES

17 August 1945 Indonesian nationalists declared the independence of the Dutch East Indies.
On **29 September** British forces occupied Java. There were clashes with the nationalists, and these increased when the Dutch reassumed control. Eventually, after two major offensives against the nationalists, the Dutch were forced to hand over power on **2 November 1949**.

MALAYA AND INDO-CHINA

The major problem in both areas was Communist insurgents, who had fought the Japanese occupiers during the war but were now determined to retain their arms and overthrow the returning British and French administrations.

In Malaya the Communist uprising did not break out until **16 June 1948**, but the Emergency would last for twelve years. In Indo-China, on the other hand, the situation was more complicated.

9 March 1945 The Japanese took total control of French Indo-China.
Two days later Japan gave it its 'independence'.

2 September Ho Chi Minh proclaimed the Democratic Republic of Vietnam in Hanoi.
His Communist regime was shortlived because nine days later British troops occupied Saigon to take the Japanese surrender. On **16 March 1946** French forces occupied Hanoi, and two months later the British had withdrawn. Initially the French were prepared to negotiate with Ho Chi Minh on the basis of limited self-independence, but this was not enough, even though they had by the end of 1949 granted Laos and Cambodia independence. They found themselves increasingly embroiled in a war with Ho Chi Minh, were defeated, and the problem then became an American one.

PHILIPPINES

Here there had traditionally been a militant peasant movement, the Huks. With significant Communist support and the immediate post-war depression, they rose against the government almost as soon as it gained its total independence from the USA on **4 July 1946**. Not until 1957 was the uprising crushed.

CHINA

It was inevitable, especially given the Russian invasion of Manchuria in August 1945, that fighting between Chiang Kai-shek and Mao Tse-tung would be renewed. By **October 1949** Mao had won, and the Nationalists withdrew to Formosa, which they renamed Taiwan. Not only had another major country joined the Communist sphere, but Mao had inspired rebel and nationalist movements in many parts of the Far East.

The Second World War had achieved its aim of eliminating the aggressive Fascism of Hitler, Mussolini and Japan. But, like its predecessor, it had not achieved a more peaceful world. If the First World War had eventually produced a polarization between democracy and dictatorship, then the Second World War evolved capitalism/imperialism versus Communism/self-determination. There might be little difference between these, but the victorious nations of 1945 took a much more pragmatic view of the world than their predecessors of 1918. Perhaps this is the main reason why there has not been a Third World War.

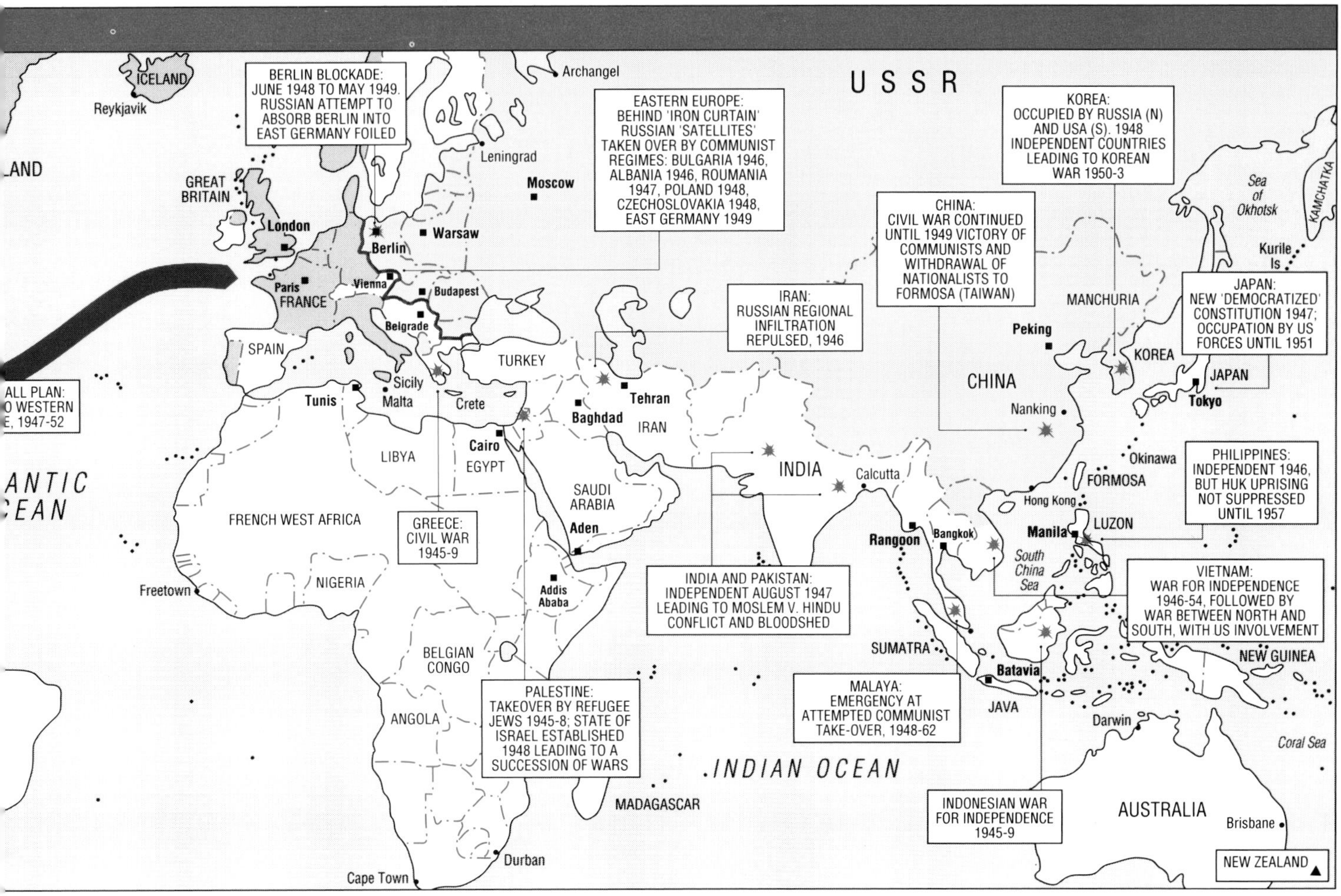

BERLIN BLOCKADE: JUNE 1948 TO MAY 1949. RUSSIAN ATTEMPT TO ABSORB BERLIN INTO EAST GERMANY FOILED

EASTERN EUROPE: BEHIND 'IRON CURTAIN' RUSSIAN 'SATELLITES' TAKEN OVER BY COMMUNIST REGIMES: BULGARIA 1946, ALBANIA 1946, ROUMANIA 1947, POLAND 1948, CZECHOSLOVAKIA 1948, EAST GERMANY 1949

KOREA: OCCUPIED BY RUSSIA (N) AND USA (S). 1948 INDEPENDENT COUNTRIES LEADING TO KOREAN WAR 1950-3

CHINA: CIVIL WAR CONTINUED UNTIL 1949 VICTORY OF COMMUNISTS AND WITHDRAWAL OF NATIONALISTS TO FORMOSA (TAIWAN)

IRAN: RUSSIAN REGIONAL INFILTRATION REPULSED, 1946

JAPAN: NEW 'DEMOCRATIZED' CONSTITUTION 1947; OCCUPATION BY US FORCES UNTIL 1951

...ALL PLAN: ...O WESTERN ...E, 1947-52

PHILIPPINES: INDEPENDENT 1946, BUT HUK UPRISING NOT SUPPRESSED UNTIL 1957

GREECE: CIVIL WAR 1945-9

INDIA AND PAKISTAN: INDEPENDENT AUGUST 1947 LEADING TO MOSLEM V. HINDU CONFLICT AND BLOODSHED

VIETNAM: WAR FOR INDEPENDENCE 1946-54, FOLLOWED BY WAR BETWEEN NORTH AND SOUTH, WITH US INVOLVEMENT

PALESTINE: TAKEOVER BY REFUGEE JEWS 1945-8; STATE OF ISRAEL ESTABLISHED 1948 LEADING TO A SUCCESSION OF WARS

MALAYA: EMERGENCY AT ATTEMPTED COMMUNIST TAKE-OVER, 1948-62

INDONESIAN WAR FOR INDEPENDENCE 1945-9

Further Reading

— **The Historical Encyclopedia of World War II.** Macmillan Reference Books, London, 1981

Allen, Louis. **Burma: The Longest War, 1941–45.** Dent, London, 1984

Ambrose, Stephen E. **The Supreme Commander: the War Years of General Dwight Eisenhower.** Doubleday, New York, 1969

Andrews, Allen. **The Air Marshals.** Morrow, New York, 1970

Blumenson, Martin. **The Patton Papers, 1940–1945.** Houghton Mifflin, Boston, 1974

Brett-Smith, Richard, **Hitler's Generals.** Osprey, London, 1976

Brogan, Hugh. **Longman History of the United States of America.** Longman, London, 1985

Bekker, Cajus. **Hitler's Naval War.** Macdonald & Jane's, London, 1974

Bullock, Alan. **Hitler: a Study in Tyranny.** Hamlyn, London, 1952

Burns, James M. **Roosevelt: the Soldier of Freedom.** Harcourt Brace, New York, 1970

Calder, Angus. **The People's War: Britain, 1939–45.** Cape, London, 1969

Carver, Field Marshal Lord. **Twentieth Century Warriors: the Development of the Armed Forces of the Major Military Nations.** Weidenfeld & Nicolson, London, 1987

Cave Brown, Anthony. **Bodyguard of Lies.** W. H. Allen, London, 1976

Cooper, Matthew. **The German Air Force, 1933–1945: an Anatomy of Failure.** Jane's, London, 1981

Craig, William. **Enemy at the Gates: the Battle for Stalingrad.** Dutton, New York and Hodder & Stoughton, London, 1973

—. **The Fall of Japan.** Weidenfeld & Nicholson, London, 1958

Creveld, Martin van. **Fighting Power: German and US Army Combat Performance, 1939–1945.** Arms & Armour Press, London, 1983

D'Este, Carlo. **Bitter Victory: the Battle for Sicily, 1943.** Collins, London, 1988

Ellis, John. **The Sharp End of War: the Fighting Man in World War II.** David & Charles, UK, 1982

Erickson, John. **The Road to Stalingrad.** Weidenfeld & Nicolson, London, 1975

— **The Road to Berlin.** Weidenfeld & Nicolson, London, 1983

Feis, Herbert. **Between War and Peace: The Potsdam Conference.** Oxford and Princeton University Presses, 1960

Foot, M. R. D. **SOE: the Special Operations Executive.** BBC, London, 1984

Fraser, David. **And We Shall Shock Them: the British Army in the Second World War.** Hodder & Stoughton, London, 1983

Freeman, Roger A. **Mighty Eighth War Diary.** Jane's, London, 1981

Gilbert, Martin **The Finest Hour: Winston S. Churchill, 1939–1941.** Heinemann, London, 1983

— **The Holocaust: the Jewish Tragedy.** Collins, London, 1986

— **Road to Victory: Winston S. Churchill, 1941–1945.** Heinemann, London, 1986

Graham, Dominick and Bidwell, Shelford. **Tug of War: the Battle for Italy, 1943–45.** Hodder & Stoughton, London, 1986

Greenfield, K. R. (ed.). **Command Decisions.** Harcourt Brace, New York, 1959; Eyre Methuen, London, 1960

Hamilton, Nigel. **Monty.** 3 vols. Hamish Hamilton, London, 1981, 1983, 1986

Hart, Scott. **Washington at War, 1941–1945.** Prentice Hall, New York, 1970

Hastings, Max. **Overlord: D-Day and the Battle of Normandy, 1944.** Michael Joseph, London, 1984

Hibbert, Christopher. **Benito Mussolini.** Longman, London, 1962

Holmes, Richard and Kemp, Anthony. **The Bitter End: the Fall of Singapore, 1941–42.** Anthony Bird, UK, 1982

Horne, Alistair. **To Lose a Battle: France, 1940.** Macmillan, London, 1969

Howarth, Stephen. **Morning Glory: a History of the Imperial Japanese Navy.** Hamish Hamilton, London, 1983

Hyde, Harford M. **Stalin: the History of a Dictator.** Hart-Davis, London, 1971

Irving, David. **Hitler's War.** Hodder & Stoughton, London, 1977

Johnson, Brian. **The Secret War.** BBC, London, 1978

Jones, R. V. **Most Secret War: British Scientific Intelligence, 1939–1945.** Hamish Hamilton, London, 1978

Keegan, John. **Six Armies in Normandy.** Cape, London, 1982

Lamb, Richard. **The Ghosts of Peace, 1935–1945.** Michael Russell, UK, 1987

Le Tissier, Tony. **Battle of Berlin, 1945.** Cape, London, 1988

Lewin, Ronald. **The Other Ultra: Codes, Ciphers and the Defeat of Japan.** Hutchinson, London, 1982

— **Slim: the Standardbearer.** Leo Cooper, London, 1976

— **Ultra goes to War: the Secret Story.** Hutchinson, London, 1978

Liddell Hart, B. H. **History of the Second World War.** Cassell, London; Putnam, New York, 1970

Lord, Walter. **The Miracle of Dunkirk.** Allen Lane, London, 1982

MacIntyre, Donald. **The Naval War against Hitler.** Batsford, London, 1971

Macksey, Kenneth. **The Partisans of Europe in World War II.** Hart-Davis, MacGibbon, London, 1975

Maser, Werner. **Nuremberg: a Nation on Trial.** Allen Lane, London, 1979

Mayne, Richard. **The Recovery of Europe: from Devastation to Unity.** Weidenfeld & Nicolson, London, 1970

Mayo, Lida. **Bloody Buna.** Doubleday, New York, 1984; David & Charles, UK, 1975

Mellenthin, Friedrich von. **Panzer Battles 1939–1945: a Study of the Employment of Armour in the Second World War.** Cassell, London, 1955

Messenger, Charles. **The Art of Blitzkrieg.** Ian Allan, London; Scribner, New York, 1976

— **Bomber Harris and the Strategic Bombing Offensive, 1939–1945.** Arms & Armour Press, London; St. Martin's, New York, 1984

— **The Tunisian Campaign, 1942–43.** Ian Allan, UK; Hippocrene, New York, 1982

Middlebrook, Martin and Everitt, Chris. **The Bomber Command War Diaries: an Operational Reference Book, 1939–1945.** Viking, London & New York, 1985

Morgan, Lieutenant-General Sir Frederick. **Overture to Overlord.** Hodder & Stoughton, London, 1950

Morison, Samuel Eliot, **The Two Ocean War.** Little, Brown, New York, 1963

Mosley, Leonard. **Marshall: Organizer of Victory.** Methuen, London; Hearst, New York, 1982

Padfield, Peter. **Doenitz: the Last Fuehrer.** Gollancz, London, 1984

Pallud, Jean Paul. **Battle of the Bulge. Then and Now.** Battle of Britain International Ltd, London, 1984

Petrow, Richard. **The Bitter Years: the Invasion and Occupation of Norway and Denmark, April 1940–May 1945.** Hodder & Stoughton, London, 1974

Piccigallo, Philip. **The Japanese on Trial: Allied War Crimes Operations in the East, 1945–1951.** University of Texas Press, 1979

Pitt, Barrie (ed.). **Purnell's History of the Second World War.** 24 vols. House of Grolier, UK edition, 1981

Roberts, Walter R. **Tito, Mihailovic and the Allies, 1941–1945.** Rutgers University Press, 1973

Salmaggi, Cesare and Pallavisini, Afredo. **2194 Days of War: an Illustrated Chronology of the Second World War.** Windward Press, London, 1977

Seaton, Albert. **The Russo-German War, 1941–45.** Praeger, New York, 1970

Shirer, William. **The Rise and Fall of the Third Reich: a History of Nazi Germany.** Secker & Warburg, London, 1959

Slim, Field Marshal The Viscount. **Defeat into Victory.** Cassell, London, 1958

Smith, Bradley. **The Road to Nuremberg.** Deutsch, London, 1981

Smith, R. Harris. **OSS: the Secret History of America's First Central Intelligence Agency.** University of California Press, 1972

Snell, John L. **Illusion and Necessity: the Diplomacy of Global War 1939–1945.** Houghton Mifflin, Boston, 1963

Speer, Albert. **Inside the Third Reich.** Weidenfeld & Nicolson, London, 1970

Strawson, John. **The Battle for North Africa.** Scribner, New York, 1969

Terkel, 'Studs'. **'The Good War': an Oral History of World War II.** Hamish Hamilton, London, 1985

Terraine, John. **The Right of the Line: The Royal Air Force in the European War, 1939–1945.** Hodder & Stoughton, London, 1985

Toland, John. **The Rising Sun: the Decline and Fall of the Japanese Empire, 1936–1945.** Random House, New York, 1970

Tsipis, Kosta. **Understanding Nuclear Weapons.** Simon & Schuster, New York, 1983; Wildwood House, UK, 1985

Tuchman, Barbara. **Stilwell and the American Experience in China, 1911–1945.** Macmillan, New York, 1970

Ulam, Adam B. **Expansion & Coexistence: the History of Soviet Foreign Policy, 1917–1967.** Preager, New York, 1968

Warlimont, Walter. **Inside Hitler's Headquarters, 1939–45.** Weidenfeld & Nicolson, London, 1964

Weigley, Russell. **Eisenhower's Lieutenants: the Campaigns in France and Germany, 1944–1945.** Indiana University Press; Sidgwick & Jackson, London, 1981

Wilmot, Chester. **The Struggle for Europe.** Collins, London, 1952

Wood, Derek and Dempster, Derek. **The Narrow Margin** the Battle of Britain and the Rise of Air Power, 1939–1945. Hutchinson, London, 1961

Ziegler, Philip. **Mountbatten.** Collins, London, 1985

Index

Notes

1. Ranks and titles given are those eventually attained, where known.

(Abbreviations: FM – Field Marshal, MRAF – Marshal of the RAF, ACM – Air Chief Marshal, AVM – Air Vice Marshal, W/C – Wing Commander, S/L – Squadron Leader, Gp Capt – Group Captain, Lt Cdr – Lieutenant Commander, Adm – Admiral, Gen – General, Brig – Brigadier, Col – Colonel, Capt – Captain.)

2. While Japanese and Chinese normally put the surname first, I have followed the normal Western custom of maintaining this for Chinese names, but reversing Japanese names.

3. I am aware that the Marines are a separate service within the US Armed Forces, but have indexed them under US Army in order to save space.

4. Both the Germans and the Russians especially frequently retitled their Army Groups and Fronts. Often the same title reappeared but the formation concerned had little or no connection with its predecessor of the same name. Where this occurs I have put the number in brackets indicating whether it is the second or third formation to bear the same title. Likewise, in order to further help the reader, I have put the formation's previous title in brackets.

A